The

Zemindary Settlement of Bengal.

IN TWO VOLUMES.

VOLUME I

B.R. Publishing Corp. Delhi

Cataloging in Publication Data—DK

The Zemindary settlement of Bengal.

2 v.

Reprint.

1. Land settlement—India--Bengal. 2 Land tenure—Law and legislation—India—Bengal. 4. Allotment of land—India—Bengal. 4. Agriculture—Economic aspects—India—Bengal. 5. Farm rents—India—Bengal. 6. Farm tenancy—India—Bengal. 7. Landlord and tenant—India—Bengal. 8. Farm law—India—Bengal.

First Published 1879
Reprinted in India 1985.

Published in India by
B. R. PUBLISHING CORPORATION
461, VIVEKANAND NAGAR,
DELHI - 110052 (INDIA)

Distributed by
D. K. PUBLISHERS' DISTRIBUTORS
1, ANSARI ROAD, DARYA GANJ,
NEW DELHI-110002. (INDIA)
PHONE : 278368

Printed at
GOYAL OFFSET PRINTERS
DELHI-110035. (INDIA)

DEDICATED

WITHOUT PERMISSION

TO

THE HON'BLE SIR ASHLEY EDEN, K.C.S.I.,

LIEUTENANT-GOVERNOR OF BENGAL.

I THINK MYSELF HAPPY, KING AGRIPPA, BECAUSE I SHALL DISCOURSE THIS DAY BEFORE THEE; ESPECIALLY BECAUSE I KNOW THEE TO BE EXPERT IN ALL CUSTOMS AND QUESTIONS WHICH ARE AMONG THE JEWS; WHEREFORE I BESEECH THEE TO HEAR ME PATIENTLY.

THE AUTHOR.

INTRODUCTION.

THE effects of the zemindary settlement of Bengal will last as long as British rule in India; but already, well conceived ideas of the authors of that settlement seem to be nigh forgotten. They designed a permanent settlement for the ryot, of the same character, and under the same guarantee of its inviolability, as the permanent settlement for the zemindar, and they thought that they had effectually provided for such a settlement, at the rates of 1792, by the Regulations of 1793. Yet we find that in 1879 the Bengal Government has appointed a Committee to consolidate the substantive rent law, and to suggest amendments, as if a permanency of assessment had not been assured to the ryots in 1793 by the authors of the permanent settlement, and as if the rents paid by ryots in the present day were not already so much greater, indubitably, than the pergunnah rates, plus *abwabs* of 1792, as (at least) to assure to the ryots immunity from further enhancement of rent.

2. But the perverse fate of the authors of the zemindary settlement appears not alone in the mislaying of their brightest idea, *viz.*, a permanent assessment for the ryot, but also in the disappointment of their hopes. They hoped much, on their views of the English landed system, from large estates; and laid too little stress on the well-being of peasant properties. In the present day, the happiest condition presented by any agricultural classes is that of the peasant proprietors in Europe; the most insecure and anxious condition is that of the landed proprietors in England; and poverty and indebtedness characterise the condition of the

mass of the zemindars in Bengal; while the condition of
the ryots in one province is wretched, and over a great part
of the rest of the lower provinces it is bad.

3. Nearly the whole of the facts in the preceding paragraphs are comprised in the statement that the ryots in
Bengal, in the present day, pay, out of the value of the produce
of their lands, more, by one-half, than the land revenue obtained from the rest of British India, and that yet the zemindars are impoverished. Even without the appointment of the
Bengal Government's Committee there was sufficient in these
facts to show the urgent importance of re-considering the
lines on which the zemindary settlement was made (or its
modelling on the landed system of England), and of ascertaining whether it is really the fact that a permanent assessment for ryots was omitted from a settlement by which its
authors " hoped to secure happiness to the body of the inhabitants." The prosecution of this inquiry and a digest of
its results, involved a deal of drudgery, wading through pon-
derous volumes, much dry reading, and hard manual labour;
but if, in the result, weighty utterances of India's worthies,
well expressed, have been exhumed from an official or parliamentary literature that is practically dead and buried, and
from writings of earnest thinkers, and well-wishers of India,
who have long since passed away, the reader will perhaps consider himself a gainer by the recovery of extracts, and the
collection of information, such as he may not find within the
four corners of any other book, and such as may be very
helpful in considering that which, for Bengal, is now the
question of the day, viz., the rent question.

4. The timeliness of the publication is also assured by the
late Resolution of the Government of India, which insists on
a real, earnest, resolute reduction of expenditure. It cannot
be inopportune to bring under consideration at this time the
greatest extravagance which any government in the world has
ever committed, viz., the spending of above twenty millions

sterling a year [1] to collect a yearly land revenue of not quite four millions sterling; for such, as a simple fact, is the price paid for the collection of land revenue from Bengal ryots through Bengal zemindars. The reduction of that non-productive expenditure, at a time when a tribute of fifteen millions sterling a year demands the utmost possible development of India's productive resources, is fully as important a measure, and as urgent, as any measures of retrenchment which may be now engaging the attention of the Government.

5. The marginal references in the text of the work are to the numbers, paragraphs, and sections of the several papers in the Appendix. It seems superfluous to add a suggestion that the reader should turn to the Appendices before he reads the text of this work.

6. The papers in the Appendix were to have been limited to subjects directly connected with the zemindary settlement of Bengal; but the progress of the inquiry showed that the condition and *status* of the ryot have been injured, not alone by the mistakes of Lord Cornwallis' benevolence in 1793, but by the legislation of 1859. Accordingly, papers have been added on land tenures in the West; for nothing short of the instructive teaching, by example, of eminent Statesmen of Continental Europe could correct to any purpose legislators' ideas of the fitness of things. It would have been an advantage if the Appendices in the second volume could have been restricted to the papers on European land tenures; but the first volume would in that case have been of inconvenient bulk.

7. Nor has a logical sequence been strictly observed in the arrangement of the papers in the first volume; they are grouped in three divisions of, *1st*, the objects which Parliament and the Home and Indian authorities proposed to

---

[1] Chapter I, para. 13

themselves in the permanent settlement, and the complete failure of their purpose in one of its principal aims; *2nd,* the unsatisfactory condition and relations of zemindars and ryots in the present day, and how these have been brought about by the wrong-doing to which Government sorely tempted the zemindars by putting tremendous power in their hands through a mistaken legislation; *3rd,* the legal status of the ryots before 1793,—as then established,—as it continued to 1859,—and as it was altered for the worse by the legislation of that year. There is necessarily some repetition of subjects in the first and third divisions, because the purposes of Parliament and of the authorities in 1793 cannot be understood or critically appreciated without considering the status of zemindars and ryots before 1793, under the law and constitution of India in that day, which Parliament enjoined should be respected.

8. The most prominent feature of the second division is the creation of middlemen—a class which far more, very far more, than the zemindars, have defeated the purposes of the authors of the zemindary settlement. This remark does not apply to that small class of middlemen who personally direct cultivation, but to the great majority of the class who are farmers of rents. Lord Cornwallis and his predecessors' justly stigmatized the rapacity of these farmers of rents. He hoped, by the recognition of zemindars as proprietors of the soil, subject to a permanent rent, to get rid of this class; but he effectually provided for the disappointment of his own hopes by his creation of great zemindars, and his unfortunate gift to them of the waste lands of Bengal. Accordingly, middlemen grew and multiplied, until we find them described —in 1852, by a body of intelligent Protestant Missionaries, as the greatest tyrants,—by a member of the Legislative Council in 1856 as the scourge of the country, by zemindars of the 24-Pergunnahs in 1857 as an unmitigated evil, "it being notorious that middlemen are the most oppressive and

extortionate of landlords all over the world";—while the Bengal British Indian Association, in the same year, testified that "the worst of landlords are the middlemen." Where this class is prosperous, no other proof is wanted of how grievously the faith has been broken which was pledged by Government as solemnly to the ryot as to the zemindar in the permanent zemindary settlement.

9. At the same time, this class is peculiar to India; it has ceased from the land even in Ireland, where, for long, middlemen were the curse of the country; and nowhere else, in Europe or in the United States, are middlemen to be found; while in Bengal they will continue to abound so long as the ryots are subject to an enhancement of rent.

10. Accordingly, among the papers in the Appendix, those which discuss and affirm the position that the authors of the permanent settlement intended to fix the rent as permanently for the ryot as for the zemindar, yield to none others in the importance of their subject.

11. The gomashtas of those zemindars who collect their rents without the intervention of middlemen also oppress the ryots to a great extent on their own account, and to a further extent by misrepresenting matters to the zemindar. In common parlance these oppressions are spoken of as practised by the zemindar, because he is the embodiment of the system, though he is personally unconscious of much wrong that is done in his name.

12. That the great zemindars are by no means the worst members of the system of which they are regarded as the embodiment, is evident from two simple facts—*viz.*, that the small zemindars are generally the most oppressive landlords, and that the ryot is a worse master than the zemindar, the condition of the koorfa ryot (or a ryot's sub-ryot) being worse than that of a zemindar's ryot, insomuch that the only hope to the koorfa ryot of rising in the scale of well-being is to become the ryot of a zemindar.

13. The acknowledgments in paras. 3 to 7 have been placed here in the forefront of this volume of Appendices, as a caution to the reader to bear in mind, throughout his perusal, alike, of the extracts, as of the author's remarks on the oppressions of zemindars, that the phrase ' zemindar' is used in the sense above explained as denoting the embodiment of a system, so that the extracts and remarks should not be considered as personal to individual zemindars, or to the class of zemindars as distinguished from their gomashtas and from middlemen. The Administration Reports contain acknowledgments of the excellent administration of their estates by several zemindars; among these are names of conspicuous benefactors of their districts and of their kind, whose good deeds are an example for even England's nobility; and even the author's acquaintance with but a few zemindars has enabled him to recognise estimable characters among them. It is farthest, therefore, from his wish or thought that remarks which refer exclusively to the zemindary system should receive a narrower or a personal application. The suggestions in the text for putting an end to the unsatisfactory relations between zemindar and ryot, evidence, it is hoped, the fairness of spirit which the writer has desired to maintain on a subject of hot controversy.

Another explanation is necessary: extreme plainness of speech has perhaps been used in commenting on the proceedings of past governments, including that of Lord Cornwallis; it will be found, however, on an examination of the passages, that the strong writing derives all its force from the received view that Lord Cornwallis declared the zemindars to be proprietors of what, until 1789, was the property of the ryots. The language is a mere rhetorical device for exhibiting the extravagance of this doctrine; for if zemindars were made absolute proprietors of the land in 1793, by ex-propriating the ryots, then were the authors of the zemindary settlement of all men the most abominable. The language loses

force and applicability, if this view be rejected, and if it be
conceded (as the author maintains) that Lord Cornwallis
alienated to the zemindars a portion of only the Government's limited share in the produce of the soil, without
trenching on the property of the ryot, whose right in his
holding was the dominant right which constituted him the
proprietor,—subject to payment of only an ancient customary pergunnah rate, which Lord Cornwallis intended should
not be increased beyond the rate, plus *abwabs*, of 1793.
Understanding the zemindary settlement in this sense, there
was no confiscation of ryots' rights in 1793.

CONTENTS.

CONTENTS TO APPENDICES.

THE

ZEMINDARY SETTLEMENT OF BENGAL.

CHAPTER I.

A PERMANENT SETTLEMENT FOR RYOTS.

THE Bengal Government, on 16th August 1769, desired CHAP. I. collectors to impress upon the ryots that "our object is not increase of rents, or the accumulation of demands, but solely XVI, 4, i. by fixing such as are legal, explaining and abolishing such as are fraudulent and unauthorised, not only to redress the ryot's present grievances, but to secure him from all further invasions of his property."

2. Sir Philip Francis, in a minute written in 1776, "considered that the rate of assessment per beegah should be fixed for ever upon the land, no matter who might be the XVI, 4, iii. occupant." Warren Hastings wrote in the same strain on 1st November 1776: "Many other points of inquiry will also be useful to secure to the ryots the permanent and un-disputed possession of their lands, and to guard them against Ib., 4, ii. arbitrary exactions,"—the term "exactions" from ryots sig- Ib., 3. nifying in that day the levy of more than the established pergunnah rate of rent. On 12th April 1786, the Court of Directors wrote: " It is entirely our wish that the natives" (ryots or subjects) "may be encouraged to pursue the occu- IV, 6, i. pations of trade and agriculture by the secure enjoyment of the profits of their industry; and that the zemindars and ryots may not be harassed by increasing debts, either public or private, occasioned by the increased demands of Government." Sir John Shore, in the same spirit, was not content IV, 6, iv. that the permanent settlement should be with the zemindar alone;—he observed: "And at present we must give every possible security to the ryots as well as, or not merely, to the zemindar. This is so essential a point that it ought not to

Chap. I.
X, 1, iii. be conceded to any plan." The Court of Directors, on 19th September 1792, approving of these views, recognised it as an object of the perpetual settlement that it should "secure to the great body of the ryots the same equity and certainty as to the amount of their rents, and the same undisturbed enjoyment of the fruits of their industry, which we mean to give to the zemindars themselves." Twenty-seven years later, the Court, on 15th January 1819, deliberately re-affirmed: "We fully subscribe to the truth of Mr. Sisson's declaration that the faith of the State is to the full as solemnly pledged to uphold the cultivator of the soil in the unmolested enjoyment of his long-established rights, as it is to maintain the zemindar in the possession of his estate, or to abstain from increasing the public revenue permanently assessed upon him." And that there might be

X, 1, v. no mistake of their meaning, the Court referred, by way of illustration, to the 24-Pergunnahs and Dinagepore, in which districts the collectors had secured a permanent rent for ryots,

IX, 3, i. by recording the money amounts of their rents in pottahs, as the sole amounts thenceforward recoverable from them.

3. In confirmation of these unanimous utterances that the permanent settlement was to fix the ryots' rents for ever at the old-established pergunnah rates of 1793, the regulations of that year regarded these as the highest recognised, that is, maximum, rates of rent, and prohibited the levy of fresh *abwals*, which would have been tantamount to an enhancement of rents. While every other detail affecting the relations of zemindar and ryot was carefully elaborated in the Regulations of 1793, they contain no provision for an increase of that rent which ancient custom had determined as the established pergunnah rate of rent.

4. The intention that by the arrangement of 1793 the ryot's rent should be as permanently settled as the zemindar's,

IV, 11, xii. at the amount obtaining in 1793, was so well known that it was carried out in the similar settlements in Benares and in the zemindary tracts in the Madras Presidency; and Mr. H. Colebrooke, on the same understanding, urged in 1812 that even then "measures should be adopted, late as it now is, to

IX, 6, vii. reduce to writing a clear declaration and distinct record of the usages and rates according to which the ryots of each pergunnah or district will be entitled to demand the renewal of their pottahs, upon any occasion of a general or partial cancelling of leases." In the same conviction the Bengal Gov-

V, 10, iv. ernment, on 1st August 1822, proposed to settle the rents payable by ryots to zemindars in the permanently-settled Lower Provinces.

5. Had the recommendation of Mr. Colebrooke in 1812, or the intention of the Bengal Government in 1822, been carried out, the ryots in Bengal would have been ensured a permanent assessment, if not at the established pergunnah rates of 1793, at least at the rates which in 1812 or 1822 were recognised as the established pergunnah rates; they would thus have crept up to near the level of the more fortunate ryots in the Benares division, and in the Northern Circars in the Madras Presidency, who, through the careful painstaking work of their civil administrators, obtained the same permanency of rent as their zemindars, under a permanent settlement which was modelled on that in Bengal.

6. But judge-made law after 1845, the legislature in 1859, and Judges of the High Court in the Great Rent Case in 1865, devised a theory, or so-called principle, that the unearned increment belongs to the zemindars; till, now, Government, the law courts, zemindars, and ryots, are perplexed how to find out that proper rent which the Government of 1793 enacted should be recovered, thereafter, from the ryot at only the established pergunnah rate which was fixed by custom, *viz.*, by a custom determined by ryots who were in request in 1793, and who would not raise the pergunnah rates over their own heads by altering the custom. The simplicity of 1793 has been superseded by a complication in 1879 so embarrassing, that, as testified by the Bengal Government not long since, a man must know all about political economy, agricultural economy, trade routes and prices in Bengal, and other things besides, before he is able, and then too he can hardly know enough to be able, to determine what rent ryots should pay to zemindars. Only thus, and in no better way, has been fulfilled the pledge of the authors of the permanent settlement, from the time of Warren Hastings, that the ryot should have the same security in the possession of his holding at a fixed rent, as the zemindar has in the possession of his zemindary at a fixed rent.

7. The zemindars have known to a penny, for the last ninety years, what rent they should pay; the ryots, for whom was designed the same permanency of rent as for the zemindar, are at the expiration of those ninety years as far off as ever from knowing, for more than three to five years together, what rent they are to pay to the zemindar. The two parties are so little agreed, where Lord Cornwallis expected perfect

Chap. I. harmony, that the Bengal Government has desisted from an endeavour to pass a law for facilitating the recovery of rent until it shall be able also to pass an Act for consolidating and amending the substantive rent law.

8. The Committee for settling that law have a difficult task; nothing less than to reconcile the present with the past: the present, in which rent is an ever-recurring cause of action, with a past in which the highest rent paid was IX, 2, vi. the ancient established pergunnah rate. "The natives of India" (observed the Select Committee of 1831-32) " have a deep-rooted attachment to hereditary rights and offices, and animosities originating in disputes regarding lands descend through generations." In memories so tenacious of custom, especially of customs relating to land, the traditions of old-established pergunnah rates will not be soon obliterated; but, in the degree that they are preserved, the Committee's task of conciliation or compromise will be difficult.

9. But the question arises, even if the authors of the permanent settlement had not designed a permanent assessment for the ryot, ought not such an assessment for him to be secured now, through the exercise of the power which was reserved to the Government at the settlement of intervening at any time to secure ryots' rights? In the Madras and Bombay Presidencies, where the ryot's assessment is XXI, 12. revised every thirty years, it remains fixed for that time; in Bengal, where the Government demand has been fixed for ever since 1793, the ryot's assessment is revised in about every five years, or at shorter intervals. This frequent revision of rent destroys in the ryot all motive to improvement, or to greater exertion than suffices for a bare subsistence; it prevents, in a word, that reserve against famine which, else, every ryot could provide by earning enough to lay by something;—and yet, Lord Cornwallis gave the waste lands of Bengal to the zemindars as a free gift, that they might provide for the people against famine, and abstain from increasing ryots' rents.

10. A thirty years' lease in the temporarily-settled Presidencies of Madras and Bombay, a five years' term of assessment in permanently-settled Bengal,—such, for the real cultivators of the land in Bengal, is the singular result of a measure which was designed to secure to each cultivator of a farm or holding the entire fruits of his own industry.

11. It is not surprising that with this main consequence of the zemindary settlement, the condition of the ryots

through the greater part of Bengal should be bad, and in one CHAP. I.
province wretched; but were it not for the proverbial un-
thriftiness and indebtedness, as a rule, of classes that live
on fixed incomes from land, it would be surprising to learn,
on the testimony of the Board of Revenue, that the majority XII, 14.
of the zemindars are in debt, and that the money-lenders are
the only class who have benefited by the permanent zemindary settlement.

12. Impoverished cultivators, indebted zemindars, usurious money-lenders,—such are the instruments with which
the Government must work in its endeavours to make the
people solve the famine problem for themselves,—the only
practical solution of the problem which is possible. It cannot be said that the poverty of Bengal has created the difficulty; the annual average, from 1795-96 to 1798-99, of the
sea-borne exports of merchandise from Bengal, coasting and
foreign, amounted to Sicca Rs. 217 lakhs, including 100 lakhs
on the Company's account; in 1877-78 it amounted to
4,414 lakhs. The returns of the number of estates and
tenures of all sorts (above the ryot) valued for the road-
cess, as given in the Administration Reports to the end of
1876-77, showed, for the districts in which the cess had been XII, 5.
introduced, a land revenue of only £3,600,000, a yearly
income to zemindars and middlemen of 13 millions sterling,
(including 8 millions sterling to middlemen), or nearly four-
fold the Government revenue. At the time of the permanent settlement, the revenue of the same tracts or provinces
was a little over 3 millions sterling; one-eighth of that
amount, or £400,000, would be an outside estimate of the
income of the zemindars in 1793, that income having been VII, 7, i.
settled in 1789 at one-tenth of the Government revenue;
the 13 millions of zemindary income in 1876 is thirty-two
fold that amount. The ryots' holdings are not included in
these valuations; and in the amounts thus excluded are comprised the enormous sums paid as interest to money-lenders.

13. There are 241,346 estates (belonging to much fewer
than 241,000 zemindars) paying revenue to Government,
with an income of 13 millions sterling, or two-thirds the whole
amount of gross land revenue of British India. To it must
be added, *1st* (as we have seen), an enormous payment of
interest to money-lenders by ryots; *2nd*, the expenses of
collection and management by zemindars and middlemen,
for the road-cess is levied on the net profits of the payer of
the cess, and expenses of management and collection are there-

CHAP. I. fore deducted before entering the valuations; *3rd*, *abwabs*, or
illegal cesses levied by zemindars, a formidable item (Appendix XII, para. 14); *4th*, the ryots' expenses of litigation,
another formidable item, as zemindars very well know,
for these expenses include, besides stamp duty and other
items, a heavy percentage, as pleaders' fees, a large disbursement for travelling expenses suborning and subsistence of
witnesses, and for sacrifices exacted on a composition with
the zemindar, if the suit goes against the ryot; *5th*, payments by zemindars and ryots to or for police, outside the
expenditure from the police grant. The total payments by
the ryots in Bengal, could they be computed, would be
simply astounding, and incredible, but for the testimony
afforded by the road-cess returns; they probably do not fall
far short of 25 or 30 millions sterling; see Chapter XI,
paragraph 22; II to IV.

XVI, 9, v,   14. Apart from any question of Government's obliga-
1, 3.   tions to the ryots under the zemindary settlement,—in view,
merely, of the famine problems of the present day, and of
the tribute to England of more than 15 millions sterling a
year,—it is impossible to resist the conclusion that the ryots'
payments in Bengal should be reduced;—and this conclusion
is only strengthened by an examination of the minutes of
the authors of the permanent zemindary settlement, and of
the laws which they enacted; these show that the ryot's rent
was to have been fixed for ever at the pergunnah rates of
1793, plus *abwabs* of that year; while the facts just recited
place beyond doubt that the ryot's payments in the present
day exceed manifold the scale of his payments in 1793.

15. Hence, it should not be difficult to establish in detail,
in the observations which are to follow, that a decree of the
legislature prohibiting any further enhancement of ryots'
rents in Bengal, would not deprive the zemindars of anything
assured to them by the permanent settlement of 1793; on
the contrary, it would leave to them more than that settlement designed for them, and it would give to the ryots very
much less than a fixity of rent, at the pergunnah rates of
1793, for the securing of which the faith of Government
was as solemnly pledged to the ryot as in its corresponding
engagement to the zemindar.

16. This prohibition of further enhancement of rent would
simplify the substantive rent law, and would root out the
middlemen or farmers of rents, who are the curse of Bengal.

CHAPTER II.

ACTUAL PROPRIETORS OF LAND IN 1789 :—RYOTS.

Zemindars and the official mind in Bengal are so habituated to repeated increase of ryots' rents, that the stopping of further enhancement of rent in the permanently-settled Lower Provinces would on the first blush be regarded as a confiscation of proprietary rights of zemindars; it might be more fitly characterised as a measure for extinguishing middlemen. But its true character will be understood best after considering, *1st* the substantive position or status of the ryot at the time of the permanent settlement; *2nd*, the limited proprietary right which by a legal fiction Lord Cornwallis vested in zemindars.

2. On the threshold we meet an enquiry whether the State was not the proprietor of the land. Good authorities answer that, according to the law and constitution of India at the time of the acquisition of the dewanny of Bengal by the East India Company, the State was not the proprietor; the sovereign's right was limited to a share of the produce of the soil, and the State's ordinary demand on the ryot was fixed by custom. This answer accords with what was the state of things in other countries where the primitive usages and institutions respecting real property were precisely the same as in India. The reason of the State's existence is the security of individual rights and of private property; and it would have been strange if the State (among the millions of its subjects) had been the sole proprietor of the land, though originally it was reclaimed from waste by individuals, each family for itself, and though it was more generally distributed than other kinds of property.

3. Hence, by the law and constitution of India in 1765, which the Parliament of 1784 desired in this matter to uphold, persons other than the State were the proprietors of land in Bengal. Who those persons were, will be more clearly discerned if we look away, first, to the land tenures in other parts of India. In Southern India, in the Deccan, in Rajpootana and Malwa, and in the North-West Provinces of the Bengal Presidency, the right of property in land resided in village communities, among whom it was identical

Chap. II. with those proprietary rights in land which primitive usages, primeval jurisprudence, had established. among all Indo-European communities as the original form of rights in real property. "The tokens of an extreme antiquity" (observes Sir Henry Maine) "are discoverable in almost
1, 3. every single feature of the Indian village communities."

4. The traces of these village communities were not so distinctly marked in Bengal in 1765; but as the commu-
II, 1 & 2. nities were essentially Hindu institutions, Bengal did not differ in this regard from the rest of India, except that her
III, 10. village communities were then in a state of incipient disintegration through the usurpation of the rights of headmen of
VIII, 9. villages by zemindars; while the great body of village proprietors, or members of the village communes, were still represented by the khoodkasht ryots.

5. I. As the Indian village communities were of extreme antiquity, so, too, the proprietary rights in land of the
XVII, 17. members of the village communes constituted a perfect title (free from accidental or accessory elements), which was derived from the acquisition (or by descent from the reclaimers) of land that had been *res nullius*. The union, for mutual help, defence, and protection, in a village commune, of the holders of these perfect titles, did not derogate from those titles as against the rest of the world, including any germs, or possible embryos or germs, of zemindars. Theirs was the most perfect title to the land in each village; and any who might come after, could become proprietors of land only in the same way (*i.e.*, by reclaiming it from waste), or by carving estates out of the lands of a village commune, by purchase, violence, or fraud.

II, 13. II. The joint and several property of the members of a village commune in the lands of their own village presented insuperable obstacles to the purchase by strangers of zemindary rights in the whole or major parts of villages. Nor had any one individual sufficient money to acquire by purchase the numerous villages and extensive lands which formed great zemindaries at the date of the zemindary settlement.
VI, 2, iv, c. "Where was the capital to purchase this? It is evident no purchase ever took place; that consequently no transfer of the soil was ever made; and that, therefore, these zemindars are not owners of it."

III. Nor had the members of village communes in Bengal been dispossessed by violence; indeed, it was within living memory that the zemindars (mere office-holders) had them-

selves been dispossessed by Jaffier Khan; and in those days
when cultivators were few and waste lands extensive, the
oppressions practised upon the ryots did not take the form of
dispossession, but of exactions, apart from the pergunnah
rate of rent, and short of any point which might drive away
the ryots to other zemindaries. This is sufficiently attested
by the fact that down to the permanent settlement, and later, VIII, 9 & 10.
the bulk of the cultivators in Bengal were khoodkasht ryots,
with a tenure identical with—or not less perfect at any rate,
than—the tenure of the resident members of village communities in other parts of India. Through the usurpation by
zemindars of the functions and lands of village headmen, the
village communities in Bengal were, indeed, being disinte-
grated, but the disintegration only perfected the khoodkasht
ryot's title, by freeing him from obligations towards the other
members of the village commune which, in other parts of
India, trammeled the possessor of a holding in his transfer
of it by mortgage, sale, &c.

6. Such, then, was the proprietary right of khoodkasht
ryots at the date of the permanent zemindary settlement; it
was valid against all individuals, including zemindars; and it
was identical with that primitive proprietary right,—that
simple title as the reclaimer, or as the descendant of the
reclaimer, of waste land,—which prevailed universally as the
form of proprietary right in land among all Indo-European
communities, or in all civilised communities which have a
history and historical traditions.

7. For tracing this identity between the proprietary rights
of khoodkasht ryots and of the primitive cultivating proprietors in the West, we have excluded, as yet, any mention
of the land tax. The imposition of this tax by the State
did not alter the proprietary right of the khoodkasht ryots as
against individuals; while we have seen that the State was
not the proprietor of the land. The land tax, therefore, in
no way impaired or modified the proprietary title derived
from the reclamation of waste, or by descent from reclaimers
of waste land. The tax, moreover, was a pergunnah rate
which had been established by ancient custom, and which
was so scrupulously respected that,—in the periodical revi-
sions by which collectors of land revenue were required to
pay larger amounts into the exchequer, on account of the
increase of cultivation, in old villages, since the last revision, XVI, 5, i⁺
—the extra revenue was assessed on the new cultivation at
the old-established pergunnah rate; *2ndly*, when, in course

CHAP. II. of time, a material and permanent rise of prices, since the
fixing of the established pergunnah rate, had been definitely
ascertained, the extra revenue claimed in consequence was
demanded in the form of a separate levy of a percentage on
the old-established pergunnah rate, which was held to represent
the percentage of rise of prices, and which left intact that pergunnah rate. The limitation of the regular assessment to a
customary pergunnah rate derogated in no respect from, but
rather confirmed, the complete proprietary title of the ryot
(Appendix XXIV, para. 2, xi).

8. Furthermore, the State's repudiation of proprietary
right in land, and its recognition of the simple perfect title
which a cultivator acquired by reclaiming land from waste,
XV, 9. were also manifested in the custom or law by which the residents in a village were free to reclaim waste land subject to
payment of beneficial rates of rent which rose gradually to,
and did not exceed, the pergunnah rate. Thus, so long as
there was waste land in a village, the increase of its population was able to acquire property in the land in it.

9. This unreserved admission, by the State, against itself,
of the proprietary right of the resident cultivator who reclaimed land from waste, furnished also clear, emphatic testimony against any proprietary right in lands which zemindars,
or their ancestors, had not bought, or had not reclaimed from
waste, or had not received as a gift from reclaimers of waste,
or their descendants.

10. This testimony was fully appreciated by the govern-
XVI, 3 & 4. ment of Warren Hastings, and that which preceded his;
their indignation against the exaction of more than the
established pergunnah rates from ryots would have been
misplaced if ryots had been mere tenants-at-will; whilst
it was but the natural outburst of a feeling of outraged
justice in presence of the fact that the resident cultivators
were proprietors of the soil, subject only to payment to the
State of not more than the established pergunnah rate of
rent, plus *State abwabs*.

11. Besides the resident cultivators in each village who
were members of the village commune with proprietary
IX, 3, xii. rights in the village land, there were stranger cultivators, or
those who had been attracted to the village from other villages. These consisted of two classes, namely, one who by
long residence had acquired proprietary right on their consenting to pay the established pergunnah rate of rent in place
of a lower rate ; second, those, not so long resident in the

village, who were cultivating at less than the pergunnah rate, and were in a state of acquiring occupancy, or proprietary right, by further residence and by conformity to the established pergunnah rate. The relations of these two classes were with the resident cultivators in the village, and their status, or the eventual recognition of their occupancy rights, was determined by these resident cultivators. We infer from these circumstances, *1st*, that, even as regards stranger cultivators, proprietary right was not derived from the zemindar, until, by his usurping the functions of the head-men of villages, he broke up the village commune,—and not even thereafter, for his permission to stranger cultivators to settle in a village was formal, if they paid the full pergunnah rate; *2nd*, stranger cultivators generally entered a village as payers of less than the pergunnah rate, and they acquired occupancy rights by conforming to the established pergunnah rates paid by resident cultivators. Unless, therefore, the resident cultivators voluntarily raised the established rates over their own heads, there was no room for an enhancement of those rates, since the zemindar had no legal power to levy more than the established pergunnah rate,—the State denouncing as oppression the exaction of anything beyond what itself had fixed,—and since the State, in raising ryots' payments on account of a rise of prices, scrupulously respected the established pergunnah rates, by leaving them intact, and levying the extra impost as a percentage on the established pergunnah rate.

XX, 15, v.

12. It was well observed by Mr. Stuart Mill that "the idea of property does not necessarily imply that there should be no rent, any more than that there should be no taxes. It merely implies that the rent should be a fixed charge, not liable to be raised against the possessor by his own improvements, or by the will of a landlord. A tenant at a quit-rent is, to all intents and purposes, a proprietor; a copy-holder is not less so than a free-holder. What is wanted is permanent possession on fixed terms." We have seen that on payment of the established pergunnah rate as a maximum, the khoodkasht ryot, the pykasht (necessarily a reclaimer of waste), and the resident reclaimer of waste, were, one and all, assured of permanent possession of land by a custom which had been held sacred from time immemorial. In other words, the ryots were the real proprietors of the land at the time of the decennial settlement, and the immemorial usage which determined this proprietary title

XVI, 16 & 24.

of the ryots was faithfully observed in that part of the regulations of the decennial settlement which empowered pykasht ryots and others, who held at favoured rates on temporary leases, to claim renewal of their pottahs at the customary established rates of the pergunnah on precisely the same footing as khoodkasht ryots.

13. It appears from this investigation that of the three possible proprietors of land, the State was not the proprietor ; while the ryots possessed all those elements of original proprietary right which are derived from the reclamation of waste land, or by descent from the reclaimers of waste ; a right which the State's demand upon them,—in great part regulated by custom,—did not impair, and which was identical with the form of proprietary right in land that obtained in the rest cf India where there were no zemindars, and in all civilised communities which possess information respecting the origin, among themselves, of land tenures and proprietary rights in land. The ryot's right, thus, was a substantive definite right, such as no legislator in the present day would attempt to destroy by a mere fiat that the right (which, as a fact, inhered in the ryot) belonged to some one else.

CHAPTER III.

ZEMINDARS NOT PROPRIETORS OF THE LAND IN 1789

After having considered all the evidence tendered to
themselves, and the information collected by previous Select
Committees, or otherwise laid before Parliament, the Select
Committee of 1812, the authors of the famous Fifth
Report, recorded their conclusion that the zemindars were not
proprietors of the land; theirs was an office to which were
attached duties of administration and of the collection of
revenue. As an administrator, the zemindar had "to superintend that portion of the country committed to his charge,
to do justice to the ryots or peasants, to furnish them with
the necessary advances for cultivation," (and as collector)
"to collect the rent of Government. As a compensation for
the discharge of this duty, he enjoyed certain allotments
of land rent-free, and certain perquisites. These personal
or rather official lands and perquisites amounted altogether
to about 10 per cent. on the collections he made in his
district or zemindary. The office itself was to be traced
as far back as the time of the Hindu Rajahs. It originally
went by the name of *chowdrie*, which was changed by
the Mahomedans for that of *crorie*, in consequence of an
arrangement by which the land was so divided among the
collectors, that each had the charge of a portion of country
yielding about a crore of *dams*, or two and a half lakhs
of rupees. It was not until a late period of the Mahomedan
Government that the term *crorie* was superseded by that of
zemindar, which, literally signifying a possessor of land,
gave a colour to that misconstruction of their tenure which
assigned to them an hereditary right to the soil."

2. This conclusion of the able Select Committee of 1812,—
formed after a very extensive investigation,—that the zemindar's was an office, and that he was not proprietor of the
lands which constituted his zemindary, is abundantly established by citations in Appendix VI, which set forth various
indications that marked the purely official character of the
zemindar. Even the extract just given from the Fifth
Report shows that the administrative and judicial functions
of the zemindar were not privileges attaching to his status

CHAP. III. as sole landed proprietor in his zemindary, but duties attaching to his office of zemindar, for which he was remunerated
by perquisites, and by land that formed but a very small
part of the lands in his zemindary, which latter were not
his *neej* lands, that is, his own private lands, but the lands of
cultivating proprietors, that is, of mostly khoodkasht ryots.

VI, 17.   3. As stated in the summary at the end of Appendix VI,
various incidents of the position of a zemindar until 1793
show that the zemindar's was an office for the revenue, police,
and general administration of the area comprised in the
zemindary, *viz.*—

I. The zemindars' liability to dismissal, and the wholesale
dispossession of them by Jaffier Khan.

II. The exclusion of incompetent zemindars from the
management of zemindaries.

III. Disqualification of a zemindar to transfer or sell the
zemindary without the sanction of Government.

IV. The exceeding largeness of several zemindaries, and
the history of their growth, showed that they were not
acquired by purchase or inheritance.

V. The hereditary succession to a zemindary showed that
it was an office, for by both Hindu and Mahomedan law
real property is equally divided among children.

VI. And even hereditary succession was not effected
without great difficulty and expense to the heir.

VII. Also, while the tenth of the Government revenue
thus acquired, represented adequately the zemindar's remuneration for official duties, it fell far short of a proprietor's
income from his own lands, if of the same extent as zemindary lands.

VIII. Two other circumstances attested, in a marked manner, the purely official character of the zemindar, *viz.*, the
appointment of canoongoes and putwarees to check the
zemindars' proceedings and collections, by way of protection
to the ryots, and the levy by zemindars of transit dues
which could be leviable in only their official character.

IX. The zemindar's sunnud, the instructions of Aurungzebe to collectors of revenue, and the testimony of various
authorities—Hindu, Mahomedan, and European—attest the
purely official character of the zemindars of 1789.

XX, 12 to 14.   X. Earliest, and perhaps clearest and most emphatic of all, was the testimony afforded by the settlement
of Toodur Mull. If zemindars had been the proprietors,
his settlement would have stopped at the lump assessments

of each zemindary; but the distribution of the assessment was carried lower down to each village and to the holding of each ryot, thus proving unmistakably that the ryot's engagement was with the Government, though he paid his rent through the zemindar. This one fact, coupled with the evidences in Chapter II of the substantive proprietary rights of ryots, would be conclusive against any pretensions of the zemindar before 1793 to the proprietorship of the lands in his zemindary, even if none of the other enumerated indications of his purely official character and status had existed.

XI. The significance of this fact, as denoting unmistakably the ryot's proprietary right and the zemindar's official status, was emphasised or deepened, on each fresh imposition of State *abwabs* subsequent to Toodur Mull's settlement, by the insertion of every one of these cesses against each ryot in the official village record of what he had to pay,—a record which was kept by officials answerable to the Government, and not under the control of the zemindar.

XII. The import of the fact was fully understood by the authors of the zemindary settlement, who enacted a law commanding the zemindars to grant pottahs, and empowering the ryots to compel by suit in the civil courts the grant of pottahs, setting forth in full detail the rent payable by the ryot, and the quantity of land for which he had to pay it. Nothing beyond the amount entered in this pottah was to be recoverable from the ryot; that amount was to constitute the gross demand of the State, and the gross amount payable by the ryot, out of which the zemindar was to retain the remuneration allotted to him by Government, and to pay the rest into the public treasury.

XIII. Once more; the zemindar had no power to raise the ryot's assessment beyond the customary rate, or beyond amounts sanctioned by Government; see Chapter IV, para. 6.

XIV. Lastly, the immense extent of waste land, the sparseness of population, the scarcity of cultivators, the absence of any floating mass of labourers, precluded the possibility of zemindars cultivating large estates by means of hired labour, or of tenants-at-will. The magic of property was the only influence which could attract ryots in those days. XXIII, 2, ii. A similar state of things exists, in the present day, in the United States, of which country it is testified that "the theory and practice of the country is for every man to own

CHAP. III. land as soon as possible.   The term landlord is an obnoxious
——   one.   The American people are very averse to being tenants,
and are anxious to be masters of the soil.   Land is so cheap
that every provident man may hold land in fee."   From the
same feeling khoodkasht ryots refused pottahs from zemindars, lest they should be regarded thereby as tenants holding
from the zemindars.

4. Thus, the status of the zemindar was purely official ;
he was an officer of the Government; and we have seen in
Chapter II that neither was the State the proprietor of the
land.   The conclusion is unavoidable that the only remaining, or third party, *viz.*, the cultivating ryot, was the proprietor by a right so unmistakable that to him alone
attached incidents of proprietorship which were common to
peasant-proprietors in the rest of British India,—including
mostly tracts where there are no zemindars,—and in countries
in the West where the rights of property in land existed in
early days in the same form, and are traced to the same
origin, as in the village communities in India.

5. The ryot was proprietor of the land, subject to payment to the State of the established customary pergunnah
rate of rent, plus State *abwabs*.   Whatever was taken from
him in excess of this was extortion, from which the State
was bound—as indeed it admitted its obligation—to relieve
him.   Hence, there was no room for any claim by the zemindar on the ryot's land, unless it were carved out of the Govern-
XVIII, 9 & ment's rent or share of the produce of the soil.   The ryot's was
10.   the dominant right, which represented *dominium* or property
in his holding ; the gross amount payable by him as rent was
servitus or easement,—a fraction or particle of dominion
broken off from the ryot's property, and limited, so that the
power of user remained with the ryot, subject to this
restricted *servitus* to the State, rendered through its representative the zemindar.

6. The zemindary settlement was modelled on the division of land in England into large estates ; and analogies
between English tenures and those in Bengal were familiar
XXVIII, 17. to the authors of the settlement.   The analogy between the
khoodkasht ryot and the copyhold tenant is not complete,
inasmuch as the proprietary rights of the former were
more perfect ; but it was sufficiently close to have rendered
it the most natural thing in the world that the ancient established customary pergunnah rate of rent, which the khoodkasht ryots were then paying, should be continued as their

permanent rent, for ever, in the same regulations which, "for CHAP. III.
the first time," vested the property in the soil, by a legal
fiction, in the zemindars.   Accordingly, we find that the XVI, 37 &
Regulations of 1793 limited the demand upon the ryot to 38.
the established pergunnah rate, that is, to a rate established by a custom which, in those days of competition for XVI, 26.
ryots, was determined by the mass of khoodkasht ryots or XX, 15, v.
resident cultivators—a rate, accordingly, which, as determined
by the custom of khoodkasht ryots, would not be raised by
them, of their own motion, over their own heads.   The possibility of an increase of the established pergunnah rate was
further guarded against, *1st*, by the direction in the Regulations of 1793 that the money amount of rent payable by the
ryot for his holding should be entered in his pottah; *2ndly*, XVI, 10.
by the prohibition of the levy of fresh *abwabs*, and the
warning that such levy, whenever discovered, would be punished by a recovery from the zemindar of three times the
amount of the levy for the whole period of its imposition.
The entry of the money amount of rent for the ryot's holding,
in the ryot's pottah, was designed to secure to him the same
immunity from any future increase of rent from a rise of
prices, as was secured to the zemindar by the limitation of
the rent payable by him to a fixed money amount.   The same
object, too, was served by the prohibition of fresh *abwabs*, for
these had constituted the only form in which the State under
Mahomedan rule enhanced ryots' rents on account of a rise
of prices, while leaving intact the established pergunnah
rates of rent.

7. What the State transferred, then, to the zemindar
under the Regulations of 1793 was a gross amount of permanently limited demand upon ryots, less the permanently
limited amount which the zemindar had to pay to the Government.   Nor was the limit of the State rights thus transferred
to the zemindars confined to the State demands on the ryots
then cultivating the land; it extended also to the demands
leviable thereafter from ryots who might bring waste lands XV, 9.
into cultivation.   For all kinds of ryots, resident and non- XVI, 16 &
resident, old and new, the rent recoverable by zemindars under 24.
the Regulations of 1793 was not to exceed the ancient established pergunnah rates, *plus abwabs* of that year.

8. The authors of the permanent settlement could not
have done otherwise, that is, could not have conferred
greater privileges on the zemindars, without violating the
injunctions of Parliament, which they professed to carry

Chap. III. out by their permanent zemindary settlement; for Act 24, Geo. III, cap. 25 (2nd Sess., 1784), section 39, had required the Court of Directors to give orders for settling and establishing "in such manner as shall be consistent with justice, and the laws and customs of the country, and upon principles of moderation and justice, *according to the laws and constitution of India*, the permanent rules by which their respective tributes, rents, and services, shall be in future rendered and paid to the said United Company by the said rajahs, zemindars, polygars, talukdars, and other native landholders." The customs of the country, and the laws and constitution of India in that day, entitled the descendants of resident cultivators in a village to take up waste land for cultivation subject to payment, eventually, of not more than the established pergunnah rate of rent; and the Court of Directors recorded as the opinion of various authorities that the gift of waste lands to zemindars was necessarily accompanied by this condition, which was implied in the immemorial custom of the country and the law and constitution of India.

XV, 4, iv.

9. We find then that—

I. Of the three parties concerned—*viz.*, the State, the zemindar, and the ryot—the ryot's was the dominant right, that is, he was proprietor, and the demand upon him was that of the State for a gross amount limited by custom, and afterwards specifically limited by the Regulations of 1793, out of which the State remunerated the zemindar.

II. The State was not the proprietor of the soil; its right was limited by custom to the money value of a specific proportion of the produce of the land; and the authors of the permanent settlement limited it further by enactments which, if carried out, according to the intention of the legislature, would have given the same immunity to the ryot as is enjoyed by the zemindar, against enhancement of rent from a rise of prices.

III. The zemindar's interest in the matter was carved out of the State's gross demand upon the ryot; it was subject, therefore, to the limitations which confined that gross demand within a specific money amount, and these limitations applied alike to the lands under cultivation in 1793 and to those subsequently brought under cultivation.

IV. Thus the so-called proprietary right of the zemindar was a very limited one; it was so greatly restricted that it was not *dominium*, but *servitus*,—a rent (or, strictly speaking, a revenue) charge upon property which belonged to another,

and which the zemindar had no power of turning to any use Chap. III.
he liked without buying it from that other, who was the
proprietor.

10. The Government of 1793 was careful to explain,
"for the sake of precision," that it used the term "proprietor, or actual proprietor," in a restricted and purely technical XVIII, 13.
sense, as denoting the person who paid revenue to Government for himself and for other proprietors, and who in
consequence stood recorded in the Government books as
proprietor. Hence, in the proclamation of the permanent
settlement, the only classes spoken of as proprietors were
those who paid revenue direct to the Government. But we
know that down to the time of the decennial settlement, XVIII, 14.
the way in which proprietary rights commonly grew up
was through custom, the ever-surviving law of the East. The
Mahomedan rulers did not interfere with this custom: the
only occasions which brought them into contact with rights
in landed property created by custom were those of collecting revenue from their subjects; and on these occasions they
collected according to established custom. They collected,
too, through comparatively few officials, whom they set over
provinces, districts, zemindaries, without ex-propriating the
actual proprietors, whose title was derived from a custom more ancient than law. It were absurd, therefore, to
suppose that at the date of the settlement there were no
proprietors of land throughout the vast provinces of Bengal,
Behar, and Orissa, other than those who paid revenue to
Government under arrangements handed over by a native
rule which had always collected through officers who were
necessarily very much fewer by far than the millions whose
rights as cultivating proprietors, in a country wonderfully
tenacious of custom, were patent throughout the land as the
custom and tradition of centuries. When, therefore, the
Government of 1789 and 1793 declared that only those who
paid revenue to Government were the actual proprietors of
the land, the declaration was, on the face of it, a mere legal
fiction, and a fiction which, it was thought, was guarded
from working mischief by the simultaneous declaration that
the ryots were not to pay more than fixed money amounts
of the established pergunnah rates of rent.

11. Unfortunately the fiction proved full of harm :—

I.—Lord Hastings (*31st December 1819*)—   VIII, 7 c.

When an individual is deputed by his neighbours to bargain on their
common behalf with the Government, there is no change of relations;

CHAP. III. he is only the spokesman of the community.   *   *   *   But a new
capacity is conferred on him, if Government appoint him to be the person
with whom, year after year, it is to settle the account.   When the character
of a zemindar is assigned to him, and responsibility for the payment of
the aggre⸱⸱ ⸱⸱ rent is attached to him, Government virtually constitutes
him a pub⸱⸱ ⸱⸱officer.   It necessarily invests him with the power of compelling, from the several families of the village, the payment of their respective portions of the general contribution, and our acquaintance with the
propensities of the natives must make us sensible that such a power is
likely to be misapplied ⸱n arbitrary and unjust demands.

VIII, 7 d. 15,   II.—GOVERNMENT RESOLUTION, 22nd December 1820—
ii.

With this variety in the classes of zemindars, it can be a matter of no
surprise that very injurious consequence have followed from a system
of management under which all persons coming under engagements with
Government, and entered in the Government books as proprietors, have
often been confounded as if belonging to one class, and have frequently been considered as the absolute proprietors of the land comprised in the mehals for which they had engaged.

III.—COURT OF DIRECTORS (15th January 1819)—

VIII, 8, iii.   The Board of Revenue, in another passage of their letter, with an
express reference to these village zemindars, state that the " mistake of
making the perpetual settlement with rajahs *as the proprietors of the
whole of the lands composing their rajes,* has chiefly affected " an intermediate class, the village zemindars, to whom no compensation can now
be made for the injustice done to them by the transfer of their
property to the rajahs.   Indeed, the whole of this valuable class may
be considered to be extinct in the *Lower Provinces,* " &c., &c.

IV.—COURT OF DIRECTORS (15th January 1819)—

X, 3, i.   In the consideration of this subject it is impossible for us not
to remark that consequences the most injurious to the rights and
interests of individuals have arisen from describing those with whom
the permanent settlement was concluded as the *actual proprietors of the
land.*   This mistake (for such it is now admitted to have been), and the
habit which has grown out of it, of considering the payments of ryots as
rent instead of revenue, have produced all the evils that might have been
expected to flow from them.   They have introduced much confusion into
the whole subject of landed tenures, and have given a specious colour to
the pretensions of the zemindars, in acting towards persons of the other
classes as if they, the zemindars, really were, in the ordinary sense of
the words, the proprietors of the land, and as if the ryots had no permanent interest but what they derived from them.   *   * There can be
no doubt that a misapplication of terms, and the use of the word " rent"
as applied to the demands on the ryots, instead of the appropriate one of
" revenue," have introduced much confusion into the whole subject of
landed tenures, and have tended to the injury and destruction of the
rights of the ryots.

12. To this so baleful fiction the Government had hastily
committed itself, when it was found convenient, through

the fiction, to exempt zemindars from the jurisdiction of the CHAP. III. Supreme Court (Appendix VI, para. 12). Another object of the legal fiction is easily discerned. On the acquisition of the dewanny by the East India Company, a great number of zemindars were superseded by farmers of revenue. The dispossession of these zemindars was one of the principal "injuries and wrongs" which Parliament, in Act 24, Geo. III, Cap. 25, enjoined the Court of Directors to redress. The only complete redress was to reinstate the zemindars, and to declare that their tenure of their zemindaries was hereditary and alienable. But, as explained by Mr. Austin, in his Principles of Jurisprudence, to transmute XVIII, 14. a strictly personal privilege, such as was the zemindar's official status, into a heritable, alienable right, it was necessary to confer the right or title mediately through a fact, and the fact selected was the land in each zemindary.

13. The personal privilege thus transmuted into a herit- XVIII, 14. able alienable right did not include a right to the unearned increment, for it was that of receiving from the cultivators of land the Government's demand upon the ryot as limited, in the maximum, by the Regulations of 1793, to the established pergunnah rate, *plus abwabs* of that year, and it was limited by a strict prohibition of fresh *abwabs*. The privilege conferred was only part of what belonged to Government, *viz.*, the public tax upon the land; its bestowal on the zemindar, as a heritable alienable right, was without prejudice to the rights of cultivators or ryots, which were expressly reserved by the Government in the regulations that form the deed of the permanent settlement.

14. The zemindar can trace his heritable and alienable right of *servitus* on the ryot's holding only up to the Government grant in 1793, whereas the proprietary right of the cultivator was derived from a custom more ancient than law, and long anterior to the permanent settlement.

15. That the right conveyed to the zemindar through the legal fiction which declared him proprietor of the soil, on the strength of his being the payer, direct to Government, of the land revenue of his zemindary, was merely a *servitus*, or revenue charge on the ryots' holding, is evident, further, from the fact that there was no actual delivery of each of the XVII, 23 to ryots' holdings to the zemindar, such as would have been necessary for completion of his new title, if the proprietary rights of the ryots had been transferred in the zemindary settlement from them to the zemindar. No such confisca-

CHAP. III. tion of ryots' rights was perpetrated; accordingly, no such
— delivery was made; and accordingly the new rights vested in
the zemindar by the Regulations of 1793 were rights that
were cut off from the State's total demand upon the ryot,
as revenue (simultaneously with the State's surrender of
title to the unearned increment, and its denial thereof to the
zemindar by the prohibition of fresh *abwabs*) and were not
in supersession of the ryot's *dominium* over his holding.

CHAPTER IV.

RENT RATES ESTABLISHED BY CUSTOM.

We have seen in Chapter III that zemindars, before the permanent settlement, were officials, not proprietors of the land in their zemindaries; and that by the zemindary settlement they were constituted proprietors of the soil in a very limited technical sense, which did not trench on the rights of the ryots, and which gave them a property that was carved out of merely the Government's definitely limited share in the produce of the soil. On the other hand, it has been ascertained in Chapter II that the resident cultivators, and those non-resident cultivators who had acquired occupancy rights by long residence, were proprietors of their holdings in a sense in which *dominium* was vested in them, subject to a limited *servitus*, or rent charge to the State, through its representative zemindar.

2. A right apprehension of these two facts is essential, for they lie at the root of the rent question. If zemindars were the proprietors of the land up to the date of the permanent settlement (Regulation II of 1793 asserted XVI, 37. that "the property in the soil was never before formally declared to be vested in the zemindar"), then any increase in the value of the land, otherwise than through the agency or expense of the ryot, belonged to the zemindar. On the other hand, if the ryot was the real proprietor of the land at the date of the permanent settlement which was designed to secure to the cultivators of the soil the fruits of their own industry, then any increase in the value of the land, otherwise than through the agency or expense of the zemindar, belongs to the ryot. Chapters II and III determine the answer to these alternative questions in favour of the ryot. But one part of the subject, *viz.*, that, by the regulations of the permanent settlement, the rent payable by the ryot was permanently limited to the pergunnah rates, *plus abwabs* of that year, may be investigated in detail.

3. Authorities have been quoted in Chapter I, paras. 1 and 2, which show that the intention of the authors of the permanent settlement was to permanently limit the rent

Chap. IV. payable by the ryot; and the Regulations of 1793 are in
———. harmony with this intent.   Further quotations may be added
here :—

> I.—Lord Grenville (a member of the Board of Control, in
> 1784)—

III, 4, i & iv.   After long and apparently endless discussion on Indian politics, there
was at least one point on which all men then (1784) agreed, *viz.*, that it
was the duty, not only of the East India Company, but of the Government and the legislature, to fix the rate of revenue by which that
country was thenceforward to be governed.   *   *   He must repeat that
no system of taxation could be more detestable in any country than a tax
upon the abilities and industry of the husbandman.   This system left to
the agents of the Company all the villainous oppression of the Mahomedan Government, and imposts were levied upon the cultivators at
their discretion.   *   *   The simple question with respect to the zemindary system was, whether you would or would not say to the person on
whom you laid the tax, you shall know what the amount shall be.   The
principle of extending this system of settled taxation was what actuated
the mind of Sir Philip Francis, of Mr. Burke or Mr. Fox, and of
Mr. Pitt; it was adopted by Parliament, and makes a part of the existing
law of India.   But since this period we had acquired other provinces, and
yet it did not seem the intention of the Company to extend the principle
to them ; it was not the language of the Company, of the ministry, nor,
he was sorry to add, of the Parliament itself.   The India Company,
in one of their reports, seemed to anticipate the greatest advantage from
leaving the system unsettled, and levying the taxes according to the
increasing wealth of the districts, or even of individuals.

II.—Mr. Campbell—

IV, 5, ix.   It had been proposed by Lord Teignmouth, in Bengal, to fix the
maximum rates of the public revenue payable by the cultivators to the
zemindar at those actually assessed when the permanent settlement was
introduced, which, though confirming existing legal cesses, would at
any rate have placed a bar against further abuse, and given a precise
limitation to the Government demand.   *   *   At Madras the suggestion was strictly adopted, and the maximum rate payable by the cultivator to the zemindar on all land was limited to the actual rates levied on
the cultivated land in the single particular year which preceded the
limitation of the zemindar's own jumma to Government.

III.—Lord Cornwallis—

IV, 6, iii.   (a). A permanent settlement, *alone*, in my judgment, can make the
country flourish, and secure happiness to the body of inhabitants.

A permanent settlement for comparatively few zemindars,
with frequently revised rates for millions of ryots, could not
secure happiness " to the body of inhabitants."   Lord Cornwallis referred, perforce, to a permanent settlement extending
to the ryots.

(*b*). If Mr. Shore means that, after having declared the zemindar proprietor of the soil, in order to be consistent, we have no right to prevent his imposing new *abwabs*, or taxes, on the lands in cultivation, I must differ with him in opinion, unless we suppose the ryots to be absolute slaves of the zemindars. Every beegah of land possessed by them must have been cultivated under an expressed or implied agreement that a certain sum should be paid for each beegah of produce, and no more. Every *abwab*, or tax, imposed by the zemindar over and above that sum, is not only a breach of that agreement, *but a direct violation of the established laws of the country*. The cultivator, therefore, has in such case an undoubted right to apply to Government for the protection of his property; and Government is at all times bound to afford him redress. I do not hesitate, therefore, to give it as my opinion that the zemindars, neither now nor ever, could possess a right to impose taxes or *abwabs* upon the ryots; and if, from the confusion which prevailed towards the close of the Mogul Government, or neglect, or want of information, since we have had possession of the country, new *abwabs* have been imposed by the zemindars or farmers, the Government has an undoubted right to abolish such as are oppressive and have never been confirmed by a competent authority, and to establish such regulations as may prevent the practice of like abuses in future.

(*c*). Neither is the privilege, which the ryots in many parts of Bengal VII, 2, i. enjoy, of holding possession of the spots of land which they cultivate, so long as they pay the revenue assessed upon them, by any means incompatible with the proprietary rights of the zemindars. Whoever cultivates the land, the zemindars can receive no more than the established rent, which in most cases is fully equal to what the cultivator can afford to pay. *To permit him to dispossess one cultivator for the sole purpose of giving the land to another, would be vesting him with a power to commit a wanton act of oppression from which he could derive no benefit.*

The italics show that the established pergunnah rate was the maximum rate leviable, whoever might be the cultivator of the land, whether khoodkasht or pykasht; for it is explicitly stated that the zemindar could not gain, that is, could not get a higher rent, by ejecting one cultivator and putting in another. The passage shows unmistakably that, according to Lord Cornwallis' reading of his own permanent settlement, no zemindar could have legal power to exact higher than the pergunnah rate, even from any who might become cultivators after that settlement.

(*d*). The rents of an estate are not to be raised by the imposition of VII, 2, . new *abwabs*, or taxes, on every beegah of land in cultivation. They can only be raised (1) by inducing the ryots to cultivate the more valuable articles of produce; (2) by inducing them to clear the extensive tracts of waste land which are to be found in almost every zemindary in Bengal.

(*e*). With regard to the rates at which landed property transferred by XVI, 9, iii. public sale, in liquidation of arrears, and, it may be added, by private sale or gift, are to be assessed, I conceive that the new proprietor has a right to collect no more than what his predecessor was legally entitled to;

for the act of transfer certainly gives no sanction to illegal impositions. I trust, however, that the due enforcement of the regulations for obliging the zemindars to grant pottahs to their ryots, as proposed by Mr. Shore, will soon remove this objection to a permanent settlement. For whoever becomes a proprietor of land after these pottahs have been issued, will succeed to the tenure under the condition, and with the knowledge, *that these pottahs are to be the rules by which the rents are to be collected from the ryots.*

We saw in extract (*c*) that a change of cultivators, from khoodkasht to pykasht, would not, in Lord Cornwallis' view, entitle a zemindar to raise the rent of the latter beyond the established pergunnah rate ; and in this extract (*e*) we are told that neither could a change of zemindars qualify the new zemindar to levy more than the established pergunnah rate. Thus, the two statements guarded the pergunnah rate from enhancement, under every contingency.

(*f*). By granting perpetual leases of the lands at a fixed assessment, we shall render our subjects the happiest people in India; and we shall have reason to rejoice at the increase of their wealth and prosperity, as it will infallibly add to the strength and resources of the State.

Reading this with the context, Lord Cornwallis' meaning was clearly that a permanent assessment for the ryots would " render our subjects the happiest people in India." His Lordship never supposed that this result would ensue upon a permanent settlement with the zemindar, and a frequent enhancement of ryots' rents.

VII, 2, iii. IV.—Mr. Hodgson, Member of the Madras Board of Revenue (*26th March 1808*)—

It is declared to be inconsistent with "proprietary right" that the proprietor should be guided by any other rule than his own will in demanding his rent. * * This mode of reasoning would not, perhaps, have gained so much ground if it had been within the means of all to have obtained the perusal of the interesting discussions on the subject between the Right Hon'ble Marquis Cornwallis and Sir John Shore, the Bengal Regulations, and the proceedings of the Board at Madras, on proposing the introduction of the permanent system. It could have been distinctly seen from these documents that the first principle of the permanent settlement was to confirm and secure *the rights of the cultivators* of the soil. *To confirm and secure* are the terms which must be used, because no new rights were granted, or any doubt entertained upon the following leading features of their right, *viz.* :—

1st.—That no zemindar, proprietor (or whatever name be given to those persons), was entitled by law, custom, or usage, to make his demands for rent according to his convenience ; or, in other words—

2nd.—That the cultivators of the soil had the solid right, from time immemorial, of paying a defined rent, and no more, for the land they cultivated. This right is inherent in all the cultivators, from the most northern parts of India to Cape Comorin.

3rd.—The "proprietary right" of zemindars, in the regulations, is, therefore, no more than the right to collect from the cultivators that rent which custom has established as the right of Government; and the benefit arising from this right is confined, *first*, to an extension of the amount—not of the rate—of the customary rent by an increase of cultivation; *secondly*, to a profit on dealings in grain, where the rent may be rendered in kind; *thirdly*, to a change from an inferior to a superior kind of culture, arising out of a mutual understanding of their interest between the cultivator and proprietor.

Mr. Hodgson recorded his minute on the occasion of discussing the measures for the introduction of a permanent zemindary settlement, into the northern circars of the Madras Presidency, after he had read an exposition by the Governor General in Council of Lord Cornwallis' similar measure for Bengal. Neither the Governor General nor the Court of Directors impugned the correctness of Mr. Hogdson's statement of the objects of the permanent settlement,—a statement which was implicitly followed in fixing permanently the ryot's rent in the permanently settled zemindary tracts in the Madras Presidency.

V.—MILL'S HISTORY OF BRITISH INDIA— VII, 13, vi.

It is wonderful that neither Lord Cornwallis nor his masters, either in the India House or the Treasury, saw that between one part of his regulations, and the effects which he expected from another, there was an irreconcilable contradiction. He required that fixed unalterable pottahs should be given to the ryots; that is, that they should pay a rent which could never be increased, and occupy a possession from which, paying that rent, they could never be displaced.

The historian of British India took the same view as the Madras Government of the permanent zemindary settlement in Bengal, *viz.*, that it was designed to fix permanently the ryot's rent, so that, like the zemindar's, it should be unalterable for ever.

VI.—COURT OF DIRECTORS (*15th January 1819*)— X, 11, iii.

The original pottah regulation (VIII of 1793) was also very materially defective, in making no sufficient provision for the ascertainment of the rights in which it professed to secure the ryots by their pottahs. It was of much more importance for the security of the ryot to establish what the legitimate rates of the pergunnah were, according to the customs of the country, or at all events to have ascertained the rates actually existing, and to have caused a record of them in either case to be carefully preserved, than merely to enjoin the exchange of engagements between them and the zemindars, leaving in total uncertainty the rules by which those engagements were to be formed. It is true that to have taken the rates at which the ryots were actually

CHAP. IV. assessed by the zemindars, at the period of the permanent settlement, as
the maximum of future demands, would have had the effect, as Mr. Shore
observed in one of his minutes, of confirming subsisting abuses and
oppressions ; but it would, at least, have fixed a limit to them.

The Court clearly understood that the Regulations of
1793 made the pergunnah rate of that day the maximum of
future demand.

VII.—BENGAL GOVERNMENT (*1st August 1822*)—

X, 12, i c.   We freely, indeed, admit that, even though the ryots of Bengal had
possessed no right of holding their lands at determinate rates, considered
in their relation to the Sovereign, it was unquestionably competent to the
Government, in fixing its own demands, to fix also the rates at which the
malguzar was to make his collections ; and it was, we think, clearly
intended to render perpetual the rates existing at the time of the
perpetual settlement. The intention being declared, the rule is of course
obligatory on the zemindars.

X, 3, id.   VIII. MR. COLEBROOKE asserts from his own experience that disputes between zemindars and ryots, in the Lower Provinces, were less
frequent and more easily determined anterior to 1793 than they now
are ;—and he further states that "the provisions contained in the general
regulations for the permanent settlement, designed for the protection of
ryots or tenants, are rendered wholly nugatory," and that "the courts
of justice, for want of definite information respecting their rights, are
unable effectually to support them. I am disposed, therefore," he adds,
"to recommend that, late as it now is, measures should be taken for the
re-establishment of fixed rates, as nearly conformable to the anciently
established ones as may be practicable, to regulate distinctly and definitely the relative rights of the landlord and tenantry."

There was thus a general agreement, among those who
were in a position to know, that it was intended by the
permanent settlement to fix permanently the assessment payable by the ryot as well as the rent payable by the zemindar ;
and this intention was affirmed as well in minutes recorded
before the settlement, by its authors, as in other minutes or
despatches by those who wrote after the Regulations of 1793.

4. The fifteen Judges of the High Court, in the Great
Rent Case, thought differently indeed from the earlier
authorities, who, two generations nearer to the facts of 1793,
had held that the permanent settlement of that year was
designed as a permanent settlement for the ryot. It would
be strange if an examination of the Regulations of 1793 did
not confirm the testimony of the earlier authorities.

XIX, 10.   5. Sir George Campbell noticed that in those Regulations no provision was made for enhancing ryots' rents on
XX, 16. account of a rise of prices. He missed the obvious inference
that as zemindars had no power, until 1793, to raise ryots'

rents beyond rates sanctioned by Government, so the omission, in the Regulations of that year, to arm them with a new power of enhancing rent showed unmistakably that the Government intended that the established pergunnah rate of rent as existing in 1793 should not be enhanced. On this point it may, firstly, suffice to refer to the abundant testimony in Appendix XVI, para. 3, that anything beyond the rates established by long usage, and the amounts sanctioned by Government, was not demandable from the ryots, and could be levied only by oppression or as an exaction. Secondly, a citation from the Report of the Select Committee of Secrecy appointed by the House of Commons to enquire into the state of the East India Company in 1773, may be reproduced here from Appendix XVI, para. 35, I—

And Mr. Verelst informed your Committee that, by the ancient rule of Government, agreements with the ryots for lands, which they and their families have held, were considered as sacred, and that they were not to be removed from their possession as long as they conformed to the terms of their original contracts;—but that this rule had not always been observed. And your Committee having enquired whether the rajas, zemindars, farmers, or collectors, have a right to levy any duties, or augment the old ones by their own authority, they find that they have no such right:—though the books and correspondence of the Company afford many instances of the country having been exceedingly distressed by additional taxes levied by the zemindar, farmer, or contractor, but not so much by the two former as by the latter. And Mr. Verelst informed your Committee that the Government *have a right to call upon them for everything so collected*, and that they have been called to an account, since the Company held the Dewanee, in several instances.

The passage in italics, which shows that whatever the zemindar levied in excess of the dues sanctioned by law or by Government was exaction, was closely followed in Regulation VIII of 1793. Section LIV of that Regulation enjoined that the dues payable by each ryot should be consolidated in one specific sum, and that "no actual proprietor of land, &c., shall impose any new *abwab* or *mahtoot* upon the ryots, under any pretence whatever. Every exaction of this nature shall be punished by a penalty equal to three times the amount imposed; and if, at any future period, it may be discovered that new *abwab* or *mahtoot* have been imposed, the person imposing the same *shall be liable to this penalty for the entire period of such impositions*," as in the instances cited in the Report of the Select Committee of 1773.

6. The facts we note here are :—

1st.—As reported by the Select Committee of 1773, and

CHAP. IV. until the permanent settlement, zemindars had no power to
levy from ryots more than the established pergunnah rate of
rent, as sanctioned by custom, *plus* State *abwabs*, as sanctioned by Government.

2nd.—Whatever the zemindars levied in excess was
exaction, and they were liable to refund the whole of such
exaction for the full period of its levy.

3rd.—The regulations of the permanent settlement
directed that the pergunnah rates established by custom,
and the State *abwabs*, should be consolidated for each ryot
in one sum, and entered in his pottah as the sole amount
recoverable from him for his holding.

4th.—Those regulations contain no provision enabling the
zemindar to enhance ryots' rents beyond the amount stated
in the preceding section; any such new power would have
been a departure from established custom. On the contrary,
whereas the old form of enhancement, without prejudice to
the pergunnah rate, was by *abwabs*, the Regulations of 1793
expressly prohibited the levy of any fresh *abwabs*, and (as
in 1773 to 1793) they held the zemindar liable to refund
thrice the amount of any exactions for the whole period
of their levy.

5th.—The conclusion seems irresistible that as zemindars
had no power before 1793, and were not armed with any
power by the Regulations of 1793, to raise ryots' rents beyond the established pergunnah rates,—as the pottah containing mention of the money amount of those rates was the sole
rule or voucher of the amount recoverable from the ryot,—
and as the separate levy of fresh *abwabs* was prohibited,—
the Regulations of 1793 did unmistakably provide that the
rent of the ryot should not be increased beyond the ancient
customary pergunnah rates existent in 1793, *plus* State
abwabs of that year. The authorities cited in Chapter I
and in para. 3 of this Chapter, confirm this conclusion.

7. Discussions in the present day on the Rent Question
in Bengal are concerned more with persons, or the several
classes of ryots, than with a uniform assessment on land,
no matter who occupies it. In this respect the assessment
upon ryots in Bengal differs (and the difference is serious)
from the assessment in the ryotwar districts of the Madras
and Bombay Presidencies. In those districts the assessment
is laid upon the land, no matter who cultivates it. This
precisely was what the author of the permanent settlement
XVI, 4, iii. Sir Philip Francis, designed for Bengal. In his minute of

1776 he "considered that the rate of assessment per beegah should be fixed for ever upon the land, no matter who might be the occupant." And the Regulations of 1793 faithfully followed Sir Philip Francis on this point. They XVI, 16. prescribed, as a general rule, what is now and has always been the rule in ryotwari provinces, *viz.*, that the rate of assessment for the ryot should be fixed upon the land, irrespective of the persons who cultivate it. This general rate was fixed at the pergunnah rate established by custom for each locality; and the rate established by custom was immutable for the particular class of land, and particular kind of special produce of the soil. The exceptions from this general rate, in favour of persons, were only two,—the one a permanent, the other a temporary exception. The permanent exception was in favour of those khoodkasht ryots who had held, for three years before the decennial settlement, at rates lower than the pergunnah rates, and the hereditary successors of these ancient khoodkashts in these excepted holdings. The temporary exception was in favour of pykasht ryots (until the expiration of their leases) and the cultivators of newly reclaimed waste lands (until the expiration of the term for which privileged rates may have been allowed to them as an inducement to cultivate). Practically, the tendency of the principle of assessment established by the Regulations of 1793, for ryots, old and new, was to bring the whole body of cultivators under the ancient established pergunnah rates as maximum permanent rates of rent.

8. We have seen (para. 3, IIIc and *e*) that, with regard to lands under cultivation in 1789, neither change of ryots nor change of zemindars afforded opportunity for enhancing beyond the established pergunnah rate of rent. And as regards new cultivation since 1789, there was no warrant in the Regulations of 1793, or in later Regulations down to 1859, for exceeding that established rate. By the law and constitution of India, as existing in 1765, which Parliament enjoined should be respected, the cultivators in a village were entitled to reclaim land from waste, subject to payment, eventually, of not more than the established pergunnah XV, 9. rate. This custom was not interrupted by the permanent XV, 5, i. settlement; for the Regulations of 1793 provided that the Civil Courts should settle disputes between zemindars and ryots in accordance with custom, and Regulation IV of 1794 XVI, 13, d. 2. expressly enacted that among others the cultivators of

CHAP. IV. waste lands should receive a renewal of their pottahs at not
XV, 4, iv. more than the established rates of the pergunnah for lands
of the same quality and description. In January 1819 the
Court of Directors pointed out that "it is the opinion of
many considerable authorities that on the leases of waste,
as well as of other lands, the pergunnah rates form a standard not to be exceeded." This custom, by which the cultivators of waste land were protected from paying more than
the established pergunnah rate, negatives the pretensions of
zemindars to raise the rents of those who became ryots after
1793, seeing that the custom was perpetuated by the Regulations of that year.

9. And as with new lands so with new ryots, the Regu-
XVI, 14 & lations of 1793 made no distinction between new and old,
15. save to protect new ryots from enhancement to the level
of the pergunnah rate during the currency of any lease
existent at the time of the permanent settlement, which may
XVI, 24. have secured to them a lower rate.

10. Thus, under the Regulations of 1793, the established
customary pergunnah rate was the eventual rate for old lands
or new, for resident cultivators or non-resident, excepting
the comparatively few who held at favoured rates. This
pergunnah rate continued, in law, the standard maximum
rate from 1793 to 1859; as such it was recognised in the Sale
XVI, 13 c. & Laws, and in those relating to distraint and the collection of
29, II. the revenue: thus—

I. Regulations XLIV of 1793, XX of 1795, VII of 1799,
VIII of 1819, prescribed that a person acquiring an estate by
purchase at a public sale for arrears of revenue, or in execution of a decree of court, or at a private sale, could not raise
the rent of any ryot above the established pergunnah rates,
or beyond the lower amount fixed in any unexpired engagement with the original proprietor, if the estate was bought
at a sale for arrears of revenue, or with the vendor, if bought
from him at any other sale.

XVIII, 24.   II. Regulation XI of 22nd November 1822, which was
passed to correct alleged defects in previous regulations, "inasmuch as they do not * * * define with sufficient precision
and accuracy the nature of the interest and title conveyed to
the persons purchasing estates sold for arrears of revenue,"
recognised, as the maximum rate of assessment, that demandable "according to the custom of the pergunnah, mouzah, or
other local division." In another section (XXXIII) the
maximum rents were spoken of as "fixed rents, or rents

determinable by fixed rules, according to the law and usage CHAP. IV.
of the country."

11. Of course it was too late in the day, in 1822,[1] for the
Government to attempt to alter a regulation of the *permanent settlement* of 1793, which restrained zemindars from exacting more than the established pergunnah rate from ryots;
but it is satisfactory to find that no new standard of rent was
set up in 1822; the ancient usage of the country continued to
determine the rate.

12. It has indeed been contended (by Sir Barnes Peacock XX, 9, iii.
among others) that Regulation V of 1812 abrogated the law
of 1793, respecting ryots' rents, and empowered the zemindars
to grant to all ryots, old and new, excepting certain protected
ryots, leases at any rent that might be specifically agreed
upon between them. But the contention is not of any worth,
for various reasons, *viz.*—

I. As regards ryots, this part of Regulation V of 1812 XVIII, 19 to
was practically inoperative; it could come into force only 24.
on mutual agreements between the zemindar and the other
parties; but the British Indian Association testified in 1859
that even so late as that year fifteen-sixteenths of the ryots
held without pottahs. Moreover, the latitude which the
Regulation gave related to the period of the lease, and a
subsequent Regulation, which legislated about the rent payable under Regulation V of 1812, was restricted to the rents
payable by *middlemen;*—such rents alone were matters of
contract between zemindar and tenant.

II. If the Regulation of 1812 rescinded the most essential
safeguard of ryots' rights in the Regulations of 1793, then
nineteen years old, it was *ultra vires;* if any power could
thus abrogate an essential safeguard of ryots' rights under
the permanent settlement, such power was equally competent
to annul the settlement with zemindars.

III. The Regulation of 1812 did not rescind any part of
the Regulations of 1793, which limited the demand upon ryots
to the established pergunnah rates, for, in that very year, the
Select Committee of 1812, which wrote the Fifth Report, was
reporting that unheard-of rights had been given to the zemindars, and that ryots' rights needed protection. The Government in 1812 would not have flown in the face of the Select
Committee of that year by passing a law empowering zemindars to levy whatever rent they liked from ryots.

---

[1] Alas! not of course, for the thing was done in 1859.

Chap. IV.
XVIII, 23.   IV. As pointed out by Mr. Justice Morgan, " these Regulations of 1812 were no part of the permanent settlement; " and, moreover, as shown in Appendix XVIII, paragraphs 19 to 23, the provisions respecting rent in the Regulations of 1812 referred to the rents paid by middlemen; the Regulation did
XVIII, 24. not abrogate any safeguard of ryots' rents. In section XXXII, Regulation XI of 1822, it was stated that nothing in section 9, Regulation V of 1812, was intended "in any respect to annul or diminish the title of the ryots to hold their land subject to the payment of fixed rents, or rents determinable by fixed rules, according to the law and usage of the country."

13. Again, it has been held that the Sale Law, Act XII of 1841, empowered purchasers of estates at sales for arrears of revenue to enhance at discretion the rents of any middlemen or ryots, saving certain excepted classes. But for various reasons this contention does not prove that zemindars became entitled to enhance the rents of ryots generally beyond the established pergunnah rates. For—

I. If the Government in 1841 could thus raise ryots' rents beyond the established pergunnah rates which had been assured to them in the permanent settlement of 1793, they were competent, and, in justice to the tax-payers in British India, were even bound, to similarly raise the rents of zemindars, by reason of the extra income thus accruing to
XVIII, 31 to them from enhancement of rents beyond the established
33. rates, which were alone taken into account in the fixing of their assessment in 1793.

II. The status of ryots on estates which were not sold under Act XII of 1841 was not affected by that Act; and even on estates sold under the Act, the status of ryots
XVIII, 25 to remained unaffected if the auction-purchaser did not, within
28. a reasonable period, exercise his right to enhance rents in accordance with the law.

III. Furthermore, the power conferred on auction-purchasers (not on zemindars generally) by Act XII of 1841 of enhancing rents at discretion was restricted to the rents of middlemen; all resident cultivators or khoodkasht ryots were within the classes who were protected from enhancement,
XVIII, 29. as shown in detail in paras. 25 to 28 of Appendix XVIII.

14. A detailed examination of the Sale Laws shows that until 1859 they recognised the established pergunnah rate as the maximum of rent recoverable from ryots. As the avowed theory of the Sale Laws was to place the auction-

purchaser in the same position as the original engager in Chap. IV. 1793 for the Government revenue,—as auction-purchasers of zemindaries, in the present day, pay on their estates the same amount of rent which was fixed for those estates in 1793,— and as the resources of the estates have increased since by the cultivation of waste lands,—there could, on the theory of the Sale Laws, have been neither reason nor equity in subjecting ryots to enhancement of rent beyond the established pergunnah rates of 1793, which were assured to them in the permanent settlement.

15. The conclusion we arrive at is, that until 1793 the zemindars were not entitled to raise ryots' rents beyond the established pergunnah rates, *plus* State *abwabs*; that the Regulations of 1793 did not confer on them any such power, but, on the contrary, restrained them from exacting from ryots more than the established pergunnah rates, *plns* State *abwabs* of that year; and that from 1793 to 1859 the law recognised no other than the established pergunnah rate, according to the usage of the country, as the maximum rent recoverable from ryots.

16. We have seen, also, that the authorities who framed, or who carried out, the permanent settlement, and others who were in a position to know, understood that a permanent settlement with the ryot was a part of the plan of the settlement of 1793. We have accordingly to consider now whether there inhered in the ancient established pergunnah rate, existent in 1793, any element of change through the working of which that ancient customary rate could have been altered, to the ryot's prejudice, without a breach of the law which, in 1793, limited the demand on him to the established pergunnah rate, and which, down to 1859, recognised that rate as the maximum recoverable from him.

CHAPTER V

PERMANENT PERGUNNAH RATES OF RENT.

CHAP. V.   Lord Cornwallis, in the regulations of the permanent
settlement, framed (Chap. IV, para. 5) the sections which
prohibited the levy of fresh *abwabs*, upon the Report of the
Select Committee of Secrecy appointed in 1773 by the House
of Commons to enquire into the state of the East India Company. His Lordship followed an earlier model in his determination that the pottah should guide the payment of rent
by the ryŏt to the zemindar. On the 16th August 1769, the
President and Select Committee wrote :—

XVI, 4, i.   For the ryot being eased and secured from all burthens and demands
but what are imposed by the legal authority of Government itself, and
future pottahs being granted him specifying that demand, he should be
taught that he is to regard the same as a sacred and inviolable pledge.
to him that he is liable to no demand beyond their amount. There
can, therefore, be no pretence for suits on that account—no room for
inventive rapacity to practise its usual arts.

The ryot, too, should be impressed in the most forcible and convincing manner * * that our object is not the increase of rents or
the accumulation of demands, * * but to secure him from all further
invasions of his property.

2. Lord Cornwallis, Sir John Shore, and the Regulations
of 1793, proceeded on this model.

I.—LORD CORNWALLIS—

XVI, 9, iii.   (See extract in Chapter IV, para. 3, III*e*) "whoever becomes a
proprietor of land after these pottahs have been issued, will succeed to
the tenure under the condition, and with the knowledge, *that these
pottahs are to be the rules by which the rents are to be collected from the ryots.*
By granting perpetual leases of the lands at a fixed assessment we shall
render our subjects the happiest people in India.

X, 6, ii.   It is with pleasure we acquaint you (Court of Directors) that
throughout the greater part of the country specific agreements have
been exchanged between the landholders and the ryots, and that where
these writings have not been entered into the landholders have bound
themselves to prepare and deliver them by fixed periods. We shall
here only observe that under the new arrangements to which we shall
presently advert, the ryots will *always* have it in their power to compel
an adherence to these agreements by an appeal to the Courts of Justice
whenever the landholders may attempt to infringe them.

II.—Sir John Shore—

When the jumma of a ryot has been ascertained and settled, he shall be authorised to demand a pottah from the zemindar, or person acting under his authority, &c., and any refusal to deliver the pottah shall be punished by fine proportioned to the expense and trouble of the ryot in obtaining it. That the zemindar be not authorised to impose any new *abwab* or *muthote*, on any pretence whatever, upon the ryots.

III.—Regulation VIII of 1793—

The impositions upon the ryots, under the denominations of *abwab*, *mahtoot*, and other appellations, from their number and uncertainty, having become intricate to adjust, and a source of oppression to the ryots, all proprietors of land and dependant talookdars shall revise the same in concert with the ryots, and consolidate the whole with the *assul* in one specific sum. "The work to be completed for the whole of the lands in the zemindaries" by the end of the Bengali year 1198 in Bengal districts, and of the Fusli and Wullaity year 1198[1] in the Behar and Orissa districts, these being the periods fixed for the delivery of pottahs, as hereafter specified. No actual proprietor of land, &c., shall impose any new *abwab* or *mahtoot* upon the ryots, under any pretence whatever.

3. From these extracts in paras. 1 and 2 we gather:—

I. The President and Select Committee of 1769 considered that the pottah to be issued to the ryot would be a sacred and inviolable pledge to him of the amount of rent permanently payable by him, so as "to secure him from all further invasions of his property."

II. Lord Cornwallis regarded the pottah in the same light. "Whoever becomes proprietor of the land after these pottahs are issued, they will be the sole rule for the recovery of rents from the ryots."

III. Sir John Shore, in the same spirit, required, for ensuring the permanency of the rent, that the amount payable by the ryot for his holding should be entered in the pottah in one consolidated sum. This form of stating the rent precluded its increase from a rise of prices.

IV. The regulations of the decennial settlement enjoined the delivery to the ryots by 1792 of pottahs stating in one specific sum for each holding the amount payable by the ryot, and simultaneously prohibited the levy of fresh *abwabs*, the only form of impost by which increase of rent beyond the ancient established pergunnah rate had been levied till then on account of a rise of prices.

V. Thus, one and all of these authorities indicated that the ryot's rent, as entered in the pottah in a specific consol-

---

[1] Christian year 1792.

Chap. V. idated sum, was to be the permanent rent; also, that it was to be an extra security to the ryot of that right of property in his holding which existed independently of the pottah.

VI. And as the period fixed for the delivery of pottahs was the year 1792, it was a part of the new zemindary settlement, with its bestowal on zemindars of, till then, unheard-of privileges, that the rent payable by ryots should, before the proclamation of the permanent settlement, have been recorded in pottahs, without power to zemindars to increase the rent thereafter on any pretence whatever.

VII. With a rent thus permanently fixed, first, for the ryot, a proclamation of the zemindars as actual proprietors of the soil could not have involved any encroachment upon ryots' rights. The zemindar's property would have been carved out of the Government's (outside the ryot's fixed) share of the produce of the soil.

XVI, 32 & 33. VIII. This was the intent of the authors of the permanent settlement; and with the execution of this intent there could not have been any confiscation of rights of ryots.

4. Thus, and from the extracts in Chapter IV, para. 3, it is evident that the amount of established pergunnah rate of rent, *plus abwabs* of 1793, imposed on the ryot by the Regulations of that year, was a permanent rent, which was to remain fixed at that amount for ever, exactly in the same way as the rent payable by the zemindar.

XVI, 24 to 27. 5. It was, too, in the nature of a pergunnah rate established by ancient custom, that it should not be liable to increase. It is the practice of the majority which determines custom; and the great majority of the cultivators were the khoodkashts, who paid the maximum pergunnah rates; 1*stly*, it was not to their interest to vary the custom by consenting to higher rates; 2*ndly*, the pykasht ryots, or non-resident cultivators, were enjoying less than the pergunnah rate, with liability to enhancement up to that rate, and no higher;—it was clearly against their interest to pay more than the pergunnah rate; 3*rdly*, the cultivators of land newly reclaimed from waste had the advantage of favourable rates to induce them to cultivate;—they, too, were assured by immemorial custom of immunity from more than the pergunnah rate, and it was not their interest to conform to a still higher rate.

6. Or, as stated in Appendix XX, para. 15, v:—In 1793, and for the several generations during which the pergunnah rates had acquired the sanctity of ancient custom, there was

a competition of zemindars for ryots; the *custom* of the pergunnah rate was necessarily imposed, therefore, by the ryots,
who were in myriads; not by the zemindars, who were few.
The latter could not create the custom; the former, perforce, would not destroy it. The resident cultivators had
a right to take up land in their own village at the customary
rate, and non-resident cultivators were attracted to the
village only by less than the customary rate. The zemindars,
too, were not entitled to raise the pergunnah rate, either
under the custom till 1793, or under the Regulations of that
year. Where, thus, there was no way of enhancement of the
pergunnah rate, unless through violence or oppression by
the zemindar, it was natural that the Regulations of 1793
should treat the pergunnah rate as permanent.

7. But the authors of the permanent settlement did not
rely for the permanent continuance of the pergunnah rate
at its amount in 1793 solely on the consideration that the
ryots, who determined the custom which fixed the rate,
would not raise the rate over their own heads. There was
a further well-conceived security, if only the pottah regulation had been carried out, namely, that the several dues of
the ryot should be consolidated in one demand, and be converted into a money amount of rent for the ryots' holding,
which specific sum should be entered in the pottah as the
amount thereafter payable by the ryot. So concerned were
the authors of the settlement to reduce the entry in the pottah XVI, 17.
to a fixed amount of money, that even in the case of a rotation of crops, where the rent varied each year with the crop,
they counted upon the zemindar and ryot coming to an
agreement for entering in the pottah the amount of annual
average rent for the whole term of the rotation of crops, as
the rent permanently payable by the ryot.

8. Money rents had prevailed in Bengal at least from XX, 15.
the time of Akbar, and it is of the nature of a money rent,
when it is fixed for even several years, only, that it ceases to
represent the value of a fixed proportion of the year's produce. Where such fixed proportion of the produce is taken
as rent at the current price, the amount taken varies yearly
with the quantity of produce and with the market price; that
is, the risks of bad seasons and of low prices are shared by
the zemindar. Where, however, rent is fixed at an amount of
money which does not vary from year to year, its character
is changed; it ceases to be a fixed proportion of the produce
of each season, and in course of time, as prices alter, it

CHAP. V. represents less and less the old proportion of the yearly produce in days when the rent was taken in kind and was commuted at the current price of the year. At the same time rent payable for a number of years, at a fixed amount of money, is not liable to enhancement from a rise, or to reduction from a fall, of prices. Hence, the enactment in the Regulations of 1793, that the ryot's rent should be entered in a pottah, in a specific amount of money, and that this amount alone should be recoverable, thereafter, from him, implied that the rent did not represent the value of a fixed proportion of the produce, and that it was not liable to increase on account of a rise of prices ; in short, it implied that the proportion of the produce belonging to the zemindar should vary inversely with the rise or fall of prices ;—the assumption which underlies the reasoning of the fourteen judges in the Great Rent Case was in the teeth of this clear inference from the fact that, from a time long prior to the British rule, money rents prevailed in Bengal, and from the condition imposed on the zemindars in 1793, with their other obligations, that they should clearly specify in pottahs the fixed money amounts of rents payable by the ryots. In other words, the Regulations of 1793 provided a permanent settlement for the ryot, when they limited the demand upon him to the established pergunnah rate of rent, *plus abwabs* of 1793,—required the consolidation of these dues in a specific amount of money,—and directed the insertion of this amount in a pottah which was to be the sole guide, standard, or instrument, for the recovery of rent from the ryot.

9. Having ascertained *1st*, in Chapter IV, that the established pergunnah rate of rent constituted, from 1793 to 1859, the maximum rent payable by the ryot, and *2nd*, in this Chapter, para. 4, that the custom on which rested the established pergunnah rate was not varied by ryots raising the rent over their own heads, while zemindars had no legal power of raising it; *3rdly*, that the pottah and other Regulations of 1793 prescribed a permanent assessment for the ryot,—it follows that the legal status of the ryot from 1793 to 1859 was one of immunity from enhancement of rent beyond the pergunnah rate of 1793, *plus abwabs* of that year. The ryot's actual position was indeed different from his legal status, owing partly to the inefficiency of the police, the corruption of the courts, the weakness of the executive, but principally to the wrong-doings of zemindars. But as XVI, 32. no man should be allowed to profit by his own wrong, both

zemindar and Government are bound to accept the legal CHAP. V.
status, instead of the actual condition, of the ryot from 1793
to 1859. That status, as we have seen, was one of immunity
from enhancement of the rate of rent which obtained in
1793.

10. It follows that two capital errors pervaded, respectively, the legislation of 1859 and the decision of the fourteen
judges of the Full Bench of the High Court in the Great
Rent Case in 1865; *1st*, the provisions in Act X of 1859
which enabled a zemindar, on certain grounds specified in
the Act, to enhance generally the rents in his zemindary
beyond the ancient established pergunnah rates, were a
violation of the permanent settlement with the ryot; *2nd*,
the fourteen judges in 1865 based their judgment on the XX, 18 & 19.
assumption that the money amount of rent paid by the
ryot represented the value of a fixed proportion of the produce of the soil, and that accordingly, the ryot was liable to
pay an increased rent, on account of an ascertained rise of
prices, in the proportion which the new scale of prices bore
to the old scale. This assumption, we have seen, was at
variance with the Regulations of 1793; and this fundamental
error vitiated the ruling of the fourteen judges, which, thus
wrong in law, has also proved unworkable in practice.

CHAPTER VI.

PERMANENT SETTLEMENT BROKEN IN 1859.

The Regulations of 1793, adhering to the intentions of the authors of the permanent settlement, prescribed a permanent assessment for ryots; the legislators of 1859, on the other hand, laid down rules for a general enhancement of ryots' rents to amounts known to be beyond the ancient established rates which existed in 1793. How was this change brought about? and that too by legislators who were so very well pleased with their own benevolence towards the ryots, that they broke out into a chorus of self-gratulation, while one of them assured the author of Act X of 1859

XIX, 20, iii. that "The Bill, if passed, would benefit all those who in this country were connected with the land; that is, it would benefit about thirty millions of people. That was a pleasant thought for the Honorable Member to put under his pillow and go to sleep upon in a snug little room in the old country." Judging by results, however, uneasy must lie the head which wears a crown made up from Act X of 1859.

XI, 15. 2. The wide departure in 1859 from the legislation of 1793 is easily explained; in that long interval of lawlessness, zemindars, gomashtahs, and middlemen, had been educating their rulers, by teaching them, as they had also taught the ryots, the uselessness of kicking against the pricks. The lesson was conveyed through oppression of the ryots. Oppression marches with no halting steps, and that practised with the help of *Huftum* and *Punjum*, of a corrupt police, and of corrupt subordinates in the civil and criminal courts, was high-handed; but still the lesson, though readily learnt by and deeply impressed upon the ryots, was more slowly apprehended by the Government. The education by zemindars, &c., of their rulers was more gradual; the murmurings of the unquiet conscience of the rulers, on account of broken pledges to ryots, were not silenced until one generation had passed away, giving place to another of a more docile disposition, that is, more disposed to acquiesce in accomplished facts which it had not helped to bring about. Thus:—

I.—Mr. Colebrooke (1812).—

X, 3, id. I am disposed, therefore, to recommend that, late as it now is, measures should be taken for the re-establishment of fixed rates, as nearly conformable to the anciently established ones as may be yet practicable, CHAP. VI. to regulate distinctly and definitely the relative rights of the landlord and tenantry.

II.—BENGAL GOVERNMENT (*1st August 1822*)—

It was, we think, clearly intended to render perpetual the rates X, 12, i. existing at the time of the perpetual settlement. The intention being declared, the rule is of course obligatory on the zemindars.   *   *   *

We are not insensible to the disadvantages of fixing rates, though the perpetual adjustment of them might still of course leave rents to vary; but our conviction certainly is, that the custom of the country gives to the ryots rights limiting the right of Government, and that the rights so possessed could not be set aside by the supreme authority without the imputation of injustice.

III.—COURT'S REPLY TO PRECEDING (*10th November 1824*)—

It is in the highest degree important that your design of adjusting the rights and interests of the ryots in the villages as perfectly in the Lower as in the Upper Provinces should be carried into effect. The doubts we have expressed as to the sufficiency of the Collector's agency will receive from you a due degree of attention.   *   * Should you succeed in securing to the ryots those rights which it was assuredly the intention of the permanent settlement to preserve and maintain, and should you, in all cases where the nature and extent of those rights cannot now be satisfactorily ascertained and fixed, provide such a limit to the demand upon the ryot as fully to leave them the cultivator's profits, under leases of considerable length, we should hope the interests of that great body of the agricultural community may be satisfactorily secured.

3. In the next generation all this was forgotten; the high-handed oppression by zemindars (Appendices IV, VII, X, and XI),—continued for more than fifty years,—had deeply impressed the Government with their power, insomuch that if any members of the Government wrote law with a big L, like Sir George Campbell, still, like him, they had more respect XX, 16. for the zemindar's power than trust in the power of the law. As observed by Sir George Campbell, the powerful zemindar "could do much without law;" and Sir Frederick Halliday began the correspondence which issued in Act X of 1859 by quoting, with approval, for its applicability to XIX, 20, i. the Lower Provinces generally, the testimony of a district officer: "The curse of this district is the insecure nature of the ryot's land tenure. The cultivator, though nominally protected by regulations of all sorts, has practically no rights in the soil. His rent is continually raised; he is oppressed and worried by every successive tickadar, until he is actually forced out of his holding, and driven to take shelter in the Nepal Terai."

CHAP. IV.   4. The discussion began thus with deep sympathy for the ryot; but past official correspondence, of the tenor of that of the extracts in paragraph 2, was clean forgotten, and had dropped out of the official mind. Mr. Sconce, with a sagacity in which he stood alone among his contemporaries, did indeed write :—

XIX, 18, ii *g.*   " We offend utterly against the broadest and deepest justice, and considering the character and operation of the permanent settlement, I will even say against our constitutional law, if we depreciate and sink out of sight the rights and property of resident cultivators, and elevate at their expense mere middlemen invested with power to absorb as increasing rent whatever substantial profit the land and labour of the ryot and improving markets may in the progress of time yield. It cannot be our deliberate purpose that the jumma of everybody should be fixed, but the jumma of the khoodkasht ryot; that the sudder jumma should be perpetually unalterable, and so the jumma of a talukdar, and the jumma of one or more in succession to him, and yet that season by season, like a ripe fruit, the ryot should be pecked at till the stone be bared."

5. Mr. Sconce thus went to the root of the matter; but even he seemed not to know the strong support which he could have found for his views in the extracts which have been cited in this and preceding chapters, from writings of the authors of the permanent settlement, and of authorities who were in a position to know that the purpose of that settlement was to ensure the same permanency for the assessment of the ryot as for that of the zemindar. Certainly the statement of this fact lost nothing in strength or point, as it flowed from Mr. Sconce's pen: the utter failure of the purpose of the authors of the permanent settlement, and the complete subversion of the grounds on which they had justified and enforced the alienation of what has proved to be some millions sterling of public revenue, cannot be more pointedly stated than in Mr. Sconce's remark that the Regulations of 1793 have resulted in fixing a permanent assessment for the zemindar, and for several grades of middlemen, but not for the ryot. A permanent settlement which was designed to extend and improve cultivation, and to promote the happiness of millions of the people, has fixed permanently the assessment of the zemindars and of numerous middlemen, who have successively pecked at the cultivators or ryots, but it has left the cultivators' rents unsettled and subject to incessant enhancement.

6. As already observed, no one followed Mr Sconce in discussing the important issue which he raised of a per-

manent settlement for the ryot : no one enquired whether Chap. **VI.**
the faith of Government had not been pledged to the ryot
in 1793 to give him such a settlement; and no one seemed XIX, 25.
to be aware that this pledge and obligation of Government
had been distinctly recognised by later Governments as one
of the unfulfilled but bounden duties of the State, in which
the honour and good name of English rule were con- X, I, iv *a*.
cerned. X, I, vii.

7. The subject was settled in a spirit of compromise;
Huftum and *Punjum* were to be repealed; the police was to
be reformed, more deputy magistrates were to be appointed,
so as to bring justice nearer to the poor. The underlings in
the courts were not, as yet, to be reformed; but still it was
hoped that much would be done to deprive the zemindars, &c.,
of facilities of high-handed oppression. At the same time,
the enhancing of rents, whether directly or in the form of
abwabs, had become a second nature for middlemen and
zemindars' gomashtahs, and they were allowed, therefore, to
obtain their old excitement, but in a more legitimate way,
under colour of a new-fangled law, which the legislators
had to borrow from the temporarily-settled North-Western
Provinces. In those provinces, when the zemindar's rent
is raised in proportion to a rise of prices, perforce his
ryots' rents must be raised in the same proportion, to enable him to pay his new rent. But this consideration was
wholly inapplicable in the Lower Provinces, where the
zemindar's rent is not subject to enhancement from a rise
of prices. The regulations of the permanent settlement
fixed the zemindar's rent for ever, at the amount paid in
1793; and in limiting, simultaneously, the rent payable
by the ryot, to the pergunnah rate of 1793, they consistently withheld from the zemindar a power which he had
not till then enjoyed, of raising ryots' rents beyond the
pergunnah rate, on account of a rise of prices, seeing that
his own rent was not to be raised on that account.

8. When once the idea was entertained of a compromise,
that is, a compromise of the rights of ryots whose voice was
not heard in the Legislative Council, the legal status of the
ryot from 1793 to 1859 was put aside, and scope was
afforded to legislators to let their ideas run riot, about the
fitness of things.

I. The author of the Bill led the way of departure
from the compact with the ryots in the permanent settlement. The Regulations of 1793 prescribed that the ryot

CHAP. VI.
——
XVI, 13 d.
XVI, 14, iii
and iv.
should not pay as rent more than (variously) (1) the established pergunnah rate (2) according to the established rates and usages of the pergunnah, (3) rates established in the pergunnah for lands of the same description and quality as those respecting which disputes between zemindar and ryot may arise. We have seen that by these expressions, and by the directions for entering in the pottahs which were to have been granted to the ryots before proclamation of the zemindary settlement, the specific amount, in money, of the rent ever after payable by the ryot, it was implied that the established pergunnah rates were immutable rates. Resting as they did on custom, they rested perforce on a custom dating from the past, which was not alterable by a custom to be created in the future, seeing that the ryots who had created the customary rate would not vary the custom so as to raise the rent over their own heads. Yet the Bill introduced in 1855, which, with amendments, was passed into law as Act X of 1859, provided that "hereditary ryots holding lands *at fixed rates of rent*, are entitled to receive pottahs at those rates. All other ryots and cultivators of land are entitled to receive pottahs according to the rates of rent *for the time being* established in the pergunnah." The phrase "*for the time being*" (which meant, a rate increasing from time to time after it had been accepted in 1793 as a settled pergunnah rate established by ancient custom) was not warranted by the Regulations of 1793;—nor was there any warrant for using the term "fixed rents" as in contradistinction to the rent payable by khoodkasht ryots at the (legally immutable) established pergunnah rates of 1793. As, in 1859, fifteen-sixteenths of the ryots held without pottahs, but in accordance with custom, that is, held without any document specifying a fixed amount of rent, this form of expression disestablished nearly all the ryots in Bengal.

XIX, 18, ii.
II. Even Mr. Sconce, who had so clearly asserted the ryot's title to a permanent assessment under the Regulation of 1793 (necessarily at the established pergunnah rate of that year), was drawn into speaking of "fair rents" instead XIX, 22, iv. of established pergunnah rates; while the Select Committee which settled the Bill as it was finally passed into law, imported from the North-Western Provinces the expression "fair and equitable rates." The use of "fair rent" and "fair and equitable rates" as substitutes or equivalents for the "established pergunnah rates" of the Regulations of 1793, implied a confusion of ideas, the confounding of ren

with revenue, which the Court of Directors had rebuked in the passage quoted in Chapter III, paragraph 11, iii. As pointed out by the Court, what the ryot paid was revenue, not rent.

III. The distinction was material. Revenue can be increased only according to the exigencies of the State, not at the discretion of individuals; and, at the permanent settlement, the State surrendered all claim to increase the revenue from land, whether from a rise of prices or any other cause. Having exempted the revenue paid by the zemindars which they collected from the ryots (that is, the revenue paid by the ryots) from increase on account of any exigency of State, the Government proceeded, in the Regulations, *1st*, to limit the demand upon the ryot to the established pergunnah rate, *plus* cesses, of 1793; *2nd*, to prohibit the levy by zemindars of fresh *abwabs*. The limitation and the prohibition were justified, and indeed called for, by the limitation of the Government's revenue from land. The established pergunnah rate payable by the ryot was an immutable rate derived from a custom of long standing; the amount payable at that rate was a *question of fact*, determinable by reference to the custom in each locality. In determining it there was no room for *opinion*, such as is afforded by the use of the words fair and equitable.

IV. Had the ryot's payment been rent and not revenue, it would then have been liable to increase, not alone for meeting exigencies of the State, but for meeting additional demands of a landlord, supposing that the zemindar were the ryot's landlord. In such case, the limit of the demand might be determined by considerations of what was fair and equitable. But the ryot, as we have seen in a previous chapter, was the proprietor of his land; his was the dominant, and the zemindar's was the servient right. In accordance with this fact, the Court of Directors correctly observed that what the ryot paid was revenue, and not rent. This confounding with rent of the revenue payable by the ryot has led to the subsequent obscurity and difficulties in the substantive rent-law. In the first place, it imported into the law the expressions "fair and equitable," which attach to ideas of rent; and by a re-action the idea of rent got firmly lodged, *1st*, in the mind of the Legislature in 1859, which exhausted ingenuity in devising grounds for enhancing that rent which the Regulations of 1793 had determined to be payable at the amount prevailing in that year; *2nd*, in the minds of judges of the High Court, among whom Sir Barnes Peacock was

CHAP. VI. driven to Malthus' Political Economy to find out what
Lord Cornwallis meant in 1793; and 3rd, in the mind
of the Bengal Government, which not long since was
XIX, 16 to disposed to believe that a great deal which passes man's
18. understanding is necessary for knowing what rent a Bengal
ryot should pay to his zemindar.

9. It may be said that the expression " fair and equitable
rates" was adopted because the established pergunnah rate
had been obliterated, and some standard for determining the
amount payable by the ryot was necessary ; but—

I. The fact remains that the use of the expression involves, and has created, a confusion between revenue and
rent, as payable by the ryot, with the results above indicated.

II. The obliteration of the pergunnah rate was no reason
for adopting a new standard of payment by the ryot, the
permanency of whose assessment, as it existed in 1793, was
as solemnly guaranteed to him as the similar assessment of
the zemindar was guaranteed to the latter. If the pergunnah rate was obliterated, at least it was known, or was
easily susceptible of proof, that the rent paid in 1859 was
higher than the established pergunnah rate paid in 1793.
Fidelity to the solemn pledge given to the ryot in 1793,
required that he should at least have been secured from paying more than the rent which was being paid in 1859, and
that a new standard should not have been devised for regulating the zemindar's departure in a fresh career of enhancing
ryots' rents and reaping profit from his own wrong-doing in
the obliteration of the permanent rate.

III. If, notwithstanding the permanency of assessment at the amounts of 1793, which was assured to the
ryot, it was proper, in violation of the deed of the permanent
settlement, that his rent should be increased to fair and
equitable rates, thereby securing to the zemindars an increase of income which had not been contemplated for
them in 1793 by the authors of that settlement;—then it
was barely just to the tax-payers in British India that, in
consideration of this increase of zemindars' income from
a source outside the deed of their permanent settlement,
their own assessment should be increased, in like manner, to
fair and equitable rates.

10. The two cardinal privileges of ryots before the permanent settlement were, 1st, that they could not be disturbed
in possession so long as they paid the established customary
revenue; 2nd, that resident cultivators and their descendants

could take up waste land in their own villages subject to CHAP. VI.
payment of the established pergunnah rates of rent for land
of the same kind. These privileges were secured by immemorial usage or custom: and both these, with an assurance
of permanency of rent, were continued by the permanent settlement. Act X of 1859, we have seen, abrogated the first
of these privileges, by importing into Bengal a law suitable for the temporarily-settled North-Western Provinces,
which was inapplicable to permanently-settled Bengal. It
also rescinded the second privilege, under which the class of
resident cultivators had continued to receive yearly accessions.
This second breach of engagement with the ryot was brought
about by again importing from the North-Western Provinces a law which in those provinces had favoured the growth
of occupancy rights among non-resident cultivators. The
result in Bengal was that the ancient division of ryots into two
classes of resident and non-resident cultivators ceased, and
that of occupancy and non-occupancy ryots was substituted.
The whole contention of the zemindars against the ryots had
been to discontinue their residence; and in 1859 the law
helped the zemindars by abrogating the privilege that had
attached to residence under an immemorial usage which the
regulations of the permanent settlement had continued in
obedience to the command of Parliament. Under that custom a resident cultivator, or the offspring of a resident cultivator, had an indefeasible right to take up waste land in his
village, paying for it the established pergunnah rate. The
zemindar could not hinder him;—but under the new law he
can be hindered by the zemindar, or if the latter allows him to
cultivate, still, by varying his rent in less than twelve years,
the zemindar prevents the growth of occupancy right in the
ryot. Thus, the old class of occupancy ryots, who were
independent of the zemindar, must become extinct; while the
hybrid class, modelled on a very different condition of things in
the North-Western Provinces, are less esteemed, as creatures
of Act X of 1859, whose occupancy right can mature only
on sufferance from the zemindar. Thus, the tendency of the
legislation of 1859 is to reduce, in time, all ryots to the position of tenants-at-will, or tenants by permission of the
zemindars; in other words, excepting those engaged in the
professions of law and medicine, and in mercantile or bank- XXIX, 10,
ing pursuits, and excepting handicraftsmen and labourers, II e.
the entire population of Bengal, a country almost entirely
agricultural, will in time consist of servants of Government,

CHAP. VI.

or servants or dependents of zemindars. Mr. Froude observed—respecting Ireland—"The good landlords, it may be said, are few, and whether good or bad, free men ought not to be at the mercy of mortals. A free man should own no master but the law of his country, and depend on nothing but his own industry."

XIX, 33.

11. Act X of 1859 brought about another change which is prolific of evil fruit to this day, by facilitating indirect suits for enhancement of rent, in a form which the zemindars often find more convenient and advantageous than a direct suit for that purpose. After the Regulations of 1793, the zemindars turned their obligation, under those Regulations, to grant pottahs to ryots, into an engine of oppression. Forgetful of this part of the history of the relations between zemindar and ryot, the Legislature in 1859 gratuitously empowered zemindars to demand kabulyuts from ryots. This power affords to zemindars the same advantage as if they could force pottahs upon ryots.

XIX, 39 & 40.

12. Thus, the legal status of the ryots, as fixed in 1793, and as it remained unaffected until 1859, was altered in three vital points, by Act X of that year, without the least discussion of the change, though Mr. Sconce had pointedly drawn attention to the assurance of a permanent assessment which was given to the ryots in the Regulations of 1793. There was eager strife in the Legislative Council, whether the Civil or the Revenue Courts should have the body of the ryot, but his legal status did not receive the slightest notice, and it was seriously altered for the worse without the least discussion, and without any reference to what had been recorded by greater authorities than those in the Legislative Council in 1859. This was not a nice thought for any Honorable Member to put under his pillow and go to sleep upon in a snug little room in the old country; it would give less pain to put a scorpion there instead.

CHAPTER VII.

BARREN RESULTS OF THE PERMANENT SETTLEMENT.

Act X of 1859 broke the deed of the permanent settle- ment against the ryot, among other ways, by introducing a new standard of the rent payable by him, though the Regulations of 1793 had assured to him a permanency of the assessment of that year. The legal status of the ryot from 1793 to 1859 was one of immunity from enhancement of rent. Through the high-handed oppression of zemindars, down to near modern times, this immunity was set at nought, and ryots' rents were increased; but still, the force of custom, the ever-surviving law of the East, is strong; and the sense of ryots' rights under the Regulations of 1793 must have moderated, in a measure, the exactions by zemindars.

2. Act X of 1859 destroyed this restraining force of custom; breaking, to the ryot, a pledge under the permanent settlement, it empowered zemindars to demand legally an increase of rent, in circumstances in which, till then,—on account of the since broken pledge,—they could not have demanded it legally, or without violence to custom. So far as the law formed a standard for the zemindar's conduct,— where formerly he laboured with an uneasy conscience, he could now engage with a clear conscience in proceedings for enhancing rent. Accordingly his demands under the law would be more unrestrained than his previous demands beyond the law. This feeling was strengthened by the great rise of prices since 1854; and thus it came about that, whereas formerly the increased demand had some regard to past usage, the new demand had none. This outraged the ryots' sense of equity, and increased the difficulties which embarrassed the courts in arriving at a satisfactory judgment on disputes about rent.

3. An unusual, special effort was made to obtain, through the Great Rent Case, a satisfactory rule of enhancement of rent, but the result was disappointing. Sir Barnes Peacock had passed, and in the Great Rent Case he upheld, a decree which adjudged to the zemindar a rent so high that the latter

CHAP. VII. would not enforce his decree. Sir Barnes erred from having regarded the ryot as reduced, by the Regulations of 1793, to the condition of a mere tenant-at-will. The other fourteen judges were unanimous in another decree which put Sir Barnes Peacock into a minority of one, but which, like his decision, has also proved to be unworkable. The fourteen judges erred in considering that the ryot's rent, though fixed in a money amount, represented the value of a fixed proportion of the produce of his land. The fallacy of this view has been exposed in Chapter V, para. 7, and in Appendix XX, 15. The result of these two unworkable decisions is that neither zemindar nor ryot can tell what the ryot should pay as rent.

4. Among the results of Act X of 1859 we may note :—

I. The broken faith of Government, which was as solemnly pledged-to the ryot as to the zemindar, for a permanency of assessment.

II. Destruction of a custom which from time immemorial had secured to resident cultivators occupancy rights in their own village.

XIV.   III. Multiplication of middlemen, who, when mere farmers of rents, are the scourges of the ryots of Bengal.

IV. Increased expense to zemindars for enlarged village establishments, *1st*, for preventing the growth of occupancy rights; *2nd*, for the frequent enhancements of rent which have been caused by the Act.

V. Increased rents laid on ryots, who have to bear, in addition, increased exactions by the larger village establishments which zemindars now keep.

VI. Increased litigation and heavy law expenses to the ryots, of which the smallest part is that incurred in court for stamp duties and pleaders.

VII. Uncertainty, amounting almost to impracticability, of application of the rent law, *i.e.*, a present deadlock between zemindar and ryot as regards rent, which is a vital point for prosperous agriculture or the reverse.

VIII. A belief among zemindars that they get less than they should from the ryots, and a belief among ryots that they pay more than they should, and a dread that they may have to pay still more, to the zemindars.

5. The Government, in regarding this its handiwork through Act X of 1859, may, if it has thought on the matter, add a bitter reflection that, for no earthly good whatever, from the zemindary settlement, several millions sterling a year of revenue (more than the yearly taxation

for the Famine Insurance Fund) have been alienated to the CHAP. VII. zemindars, who yet, as a body, are impoverished or in debt, while the condition of the greater part of the ryots in the Lower Provinces is bad. All but the first of the ill effects of Act X of 1859, as detailed in the preceding paragraph, have flowed from the enhancement of rent, consequent on forgetfulness of the pledges of the Government.

6. From the ryot's point of view the retrospect is still more disheartening; all that the Government has lost, he has lost too, and more. Besides four millions sterling (nearly) of land revenue to the Government, the ryots pay above thirteen millions sterling, net income, to zemindars and middlemen; over and above that they pay all the expenses of management and of collection, and formidable amounts of law expenses for both sides, of arbitrary cesses and exactions, and of interest to money-lenders. In exchange for these enormous payments they have a state of things in which the condition of their class, in at least one entire province, is wretched, and over a large portion of the remainder of the Lower Provinces is bad. And who can estimate the further immense loss to ryots from the moral degradation which is an incident of their material condition?

7. From the point of view of the general tax-payers in British India, the retrospect, if not so saddening as the above, is perhaps more humiliating to the wisdom by which the world is governed. At the time of the acquisition of the Dewanny of Bengal, Behar, and Orissa, by the East India Company, the zemindars were administrators of districts and collectors of revenue. Under British rule they were relieved from duties of administration, but, though separate European collectors of revenue were appointed, the zemindars, in an evil day for Bengal, were still utilised as collectors of revenue. In that capacity they became payers of the Government revenue into the public treasuries; and, by reason of their being these payers of revenue, they were constituted proprietors of the soil, with an allotment of certain perquisites and lands as remuneration for the duties of collecting the revenue; and with a further gift to them of the waste lands of Bengal, which then constituted about one-third of the culturable land in the Lower Provinces. It was, indeed, hoped that in return for these immense concessions the zemindars would take a preponderating share in improving cultivation. Here and there, they have spent money in digging or filling up jheels and

CHAP. VII. erecting embankments; but the expenditure is as a mere flea-bite out of the enormous millions sterling that they have derived from the land; and the testimony of good authorities, extending over a long period, is, that the zemindars have done little or nothing, the ryots everything, for the extension and improvement of cultivation. Thus it has happened that where the authors of the permanent settlement hoped that the improved cultivation of the land would be the primary, and the collection of revenue the secondary function of the zemindars, the only duties, substantially, which they have rendered for the enormous concessions to them in 1793 have been as collectors of revenue. We have seen that they and middlemen receive above 13 millions sterling, besides expenses of collection and management, from the ryots. This amount, then, and the Government's expenses of collection, with the *abwabs* exacted by zemindars, constitute the real charges which are incurred for the collection of a revenue of only four millions sterling. That is a cheering thought for the tax-payers in British India to put under their pillows and go to sleep upon, in their huts or houses, when they are disposed to feel an ignorant impatience of taxation for providing in Bengal an insurance against famine! and they may couple with it a second thought that the Bengal ryots could not only dispense with help in time of famine, but voluntarily contribute to famine relief in other parts of India, if they were spared the crushing charges of collection which have been gratuitously laid on them since 1793.

8. Need we go into greater detail?

VI, 15, v.   I. Necessitous zemindars are the most oppressive landlords—*i.e.*, after the above-mentioned enormous payments by ryots, the cultivators might hope to find themselves under wealthy liberal zemindars; yet it was reported in 1868 that—

XII, 7, ii. the zemindars as a body are not wealthy men. There are *some* rich men among them, a few *very* rich men, but the bulk of the class are men of very limited income, and too many of them of embarrassed circumstances."

Again—

The vast majority of the estates for which revenue is paid direct to the Government are *petty* properties, and the larger ones are almost all so charged with subordinate tenures of a more or less permanent character, as often to leave the so-called owner with only a moderate annuity."

II. Five years later, or in 1873, the Board of Revenue Chap. VII. reported in effect that the condition of zemindars was that of Irish landlords before the Encumbered Estates' Act, while XII, 14. the condition of ryots was that of Irish cottiers; thus:—

"It is not too much to say that, while the ancestral landholders have, by their apathy and short-sightedness, fallen out of the race and lost their share of the growing wealth of the country, the money-lenders have by thriftiness, care, and rapacity that could never have been tolerated by a less patient and indolent race, amassed such riches and such influence as to have become the most powerful class in the community. The condition of the ryot all over Bengal is that of hopeless indebtedness to his mahajun. The cultivation of the country is carried on upon advances made by them, and the well-being and comfort of the lower classes, and of a large portion of the higher classes also, is in their hands. Fortunately for all parties they are wise in their generation; and though they exact usury at rates unknown in other parts of the world, they know how to adjust their demands to the immediate capacities of their debtors, and so avoid the catastrophe of a general bankruptcy, which would involve themselves.

III. Of one Province, Behar, the Bengal Government XIII, 9, viii. reported in 1874-75 :—

" So far, then, we may hope that the lot of the labourer, which was always very hard, has not become harder of late. But we must sorrowfully admit that it is almost as hard as can be borne. A plain calculation will show that the wages will suffice for little more than the purchase of food, and leave but a slender margin for his simplest wants. In Behar, indeed, a comparison of prices with wages might indicate that his lot must be hard beyond endurance.

The condition of the labourer, in the territories under the Bengal Government, takes its hue from that of the ryots. The Bengal Government added on 7th September 1878 :—

Nearly every local officer consulted is agreed that while a system of summary and cheap rent procedure is required in the interests of both zemindar and ryot, the most urgent requirement of Behar is an amelioration of the condition of the tenantry.

IV. We have seen that the majority of the zemindars are XIII, 8. in debt and are petty zemindars, and wherever this is the case—

the condition of the ryots is bad. They are prosperous in the 24-Pergunnahs, or suburban district of the Presidency division (and in Chittagong), where they enjoy fixed rents; in the eastern districts, where, through intelligence, strength of character, and force of circumstances, they have successfully asserted rights against undue enhancement of rent; in parts of the central districts, and in some northern districts where there is a demand for labour. But elsewhere the condition of the ryots is one of deep indebtedness and poverty.

V. Wherever, through fixity of rents, as in the 24-Pergunnahs and Chittagong, or through exemption from undue enhancement and from rack rents, the ryots are prosperous, wages are high, and labour is efficient. In other parts of Bengal, where the ryots are oppressed, wages are low; they are lowest in Behar, next in Orissa (2 annas a day), 3 annas in Northern Bengal, 4 annas in Central and Eastern Bengal, and 6 annas in Calcutta; and the intensity of ryot's indebtedness is distributed in the same order.

9. This is a melancholy chapter; it tells us of a self-abnegation by Government which gave up some millions sterling of yearly revenue, and that the sacrifice has been useless;— of zemindars and middlemen who divide an income (including cesses) equalling the land revenue of the rest of British India, and of whom, notwithstanding, the zemindars, as a class, are poor and in debt;—of ryots, of whom a large proportion are reduced to cottierism, and a yet greater number are in deep indebtedness, while, of the remainder, only those are prosperous who pay rents as fixed at the time of the permanent settlement, or low rents. We close the chapter with an enquiry of what earthly use to any but the money-lender, and to a very few zemindars, is the existing zemindary settlement? Would not the small minority of ryots who are in tolerable or in good circumstances, have been equally well off, and would not the rest have been better off, without it, seeing that to the great majority of both zemindars and ryots it has brought nothing but indebtedness and impoverishment, notwithstanding an increase of the quantity and of the value of the produce of Bengal, since 1789, manifold greater than the increase of population? Great cities have decayed, not one new city has arisen, in Bengal since the zemindary settlement of 1789.

CHAPTER VIII.

MISTAKES OF THE GOVERNMENT.

But little good has come of the permanent zemindary
settlement, notwithstanding the benevolence in which it was conceived, and the rare self-abnegation by which it was accompanied. Through what mistakes of the Government have its benevolence and self-sacrifice proved abortive?

2. Four years after the acquisition of the Dewanny, the XVI, 4, i. President and Select Committee in Bengal issued instructions to the collectors with the view of eventually concluding a permanent settlement with the ryots. Fifteen years later, Parliament enjoined that permanent rules should be laid III, 5. down for regulating the payments or services due from all classes of landholders. These rules were to be permanent, and they were to be in accordance with the law and constitution of India, as these had been received, with the Dewanny, from the native rule; in other words, the status of the landholders, as fixed by the laws and usages under native rule, was to be perpetuated.

3. The most ancient Indian form of proprietary right in land, one which law and immemorial usage under native rule had respected, was that of the members of village communities and khoodkasht ryots, who were entitled to hold their lands without disturbance in possession, so long as they paid the ancient customary rate of rent. The authors of the permanent settlement recognised this right of the khoodkasht ryot, and in obedience to the injunction of Parliament, that rights in accordance with the law and constitution of India under the native rule should be perpetuated, they placed on record, in minutes, and in the Regulations of 1793, that the ryots in Bengal, khoodkasht and pykasht, should not be required to pay more than the established pergunnah rates, and that, paying these rates, they should be maintained in their holdings. Furthermore, they directed that the dues payable by the ryot should be consolidated in one specific sum, which was to be the sole amount recoverable ever after from the ryots' holdings.

4. Thus, a permanent assessment for the ryot was made a part of the permanent zemindary settlement of 1793.

The ample testimony to this effect, in Chapters I to V, leaves no doubt on this point, respecting which only those can be sceptical who would venture to maintain that the members of the Government of Lord Cornwallis and of his successors, including respected and honoured names, deliberately confiscated the rights of the mass of cultivators in Bengal. It was well observed by Sir John Peter Grant in 1840, that "the right to enhance according to the present value of the land differs not in principle from absolute annulment of the tenure." Fully aware of this, the authors of the permanent settlement limited the demand upon the zemindars, in whose favour they created a new property out of the Government's limited share in the produce of the soil; and they directed a similar limitation, to the established customary pergunnah rate, of the demand upon the ancient proprietors of the land, namely, the ryots.

5. They thought that the limitation of the future demand upon the ryot, to the amount then existing, simultaneously with the issue of a proclamation which gave a limited proprietary right in the soil, in only a technical sense, to the zemindars, would secure the former from encroachment on their ancient undoubted privileges. And they strengthened themselves in this belief by a provision in their regulations that the zemindars should grant pottahs to the ryots, setting forth in one specific sum, consolidated from the dues then being paid, the amount thereafter recoverable from each ryot.

6. Their purposes, plans, and precautions, have failed; the ryots in the present day are subject to enhancements of rent in about every five years; through what mistakes was the failure brought about? they were many.

I. The ryot was required to pay his revenue through the zemindar. As pointed out by Lord Hastings (Chapter III, para. 11, section I), the zemindar "was thereby invested with the power of compelling, from the several families in the village, the payment of their respective portions of the general contribution, and our acquaintance with the propensities of the natives makes us sensible that such a power is likely to be misapplied in arbitrary and unjust demands."

II. This temptation to an oppressive abuse of power would, in 1793, when the law was weak, have been strong even with zemindars of average qualities; but the persons VI, 18, iv. selected by Lord Cornwallis as zemindars were, as a body, worthless characters, unworthy of trust.

III. They were exactly the persons who would turn, as they did turn, into an engine of oppression, the regulations which required them to give pottahs to ryots who had, from immemorial usage, held without pottahs independently of the zemindars. In this mistake Lord Cornwallis erred with knowledge.

CHAP.
VIII.
——

IV. Lord Cornwallis' Government knew that the ryots XVI, 9, ii. held without pottahs: and that the only record of the ancient customary rates which determined the payment of their dues was the official record kept by canoongoes and putwarries, who were servants of the Government, not of the zemindars. The canoongoe's office was abolished, and the putwarries were made the servants of the zemindars.

V. This was done before the existent dues of each ryot had been consolidated and entered for him in a pottah stating the specific amount which alone was to be recoverable from him after 1793. Lord Cornwallis did indeed report to the Court of Directors on 6th March 1793—

"We have anticipated your wishes respecting the pottahs to be granted by the landholders to the ryots. It is with pleasure we acquaint you that throughout the greater part of the country specific agreements have been exchanged between the landholders and the ryots, and that where these writings have not been entered into, the landholders have bound themselves to prepare and deliver them by fixed periods :"—

But His Lordship was grossly misinformed; the Bengal British Indian Association testified in 1859 that, then, fifteen-sixteenths of the ryots in Bengal held without pottahs. The omission to record the amount of rent of each ryot was not unavoidable. In the similar permanent zemindary settlements in the Madras Presidency, and in the Benares Division, the record was carefully made, with the result that the ryots in those zemindaries are to this day protected from enhancement of rent. The same result was secured by like care and pains-taking work in three or four districts in Bengal, a sufficient proof that what was effected there could have been carried out in the rest of the Lower Provinces.

VI. The gift of waste lands to the zemindars in Bengal, XV, 4. in spite of the views of Sir John Shore and the Court of Directors who had deprecated the gift, soon endangered the permanent settlement by enabling those zemindars who had plenty of waste land to attract ryots from older zemindaries by low rents.

VII. To prevent this mischief to the public revenue, laws XVI, 43 & 44. were passed with the object of preventing zemindars from letting lands on low rents, except for short periods; but they were so ambiguously worded that they were interpreted, to the prejudice of ignorant ryots, as destructive of the ryot's privilege to hold his land permanently if he paid the established rent.

VIII. The ryot having been required to pay revenue through the zemindar (Section I), a principle was set up that powers of distraint and coercion (without heed of the hazard to ryots' rights) should be given to zemindars, even to the extent of summoning ryots to zemindars' cutcherries, for the sake of the security of the public revenue.

IX. These powers were given when the police was corrupt, and the executive too weak to watch the exercise,— still less to prevent an abuse—of the powers, under the guise of which rascality and tyranny spread over the country.

X. The evil of these mistakes was fully apparent in 1812, when Mr. Colebrooke recommended that even at that late period the rents of the ryots should be ascertained and fixed, at amounts approximating as nearly as possible to the established rates of 1793. The evil was again forced on the attention of the Bengal Government in 1822, when they stated their intention of having a detailed survey and assessment with the view of fixing the ryots' rents. Had this measure been adopted at either of these periods, the rents which might then have been fixed for the ryots would have been permanent rents greatly below the amounts now paid by them. The omission to carry out the measure was a mistake; and the error was committed with knowledge of what was the Government's duty in the matter.

XI. The creation of middlemen, on permanent tenures, down to the third and fourth degrees, and lower, was permitted without stint. There was excuse for the creation of a class of cultivating middlemen where waste lands had to be brought under cultivation; but the permission of numerous grades of middlemen between zemindar and ryot, on old estates, all of whom, as well as the zemindar, derived their income out of the ryot's payments, only set in train so many agencies for repeated illegal enhancements of rent, beyond the amount warranted by established custom. These middlemen, or farmers of rents, have proved a scourge of the country.

XII. A section of the Sale Law of 1841, which entitled auction-purchasers of estates, at sales for arrears of revenue, to enhance the rents of tenures on the estates, was ambiguously worded. The correspondence which led to the passing of that Act began with a declaration that to prevent frauds by zemindars, the annulling of leases on sale of an estate for arrears of revenue should be greatly restricted. It ended with a law which, by one section of Act XII of 1841 empowered, auction-purchasers of zemindaries to enhance "at discretion" the rents of all under-tenures with certain exceptions. From the ambiguous wording of the exceptions, their scope was misunderstood; and in course of time, erroneous interpretations by the courts so restricted the exceptions as to create a wrong belief that under the Act all zemindars were empowered to enhance the rents of nearly all ryots at discretion. Even had the wrong interpretation of the exceptive clauses of the Act been correct, this exercise of the power should have been limited to sales of estates under that specific Act XII of 1841, and among these, to those estates only the auction-purchasers of which exercised, within a reasonable period after their purchase, the power of annulling tenures under the Act. But the wrong interpretation only generated fresh error.

XIII. The courts came to consider that if auction-purchasers had the power of enhancing rents at discretion, all zemindars necessarily had the same power, though they had it not before 1793, while the Regulations of that year did not confer on them any such power; and thus the fixity of the established pergunnah rates of 1793, which were obligatory on all zemindars, was upset by ambiguous phrases in Sale Laws respecting the general powers of auction-purchasers to enhance rents. It was overlooked that the theory of the Sale Law, from 1793 to 1841, went no farther than this, namely, that to enable the auction-purchaser to pay the amount of Government revenue which was fixed on the zemindary in 1793, he should be empowered to recover from privileged dependent talukdars merely the amount of revenue which their taluks paid in 1793, and from ryots the ancient established pergunnah rates, and no more. The receipts thus assumed, and the rents from resumed lands and from waste lands reclaimed since 1793, afforded ample resources for paying the Government revenue, which remained the same as in 1793; and, therefore, no ground for enhancement, to a rate higher than the pergunnah rate of 1793, was justifiable under Sale Laws which professed to do no more than to place the auction-purchaser in the position occupied in 1793 by the original engager with Government.

XIV. A tacit assumption, however, that the Sale Laws had enlarged the zemindar's power of enhancing rent beyond the established pergunnah rate of 1793, on all estates, including those not sold for arrears of revenue, pervaded the decisions of the courts, insomuch that even Judges of the High Court, in the decisions on the Great Rent Case, sought to explain the general character of the established pergunnah rates, under the Regulations of 1793, by their interpretation of the Sale Laws.

XV. This too prevalent error, and the actual facts of zemindars having, through their power beyond the law, enhanced ryots' rents beyond the established pergunnah rates of 1793, brought about a state of opinion in which all persons, except Mr. Sconce, who took part in the discussions which preceded the passing of Act X of 1859, considered it as a matter of course that zemindars should have the power of increasing ryots' rents, notwithstanding the permanent settlement which was prescribed for the ryot in the Regulations of 1793.

XVI. The crowning mistake was next committed of borrowing the temporarily settled North-Western Provinces' rules of enhancement of rent, which were necessarily inapplicable to permanently settled Bengal. This error was committed by confounding the distinction between rent which the ryot did not pay and revenue which the ryot did pay. Had that distinction been observed, it would have been seen that, though the ryot's revenue or jummah was properly increased on account of a rise of prices where his zemindar's jumma was increased from the same cause, namely, in the North-Western XIX, 36. Provinces,—the precedent or example was irrelevant in Bengal, where the zemindar's jumma was not increased on account of a rise of prices, or from any other cause.

XVII. A further error was committed in Act X of 1859, viz., that of substituting a hybrid occupancy right for non-XXI, 3. resident cultivators, for the genuine occupancy right, resting on an immemorial custom, perpetuated by the Regulations of 1793, which had prevailed in Bengal.

XVIII. Law expenses for the ryot were increased in 1862, by allowing the recovery of charge for zemindars' pleaders, as costs of suit, in suits for the recovery of arrears of rent.

7. Of these numerous mistakes it may be said that the earlier ones did not conflict with the plan and law of 1793, that there should be a permanent settlement with the ryot; they show merely how the intentions of Government proved

abortive. In the later errors, on the other hand, especially those of the courts and of the legislation in 1859, there is a tacit assumption that no one could dream of fixity of rent, or a permanent settlement for the ryots : in other words, it was considered the proper thing that ryots' rents should be repeatedly increased, with the result of creating fresh grades of middlemen. The legislators of 1793 went no farther than to affirm a predilection for great zemindars, without encroaching on the rights of peasant-proprietors ; the later legislation could not conceive that the cultivators in Bengal, once a country of peasant-proprietors, should have the same tenure as the peasant-proprietors in Europe, or at least fixity of rent, though their status and primitive rights of property once correspond-ed ;—or should be exempt, like the latter, from the scourge of middlemen. Thus it has come about that, whereas the Regulations of 1793 limited the demand upon the ryots to a pergunnah rate established by ancient customs which were formed by ryots, it was reported in 1872-73, of the district of Gya, that " the rates current in the village are varied at the will of the landholder. No one single individual XIII, .7, iv, ryot is subjected to an isolated invasion of the village usage, 6. but a wholesale enhancement upon all brings all to a com-mon level, and such enhancement may take place, as it were, in a single night." This is the modern interpretation of the ancient established pergunnah rate of rent,—as determined by the custom of ryots, not by the fiat of zemindars,—which the Regulations of 1793 assured to the ryots.

CHAPTER IX.

ZEMINDARS AND PEASANT-PROPRIETORS.

CHAP. IX.   In the preceding Chapter the mistakes committed by Government in and since the permanent settlement have been enumerated. May we say that one, the greatest mistake, has been omitted from the enumeration, *viz.*, the creation of great zemindars?

2. Lord Cornwallis modelled his scheme of zemindary proprietors on the English system of large landed estates. That system is still on its trial, and it seems to be falling on evil days. But in its best days its success was greatly promoted by the existence, and the increasing growth and prosperity, of large towns, of great manufacturing industries, and generally of manufactures. Moreover, for long, the high price of wheat during the war, and afterwards the Corn Laws, also abuses of the Poor Laws, gave a factitious support to the system of large estates. Even now, the Poor Laws indirectly help land-owners and farmers to work large farms at a minimum cost of labour. Not one of these circumstances which have promoted the success of large estates in England is present in Bengal, where the only compensating circumstance is a large export of agricultural produce which unequally affects its forty-four districts.

3. On the other hand, vicious incidents of that system, which prevail in England and Ireland, have appeared in Bengal, with one or two others of a like character.

XXVIII, 14, 1.   I. Mr. Caird was in raptures with the great increase of income of English land-owners, and of the gross annual value of land. But it is also known that the indebtedness of *ibid*, 12, iv. land-owners, which he mentioned in his work in 1850, and the burdens of rent charge on estates, are great. The annual value of zemindaries in Bengal is in like manner very large, and it shows a prodigious increase on the value in 1793; but zemindars as a body are poor and in debt.

VI, 15, iv.   There appears to be only too much truth in Mr. J. Mill's remark in 1831, that—

"it may be predicated generally of persons that live upon rent, that they are not saving men. I know no country in which the class of men whose income is derived from rent can be considered as accumulators;

Chap. IX.

they are men who spend their incomes, with a very moderate portion of exceptions. * * In general, the persons who own rent, and live upon rent, consume it all; that is the rule almost universally with them in India, and very generally, I believe, elsewhere."

II. Entails, settlements, and the right of primogeniture create difficulties or impose burdens, which in England check improvements of the land. Similar difficulties are created in Bengal by the sub-division of estates and tenures (or of interests therein without an actual partition of the land) under the laws of inheritance, qualified by the system of joint family property. The consequent complications, in the re- VII; 12. lations of landlord and ryot, are oppressive to the latter, and unfavourable to economical and improving management of lands.

III. While Lord Cornwallis thought that he was modelling his zemindary system on the English, he really framed it on the Irish system, and thus introduced two special evils which are absent from the English system of large estates. In England there are no middlemen or farmers of rents; the farmers are those who engage in actual cultivation, with the help of capital, either fully sufficient, or so nearly sufficient as to be eked out by moderate loans from banks. The English agricultural system is thus free from two ruthless oppressors of Bengal ryots, *viz.*, middlemen and money-lenders; and this great difference, to the ryot's prejudice is widened by the further difference in the rates of interest. Seven per cent. a year would be considered a high rate in England; while 36 per cent. a year would be a moderate charge to the Bengal ryot by his zemindar or by the money-lender. The lending of money to the ryot by his landlord, at usurious interest, is another material difference in the characteristics of the two systems.

IV. By a legal fiction, similar to that by which Lord Cornwallis turned the zemindars into proprietors of the soil, in a restricted technical sense, the Irish chieftains were recognised as proprietors in a similar sense of the lands of their respective tribes. But the law courts, ignoring the custom by which the land belonged to the tribe at large, regarded the chiefs as sole proprietors of the soil. Precisely the same thing happened in Bengal. In Ireland the results in time were middlemen and cottierism; in Bengal they have been the same: if the ryots have not everywhere been reduced to a state of cottierism, the tendency of the laws, and of the policy of numerous zemindars, if not of zemin-

CHAP. IX. dars generally, is to reduce them to that condition. In Ireland middlemen have happily well nigh ceased from the
land ; in Bengal they multiply with every fresh opportunity
or prospect of enhancing ryots' rents.

V. In Ireland the tradition among the cultivators that
the land once belonged to them, keeps up that resentful feeling towards landlords which is the Irish difficulty. In Bengal there is the same tradition among ryots who have a
deep-rooted attachment to the land, and who have not to
trace back their traditions for even a century. In Ireland
the chronic feeling of resentment is fed by evictions which
would not be so freely, if at all, enforced, if the evicted
could not emigrate, but remained a burden on the poor rates.
In Bengal the struggle is not to evict, but to enhance rent ;
and enhancement of rent is accepted as the lesser of two
evils, the preferable alternative to eviction, for Bengali ryots
and their families are not fitted to emigrate by tens of
thousands, and there is no Poor Law by which zemindars,
possessed of the Oriental Poor Fund, *viz.*, waste lands, could
be burdened with their support, as the worse alternative
to observing moderation towards their ryots.

VI. A resentful feeling towards zemindars has shown
itself more than once in parts of Bengal.

VII. Mostly indebted landlords, oppressive middlemen,
many masters over ryots where interests in estates or tenures
are sub-divided without an absolute partition of the lands,
frequent enhancements of rent, consequent deep indebtedness
aggravated by usurious interest, and strained relations between
zemindar and ryot,—such are the helps to improved management and cultivation of the land which the zemindary settlement has provided for Bengal.

4. Nor can better things come of a closer adherence to
Lord Cornwallis' model. In a regular sequence, high prices
during the war till 1815, the corn laws, the outburst of prosperity, on their abolition, which synchronised with the gold
discoveries, the long-sustained inflation of prices from a great
and progressive expansion of credit, which collapsed in
1873, helped to keep up in England high prices of agricultural produce throughout this century, until 1873. In this
long period of continuous prosperity for landlords, rents
advanced with a steady progression ; but from the characteristic quality of the class that lives upon rents, which Mr.
Mill noticed, their expenditure also increased. Settlements,
rent-charges, debts, have increased the fixed yearly burdens

on land, in a percentage corresponding in a sensible measure Chap. IX. to the percentage of rise of rents. But the remarkable fall in prices of agricultural produce has now continued for several years; the depression of the great manufacturing industries which provide a market for the farmers still prevails; the sources from which farmers were able to provide the long-continued progressive increase of rents have in great measure dried up; there has been a considerable fall of rents, but not sufficient, it would seem, to meet the fall of prices and diminution of markets, for farms continue to be thrown up, and many remain at present without tenants. But the yearly charges which landlords laid as a burden on their estates during the long period of high and advancing rents remain. A break-up of numerous, of course not all, large estates is inevitable. If sold entire, the estates during the present depression, with farmers relinquishing their tenancies, would be sold at a loss, such as would neutralise the expected relief to landlords. The present agricultural distress is most clearly manifested in the difficulty of paying rent; the weight which oppressively handicaps the English farmer in his struggle with foreign competition is rent; and if the sale of estates is to bring effectual relief to landlords, they must be sold in plots large and small, including small lots, to persons who will cultivate their own properties. Selling in this form, landlords will probably realise from the sale of part of their estates sums sufficient, if invested, to make up, with the rent on the remainder of their estates, nearly their present amounts of income. At the same time the old class of peasant proprietors will be revived; and with them the produce of the land will be increased, in accordance with the ample testimony that small farms realise larger returns than large farms; in other words, the conditions of the struggle with foreign competition will be much improved.

5. This apparently should be the result, if, under the blessing of Heaven, England is to retain her heritage among the nations. Taking the progress of land tenures in France as a type of that on the Continent of Europe, at least among the great States, and the richer among the secondary States, one is struck with the divergence between the lines of progress in England and on the Continent. In both, the same forms of proprietary right prevailed in the early histories of the States; i.e., the right lodged in the members of village communities, or in peasant proprietors as individual rights got separated from the joint rights in the commune.

Chap. IX. In both, feudalism overlaid these rights, and the land, with its heavy burdens; but in a lesser degree in England, where there continued for long a class of sturdy peasant-proprietors, which was recruited from those who from time to time gained enfranchisement from the heavier of the feudal burdens. On the Continent those burdens pressed with steadily accumulating weight until the French Revolution; then there was complete enfranchisement;—feudal rights were simply swept away;—and the peasant cultivators obtained a complete and perfect title as peasant-proprietors. In the other great European States on the Continent, the enfranchisement was later, and it was effected by the act of each State itself, not by a Revolution, but still with the same result as in France.

6. In England the progress of land tenures was very different. The yeomanry who won her liberties for England engaged in the contest, in the same ranks and on the same side with the aristocracy; thereby these latter preserved and increased their privileges and acquisitions, till they became rich and powerful enough to gradually buy out or ex-propriate the yeomen. Thus was brought about in England the aggregation of small farms in large estates, and a disappearance of the class of peasant-proprietors. Feudal burdens ceased in England with the extinction,—they were removed on the Continent by the enfranchisement,—of peasant cultivators. The political and social results of the two systems are that, on the Continent, the cultivators of the land, its peasant-proprietors, are the most conservative force in the State; the fate of the present republic in France trembled in the balance until the peasant-proprietors gave their adhesion to it; and then it received the character of a conservative republic. In England, on the other hand, there is a growing and an alarming severance of the people from the land. Mr. John Macdonell wrote:

XXVIII, 9, vi b. "In his celebrated essay on M. de Tocqueville's book, Mr. Mill has, with similar prescience, remarked that without a large agricultural class, with an attachment to the soil, a permanent connection with it, and the tranquillity and simplicity of rural habits and tastes, there can be no check to the total predominance of an unsettled, uneasy, gain-seeking commercial democracy." * * "So in a late debate upon Irish tenures in Parliament, it was argued with unanswerable force by Mr. Gregory, in reference to the tenure now generally prevalent in the island—"There could be no attachment to the institutions of a country in which the whole of a peasantry existed merely on sufferance; certainly there was nothing conservative in tenancies-at-will, indeed he believed such tenancies to be the most revolutionary in the world." In England, an agricultural class dissevered from the land; on the Continent the cultivating classes proprietors of the land; in which of these will the distribution of land conduce more, and effectually, to the happiness of the people, the stability of the country's institutions, its power of defence, and of making itself respected abroad? As the years roll on, Mr. Caird advises the agricultural population of England to go to Australia, and to leave the land in fewer hands than ever, in presence of monarchies and States mightier than ever;—for his solution of the famine problem is a system of large estates which flourish best when they support on the estates the smallest possible number of people.

7. This may be good advice for the very advanced type of civilisation which sinks the country's good, and is nothing if not cosmopolitan; but agricultural Bengal, with few and poor manufacturing industries, and a population not fitted to emigrate, resembles more the countries on the Continent which are blessed with peasant-proprietors, than England with her large estates, of which there should soon be a break-up into smaller properties, including numerous peasant-properties, if the happiness and prosperity of her people and the conservative forces of the State are to be preserved. Taking Mr. Caird's advice, England's agricultural population went to Australia and the United States in such numbers as to force England to send forth striplings to the battle for the Zulu war; and now England appoints a committee to report on the shrinking of thews and sinews in the British Army. What interminable reporting by military committees there must have been during the decline of the Roman Empire, when the ablest and most energetic of Italy's agricultural population was emigrating; the reports were indeed of no avail against the barbarians, else they would have come down to posterity; but we may be sure that committees submitted able reports which failed to bring able-bodied Roman recruits only because none were to be had.

8. We may sum up:—

1st.—Lord Cornwallis modelled the zemindary system in Bengal on the English system of large estates; the results

CHAP. IX. have been barren of any good, and fruitful in special mischiefs incidental to the system. At the same time the English system which furnished the model is in a precarious state; its best chance of safety is in a renovation through a break-up into smaller properties, principally peasant-properties.

2nd.—On the Continent the cultivating classes are mostly peasant-proprietors, of the class into which Lord Cornwallis would have transformed the ryots in Bengal, if the perpetual assessment for them which he provided in his permanent settlement had been faithfully observed. The peasant-proprietors on the Continent are prosperous; the condition of the ryots in Bengal is bad, except where they pay low rents which have not been greatly increased since the settlement.

3rd.—The ryots in Bengal formed a cultivating class similar in legal status to the peasant-proprietors on the Continent, inasmuch as liability to an established customary rate of rent did not detract, in any essential point, from their status as proprietors. The unnatural forcing of the landed system of Bengal into a conformity with an inapplicable English system of large estates which is now failing in England, has, through subsequent legislation, divested the Bengal ryots of their ancient rights, and subjected them to about quinquennial enhancements of rent, while they are staggering under the burden of the stupendous, almost incredible, payments by them which have been mentioned. Despite their rights, once identical with those of the class who are now peasant-proprietors in Europe, and notwithstanding the permanent assessment provided for them by Lord Cornwallis, it seems to be considered the most natural thing in the world that they should not have fixity of rent.

9. We have traced analogies and contrasts between the zemindary system and ryots' rights in Bengal, and the English system of large estates and the Continental system of peasant-proprietorship in Europe. We may close this chapter with a note of the resemblance between some of the steps in the descent of the Russian peasant to serfdom, and the mistakes—destructive of ryots' rights—which were committed by Lord Cornwallis and his successors in the zemindary settlement.

XXVII, 12 a.   I. The Czar granted waste lands to Russian land-owners, as Lord Cornwallis made a similar free gift to zemindars, when there was a scarcity of labourers and a competition for

them. The same result ensued from both grants, *viz.*, an Chap. IX.
endeavour by some land-owners or zemindars to draw away
cultivators from others. In Russia this caused discontent
among the land-owners ; in Bengal it endangered the security
of the revenue under the permanent settlement. In both
countries alike, the remedy adopted was to set aside summarily a right of the cultivator. In Russia "severe fugitive XXVII, 12 c.
laws were issued against those who attempted to change
their domicile, and against the proprietors who should harbour
the runaways." In Bengal, as a check upon giving land at
low rents, zemindars were restrained from letting for more
than ten years, and this was interpreted to the destruction
of the ryots' right to hold for ever so long as he paid the
established rent. A little later, from difficulties in paying
rent, arising partly out of the gift of waste lands, partly
from other causes, the *Huftum* and *Punjum* Regulations
were passed, which conferred great powers upon zemindars,
and the ryots became *adscripti glebæ*.

II. Mr. Wallace writes of Russia in those early days :
"The force of custom prevented the proprietors for a time from
making any important alterations in the existing contracts ;—"
(the same thing happened with the zemindars.) "As time
wore on, however," exactions increased :—"So far from endeavouring to protect the peasantry from the oppression of *Ibid,* 12 e.
the proprietors, the Government did not even determine by
law the mutual obligations which ought to exist between the
two classes ;" (precisely in the same way, the government
of Lord Cornwallis omitted to ensure a record of the specific
amount of rent payable by each ryot).

III. "Taking advantage of this omission, the proprietors
soon began to impose whatever obligations they thought fit,
and as they had no legal means of enforcing fulfilment, they
gradually introduced a patriarchal jurisdiction, similar to
that which they exercised over their slaves, with fines and
corporal punishment as means of coercion." (This describes
exactly the origin of the *Huftum* and *Punjum* Regulations,
and the coercion practised by zemindars in their private
cutcherries under colour of those Regulations.)

IV. "The proprietor could easily overcome any active
resistance by selling or converting into domestic servants
the peasants who dared to oppose his will." (In Bengal the
law did not allow the sale of peasants, but a permission to
sell would not have been availed of : the refractory ryot
was soon coerced by other more effectual means, and he was

Chap. IX. of more value in a state of predial bondage than the money which he could have fetched if sold as a slave).

V. "To facilitate the collection of the poll tax, the proprietors were made responsible for their serfs. * * These measures had a considerable influence, if not on the actual position of the peasantry, at least on the legal conceptions regarding them. By making the proprietor pay the poll tax for his serfs, as if they were slaves or cattle, the law seemed to sanction the idea that they were part of his goods and chattels." Of Bengal, Lord Hastings observed that the appointment of zemindar as collector of revenue from the Chap. III, para. 11. ryots invested him with power to oppress, and with a character in which his position as collector was confounded with that of proprietor.

VI. "From an historical review of the question of serfage, XXVII, 20. the Emperor drew the conclusion that "the autocratic power created serfage, and the autocratic power ought to abolish it." Here, the parallel fails, as yet, in Bengal; for there has not been any corresponding declaration by the Bengal Government regarding the restoration of ryots' rights. But the Lieutenant-Governor of Bengal thinks for himself, and has the courage of his convictions; and England will not be less virtuous than the Czar in confessing error and making amends for nigh one century of wrong.

CHAPTER X.

LIBERATION OF CULTIVATORS IN EUROPE.

From the facts which have been ascertained in previous Chapters we select four, *viz.* :—

I. Ryots were proprietors of their holdings under the Law and Constitution of India, which the permanent settlement was designed to perpetuate for Bengal.

II. A broken pledge of a permanent assessment for the ryots, to whom the faith of Government was as solemnly pledged as to the zemindars in the permanent settlement with them. Solemnity would have ill beseemed the transfer by Government to a few office-holders, mostly worthless characters, of the property of its subject millions ;—but in a compact between rulers and people which assured to the ryots the same permanency of assessment as to the zemindar, there is a grandeur of conception to which the solemnity of the engagement of 1793 was befitting.

III. Over the greater part of Bengal ryots' rights have been destroyed, the zemindars seeming to be regarded as the proprietors of all except a bare subsistence which is left for the ryot.

IV. Ryots in Bengal pay to Government, to zemindars, and to middlemen, more, by at least one-half, than the land revenue of the rest of British India, whilst the population of Bengal is not one-third and its area slightly over one-sixth of the totals for British India.

V. With these, especially with I and III, we may couple a fact not before noticed in these remarks, namely, the notoriously litigious character of the people of Bengal, which shows itself more particularly in the preponderance, in the Civil Courts, of suits connected with rent and land. Nearly fifty years ago, the Select Committee of 1831-32 reported that " the natives of India have a deep-rooted attachment to hereditary rights and offices, and animosities originating in disputes regarding lands descend through generations." The tradition of the ryot's proprietary right in the land is as strong as in 1793; but the zemindar's power to enhance rent, a power destructive of proprietary right, is such as was

Chap. X. unheard of in 1793. A deep-rooted, undying tradition is in
—— conflict with facts in 1879. The conflict rages in the civil,
and often in the criminal courts, with a bitterness peculiar
to disputes about land, with an intensity of hate that, if
spread over a great part of Bengal, is a conception of a kind
to make the flesh creep; and with results ruinous to both
parties, ruinous to the ryots in the degree of the ill-success
of a poor man contending against a rich man in a court of
law; ruinous to both ryot and zemindar in respect of the
corroding effect of hatred on the moral qualities of our better
nature. This melancholy strife, continued through three
generations, but intensified since 1859, has confirmed the
people of Bengal in a habit of litigation which means the
play of the worst passions; but under the euphemism of a
tax upon litigation we sweep into the public treasury, as
the gold into the bank at a roulette table, a flourishing
stamp revenue, and thank God for our beneficent, healthful,
moral rule of British India.

2. Those who are concerned for the honour and good
name of the British rule, and who have imagination and
sympathy to realise what must be the baneful influence of the
preceding facts on the happiness, and on the social and moral
condition, of the myriads of ryots whom they affect, will not
gainsay the conclusion that a remedy—full, substantial, real,
searching, effective, and thorough—must be found, even if that
to be presently suggested should not meet acceptance.

3. In an earlier Chapter, to get a clear view of ryots'
rights in Bengal before the permanent settlement, we looked
first in the direction of the village communities outside
Bengal, and examined their proprietary rights. In like
manner, we may find out a way of restoring ryots' rights in
Bengal if we look first at what other States have done for
the liberation of the same class of cultivators in Europe.

4. The principal examples are afforded by Denmark,
Baden, Austria, Prussia, Bavaria, Russia.

I.—DENMARK—

XXVI, 1. The measures of liberation were confined to promoting
the purchase of their farms in fee simple, by the peasant
cultivators. Mr. G. Strachey reported on 18th December
1869 :—

The tenures of Denmark are not the tenures of England. The
Danish landlord is not, except as regards his demesne, the complete
legal or customary master of his own. To the tenemental lands he

stands, roughly speaking, as did the zemindar to the ryot before the permanent settlement. From another point of view the analogy between the Bengalee and the Scandinavian would be close enough. If the zemindar-proprietor, or tax-gatherer, was not the mildest of masters, the Danish Jorddrot was, till recent times, the scourge of the peasantry. Under his parental love the Danish " bönde," now the freest, the most politically wise, the best educated of continental yeomen, was a mere hewer of wood and drawer of water. His lot was no better than that of the most miserable ryot of Bengal.

What has been changed in Denmark, should admit of as thorough and beneficial a change in Bengal.

II.—BADEN—GRAND DUCHY OF—

The tithes, dues, and various charges with which the land was at one time burdened, were all abolished by law during the period from 1833 to 1848, and compensation awarded to the land-owners for the losses thereby sustained. The burdens were commuted for a capital sum, generally 16 to 18 times the amount of their annual value.

III.—AUSTRIA—

The application of a feudal system to land and labour lasted in Austria till the year 1848, when it was abolished by revolutionary legislation. * * The manner in which this change was effected was by compensation from the State to the great proprietors for the pecuniary value of the feudal rights of which the State deprived them. * * A commission, in which all the great proprietors were fully represented, having calculated the pecuniary value of the feudal rights enjoyed by each proprietor, and the consequent compensation due to each proprietor for the abolition of those rights, presented to the Government its estimate of the total amount. From this estimated total the Government cancelled one-third. * * The result of this arrangement is, that of the total amount of compensation assigned by the Land Commission to the great proprietors, one-third has been altogether disallowed by the State, and one of the remaining two-thirds is raised by a tax levied upon the great proprietors themselves. Virtually, therefore, the compensation they receive for the abolition of their feudal rights is only one-third of their estimated pecuniary value. The great proprietors generally complain of this. But there are, at the present moment, very few of them who are not ready to admit that (despite also of the great inconvenience and heavy pecuniary loss to which they were subjected by the suddenness of the change through which they have passed) that change has been on the whole decidedly beneficial to themselves, as well as to all other classes of the population, from an agricultural no less than from a social point of view.

IV.—FRANCE—

Feudal burdens were abolished in the Revolution without compensation.

CHAP. **X.**

XXVI, **3.**

XXVI, **4.**

V.—Prussia—

(a). The edict of 1807 abolished villeinage, without compensating land-owners.

(b). The edict of 1811 set itself to substitute allodial ownership for feudal tenure. Tenants of hereditary holdings shall by the present edict become the proprietors of their holdings, after paying to the landlord the indemnity fixed by this edict. * * We desire that landlords and tenants should of themselves come to terms of agreement, and give them two years from the date of this edict to do so. If within that time the work is not done, the State will undertake it. * * To obtain, therefore, a solid foundation for the work of commutation, and not to render it nugatory by difficulties impossible to be overcome, we deem it necessary to lay down certain rules for arriving at this estimate of the value of the services due from the tenant to the landlord,—and to deduce those rules from the general principles laid down by the laws of the State.

These principles are :—

(1). That in the case of hereditary holdings, neither the services nor the dues can, under any circumstances, be raised.

(2). That they must, on the contrary, be lowered if the holder cannot subsist at their actual rate.

(3). That the holding must be maintained in a condition which will enable it to pay its dues to the State.

From these three principles, and from the general principles of the public law, it follows that the right of the State, both to ordinary and extraordinary taxes, takes precedence of every other right, and that the services to the manor are limited by the obligation which the latter is under to leave the tenant sufficient means to subsist and pay taxes.

(c). What the statesmen did in Prussia in 1811 was this :—they took half (from temporary) or one-third (from hereditary) holdings, of the land possessed by the tenants of Prussia, and handed it over in full possession to the landlords of Prussia. The land occupied by these tenants was land on which, *except in case of devastation and in virtue of a judgment passed by a Court of law*, the Lord of the Manor had no right of re-entry. What the law of 1811 did was to force the Lord of the Manor to sell to the copyholder his manorial overlordship, (that is, his rights of ownership, and to ordinary services and dues from the tenants) for one-half or one-third of the copyhold. By this process he was put in possession of more land than he was possessed of before; what he was deprived of was labour. The tenant lost one-half or one-third of the land he possessed before, but obtained the *dominium directum* as well as the *dominium utile* over the remaining half or two-thirds : what was, however, much more important, he got back the free use of his own labour. The landlord sold labour and bought land; the tenant sold land and bought labour.

(d). A separate edict enacted as a supplementary measure that in the case of hereditary leaseholds, the services and fines may be commuted into rent charges, and these rent charges redeemed by a capital payment calculated at 4 per cent.

(e). After 1811, the most directly retrogressive step was the declaration of the 29th May 1816, which limited the action of the edict of 1811 to farms of a comparatively large size, without abrogating the provisions of the separate " Edict for the better cultivation of the land," which did CHAP. X. away with the constitutional difference between peasant's land and demesne land, and established the principle of free trade in land. By the combined effects of these two principles, the " so-called small folk " whom the latter edict so ostentatiously took under its protection, *i.e.*, the great mass of small holders, who did not cultivate with teams,—were placed at a huge disadvantage, for where their tenures were hereditary, they continued burdened with feudal services and dues ; where they were not hereditary, they were evicted wholesale.

(*f*). The legislation of 1850 included a law for the redemption of services and dues, and the regulation of the relations between the lords of the manor and their peasants. This law abrogated the "*dominium directum*," or overlordship of the lords of the manor, without compensation; so that from the day of its publication all hereditary holders throughout the Prussian monarchy, irrespectively of the size of their holdings, became proprietors, subject, however, to the customary services and dues, which by the further provisions of the law were commuted into fixed money rents, calculated on the average money value of the services and dues rendered and paid during a certain number of years preceding. By a further provision these rent-charges were made compulsorily redeemable, either by the immediate payment of a capital equivalent to an 18 years' purchase of the rent-charge, or by a payment of $4\frac{1}{2}$ or 5 per cent. for $56\frac{1}{1f}$ or $41\frac{1}{12}$ years, on a capital equivalent to 20 years' purchase of the rent-charge.

VI.—BAVARIA—

(*a*). The law of 1848 decreed (1) that after the 1st January XXVI, 8. 1849, personal services[1] of every description rendered in respect of the occupancy of lands, houses, &c., should be absolutely abolished, without any indemnity being made to the ground landlord; (2) that every peasant should be competent to buy off or commute, by means of a money payment once for all, or a yearly sum to be paid during a certain number of years, all charges, tithes, or burthens, of whatsoever description, subject to which he held his land from the ground landlord; and that, having done so, he should become the freehold proprietor of the land.

(*b*). The net annual money value of the burdens to be commuted was to be ascertained and fixed by a commission specially appointed for this purpose for each administrative district, the basis assigned for the valuation of all tithes in kind being the average of the ascertained value during the period of eighteen years from 1828 to 1845.

(*c*). The value having been thus fixed in the form of an annual money payment, the peasant was in each case left at liberty to redeem the payment :—

(1). By settling direct with the landlord, paying him either a lump sum, once for all, equal to eighteen times the amount at which his yearly money payment has been assessed by the Commissioners; or, by annual instalments spread over 34 or 43 years.

---

[1] *Viz.*, a certain number of days' work, with or without the peasants' cattle, the providing of beaters for the chase, &c.

(2). By creating in favour of the State a mortgage bearing 4 per cent. interest on his land, for a sum representing (as in the first-mentioned mode of commutation) eighteen times the amount of the annual assessed payment.

VII.—RUSSIA—

XXVII, 27.   (*a*). The leading principles on which the Emancipation Act is now based are as follows :—

(1). The cession by the landlord of the perpetual usufruct (tenancy) of the serf's homestead, and of certain allotments of land, on terms settled by mutual agreement, or, failing which, on conditions fixed by law.

(2). The compulsory sale by the lord, at the desire of the serf, of the serf's homestead, either on terms fixed by mutual agreement, or on terms fixed by law, the right of refusing to sell the homestead without the statute land allotment being reserved by law.

(3). State assistance in the redemption (purchase) by the serf of his homestead and territorial allotment, provided the lord shall agree to sell the latter.

(*b*). As regards, therefore, the interests of the serf, the Emancipation Act confers upon him the right of—

(1). a freeman ;

(2). enjoying on terms fixed by law the perpetual usufruct of the homestead, and of certain maximum and minimum territorial allotments, based on the quality of land which he cultivated prior to the emancipation ;

(3). converting his liability to service (socage) into a money rent, on terms fixed by law ;

(4). demanding the sale of his homestead from the lord, and (subject to the consent of the lord) purchasing his territorial allotment also ;

(5). fully and finally terminating (with the help of the State) his relations of dependence towards the lord of the soil, by the redemption of homesteads and territorial allotments.

(*c*). The interests of the landed proprietors were protected by the following provisions of the Emancipation Act :—

(1). Whether the lord grant the perpetual usufruct (tenancy), or the freehold, of the peasant homesteads and land allotments, a money payment, more or less equivalent, based on the rents which he previously enjoyed, is secured to him, and he is therefore called upon to cede without compensation only his political rights over the serf, and his right to the gratuitous labour of the domestic serf.

(2). He can insist on the serf purchasing his territorial allotment as well as the homestead ; and he can refuse to sell the former without the latter.

(3). He can avoid the cession of the perpetual usufruct of the territorial allotments fixed by law, by bestowing, as a free gift on the peasantry who shall consent to receive the same, a quarter of the maximum allotment of which they are entitled to enjoy the usufruct, with the homestead on it.

5. The nature of the burdens on the peasant cultivators and the measures for their liberation, were substantially o

the same character in all the States. The burdens were reduced to a money amount of yearly value. This money amount, or a lower one, was then fixed as the permanent assessment on the cultivator, with liberty to him to redeem the money payment by a lump payment, or payments, of so many years' purchase of the money value. The first of these arrangements, *viz.*, a permanent assessment for the cultivators, was a novelty,—a great innovation,—in Europe. It was no novelty in Bengal, for the ryots had paid ancient customary rates of rent until the permanent settlement, and they were assured by the authors of that settlement, and by the Regulations of 1793, of a permanent assessment of their holdings. The novelty or great innovation has settled into law and custom in Europe—precisely the same arrangement which in Bengal accorded with ancient custom, and for which the faith of Government was as solemnly pledged to the ryot as the faith pledged to the zemindar has been put aside and subverted in Bengal,—the ryots being now subject to about quinquennial enhancements of rent. The ryots in Bengal were the real proprietors of land in 1789; but the majority of them now bear at least as heavy burdens as did, in that year, the cultivators in Continental Europe, who, through liberation from their burdens, are now peasant-proprietors, in a condition of prosperity with which the worse condition of the Bengal ryot can only be contrasted, not compared. In matters agrarian, which, after all, lie nearest to the hearts of the people, the rule of despotic States on the Continent, during this century, has been more considerate, beneficent, conservative, and restorative of ancient rights of the cultivators of the soil, than the English rule in Bengal for the same period.

6. In commuting the feudal services and burdens on land into money payments, credit was not allowed to the landowner for unearned increment; the valuations were based on past actual collections, and even the average amount thus obtained was not, in every case, given to the land-owner without abatement. Furthermore, though the cultivators had been *adscripti glebæ* for periods compared with which the ninety years elapsed since the decennial settlement of 1789 are but a brief interval, the governments of the five States were not deterred from their measures of bare justice and humanity by pleas of prescription and vested rights, and of injury to persons who had bought estates in the inhuman belief in a perpetuity of exaction and oppression.

_____

7. The measures of liberation included, we have seen, the option of redeeming a new perpetual assessment by a capital payment. Some of the States helped the peasants in providing the redemption money.

I.—Austria—

XXVI, 4.   (*a*). From the estimated annual value of the feudal rights that were to be abolished, the Government cancelled one-third. Two-thirds remained to be provided for. The amount represented by these two-thirds, the State undertook to pay, in 5 per cent. bonds, the whole debt being redeemable in 40 years, by annual drawings at par. To carry out this engagement, therefore, it was necessary to provide, not only for the annual interest on the debt, but also for its redemption by means of a sinking fund within forty years.

(*b*). One-third of the amount necessary for this purpose is provided for by a tax levied exclusively on the new peasant-proprietors, and regarded as the price payable by them to the State for the immense advantage which they derived from the Legislation of 1848. The remaining one-third is assessed as a sur-tax on the local taxation of each province, and annually voted as part of the local budget by each of the provincial diets. The result of the arrangement is, &c. (see quotation in para. 4, II).

II.—Baden—

XXVI, 3.   The burdens were commuted for a capital sum, generally 16 to 18 times the amount of their annual value. The law further provided that this capital, of which the State undertook to discharge one-fifth, should be paid off in equal portions annually (shorter periods not being excluded), together with 4 per cent. interest during 25 years.

III.—Prussia—

XXVI, 6, X.   (*a*). The rent charges having been permanently fixed were made compulsorily redeemable, either by the immediate payment of a capital equivalent to an eighteen years' purchase of the rent charge, or by a payment of $4\frac{1}{2}$ or 5 per cent. for $56\frac{1}{12}$ or $41\frac{1}{12}$ years, on a capital equivalent to 20 years' purchase of the rent charge.

(*b*). The law for the establishment of rent-banks provided the machinery for this wholesale redemption. By it the State, through the instrumentality of the rent banks, constituted itself the broker between the peasants by whom the rents had to be paid and the landlords who had to receive them.

(*c*). The bank established in each district advanced to the landlords, in rent debentures paying 4 per cent. interest, a capital sum equal to 20 years' purchase of the rent. The peasant, along with his ordinary rates and taxes, paid into the hands of the district tax-collector, each month, one-twelfth part of a rent calculated at 5 or $4\frac{1}{2}$ per cent. on this capital sum, according as he elected to free his property from encumbrance in $41\frac{1}{2}$ or in $56\frac{1}{2}$ years, the respective terms within which, at

compound interest, the 1 or $\frac{1}{2}$ per cent. paid in addition to the 4 per cent. CHAP. X.
interest on the debenture would extinguish the capital.

IV.—BAVARIA—

(*a*). If the peasant elected to redeem the permanent yearly rent charge XXVI, 8, v.
with the State's help, the transaction was between the peasant and the
State, and the latter, having obtained the mortgage on the peasant's
land, undertook to indemnify the ground landlord for the dues or tithes
which he relinquished.

(*b*). For the latter purpose the law authorised the Government to create
" Land charge redemption debentures," bearing 4 per cent. interest,
and to make over to each ground landlord a sum, in these debentures,
reckoned at their full par value, equal to twenty times the annual value
as fixed by the Commissioner of the land charges or tithes to be commuted.

(*c*). It will thus be seen that whilst the peasants were permitted to
compound for their land burdens, by means of mortgages created in
favour of the Government, on the basis of eighteen years' purchase of
those burdens, the Government undertook to indemnify the ground landlords on the basis of twenty years' purchase, the State having been
consequently a loser under this arrangement to the extent of the difference between the two rates assumed.

(*d*). The law of 1848 further provided that a sinking fund for the
voluntary amortization of the peasants' Land Charge Redemption Mortgages should be established, and that the payments made annually by
the peasants as contributions towards that fund should be devoted to the
redemption, every year, of a corresponding amount of the debentures
issued by the Government as indemnity to the ground landlords.

V.—RUSSIA—

(*a*). The work of concluding contracts for the redemption of the dues,
or, in other words, for the purchase of the land ceded in perpetual usufruct,
proceeded slowly, and is, in fact, still going on. The arrangement was
as follows :—The dues were capitalized at 6 per cent., and the Government paid at once to the proprietors four-fifths of the whole sum. The
peasants were to pay to the proprietor the remaining fifth, either at once
or in instalments, and to Government 6 per cent. for 49 years on the
sum advanced. The proprietors willingly adopted this arrangement, for
it provided them with a sum of ready money, and freed them from the
difficult task of collecting dues.

(*b*). The advances of redemption money by the State were protected
by the introduction of a system of collective responsibility under which
the peasantry were made to guarantee mutually the exact payment of their
quit-rents, taxes, and " redemption dues." That collective responsibility
was laid on the village communes, which, as corporate bodies, became
purchasers of the land ceded to the peasantry, who thus became in a
measure only tenants in common.

8. In this account of the manner in which funds for the
redemption of peasants' dues, or the purchase of free-hold

CHAP. X. rights, were provided in five States, the following noteworthy
—   points are observed :—

I. The sum advanced by the State to the proprietors was
recoverable from the peasants, whose lands were mortgaged
to the State till repayment of its advances.

II. The rate of interest charged on the advances was as
low as possible, in two instances 4 per cent. per annum;
with a further percentage for forming a sinking fund for
liquidation of the debt in twenty-five to fifty years.

III. One of the States found it expedient to make each
village jointly responsible for the sum advanced for each
peasant's holding.

IV. The payments to the proprietors were not in cash,
but in bonds redeemable at distant or indefinite periods ;—
recoveries from peasants were set apart for the redemption
of the bonds.

V. When the dues by the peasants were once permanently
assessed, the statesmen who secured this result could have
urged, in the platitudes of safe men, that they had done
enough; but they arranged further for the redemption of
the dues ;—evidently, it was felt that, even with a permanent
assessment, the peasant would not be free from risk of oppression, if his relations of tenant towards a landlord continued.
The feeling would have found justification in Bengal, where,
no matter what the law might exact, its decrees affecting
the relations of zemindar towards ryot may be ineffectual,
through the overpowering influence of the zemindar. And
so, European States, including some with a credit not so
good as India's, and all of them with a credit inferior to
England's, deemed it their duty to help the peasant-proprietors with the State's credit in buying freehold properties.

CHAPTER XI.

REDEMPTION OF BENGAL RYOTS' DUES.

We have seen in the previous chapter how cultivators bending under feudal burdens were liberated by European States, sometimes at a cost to those States which they could not afford with the same facility as England or India. The burdens from which they relieved the peasants had accumulated during centuries. It is only during the present century, under British rule, and under Regulations and Acts since 1793, that similar burdens have accumulated on Bengal ryots, who have lost the status they had in the last century as peasant-proprietors.

2. The destruction of ryots' rights has occurred from a series of mistakes, and through the influence of the first and greatest mistake, viz., the formation of a zemindary settlement for Bengal. The Parliament of England shares responsibility for that error. There was a dispossession of zemindars from their offices in which they were replaced by farmers of rents. Mistaking the zemindars for landholders, Parliament directed their reinstatement; and in carrying out its behests, Lord Cornwallis devised for Bengal a zemindary settlement. A Select Committee of the House of Commons stated, in 1812, in their Fifth Report, that unheard of rights had been conferred on zemindars in the settlement of 1789-93, and that the ryots possessed definite substantial rights: "with respect to the cultivators or ryots, their rights and customs varied so much in different parts of the country and appeared to the Government to involve so much intricacy, that the Regulation VIII, 1793, only provides generally for engagements being entered into, and pottahs or leases being granted by the zemindars, leaving the terms to be such as shall appear to have been customary, or as shall be particularly adjusted between the parties; and in this *it is probable* that the intentions and expectations of the Government *have been fulfilled, as no new regulation yet appears, altering or rescinding the one alluded to.*" In the passage italicised, the Select Committee were content, on so important a matter as the permanent assessment of

CHPA. XI. the ryot's holding, to accept as sufficient evidence of everything being as it should be, that no new regulation had been
issued amending that of 1793.

3. Nineteen years later, the Select Committee of the
House of Commons in 1831-32 observed that

IV, 9, iii. " in the permanently settled districts in Bengal, nothing is settled and
little is known, but the Government assessment. The causes of this
failure may be ascribed in a great degree to the error of assuming, at
the time of making the permanent settlement, that the rights of
all parties claiming an interest in the land were sufficiently
established by usage to enable the Courts to protect individual
rights; and still more to the measure which declared the zemindar
to be the hereditary owner of the soil; whereas it is contended
that he was originally, with few exceptions, the mere hereditary
steward, representative, or officer of the Government, and his undeniable hereditary property in the land revenue was totally distinct
from property in the land itself. Whilst, however, the amount of
revenue payable by the zemindar to Government became fixed, no
efficient measures appear to have been taken to define or limit the
demand of the zemindar upon the ryots who possessed a hereditary
right of occupancy, on condition of their cultivating the land or finding
tenants to do so. Without going into detail to show the working of
the system, it may be proper to quote the opinion of Lord Hastings,
as recorded in 1819, when he held the office of Governor General of
India. " Never," says Lord Hastings, " was there a measure conceived
in a purer spirit of generous humanity and disinterested justice, than
the plan for the permanent settlement in the Lower Provinces. It was
worthy the soul of Cornwallis. Yet this truly benevolent purpose,
fashioned with great care and deliberation, has to our painful knowledge
subjected almost the whole of the lower classes throughout these provinces to most grievous oppression, an oppression, too, so guaranteed
by our pledge, that we are unable to relieve the sufferers—a right of
ownership in the soil, *absolutely gratuitous*, having been vested in the
person through whom the payment to the State was to be made,
with unlimited power to wring from his co-parceners an exorbitant rent
for the use of any part of the land." * * " If, then, the conclusion
may be formed that the permanent settlement of Lord Cornwallis has
failed in its professed object, it must be a matter of anxious enquiry to
ascertain how far the evils of the system are capable of being remedied."

4. Thus, for the second time was the subject brought
before Parliament, with a distinct report that ryots' rights
had been destroyed, and that the permanent settlement had
failed in its professed object; but nothing was done. Even
had rates of rent been then fixed permanently for the ryots,
their legal status, though worse than that conferred on them
by the Regulations of 1793, would have been better than
their *status* in the present day.

5. In respect of these two Reports of the Select Committees of 1812 and of 1831-32, Parliament had a special responsibility; but for the mistakes enumerated in Chapter VIII, para. 6, it had also a general responsibility.

6. These errors are no light thing; they mean the stupendous, almost incredible burdens, laid upon the ryots in the present day, which are enumerated in Chapter I, para. 13:—above forty millions of people impoverished by a settlement formed in execution of orders by Parliament;—and the British nation's grave responsibility for the errors is not set aside by merely talking of the benevolence of Lord Cornwallis, and with superior wisdom bewailing the mistakes of himself and his successors. Confessions of impotence will not relieve one iota of the ryots' burdens, whilst the governments of many European States have shown the way how to remove them.

7. Those European States liberated cultivators of the soil whose proprietary rights were weaker than the ryots' rights which British rule has destroyed; therefore is there a greater stress of obligation and duty on England, and on the Government in India, to do not less than several European States have done.

8. In proportion as the duty of the Government is imperative, the zemindars have to accept the inevitable, viz., any measure for clearing the conscience of British rulers of the sin by which, though unwittingly, they destroyed ryots' rights, incurring the reproach of broken pledges. The examples of European States, and the principles which XXXI, 5. determine compensation for putting aside private rights, will command the acquiescence of zemindars; while again, the burden which is oppressing the liberated Russian serfs, from the redemption of their dues at too high a price, inculcates moderation, and zemindars are aware that ryots received no compensation whatever for the mutilation, in favour of the zemindars, of ryots' rights which were supported by the prescription of centuries, while the zemindars cannot plead the prescription of even one century.

9. As a first step there might be stopped all further enhancement of rent, thus carrying out, some ninety years after it was conceived, the clear unmistakable purpose of the authors of the permanent settlement that there should be a permanent assessment for ryots. This measure might be general throughout the permanently-settled districts under the Bengal Government; though the redemption of

CHAP. XI. the rent, or purchase by ryots of the fee-simple of their
—— holdings, might be gradual, being extended, beyond a few
districts at a time, only according to the agency at the
command of Government.

10. By stopping further enhancement of rent, the multiplication of middlemen would cease; and the factitious
value that attaches to zemindaries from any scope which they
afford for raising ryots' rents, would also fall away; though
perhaps not to any thing like the extent it should; for, as
observed by Sir George Campbell, law or no law, the
zemindar can do much without law or against law. Hence,
it would not be safe to rest content with prohibiting
further enhancement of rent; the supplemental measure
of redemption should be introduced without avoidable delay:
it might include a sale of zemindary rights in Bengal by
zemindars to the ryots, and a mortgage of Bengal by ryots
to the Government as security for the purchase-money to be
advanced by Government.

11. The outside compensation to zemindars might be
about 16 years' purchase, for, in parts of the country where
the price is higher, the exactions of zemindars enhance their
income and the value of their estates, and it would be
against sound principle to allow compensation for exactions.
The road cess returns give 13 millions sterling as the yearly
value of estates, and 8 millions as the annual value of
middle tenures. To lay apprehension it might seem that a
total yearly profit of 21 millions sterling is obtained out of
the payments by ryots; but it appears that the 8 millions of yearly value of tenures are included in the 13 millions of valuation of estates. Taking the yearly value of
estates, including that of middle tenures, at 13 millions
sterling, the total, at 16 years' purchase, would be 208 millions
sterling. At the same time the zemindars might be required
to capitalise their payment of land revenue at twenty years'
purchase; this for $3\frac{2}{3}$ millions sterling would amount to
73 millions. On this calculation, the outside payment to
zemindars and middlemen for reducing ryots' dues would
be 135 millions sterling. But very large abatements can be
made.

I. Immediately above the ryot is the middleman who has
farmed rents with the view of enhancing them; he must be
bought out; at the top is the zemindar, whose revenue to
Government has to be capitalised; he too must be bought
out; but grades of middlemen, intermediate between these

two, have no authority over the ryots, and they may be left Chap. XI. as they are, unless it be convenient to redeem the annuities payable to them. If these annuities be not capitalised, the outlay required will be much reduced.

II. Among the farmers immediately above the ryots, there are many who have only temporary leases ; a number of these leases might on scrutiny be cancelled ; others, on account of their short term, may 'be left to expire ; the remainder would be redeemable for fewer years' purchase than the permanent interest of zemindars.

III. Like discrimination may be observed in dealing with zemindars, among whom are many who have extensively purchased estates on foreclosure of mortgages, or on other forced sales during the past ten or twenty years. It will bear consideration whether the compensation to these should be limited to about the sums which they paid for their estates, or should be regulated by the market value of the estates ; if the former be a fair adjustment, then some material abatement of the total outlay would be effected under this head.

IV. In most zemindaries, the income is swollen by the levy of cesses, market dues, &c. The Regulations of 1793 warned zemindars that three times the amount of any fresh cesses imposed by them would be recovered from them for the full period that the cesses may have been imposed. There would be no call to redeem the payment of these unauthorized cesses at so many years' purchase of their annual yield. Were the law strong enough and searching enough, all these would be discontinued now, under present arrangements, without any compensation. The plea has been set up for zemindars, that the fresh cesses levied since 1793, in defiance of the Regulations of that year, are only an irregular form of raising ryots' rents ; but the raising of rents is also repugnant to those regulations which provided a permanent assessment for ryots ; therefore, in this matter, a too facile disposition to yield everything to zemindars by way of a compromise, which, if really a compromise, ought to include some equivalent surrender by them, should be restrained, it being borne in mind that extra payments to zemindars from undue concessions would be recovered from the ryots. The former should have justice, and in addition such liberal measure as will leave liberal measure also for the ryots, compared with their present condition.

CHAP. XI.   V. There are good zemindars, and there are bad zemin-
—————   dars who rack-rent the ryots, taking from them the uttermost farthing. The annual value of the estates of these
latter is, by reason of the oppression they practise, greater
than that of other estates of the same class and size. On
sale, they probably fetch, also, many more years' purchase
of the income of the zemindaries than the estates of good
zemindars; estates in Behar are worth above twenty-five
years' purchase; in Eastern Bengal only fourteen or sixteen
years' purchase. Were there to be no discrimination between
the sheep and the goats, the good zemindar would simply get
the reward of his own conscience; while the oppressive rack-
renting zemindar would get Benjamin's portion. It would
be for the district officers to cut down the annual value of the
estates of bad zemindars, or to allow them fewer years' purchase than the standard compensation. A very nice adjustment would not be necessary; nothing more than the removal
of glaring inequalities need be attempted in the scrutiny and
revision, preparatory to payment of compensation.

VI. The rents paid in the present day greatly exceed the
established pergunnah rates of 1793, which were assured to
the ryots in the permanent settlement. The only case in
XVI, 17. which, consistently with the assurance of 1793, the ryot's
rent could be raised, was on his changing, after that year, to
a more valuable produce; but in that case his new rent had
to be adjusted to the established rate for the new produce
at the time that the change was effected. The rate of that
time, for the more valuable produce, became the permanent
rate for the ryot; and any subsequent enhancement of it was
a breach of the settlement of 1793. Hence, in the present
day, a large part of the income of zemindars is derived from
the excess of the rates paid by ryots over the permanent rates
which were assured to them at the permanent settlement. It
may bear consideration whether the zemindar's income should
not be distinguished into (*1st*) the portion which is conformable with the spirit of the permanent settlement; and (*2nd*)
the portion which has accrued from a violation of the
Government's solemn engagement to the ryot. The compensation for the first and second parts could then be regulated on different principles. For the first, there would
be full compensation; for the second, under English law an
entail of an estate to which there is a good title can extend
"ordinarily for fifty, but possibly for eighty or even ninety
years. In common parlance—for the practice is that now in

force—estates in land may be settled upon any number of CHAP. XI.
lives in being, *and twenty-one years afterwards.*" It is for
lawyers and actuaries to say whether, the foregoing distinction XXXI, 7 & 8.
being recognised, an inferior compensation for the second
part of the zemindar's income would not be fair, nay, imperative, in justice to the ryot.

VII. Existing rents have been adjusted to a considerable
rise of prices since 1793, in violation of the permanent
assessment which was designed for the ryot: it is probable
that prices will fall, and this consideration should induce
caution in appraising the value of estates.

VIII. To Bengal officers, who are familiar with details of
zemindary management, and of the relations between zemindars and middlemen, and zemindars and ryots, other equitable
grounds of abatement will perhaps occur; and some considerations in favour of zemindars may also arise. One large
exception, for instance, must be made regarding minerals; but
with respect to these there is no tension in the relations of
zemindar and ryot, and accordingly it is not necessary to
buy out zemindars' rights in respect of coal fields, mines,
quarries, &c.

12. We assumed, in para. 11, that an outside sum of 135
millions sterling, *viz.*, 208 millions gross, less 73 millions of
capitalised land revenue, might be required to buy out the
rights of zemindars and middlemen. With the preceding large
abatements, the net amount would probably be reduced
below 100 millions, for the gross amount includes 128 millions
of compensation to middlemen alone, or a sum which at $4\frac{1}{2}$
per cent. interest would give them an income of one and a
half times the land revenue of Bengal. Making, however,
the large assumption that 100 millions sterling net would be
required to buy out the zemindars of Bengal; and adding
100 millions more for paying off ryots' debts to village
bankers (Chapter XII), thus raising the total to 200
millions,—how is that money to be provided?

13. Following the example of the European States which
have liberated their cultivators of the land, the money for
redeeming the dues to zemindars might be provided in paper,
namely, in bonds to be issued to the zemindars; but as the
entire Public Debt of India, bearing interest, in both England and India, may be reckoned at 143 millions, would not
the issue of a stock of 100 millions sterling depreciate
Indian securities? England and the British rule in India are
jointly responsible for the present unsatisfactory condition of

CHAP. XI. Bengal, and of the relations between zemindar and ryots; and
they must jointly take the bull by the horns, and pay off
existing Public Debt in India, by measures which would, for
many years to come, supersede the existing Rupee Debt in
India by a new sterling Loan in London; in that case, the
payment of zemindars by bonds would not cause any difficulty.

14. In discharge of weighty moral obligations, and without real or more than nominal risk, England might guarantee
a loan for India to the extent required for redemption of
ryots' dues. As the full amount would be eventually recovered from the ryots, and the recoveries would be appropri-
able for gradually extinguishing the guaranteed Loan, England's guarantee would diminish yearly, after provision of
the full amount of loan, and would cease within the term of
the next generation. The English Government might, however, be asked to agree to an arrangement by which the full
advantage of the Imperial guarantee on the whole amount
of the guaranteed loan, might be continued to India throughout the period of liquidation of the ryots' debt to Government, on the condition that the sinking fund formed from
ryots' repayments of capital is invested in Indian securities.
By observing this condition the guaranteed stock could eventually be withdrawn in bulk, or in three or four instalments,
by the issue of unguaranteed stock.

15. The 200 millions sterling of guaranteed loan would
not be wanted at once; the redemption of ryots' dues
would be gradual; if, when the work is in full swing,
it proceeded at the rate of 10 or 12 millions sterling a
year, that would perhaps be considered very satisfactory
progress. France raised 220 millions sterling for the War
Indemnity in two years. The Imperial guarantee of the
English Government would ensure 200 millions sterling. at
not more than $3\frac{1}{4}$ per cent. interest, if spread over twelve or
fourteen years.

16. The gross amount required for paying the zemindars
would, at the outside, be 135 millions sterling, *plus* the 73
millions of capitalised land revenue which they would have
to return; total 208 millions gross. As already observed, the
progress of redemption of ryots' dues would be gradual; so
that recoveries from ryots who have redeemed their payments would be concurrent with outlay in other districts for
fresh redemption. In this way, in the long run, the actual
guaranteed loan would not exceed 200 millions sterling.

17. The assets for meeting the obligations to be guaranteed

by the British Government would be the capitalised land CHAP. XI.
revenue, recoveries from ryots, and a surplus of yearly
revenue over expenditure which would incidentally ensue
from the redemption measures. This last being assured, as
will be presently seen, and on the condition that these assets
would be reserved for discharging the imperial guarantee,
the loan under that guarantee might proceed at the rate of
15 millions sterling a year, irrespective of the actual yearly
progress of the redemption measure, while the honour of the
Indian Government would be committed to maintaining
satisfactory progress.

18. The 15 millions sterling of yearly borrowing under
the imperial guarantee could be applied in payment of home
charges. It would thus liberate 19 crores of rupees
yearly for the extinction of a corresponding amount of the
Public Debt in India—with the two results that loss by exchange to the amount of 4 millions sterling a year would
cease, and the 4 per cent. Government securities of the
existing Indian stocks would rise above par. Of the saving
of 4 millions sterling in loss by exchange, a portion would
cover present deficit or prevent new taxation; but the bulk
would, as a saving from the redemption measure, be strictly
appropriated to the reduction of debt, or to providing without fresh borrowing for the 2 millions a year of Productive Public Works expenditure.

19. In issuing stock to zemindars, the amount of the
issue might be restricted by issuing it at a high rate of
interest, namely, 6 per cent., guaranteed for a fixed period.
In theory, if two stocks bear, respectively, 4 and 6 per cent.
interest, each in perpetuity, the 6 per cent. stock would
command a premium of only 50 per cent. compared with
the 4 per cent. stock; but in practice, where the perpetuity of the stock bearing the lower interest is not assured,
while the higher interest on the other stock is guaranteed for
a fixed term, the latter commands a proportionately higher
premium than that obtainable with the common perpetuity
of the two stocks. Thus, if the interest on 4 and $4\frac{1}{2}$ per
cent. stocks, respectively, were alike perpetual, the $4\frac{1}{2}$ per
cent. stock would command a premium of $12\frac{1}{2}$ per cent.;
whereas the ordinary difference between the market values
of 4 and $4\frac{1}{2}$ per cent. stock, of which the latter is guaranteed
for only 14 years, is 5 or $5\frac{1}{4}$ per cent., the premium or difference being the present value of the yearly amount of the
extra interest for the number of years for which it is guaran-

teed. With this fact we may, for the matter in hand, couple the consideration that with the temporary help of a $3\frac{1}{4}$ per cent. loan, under the imperial guarantee, for paying off the existing loans which bear 4 per cent. or higher interest, the perpetuity of 4 per cent. as the lowest interest for Indian stock is by no means assured; on completion of the operations here discussed, including the eventual repayment of the loan under the imperial guarantee, future unguaranteed Indian loans would bear less than 4 per cent. interest. Indeed, the average price of 4 per cent. India stock, in London, in 1874, gave a return of only 3·82 per cent.

20. Coupling, then, these two considerations, namely, the guarantee of 6 per cent. interest for a fixed period, and the strong probability that the rate of interest on Indian loans would settle down at below 4 per cent. a year, zemindars might be paid in bonds bearing 6 per cent. interest, in respect of which that rate of interest may be guaranteed for a period so fixed that the stock would, on its issue, command a premium of 50 or 40 per cent., the 4 per cent. being then at a premium, under the influences in para. 18. Hence to a zemindar who has to receive 7 lakhs as compensation, the Government (with 6 per cent. paper at a premium of 40 per cent.) could tender, as full discharge, 5 lakhs of paper bearing 6 per cent. interest, for, by selling it in the market he could realise 7 lakhs. We have assumed that the compensation payable to zemindars, &c., would amount to 135 millions. In this manner, the actual issue of stock could be restricted to 96 millions, or about two-thirds of the present amount (143 millions) of the Public Debt of India, at home and in this country, which will have been paid off during the operation.

20a. There would be great gain to Government, without loss to anybody, from the issue of 6 per cent. stock. The zemindar, as we have seen, would get full value for his estate by selling the stock. In paying 6 per cent. on the stock issued to the zemindar to the extent of two-thirds amount value of his estate, the Government would not lose, because the ryot would pay the whole of that interest in the rate of 4 per cent. on the full amount value of the zemindary. On the contrary, the Government would gain, because on expiration of the period for which 6 per cent. interest is guaranteed, the Government, by reduction of the interest from 6 to 4 per cent., or less, would continue liable for only two-thirds or four-sevenths the amount value of the zemindaries, instead of for the whole value, which latter liability would attach to the issue of 4 per cent. instead of 6 per cent. stock to the zemindar. At the end of the period for which 6 per cent. interest may have been assured, the Government would gain 45 or 39 millions sterling, on the assumption of 135 millions as the full value of the compensation to zemindars which Government will have discharged with 90 or 96 millions of 6 per cent. stock; the extra 2 per cent. of interest having been paid in the interval by the ryots in the reckoning of their debt at 4 per cent. on the full value of the estate.

21. By the measures suggested in paragraphs 18 and 19, the 6 per cent. stock would be issued in arrear of the *vacuum* to be caused by the discharge of 15 millions sterling a year of existing debt; and it would be issued to the extent probably of two-thirds the yearly discharge of the present debt. The issue, therefore, could not depreciate Indian rupee securities in this country; they would rise in value.

22. The recoveries from the ryots might be in the form of a percentage on the gross valuation of the dues by them,—other than the road cess,—which are to be redeemed by the capital payments to zemindars, *viz.*—

1*st*.—Four per cent. annual interest on the gross valuation of their dues, at sixteen years' purchase, which would exceed 6 per cent. on the amount to be paid to zemindars.

2*nd*.—One per cent. to cover charges of collection.

3*rd*.—One per cent. to cover loss to Government from capitalising at twenty years' purchase the land revenue now paid by zemindars.

4*th*.—Two per cent. for a sinking fund.

22*a*. The third and fourth items could be reserved for buying up and cancelling stock of the loan bearing the Imperial Guarantee, or (para. 14) Indian stock. It would bear discussion whether the ryots' sinking fund should be credited with interest at 3 or at 4 per cent. In favour of the former would be the very solid advantages to accrue to the ryots from the redemption of their dues, *viz.*—

I. Exemption from enhancement of rent, and cessation of rent payments.

II. Saving to the ryot of the zemindars and middlemen's charges of collection and management, which are included in the rent now paid by the ryot, but which would be excluded from the composition with the zemindar. This saving would be considerable; for under the present sys-

CHAP. XI tem it often happens that more than one person incurs expense for collecting from the same ryot.

III. A saving of law expenses; for these would cease, on discontinuance of enhancements of rent, and of disputes about land. It would perhaps be found on enquiry that, if law expenses and other charges on account of litigation, which the ryot now pays, were to be thrown on his holding at a rate per beegah, the ryot's rent would in many cases be doubled.

IV. Discontinuance of *abwabs*, irregular cesses or exactions, market dues, &c.

V. Cessation of certain other payments, when there is no longer a zemindar or middleman to dispute with the ryot about land.

VI. The acquisition by the ryots, as the joint property of their village, of all the waste land in it;—for, the whole estate being purchased from the zemindar, the waste land in it would go with the estate.

23. The charges of collection, which in para. 22*a* are reckoned at 1 per cent., may seem a low estimate; but it is assumed that the advantages to the ryots, which are enumerated in para. 22, would be so considerable, that the joint responsibility of the ryots in each village, for the Government's capital payments in redemption of the village's dues to the zemindar, could be exacted by Government as a condition of its help in purchasing the zemindar's rights. This would assimilate the villages in Bengal with the village communities in the North-Western Provinces; failing this, the duty of realising dues to Government might be exacted from the village officers as a condition of the Government's help. This would assimilate the village organisation with that in the Madras and Bombay Presidencies. If each village arranged to pay its dues on the appointed dates into the nearest sub-divisional treasury, the charges of collection might be less than 1 per cent.; and they would cease on liquidation of their debt to Government by the ryots. The charges of collection would at any rate be less than the present charges of that kind, and of management, which zemindars and middlemen now recover from ryots. The existing expenditure would thus limit the charge, and the Government would not seek to profit by a higher percentage than may be sufficient.

24. With the joint responsibility of each village for its ryots, loss from bad debts need not be apprehended, espe-

cially as, through the redemption measure, by the cessation of enhancements of rent and of arbitrary cesses, and by the amount of money which would be thrown into circulation through the capital payments to zemindars, and to village bankers in discharge of ryots' debts, the value of land and of each ryot's holding would increase. Even if joint responsibility of the village be not formally established, the Government could reserve the power of recovering losses from bad debts written off in one year, by raising the rate of interest on the village's debt till the loss is recovered: this would ensure the joint responsibility of the village.

25. If a ryot pays rent for his land at 2 rupees a beegah, the capitalised value for redeeming his dues would be Rs. 32. According to para. 21 he would pay 8 per cent. interest on that, or Rs. 2·56, and thus his yearly burden would be seemingly greater than now. But firstly, the Rs. 2·56 include 2 per cent. for a sinking fund, or ·64, which in time would entirely terminate his payment of Rs. 2·56; secondly, his gross payment would not be Rs. 2·56, by reason of the large abatement to be made from the gross valuation of estates (para. 11); thirdly, the solid advantages detailed in para. 22 would outweigh the greater part, if not the whole, of the direct payments mentioned in para. 21. Lastly, the zemindars in the present day receive rents much higher than the pergunnah rates of 1793, plus cesses of that year; that is, they receive more than their just dues: if, therefore, a test like the above, applied to the scale of recoveries from ryots sketched in para. 21, should show a disadvantage to the ryot, under the scale, the remedy would lie in reducing the valuations of zemindars' estates.

26. The main features of the scheme may be summarised as follows :—

I.—ZEMINDARS—

MILLIONS STERLING.

To receive 13 millions × 16 years' purchase = 208
„ pay 3⅔ „ × 20 „ „ = 73

135 in 6 °/$_o$ paper = 96.

II.—VILLAGE BANKERS TO RECEIVE—

In cash, say ... ... 73 see Chapter XII.
Balance in 4 °/$_o$ bonds x

III.—RYOTS TO PAY TO GOVERNMENT—

(a). 208 millions at 4°/$_o$ for redeeming dues to zemindars.
(b). 18 „ or loss on capitalising land revenue at 20 instead of 25 years' purchase. In the text the recovery has been stated in the

CHAP. XI form of 1 per cent. a year on 208 millions, but it would be so adjusted as to cease on recovery of 18 millions with interest at 4 per cent. a year.

(c). 73 millions towards cash payments to village bankers, plus x millions of balance of ryots' debts, settled by Government bonds to bankers.

IV.—GOVERNMENT TO BORROW—

| | MILLIONS STERLING. | |
	Cash.	Paper.
Under Imperial Guarantee	208	...
To issue in 6 % bonds to zemindars ...		90
„ „ in 4 % bonds to village bankers ...		x

V.—GOVERNMENT TO APPLY PROCEEDS OF IV FOR—

Paying off village bankers in cash ...	73
„ „ existing debts (out of 143 millions —remainder being paid off yearly surplus of revenue)	135

VI.—FINANCIAL RESULT—Government will

(1). Have paid off imperial guaranteed loan, on recovery of 208 millions from ryots, partly by issue of unguaranteed stock bearing interest at 4 per cent. or less, and the remainder in cash by the appropriation of capitalised land revenue and other surplus assets.

(2). Have paid off 143 millions of existing debt.

(3). Have outstanding 96 millions of bonds issued to zemindars at 6 per cent. interest, but reduced by the end of the redemption operation to 4 per cent.; Government gaining 39 millions.

(4). Have paid off 96 millions of other debt, as a set-off to 3, on receiving III $b + c$ from ryots.

27. To the Government the advantages would be considerable :—

I. A saving of 4 millions sterling a year in loss by exchange for a period of perhaps twelve or more years; in that time measures would surely be devised for making the saving permanent.

II. A saving, until repayment of the loan bearing the imperial guarantee, of the difference between the interest on that loan, and the higher interest on the existing loans which will have been paid off.

III. A reduction of 39 millions of debt, without any cash payment, simply by utilising the Government's credit in the issue of 6 instead of 4 per cent. stock to zemindars.

IV. It has been said in para. 23 that the solid advantages to ryots from a redemption of their dues would be so very great that the Government would be in a position to exact conditions for extending its help; one of these might be the acceptance by each village of the system of frank-pledge,—a system with which the traditions of the people have familiarised them. In this way a deal of existing police charge, and some expenditure for adjudicating petty suits and minor criminal offences, would be saved. On extinction of the ryot's debt to Government a further great reduction of expenditure might be made; and even earlier, the cessation or considerable diminution of disputes relating to land, would relieve the civil and criminal courts, and the police, and facilitate reductions of charge.

V. With a more equable distribution of property, and a more general diffusion of prosperity, the revenue from other sources would become more productive.

VI. The moral progress of the people would be promoted by their material progress.

VII. Means for the education of the masses would be forthcoming; the ryots would then cheerfully pay an educational cess which their village officers could administer, subject to government inspection of results; indeed, assent to such a cess might be exacted as a condition of Government help in the redemption measure; for, unless the ryots be fitted by education to maintain their rights, it might be found, in course of time, that they had only exchanged one set of masters for another—the zemindars for the leading village officials.

VIII. With the joint responsibility of each village for liquidation of the debt to Government, for police, for justice in petty cases, civil and criminal, for education, and for administering the village poor fund, *viz.*, the village waste lands, it would be possible to revive the old village organisation of which remains still exist in Bengal. (*See Bengal Government Selections, 1872.*)

IX. There is over-population, with minute sub-division of holdings, in some parts of Bengal; this, however, is an incident of cottierism or of rack-renting, not of peasant-proprietorship; there is not a more restraining check on the growth of population than peasant-proprietorship; and that check the redemption measure would provide.

28. In connection with the famine problem, the Government would have to define the obligations of each village with respect to the support of its poor when it becomes proprietor of the waste lands in the village. As part of this subject, it might be expedient to limit, prospectively, the sub-division of holdings. The tendency to this is indeed greater under the present system, whilst that of peasant-proprietors restrains the tendency by promoting the aggregation, or the enlargement, of small holdings. Still, the subject

CHAP. XI. might require special provision and legislation, in directions
which are indicated in the Appendix.

29. A survey of ryots' holdings, that is, a cadastral survey
of Bengal, would be necessary. The outside cost would be
8 annas an acre, or $2\frac{2}{3}$ annas per beegah. This could be
recovered from the ryots, while the survey could absorb
much of superfluous public works establishments.

30. Doubts may occur that the borrowing of 150 to 200
millions sterling in England, whereby the rupee debt now
held in India would be temporarily transferred to England,
will not be tolerated by the Home authorities.

31. The answers are :—

1st.—Which is worse,—the broken pledge of a permanent
assessment for the ryot; the moral responsibility for unsatisfactory relations between zemindars and ryots, and for
the poverty, distress, and moral degradation in which the
mass of the cultivators in Bengal live, as the result of ninety
years of their British rulers' gift of a zemindary settlement;
or a borrowing in England which will not increase the total
debt of India, and which, by discontinuing 4 millions sterling a year of loss by exchange, would save the country an
else inevitable amount of fresh taxation which it is perhaps
not able to bear?

2nd.—Though the loan under the imperial guarantee
would be raised in England, yet it would not form an addition
to the amount of Indian stock of all kinds now held in England. Exchange would improve with the cessation of Council
drafts; and when that happens, and a void in the money
market in India is created by the discharge of Rupee loans
and the cessation of borrowing in India, the Indian Government could arrange for paying in India at a favourable
exchange the interest on the existing sterling loans and on
guaranteed railway stock. The former may be reckoned at
65 millions sterling, the latter at 97 millions, total 162 millions sterling of stock bearing 4 per cent. or higher interest. There are other 16 millions sterling of Rupee paper
enfaced for payment of interest in London, making the gross
total 178 millions. A portion of this would be paid off from
the new loan under the imperial guarantee; the remainder
would be transferred to India, where there would be a special
demand for it, under the suggested facilities for the payment of interest, from the scarcity of paper in the Indian
market on the discharge of the existing Rupee loans, from
the accumulation, in village bankers' hands, of the money

paid to them in discharge of ryot's debts, and from the Chap. XI.
yearly savings of the ryots when they are liberated from
the burdens mentioned in para. 22. Hence, the result,
at the close of the operation for raising 200 millions
sterling in London, under an imperial guarantee, would be
that the amount of Indian stocks of all kinds held in England would, in some fifteen years from the present time,
exceed the present amount by only 22 millions, or a degree
of growth which might be predicated from the ordinary rate
of increase of English investments in Indian securities, even if
there were not to be any borrowing of 200 millions under the
imperial guarantee. Furthermore, the interest payable in
England on those 200 millions sterling, would be less than the
interest now paid there on Indian stocks of all kinds.

32. As to the imperial guarantee, the English Government would certainly not withhold it when pressed with
the following considerations, *viz.*—

I. England's special and general responsibility for the
evils which have happened in Bengal from the zemindary
settlement.

II. The great advantages to the Government, the country, and indirectly to England, from the redemption of ryots'
obligations to zemindars.

III. The inappreciable risk to England from guarantee-
ing the redemption loan, and the certainty of its discharge
in the next generation.

IV. A recollection of how much was added to the present debt of India, from causes for which Parliament or
the English Government was responsible, *e.g.*, the mistake
which was committed in funding the provision for the discharge of East India Stock in consols instead of in the
stock itself; *2nd*, the expenses of the first and second Afghan
wars; 3rd, an undue debit to India of home charges of the
British troops in India.

V. The mistake committed in the zemindary settlement:
until 1765, and later, the zemindars were administrators of
districts, and not merely collectors of revenue. Their duties
of administration were transferred to separate European
agency at considerable expense; their duties as collectors
were also partially transferred to like agency, at further
expense; but their official remuneration was not reduced
for the residue of their duties as collectors. On the contrary,
a settlement was concluded with them, in circumstances, and
with after-mistakes of legislation, which gave them power

CHAP. XI. over ryots that was abused for enhancing rents and levying
exactions, till, in the present day, much more than 20
millions sterling a year is spent in collecting not quite 4
millions a year of land revenue. This enormous expenditure, on a lesser scale it is true, in earlier years, has continued for three generations, with the results which we have
seen. Parliament is responsible for the mistake of the
zemindary settlement, equally with the Indian Government.
The duty of making amends was never more urgent than
now, when there is felt great embarrassment and difficulty
in remitting to England India's tribute of 15 millions sterling
a year, most of it for unproductive expenditure. India, to
provide that tribute, has to send 15 millions sterling of exports beyond the exports which are interchanged against
imports or for other equivalents. In other words, she, in
the final result, receives nothing for those 15 millions sterling
of exports beyond the discharge by that means of the
tribute, save in respect of stores purchased, and interest on
the capital of Guaranteed Railways. Hence, in providing
the tribute she does sustain a loss in one form or another;
partly, in increase of taxation, which, unlike " the fertilising
rain from heaven," does not return to Indian earth, but is
spent in a distant country; partly in higher prices of articles
consumed in India; partly in further diminished incomes of
her people. There is an especial obligation on England to
lessen to India the pressure of this burden, and she can
afford relief by now performing a too long deferred act of
reparation and atonement.

CHAPTER XII.

RYOTS' DEBTS AND EXPENSES.

Perhaps the liberation of the Bengal ryots would not be complete without their further enfranchisement from village bankers. Much of what the zemindar spares, the money-lender takes from the ryot, and the work of stopping enhancement of rent may be but partially done, if the village banker be allowed to run up his score against the ryot. The re-organisation of village communities would help a reform in this matter.

2. In another view, also, some action of Government might be unavoidable, if it helped the ryots in buying out zemindars' rights. The Government's advance of the purchase money would be virtually on mortgage of the ryots' holdings; and that security might be imperfect if the money-lender retained power of attaching each season's crops. It were better for Government to settle with the money-lenders, and having made itself the sole creditor of the ryot, to cry down his credit to others, and prohibit the sale of his holding to others, so long as he remained indebted to the Government.

3. It would be necessary, in that case, for the Government to advance money to the ryot for expenses of cultivation, and for marriages and funerals, besides paying off his debts.

4. A great deal of the ryot's indebtedness is for compound interest, at usurious rates. The usury has been justified on grounds which have force, if the present system is to continue; it is held that the rate of interest is high because it covers a great risk. It may be so; but when once the Government determines on paying off the ryot's debts, the risk is at an end, and all the past fear of risk, under the influence of which a high rate was charged, *and simply carried to account against the ryot*, proves to have been unnecessary; a mere sentiment, or timorous feeling. To pay the money-lender the compound interest he had heaped up on paper, against the ryot, under needless fear, would be Quixotic. He would himself acquiesce in the propriety of a revision, and a considerable reduction, of his account by the district officer, when he is assured payment in full of the real principal of his claim with reasonable interest.

CHAP. XII.   5. The village bankers might be paid the reduced amount of their claims in Government paper, carrying 4 per cent. interest and 2 per cent. sinking fund, which the Government could receive at par in payment of dues, re-issuing it to others in discharge of similar claims against ryots. The ryots, in addition to the payments detailed in para. 21 of Chapter XI, would pay to Government, on this new account, 8 per cent. upon the amount of the paper issued by Government to the village bankers. The village would be jointly responsible for this, as for the payments in Chapter XI above quoted.

6. Respecting marriage expenses, the Government might add to the conditions of its help, in the redemption measure, an engagement by each village, and an acknowledgment by the heads of villages, of a special responsibility for using their influence to restrict such expenses within a moderate amount; subject to an increase of the rate of interest on the village's debt to Government, should there be no improvement in this respect. This measure, and the prohibition of credit to ryots by private individuals while their debt to Government remains undischarged, might be efficacious.

7. The expenses for cultivation and for marriages and feasts might be advanced on interest at 6 per cent. per annum, through the representatives of the village, on its joint responsibility with the ryots; and the waste lands of the village might be considered hypothecated for all the ryot's dues to Government for which the villagers are jointly responsible, and as an incident of that their responsibility. It would be for the Government to consider whether the villages might be grouped in an organisation of circles smaller than a sub-division.

8. Advances by Government for the expenses just mentioned might be issued in district currency notes, without silver having been deposited in the district for the notes, which would be legal tender, and would be received in the district in payment of dues to Government.

9. The principal work of the village headmen or representatives would be that of receiving the payments mentioned in Chapter XI, paragraph 21. The duty would be analogous to that now performed in the ryotwar territories of the Madras and Bombay Presidencies: the issue and recovery of advances for expenses of cultivation, &c., would be added as an incidental duty to the other more onerous func-

tions. The same legal power and the same administrative Chap. XII.
agency which the Government has in the Madras and Bombay
Presidencies for the recovery of its land revenue, the Bengal
Government would have for the realisation of its dues from
villages.

10. The duties here suggested for Government functionaries, though new in Bengal, would not be novel; the ryots'
payments towards their debt for the purchase of zemindars'
rights would be in the place of rent; the advances to them
for expenses of cultivation would be the same as now, only
on a larger scale, and through a re-organised body of village
officers; the advances for marriage expenses, &c., are not
new in the experience of Government, inasmuch as advances
for like and for additional purposes are made on the Continent
of Europe to peasant-proprietors by district banks, which are
Government institutions or are controlled by Government.
Only through such advances, and by the means above suggested, can the Government escape the reproach, which it
incurs in some other parts of India, of realising its land
revenue and dues only by plunging its ryots into debt on
usurious interest.

11. In short, the duties which would devolve on the Government of Bengal would be no other than those which, for the
most part, form the ordinary routine of work in districts in
the Madras and Bombay Presidencies, and for the remaining
part, in some countries on the Continent of Europe. A
heavy weight of obligation for duties unfulfilled for nearly
a century supplies to the Bengal Government an overpowering motive, and would inspire it with a determined spirit in
the matter, without which the other Governments appear to
have succeeded with ease.

12. It has been urged that the village banker is indispensable, even though the Government were to pay ryots'
debts and advance them money for expenses of cultivation
and for current expenses, for he provides seed, takes over the
crops at a valuation, sends the produce to market, &c.; but
the answer to this is that in parts of the Lower Provinces
where the ryots pay low rents they do without a village banker;
in other zemindaries he is not allowed on the estate by the
zemindar, though the latter does not carry the ryots' produce to market; there are parts of India, under ryotwar
settlement, in which the village banker is dispensed with; and
in the peasant-proprietorships on the Continent, he is not a
necessary institution. Moreover, when the village banker is

CHAP. XII. encumbered with the money paid to him by Government in discharge of ryots' debts, he would soon discover that there was no better way of employing it than in buying produce from the ryots, and finding new markets for it;—he would buy as hitherto, with only this difference, that, instead of taking over the produce at his own valuation, he would have to give a fair price for it to the ryots.

13. It is not possible to estimate the amount of ryots' debts; but a very rough idea of the minimum may be attempted for assisting the consideration of our subject. The annual value, *i.e.*, the bare profits, of zemindars' estates, as returned for the road-cess, is 13 millions sterling. Charges of collection and management might increase that amount to nearly 14 millions, and the land revenue adds nearly 4 millions, total, nearly 18 millions. If we assume this as representing one-sixth of the total value of the yearly produce, there remain nearly 90 millions sterling for division between the ryots (for their subsistence) and the money-lenders, as interest and for advances for seed, cattle, &c. The high rate of interest charged to the ryot, *viz.*, 36 to 50 per cent., must prevent the money-lender from letting the debt increase to many years' gross income of the ryot; on the other hand, the yield from seed is very large, though the soil of Bengal has perhaps deteriorated greatly since the beginning of this century. The larger the yield the greater the number of years for which the village banker would allow the ryots' debts to accumulate, and it seems within bounds of possibility that ryots' debts to village bankers exceed 100 millions sterling, even when reduced by the abatements mentioned in Chapter XI, para. 4, and by limiting the need of advances for current expenses to six months in each year.

14. Or to apply another test. The adult male population of Bengal engaged in agriculture is 11 millions; the adult male labourers are 2½ millions; and the adult males in industrial occupations, 2 millions. Omitting these last, we have a total of 13½ millions: multiplying that by 3, we have 40 millions of souls whose yearly subsistence has to be provided out of the holdings of the ryots. At Rs. 2-8 per month, or 30 rupees a year, the annual amount becomes 120 crores, or 120 millions sterling. If we assume that one-half of this has to be advanced by the village banker, we have 60 millions sterling, to which we must add interest, advances for seed and cattle, and accumulations of past years' debts; and then we arrive at the same conclusion

as in the preceding paragraph, namely, that the ryots' debts, CHAP. XII.
even if reduced by striking-off compound interest at usurious
rates, must exceed 100 millions sterling.

15. The reduced claims of the village bankers might be
discharged partly in cash, partly in paper. For the cash
payments there would be available 73 millions sterling from
the amount to be borrowed in England under imperial
guarantee, conformably with the suggestion in Chapter XI,
para. 14. The balance might be paid in Government bonds
bearing 4 per cent. interest, with a sinking fund of 2 per cent.,
attached: while the ryots might pay 8 per cent. interest,
including 2 per cent. sinking fund. The payment would be
additional to the payments detailed in para. 21 of Chapter
XI, and the village would be jointly responsible for this as
for the payments in Chapter XI.

16. The bonds issued by Government to village bankers
might be received at par freely in payment of Government
revenue. The bonds thus received in payment of revenue
could be re-issued in fresh discharge of other similar claims
against ryots during the course of the redemption operations.

17. The 73 millions sterling of cash payment need not be
made in silver; a great part might be paid in a new series of
district currency notes (including tentatively notes of smaller
denominations than the present) for which silver would be
payable in the district of issue, and at the Presidency town.
The notes would be issued against the 73 millions sterling of
silver available from the proceeds of the loan to be raised
under imperial guarantee; but the whole of the silver need
not be carried to the several districts whence the notes against
it issue; the bulk of it may, at the outset, be kept in the
Presidency town, at the Head Office of Issue; for some incidents of the redemption operation would render it probable
that most of the notes issued in the interior would be
remitted to Calcutta,—while of the remainder another large
part would remain outstanding in active local circulation,
thereby making it safe to keep the smaller part of the silver
in the district offices of issue.

18. The activity of the local circulation would be maintained by the following circumstances :—

I. At the season for sowing, the ryots would receive
advances for cultivation ; and, during the year, for marriages,
deaths, &c.

II. The payments of ryots' dues to village bankers might
be made principally about the time of harvest; while the

CHAP. XII. yearly repayments of their dues to Government by ryots would ensue after harvest.

III. If the payments from Government treasuries under I and II be made principally in district currency notes, the paper money issued in both kinds of payments would, to a great extent, accumulate with ryots during harvest, and would be by them returned to the district treasury in payment of their yearly dues. Thus a great part of the district note circulation would be local; and the bulk of this would return to the treasury, not to be exchanged for silver, but in payment of dues to Government. Another large part would go to the Presidency town, and these two large divisions of the total issue of district notes would leave a small residue against which the district treasuries need hold silver, not to the full amount of such residue, but with due advertence to its distribution over the several months of the year.

19. The district notes remitted to the Presidency town would be discharged from the silver reserved there for the purpose out of the 73 millions obtained from the proceeds of the loan under the imperial guarantee. The notes might be held there until the season came round for buying produce afresh from the ryots, when they would be taken out by merchants who would pay silver instead into the Currency Office at the Presidency.

20. On the surface, it would seem that on the silver retained in the Currency Office at the Presidency, the Government would be sustaining a loss of interest. But it would not be so. The interest paid by Government at the rate of $3\frac{1}{4}$ per cent. per annum would be more than covered by the 6 per cent. interest leviable from ryots, for whether the district notes be issued to the ryots, or to village bankers in discharge of ryots' debts, the ryots will pay the higher rate of interest on the amounts advanced or discharged by the notes.

21. We have also seen that by keeping the bulk of the silver in Calcutta, and having regard to the small demand upon the silver reserve in the district treasuries for cashing district currency notes which would be returned to the treasury in payment of dues to Government, the cost of moving silver about for maintaining the convertibility of the notes would be small. The difference between the 6 per cent. interest leviable from ryots, and the $3\frac{1}{4}$ per cent. payable by Government, would very much more than cover it. Thus during the long period of the redemption opera-

on, the people would be educated in the use of paper money CHAP. XII.
; a considerable gain to the Government, for, eventually, a
ortion of the amount of district currency notes that may
rove to be permanently outstanding, will have permanently
splaced silver, and it could be invested in Government
curities.

CHAPTER XIII.

ENGLAND'S OBLIGATIONS OF HONOUR AND DUTY.

Making a second selection (Chapter X) of the fact
established in the course of these remarks, we choose th
following:—

I. Ninety years after the permanent settlement (1) th
majority of the zemindars are poor and in debt, and, throug
the continual sub-division of estates under the Hindoo law
of inheritance, the poverty of the class is increasing, inso
much that estates in large numbers are passing into th
proprietorship of bankers (sometimes foreigners in Bengal)
(2) the condition of the ryots through the greater part of th
Lower Provinces is bad, and in one province it is wretched.

II. The amounts paid by ryots to zemindars and middl
men give to these two latter net profits equal to two-thir
the gross land revenue of British India; if cesses, charges
collection and management, law expenses, and other paymen
be added, the Bengal ryots pay an amount more by one-ha
than the amount of the land revenue from the rest of Britis
India.

III. With all these enormous payments the ryots are n
assured of continuing on the same assessment for more than fi
years where Lord Cornwallis assured them of a fixity of rent

IV. Of late years, with these conditions so unfavourab
to the proper cultivation of the land, the possibility, an
the actual visitations, of famine have increased.

V. The frequency of revision by zemindars of ryot
assessments has multiplied the gomashtahs of zemindars an
middlemen, and their tremendous power of oppressing ryot
from whom they levy cesses on their own account, witho
the zemindar being able to prevent them, though he incu
the reproach of all their oppressions.

VI. In a country almost purely agricultural, the cond
tion, as a whole, of both zemindars and ryots is bad, and, to
great extent, the ryots are dissevered from the great zemi
dars (the ideal zemindars of Lord Cornwallis), and a
practically under subjection to gomashtahs, farmers of ren
and petty zemindars. The peasantry of the country, inste

f being peasant-proprietors, are the servants of tyrannical
ervants.

VII. Such is the condition of the class whose labours
vere the riches of the State in the estimation of those who
onceived the zemindary settlement for the ryots' benefit;
nd such are the prospects of the class which in other coun-
ries are the bone and sinew, the strength and manhood, of
he nation. The career which in Continental Europe this
lass finds in a growing prosperity from the improvement of
heir own land, and the acquisition of more of it, is shut to the
yots of Bengal; that is, the mass of the population have no
areer open to them;—servants of servants they are, and
hey see that such they must remain.

2. With some perception of this longing for a career, the
overnment is reserving all offices or appointments below a
ertain value for the natives of the country; but the Govern-
nent cannot work a miracle, and what are these few loaves
nd fishes among so many! *2ndly*, the new career will not
hange the character of the condition of the people;—one kind
f service will be simply exchanged for another kind, by a
w thousand natives, and that is all: the people will conti-
ue a population of servants, instead of holding, as peasant-pro-
rietors, a position of social independence, without which it is
ot reasonable to look among Bengalees for the truthful, open,
rm, and manly character which they are reproached with
cking. Service under masters, even though those masters be
Government, does not foster these qualities. In other
ords, so far as British rule is responsible for a condition
the ryots of Bengal, in which they have no hope, and no
cial independence, it is also answerable for their moral
egradation.

3. Glory to God on high, on earth peace, good will to-
ards men! was the strain which announced salvation
a shortly-to-be-redeemed world. But, confused by the
hoes of nineteen centuries, the strain, so dear to English
sociations, strikes with a harsh dissonance on the ears of
engal ryots. "What peace and good will! with these unhap-
y relations with our zemindars, these incessant disputings
out rent, which leave life without hope or rest, and with
it little sustenance! British messengers of salvation do
deed bring to us its news of peace and good will, but
ritish rule has destroyed our peace, and keeps us in perpe-
ial unrest, feverish anxiety, many of us in a demoralising
ite, and, several millions of us, on the verge of famine!"

4. During the greater part of this century, Bengal has been the field of labour of missionaries, including some of a rare self-devotion and resolute will, of brave hearts and steadfast purpose, which a life-long ill success could not weaken or discourage, and not intellectually inferior, perhaps, to some Bengal Governors. These qualities, exerted in some other sphere, could have borne rich fruit of good to others; but labouring as these men did among a people whose moral degradation was an incident of a material condition which every year was deteriorating, their life, so far as it concerned others, was on the surface a mistake; and if a mistake, not the least sad in the list of mistakes which accompanied and followed the zemindary settlement. Excepting here and there, can missionary power break any other than its own strength, in its efforts to bring home a religion of hope to the hearts of a people whose deteriorating condition, over the greater part of Bengal, is ever sinking them deeper into a stolid unreasoning materialism?

5. Peace on earth, good will towards men! is, however, only one-half of the Christmas strain, sweet to English hearts, which strikes as dissonance on the ryots' ears. "For unto you this day is born a Saviour, who is Christ the Lord!" Peace the ryots have not known, for well nigh a century, in the incidents affecting land, which make the sum of their happiness or misery. But Saviour! Redeemer!—partly the tradition, partly the experience of a century of suffering, will fill the ryots with rapture at the strange music of the word Redemption. Bring but the word home to them! at first they may have but a glimmering of its meaning, when they see their redemption from demands which, as things have gone on for ninety years, might, else, never end; but, escaped from bonds which now keep them in a low grovelling materialism, freed from carking care, and from an enmity to their zemindar which now corrodes the better qualities of their nature, free to think and feel like men who have hope, new tendrils of feeling, a new sympathy for the English rule and race, will help them to apprehend the higher Redemption wrought for them by their and their deliverers' common Lord and Saviour.

6. Christmas thoughts in June are behind their time. During Christmas the writer was engaged on the Chapter in the Appendix about zemindars and ryots from 1793 to 1859; from repulsion of his thoughts in that season by the facts in that Chapter, the thoughts had to be laid aside;—

but they have come back with a force which he has not been able to resist, and the reader will pardon the digression if there be one ; but perhaps there is none.

7. For the redemption which inspires Christmas thoughts rebukes any feeling that the rule of wrong should not be destroyed because it has lasted for four thousand years or for a hundred years, and that there is no call upon us to extirpate evil which we had no part in bringing about. Nor may we dissociate ourselves from any errors of the authors of the zemindary settlement. We have received a noble heritage from the past rulers of Bengal and of India; we are proud of their glory. Let us make their errors our own, and with loving care of their memory undo their mistakes! What they did worthily has redounded more to England's honour and glory than to theirs; what they did wrong unwittingly, let us with loyalty to worth which with all its blemishes was better than ours, set right, not alone in their memory, but because the reputation of England's sons is her own. Their deeds are her deeds; and if they have passed away, without redress of wrong unwittingly done, be it hers with profound feeling to confess error, and to the utmost of a power which abolished slavery in her West Indies, make amends to a whole people that, in a province of her East Indies, depend upon her and look only to her for delivery from else hopeless misery and moral degradation.

8. England has to purge her conscience from the sin of the zemindary settlement as she purged it from the sin of slavery. She is incited to the work by her honour and good name, the memory of her sons (Indian worthies of a not remote past), her duty to her subjects, her heavy moral obligations in the matter, on account of the terrible burden which has been unwittingly laid on the ryots, and by the claim before God of a whole people in agricultural Bengal, that they should have the same freedom and security as the peasant cultivators in Europe for the growth of their moral life. The work is not beyond England's strength, for poorer States have done the like, while the obligations of honour and duty, which leave her no escape, are seconded by material considerations of great moment and practical concern to the teeming millions in British India.

APPENDIX I.

ORIGIN AND COURSE OF PROPERTY IN LAND.

The statutory rights of property in Bengal, which App. I. the Government created in 1793, and by subsequent legislation, should be considered in connexion with the origin and course of the right of property in land, and with the law and constitution of India as they existed at the time of the acquisition of the Dewanee by the East India Company, in 1765. Sir Henry Maine's treatises on Ancient Law and on Village Communities in the East and West throw a light on the first of these subjects, which was much needed by the authors of the zemindary settlement.

2. The Family—

I.—Agnatic and cognatic relationships.

(*a*). The old Roman law established; for example, a fundamental Maine's Ancient Law, page 59. difference between "agnatic" and "cognatic" relationship; that is, between the family considered as based upon common subjection to patriarchal authority, and the family considered (in conformity with modern ideas) as united through the mere fact of a common descent.

(*b*). *Cognatic* relationship is simply the conception of kinship familiar *Ibid*, pp. 146-47. to modern ideas : it is the relationship arising through common descent from the same pair of married persons, whether the descent be traced through males or females. *Agnatic* relationship is something very different: it excludes a number of persons whom we, in our day, should certainly consider of kin to ourselves, and it includes many more whom we should never reckon among our kindred. It is, in truth, the connexion existing between the members of the family, conceived as it was in the most ancient times.

(*c*). *Cognates*, then, are all those persons who can trace their blood to a *Ibid*, p. 147. single ancestor or ancestress; or, if we take the strict technical meaning of the word in Roman law, they are all who trace their blood to the legitimate marriage of a common pair. "Cognation" is, therefore, a relative term ; and the degree of connexion in blood which it indicates depends on the particular marriage which is selected as the commencement of the calculation. If we begin with the marriage of father and mother, cognation will only express relationship of brothers and sisters : if we take that of the grandfather and grandmother, then uncles, aunts, and their descendants will also be included in the notion of cognation

1

and, following the same process, a larger number of cognates may be continually obtained by choosing the starting-point higher and higher up the line of ascent.

(d). All this is easily understood by a modern :—but who are the agnates? In the first place, they are all the cognates who trace their connexion exclusively through males. A table of cognates is, of course, formed by taking each lineal ancestor in turn, and including all his descendants of both sexes in the tabular view: if, then, in tracing the various branches of such a genealogical table or tree, we stop whenever we come to the name of a female, and pursue that particular branch or ramification no further, all who remain, after the descendants of women have been excluded, are agnates, and their connexion together is agnatic relationship. I dwell a little on the process which is practically followed in separating them from the cognates, because it explains a memorable legal maxim, *Mulier est finis familiæ*—a woman is the terminus of the family. A female name closes the branch or twig of the genealogy in which it occurs. None of the descendants of a female are included in the primitive notion of family relationship.

(e). If the system of archaic law at which we are looking be one which admits adoption, we must add to the agnates thus obtained all persons, male or female, who have been brought into the family by the artificial extension of its boundaries. But the descendants of such persons will only be agnates, if they satisfy the conditions which have just been described.

(f). What, then, is the reason of this arbitrary inclusion and exclusion? Why should a conception of kinship, so elastic as to include strangers brought into the family by adoption, be, nevertheless, so narrow as to shut out the descendants of a female member? To solve these questions, we must recur to the *Patria potestas* (section III, below). The foundation of agnation is not the marriage of father and mother, but the authority of the father. All persons are agnatically connected together who are under the same paternal power, or who have been under it, or who might have been under it, if their lineal ancestor had lived long enough to exercise his empire. In truth, in the primitive view, relationship is exactly limited by patria potestas : where the potestas begins, kinship begins; and therefore adoptive relatives are among the kindred. Where the potestas ends, kinship ends; so that a son, emancipated by his father, loses all rights of agnation. And, here, we have the reason why the descendants of females are outside the limits of archaic kinship. If a woman died unmarried, she could have no legitimate descendants. If she married, her children fell under the patria potestas, not of her father, but of her husband, and thus were lost to her own family. It is obvious that the organisation of primitive societies would have been confounded, if men had called themselves relatives of their mothers' relatives. The inference would have been that a person might be subject to two distinct patriæ potestates; but distinct patriæ potestates implied distinct jurisdictions, so that anybody amenable to two of them at the same time would have lived under two different dispensations. As long as the family was an *imperium in imperio*, a community within the commonwealth, governed by its own institutions, of which the parent was the source, the limitation of relationship to the agnates was a necessary security against a conflict of laws in the domestic forum. * *

APP. I.

(*g*). In Hindoo law, for example, which is saturated with the primitive notions of family dependency, kinship is entirely agnatic; and I am informed that in Hindoo genealogies the names of women are generally omitted altogether. The same view of relationship pervades so much of the laws of the races who overran the Roman empire as appears to have really formed part of their primitive usage; and we may suspect that it would have perpetuated itself even more than it has in modern European jurisprudence, if it had not been for the vast influence of the later Roman law on modern thought.

THE FAMILY.
Para. 2, I.
Ibid, p. 151.

II.—PROGRESS OF THE FAMILY TOWARDS FORMATION OF SOCIETY.

(*a*). It is just here that archaic law renders us one of the greatest of its services, and fills up a gap which otherwise could only have been bridged by conjecture. It is full, in all its provinces, of the clearest indications that society in primitive times was not, what it is assumed to be at present, a collection of *individuals*. In fact, and in the view of the men who composed it, it was *an aggregation of families*. The contrast may be most forcibly expressed by saying that the *unit* of an ancient society was the family,—of the modern society, the individual. * *

Ibid, p. 126.

(*b*). If very general language were employed, the description of the Teutonic or Scandinavian village community might actually serve as a description of the same institution in India. * * There is the village, consisting of habitations, each ruled by a despotic pater-familias. And there is constantly a council or government to determine disputes as to custom. * * I now pass to the village itself, the cluster of homesteads inhabited by the members of the community. The description given by Maurer of the Teutonic mark of the township, as his researches have shown it to him, might here again pass for an account, so far as it goes, of an Indian village. The separate households, each despotically governed by its family chief, and never trespassed upon by the footstep of any person of different blood, are all to be found there in practice. * * While it is quite true of India, that the head of the family is supposed to be chief of the household, the families within the village township would seem to be bound together through their representative heads by just as intricate a body of customary rules as they are in respect of those parts of the village domain which answer to the Teutonic common mark and arable mark. The truth is, that nothing can be more complex than the customs of an Indian village, though, in a sense, they are only binding on heads of families.

Village Communities, page 107.

Ibid, p. 113.

(*c*). In most of the Greek states, and in Rome, there long remained the vestiges of an ascending series of groups, out of which the state was at first constituted. The family, house, and tribe of the Romans may be taken as the type of them; and they are so described to us, that we can scarcely help conceiving them as a system of concentric circles, which have gradually expanded from the same point. The elementary group is the family, connected by common subjection to the highest male descendant. The aggregation of families forms the gens or house. The aggregation of houses makes the tribe. The aggregation of

Ancient Law, p. 128.

tribes constitutes the commonwealth. Are we at liberty to follow these indications, and to lay down that the commonwealth is a collection of persons, united by common descent from the progenitor of an original family? Of this we may at least be certain, that all ancient societies regarded themselves as having proceeded from one original stock, and even laboured under an incapacity for comprehending any reason except this for their holding together in political union. The history of political ideas begins, in fact, with the assumption that kinship in blood is the sole possible ground of community in political functions; nor is there any of those subversions of feeling, which we term emphatically revolutions, so startling and so complete as the change which is accomplished when some other principle,—such as that, for instance, of *local contiguity*,—establishes itself for the first time as the basis of common political action. It may be affirmed, then, of early commonwealths, that their citizens considered all the groups in which they claimed membership to be founded on common lineage. What was obviously true of the family, was believed to be true first of the house, next of the tribe, lastly of the state.

(*d*). And, yet, we find that, along with this belief, or, if we may use the word, this theory of common lineage, each community preserved records or traditions which distinctly showed that the fundamental assumption was false. Whether we look to the Greek states, or to Rome, or to the Teutonic aristocracies in Ditmarsh, which furnished Neibuhr with so many valuable illustrations, or to the Celtic clan associations, or to that strange social organisation, the Slavonic Russians and Poles, which has only lately attracted notice,—everywhere we discover traces of passages in their history when men of alien descent were admitted to, and amalgamated with, the original brotherhood. Adverting to Rome singly, we perceive that the primary group, the family, was being constantly adulterated by the practice of adoption; while stories seem to have been always current respecting the exotic extraction of one of the original tribes, and concerning a large addition to the houses, made by one of the early kings. The composition of the state, uniformly assumed to be natural, was, nevertheless, known to be, in great measure, artifical. This conflict between belief or theory and notorious fact is, at first sight, extremely perplexing; but what it really illustrates is, the efficiency with which legal fictions do their work in the infancy of society.

(*e*). The earliest and most extensively employed of legal fictions was that which permitted family relations to be created artificially; and there is none to which I conceive mankind to be more deeply indebted. If it had never existed, I do not see how any one of the primitive groups, whatever were their nature, could have absorbed another; or on what terms any two of them could have combined, except those of absolute superiority on one side and absolute subjection on the other. No doubt, when, with our modern ideas, we contemplate the union of independent communities, we can suggest a hundred modes of carrying it out; the simplest of all being that the individuals comprised in the coalescing groups shall vote or act together according to local propinquity. But the idea that a number of persons should exercise political rights in common, simply because they happened to live within the same topographical limits, was utterly strange and monstrous to primitive antiquity. The expedient which in those times commanded favor was that the incoming population should *feign themselves* to be descended from the same stock as the people on whom they were engrafted; and it is precisely the good faith of this fiction, and the closeness with which it seemed to imitate reality, that we cannot now hope to understand.

(*f*). One circumstance, however which it is important to recollect, is, that the men who formed the various political groups were certainly in the habit of meeting together periodically for the purpose of acknowledging and consecrating their association by common sacrifices. Strangers, amalgamated with the brotherhood, were doubtless admitted to these sacrifices; and when that was once done, we can believe that it seemed equally easy, or not more difficult, to conceive them as sharing in the common lineage. The conclusion, then, which is suggested by the evidence is, not that all early societies were formed by descent from the same ancestor, but that all of them which had any permanence and solidity were either so descended, or assumed that they were. An indefinite number of causes may have shattered the primitive groups; but wherever their ingredients recombined, it was on the model or principle of an association of kindred. Whatever were the fact, all thought, language, and law adjusted themselves to the assumption. But though all this seems to me to be established with reference to the communities with whose records we are acquainted, the remainder of their history sustains the position before laid down, as to the essentially transient and terminable influence of the most powerful legal fictions. At some point of time, probably as soon as they felt themselves strong enough to resist extrinsic pressure, all these states ceased to recruit themselves by factitious extensions of consanguinity.

(*g*). They necessarily, therefore, became aristocracies, in all cases where a fresh population from any cause collected around them which could put in no claim to community of origin. Their sternness in maintaining the central principle of a system under which political rights were attainable on no terms whatever except connexion in blood, real or artificial, taught their inferiors another principle, which proved to be endowed with a far higher measure of vitality. This was the principle of *local contiguity*, now recognised everywhere as the condition of community in political functions. A new set of political ideas came at once into existence, which, being those of ourselves, our contemporaries, and in great measure of our ancestors, rather obscure our perception of the older theory, which they vanquished and dethroned.

(*h*). The family, then, is the type of an archaic society in all the modifications which it was capable of assuming: but the family here spoken of is not exactly the family as understood by a modern. In order to reach the ancient conception, we must give to our modern ideas an important extension, and an important limitation. We must look on the family as constantly enlarged by the absorption of strangers within its circle, and we must try to regard the fiction of adoption as so closely simulating the reality of kinship, that neither law nor opinion makes the slightest difference between a real and an adoptive connexion. On the other hand, the persons theoretically amalgamated into a family by their common descent are, practically, held together by common obedience to their highest living ascendant, the father, grandfather, or great-grandfather. The patriarchal authority of a chieftain is as necessary an ingredient in the notion of the family group as the fact (or assumed fact) of its having sprung from his loins; and, hence, we must understand that, if there be any persons who, however truly included in the brotherhood by virtue of their blood-relationship, have nevertheless, *de facto*, withdrawn themselves from the empire of its ruler, they are always, in the beginnings of law, considered as lost to the family. It is this patriarchal aggregate,—the modern family thus cut down on one side and extended on the other,—which meets us on the threshold of primitive jurisprudence.

Ibid, p. 162.

(*i*). The law of persons contains but one other chapter which can be usefully cited for our present purpose. · The legal rules by which systems of mature jurisprudence regulate the connection of *master* and *slave*, present no very distinct traces of the original condition common to ancient societies. But there are reasons for this exception. There seems to be something in the institution of slavery which has, at all times, either shocked or perplexed mankind, however little habituated to reflection, and however slightly advanced in the cultivation of its moral instincts. * * The relation in which servitude had originally stood to the rest of the domestic system, though not clearly exhibited, is casually indicated in many parts of primitive law, and more particularly in the typical system—that of ancient Rome. It is clear from the testimony both of ancient law and of many primeval histories, that the slave might, under certain conditions, be made the heir or universal successor of the master. * * When we speak of the slave as anciently included in the family, we intend to assert nothing as to the motives of those who brought him into it, or kept him there :—we merely imply that the tie which bound him to his master was regarded as one of the same general character with that which united every other member of the group to its chieftain. This consequence is, in fact, carried in the general assertion already made, that the primitive ideas of mankind were unequal to comprehending any basis of the connexion *inter se* of individuals, apart from the relations of family.

Ibid, p. 165.

(*k*). The family consisted primarily of those who belonged to it by consanguinity, and next, of those who had been engrafted on it by adoption; but there was still a third class of persons who were only joined to it by common subjection to its head—and these were the slaves. The born and the adopted subjects of the chief were raised above the slave by the certainty that, in the ordinary course of events, they would be relieved from bondage, and entitled to exercise powers of their own : but that the inferiority of the slave was not such as to place him outside the pale of the family, or such as to degrade him to the footing of inanimate property, is clearly proved, I think, by the many traces which remain of his ancient capacity for inheritance in the last resort. It would, of course, be unsafe in the highest degree to hazard conjectures how far the lot of the slave was mitigated in the beginnings of society by having a definite place reserved for him in the empire of the father. It is, perhaps, more probable that the son was practically assimilated to the slave, than that the slave shared any of the tenderness which, in later times, was shown to the son. But it may be asserted with some confidence of advanced and matured codes that, wherever servitude is sanctioned, the slave has uniformly greater advantages under systems which preserve some memento of his earlier condition, than under those which have adopted some other theory of his civil degradation.* * The Roman law was arrested in its growing tendency to look upon him more and more as an article of property by the theory of the law of nature; and hence it is that, wherever servitude is sanctioned by institutions which have been deeply affected by Roman jurisprudence, the servile condition is more intolerably wretched.

III.—Patria potestas.

(a). The effect of the evidence derived from comparative jurisprudence *Ibid*, p. 122. is to establish that view of the primeval condition of the human race which is known as the patriarchal theory. There is no doubt, of course, that this theory was originally based on the scriptural history of the Hebrew patriarchs in Lower Asia.* * It is to be noted, however, that the legal testimony comes nearly exclusively from the institutions of societies belonging to the Indo-European stock, the Romans, Hindoos, and Sclavonians supplying the greater part of it; and indeed the difficulty, at the present stage of the inquiry, is to know where to stop, to say of what races of men it is *not* allowable to lay down that the society in which they are united was originally organised on the patriarchal model. The chief lineaments of such a society, as collected from the early chapters of Genesis, I need not attempt to depict with any minuteness.* * The points which lie on the surface of the history are these. The eldest male parent, the eldest ascendant, is absolutely supreme in his household. His dominion extends to life and death, and is as unqualified over his children, and their houses, their marriage, divorce, transfer, and sale, as over his slaves;—indeed, the relations of sonship and serfdom appear to differ in little, beyond the higher capacity which the child in blood possesses of becoming one day the head of a family himself. The flocks and herds of the children are the flocks and herds of the father; and the possessions of the parent, which he holds in a representative rather than in a proprietary character, are equally divided at his death among his descendants in the first degree, the eldest son sometimes receiving a double share under the name of birthright, but more generally endowed with no hereditary advantage beyond an honorary precedence.

(b). On a few systems of law the family organisation of the earliest *Ibid*, p. 135. society has left a plain and broad mark in the life-long authority of the father or other ancestor over the person and property of his descendants—an authority which we may conveniently call by its later Roman name of *patria potestas*.* * In every relation of life in which the collective community might have occasion to avail itself of his wisdom and strength, for all purposes of counsel or of war, the *filius familias*, or son under power, was as free as his father.* * But in all the relations created by private law, the son lived under a domestic despotism, which, considering the severity it retained to the last, and the number of centuries through which it endured, constitutes one of the strangest problems in history.* *

APP. I.
———
DECAY OF
PATRIA
POTESTAS,
Para. 2, III.
Ibid, p. 141.

The ancient law of Rome forbade the children under power to hold property apart from their parent, or (we should rather say) never contemplated the possibility of their claiming a separate ownership. The father was entitled to take the whole of the son's acquisitions, and to enjoy the benefit of his contracts, without being entangled in any compensating liabilities. So much as this we should expect from the constitution of the earliest Roman society; for we can hardly form a notion of the primitive family group, unless we suppose that its members brought their earnings of all kinds into the common stock, while they were unable to bind it by improvident individual agreements. The true enigma of the patria potestas does not reside here, but in the slowness with which these proprietary privileges of the parent were curtailed, and in the circumstance that, before they were seriously diminished, the whole civilised world was brought within their sphere.

IV.—DECAY OF PATRIA POTESTAS.

(*a*). The active discharge of the most important among the duties which the son owed to the state must have tempered the authority of his parent, if they did not annul it. We can readily persuade ourselves that the paternal despotism could not be brought into play without great scandal against a man of full age, occupying a high civil office. During the earlier history, however, such cases of practical emancipation would be rare compared with those which must have been created by the constant wars of the Roman republic. The military tribune and the private soldier, who were in the field three-quarters of a year during the earlier contest,—at a later period the proconsul in charge of a province and the legionaries who occupied it,—cannot have had practical reason to regard themselves as the slaves of a despotic master; and all these avenues of escape tended constantly to multiply themselves. Victories led to conquests, conquests to occupations; the mode of occupation by colonies was exchanged for the system of occupying provinces by standing armies. Each step in advance was a call for the expatriation of more Roman citizens, and a fresh draft on the blood of the failing Latin race. We may infer, I think, that a strong sentiment in favour of the relaxation of the patria potestas had become fixed by the time that the pacification of the world commenced on the establishment of the empire. * *

(*b*). No innovation of any kind was attempted till the first years of the empire, when the acquisitions of soldiers on service were withdrawn from the operation of the patria potestas, doubtless as part of the reward of the armies which had overthrown the free communities. Three centuries afterwards the same immunity was extended to the earnings of persons who were in the civil employment of the state. Both changes were obviously limited in their application; and they were so combined in technical form, as to interfere as little as possible with the principle of patria potestas.

(*c*). A certain qualified and dependent ownership had always been recognised by the Roman law in the perquisites and savings which slaves,

App. I.

Disintegra-
tion of the
Family.
Para. 2, IV.

and sons under power, were not compelled to include in the household accounts; and the special name of this permissive property, *peculium,* was applied to the acquisitions newly relieved from patria potestas, which were called in the case of soldiers Castrense Peculium, and Quasi-castrense Peculium in the case of civil servants.

(*d*). Other modifications of the parental privileges followed, which showed a less studious outward respect for the ancient principle. Shortly after the introduction of the quasi-castrense peculium, Constantine the Great took away the father's absolute control over property which his children had inherited from their mother, and reduced it to a *usufruct,* or life interest. A few more changes of slight importance followed in the Western Empire, but the farthest point reached was in the East, under Justinian, who enacted that, unless the acquisitions of the child were derived from the parent's own property, the parent's rights over them should not extend beyond enjoying their produce for the period of his life.

(*e*). ** Perpetual guardianship is obviously neither more nor less than an artifical prolongation of the patria potestas, when for other purposes it has been dissolved. In India the system survives in absolute completenes, and its operation is so strict, that a Hindoo mother frequently becomes the ward of her own sons.

V.—Disintegration of the Family.

(*a*). Ancient jurisprudence—if, perhaps, a deceptive comparison may be employed—may be likened to international law, filling nothing, as it were, excepting the interstices between the great groups which are the stones of society. In a community so situated, the legislation of assemblies and the jurisdiction of courts reaches only to the heads of families; and to every other individual the rule of conduct is the law of his home, of which his parent is the legislator.

Ibid, p. 176.

(*b*). But the sphere of civil law, small at first, tends steadily to enlarge itself. The agents of legal change, fictions, equity, and legislation, are brought, in turn, to bear on the primeval institutions; and at every point of the progress, a greater number of personal rights and a larger amount of property are removed from the domestic forum to the cognizance of the public tribunals. The ordinances of the government obtain gradually the same efficacy in private concerns as in matters of state, and are no longer liable to be overridden by the behests of a despot, enthroned by each hearthstone. We have in the annals of Roman law a nearly complete history of the crumbling away of an archaic system, and of the formation of new institutions from the recombined materials—institutions some of which descended, unimpaired, to the modern world, while others, destroyed or corrupted by contact with barbarism in the dark ages, had again to be recovered by mankind.* *

(*c*). The movement of the progressive societies has been uniform in one respect. Through all its course it has been distinguished by the gradual dissolution of family dependency, and the growth of individual obligation in its place. The individual is steadily substituted for the family, as the unit of which civil laws take account. Nor is it difficult

App. I.

CO-HEIRS OR
EQUAL PARTI-
TION OF PRO-
PERTY.

Para. 2, V.

to see what is the tie between man and man, which replaces by degrees those forms of reciprocity in rights and duties which have their origin in the family. It is contract. Starting, as from one terminus of history, from a condition of society in which all the relations of persons are summed up in the relations of family, we seem to have steadily moved towards a phase of social order in which all these relations arise from the free agreement of individuals. In Western Europe the progress achieved in this direction has been considerable.

VI.—CO-HEIRS OR EQUAL PARTITION OF PROPERTY.

Ibid, p. 227.

(a). We know of no period of Roman jurisprudence at which the place of the heir, or universal successor, might not have been taken by a group of co-heirs. This group succeeded as a single unit, and the assets were afterwards divided among them in a separate legal proceeding. When the succession was *ab intestato,* and the group consisted of the children of the deceased, they each took an equal share of the property ; nor, though males had at one time some advantage over females, is there the faintest trace of primogeniture. The mode of distribution is the same throughout archaic jurisprudence. It certainly seems that when civil society begins, and families cease to hold together through a series of generations, the idea which spontaneously suggests itself is, to divide the domain equally among the members of each successive generation, and to reserve no privilege to the eldest son or stock.

(b). Some peculiarly significant hints as to the close relation of this phenomena to primitive thought are furnished by systems yet more archaic than the Roman. Among the Hindoos, the instant a son is born, he acquires a vested right in his father's property, which cannot be sold without recognition of his joint ownership. On the son's attaining full age, he can sometimes compel a partition of the estate, even against the consent of the parent; and should the parent acquiesce, one son can always have a partition, even against the will of the others. On such partition taking place, the father has no advantage over his children, except that he has two of the shares, instead of one. The ancient law of the German tribes was exceedingly similar. The *allod* or domain of the family was the joint property of the father and his sons. It does not appear, however, to have been habitually divided, even at the death of the parent; and in the same way the possessions of the Hindoo, however divisible theoretically, are so rarely distributed in fact, that many generations constantly succeed each other without a partition taking place ; and thus the family in India has a perpetual tendency to expand into the village community. All this points very clearly to the absolutely equal division of assets among the male children at death, as the practice most usual with society, at the period when family-dependency is in the first stages of disintegration.

(c). Although, in India, the possessions of a parent are divisible at his death, and may be divisible during his life, among all his male children in equal shares ; and though this principle of the equal distribution of *property* extends to every part of the Hindoo institutions, yet, wherever *public office* or *political power* devolves at the decease of the last incumbent, the succession is nearly universally according to the rules of primogeniture. Sovereignties descend, therefore, to the eldest son; and where the affairs of the village community, the corporate unit of Hindoo society, are confided to a single manager, it is generally the eldest son who takes up the administration at his parent's death. All offices, indeed, in India tend to become hereditary, and, when their nature permits it, to vest in the eldest member of the oldest stock. Comparing these Indian successions with some of the ruder social organisations which have survived in Europe almost to our own day, the conclusion suggests itself that, when patriarchal power is not only *domestic*, but *political*, it is not distributed among all the issue at the parent's death, but is the birthright of the eldest son.

App. I.

———

Hindu and European institutions of property the same up to the formation of village communes.

Para. 3.

3. These extracts show that primitive usages, primeval jurisprudence respecting property, were the same among the Hindoos as in the other Indo-European communities; and that, in the progress of society, one and all reached in the village commune a stage of development of such complete uniformity, that the resemblance extends down even to the presence, in the communities, of a servile class, below the proprietary members of the commune, who, yet, had proprietary rights. The incidents or steps leading to this stage of development, *viz.*, the family, the patria potestas, its decline, the disintegration of the family, the equal distribution of proprietary right among children without, generally, an actual division of the property, and the consequent growth of village communities, consisting of families with these joint and several rights in property,—these incidents precluded the possibility or idea of the growth of the Cornwallis type of Bengal zemindars. At the date of the zemindari settlement in 1793, these village communes existed throughout India, as we shall see in the next appendix, in a perfect form outside the Lower Provinces of Bengal, Behar, and Orissa, and in those provinces in only an incipient state of disintegration, in which the zemindars had usurped the functions and proprietary rights of the heads of village communities, while the members of the village communes yet retained proprietary rights of a perfect kind. "The tokens of an extreme antiquity are discoverable in almost every single feature of the Indian village communities."—(*Maine*.)

The history of property in land in Europe diverges from that in India after reaching this point, *viz.*, the village commune. If we follow that history in Europe, we trace the course of property through centuries of war, misrule, spoliation, and social degradation of the original millions of cultivating proprietors; yet the best part of Europe is covered, still, by peasant proprietors. In India, on the other hand, custom which had embodied the rights of property in land

App. I.

Disintegration of
joint property.

in the village commune remained crystallized for centuries
of misrule, down to 1793; but though the Lower Provinces
have enjoyed, since, an uninterrupted peace, yet the proprietary rights of millions have disappeared in that brief
period. What, in Europe, centuries of war, rapine, spoliation, and wrong or misrule could not destroy, or benevolently
spared, in India not quite one century of benevolence and
law has dissolved in Bengal.

4. The tenures of land in Europe will be noticed in a
separate appendix: the following extracts will help to maintain the connexion between it and this appendix.

I.—Progress from joint towards individual property.

Ancient Law,
p. 269.

(a). We have the strongest reasons for thinking that property once
belonged not to individuals, nor even to isolated families, but to larger
societies, composed on the patriarchal model; but the mode of transition
from ancient to modern ownerships, obscure at best, would have been
infinitely obscurer if several distinguishable forms of village communities had not been discovered and examined. It is worth while to
attend to the varieties of internal arrangement within the patriarchal
groups, which are, or were till recently, observable among races of Indo-
European blood. The chiefs of the ruder highland clans used, it is
said, to dole out food to the heads of the households under their jurisdiction at the very shortest intervals, and sometimes day by day. A
periodical distribution is also made to the Sclavonian villagers of the
Austrian and Turkish provinces by the elders of their body; but then it
is a distribution, once for all, of the total produce of the year. In the
Russian villages, however, the substance of the property ceases to be
looked upon as indivisible, and separate proprietary claims are allowed
freely to grow up; but then, after a given, but not in all cases of the
same, period, separate ownerships are extinguished, the land of the village
is thrown into a mass, and then it is redistributed among the families
composing the community, according to their number. In India, not
only is there no indivisibility of the common fund, but separate proprietorship in parts of it may be indefinitely prolonged, and may branch
out into any number of derivative ownerships; the *de facto* partition of
the stock being, however, checked by inveterate usage, and by the rule
against the admission of strangers without the consent of the brotherhood.

(b). It is not, of course, intended to insist that these different
forms of the village community represent distinct stages in a process of
transmutation, which has been everywhere accomplished in the same
manner. But though the evidence does not warrant our going so far
as this, it renders less presumptuous the conjecture that private property,
in the shape in which we know it, was chiefly formed by the gradual
disentanglement of the separate rights of individuals from the blended
rights of a community. Our studies in the law of persons seemed to
show us the family, expanding into the agnatic group of kinsmen; then

the agnatic group, dissolving into separate households; lastly, the household, supplanted by the individual;—and it is now suggested that each step of the change corresponds to an analogous alteration in the nature of ownership; and by far the most important passage in the history of private property is its gradual elimination from the co-ownership of kinsmen.

II.—POSSESSION AND PRESCRIPTION.

(*a*). There is no principle in all law which the moderns, in spite of its beneficial character, have been so loath to adopt, and to carry to its legitimate consequences, as that which was known to the Romans as 'usucapion,' and which has descended to modern jurisprudence under the name of prescription. It was a positive rule of the old Roman law, a rule older than the Twelve Tables, that commodities which had been uninterruptedly possessed for a certain period became the property of the possessor. The period of possession was exceedingly short—one or two years, according to the nature of the commodities—and in historical times usucapion was only allowed to operate when possession had commenced in a particular way. * *

Ibid, page 284.

(*b*). In order to have the benefit of usucapion, it was necessary that the adverse possession should have begun in good faith—that is, with belief on the part of the possessor that he was lawfully acquiring the property; and it was further required that the commodity should have been transferred to him by some mode of alienation, which, however unequal to conferring a complete title in the particular case, was at least recognized by the law. In the case, therefore, of a mancipation, however slovenly the performance might have been, yet, if it had been carried so far as to involve a tradition or delivery, the vice of the title would be cured by usucapion in two years at most. * * Usucapion did not lose its advantages till the reforms of Justinian. But as soon as law and equity had been completely fused, and when mancipation[1] ceased to be the Roman conveyance, there was no further necessity for the ancient contrivance; and usucapion, with its periods of time considerably lengthened, became the prescription which has at length been adopted by nearly all systems of modern law.

Ibid, page 287.

III.—DISTINCTION BETWEEN PROPERTY AND POSSESSION.

The language of the Roman jurisconsults on the subject of possession long occasioned the greatest possible perplexity. * * Possession, in fact, when employed by the Roman lawyers, appears to have contracted a shade of meaning not easily accounted for. The word, as appears from its etymology, must have originally denoted physical contact, or physical contact resumable at pleasure; but as actually used, without any qualifying epithet, it signifies, not simply physical detention, but physical detention, coupled with the intention, to hold the thing

---

[1] Delivery before witnesses, by certain gestures, symbolical acts, and solemn phrases, and an intricate ceremonial, in days before written instruments of conveyance were used.

detained as one's own. Savigny, following Neibuhr, perceived that for this anomaly there could only be a historical origin. He pointed out that the patrician burghers of Rome, who had become tenants of the greatest part of the public domain at nominal rents, were, in view of the old Roman law, mere possessors ; but, then, they were possessors intending to keep their land against all-comers. They, in truth, put forward a claim almost identical with that which has recently been advanced in England by the lessees of church lands. Admitting that, in theory, they were the tenants-at-will of the state, they contended that time and undisturbed enjoyment had ripened their holding into a species of ownership, and that it would be unjust to eject them for the purpose of redistributing the domain. The association of this claim with the patrician tenancies permanently influenced the sense of " possession. "

IV.—EMPHYTEUSIS (OR TENANCY SUBJECT TO A FIXED PERPETUAL RENT).

(*a*). Emphyteusis, not probably as yet known by its Greek designation before the middle ages, marks one state in a current of ideas, which led ultimately to feudalism. The first mention in Roman history of estates larger than could be farmed by a paterfamilias, with his household of sons and slaves, occurs when we come to the holdings of the Roman patricians. These great proprietors appear to have had no idea of any system of farming by free tenants. Their *latifundia* seem to have been universally cultivated by slave-gangs, under bailiffs, who were themselves slaves or freedmen ; and the only organisation attempted appears to have consisted in dividing the inferior slaves into small bodies, and making them the *peculium* of the better and trustier sort, who thus acquired a kind of interest in the efficiency of their labour.

(*b*). This system was, however, especially disadvantageous to one class of estated proprietors—the municipalities. Functionaries in Italy were changed with the rapidity which often surprises us in the administration of Rome herself ; so that the superintendence of a large landed domain by an Italian corporation must have been excessively imperfect. Accordingly, we are told that with the municipalities began the practice of letting out *agri vectigules*—that is, of leasing land for a perpetuity to a free tenant, at a fixed rent, and under certain conditions. The plan was afterwards extensively imitated by individual proprietors, and the tenant, whose relation to the owner had originally been determined by his contract, was subsequently recognized by the *Prætor* as having himself a qualified proprietorship, which in time became known as emphyteusis.

(*c*). From this point the history of tenure parts into two branches. In the course of that long period during which our records of the Roman empire are most incomplete, the slave-gangs of the great Roman families became transformed into the *coloni*, whose origin and situation constitute one of the obscurest questions in all history. We may suspect that they were formed partly by the elevation of the slaves, and partly by the degradation of the free-farmers ; and that they prove the richer classes of the Roman empire to have become aware of the increased value which landed property obtains when the cultivator has an interest in the produce of the land. We know that their servitude was predial; that it wanted many of the characteristics of absolute slavery; and that they acquitted their service to the landlord in rendering to him a fixed portion of the annual crop. We know further that they survived all the mutations of society in the ancient and modern worlds. Though included in the lower courses of the feudal structure, they continued in many countries to render to the landlord precisely the same dues which they had paid to the Roman *dominus ;* and from a particular class among them, the *coloni medietarii,* who reserved half the produce for the owner, are descended the *metayer* tenantry, who still conduct the cultivation of the soil in almost all the south of Europe.

(*d*). On the other hand, the Emphyteusis, if we may so interpret the allusions to it in the Corpus juris, became a favourite, and beneficial modification of property; and it may be conjectured that, wherever free farmers existed, it was this tenure which regulated their interest in the land. The *Prætor,* as has been said, treated the Emphyteuta as a true proprietor. When ejected, he was allowed to reinstate himself by a real action, the distinctive badge of proprietary right, and he was protected from disturbance by the author of his lease, so long as the *canon,* or quit rent, was punctually paid. But, at the same time, it must not be supposed that the ownership of the author of the lease was either extinct or dormant. It was kept alive by a power of re-entry on non-payment of the rent, a right of pre-emption in case of sale, and a certain control over the mode of cultivation.

APPENDIX II.

THE LAW AND CONSTITUTION OF INDIA IN 1765.

Bengal was not a *tabula rasa* on which the authors of the permanent zemindary settlement were free to construct any system of land tenures that pleased them. As shown in the previous appendix, proprietary rights in land had grown up in India under a custom of singular uniformity with the customs which had shaped landed tenures in Europe; and the injunction of Parliament, that the rights of landholders in Bengal should be determined in accordance with the law and constitution of India, emanated from a body of landed proprietors whose political gospel was a tenacious adherence to the customs supporting proprietary rights in land which are a part of the law of the United Kingdom. In directing a land settlement in accordance with the law and constitution of India, Parliament intended the maintenance of local usage, and of established custom, and not the creation of landed proprietors with mere statutory rights.

2. Indeed, Parliament, had it so wished, could not have sanctioned a subversion of the rights of property in land in India, considering that even conquest could not have conferred such power of sanction, and that the Dewanny of Bengal, Behar and Orissa was acquired by the East India Company in 1765, through a bargain. The Governor and Council of Bengal wrote to the Court of Directors on 30th September 1765—

By establishing the power of the Great Mogul we have likewise established his rights; and his Majesty, from principles of gratitude, equity and policy, has thought proper to bestow this important employment of Dewan on the Company, the nature of which is, the collecting all the revenues, and after defraying the expenses of the army, and allowing a sufficient fund for the support of the Nizamut, to remit the remainder to Delhi, or wherever the King shall reside or direct.

Manifestly the Company did not acquire any right of property in land superior to that of the Great Mogul.

3. Whatever was the law and constitution of India at the time of the acquisition, in 1765, by the East India Company of the Dewanee of Bengal, Behar and Orissa, it remained unchanged in 1784, when the Parliament of England

App. II.

directed the East India Company to settle and establish permanent rules for the payment of rents in accordance with "the laws and constitution of India."

4. Sir Broughton Rouse, in his *Dissertation concerning the landed property of Bengal, 1791,* observed :—

I. The rise and progress of private property in land have been nearly Introduction, page similar throughout the world, always keeping pace with civilization, and an enlarged policy ; and frequently, when established, resting more upon construction and usage, than upon the strict letter of written law, or deeds of tenure ;—conquest seldom did, in ancient times, and is now never understood to, annihilate it ; where we now find it ever so firmly fixed, it was once slender and precarious ; but every mode of possession has gradually become permanent and hereditary, modified only by such arrangements as might arise from peculiar circumstances and situations.

II. I shall conclude the present digression upon the rights of con- Pages 128 to 130. quest with reciting the judgment which this eminent writer (Grotius) has really given to all civilized nations, that the conquest is no more than a simple transfer of the sovereignty, not an annihilation of private property. Now, with respect to the British territories in India, a question may arise, whether they were not obtained more by compact than conquest. If they be so considered, it would surely be an aggravation of injustice to practise a severity which even conquest would not sanction (Rousseau, Social Compact, chapter IV), and to wrest from those who had been tolerated and protected by our predecessor in power, the possessions they had peaceably enjoyed under his jurisdiction. How much more is it incumbent on us to observe this tenderness towards our Indian subjects, when it is considered that the cession of the country, although it is now held, and will be maintained, by Great Britain in a state of sovereign dominion, was made at the time under the name of an ancient office of the Moghul Empire ; the public seals and forms of which were then adopted, and have been used in all the subsequent acts of the administration, so that the people seemed only to change their governors, not their government.

5. Sir Broughton Rouse argued against the contention that the State was the sole proprietor of the land, both cultivated and uncultivated. His reasoning was conclusive, at least against the right of the Parliament of 1784 to give away to zemindars any property in land which belonged to ryots or cultivators ; while the declarations and the Act of that Parliament show that any such spoliation of the property of the subjects of the Crown in India was far from its intention. No proprietary right which the ryot or the cultivator possessed would Parliament have deliberately transferred to some one else as zemindar without giving full compensation to the former. The rights of the so-called zemindars of 1765, and of ryots or cultivators, according to the laws and constitution of India in that day, have to be ascertained.

APP. II.
——
Para. 6.

6. Perhaps the ablest work on this subject is Colonel Galloway's " *Observations on the Law and Constitution of India, on the nature of landed tenures, &c., &c., as established by the Muhammadan Law and Moghul Government, 1825.* " This work will be quoted as " Law and Constitution of India."

Page 6.

I. What is the 'law and constitution of India' to which the Legislature refers as above, by which it declares that the rights of the natives shall be protected? There are two codes of law or constitutions known to us in India—the Hindu and the Muhammadan—totally distinct, however, in themselves; so that, as they never could have been, and certainly never were, *combined*, either the one or the other must be distinctly pointed at. Is it the Hindu 'law and constitution,' then, or the Muhammadan 'law and constitution,' that is meant by the Legislature as the law, &c., of India?

Page 7.

II. I must, however, pause here, and observe that, when we speak of a 'Hindu law of India,' we assume the previous existence of a paramount Hindu Government,—a fact which ought first to be established. I ask for records to show that there ever was a regular Hindu Government established over India. We know that a number of petty States, or Rajahships, existed at a late period, and even now exist. These have been magnified into kingdoms and independent principalities. Independent, indeed, they may have been who held them, as in a rude state of society every head of a family is independent and absolute; but we have no authentic account of a Hindu paramount monarchy, whilst, on the contrary, Mr. Ward notices the names of " 53 separate kingdoms " in India. * * Ferishta declares that the Hindus have no written history better than the heroic romance of the Mahabarat. It is, indeed, contrary to the analogy of history to believe, if there had been a regular Government over India, that in the course of 2,000 years no one prince should have appeared to rescue his country from the Persian yoke; for that is the period between the eras of the Persian and Mahomedan conquest of India by Mahomed.

Page 10.

III. * * Supposing the Hindus to be in possession of an authentic body of law, the point would still remain—Is it the *Hindu* 'law and constitution,' or the Mahomedan 'law and constitution' which is the 'law and constitution of India.' That it is not the former I have undertaken to prove. All must deem this at least *probable*, who advert to the mere fact that six to eight centuries have elapsed since the country has been ruled by the triumphant and intolerant Moslems. We cannot believe, indeed, that a Moslem who had the *power*, even the legal power, to exterminate the Hindus as idolaters, would have the *will to adopt* and to *administer* their law and constitution, *and to subject his Moslem conquerors to it.* * * During the whole period of the Mahomedan history in India, though we have seen that Hindus were employed even at the head of other departments, we have never heard of a *Hindu Judge*, and assuredly no Mahomedan Kazi could even have been found to administer the laws of Menu.

Page 11.

IV. The public law (I mean that publicly administered, as well as that to which the sovereign could be a party, that between the sovereign and the people) I conclude, therefore, was indisputably Mahomedan;

App. II.

Paras. 6 & 7.

and that is the only law with which, in a question of this nature, we have anything to do. The more tolerant princes may have sanctioned indulgences in cases of private succession, where the interests of the Hindus alone were the subject of discussion, but *in foro judice*, a question of private right, even of inheritance among Hindus, could not have been decided except by the Mahomedan law, which accordingly provides for such questions, and declares that "they are to be determined as between Moslems," with certain limitations however, which are applicable alike to *all* non-Moslem subjects.

V. It is of importance to note that in the *Futava-ool-Aalumgeeree,* a celebrated work on the Mahomedan law, compiled in India under the patronage of Aurungzebe expressly for the government of his Indian subjects, the chapter on the law of Inheritance, entitled "Of Inheritance among non-Moslem Subjects," is preserved entire, as compiled from the original law of Arabia. "They shall *take*," says this work, "among themselves, by *blood* and by *compact*, as Moslems *take* among themselves. The *progeny* of a marriage which is legal by *their sacred books*, though illegal by *our* law, shall not be debarred from inheriting, but the parties to a marriage, which is illegal by *our* law, shall not take in virtue of such marriage." And the test of an illegal marriage, as we find in the *Surauj*, is, "were the parties to become Moslems, would the marriage be legal?" Here, then, the Mahomedan law on the most delicate point is maintained, and an exemplary liberality at the same time shown to the innocent progeny. The same is found in the other works on the Mahomedan law; but I mention this work in particular on account of the peculiarity of its origin.

(*f*). This is the written "law and constitution of India," as published, under the sanction of the Emperor himself, little more than fifty years before the English power became paramount in Bengal.

7. The writer's conclusion from the foregoing, and from history, that the "law and constitution of India" was Mahomedan, may be admitted without derogating from the authority of the Hindu law, among Hindu subjects of the Mahomedan rule, in respect of proprietary right in land, and of inheritance of real and personal property. The writer himself shows that though, in theory, under the Mahomedan law, all civil rights in real property were annulled by conquest, yet the inhabitants were allowed to retain their lands; that is, they retained their proprietary rights by paying the *khirauj*, and submitting to the capitation tax; and rights thus secured were transmitted under the Hindu law of inheritance, as shown in section iv. of the preceding paragraph. But for this large exception in favour of Hindu rights and laws, the existence of village communities throughout Hindustan during seven centuries of Mahomedan rule would vitiate the author's conclusion, those communities, with their rights in real property, being Hindu institutions.

HINDU LAW.

1. ORIGIN OF PROPERTY IN LAND.
2. INHERITANCE.
3. OTHER SOURCES OF TITLE.
4. ADMINISTRATION, AND VILLAGE COMMUNITIES.

ORIGIN OF PROPERTY IN LAND.

8. In the following quotations, the extracts from Menu are from Mr. N. J. Halhed's "*Memoir on the Land Tenure and Principles of Taxation in the Bengal Presidency*," &c., or from other authorities indicated :—

Halhed, page 1.

I. "Sages who know former times consider this earth (Pristhivi) as the wife of King Prithu, and thus they pronounce cultivated land to be the property of him who cut away the wood, or who cleared and tilled it, and the antelope of the first hunter who mortally wounded it' —(*Menu*).

Origin of property in land. Halhed, page 1.

II. The right so acquired might be sold, given, bequeathed, or otherwise alienated at the discretion of the individual—(*Halhed*).

Tagore Law Lectures, 1874-75, page 4.

III. (referring to I). This general principle has been recognized in Germany, Java and Russia, and indeed, in most countries, and is expressly enunciated in Muhammadan law also, but it does not enable us to advance much on our present enquiry. It leaves open the question, what right of property is acquired; whether absolute and exclusive, or only limited; whether in the soil itself, or only the right to cultivate it? This question has to be answered in the silence of express law by a reference to the actual practice and the ideas of the time. Menu also speaks of the owner of land, and appears to contemplate exclusive, and perhaps individual, rights in land; although we get no further information as to their nature. The owner of a field is directed, or advised, to keep up sufficient hedges: he is entitled to the produce of seed sown by another on his land, unless by agreement with him; and to the produce of seed conveyed upon his land by wind or water. The case of a dispute between neighbouring landholders or villages as to boundaries is contemplated; and a penalty provided for forcible trespass upon another's land. These passages show that some kind of exclusive right was contemplated, and appear to recognize a right beyond that of the village; but whether in the family or the individual is not clear. The sale of lands is also spoken of in connexion with the sale of metals. (*Mr. Arthur Phillips.*)

9.—INHERITANCE.

Patton's "Asiatic Monarchies."

Pages 168—171.

I. *Equal division among equal kindred.*—By the ordinances of Menu, the eldest son is entitled to greater respect than the others, and to some particular marks of attention. "After the death of the father and the mother, the brothers, being assembled, may divide among themselves the

patrimonial and matrimonial estate (Chapter IX, Art. 104). The
eldest brother may take entire possession of the patrimony; and the
others may live under him, as they lived under their father, *unless they*
choose to be separated (Article 105)." In Article 106 it is said: "The eldest
son ought, before partition, to manage the whole patrimony." In case of
extraordinary acquirements and distinguished excellence in the eldest
son, particular marks of distinction are enjoined, the performance of
which, however, seems to depend upon the inclination of his brothers.
By the 115th Article, equality of division seems to be the general rule;
the words are: "But among brothers equally skilled in performing the
several duties, there is no deduction of the best in ten, or the most excellent chattel, though some trifle, as a mark of greater veneration,
should be given to the first-born." *The Code of Gentoo Laws,* published by
Mr. Halhed, which have a wonderful agreement with the *Ordinances* of
Menu, considering a difference in their dates of about three thousand
years, and which, therefore, may be regarded as the modern explication
and interpretation of those laws, are clear and explicit on this subject.
The following quotations are from the second chapter, entitled *Of the
Division of Heritable Property,* section 1st: "If a man dies, or renounces
the world, &c., all his possessions, be they *land* or money, or effects,
or cattle, or birds, go to his son. If there be several sons, *they all shall
receive equal shares.*" Again, "if there be no brother, property goes to
the son of the brother by blood." "If there are several sons, *they all
shall have equal shares.*" In this Code the rule seems to be, without an
exception, that equal kindred share equally of land, money, or effects.
In the same Code and chapter, section XI, it is said: "If a father divides
among his sons the glebe, orchards, houses, rents, slave-girls, and slaves
of his father and ancestors, &c., he hath no authority to give to some
more, or to others *less.*" It, therefore, appears that, if the *zemindary* had
been *a landed estate,* continuing by hereditary descent in the same family,
it would not, by the Hindu law (which alone could be applicable), have
descended to *one son,* where there were *many,* nor to *one relative,* where
there were others of *equal kindred;* but it would have been equally
divided among all the equal relatives of the last occupant; which, not
having been the case, demonstrates, I think, that it could not be
esteemed *landed property.* So that the circumstance upon which the
European idea of landed property is founded, actually infers an opposite
conclusion; and establishes with certainty that the zemindary appointment must have been an *office,* which, not admitting of division, could
only be continued (when given to persons of the same family) in the
manner that has been followed."

II. One of the principles of the Hindu law of inheritance is, that
all the male heirs possess a joint interest in patrimonial property, which
is absolutely inseparable without the consent of all the parceners.

III. The Hindu law indicates to Hindu heritors their several
interests in ancestorial property, the alienation of any part of which, to
their prejudice, without their consent, is expressly prohibited. A Hindu
cannot dispose of anything by will, as the law stands, except such
personal property as he may have himself acquired; the commentators,
however, are at variance, and the pundits find no difficulty in finding
arguments favouring either side of a question of inheritance or bequest

from their works. In the Supreme Court, wills by Hindus have long been considered legal documents, and the disputes which arise in the course of administration prove never-failing sources of litigation.

10.—Other modes of acquiring property in land.

Halhed, page 2.   There are seven virtuous means of acquiring property : succession, occupancy or donation, and purchase or exchange, which are allowed to all classes ; conquest, which is peculiar to the military class ; lending at interest, husbandry or commerce, which belong to the mercantile class ; and acceptance of presents by the sacerdotal class *from respectable* men.—(*Menu*).

11.—Administration.

Halhed, page 6.   I. The collection of a tax of grain in kind demanded the employment of a great number of officers, and, under any other than the system adopted, their allowance would have taken up the greater portion of the revenue. The legislator, however, seems to have been fully aware that the agency of individuals employed *in the vicinity of their homes may be purchased at a cheaper rate than when their duty calls them to a distance from their families*. The public officers of revenue and police in each district were, accordingly, selected from among the proprietors of the immediate neighbourhood.

These officers, denominated *gram adhiputi*, were appointed in every parish, and were amenable to overseers of ten parishes, who were under the direction of superintendents, whose jurisdiction extended over 20 parishes, who were subject to the authority of presidents of districts containing 100 parishes, who, in their turn, were subordinate to governors of provinces consisting of a thousand parishes. "Let him appoint a lord[1] of one town[2] with its districts ; a lord of ten towns, a lord of twenty, a lord of a hundred, and a lord of a thousand ".—(*Menu*).

II. The system under which these functionaries were remunerated for their trouble and responsibility was as follows :—

The *gram adhiput*, or overseer of a single parish,[3] received as his allowance the quantity of food, drink, firewood, and other articles which the other inhabitants of his parish were bound to provide daily for the public service.[4] The superintendent of ten villages enjoyed the whole produce of as much land as could be tilled by two ploughs (drawn by six bullocks each), that is to say, the proportion of the land tax for so much of his own land was remitted ; the superintendent of twenty villages paid no tax for five plough-lands of his property ; the rulers of districts appropriated the tax of a small parish ; the governors of provinces, the tax of a large one, to their own purposes. Thus—

(*a*). " Such food, drink, wood and other articles as, by law, should be given each day to the king by the inhabitants of the township, let the lord of one town receive *as his perquisite*."

---

[1] *Adhiput* does not mean lord, but superintendent.
[2] The word *gram* signified not a town, but a tract of country in cultivation with its village ;—it means, rather, a parish.
[3] The word *gram* signifies grange or village, with the land belonging to it.
[4] This food, &c., is by the commentators upon the laws of Menu admitted to be independent of, and in excess of the land tax.

(*b*). " Let the lord of ten towns enjoy the produce of two plough-
lands (or as much ground as can be tilled with two ploughs, each drawn
by six bulls) ; the lord of twenty, that of five plough-lands ; the lord of
hundred, that of a village or small town ; the lord of a thousand, that of
a large town. "—(*Menu*).

The reading in the here quoted slokh may seem somewhat obscure, as a grant of the land itself might be inferred from the translation : this, however, was not the case. There is, however, a slight obscurity in the text (" two plough-lands' *produce*[1] let him enjoy ") ; and perhaps this obscurity may be attributed to a sacrifice made in favour of conciseness and versification. The Government could not transfer that which it never possessed, *viz.*, a paramount exclusive proprietary interest in the soil ; it could lay claim to a portion of the produce only, not as rent, but as tax revenue, and it provided for its officers, who collected it by an assignment of a portion of the revenue it was entitled to by law. By the remission of a portion of the tax to the proprietors who held official situations, an amount of individual and local influence by no means trivial was secured to the State for a very inconsiderable sacrifice. As these functionaries were appointed by the ruling power, they were also liable to dismissal from office for irregularities or misconduct, and to very heavy penalties in addition.

(*c*) " Since the servants of the king, whom he has appointed guardians of the districts, are generally knaves, who seize what belongs to other men, from such knaves let him defend his people."

(*d*) " Of such evil-minded servants as wring wealth from subjects attending them on business, let the king confiscate all their possessions, and banish them from his realm".—(*Menu*).

12.—VILLAGE COMMUNITIES.

I. As the most numerous class of the Hindu population, that of the Sudras, was declared incapable of possessing any property whatever, it follows that no member of it could be a landholder, under the ancient Hindu Governments. The proprietary interest in the soil was vested in the Brahmins, Kheytres, and Byres, and the Burrun Shunker or intermediate class, under the original Hindu Governments.

(*a*). " But a man of the servile class, whether bought or unbought, he may be compelled to perform servile duty, because such a man was created by the self-existent for the purpose of serving Brahmins."

(*b*). " A Sudra, though emancipated by his master, is not released from a state of servitude ; for of a state which is natural to him, by whom can he be divested ?"—(*Menu*).

II. The Brahmins and Khetries, considering manual labour as in- consistent with their dignity, and, to a certain extent, with their religious purity, avoided all personal interference with agricultural operations as degrading and even sinful, and not to be resorted to, except in cases of extreme necessity ; but they had no objection to profit by the advantages afforded by landed possessions, and were content to realize all

---

[1] Colonel Briggs, quoting this text, adds in a note :—" By the produce is meant the revenue derivable from the land to the Crown. "—*Land Tax*, page 23.

App. II.
———
Hindu Law.
Village communities.

Para. 12, section
III, contd.

the benefits which the legislator would seem (by declaring agriculture as a profession, their peculiar calling) originally to have designed to secure to the Byre caste, by imposing on their Sudra servants and slaves the labours of tillage, while they appropriated the crops.

III. Lieutenant-Colonel Briggs—

Land tax in
India.
Page 35.

(*a*). Although Menu has embraced all subjects of legislation, and has entered into much detail regarding the rights of landed property, he has laid down no rules for the internal economy of villages and towns ; a circumstance the more remarkable, as this part of the Hindu constitution appears once to have been universal throughout the country.

Ibid.

(*b*). Each village in India contains within itself the seeds of an entire republic or government ; wars, deluges, pestilence or famine may break it up for a time, but it has a tendency to re-unite, which nothing can prevent. It consists of an agricultural corporation, owning all the land, at the head of whom is a chief elected by the corporation. It has also at least one individual of all the crafts necessary to agriculture and essential to the comforts of rural life, *viz.*,—(1) the carpenter ; (2) blacksmith ; (3) shoemaker ; (4) juhar (acts as scout guide, frequently as watchman) ; (5) cordwainer,—provides all leather ropes, thongs, whips, &c., used by the cultivators ; (6) potter ; (7) barber ; (8) washerman ; (9) priest of the temple, or (10) school master and astrologer, (11) bard or village poet ; (12) distributor of the water.

Land tax in
India, page 37.

(*c*). The land belonging to every township is accurately defined, and the village officers above-mentioned are retained on the spot by the assignment of a portion of it to each. These lots are usually situated on the borders of the village limits, in order to give to the hereditary officers a perfect knowledge, under all circumstances, of the boundary of the township.

Page 39.

(*d*). The whole land seems originally to have been divided into ten, twenty, or more shares, each bearing the names of the first settlers.

Ibid.

(*e*). The Government portion was originally paid in kind, and its amount was taken from the gross produce, estimated according to the quantity of seed sown, or according to the actual crop. Each cultivator also contributed something as fees to all the village officers who received these fees in addition to the lands they occupied free of tax to the king, *viz.*,—

Report, page 40.

(1).—The *gram-adikar*, or village mayor, originally elected by the people, was at the same time the representative of the inhabitants and of the Government. He decided disputes, either in person or by convening a court of arbitration ; he was the head of the police ; and the whole community was bound to produce to the Government either the property or the thief, in case of robberies, and the guilty in more serious cases, such as of murder.

(2).—*Gram-lekuk.*—Besides the Government tax, an extra contribution was made for village expenses, not unlike that of the parish rates in Europe. The most minute details of the transfer and sale of land, of rents and contracts, as well as of receipts and disbursements, were recorded by the village clerk, or gram-lekuk, under authority of the gram-adikar, whose accounts were always open to inspection.

APP. II.

Hindu Law.
Village commu-
nities.
Para. 12, section
III, contd.
Report, p. 40.

(*f*). Thus each village was in itself a small state; several villages formed a district, over which also presided a chief denominated *Des adikar*, and under whom was also a record-keeper denominated *Des lekuk*.[1] The former superintends all the villages of his department as the *gram-adikar* presided over the concerns of his village, and the des lekuk received from the village clerks their accounts, and presented an abstract to the Government. These latter officers were usually conciliated by the villages by assignments of land from each, and were paid by the Government by a percentage of the collections. The proportion of each was not defined, and seems to have varied in different parts; though for the most part a tenth of the revenue divided between these district chiefs appears to have been the fee of office.

(*g*). It was not unusual for the king to maintain his army, and to reward the officers and nobles of his courts, by assignments on the revenue; and, although those chieftains resided in the districts themselves, they had no authority to interfere in the ancient usages of the people, but merely to receive the king's dues, permitting the village communities to manage their own concerns.

IV. — *Deccan.* ELPHINSTONE (HON'BLE MOUNTSTUART).—

Land tax in
India,
page 41.
Colonel Briggs
Land tax in
India,
pages 7 & 8.

(*a*). In whatever point of view we examine the native government in the Deccan, the first and most important feature is the division into villages or townships. These communities contain in miniature all the materials of a State within themselves, and are sufficient to protect their members if all other governments were withdrawn.

(*b*). Each village has a portion of ground attached to it, which is committed to the management of the inhabitants. The boundaries are carefully marked and jealously guarded. They are divided into fields, the limits of which are exactly known; each field has a name, and is kept distinct, even when the cultivation of it has been long abandoned. The result of the several reports received from Mr. Elphinstone is his conviction " that a large portion of the ryots (cultivators) are the proprietors of their estates, subject to the payment of a FIXED LAND-TAX to Government, that their property is hereditary and saleable, and they are never dispossessed while they pay their tax; and even then they have for a long period (at least thirty years) the right of re-claiming their estate on paying the dues of Government." Again, an opinion prevails throughout the Mahratta Country, that under the old Hindu government all the land was held by (meerassies) hereditary landlords, and that the oopries (tenants) were introduced as the old proprietors sunk under the tyranny of the Mahomedans.

(*c*). (*Colonel Briggs continues*).—" The Collector of Poonah states, the general divisions of husbandmen are two: *tulkaries,* men who cultivate their own fields; and *oopries,* or tenants who cultivate lands not their own. A third class exists, called *wawandkary,* a temporary tenant, who, residing in one village, comes for a season to take land

---

[1] The appellation of the village headmen and clerks, and of the district chiefs and their record-keepers, differs in the various tongues of the several nations where they are found, though the duties and perquisites are everywhere of a similar nature. The general term here given is derived from the Sanskrit law books.

App. II.

Hindu Law.

Village communities.

Para. 12,
section IV,
contd.

in another. The *tulkary* is a mirasdar. *Tul* signifies a field, and *tulkary* the owner of land; he is considered, and universally acknowledged by the Government, to have the property of the lands he cultivates. I am yet uninformed," says the Collector, " and perhaps it may never be clearly established, at what period the Deccan landlords acquired their rights to the property of the soil, by purchasing it from the Government, or the village; or whether it has always been inherent in them, and that the Government has either usurped their rights in some instances, or broken through a custom of allowing lands *lying waste from a deficiency of population*, afterwards to become the inheritance of the multiplying *descendants of the original number of landed proprietors*."

(*d*). By the original proprietors (continues Colonel Briggs), no doubt is meant those persons who obtained the first possession of the land of the village; and thus we perceive the remains of the ancient agricultural body corporate to exist in the Deccan, though for several centuries the country was under the foreign yoke of the Mahomedans. Again, " The Deccan landlord is proud of his situation, and is envied among his brethren, who are the cultivators of lands not their own; the feeling of attachment to their fields is remarkably keen, and no consideration but the utmost pecuniary distress will induce them to abandon their rights of proprietorship. These rights are either inherited or purchased; and it is a remarkable circumstance, that in the body of the deed of sale it is invariably recorded that he who sells his land has begged of him who buys to become the proprietor. It would seem that this insertion is deemed requisite as a safeguard to the buyer, in consequence of the well-known reluctance of all landlords to part with their lands, and to show that no subterfuge was used to force or trick them from the original proprietor. The *tulkary* pays a land-rent to Government according to the extent and quality of his lands. *This land-rent is supposed to admit of no increase*. Such is this acknowledged right of the proprietor in most parts of the country."

(*e*). In the administration of the office of Magistrate, the potel, or chief of the landed corporation, was here, as in other parts, the head of the village and the representative of the people as well as of the Government. The existence of the local officers in the Mahratta Country is thus described,—" A *turuf* is composed (Mr. Elphinstone's Report) of an indefinite number of villages; it is under no particular officer. Several *turufs* make a *pergunnah*, which is under a *desmook* (literally, chief of the district) who performs the same functions towards the pergunnah as the potel towards the village. He is assisted by a *des pandia*, (writer of the district) who answers to the *koolkurney* or village register.

(*f*). It is universally believed in the Mahratta Country, that the *des mooks*, *des pandias*, &c., were all officers appointed by some former government; and it seems probable that they were the revenue officers of the Hindu government. These officers still hold the lands and fees that were orginally assigned them as wages, and are considered as servants of the Government; but the only duty they perform is to produce these old records, when required, to settle disputes about land by a reference to those records, and to keep a register of all new grants and transfers of property either by Government or by individuals. Mr. Elphinstone rates the *des mook's* profits at 5 per cent. of the collections, together with as much more in rent-free land ; and half of these perquisites to the *des pandia* or district register.

App. II.

HINDU LAW.

Village communities

Para. 12, section VI, contd.

Pages 81 to 107.

Report of Select Committee, E. I. Affairs, Sess. 1831-32, vol. xi.

V. RAJPOOTANA AND MALWA.—Colonel Briggs describes the existence in these States of the same village system as in the Deccan, but with this modification, that under a feudal system which prevailed, the Hindu landholders who constituted the hereditary village landed proprietary paid revenue to feudal superiors to whom the revenue had been assigned as a reward for services, or as a provision for the support of military establishments.

VI. NORTH-WESTERN PROVINCES.

(*a*). *Mr. Thomas Fortescue, Commissioner for Civil Affairs of Delhi, 12th April 1832.* Q. 2230.—Did the village officers, who appear to have existed in early times throughout the East, continue in authority and power under the Mahomedan government ? In no part of our provinces where I have served (Midnapore, Dacca, Moorshedabad, Patna, Benares, Allyghur, Mynpooree), have I seen the organization of society so good as it was in the territory of Delhi. The nature of the Mahomedan government, before we got possession of the Delhi territory, was such that the villages, many of them, united together for their own protection, and they organized themselves entirely with reference to every point connected with their security and their advantage. Almost every individual in the village had an acknowledged portion of the soil, and a right to it ; and the revenue which the Government obtained was generally in proportion to its power to collect.

Q. 2234.—Have the villages themselves any records of the property before our conquest ? The property was so strongly recognized in the territory, that the families who had absented themselves from various causes for years, returned, claimed, and got possession of their lands without any opposition, in the old villages which they had formerly occupied.

Q. 2235.—Was there any dispute with respect to boundaries ? None. There were, as well as I recollect, about 600 villages, the names of which were on the records when we got possession uninhabited ; and when I had to report upon the province, there were 400 of them re-peopled, and chiefly by persons who had themselves, or as the descendants of former occupants, hereditary and admitted property in those villages.

Q. 2238.—Was there in those villages any class of persons living upon rents, and not actually cultivating the soil ? There was no person between the proprietors and the Government.

Q. 2239.—Will you be so good as to define what you mean by the term proprietor ? In Delhi a person who has had hereditary possession from time immemorial of certain portions of land, included within the nominal boundaries of the village, that hereditary possession gives him the right to dispose of the same as he pleases, to hire it, or lend it, subject only to certain local customs of their own, and his heirs become the proprietors : such constituting what I call a proprietor.

Q. 2240.—Are the Committee to understand that in the answer you have given you allude to the right of possession which is inherent in the actual cultivator of the land, or do you allude to a class of persons living upon rents paid to them by persons residing upon the land? No; I mean the former, though they have persons often assisting them in their cultivation. The most perfect description of property that I have personally met with in India is found in that territory in the manner I have endeavoured to describe.

(*b*). *Mr. Holt Mackenzie, 1832.*—In many places extensive tracts are held by communities of cultivating zemindars (commonly called with us *biswadars*) who assert, as colonists or conquerors, a property, several or common, in the lands lying within defined boundaries, whether cultivated or waste, subject, in certain cases, to the rights of the preceding class (*khodkhast,* or cultivators having rights of proprietors in the fields they occupy). From these latter they are to be distinguished chiefly by this, that besides a fixed title of occupancy in the fields actually cultivated by them, they have a right, corporate or several, in all lands lying within a specific division of territory, not appropriated to the use of others, and in the advantages, actual or reversionary, derivable from occupied land, not taken by Government to itself, nor specifically admitted to belong to others, which right, though it does not go the length of barring Government from the appropriation or assessment of the waste (the prerogative of drawing revenues from every acre not alienated seems to outweigh all private interests), gives a preferable title of occupancy and a preponderating influence in the management of village affairs. * * * The two classes I have last mentioned, *viz.,* the fixed occupants of fields, and the biswadars, or co-parcenary occupants of villages, appear to be the only ones who have a permanent title of property, independently of grant from, or permanent engagement with, the Government. (Rajahs or chiefs continued in the management of extensive tracts from political motives, or from a regard to their hereditary exercise of power, I regard as a part of the Government.)

(*c*). *Sir C. T. Metcalfe.*—The village communities are little republics, having nearly everything that they want within themselves, and almost independent of any foreign relations. They seem to last where nothing else lasts. Dynasty after dynasty tumbles down : revolution succeeds to revolution; Hindoo, Patan, Mogul, Mahratta, Sikh, English, are all masters in turn, but the village communities remain the same. In times of trouble they arm and fortify themselves; an hostile army passes through the country : the village communities collect their cattle within their walls, and let the enemy pass unprovoked. If plunder and devastation be directed against themselves, and the force employed be irresistible, they flee to friendly villages at a distance, but when the storm has passed over, they return and resume their occupations. If a country remain for a series of years the scene of continued pillage and massacre, so that the villages cannot be inhabited, the scattered villagers nevertheless return whenever the power of peaceable possession revives. A generation may pass away, but the succeeding generation will return. The sons will take the place of their fathers, the same site for the village, the same positions for the houses, the same lands will be re-occupied by the descendants of those who were driven out when the village was depopulated, and it is not a trifling matter that will drive them out, for they will often maintain their post through times of disturbance and convulsion, and acquire strength sufficient to resist pillage and oppression with success.

(2). The village constitution which can survive all outward shocks, is, I suspect, easily subverted with the aid of our regulations and courts of justice; by any internal disturbance; litigation above all things, I should think, would tend to destroy it.

(3). In many instances there are resident cultivators who, though not claiming ownership, have a right, by the usage of the village, to retain the land which they cultivate.

VII. Madras Presidency.

(a). *Fifth Report.*—Of the internal form and constitution of the village communities in the Northern Circars, the Committee of Circuit have afforded only an imperfect account, but later and more particular enquiries have clearly shown that they do not differ in their nature from those existing in the modern territories in the Peninsula. A village, geographically considered, is a tract of country comprising some hundreds or thousands of acres of arable and waste land; politically viewed, it resembles a corporation or township. Its proper establishment of officers and servants, consisting of the following descriptions (the detail is of the same classes of village officers as in Hindoostan generally, see Section III b). Under this simple form of municipal government, the inhabitants of the country have lived from time immemorial. The boundaries of the villages have been but seldom altered; and though the villages themselves have been sometimes injured, and even desolated by war, famine and disease, the same name, the same limits, the same interests, and even the same families, have continued for ages. The inhabitants give themselves no trouble about the breaking up and division of kingdoms; while the villages remain entire, they care not to what power it is transferred, or to what sovereign it devolves; its internal economy remains unchanged; the Potail is still the head inhabitant, and still acts as the Petty Judge and Magistrate and Collector or renter of the village.

(b). *Mr. Place, 6th June 1799 (Fifth Report).*—I draw my first argument in favour of the hereditary right of the indigenous natives and husbandmen to the usufructuary property of the soil, from the division of the land into shares, and from the appointment of a distinct class of people to record them; to note down every variation that takes place, and to keep all accounts of the cultivation and produce. As I have already said, these divisions are supposed to have taken place at the original settlement of each village, and were, to a greater or smaller number, according to the number of original settlers or of labouring servants that they brought with them; for I presume I need not explain that the latter, doomed to the meanest offices, can acquire no property in land. Had they been regulated by any other rule, villages of the same extent would have been divided into the same number of shares; whereas whilst one is divided into ten, another having the same quantity of land annexed to it may be divided into 100 shares, but all equal. Every

APP. II.
——
HINDU LAW.
Village commu-
nities.
——
Para. 12 contd.
Land Tax, page
175.

original share may be reckoned a freehold, which, although it may have been subsequently sub-divided into several similar ones, they all hold of the proprietor of the original remainder, who retains a pre-eminence over them, and to whom, I imagine, they were originally considered to owe service, for his right of pre-eminence is still so tenaciously asserted, and so unequivocally acknowledged, that when making the late settlement of the Jughire, a few *meerasadars* only of villages, where I know them to be very numerous, appeared to rent them. I was told that they were the proprietors of the original shares; that all other were sub-meerasadars and would agree to whatever terms their principals entered into: and although I thought it proper that all should give their consent personally or in writing, yet I found that the sub-meerasadars invariably considered themselves dependent upon the proprietor of that share from which they had ramified, if I may use the expression.

VIII. BENGAL—LOWER PROVINCES.

1. *Colonel Briggs.*—The system of the former government embraced the realization of the revenue from the value of the crops annually raised, a scheme which continued under the Mahommedans, though evidently belonging to a period anterior to their invasion. By this rule the produce of the land, whether taken in kind, *or estimated in money*, was understood to be shared in distinct proportions between the cultivator and the Government. In Bengal it was estimated that the husbandman received only two-fifths, and the remainder was sub-divided between the latter and the zemindar and village officers; of this the zemindar received, as COLLECTOR, one-tenth, or about 3-50ths of the whole. Smaller portions went to the mocuddum (the village Hereditary Magistrate), the Patwarry (village accountant), &c. Provision was also made in the same way for the Canoongoe, or district registrar.

2. [Thus far the extract from Colonel Briggs' *Land Tax, &c.*, shows merely that, in the Lower Provinces of Bengal, there was an organization of village officers similar to that in the rest of Hindoostan; but it does not state explicitly that there was a village proprietary corresponding to that in other parts of India. The duties of the principal village officers, however, imply the existence of a village proprietary, and it will be seen in a subsequent paper in the appendix, that the rights of the khodkasht and pykasht cultivators in the Lower Provinces were identical with those of corresponding members of village communities in the North-Western Provinces and the Madras Presidency.]

3. In making the new settlement for Benares, a due respect was paid to the experience of the Resident, Mr. Jonathan Duncan, and it is a remarkable fact that, with all Lord Cornwallis' repugnance to the principles and practice of Asiatic governments, he adopted them entirely in the settlements of Benares, as will be seen in the sequel. It is pretended that the Hindoo institutions here *were more perfect than in*

Bengal, but there is no just reason for supposing so. Here the Resident had enquired and made himself master of the subject ; in other parts the public officers were absolutely *" prohibited "* as we have seen *" from going into local scrutiny."* Here we find the village occupants of the land termed zemindars. They are thus described in the Fifth Report,—" the village zemindars paying revenue to Government are said to belong to a joint partnership, denominated *putteedar* or sharers, descended from the same common stock. Some, however, had their separate shares, while others remained united with the principal of the family, or the headmen of the brethren, one or more, whose names were usually inserted in all agreements for land revenue. Besides these village zemindars, there were others denominated talukdars, who have the management of a greater or lesser number of villages, with the heads of whom, *in conjunction with the partners*, they make their settlements.

IX. Summary—India.

Maine's Ancient Law.—There is, however, one community which will always be carefully examined by the inquirer who is in quest of any lost institution of primeval society. How far so-ever any such institution may have undergone change among the branch of the Indo-European family which has been settled for ages in India, it will seldom be found to have entirely cast aside the shell in which it was originally reared. It happens that among the Hindoos we do find a form of ownership which ought at once to rivet our attention from its exactly fitting in with the ideas which our studies in the law of persons would lead us to entertain respecting the original condition of property. The village community of India is at once an organized patriarchal society and an assemblage of co-proprietors. The present relations to each other of the men who compose it are indistinguishably confounded with their proprietary rights, and to the attempts of English functionaries to separate the two may be assigned some of the most formidable miscarriages of Anglo-Indian administration. The village community is known to be of immense antiquity. In whatever direction research has been pushed into Indian history, general or local, it has always found the community in existence at the farthest point of its progress. A great number of intelligent and observant writers, most of whom had no theory of any sort to support concerning its nature and origin, agree in considering it the least destructible institution of a society which never willingly surrenders any one of its usages to innovation. Conquests and revolutions seem to have swept over it without disturbing or displacing it, and the most beneficent systems of government in India have always been those which have recognized it as the basis of administration.

The mature Roman law, and modern jurisdiction following in its wake, look upon co-ownership as an exceptional and momentary condition of the rights of property. This view is clearly indicated in the maxim which obtains universally in Western Europe, ' *Nemo in communione potest invitus detineri*' ('No one can be kept in co-proprietorship against his will'). But in India this order of ideas is reversed ; and it may be said that separate proprietorship is always on its way

App. II.
———
Hindu Law.

Village commu-
nities.

Para. 12, section
IX, contd.

Page 262.

to become proprietorship in common. The process has been adverted to already. As soon as a son is born, he acquires a vested interest in his father's substance; and on attaining years of discretion, he is even, in certain contingencies, permitted by the letter of the law to call for a partition of the family estate. As a fact, however, a division rarely takes place even at the death of the father, and the property constantly remains undivided for several generations; though every member of every generation has a legal right to an undivided share in it. The domain thus held in common is sometimes administered by an elected manager, but more generally, and in some provinces always, it is managed by the eldest agnate, by the eldest representative of the eldest line of the stock. Such an assemblage of joint proprietors, a body of kindred holding a domain in common, is the simplest form of an Indian village community; but the community is more than a brotherhood of relatives, and more than an association of partners. It is an organized society, and, besides providing for the management of the common fund, it seldom fails to provide by a complete staff of functionaries for internal government, for police, for the administration of justice, and for the apportionment of taxes and public duties.

The process which I have described as that under which a village community is formed may be regarded as typical. Yet it is not to be supposed that every village community in India drew together in so simple a manner. Although in the north of India the archives, as I am informed, almost invariably show that the community was founded by a single assemblage of blood relations, they also supply information that men of alien extraction have always from time to time been engrafted on it; and a mere purchaser of a share may generally, under certain conditions, be admitted to the brotherhood. In the South of the Peninsula there are often communities which appear to have sprung, not from one, but from two or more families; and there are some whose composition is known to be entirely artificial;—indeed, the occasional aggregation of men of different castes in the same society is fatal to the hypothesis of a common descent. Yet in all these brotherhoods either the tradition is preserved, or the assumption made, of an original common parentage. Mountstuart Elphinstone, who writes more particularly of the southern village communities, observes of them (*History of India, I, 126*) :—" The popular notion is, that the village landholders are all descended from one or more individuals, who settled in the village; and that the only exceptions are formed by persons who have derived

their rights by purchase, or otherwise, from members of the original stock. The supposition is confirmed by the fact, that, to this day, there are only single families of landholders in small villages, and not many in large ones; but each has branched out into so many members, that it is not uncommon for the whole agricultural labour to be done by the landholders, without the aid either of tenants or of labourers. The rights of the landholders are theirs collectively; and though they almost always have a more or less perfect partition of them, they never have an entire separation. A landholder, for instance, can sell or mortgage his rights; but he must first have the consent of the village, and the purchaser steps exactly into his place, and takes up all his obligations. If a family becomes extinct, its share returns to the common stock."

The village community, then, is not necessarily an assemblage of blood relations; but it is *either* such an assemblage, or a body of co-proprietors, formed on the model of an association of kinsmen. The type with which it should be compared is evidently not the Roman family, but the Roman *Gens*, or House. The *Gens* was also a group on the model of the family; it was the family extended by a variety of sections, of which the exact nature was lost in antiquity. In historical times, its leading characteristics were the very two which Elphinstone remarks in the village community. There was always the assumption of a common origin, an assumption sometimes notoriously at variance with fact; and, to repeat the historian's words, "if a family became extinct, its share returned to the common stock." In old Roman law, unclaimed inheritances escheated to the Gentiles. It is further suspected by all who have examined their history, that the communities, like the Gentiles, have been very generally adulterated by the admission of strangers, but the exact mode of absorption cannot now be ascertained. At present they are recruited, as Elphinstone tells us, by the admission of purchasers with the consent of the brotherhood. The acquisition of the adopted member is, however, of the nature of a universal succession; together with the share he has bought, he succeeds to the liabilities which the vendor has incurred towards the aggregate group. He is an *emptor familiæ*, and inherits the legal clothing of the person whose place he begins to fill.

13. Thus, **the Hindu law of real property found a clear and distinct expression in the village communities, which were co-extensive with, and peculiar to, the Hindu system throughout India. The joint and several property of members of the village commune in the land of one's own village is incompatible with the theory of the exclusive proprietary right of a zemindar in several villages. Hence, the prevalence of village communities throughout India raises a presumption of full proprietary right of members of the village commune, that is, of the village cultivators, and throws the burden of proof on any zemindar who might claim absolute and exclusive proprietary right in the lands of several villages, or of a village. In the permanent settlement, however, the zemindar was relieved of this burden of proof by the Government laying the burden on the ryots.**

MUHAMMADAN LAW.

1. ORIGIN OF PROPERTY IN LAND.
2. INHERITANCE.
3. OTHER SOURCES OF TITLE.
4. ADMINISTRATION AND VILLAGE COMMUNITIES.

14.—ORIGIN OF PROPERTY IN LAND.

I. The explanation of the origin of landed property which is delivered by Menu is not exceeded in correctness by any of the writers of the West. "Cultivated land is the property of him who cut away the wood, or

(margin: App. II. — MAHOMEDAN LAW. Para. 14.)

(margin: Wilks' Mysore. page 108.)

who first cleared and tilled it;" and the exact coincidence of this doctrine with that of the early Muhammadans is worthy of particular remark. " Whosoever cultivates waste lands does thereby· acquire the property of them; a zummee (infidel) becomes proprietor of them in the same manner as a Mussulman."

Halhed, p. 39.
II. " He who brings into life land which was dead, he is the owner thereof."

15.—INHERITANCE.

I. The law of equal division holds both with respect to Muhammadans and with Hindus (*James Mill*).

Inheritance.
3rd Report, Se-
lect Committee,
1832, Q. 3235.
H.E. Cole-
brooke's Hus-
bandry of
Bengal, page 91.
II. Estates of Muhammadans are more rapidly subdivided than those of Hindus. The law of family partnership generally preserves the unity of the estates held by the Hindus. This, however, is not the most material difference. The Hindu law divides property in equal shares among heirs of the same degree, but without commonly admitting the participation of females. In general, these only inherit in default of male heirs. The Arabian law assigns to several relations their specific portion as allotted by the Koran, and divides the remainder of the inheritance among the residuary heirs, giving equal shares to all males of the same degree, and half the portion of males to females in the same degree of consanguinity.

16.—OTHER TITLES TO LAND.

Law and Consti-
tution of India,
page 32.
I (*a*). The Mahomedan laws which were in force in Hindoostan were those of the Huneefecah Soonees. With the laws relating to land, which prevail in Arabia, India was not concerned, because all countries conquered by the Mahomedans were brought under the law laid down by them on the occasion of their first conquests, *viz.*, of the Sūwaūd of Erauk, Syria and Egypt.

20. (*b*). " The land of the Sowad is the property of those who live in it, they have a right to sell it, or to hold it in possession. Because the Imam, when he has conquered a country by force of arms, may confirm the people in possession of it, and may impose upon it, and upon the heads of the people, a tax or tribute, after which the land remains the property of the people." The land or Sowad of Irak is here mentioned, but it was not the intention of the author of the Hidayah to declare

Ibid, pages 13
and 32.
proprietary rights restricted to the inhabitants of that country. He quotes the principles obtaining in Irak, because, in that province, after its subjection by the Khalif Oomar, they were there first settled by the Subaheh, or council, and thus became the precedent for establishing the khiraj in other countries. India was brought under the principles of law of settlement of the land of the Sowad of Irak, because the people paid the *Jizeeat* or capitation tax, and consented to pay the khiraj.

Page 32.
Briggs, pages
109, 110, 112.
(*c*). " The land of the Sūwaūd of Erauk is the property of its inhabitants. They may alienate it by sale and dispose of it as they please; for when the Imaum conquers a country by force of arms, if he permit the inhabitants to remain on it, imposing the *kurauj* on their lands and the *jizeeat* on their heads, the land is the property of the inhabitants, and since it is their property, it is lawful for them to sell it, or to dispose of it, as they choose."

(*d*). On the whole, then, according to the Hunecfecah law, if a Moslem army conquered a non-moslem province or kingdom by force of arms, and the conqueror chose to suffer the inhabitants to remain in it, his duty would be, either himself, or by Commissioners (as Oomar did in settling the khurauj of the province of Erauk) to partition the land among them and to fix the land tax. Those who share in this partition are the proprietors of the soil for ever, and may not be disseized of it, without their consent, so long as they pay the land tax. App. II.
———
MAHOMEDAN
LAW.
———
Para. 17.
Law and Con-
stitution, &c.,
page 40.

II. I shall now notice the different kinds of tenures or modes by which property in lands can be acquired, as recognized by the Mahome- dan law. These are— Law and Con-
stitution of
India, pages 63
to 67.

   a. Partition among the conquerors, when the lands are conquered.

   b. By fixing the *khirauj* upon the lands of conquered inhabitants, by specific assessment (and imposing also the capitation tax), they being suffered to remain upon the lands.

   c. By *compromise* entered into with the inhabitants of a country *before conquest.* Other titles to
land.

   d. By the *cultivation of waste land,* when with the express sanction of Government. These four are the original tenures of land.

   e. Purchase, exchange, or other *mutual compact* for equivalents.

   f. Dower.

   g. Gift; bequest.

   h. Inheritance.

   i. Wuqf or endowment.

It will be perceived that none of these tenures convey any right whatever to exemption from the public revenue.

17.—ADMINISTRATION.

LAW AND CONSTITUTION OF INDIA.

   I *a.* The great Hunefeeah lawyer, Shums-ool-Aymah-oos-Sumkohee, adds : " It is proper that the sovereign appoint an officer for the purpose of collecting the khurauj from the people in the most equitable manner. He shall collect the khurauj to the best of his judgment, in proportion as the produce is reaped. When lands produce both a rubbeaa crop and a khureef crop, when the rubbeaa crop is gathered, he shall consider, according to the best of his judgment, how much the khureef crop is likely to produce, and if he think it will yield as much as the rubbeaa, he shall take half the khuraj from the produce (lit. : "the grain") of the rubbeaa, and postpone the other half to be taken from the produce of the khureef." Here we see the minutest detail, and who are the parties? the sovereign, or his servant, and the cultivator.

   b. The truth is, that between the sovereign and the *rubb-ool-arz* (who is properly the cultivator or "lord of the land") no one intervenes who is not a servant of the sovereign ; and this servant receives his hire, not out of the produce of the lands over which he is placed, but from the public treasury, as is specially mentioned by every lawyer.

   c. And the only servant that intervenes between the sovereign and the cultivator is one collector. Thus—

   " It is proper," says the learned *Shums-ool-Aymah,* " that the sovereign appoint collectors to collect the khurauj in the most equitable manner from the people." These collectors were called *amil-een* (the plural of *amil*); and accordingly Akbar appointed a collector over every crore of dams, who was called *amilguzzar*, and the name is preserved to this day (1825) in the province of Oudh and other parts of India beyond the Company's territories. "And," says Akbar, "let the amilguzzar transact his business with each husbandman separately, and see that the revenues are demanded and received with affability and complacency. And again, "let him agree with the husbandman to bring his rents himself, that there may be no plea for employing intermediate mercenaries. When the husbandman brings his rent, let him have a receipt for it signed by the treasurer" (*Ayeen Akbaree*). Here the written law says the people shall pay to the Government collectors, "and the practice of India was such." *No intermediate mercenaries shall be suffered*, says Akbar, to come between the sovereign and the cultivator.

II (*a*). The conquerors found the agency of the officers of the Hindu governments useful in more respects than one; by availing themselves of it, they secured the payment of the tribute in money without materially interfering with the established system of collection, or with the vested rights of proprietors of the soil.

(*b*). It is unlikely that any of the foreigners could have been capable of entering into the minutiæ of village detail and management; the contracts with the Government for the revenue must necessarily have been made with those natives who had previously superintended extensive jurisdictions, consisting of ten, twenty, or more parishes, leaving them to make their arrangements with the headmen of single villages, a procedure calculated to meet the wishes of the agriculturists at large; for, with the exception of parishes of large extent, in a high state of cultivation, and thickly populated by people of the same class, firmly bound together by the ties of blood and common interest, able and willing to resist oppression or open violence (and of this description there were, and are many such in the western provinces), it was certainly more advantageous to proprietors of single villages to place themselves under the protection of a powerful contractor, connected with the ruling power, able and willing to support them and their constituents, by acknowledging him as their over-lord, and paying, through him, their quota of taxation, than to enter into engagements direct with Government officers, who would have fewer scruples in extracting money from poor persons, ill able to afford the time necessary to seek justice, than in demanding, or exacting, fees from men whose rank and station in life enabled them to insist upon redress for acts of gross violence and rapacity. These extensive contractors were denominated talookdars, or zemindar talookdars, and some of them contracted for the revenue of tracts of country comprising two or three hundred villages, or of whole provinces.

III. *Colonel Briggs.*—It has been already shown that each Hindu village had its distinct municipality, and that over a certain number of villages or districts was an hereditary chief and accountant, both possessing great influence and authority, and certain territorial domains or estates. The Mahomedans early saw the policy of not disturbing an institution so complete, and they availed themselves of the local

fluence of these officers to reconcile their subjects to their rule. In
the long contest of the Hindu Rajahs against the Mahomedans, it
seems likely that the former had levied the fourth of the crop from
all their subjects, to which by law they were entitled; and it is probable that in their necessities they might even have exacted more. We
have no account of the mode the Mahomedans adopted to raise supplies,
but we may conclude from what we have seen in later times
that, without going into details, they assessed whole districts at a
certain sum, and required the *des adikars,* whom they subsequently
entitled zemindars, to levy the amount from the respective villages or
towns under their charge. From the existence of these local Hindu
chiefs, at the end of six centuries, in all territories conquered by the
Mahomedans, it is fair to conclude they were cherished and maintained
with great attention as the keystone of their civil government. While
the administration of the police, and the collection of the revenue, were
left in the hands of these local chiefs, every part of the new territory
was retained under military occupation by an officer of rank, and a considerable body of Mahomedan soldiers.

V. Mr. Arthur Phillips—

(*a*).—Hindu custom appears to have held its own against Mahomedan theory, but to have succumbed in a great measure before the rude
shocks of Mahomedan practice and the rapacity of conquerors. The
machinery for collecting the revenue, indeed, long continued the same.
From motives of policy and convenience, such as afterwards influenced the
English, the conquerors, as I have said, were content to realize the revenue
in the ancient way, and through the established agencies, * * * but eventually the village officers and communities sank before the zemindars.

Tagore Law Lec-
tures, 1874-75

Pages 57 to 61.

18. From this account, and from the whole of this
appendix, it appears that—

I. The system of village communities prevailed throughout India before the Mahomedan rule, and it survived under
that rule of seven centuries.

II. This universal system of village communities was
based on the joint and several proprietary rights of the original
cultivators of the land in a village,—and of their descendants,
in the waste lands of their own village, subject to the
payment of a Government tax according to rates fixed by
custom.

III. The Mahomedan rulers left the village communities
intact, utilized the village and district officers, and in only
some parts of Hindustan superadded other officers as zemindars; or, rather, allowed the district officers or their immediate supervisors to become, through encroachments, great
zemindars.

IV. Apart from this encroachment on the rights of
the real proprietors, neither the Hindu nor the Mahomedan

law and constitution favoured the growth of large zemindaries.

V. The Mahomedan law of inheritance, which directs an equal division of real estate among the heirs, favours a disintegration of estates; and though the similar tendency of the Hindu law of division of property among the male issue, or (failing them) the female issue, is qualified by the system of the joint family property, yet the Hindu law, if it thus prevents the disintegration of estates, did also hinder the aggregation in one person of property in several villages, through the difficulties which the village communities interposed against the acquisition of land in a village by strangers from another village. The purchase of a holding in a village, as distinguished from shares in the whole village regarded as one estate, with the consent of the village community, was indeed practicable at all times, but not by such purchases could a large zemindari have been acquired by a proprietor.

VI. The essence of the village system was the proprietary right of the members of the village communities in the lands of their village, a right which included that of allotting waste lands of the village to their sons, or to purchasers, from other villages, of occupancy rights as resident cultivators, subject, in both cases, to the payment of the Government tax. This limited power of appropriating waste lands of the village was the provision, under, virtually, the Oriental Poor Law, for the growth of population, and for employing the increase in the village work-house, that is in the village waste lands, while the provision for receiving strangers from other village communities promoted immigration from overstocked to thinly peopled villages. But this facility for immigration did not promote vagrancy; the sense of peasant proprietorship was strong in the village community, so strong that, though a generation might have passed away since the village was over-run and for a time partially destroyed by conquest, the descendants of the original proprietors would return to the inheritance of their fathers, under the influence of that feeling of peasant, proprietorship which proved a more effectual and salutary law of settlement than England has been able to devise under the Poor Law.

VII. Sir Charles Metcalfe observed that the vitality of the village community was such that nothing could destroy it except the regulations which could easily subvert it. This the Regulations have done in Bengal; the zemindary settlement, with the evils in its train of *huftum punjum*, nhancement of rents, the control by zemindars, for more han two generations, of a weak, inefficient, corrupt police, nd of corrupt subordinate officials in an insufficient number f courts, also the transfer of village waste lands, or the 'oor Law Fund, from the villages to the zemindars, have welligh obliterated all trace of proprietary rights such as they xisted at the time of the Permanent Settlement. Under he working of the village system and its Poor Law Fund f waste lands, as explained in VI, the allotment of waste ands to new population could not prejudice the rents of the arent proprietors, by raising the pergunnah rates of rent; ut under the zemindary system, with the waste lands urned into a monopoly in the zemindar's hands, a growth f population and a rise of prices, (brought about "otherwise han by the agency or at the expense of the" *zemindar*,) ave created competition rates of rent which enable him, nblushing inconsistency, through Law's to demand from proected ryots (so called) an increase of rent because, forsooth, he value of the produce of the land "has been increased therwise than by the agency or at the expense of the *ryot*," ord Cornwallis' misappropriation of the Poor Law Fund ɔ zemindars, and the legislation in Act X of 1859, have nabled the zemindars to make this demand and to throw pon the tax-payers of British India the cost of meeting two f the economic results of those measures, *viz.*, a famine in Orissa, in 1866, when the condition of oppressed ryots was retched; and another in Behar, where the ryots in the resent day are in a deplorable condition, much worse than 1 any part of Bengal or Orissa.

VIII. Another feature of the native administration hrough village communities was the maintenance of the dministrative staff of districts and sub-divisions, and not nusually the maintenance of the troops, by grants of land hich localised the expenditure, causing the greater part of to be spent or saved within the district. In the present ay, the usufruct and the unearned increment of the lands hich maintained the Civil administration and the army ave passed away from cultivating proprietors to zemindars mostly non-resident) and money-lenders, and, additional ereto, is an expenditure for a costly administrative machiery of which the largest part, *viz.*, that for European gency, is but partially spent in the district.

APPENDIX III.

THE PERMANENT SETTLEMENT AS DESIGNED BY PARLIAMENT.

App. III.
—

The permanent settlement in the Lower Provinces of Bengal was the actual, though not the logical or necessary, issue of a Resolution of the House of Commons in 1784.

Mr. J. Mill.

2. (I) *1783, Fox's India Bill.*—The project of declaring the zemindars and other managers of the land revenue hereditary proprietors of the land, and the tax fixed and invariable (orginally started by Mr. Francis, and in part proposed for enactment in the late Bill of Mr. Dundas), was adopted.

Mr. W. Pitt's
speech, 6th July
1784.

(II) *1784, Pitt's India Bill.*—Another object of investigation, and an object of considerable delicacy, was the pretensions and titles of the landholders to the lands at present in their possession ; in the adjustment of this particular, much caution must be adopted, and means found that would answer the ends of substantial justice, without going the length of rigid right ; because he was convinced, and every man at all conversant with Indian affairs must be convinced, that indiscriminate restitution would be as bad as indiscriminate confiscation.

Speech of
Sir P. Francis,
16th July 1784.

(III). He spoke of the clause respecting tribute, rents, &c., to be hereafter paid by the landholder, and the plan proposed in clause 57 for the servants abroad to devise the methods of fixing the tribute, rent, &c., of each landholder. He asked, were these sort of enquiries never to end ? They might, he said, be determined at home, and the rule

The rate of land
assessment in
India should be
permanently
settled from
Leadenhall
Street, without
local enquiry.

might be easily fixed, by taking an average of them for some years past. Any further enquiry to be set on foot now would tend greatly to delay, and to the utter ruin of the people, and would be open to violent and dangerous abuse. * * The next clause, *viz.*, that enacting that the Government abroad should not alter the rents after they had been fixed by the Directors, he highly approved. The clause respecting the pension of the zemindars he reprobated, because he considered the forcing those pensions on the zemindars as a gross oppression.

Mr. C. J. Fox,
16th July 1784.

(IV). In regard to the second part of the Bill, consisting of the regulations, I think, and always did, that the zemindars and polygars ought to be restored to their possessions, and that the rents should be fixed and settled by a rule of past periods, and not of future enquiry. Begin fresh enquiries and assessments, and you give authority to the very evils which you profess to remove.

Mr. J. Mill.

(V). *Pitt's India Bill (passed into an Act on 13th August 1784).*—The zemindars who had been displaced were to be restored, and their situation, as much as possible, rendered permanent, though nothing was said about their hereditary rights, or a tax incapable of augmentation.

(VI). *Act 24, Geo. III, cap. 25 (2nd Sess., 1784), sec. 39.*—And whereas complaints have prevailed that divers rajahs, zemindars, polygars, talookdars, and other native landholders within the British territories in India have been unjustly deprived of, or compelled to abandon and relinquish, their respective lands, jurisdictions, rights and privileges ; or that the tributes, rents, and services required to be by them paid or performed for their respective possessions to the said United Company are become grievous and oppressive ; And whereas the principles of justice and the honour of this country require that such complaints should be forthwith enquired into and fully investigated, and, if founded on truth, effectually redressed ;—Be it therefore enacted

that the Court of Directors of the said United Company shall, and they APP. III.
are hereby accordingly required, forthwith, to take the said matters into
their serious consideration, and to adopt, take, and pursue such methods Para. 3.
for enquiry into the causes, foundation, and truth of the said complaints,
and for obtaining a full and perfect knowledge of the same, and of all
circumstances relating thereto, as the said Court of Directors shall
think best adapted for that purpose; and thereupon, according to the
circumstances of the respective cases of the said rajahs, zemindars,
polygars, talookdars, and other native landholders, to give orders and
instructions to the several governments and presidencies in *India*, for
effectually redressing, in such manner as shall be consistent with justice
and the laws and customs of the country, all injuries and wrongs which
the said rajahs, zemindars, polygars, talookdars, and other native landholders may have sustained unjustly in the manner aforesaid, and for
settling and establishing, upon principles of moderation and justice, according to the laws and constitution of *India*, the permanent rules by
which their respective tributes, rents, and services shall be in future
rendered and paid to the said United Company by the said rajahs,
zemindars, polygars, talookdars, and other native landholders.

(VII). The Act, under the authority of which the permanent settle- Observations on
ment was made, gave no power to grant waste land. It is the 24th, the law and
Geo. III, cap. 25, sec. 39. By this section, the Court of Direc- constitution o
tors were required to give orders for settling and establishing, " upon India, 1825, page
95.
principles of moderation and justice, *according to the laws and constitution
of India*, the permanent rules by which the tribute, rents, and services
of the rajahs, zemindars, polygars, talookdars, and other native landholders should be in future rendered and paid to the united Company."
Here there is no authority to give away waste land, or uncultivated
land, or indeed land at all; nothing in the most remote sense authorising
the giving any *permanent right* to land of any kind. It is " to fix
permanent rules for the payment of *rents*, tributes, and services due
from native landholders," such as rajahs, zemindars, polygars, talookdars, to the Company; affording a presumption, indeed, in direct opposition to the idea of property in the soil existing in any of the classes
of persons mentioned. And these "rules for paying rents" were ordered
to be fixed " according to the law and constitution of India;" which
" debars even the Emperor himself from giving away one inch of waste,
or any other land, without an equivalent."

3. The Court of Directors, in a letter to the Government
of Bengal, dated 12th April 1786 (second report from Select
Committee, 11th May 1810), stated that " we have entered
into an examination of our extensive records on the subject
of the revenues of Bengal, from a wish to adopt some
permanent system compatible with the nature of our Government, the actual situation of the Company, and the ease of
the inhabitants." The despatch, which embodied the results
of this examination, constituted the orders of the Court subsidiary to the Resolution in 1784 of the House of Commons.
The despatch treats fully of the assessment and collection
of the land revenue. The following extracts relate more
especially to the Parliamentary legislation of 1784.

I. (*a*).—In ordering the settlement to be made *in every practicable* Paras. 39 to 42.

APP. III.

Para. 3.

instance with the zemindar, we conceive that we adopt the true spirit of the 39th section of the Act of 24th George 3rd. Various objections may be urged against a zemindar, which will absolutely be a deviation from the general rule in their favour, such as incapacity from age, sex, or lunacy, contumacy, or notorious profligacy of character. In such instances, a discreet and reputable relation, by way of guardian or dewan, is to be preferred before any temporary farmer or servant of Government. But we know that there are great difficulties in this matter, and that cases may occur in which the letting of lands to a farmer is the only means of securing the revenues of Government and preserving the inheritance of the zemindar inviolate.

(*b*).—The Committee of Revenue acted perfectly right in stating to you, before they proceeded to the settlement of Bengal year 1192, their queries, entered on your Revenue Consultations of 6th June 1785, and we are satisfied with the construction of the Statute which you gave them for their guidance.

(*c*).—We apprehend the design of the Legislature was merely to declare general principles for the regulation of our conduct towards the natives, not to introduce any novel system, or to destroy those rules and maxims which prevailed in the well-regulated periods of the Native Princes; an adherence to these must be most satisfactory to the natives, and most conducive to the security of our dominion. In our system, however, there will be this difference and advantage: that every deviation from an established usage or principle is to be made an article of record, with the justification arising from the necessity of the occasion.

Para. 52.

II. It is therefore our intention that the jumma now to be formed shall, as soon as it can have received our approval and satisfaction, be considered as the permanent and unalterable revenue of our territorial possessions in Bengal; so that no discretion may be exercised by our servants abroad in any case, and not even by us, unless in some urgent and peculiar case, of introducing any alteration whatsoever.

Para. 61.

III. (*a*).—The condition of the various descriptions of landholders throughout our provinces has been brought under the consideration of Parliament in a manner that has produced much reproach against the British Government in India; and every plan which has been proposed has been directed to this object as one which called urgently for the interposition of the Legislature, although in the result a considerable degree of latitude is left to us as to the mode of effectuating the redress of those grievances stated to exist:—you will perceive that by the 39th section of the Act passed in the year 1784, we are explicitly commanded forthwith to enquire into the causes, foundation, and truth of the said complaints, and to send orders and instructions to our Governments in India for effectually redressing the same, in such manner as may be consistent with justice and the laws and customs of the country.

Para. 62.

(*b*).—We desire that you will consider this clause of the Act of Parliament with a most minute and scrupulous attention, and take especial care that all the measures adopted by you, in the administration of our revenues, may be consonant to the sense and spirit thereof. We entertain strong hopes on our part, that the instructions we have already given upon a general view of the subject, and founded upon such materials as we now possess, will essentially contribute to carry into effect the humane intentions of the Legislature towards the native land-holders.

Paras. 66-67.

IV. (*a*).—Another essential object of the above recited section is " to settle and establish upon principles of moderation and justice, according to the laws and constitution of India, the permanent rules by which

their tributes, rents, and services shall be in future rendered and paid App. III.
to the said united Company by the said rajahs, zemindars, polygars, ———
talookdars, and other native landholders." In this point of view we Para. 4.
flatter ourselves that the mode we have directed you to pursue, for
the purpose of settling the *permanent* revenue for each zemindar, either
for perpetuity *or a long term of years,* and giving him the uninterrupted
management of his district, will prove extremely satisfactory to the
landholders in general, and far more so than any new enquiries into the
value and the produce of the lands. At the same time we are desirous
of ascertaining, as correctly as the nature of the subject will admit, what
were the real jurisdictions, rights, and privileges of zemindars, talookdars, and jaghirdars under the constitution or customs of the Mahomedan or Hindu Government; and what were the tributes, rents, and
services which they were bound to render or perform to the sovereign
power; and, in like manner, those from the talookdars to their immediate liege lord, the zemindar, and by what rule or standard they were,
or ought, severally to be regulated.

(*b*).—This object will be best attained by a set of queries drawn out Para. 68.
by you, accommodated to local circumstances, and proposed to the most
intelligent and experienced natives, Hindu or Mahomedan, either by
yourselves or by our servants stationed in different parts of our provinces,
or in any other parts of Hindustan, who will transmit the several
answers to you, with such further illustrations as they may derive from
their own enquiries.

V. (*a*).—We have seen the striking want of uniformity which has of Para. 83.
late pervaded every part of your revenue system; we have at the same
time had under our view the various regulations formed at different
periods by our administrations in Bengal, as founded upon the old constitutions of the country, or arising from the necessity of the case, in
order to prevent the clashing of authorities, the injury of the revenue,
or the inconvenience of the ryots.

(*b*).—This inquiry has shown us that almost every individual Para. 84.
throughout the country is concerned in the farming or cultivation of
land, and consequently implicated in the immediate demands of Government, or those of the zemindars; insomuch that, in numberless instances,
justice would be defeated if the magistrate were withheld from the
inspection of revenue accounts which, under the prevailing customs and
prejudices, could not be obtained but by that authority which superintends the collections and the general administration of the district.

4. The subsequent discussions in India, and the final
orders of the Court of Directors relating to the permanent
settlement in Bengal, are noticed in other Appendices. In
1813, the following observations were made in the House
of Lords :—

I. LORD GRENVILLE (*16th March 1813*).—Much important
matter for the instruction of the House would be found in a perusal
of the progress of events in India from the year 1765 to the year 1784.
At the latter period a termination was put to the false, fluctuating
policy which had before prevailed, especially in the rate and collection of the land revenue. After long and apparently endless disputes on Indian politics, there was at least one point on which all men
then agreed, *viz.*, that it was the duty, not only of the East India Company, but of Government and the Legislature, to fix the rate of revenue

App. III.

Para. 4.

by which that country was thenceforward to be governed. Contemplating, as he did, with pride and satisfaction the beneficial tendency of that measure, which he had assisted in framing, it was with deep concern and alarm that he perceived by the Fifth Report of the Committee of the House of Commons, that a purpose was entertained of altering, or unsettling, that equitable and salutary measure, the benefits of which had been so conspicuously exemplified in 1786, by the wise and exemplary administration of Lord Cornwallis. Departing from that wise system, the Court of Directors had sent out orders to their servants not to be in a hurry to make the new settlements according to the arrangement of 1784, which had tended so much to the prosperity, glory, honour, and advantage of the subjects in India.

The permanent settlement was designed for the prosperity, glory, honour, and advantage of the subjects in India.

II. Marquis of Wellesley (*16th March 1813*).—With respect to the measure referred to by his noble friend, of making the revenue in India defined and permanent, that, too, was his opinion and his policy; and however he might appear to differ from the Directors at one time, upon that subject, he differed only in requiring due and necessary time. Some delay was absolutely necessary to effect that security and right of property which it was his wish and endeavour to establish. He did establish it before he departed from Fort St. George; and the act was so eminently and solidly beneficial to the country, that he professed himself proud of it, and should be ambitious to have the record of it inscribed upon his tomb.

III. Lord Grenville (*16th March 1813*).—In explanation, stated that it was not of the delay in taking time to consider this law of settlement being extended to new provinces, but of the expressed reluctance to grant this benefit that he complained. In the Fifth Report of the Committee to which he had referred, he, with regret, perceived this statement; and he must repeat that no system of taxation could be more detestable in any country than a tax upon the abilities and industry of the *husbandman*. This system left to the agents of the Company all the *villainous oppression* of the Mahomedan Government, and *imposts were levied upon the cultivators* of the ground according to their discretion.

The italics show that a leading member of the Board of Control, who actively promoted the permanent settlement, considered that it would permanently limit the demands upon the ryot or cultivator.

IV. Lord Grenville (*21st June 1813*).—The revenue of India had been spoken of to ascertain whether it exceeded the expenditure; *but a very important question was to know how it was raised*—whether by taxes that pressed on the people, or afforded a temptation to corruption? Whether a great part did not arise from *a most oppressive and ruinous land tax?* It had been stated, somewhere, that his (Lord Grenville's) opinion was that this tax was not excessive; but this opinion he had never uttered, because he was not ever able to know what the proportion was. This last problem he should be obliged to any one to solve. It had been stated by high authorities that the proportion was excessive, and the system, it was said, was not to be extended to the conquered provinces. The simple question with respect to the zemindary system was, whether you would, or would not, say to the person on whom you laid the tax, you shall know what the amount shall be. The principle of extending this system of settled taxation was what actuated the mind of Sir Philip Francis, of Mr. Burke, of Mr. Fox, and of Mr. Pitt; it was adopted by Parliament, and makes a part of the existing law of India. But since this period we had acquired other provinces, and yet it did not seem the intention of the Company to extend the principle to them;

it was not the language of the Company, of the ministry, nor, he was sorry to add, of the Parliament itself. The India Company, in one of their reports, seemed to anticipate the greatest advantage from leaving the system unsettled, and levying the taxes according to the increasing wealth of the districts, or even of individuals.

V. Earl of Liverpool agreed with the noble Lord in the propriety of extending a permanent system of regular taxation to all the provinces of India.

5. It appears that—

I. Parliament in 1784 did not prescribe a permanent settlement, but that permanent rules for the payment of rent should be established; nor did Parliament direct that zemindars other than actual proprietors should be declared proprietors of the land, to the exclusion of other proprietary rights; but that the titles of all rajahs, zemindars, polygars, talookdars, *and other native landholders*, should be recognized, if found to be valid.

II. The permanent rules for the payment of rent were to be consistent with justice, and in accordance with the laws, customs, and constitution of India; that is to say, proprietary rights, which that law, custom, and constitution recognized, were not to be destroyed or confiscated, but to be maintained; and the rent for the State was to be fixed in accordance with the share or proportion of quantity, or of amount value of produce which, in accordance with those laws, customs, and the constitution of India used to be taken from the cultivator.

III. The settlement was not to be one of spoliation of rights, but such as should vindicate the principles of justice and the honour of England; should redress wrongs instead of multiplying them, and so should redound to the glory and honour of England, and to the prosperity and advantage of the subjects in India.

IV. The Court of Directors in 1786 ordered that the settlement of the land revenue should, in all practicable cases, be made with the zemindars, and that the settlement, after approval by them, should be permanent only so far that it should not be alterable by the Government of India, in any case, nor even by the Court of Directors, except in some urgent and peculiar case.

V. One, at least, of the authors of the permanent settlement, Lord Grenville, who was a member of the Board of Control, considered that in permanently limiting the rent payable by the zemindar, that payable by the husbandman or cultivator would also be permanently limited.

VI. Another, the most violent advocate of a permanent settlement, Sir Philip Francis, was so self-sufficient, and so ill-informed about the proprietary rights involved, that he gravely averred that the settlement for all Bengal might be easily made in England; in the present day the revision of the settlement of but one district is a work of some years, from the necessity of distributing the total assessment among cultivators and recording their rights.

VII. In 1784, the permanent settlement of Bengal appeared to Sir Philip Francis so easy of accomplishment, that it could be arranged from Leadenhall Street :—in the present day the question which most perplexes the Government of Bengal is how to settle the unsatisfactory relations between zemindar and ryot.

VIII. In 1813, Lord Grenville considered that the permanent settlement had greatly redounded to the glory and honour of England, and to the prosperity and advantage of the subjects in India :—In 1873, the Bengal Board of Revenue reported that, under that settlement, the majority of the zemindars were impoverished; the condition of a large proportion of the ryots was bad; and the only class that had signally and chiefly benefitted was that of the money-lenders, who thus crown the pinnacle of England's honour and glory from the permanent zemindary settlement (Appendix XII, para. 14.)

IX. In 1784 the principles of justice and the honour of the country required that charges of the dispossession of landholders should be fully investigated, and, if founded on truth, effectually redressed. The investigation ended in a permanent zemindary settlement, hurriedly passed, which expropriated by the million, and under which the rights of millions of cultivating proprietors have passed away " *sub silentio*."

X. In 1813, Lord Grenville felt constrained " to repeat that no system of taxation could be more detestable in any country than a tax upon the abilities and industry of the *husbandman*. This system left to the agents of the Company all the *villainous oppression* of the Mahomedan Government, and *imposts were levied upon the cultivators* of the ground according to their discretion."—In 1879, the Bengal Government's political economy is much exercised how to settle the question of lop-sided competition rents in a country where towns are few, manufactures scant, land a monopoly, and population dense and so overgrown, that competitive rents have reduced the cultivators in Behar to a state at least not better, apparently worse, than under " the villainous oppression of the Mahomedan Government."

APPENDIX IV.

PERMANENT SETTLEMENT; ITS OBJECTS AND RESULTS.

1. Mr. Philip Francis arrived in India on 19th October 1774. On 22nd January 1776 he put forward his scheme of a permanent settlement for Bengal with a self-sufficiency which has unamiable prominence in his minute. In 1786 he, with others, drafted the instructions respecting a permanent settlement, in the letter from the Court of Directors dated 12th April 1786;—in 1789 and 1790, the Government in India introduced the decennial settlement;—and in March 1793 they declared it a permanent settlement. App. IV. — The permanent settlement was conceived in ignorance, and was carried out with precipitancy.

2. In the North-Western Provinces, a revision of settlement was begun in 1855; it was interrupted by the mutiny and was resumed in 1862; it is not yet finished, though an increase of the land revenue by about half a million sterling as the total result, is expected from the complete revision of a settlement which is to last for only 30 years. Of this amount, the greater part has been gradually realized, only as two or more of the districts have been successively settled. The slowness of the government of the present day to realise an additional revenue of fifty lakhs a year by gradual steps, instead of by a lump re-assessment of the district or of the province, as in the permanent settlement, proceeds from a foolish idea that the amount of the revised assessment should first be distributed individually among the ryots, and their rights be recorded. The enlightened benevolence, the wise philanthropy of 1793 was not fettered by stupid considerations of this kind, which would have interfered with the creation of great zemindars. An artificial class of proprietors was created with indecent haste.

3.—COURT OF DIRECTORS, *12th April 1786* (*paras. 41 and 42.*)

(1). We apprehend the design of the legislature was merely to declare general principles for the regulation of our conduct towards the natives, not to introduce any novel system, or to destroy those rules and maxims which prevailed in the well-regulated periods of the native princes; an adherence to these must be most satisfactory to the natives and most conducive to the security of our dominions. Report of Select Committee, 1810, page 160.

APP. IV.

(2). In our system, however, there will be this difference and advantage, that every deviation from an established usage or principle is to be made an article of record, with the justification arising from the necessity of the occasion.

4.—As to the Permanency of a Settlement.

I.—Mill's History of British India, (Chapter on the year *1775*).

A permanent settlement, as originally ordered, did not mean that the Government demand should be fixed for ever.

By certainty in matters of taxation is not meant security for ever against increase of taxation. Taxes may be in the highest degree certain, and yet liable to be increased at the will of the legislature. For certainty, it is enough that, under any existing enactment of the legislature, the sum which every man has to pay should depend upon definite cognizable circumstances.

II.—Court of Directors, *12th April 1786, paragraphs 51 and 52.*

Report of Select Committee, 1810, page 161.

(*a*).—We speak next as to the duration. We are not insensible that the mode of making settlements to continue only from year to year has, in many points of view, been impolitic and prejudicial. For this we impute no blame to our Governor General and Council, as your sentiments on this subject were very wisely and fairly stated to us in the 22nd paragraph of your general letter dated 10th January 1780; but as the subject has now undergone so complete an investigation, we trust that a steady system of conduct will now be adhered to, both at home and abroad.

(*b*). It is therefore our intention that the jumma now to be formed shall, as soon as it can have received our approval and ratification, be considered as the permanent and unalterable revenue of our territorial possessions in Bengal, so that no discretion may be exercised by our servants abroad in any case, and not even by us, unless in some urgent and peculiar case, of introducing any alteration whatsoever.

III.—Mr. J. Mill, *23rd August 1831.*

3rd Report, Select Committee.

(*a*). If I understand the purport of section 39 of the 24th of Geo. 3rd, C. 25, which has just been read, it has nothing to do with the permanent settlement; it merely ordains that such rights as actually belonged by the law of India to various parties named should be secured to them. *Q, 4046.*—You do not think it applies to a permanent settlement of the revenue? Decidedly not.

(*b*). I think the leases should be of considerable duration; a few years more or less I consider of no material importance; but I conceive that the principle of duration of the lease is, that there should be full time during the currency of the lease to derive the full benefit of any ordinary expenditure of capital which the cultivation may require. I think it ought not to be less than 20, and I should not make it more than 30 years as a general rule (Qs. 3911 and 3912).

5. The author of the scheme of a permanent settlement had advocated in 1776 principles but slightly different from those enjoined by the Court of Directors in 1786, as shown

in the following extracts from his Plan of a Permanent Set- APP. IV.
tlement, dated 22nd January 1776 :—

a. The jumma once fixed, must be matter of public record. It
must be permanent and unalterable; and the people must, if possible, be
convinced that it is so. This condition must be fixed to the lands themselves, independent of any consideration of who may be the immediate
or future proprietors. If there be any hidden wealth still existing, it
will then be brought forth and employed in improving the land, because
the proprietor will be satisfied he is labouring for himself (paragraph
48).

b. When the gross sum to be levied from the country is determined,
as well for the revenue as all charges incident to it, each zemindary
should be assessed its proportion according to the rule in the first
article, and let that sum be declared the gross rent of those particular
lands in perpetuity. This distribution should be called the tumar
jumma, a term sanctified among the natives from the idea of security
which they had long been accustomed to annex to it. There is no case
of necessity, no emergency whatsoever, which in my opinion should
induce Government to increase the jumma (paragraph 53).

c. Temporary distresses may be provided for by temporary contributions which a flourishing country does not feel. If these are once
added to the jumma, according to modern practice, they become perpetual, and drive the proprietor, who sees no limit or period to the impositions on his land, to fraud, indolence, or despair.

d. When the zemindar has given a lease of any part of his land to
a ryot, the conditions of such lease should be invariably adhered to. In
other words, the same security which Government gives to the tenant in
chief, should, for the same reason, descend to the under-tenants in their
several gradations; so that every rank of society, and every member
of it, may have something to call his own. Government should present
a form for the pottah, which may be deemed the legal one, and no other
be held valid (paragraph 60).

Marginal notes: Even Sir Philip Francis proposed that ryots should have from zemindars precisely the same permanent settlement as the Government was to give to the zemindars. Para. 6.

6.—OBJECTS OF THE PERMANENT SETTLEMENT.

I.—COURT OF DIRECTORS, *12th April 1786.*

It is entirely our wish that the natives may be encouraged to pursue
the occupations of trade and agriculture by the secure enjoyment of the
profits of their industry; and that the zemindars and ryots may not
be harassed by increasing debts, either public or private, occasioned by
the increased demands of Government (paragraph 29).

Marginal note: Report of Select Committee of 1810, page 158.

II.—LETTER FROM GOVERNOR GENERAL TO COURT OF DIRECTORS, *6th March 1793.*

a. It is necessary to apprise you (of what you could not have been
aware) that all waste lands form a part of the estate of the different
landholders, and the boundaries of the portions of these lands that
belong to each individual are as well defined as the limits of the culti-

Marginal note: *Ibid*, page 101.

App. IV.
—
Para. 6, contd.

vated parts of their property, and that they are tenacious of their right of possession in the former as the latter.

b. The waste lands may in general be comprehended under two descriptions: first, those in the level country, which are interspersed in more or less extensive tracts amongst the cultivated lands; and secondly, the Sunderbuns (the country along the sea-shore between the Hooghly and Megna rivers) and the foot of the vast range of mountains which nearly encircle your Bengal provinces (paragraph 14).

c. The first mentioned description of waste grounds will be easily brought into cultivation when the zemindars have funds for that purpose, and provided they are certain of reaping the profit arising from the improvement. These lands, however, are not wholly unproductive to them at present; they furnish pasture for the great herd of cattle that are necessary for the plough, and also to supply the inhabitants with ghee (a species of butter) and milk, two of the principal necessaries of life in this country (paragraph 15).

d. It is true that the lands (*c*) in this desolate state far exceed what would suffice for the above purposes, but it is the expectation of bringing them into cultivation, and reaping the profit of them, that has induced many to agree to the decennial jumma which has been assessed upon these lands. It is this additional resource alone which can place the

Provision for famine.

landholders in a state of affluence, and enable them to guard against inundation or drought, the two calamities to which this country must ever be liable, until the landholders are enabled to provide against them (as we are of opinion they in a great measure might) by the above-mentioned and other works of art. To stipulate with them, therefore, for any part of the produce of their waste lands would not only diminish the excitement to these great and essential improvements in the agriculture of the country, but deprive them of the means of effecting it (paragraph 15).

e. With respect to the second description of waste lands (the lower parts of the Sunderbuns perhaps excepted), they also include the estates of individuals with whom the settlement is made; but supposing these lands to be at the disposal of Government, as they have for the most part been covered with forest or underwood from time immemorial, and as the soil is in itself, compared with that of the open country, unproductive, * * we are of opinion that any attention to them would be premature for a long period of years to come (paragraph 16).

III.—Lord Cornwallis, *18th September 1789.*

Fifth Report, page 472.

Page 473.

a. A permanent settlement, *alone,* in my judgment, can make the country flourish, and secure happiness to the body of the inhabitants.

b. Where the landlord has a permanent property in the soil, it will be worth his while to encourage his tenants, who hold his farm in lease, to improve that property; at any rate he will make such an agreement with them as will prevent their destroying it.

Ibid.

c. I may safely assert that one-third of the Company's territory in Hindostan is now a jungle, inhabited only by wild beasts; without a permanent settlement, the zemindars will not be incited to clear

away that jungle and bring it into cultivation, and effect other substantial improvements.

d. With a permanent settlement, the zemindars will do all such acts The authorities joined in crying for the moon.
as are calculated to promote the improvement of the country, such as
assisting ryots with money, refraining from exactions, foregoing small Para. 6, contd.
temporary advantages for future permanent profits, such as must *Ibid.*, page 474.
ultimately redound to the benefit of the zemindars, and ought to be
performed by them.

e. It is for the interest of the State that the landed property should
fall into the hands of the most frugal and thrifty class of people, who
will improve their lands and protect the ryots, and thereby promote the
general prosperity of the country.

f. It is immaterial to Government what individual possesses the
land, provided he cultivates it, protects the ryots, and pays the public
revenue.

g. Although, however, I am not only of opinion that the zemindars
have the best right, but from being persuaded that nothing could be so
ruinous to the public interest *as that the land should be retained as the
property of Government,* I am also convinced that, failing the claim of
right of the zemindars, it would be necessary for the public good to
grant a right of property in the soil to them, or to persons of other
descriptions. I think it unnecessary to enter upon any description of
the grounds upon which their right appears to be founded. The
recognition of the right is the most effectual mode for promoting the
general improvement of the country, which I look upon as the important
object for our present consideration.

This last ought Lord Cornwallis not to have done, but his
Lordship did it; and the zemindars left the others undone.
Failing the zemindar's right, Lord Cornwallis saw no proprietary right except that of the Government, who, as
shown in Appendix V, were not the proprietors of the soil.
There is, indeed, another, and evidently the proper, though
not the received view, which divests Lord Cornwallis's
benevolence of heartlessness, *viz.,* that his Lordship contemplated a permanent assessment or fixed rent from the
ryot to the zemindar of exactly the same character as the
permanent settlement with the zemindar. In this view his
Lordship's indifference about the question of proprietary
right becomes, at least, intelligible.

IV.—Sir J. Shore.

a. The surest way to retain our dominion in Bengal is by establishing June 1789, para. 257.
a system of government calculated to promote the happiness of our
subjects, by affording them security in their property, relief from oppression, and a reasonable indulgence to their prejudices.[1]

---

[1] A sense of their proprietary rights was a very strong prejudice or conviction in the
khodkhast ryots.

App. IV.

All the authorities joined in crying for the moon.

Para. 6, contd.

Paras. 268 and 270.

Para. 531.

b. In restoring and confirming the confidence of our subjects, we assume one solid principle of reform, a principle without which no system can be successful. It now remains to trace the several considerations connected with the principle; to form the best possible regulations consistent with it for guarding against the evils arising from the incapacity of the zemindars, for the security of the ryots, and for preventing oppression on the ryots by the farmers and zemindars.

c. With respect to ryots, however, their security requires that the settlement made with them should become matter of record. In every zemindary, *where the established laws of collections have not been infringed,* this is the case at present. But we know also, that the zemindars continually impose new cesses upon their ryots, *and having subverted the fundamental rules of collection,* measure their exactions by the abilities of the ryots. This is a very serious evil; for, exclusive of the injury which the unprotected subjects of Government sustain from it, a necessity follows *of our interference to regulate the assessment upon them* * * Some time will now be required to convince the zemindars that we are serious; * * to eradicate those habits and impressions which have been continued through life, is scarcely to be expected during the present generation * * In relying, therefore, on the example of good faith which the Government gives to the zemindars, we ought not, while the example is taking effect, to abandon the ryots to caprice or injustice, the result of ignorance and inability. With knowledge, or the means of obtaining it, we may correct the consquences of both. And at present, we must give every possible security to the ryots as well as, or not merely, to the zemindars. This is so essential a point that it ought not to be conceded to any plan.

September 1789, page 476.

d. But if this were the place for discussing the perpetuity of the assessment, I should suggest another question, whether we ought not to have some experience, that the regulations which we mean to establish are found in practice sufficient to correct the various abuses existing in the detail of the collections? If these regulations are generally necessary, as I suppose them to be, it is very evident that they must be enforced before we can expect improvement from the labours of the ryots for whose ease and security they are principally calculated.

The foregoing extract shows that ryots were not to become tenants-at-will under the zemindary settlement. Every possible security against the exactions of zemindars was to be provided.

V.—Lord Cornwallis, *3rd February 1790.*

Page 492.

In case of a foreign invasion, it is a matter of the last importance, considering the means by which we keep possession of the country, that the proprietors[1] of the lands should be attached to us from motives of self-interest. A landholder, who is secured in the quiet enjoyment of a profitable estate, can have no motive for wishing for a change. On the contrary, if the rents of his lands are raised in proportion to their improvement, if he is liable to be dispossessed should he refuse to pay the increase required of him, or if threatened with imprisonment

---

[1] Read "cultivating proprietors."

or confiscation of his property, on account of balance due to Government,[1] upon an assessment which his lands were unequal to pay, he
will readily listen to any offers which are likely to bring about a
change that cannot place him in a worse situation, but which holds out
to him hopes of a better. * * There is nothing new in this plan,
except the great advantages which are given to the zemindars, talookdars,
and *ryots*.

App. IV.

—

All the authori-
ties joined in
crying for the
moon.

—

Para. 7.

VI.—Court of Directors, *1st February 1811.*

The objects of that settlement were to confer upon the different
orders of the community a security of property which they never before
enjoyed; to protect the landholders from arbitrary and oppressive
demands on the part of Government; to relieve the proprietors of small
estates from the tyranny of the powerful zemindars; and to free the
whole body of merchants and manufacturers, and all the lower orders
of the people, from the heavy impositions to which they have long
been subjected (paragraph 27).

Revenue Selec-
tions, Vol. 1,
page 3.

VII.—Mr. Sisson's Report, *2nd April 1815.*

The expected result of the decennial settlement was that " individuals would thereby be certain to enjoy the fruits of their industry;
that it would dispense prosperity and happiness to the great body of
the people, and increase the power of the State, which must be proportionate to the collective wealth that, by good government, it might
enable its subjects to acquire.

Revenue Selec-
tions, Vol. ,
page 385.

7.—Mistakes in the Permanent Settlement.

I.—Mill's History of British India.

Without much concern about the production of proof, Mr. Francis
assumed as a basis, two things: first, that the opinion was erroneous,
which ascribed to the sovereign the property of the land; and secondly,
that the property in question belonged to the zemindars. * * It is only
necessary to state that Mr. Francis proposed to protect the ryots from
the arbitrary exactions of zemindars by prescribed forms of leases, in
India known by the name of pottahs. (Vol. 4, 1775, page 6.)

II.—Lord Cornwallis, *3rd February 1790 (replying
to Sir J. Shore's* objection that there was great uncertainty
about ryots' rights, and ignorance on the part of the ryot
himself of what he should pay):—

Fifth Report,
page 486.

(*a*). If the officers of Government possessing local control
are imperfectly acquainted with the rules by which the rents are
demanded from the ryots, and their superiors, farther removed from the
detail, have still less information about them, at what period are we to
hope that Government and its officers will obtain a more perfect
knowledge of them? The collectors have now been three years acting

---

[1] For " Government" read " zemindar."

APP. IV.

Nothing is known about ryots, but everything will come right with a permanent settlement.

Para. 7, contd.

under positive instructions to obtain a more perfect knowledge of them * * It is to be supposed that they have communicated all the information which they possessed; and no further lights are, therefore, to be expected from them. * * Shall we calmly sit down discouraged by the difficulties which are supposed to exist, and leave the revenue affairs of this country in the singular state of confusion in which they are stated to be by Mr. Shore?

(b). In order to simplify the demand of the landholder upon the ryots, or cultivators of the soil, we must begin with fixing the demand of Government upon the former; this done, I have little doubt[1] but that the landholders will, without difficulty, be made to grant pottahs to the ryots upon the principles proposed by Mr. Shore for the Bengal settlement. The value of the produce of the land is well known to the proprietor or his officers, and to the ryot who cultivates it; and is a standard which can always be reverted to by both parties for fixing equitable rates.

Ibid, page 490.

(c). I must declare that I am clearly of opinion that this Government will never be better qualified, at any given period whatever, to make

* Equitable.

an equivalent* settlement of the land revenue of these provinces; and that if the want of further information was to be admitted now, or at any future period, as a ground for delaying the declaration of the permanency of the assessment, the commencement of the happiness of the people and of the prosperity of the country would be delayed for ever.

(d). The question that has been so much agitated in this country, whether the zemindars and talookdars are the actual proprietors[2] of the soil, or only officers of Government, has always appeared to me to be very uninteresting to them; whilst their claim to a certain percentage upon the rents of their lands has been admitted, and the right of Government to fix the amount of those rents at its own discretion has never been denied or disputed.

III.—SELECT COMMITTEE *of 1812.*

Your Committee have been induced to mention these and other circumstances of a similar nature from an impression that in settling the revenue, and introducing new regulations of a permanent nature, into the new acquisitions of territory under the different presidencies, in which important service the India Government is now actually employed, the operation of the new system, introduced into Bengal, should be kept constantly in view, in order that any errors[3] which may have been committed through inadvertency or precipitancy, or want of experience in those possessions, may be avoided on future occasions.

---

[1] Two paragraphs previously His Lordship had observed: "We have found that the numerous prohibitory orders against the levying of new taxes, accompanied with threats of fine and punishment for the disobedience of them, have proved ineffectual; and indeed how could it be expected that whilst the Government were increasing their demands upon the zemindars, that they, in turn, would not oppress the ryots."

[2] Lord Cornwallis contemplated the alternative, that if the zemindars were not the proprietors, then the Government was the proprietor. The possibility of the ryot being proprietor did not occur to His Lordship.

[3] Errors by which the property of millions of proprietors was confiscated.

IV.—Court of Directors, *6th January 1815.*

App. IV.

If mistakes occurred (and great mistakes unquestionably did) in forming the permanent settlement of Bengal, the proper inference is not that they are wholly unavoidable in great transactions of a similar character, but that the utmost care and caution ought to be used to prevent their recurrence. * * It is important also not to lose sight of the causes from which those mistakes arose; and we are warranted, not only by general probability, but by the recorded confession of some of our revenue servants at the time, in imputing the errors in question to the want of information by the collectors, who were positively prohibited from resorting to minute local scrutinies for the purpose of ascertaining the resources of the country. * * In the state of darkness and uncertainty above described, it is not surprising that errors were committed in the formation of the settlement (paragraphs 34 and 35).

Confession of error by which the proprietary rights of millions were destroyed.

Para. 7, contd.

Revenue Selections, Vol. I, page 281.

V.—Sir E. Colebrooke, *12th July 1820.*

The errors of the permanent settlement in Bengal were two-fold: *first*, in the sacrifice of what may be denominated the yeomanry, by merging all village rights, whether of property or occupancy, in the all-devouring recognition of the zemindar's paramount property in the soil; and, *secondly*, in the sacrifice of the peasantry by one sweeping enactment, which left the zemindar to make his settlement with them on such terms as he might choose to require. Government, indeed, reserved to itself the power of legislating in favour of the tenants; but no such legislation has ever taken place; and, on the contrary, every subsequent enactment has been founded on the declared object of strengthening the zemindar's hands.

Revenue Selections, Vol. III, page 167.

VI.—Mr. Holt Mackenzie, *2nd January 1822.*

(a). Subsequently to the perpetual settlement (11th February 1793), Lord Cornwallis, in the minute in which he brought forward his great scheme for regulating the judicial and revenue establishments of the provinces, proposed the abolition of the office of canoongoe. The grounds on which the measure is recommended it would be superfluous to notice here, excepting in so far as it is instructive to observe how much the distinguished person with whom it originated was misled in regard to the facts on which his reasoning is founded (paragraph 53).

Revenue Selections, Vol. III, page 41.

(b). It seems now scarcely credible that Lord Cornwallis should have been led to believe that all the needful particulars regarding the relative claims of Government and of individuals had been recorded; and still less that " the rights of the landholders and cultivators of the soil, whether founded upon ancient custom or on regulations, which have originated with the British Government, had been reduced to writing." The contemplation of such declarations, made by so eminent a person, may naturally lead to the cautious and even suspicious examination of any general statements in regard to the present state of things (paragraph 54).

VII.—LAW AND CONSTITUTION OF INDIA.

The author of that work, after quoting the statement in the proclamation of 22nd March 1793, that the permanent settlement was made with the actual proprietors of the soil, observed as follows :—

(*a*). It would, therefore, appear, were we to attend to this alone, that the local Government intended to admit to the settlement only the "actual proprietors of the soil," excluding such possessors of land as by their own act were *known not to be actual proprietors*, as talookdars holding by special deeds, or holders under crown grants, or persons incapacitated by their sex, or by the hand of God, from entering into such settlement.

(*b*). Why this intention was departed from it is not easy to imagine. Necessity alone could warrant a proceeding so arbitrary; and it so happened that not only no such necessity existed, but that the ablest by far, as well as the best-informed member of the Bengal Government at the time, Mr. Shore, the present Lord Teignmouth, strenuously opposed the precipitancy with which the permanent settlement was urged to a conclusion. * *

(*c*). Lord Cornwallis was an amiable and a virtuous man, and in carrying into effect the permanent settlement no doubt thought that he was conferring a great blessing upon India. But it was one of those short-sighted benevolent-like acts which men with good hearts sometimes rush upon without seeing, in all its bearings, what they are about ; and while they effect a partial good, they entail an enormous general evil. Lord Cornwallis and his concurring colleagues at home and abroad of that day have the pre-eminent satisfaction of knowing that, by their celebrated proclamation of 1793, they deprived the whole population of the three finest provinces of India of their hereditary and hitherto undoubted right of property in the soil, the land of their fathers, the only thing which the anarchy of their country had ever suffered them to recognise as property, and vested this sacred right, *not* in the honourable, the benevolent, and the humane breasts of the English Government, but they transferred the real owners of the soil, like a herd of the inferior creation, into the hands of what we call the zemindars, a set of men proverbial throughout the country for their tyranny, profligacy, and incapacity. This was the blessing for which India was expected to return thanks to those who were instrumental in bestowing it.

VIII.—MR. A. D. CAMPBELL.

Any attempt, however, to adjust satisfactorily the payments of the cultivators must necessarily fail, without a thorough reform of the office of village accountant. It has been one of the greatest errors of the permanent settlement to allow this useful office to fall into disuse, or, where it exists, to place the holders of it entirely under the zemindars. The object of the original institution of the office of putwari or curnum was, that, after the rates payable by the cultivators had been adjusted, they should register them as recorders of the Government, nominated for the mutual guidance as much of the hereditary payers as of the hereditary receivers of the land revenue; nor could any measure have been more inexpedient than the transfer of this most useful check against the exactions of the more powerful from the more helpless classes of the community from the protecting hands of the ruling power itself to the exclusive charge of the zemindars; for they thus obtained the complete surrender of the great check against their own rapacity.

IX. (*a*).—It had been proposed by Lord Teignmouth in Bengal to fix the maximum rates of the public revenue payable by the cultivators to the zemindar at those actually assessed when the permanent settlement was introduced, which, though confirming existing illegal cesses, would at any rate have placed a bar against further abuse, and given a precise limitation to the Government demand.

(*b*).—The local or pergunnah rates left undefined were, however, preferred in Bengal; and the result has been already stated. But at Madras the suggestion was strictly adopted; and the maximum rate payable by the cultivator to the zemindar on all land was limited to the actual rates levied on the cultivated land in the single particular year which preceded the limitation of the zemindar's own jumma to Government. The accounts invariably kept by the village accountants under the Madras Presidency afford a record of these rates not procurable in Bengal. It is only where these rates are not ascertainable that reference is to be had to the rates established for lands of the same description and quality as those respecting which the dispute may arise. The consequence has been that the cultivators under the Madras Government have looked to this limitation as a great security for their rights.

8.—ILLUSIONS OR VAIN EXPECTATIONS OF THE FRAMERS OF THE PERMANENT SETTLEMENT.

I. In the *Ayeen Akbari* it was directed that the amulguzzur, or collector of the revenues, "shall annually assist the husbandman with loans of money, and receive payment at distant and convenient periods," necessarily without interest, the taking of interest being absolutely prohibited by the Mahomedan law. Lord Cornwallis stated a like expectation, that the zemindar, under a permanent settlement, will "assist the ryots with money" (paragraph 5, section III*d*).

(*a*). COLEBROOKE'S SUPPLEMENT, *page 182: Proceedings, 16th August 1769—*

An advance in money is made by the zemindar to the cultivator, by the help of which he tills and improves the land. When the crops are cut and gathered in, they are generally divided between the cultivator and the zemindar; from one-third to one-half to the cultivator, and the remainder to the zemindar, when the former accounts to the latter for the amount of the advances, which are often taxed by the zemindar with a heavy interest.

APP. IV.

ILLUSIONS OF
THE FRAMERS OF
THE PERMANENT
SETTLEMENT.

Sess., 1831-32,
Vol. XI,
Q. 2737.

Para. 8, contd.

(b) Mr. H. Newnham, 7th May 1832.

Many persons advocate the zemindary cause by alleging outlay of capital, but it is seldom more than a current loan, repayable at very high interest, or, which is worse, the repayment in commodities at a very much lower price than the market price; but as for any permanent outlay of capital in digging wells and making tanks, I fear that there are very few instances of the zemindars laying out capital in that way: the great improvements in the country take place from the junction of the ryots in different labours; at least I have seen them making bunds across rivers, sinking wells, making water-courses from tanks, or collections of water, and undertaking many important works of that kind.

(c) Board of Commissioners in Behar and Benares, 8th March 1822.

Revenue
Selections,
Vol. III,
page 364.

We cannot also acquiesce in the assertion of capital, or the gains of the sudder malguzar, being laid out in agricultural improvements. It is the labour and industry of the ryots, frequently in opposition to the sudder malguzar, which has brought the country into its present state of cultivation. Wells are dug in most soils by the labour, and oftentimes by the money of the cultivator. In tracts of country where wells require cylinders of masonry or wood, the zemindars do not increase the fertility by any outlay. It is in these spots that the present Government, like all preceding Governments, should interpose with the public purse. We doubt whether a single well entailing a considerable outlay will be found to have been dug and constructed by the zemindars under the British Government, with a clear and unbiassed wish to fulfil towards it the functions of their stations. We have seen the shafts of masonry of former Governments remaining incomplete; and we venture to say that the only wells of this kind which the zemindars have constructed are merely designed to increase the produce of the private farms (*arazeeat zeer*), for which they pay nothing to Government. The advance of tuccavi can scarcely be called the employment of capital by the sudder malguzar; it is, more strictly, the employment of capital by the ryots, for it is a mere banker's loan on high interest, without risk, as the ryots' crop, the security, remains within the power of the lender. If the ryots' profits were secured by laws, the loan could be more advantageously borrowed from the village banker.

II.—It was expected that the zemindar, having the advantage of all the revenue from bringing waste lands into cultivation, would conform to the law which prohibited him from increasing the ryot's rent. Thus—

Mr. Sisson's report, 2nd April 1815.

Revenue Selections, Vol. I,
page 385.

The permanent settlement differed from the settlements which preceded it in but three points: first, in its being fixed for ever; secondly, in its formally vesting the property of the soil, under certain restrictions, in the zemindar, till then a mere ministerial officer under Government; and lastly, in its giving up to the zemindar the whole of the profit which was certain to accrue from a progressive extension of cultivation, for generations to come. The additional profits which were

App. IV.
———
ILLUSIONS OF
THE FRAMERS OF
THE PERMANENT
SETTLEMENT.
———
Para. 8, contd.

to accrue to the zemindar from the permanent settlement of his estate were confined to but one source, *i.e.*, extension of cultivation. He was vested with no power to enhance the rents of his tenants;—with reference even to the waste lands which his exertions might bring into cultivation, he was peremptorily restricted from exacting a higher rent than that which lands of a similar quality might be rated at in the nirkbundi of his estate. The profit that was to arise to him from bringing the waste lands into cultivation was the enjoyment of the Government's share of their produce in addition to his own.

Huftum and Punjum, the strained relations between zemindar and ryot, and the multitudinous suits for enhancement of rent, long since dispelled the foregoing illusion. Thus—

a.—MR. C. B. TREVOR, *13th April 1850.*

The relations between landlord and tenant should be in these Provinces founded on mutual interest, and the good-will which such a bond creates is, when realised, one of the surest marks of social happiness, if not of social progress. Indubitably, in this country, we do not see the full advantage of the system of non-interference;—circumstances, which it is needless here to detail, have tended to throw the responsible duties attaching to landholders upon persons unworthy of exercising or incapable of appreciating them; and the result has been, that the most important class of the community, the ryots, have come to look upon the zemindars simply as unreasonable demanders of rent, and aiders and abettors in all sorts of tyrannical practices; no Government can expect immediate results from any act of its own; time, however, and education will, probably, at last produce a race of zemindars keenly alive to their own rights and interests, and equally so to those of others, and at the same time fully sensible of the duties which their station as landholders entails upon them.

b.—MR. WELBY JACKSON, *July 1840.*

In the present state of the country, I look on the zemindars as the opponents of the cultivators, not the protectors, of their interests; the zemindars are continually trying to shake the permanency of the old resident ryots' tenure, the only permanent interest in the land now existing (besides that of the Government), while the ryots are endeavouring to retain it; the Government is bound to protect them, and interested too; for rack-renting, the general practice of the zemindars, where they can have recourse to it, is far from conducive to the improvement of the land.

c.—EDITOR OF THE "HINDOO PATRIOT" (BABOO HURRISCHUNDER MOOKERJEA),

BABOO SUMBHOONATH PUNDIT, AND OTHERS, *27th September 1851.*

(1). There is an almost universal absence of good feeling between landlord and tenant in this country, which leads to unceasing endeavours

APP. IV.
———
ILLUSIONS OF
THE FRAMERS OF
THE PERMANENT
SETTLEMENT.
———
Para. 8, contd.

on the part of the one to injure the other to the utmost of his power. This power is obviously greater on the side of the landlord.

(2). The new sale law (Act I of 1845) grants to landlords the power of enhancing without limit the rents of all tenures except the khood-kasht and some others of a rare description, situated in estates purchased at a sale for arrears of revenue due upon them. The removal of a khoodkasht tenant is therefore a very great advantage to the landlord whenever the holding, as it often must be, is more highly bid for by a new-comer

(3). The resumption laws in favour of zemindars have gradually placed under their power a class of men who, bred up in independent habits and amidst the associations of good birth, are generally personally obnoxious to an oppressive landlord. The removal of these *quondam* freeholders is an object of general desire among landlords

d.—REVD. A. DUFF AND 20 OTHER MISSIONARIES, *April 1857.*

The zemindars have not fulfilled the just expectations of the State, or the conditions connected with the permanent settlement. Far from accelerating the progress of the country either in civilisation or material prosperity, the zemindars have generally checked the accumulation of capital by their tenants. They have not stimulated exertion by their own example, nor encouraged confidence by generosity and kindness. On the contrary, by arbitrary exactions they have repressed the industry of their tenants, and by the exercise of their excessive powers under Regulation VII of 1799 they have destroyed every vestige of their independence. * * The oppressions of all grades of superiors, both middlemen and zemindars, have been practised, and are still practised with lamentable effect, partly with legal sanction, and partly without it, but entirely, in nearly every case, without the slightest hope on the part of the tenant of legal redress.

e.—SIR H. RICKETTS, *10th May 1850.*

The consequence is, that on a sale taking place, affrays and litigation cannot but ensue. There must always in every case be years of enmity between the new landlord and his tenantry. There being no record of the protected, he assumes that none are protected, while the tenants set up groundless claims to protection, oftentimes supported by the late zemindar. * * I can imagine no condition more pitiable than that of the inhabitants of a zemindary transferred by sale for arrears. Though the purchaser may be a man of good character, his agent may be a tyrant. All the tenures of all classes are open to revision; each inhab-itant can see before him only the feeing of peadas and ameens, "salamee" to the new owner, weary journeying to the sudder station, and at last readjustment of his rent. "Readjustment of his rent;" we can talk of it and write of it with indifference, but to the tenants of an estate a sale is as the spring of a wild beast into the fold, the bursting of a shell in the square. It is the disturbance of all they had supposed stable. The consequence must be a recasting of their lot in life, with the odds greatly against them.

f.—SIR F. HALLIDAY, *2nd September 1856.*

APP. IV.
———
ILLUSIONS OF
THE FRAMERS OF
THE PERMANENT
SETTLEMENT.

Para. 8, contd.

The *intention* of the permanent settlement was to recognise and confirm existing rights in the land, and to prevent encroachment on those rights for the future. The *effect* of the settlement was, however, to erect into landowners men who were mere tax-collectors, and to give them almost unlimited power over all the old village proprietors, thus exposing to hazard a vast mass of long existing rights and creating new and unknown rights of property where they had never been before. The consequences of this have been deeply injurious to the great body of real proprietors whose rights were sacrificed on the occasion; and the bad consequences of the measure may be traced at the present day in many of the evils which penetrate into and vitiate so much of the constitution of our rural societies. The only chance of breaking any part of this system down (and every breach of it is a blessing to thousands) is through the purchase of zemindaries by Government at auction sales * * Every zemindary so purchased is a population redeemed and regenerated.

(*g*).—SIR J. P. GRANT, *10th February 1840.*

The right to enhance according to the present value of the land differs not in principle from absolute annulment of the tenure.

III.—The rent to zemindars from bringing waste lands into cultivation (one-third of culturable land in Bengal was uncultivated at the time of the permanent settlement) and the prosperity of the ryots under fixed rents, were the State provision for famine. The famine in Behar in 1874-75 cost six and a half millions sterling; interest on that sum, at $4\frac{1}{2}$ per cent., *viz.*, £292,500, deducted from the land revenue of Behar (£970,409) leaves £677,909, or little more than the land revenue of that province in 1790-91, *viz.*, £530,918, though considerable additions were made to the land revenue of Behar, after the permanent settlement, in respect of lands not included in the settlement with the zemindars. A zemindary in Behar sells for 25 or 30 years' purchase, one in Eastern Bengal for about ten or twelve years' purchase, its value being enhanced to the zemindar in Behar partly by the more valuable produce of the province, but also by the oppression of the ryots, and their absolute subjection to the will of the zemindar.

IV.—Inland transit duties, and increased revenue from sea customs, were to compensate the State for the surrender of increase of land revenue;—thus:—

(*a*).—LORD CORNWALLIS, *3rd February 1790.*

In course of time, as commerce and wealth increase, such regulations may be made in the duties on the internal trade, and the foreign imports and exports, as will afford a large addition to the income of

Fifth Report, pages 491-2.

App. IV.

Illusions of
the framers of
the Permanent
Settlement.

Para. 8, contd.

Report, Select
Committee, 1810,
page 103.

the public, whenever its necessity may require it, without discouraging trade or manufactures, or imposing any additional rent on the lands.

(b).—LETTER TO COURT OF DIRECTORS, 6TH MARCH 1793, REPORTING THE PERMANENT SETTLEMENT.

If at any future period the public exigencies should require an addition to your resources, you must look for this addition in the increase of the general wealth and commerce of the country, and not in the augmentation of the tax upon the land. Although agriculture and commerce promote each other, yet in this country, more than in any other, agriculture must flourish before its commerce can become extensive. The materials for all the most valuable manufactures are the produce of its own lands. It follows, therefore, that the extent of its commerce must depend upon the encouragement given to agriculture, and that whatever tends to impede the latter, destroys the two great sources of its wealth. At present, almost the whole of your revenue is raised upon the land, and any attempt to participate with the landholders in the produce of the waste lands would (as we have said) operate to discourage their being brought into cultivation, and consequently prevent the augmentation of articles for manufacture or export. The increase of cultivation (which nothing but permitting the landholders to reap the benefit of it can effect) will be productive of the opposite consequences. To what extent the trade and manufactures of this country may increase, under the very liberal measures which have been adopted for enabling British subjects to convey their goods to Europe at a moderate freight, we can form no conjecture. We are satisfied, however, that it will far exceed general expectation, and the duties on the export and import trade (exclusive of any internal duties which it may in future be thought advisable to impose) that may hereafter be levied, will afford an ample increase to your resources, and without burdening the people, or affecting in any shape the industry of the country.

The inland transit duties were to supplement the permanent land revenue: but with the same precipitancy, characteristic of a rash benevolence, with which the permanent settlement had been pushed forward, because detailed enquiries would have been troublesome, the sayer duties were abolished (as "the shortest way of getting rid of the embarrassment which the resolution for the resumption of sayer had occasioned"), only to be revived, however, after a brief interval, in 1810, as transit duties, until they were finally abolished in 1836. Under sea customs, export duties, excepting, perhaps, the duty on rice, are doomed; and the prospect of free custom houses in a not remote future has been entertained.

V.—It was expected that the zemindars, with a fixed land tax (and, it might be added, with the acquisition of a new proprietary right in the properties of millions) would lay out capital in improving agriculture. The testimony recorded is, that the zemindars have done little or nothing, the ryots everything, for the extension and improvement of cultivation.

APP. IV.
———
ILLUSIONS OF
THE FRAMERS OF
THE PERMANENT
SETTLEMENT.

Para. 8, contd.

-(*a*). SEE SECTION I.

(*b*). COURT OF DIRECTORS, *9th May 1831.*

(1). The second proposition of the Commissioners, that to fix the rates of the ryots would be exceedingly mischievous, is founded on the assumption that to give the ryots more than the bare and miserable subsistence allowed them by the zemindars, would not make them more happy, but as they are indolent and improvident, would only render them less productive: and that, happily for the country, the profit left by the permanent assessment on the land " had not exclusively centred with the ryot, which it must chiefly have done had the original intentions of its author been enforced." It is assumed that the zemindar, on the other hand, is a man of a very provident disposition, and " by allowing him," they say, " to derive a fair profit by enhanced rents, a strong excitement would be given to the extension of the cultivation. Capital would be employed in the mode most conducive to augment the wealth of the country, while the advantages attendant on industry would be more generally promoted; new channels of abundance and riches would be opened, &c." All this magnificent promise, you may observe, is founded on the two suppositions that the zemindars in India are a provident, productive class, and that the ryots are the reverse. And on no better foundation than this do Messrs. Rocke and Waring place the conclusion that all the prescriptive rights of the ryots ought to be annulled. We desire to record our satis-faction at the following part of your reply: " The Vice-President in Council is little disposed to believe that any rules will be required to guard against the extension of too great advantages to the ryots; still less can he for a moment admit the position that the native of India, by a strange perversity of nature, requires the stimulus of misery to goad him to exertion, and that he must for ever remain insensible to the benefit, however great and manifest, which industry holds out to him. The in-fluence of such an opinion must extend far beyond the question now under discussion, and would, in fact, destroy all hopes of the moral improvement of the people. It appears, however, to the Vice-President in Council altogether at variance with the acknowledged principles of human nature. In point of fact, too, the experiment has never been tried; on the contrary, it may be much more justly said that the characteristic indolence and imprudence of the Indian peasantry are the necessary results of the circumstances of their situation; and it would be un-reasonable to expect the efforts of industry, or the cares of prudence, from persons who cannot but feel that the laws are insufficient to protect them in the enjoyment of fruits of the one, and still more to secure to them the more distant advantages of the other" *(paragraph* 55).

Sess. 1331-32, Vol. XI, pages 102-3.

(2). You had, indeed, express and decisive experience to which it lay with you to appeal. There is scarcely any fact to which there is more

App. IV.
—
ILLUSIONS OF
THE FRAMERS OF
THE PERMANENT
SETTLEMENT.
—
Para. 8, V, contd.

frequent testimony in your records than the improvidence and pro-
digality which characterise the zemindars. On the subject of their
inattention to the improvement of their estates, the following declaration
of Mr. Ernst, in his answer to the questions which were circulated in
1801, may serve as a specimen of the body of evidence which fills your
records: " I have never seen or heard of a zemindar in Bengal who took
any measures for the improvement of his estate on a large and liberal
scale. Landholders do not carry their views beyond granting waste lands
on the terms which are customary in the pergunnah; they hardly ever
encourage cultivation by digging a tank or making advances to the
ryots" (paragraph 56).

(3). The words of the Board of Revenue are these, and we cannot but
observe how directly the sentiments they express stand in opposition to
those maintained by Mr. Rocke on the same subject in the report now
under immediate attention: " With respect to the observation of the
Collector, that the talookdars have expended large sums of money in
bringing the lands into a productive state, we are induced to think he is
misinformed on that point. The ryots generally clear and cultivate the
lands at their own expense. The period of exemption from rent may
in some instances exceed that specified in the talookdar's grant, but the
burthen of expense, generally speaking, falls on the ryot." With
respect to the actual situation of the ryot in the permanently-settled
territories, you observe that the records of Government contain numerous
representations of the oppressed and miserable condition to which, in many
cases, they have been reduced" (paragraph 57).

c. MR. HOLT MACKENZIE, 18th April 1832.

Q. 2627.—Is the cultivation of the land supposed to have improved
since the permanent settlement? I should say rather extended than
improved; it has very greatly extended. I am not aware of any essential improvement, but I believe in some cases there has been improvement.
Whatever may be thought of the probable consequences of having the
landed property of a country divided among a multitude of petty proprietors (and I do not think we have experience enough to justify any
dogma on the subject), it is certain that the existence of large zemindaries in Bengal has had no tendency to make farms large. And if in
Ireland we find that beggarly farms and a wretched people may be
conjoined with domains of princely magnitude, still more may we look
for poverty and distress under the zemindary system of India, so long at
least as the people retain the remembrance of their rights, and cling to
their fields though rendered worthless by exaction. The injustice of
the thing, and the mischief to the individuals thus placed in subjection
to the Government assignee, are enough for condemnation. But I should
further apprehend that the system must oppose a serious obstacle to the
successful cultivation of new and better crops. The zemindar, who is
neither agriculturist nor owner of the soil, and stands in a position little
favourable to the growth of enlightened and liberal ideas, must be
expected to act as a tax-gatherer, and as a short-sighted tax-
gatherer nipping in the bud the seeds of improvement. And we cannot
hope that any new or increased demand for the produce of the country

APP. IV.
———
ILLUSIONS OF
THE FRAMERS OF
THE PERMANENT
SETTLEMENT.
——
Para. 8, V, contd.

can be met with that promptitude which might be expected if the occupants were secured in their property, so long as the contractors for the Government revenue were on the watch for every new occasion of exaction, and the ignorance or inefficiency of our courts permit them unjustly and arbitrarily to tax the industry of the country. It is a curious fact, which I have more than once had occasion to state, but -may now not uselessly repeat, that when it was an object to supply the demand for sugar in England, which existed in 1792, the Government of that day, who had doubtlessly clearly in view the *principles*[1] *which Cornwallis intended to enforce in favour of the cultivators,* did not hesitate to issue orders against the enhancement of the rent of the sugar-cane land.

d.—MR. J. MILL.—*9th August 1831.*

Q. 3347.—Is it not the fact that the cultivation has extended in those provinces where the zemindary system prevails? I believe that is the fact. Third Report, Select Committee, 1831.

Q. 3348.—To what do you ascribe that? There can be no doubt that this extension of cultivation implies an increase both of population and of capital. In order to enable the country to extend its cultivation farther, capital must have been applied to it, unless old land at the same time had gone out of cultivation. I have no doubt that there has been in Bengal considerable increase of capital and extension of cultivation;—but it is another question whether that has been owing to the zemindary system.

Q. 3349.—Would you not ascribe that accumulation of capital in any degree to the zemindary system? I should ascribe it in no degree whatever, because I have no idea that the zemindary system is favourable to the accumulation of capital in the hands of the ryots, and there is express evidence of the fact that it is the ryots, and not the zemindars, who have extended the cultivation.

Q. 3350.—By what means have the ryots extended the cultivation? Their numbers have increased; and where an estate of a zemindar borders upon waste land, it has been found that the ryots generally have advanced upon the waste and have carried on the cultivation by degrees.

Q. 3351.—Do you think the ryots have accumulated capital? The ryots cannot have done this without an extension of capital equal to those effects. They have multiplied considerably, and when the families increase, there is a sub-division of the property, and, in consequence of the sub-division of the property, there is a stimulus to the numbers of the family among whom the sub-division has been made to increase their income by attempting to cultivate the waste.

Q. 3352.—If the ryots have in any degree accumulated capital, is not that a proof that their situation has somewhat improved? Of some of them no doubt it has.

Q. 3353.—Then you would not say that the effect of the zemindary settlement has been unmixed injury to the ryots? Where the ryots have had an opportunity of obtaining fresh land under certain advantages, they have been able, under the zemindary system, to extend cultivation; but I conceive that they would have effected it better under another system.

---

[1] That is, a rent fixed for ever.

APP. IV.

ILLUSIONS OF
THE FRAMERS OF
THE PERMANENT
SETTLEMENT.

Para. 8, V, contd.

Q. 3361.—I rather think ,unless I mis-recollect, that Lord Cornwallis's statement was that there was only one-third of Bengal under cultivation; he did not, however, mean to say that there were two-thirds absolutely waste, for a large portion of that which is not under cultivation is still considered as pasture land? It is in one sense waste, but it is not absolutely useless. Lord Cornwallis may have also declared that there was a full third of Bengal that was jungle, and absolutely useless. But within a few years the declaration has been repeated, by people upon the spot, that not above one-third of Bengal is under cultivation.

Q. 3362.—Then, according to that statement, there would be one-third under cultivation, one-third in a state of jungle, and one-third in an intermediate state? That is probably something of an approximation to the fact.

Q. 3363.—Do you think that those proportions have been much changed since the time of Lord Cornwallis? The proportion, I should say, cannot be very considerably changed, because the amount of land is so great, that the increase of cultivation bears a very small proportion to it, although absolutely it is considerable.

e.—Mr. A. D. Campbell (in his "able paper," which summarised the evidence before the Select Committee of 1831).

Ibid, page 33.

There is, no doubt, ample proof that, under the permanent settlement in Bengal, as the population augmented, cultivation greatly increased, fully perhaps to the same extent as in the periodically settled districts; but in both there is express evidence that it is the cultivators alone who advanced upon the waste; and such increase of cultivation, though concomitant with the permanent settlement, was by no means caused by it. In the Lower Provinces of Bengal, indeed, the permanent settlement enabled the zemindars, by ousting the hereditary cultivators in favour of the inferior peasantry, to increase the cultivation by a levelling system, which tended to depress the hereditary yeomanry, or middle ranks of the community, and to amalgamate them with the common labourers and slaves, from whom the highest judicial authorities in Bengal are now unable to distinguish them;—a change which must have seriously depressed the middle class, the only solid basis of all further advancement or improvement.

f.—Mr. R. D. Mangles.—*3rd April 1848.*

Q. 3560.—In Bengal has there not been a large increase of cultivation, and great improvements in agriculture since the permanent settlement? Yes; a vast increase of cultivation;—but, I am afraid, not much improvement in the mode of agriculture; —almost all that has been done in the way of indigo and sugar has been done by Europeans; little, if any, improvement has taken place in the system of agriculture.

Q. 3628.—Do the zemindars make permanent improvements upon their estates? Not as a general rule.

Q. 3633.—Still, you admit that the extension of cultivation, and the growth of many articles has been greater in Bengal than in other provinces? The extension of the cultivation has been greater; but I apprehend that the growth of any articles—indigo is the principal one—has not arisen, at all, directly from the effect of the permanent settlement, but from the great fitness of the soil and the climate of that part of the country for the growth of that particular article.

App. IV.
————
ILLUSIONS OF
THE FRAMERS OF
THE PERMANENT
SETTLEMENT.
————
Para. 8, V, contd.

g.—Mr. WELBY JACKSON.—*15th November 1849.*

It is the resident cultivators who have brought the country into cultivation. It is to them that the improvement and extension of the tillage is to be ascribed. It is by their energy and toil that the Government is supported. They are the most valuable and most respectable class in the country. The zemindars, on the other hand, are mere farmers of the revenue; they may have capital, but never lay out capital on the land. They collect rigorously, often, it is believed, illegal cesses prohibited by law; but they do nothing for the improvement of the country. Rack-renting, the general practice of the zemindars where they can have recourse to it, is far from conducive to the improvement of the land.

h.—Baboo Hurris Chunder Mookerjee, Editor of the *Hindoo Patriot*, and afterwards Assistant Secretary, Bengal British Indian Association; Baboos Sumbhunath Pundit, Unnoda Prosad Bose, Govind Persad Bose, &c.—*27th September 1851.*

Frequent removals of habitation (ejectments) are proverbially injurious to the industrious classes of the Bengal peasant, who builds his own hut, irrigates and manures the land at his own expense, and owes his landlord nothing but the use of the bare natural powers of the soil, who is absolutely without a reserved capital, and is almost always encumbered with a family; a single removal completes the ruin.

i.—Revd. A. Duff and 20 other Missionaries.—(*April 1857.*)

The extension of cultivation in Bengal, for which the zemindars claim credit, your petitioners ascribe not to enterprise, capital, or public spirit of the zemindars, but to the great increase of the population during the last hundred years of domestic peace.

k.—See Appendix XIV, Middlemen, *Para. 6, Section VIII.*

l.—Mr. Justice George Campbell.—*1st June 1864.*

It is by no means the case in this country, that the improving holder is necessarily or usually the large zemindar. That is another theory borrowed from a totally different state of things in a peculiar country of great capitalists. Even there it seems not to be quite universally admitted. And in this country it is as yet absolutely and almost universally false in fact. The great zemindar, as a rule, (and the exceptions are most rare), does not spend a farthing on the improvement of his estate. He neither himself cultivates and introduces an improved agriculture, nor does he prepare farms for his tenants, build farm-houses, fence fields, drain and plant,—he does nothing whatever of all this, he performs none of the functions of a landlord in the English sense; he merely permits ryots to cultivate at their own expense, and takes from them the dues to which the law entitles him, or more if he can get it.

APP. IV.
——
ILLUSIONS OF
THE FRAMERS OF
THE PERMANENT
SETTLEMENT.
——
Para. 8, V, contd.

So far as I have been able to see and learn, the only really improving class among native agriculturists are the small holders, the better class of ryots at fixed easy rents in prosperous parts of the country, and small maafeedars, putnidars, and the like, who carry on cultivation for the most part on their own account. Men of such classes are, I understand, very numerous in some districts of Lower Bengal; and, to take a well-known instance, by them, and not by great zemindars, has a great sugar production been introduced of late years by planting date trees, a species of culture which requires some outlay of capital, since the trees produce nothing for several years.

Even as regards European " Plantation," I believe it is notorious that, as they are circumstanced in this country, it is rather commercially, and as manufacturers than as agriculturists, that Europeans can succeed and do good. To take the land into their own hands and cultivate it, is a system which never pays. Give them the most absolute right, and still they must let most of the land out to ryots after all. They may as merchants, with great advantage, advance money for an improved produce; they may with still greater advantage manufacture the indigo plant or the cleaned cotton from the pod into chests of indigo and bales of clean pressed cotton; but for the cultivation they must mainly trust to the ryots, and to the better class of ryot, with a tenure which gives him some character, some vigour, and some command of funds.

m.—MR. JUSTICE SUMBHOONATH PUNDIT.—*19th June 1865.*

In this part of the country (Bengal) the zemindars do not improve their estates by laying out any large amount of capital in draining or otherwise improving the lands. In several localities, however, they advance seed or money to their ryots, build and maintain some embankments, or dig and keep clear and in working order certain water-courses, or prepare some wells. All these works and proceedings, generally, are such matters of necessity, that, without them, it would be impossible for the ryots to make any profitable cultivation * *. In Bengal an advance by a landlord to improve his estate is a thing unfortunately a mere contingency, written in the books of laws, but not practically realized.

n.—MR. JUSTICE SETON-KARR—*19th June 1865 and 2nd June 1864.*

1. The zemindar, it is perfectly notorious, takes no part in controlling or assisting the various processes of agriculture, for I do not consider the advance of tuccavee for seed, made occasionally in frontier or jungle districts, as anything but partial exceptions not to be taken into account. He bears none of the risk. He supplies none of the capital. He makes no contribution to the ryot's stock, and he is never anywhere charged with the erection or the repairs of the ryots' houses, which do not belong to, and are never claimed by him, but which are invariably removed by the ryot when he changes his residence to some other village.

2. It is quite certain that no practical interference whatever, with the rotation of crops by the cultivator, is ever attempted to be exercised by the zemindar. He never directs the cultivator to sow early rice in one year and hemp in the next, or to make the cold weather crops alternate-

ly, mustard seed and barley. In fact he never troubles himself for a moment with such matters. The Bengal ryot, though restricted by the peculiarities of climate to the use of one single crop over a large portion of the country, cultivates his higher lands with tobacco, sugar-cane, or with oil-seeds, with indigo for seed, with vetches, with oats, with barley, or turns the same into a series of date gardens, at his own expense, and at his own choice and pleasure.

3. Excepting a few tanks dug, a few roads opened, and here and there a new haut or gunge established, after a series of disturbances by which the population had been half demoralised, the zemindars, it was notorious, had done absolutely nothing worthy of their position and name. No new products have been introduced by any native zemindars. Improvements in agriculture have not proceeded from them. Under their apathy the breed of cattle has to a certain extent degenerated.

4. On the other hand, considerable tracts of jungle have been cleared wholly at the expense of the ryots; and some of the higher kinds of cultivation, as for instance, those of the date-tree, of the sugar-cane, and of tobacco, are entirely due to the capital and the exertions of substantial ryots and jotedars; no zemindar has to this end, as far as I have been able to ascertain, contributed one farthing, or even given to the population below him the benefit of his example.

9. Results of the Permanent Settlement.

Among the foremost of the results of the Permanent Settlement must be placed the destruction of those rights of millions of cultivating proprietors which in theory were reserved in the Proclamation of the zemindary settlement.

I.—Fifth Report, Select Committee.

It must have appeared, from what has been stated, that the inhabitants of the Company's territorial possessions, whose condition was considered to be the most improved by the introduction of the new system, were the class of landholders or zemindars. * * But in India, as already has been mentioned, subordinate rights were found to exist, which justice and humanity required should be protected, before the privileges of the zemindars, under the new system, were declared fixed for ever.

This was not done.

II.—Mr. Sisson's report (2nd April 1815).

(a). The expected result of the decennial settlement was that "individuals would thereby be certain to enjoy the fruits of their industry; that it would dispense prosperity and happiness to the great body of the people, and increase the power of the State, which must be proportionate to the collective wealth that, by good government, it might enable its subjects to acquire."

(b). (There are but 202 zemindar families in Rungpore, 1793, Regulation I.) Two hundred families were not to aggrandise themselves at the expense of the rights of a million of under-tenants, but were told that "to conduct themselves with good faith and moderation towards their dependent talookdars and ryots, are duties at all times indispensably required from the proprietors of land; and that a strict observance of these duties is now more than ever incumbent upon them, in return for the benefits which they will themselves derive from the orders now issued. The Governor General in Council, therefore, expects that the proprietors of land will not only act in this manner themselves towards their dependent talookdars and ryots, but also enjoin the strictest adherence to the same principles on the persons whom they may depute to collect the rents for them."

(*c*). This was the expected result; the actual result, as it appeared in April 1815, was as follows:—

Ibid., pages 331-32.

(1). It only remains for me to represent the relative state in Rungpore of the landlord and tenant, which will be the subject of the present address.

What I shall have occasion to bring to notice may possibly prove that, in Rungpore, it is not the prevalence of gang-robbery and other public crimes which calls the most loudly for remedy. These are but the ramifications of an evil, whose root has long flourished in secret. The arbitrary oppression, under which the cultivator of the soil groans, has, at length, attained a height so alarming, as to have become by far the most extensively injurious of all the evils under which that district labours. * * In the course of the present address I shall endeavour to show to what a height rapacity, seconded by the law of distress and sale and other instruments, has attained in the district of Rungpore.

III.—SELECT COMMITTEE, *1831-2.*

Lessns. 1831-32, Vol. XI, page 4.

(1). A great body of evidence has been taken on the nature, object, and consequences of this permanent zemindary settlement, and your Committee cannot refrain from observing that it does not appear to have answered the purposes for which it was benevolently intended by its author, Lord Cornwallis, in 1792-3. The Finance Committee at Calcutta, in their Report, 12th July 1830, acknowledge that, "in the permanently settled districts in Bengal, nothing is settled and little is known but the Government assessment."

(2). The causes of this failure may be ascribed in a great degree to the error of assuming, at the time of making the permanent settlement, that the rights of all parties claiming an interest in the land were sufficiently established by usage to enable the courts to protect individual rights; and still more to the measure which declared the zemindar to be the hereditary owner of the soil, whereas it is contended that he was originally, with few exceptions, the mere hereditary steward, representative, or officer of the Government, and his undeniable hereditary property in the land revenue was totally distinct from property in the land itself.

(3). Whilst, however, the amount of revenue payable by the zemindar to the Government became fixed, no efficient measures appear to have been taken to define or limit the demand of the zemindar upon the ryots, who possessed an hereditary right of occupancy, on condition

App. IV.

RESULTS OF THE
PERMANENT
SETTLEMENT.

Para. 9, contd.

Sess. 31-32,
Vol. XI, page 83.

of either cultivating the land, or finding tenants to do so. Without going into detail to show the working of the system, it may be proper to quote the opinion of Lord Hastings, as recorded in 1819, when he held the office of Governor General of India. "Never," says Lord Hastings, "was there a measure conceived in a purer spirit of generous humanity and disinterested justice, than the plan for the permanent settlement in the Lower Provinces. It was worthy the soul of Cornwallis. Yet this truly benevolent purpose, fashioned with great care and deliberation, has, to our painful knowledge, subjected almost the whole of the lower classes throughout these provinces to most grievous oppression; an oppression, too, so guaranteed by our pledge, that we are unable to relieve the sufferers; a right of ownership in the soil, absolutely gratuitous, having been vested in the person through whom the payment to the State was to be made, with unlimited power to wring from his co-parceners an exorbitant rent for the use of any part of the land."

(4). An opinion not less strong was recorded at the same time by Sir E. Colebrooke, then a Member of the Supreme Council, who observed that "the errors of the settlement were two-fold: first, in the sacrifice of what might be denominated the yeomanry, by merging all tillage rights, whether of property or of occupancy, in the all-devouring recognition of the zemindar's permanent property in the soil; and then leaving the zemindar to make his settlement with the peasantry as he might choose to require."

(5). If, then, the conclusion may be formed that the permanent settlement of Lord Cornwallis has failed in its professed object, it must be a matter of anxious enquiry to ascertain how far the evils of the system are capable of being remedied.

IV.—Lord Moira's Revenue Minute, 21st September 1815.

Ibid, page 83.

(*a*). The situation of the village proprietors in large estates, in farms and jagheers, is such as to call loudly for the support of some legislative provision. This is a question which has not merely reference to the Upper Provinces, for within the circle of the perpetual settlement, the situation of this unfortunate class is yet more desperate; and though their cries for redress may have been stifled in many districts, by their perceiving that uniform indisposition to attempt relieving them which results from the difficulty of the operation, their sufferings have not on that account been the less acute (*para. 138*).

(*b*). In Burdwan, in Behar, in Benares, in Cawnpore, and indeed wherever there may have existed extensive landed property at the mercy of individuals, whether in farm, in talook, in jagheer, or in zemindary of the higher class, the complaints of the village zemindars have crowded in upon me without number; and I had only the mortification of finding that the existing system, established by the legislature, left me without the means of pointing out to the complainants any mode in which they might hope to obtain redress (*para. 139*).

(*c*). Of these complaints I beg leave to lay before your Honorable Board the accompanying original, received at Patna from a mookhtar on the part of the village proprietors of Tuladah, together with the abridged translation of it. I beg to assure your Honorable Board, however, that the oppressions alleged against the Rajah of Benares and Sheo Nerayun, against the Jagheerdhar Nemudar Gur Ghosain, and other large holders, were not less flagrant or apparently less substantiated than those alleged in this petition against Baber Ally Khan, the holder of the life-ijarah of Tuladah. In all these tenures, from what I could observe, the class of village proprietors appeared to be in train of annihilation, and unless a remedy is speedily applied, the class will become extinct. Indeed, I fear that any remedy which could be proposed would even now come too late to be of any effect in the several estates of Bengal, for the license of twenty years, which has been left to the zemindars of that province, will have given them the power—and they have never wanted the inclination—to extinguish the rights of this class, so that no remnants of them will soon be discoverable (*para. 140*).

(*d*). The cause of this is to be traced to the incorrectness of the principle assumed at the time of the perpetual settlement, when those with whom Government entered into engagements were declared the sole proprietors of the soil. The under proprietors were considered to have no right except such as might be conferred by pottah, and there was no security for their obtaining these on reasonable terms, except an obviously empty injunction on the zemindar amicably to adjust and consolidate the amount of his claims (*para. 141*).

(*e*). Here follow six paragraphs of which two will be found in Appendix No. X, para. 6, section I*b*)

(*f*). If it were the intention of our Regulations to deprive every class but the large proprietors who engage with Government, of any share in the profits of the land, that effect has been fully accomplished in Bengal. No compensation can now be made for the injustice done to those who used to enjoy a share of these profits under the law of the empire, and under institutions anterior to all record for the transfer of their property to the rajahs (*para. 148*).

(*g*). In Behar, however, and in Benares, the stand which was made by the mofussil zemindars has been rather more successful, and the class has not yet been entirely proscribed and hunted down; but unless some effectual measures are taken to stop the evil, the petition I have now the honor to lay before your Honorable Board is sufficient to show that such will be the ultimate consequence of our system, even in those provinces (*para. 149*).

But oppression marches with no halting pace; the condition of the ryots in Behar, in 1878, is far worse than that of ryots in any part of Bengal; it is benevolence only that has halted since it exhausted itself in creating great zemindars at the expense of millions of cultivating proprietors.

V.—RESOLUTION OF GOVERNMENT, *1st August 1822.*

(*a*). As far, therefore, as concerns the ryots, the perpetual settlement of the Lower Provinces must, His Lordship in Council apprehends, be held to have essentially failed to produce the contemplated benefits, with whatever advantages it may have otherwise been attended (*para.* 122).

(*b*). As to the expediency of maintaining the tenures of the ryots, or of allowing them to fall into the condition of tenants-at-will, the Governor General in Council cannot view it as a question debatable. Their rights, His Lordship in Council considers, it is the bounden duty of Government to maintain (*para.* 123).

RESULTS OF THE PERMANENT SETTLEMENT.
Para. 9, contd.
Sess., 1831-32, Vol. XI, page 308.

VI.—MR. HOLT MACKENZIE, *1832.*

It must also be admitted that we have hitherto failed to secure for the landowners of Bengal that precision and certainty as to the other circumstances of their property which the permanent settlement has given in respect to the Government demand. * * * The grand objection to the permanent settlement is that it has in a multitude of cases left the owners of the land subject to demands on account of Government revenue even less settled and defined than if we still retained the right of varying the assessment; and scarcely any one, I imagine, can doubt that the effect must have been very prejudicial to the interests of the community, and must have impeded the progress of national wealth. * * The zemindar, who is neither agriculturist nor owner of the soil, and stands in a position little favourable to the growth of enlightened and liberal ideas, must be expected to act as a tax-gatherer, and as a short-sighted tax-gatherer, nipping in the bud the seeds of improvement. And we cannot hope that any new or increased demand [1] for the produce of the country can be met with that promptitude which might be expected if the occupants were secured in their property, so long as the contractors for the Government revenue were on the watch for every new occasion of exaction, and the defectiveness of our revenue arrangements, and the ignorance or insufficiency of our courts permit them unjustly and arbitrarily to tax the industry of the country.

VII.—MR. CANNING, PRESIDENT OF THE BOARD OF CONTROL, *17th August 1817.*

(*a*). As I am far from feeling myself sufficiently informed upon the extensive and complicated subjects to which those paragraphs of the Court's draft letter relate, every consideration of personal responsibility induces me, above all things, to take care that no instructions which may go out under my sanction, for the present, shall either contradict the tenor or impair the efficacy of what I find, at my accession to the Board, to be the recorded intentions of the Board and the Court of Directors. The points upon which I find an agreement between the Court and the Board established (whether by coincidence or compromise of opinion) are these :—

Sess. 1831-32, Vol. XI, Appendix No. 8, page 56.

1st.—That the system of 1793, though originating in the most enlightened views and the most benevolent motives, and though, having produced considerable good, has nevertheless been attended, in the course of its operation, with no small portion of evil to the people for whose happiness it was intended.

---

[1] It is a curious fact, which I have more than once had occasion to state, that when it was an object to supply the demand for sugar in England, which existed in 1792, the Government of that day, who had doubtlessly clearly in view the principles which Cornwallis intended to enforce in favour of the cultivators, did not hesitate to issue orders against the enhancement of the rent of sugarcane land.

2nd.—That the same views and motives which dictated the original introduction of the permanent settlement 25 years ago, would not, after the experience which has been had of it, justify the immediate introduction of the same system into provinces for which a system of revenue administration is yet to be settled.

3rd.—That the creation of an artificial class of intermediate proprietors between the Government and the cultivators of the soil, where a class of intermediate proprietors does not exist in the native institutions of the country, would be highly inexpedient.

4th.—That no conclusive step ought to be taken towards a final settlement of the yet unsettled provinces until it shall have been examined, and if possible ascertained by diligent research and comparison of collected testimonies, as well as by accurate survey of the lands to be settled, how far the principles of a system which would bring the Government into immediate contact with the great body of the people can be practically and usefully applied to them.

VIII.—Mr. J. MILL, *2nd August 1831.*

Q. 3138. To what extent do you believe that the permanent settlement did affect the rights of the ryots? I believe that, in practice, the effect of it has been most injurious. The most remarkable circumstance, and that by which all the rest seem to have been influenced, was the interpretation put upon the effect of the sales of land, particularly of the sales that were made for recovering arrears of revenue. The idea came to be entertained that the purchasers at those sales were proprietors. They were denominated proprietors. A man that purchased an estate was considered to be the proprietor of that estate; and in consequence of this notion of proprietorship, and the great powers that are annexed to it in the mind of an Englishman, an idea seems to have been entertained that the purchaser of this estate purchased the rights over it as completely as a man would purchase rights over an estate by purchasing it at a public sale in England. Those auction-purchasers, as they are called, proceeded to act upon this assumption, to impose new rates upon the ryots, and even to oust them wherever they found it convenient. When applications were made to the courts, and they were not easily made, because the people are exceedingly passive, the judges, for the most part, coincided in opinion with those auction-purchasers, and decided that their rights included every thing, and that the ryots were in the condition of tenants-at-will. This had proceeded to a very considerable length, because, during the first years of the operation of the permanent settlement, a very great transfer of property took place. It appears, also, that the same sort of feeling as to the rights of the ryots, which was thus spread by the interpretation of this act of purchasing, has pervaded also the other properties which had not changed hands, and even those cases of transfer which took place by private bargain; and that generally in Bengal now there is hardly any right recognised as belonging to those inferior holders.

Q. 3139.—Do you conceive that at present the transfer of property by any means is held to give the new acquirer a complete right over the cultivators? I believe so; the thing is not so distinctly made out upon the records in other cases as in that of auction purchasers, but there is every reason to infer that the same sort of feeling, that was generated in the case of those estates that were sold, now pervades the whole of them. There is a very remarkable expression in one of the despatches from the Government of Bengal, that the rights of the ryots in Bengal, under the operation of the permanent settlement, had passed away *sub-silentio*.

IX.—Law and Constitution of India, *1825.*

" It is of the utmost importance," says Mr. Colebrooke, " to conci- Pages 169-70. liate the great body of landed proprietors, to attach to the British Government this class of persons, whose influence is most permanent and most extensive." But the fact is, that the " great body of landed proprietors," to whom the above does, *in reality*, though not intentionally, apply, are just that class of people which the permanent settlement of Bengal has completely destroyed, and instead of conciliating, has blotted out from among the different gradations of society in that province. The village cultivating zemindars, the best of the people, honest, manly, independent men, that are now to be met with in every village of the Upper Provinces, the younger branches of whose families crowd our armies and crown them with incessant victory—the permanent settlement has annihilated this class of men in the Lower Provinces, or totally and entirely changed their character.

X.—Halhed on Land Tenure and the Principles of Taxation, *1832.*

(*a*). A lamentable instance of the want of real information. in regard Page IV. to the nature of the land tenure in India, is exhibited in the legislative enactments consequent upon the discussions of the zemindary question before the Hon'ble Houses of Parliament in 1781-82, by which the allodial interests of millions of proprietors were destroyed, in order to establish on their ruins a landed aristocracy in the persons of the tax-gatherers.

(*b*). Trivial and inadequate, indeed, was the amount of redress which the judicial courts were empowered to afford to the *raeeuts ;* the judges were tied down by the Code, which limited the rights of the *raeeut* to the stipulations in his lease, and little, in the shape of retributive justice, could be granted to them. * * " The extreme propensity of the natives to litigation" has often been quoted, oftener urged in excuse for the measures of severity resorted to, with the view of preventing what appears to be an evil of unlimited extent. Perhaps the native character is not sufficiently understood; may not the overwhelming accumulation of civil causes be, with greater justice, attributed to the effects of a Code ill adapted to the genius and prejudices of the people, than to their love of legal strife ? That an increase of criminality, in Bengal especially, where the result of the operation of the Code has been more severely felt, may be ascribed to it, no one, who has had opportunities of seeing its effects upon the minor orders of the agricultural community, will deny.

(*c*).—Practical experience of its merits fully proves that it has failed to gain for the Government the love of the most quiet and submissive portion of its subjects, while the influence possessed by the very powerful class of exclusive proprietors created by the Code, has more frequently been excited to counteract the views of the ruling power, than to support its interests. Much might be said upon this branch of the subject; it is by no means clear that the transfer of the rights of the ancient allodial proprietors to a race of hereditary tax-gatherers, of clerks to British houses of agency, and of sirkars and moonshees from Writers' Buildings, has been productive of either advantage or reputation to the British name.

XI.—Sir Henry Maine—(Village Communities)—

A province like Bengal Proper, where the village system had fallen to pieces of itself, was the proper field for the creation of a peasant proprietary; but Lord Cornwallis turned it into a country of great estates, and was compelled to take his landlords from the tax-gatherers of his worthless predecessors. The political valuelessness of the proprietary right thus created, its failure to obtain any wholesome influence over the peasantry, and its oppression of all inferior holders, led to distrust of the economical principles implied in its establishment.

XII.—Editor of the *Hindoo Patriot*, Baboo Sumbhunath Pundit, and others, *27th September 1851.*

The legal condition of the tenure by which the greater portion of the land in Bengal is held has been deteriorating for the last sixty years by successive degrees, from a sort of proprietorship not much inferior to an *allodium*, and is strongly tending towards a mere tenancy-at-will. Without entering into the question of the policy of this revolution in property, it is of importance to bear in mind that of this change the peasantry as a body are wholly ignorant. Hence rights of occupancy determine in a large number of cases without the cognizance of the owners. It is but a venial offence on the part of the rural population of this country, that they are not well acquainted with the extent and limit of their rights. The fact is that the ignorance extends to the highest quarters. In a despatch to the Hon'ble the Court of Directors, dated the 22nd February 1827, the Government of Bengal "ascribe the alleged inadequacy of our civil tribunals in the Lower Provinces to meet the demands upon them to the precipitation with which the permanent settlement was carried into effect, without previously defining the relative rights and interests of the zemindars and other landholders and the various classes of the cultivating population." * * The proposed law "to facilitate the ejectment of occupiers of land whose title has ceased," if passed, will, we have ample reason to fear, complete, for the immense majority of the nation, the misery of their cottierism.

XIII.—Mr. W. G. Rose, Indigo Planter, Moorshedabad, *6th March 1841—*

Several of the most influential zemindars in Bengal have opportunities of stating their grievances to His Lordship in person, and to those in office whom His Lordship is in the habit of consulting on such matters, but the voice of the poor ryot they never hear. It is a notorious fact that the ryots of Bengal are worse off now, that is poorer, than they were fifty years ago, and are getting poorer and poorer every day, and the present Regulation, if passed, will not make them any richer. Hardly a single village in Bengal is able to pay its rents punctually. Let Government enquire into the cause of this. * Government have much to answer for in not having done more than they have to protect the interests of the agriculturists and ryots of Bengal.

XIV.—REVD. A. DUFF AND 20 OTHER MISSIONARIES, *April 1875.*

(*a*). The tenants suffer from a lax administration of laws passed for their protection; they are oppressed by the execution of other laws which arm the zemindars with excessive power; they do not share with the zemindars in the advantages derived from the development of the resources of the country; the profits thus monopolised by the zemindars are already incalculably valuable, and year after year the condition of the tenants appears more and more pitiable and hopeless. * * Ignorant of his rights, uneducated, subdued by oppression, accustomed to penury, and sometimes reduced to destitution, the cultivator of the soil in many parts of this Presidency derives little benefit from the British rule, beyond protection from Mahratta invasions.

(*b*). * * The causes to which the misery and degradation of the peasantry must be attributed are manifold; such as the long continued prevalence of Hindoo idolatry and Mahomedan oppression, of early marriages and the prejudices of caste; also the innate defects of the national character and the density of the population. Causes like these cannot well be remedied by legislative enactments; but there is another which appears to admit of such a remedy, namely, the mutual relations between the zemindars and the ryots, to which the alarming deterioration of the peasantry must be, in a great measure, attributed; whilst at the same time it places the zemindars in a position which is calculated to prolong the evil to an indefinite period without any prospect of improvement. * *

(*c*). The zemindars are almost all, however, in the habit of treating their ryots, not merely as their tenants, but as their serfs. They call themselves rajahs or kings, and the ryots their subjects. They almost universally claim either more than their due, or else they claim it in an improper manner, for it is not easy to determine what is really their due. They exact contributions from their ryots for funeral rites, annual heathen festivals, and when a marriage, or a birth, or a death takes place in the family. These practices are almost universal. In numerous localities they exact from the ryots gratuitous labour in the field or at the oar, and compel the poor people to allow them without payment the use of their cattle or their boats, if they possess any. It is not unusual (1852), especially at a considerable distance from the civil stations, for zemindars to go still further in the abuse of their power, by inflicting imprisonment and torture upon any ryot who may have incurred their displeasure.

(*d*). (In another petition in March 1858, respecting the Bill which was passed as Act X of 1859). This Bill and the Sale-Bill will, your petitioners believe, secure relief to khoodkasht ryots, and to the mass of the tenants of Bengal from extensive and grievous oppression.

XV.—MR. A. J. M. MILLS, JUDGE OF SUDDER COURT, *31st August 1852.*

The condition of the ryot in Bengal is most wretched; he has no means of obtaining redress against a powerful landlord.

10. REMEDIES.

I.—LORD CORNWALLIS, *3rd February 1790.*

(*a*). I agree with Mr. Shore that some interference on the part of Government is undoubtedly necessary for effecting an adjustment of the demands of the zemindars upon the ryots; nor do I conceive that the former will take alarm[1] at the reservation of this right of interference, when convinced that Government can have no interest in exercising it, but for the purposes of public justice. Were the Government itself to be a party in the cause, they might have some grounds for apprehending the result of its decisions.

(*b*). Many regulations will certainly be hereafter necessary, for the further security of the ryots in particular, and even of those talukdars who, to my concern, must still remain in some degree of dependence on the zemindars. * * I cannot, however, admit that such regulations can in any degree affect the rights which it is now proposed to confirm to the zemindars; for I never will allow that, in any country, Government can be said to invade the rights of a subject when they only require, for the benefit of the State, that he shall accept of a reasonable equivalent for the surrender of a real or supposed right, which in his hands is detrimental to the general interest of the public, or when they prevent his committing cruel oppressions upon his neighbours, or upon his own dependents.

II.—COURT OF DIRECTORS, *19th September 1792.*

(*a*). We therefore wish to have it distinctly understood, that while we confirm to the landholders the possession of the districts which they now hold, and subject only to the rent now settled, and while we disclaim any interference with respect to the situation of the ryots, or the sums paid by them, with any view to any addition of revenue to ourselves, we expressly reserve the right, which clearly belongs to us as sovereigns, of interposing our authority in making from time to time all such regulations as may be necessary to prevent the ryots being improperly disturbed in their possessions, or loaded with unwarrantable exactions. A power exercised for the purposes we have mentioned, and which has no view to our own interests, except as they are connected with the general industry and prosperity of the country, can be no object of jealousy to the landholders, and, instead of diminishing, will ultimately enhance the value of their proprietary rights.

(*b*). Our interposition, where it is necessary, seems also to be clearly consistent with the practice of the Mogul Government, under which it appeared to be a general maxim that the immediate cultivator of the soil, duly paying his rent, should not be dispossessed of the land he occupied. This necessarily supposes that there were some measures and limits by which the rent could be defined, and that it was not left to the arbitrary determination of the zemindar, for otherwise such a rule would be nugatory:—and, in point of fact, the original amount seems to have been annually ascertained and fixed by the act of the sovereign (*para. 46*).

---

[1] Far from taking alarm, they took advantage of *huftum* and *punjum* and other means of destroying the ryots' rights, which rights Lord Cornwallis had hoped that they would respect and cherish from self-interest.

(*c*). It was in conformity with the principles laid down in the minute of Lord Cornwallis dated 3rd February 1790 (Appendix VI, para. 2, I and II), that we, having then before us the recorded discussions which had taken place between him and Mr. Shore, made the reservations which are declared in our despatch of 19th September 1792, that " while we confirm &c., (extracts *a* and *b* above: Court's letter, 15th January 1819).

APP. **IV.**

REMEDIES.

Para. 10, contd.

III.—To COURT OF DIRECTORS, *6th March 1793*.

We shall further declare (although a clause to that effect has been inserted in the engagements with the landholders), that you do not mean, by fixing the public demand upon the lands, to debar yourselves from the exercise of the right inherent in you as sovereigns of the country, of making such regulations as you may occasionally think proper for the protection of the ryots and inferior landholders, or other orders of people concerned in the cultivation of the lands (*para. 23*).

Select Committee, 1810, Appendix No. 9, page 103.

IV.—BENGAL GOVERNMENT TO COURT OF DIRECTORS, *1st August 1822*.

(*a*). With respect to the precise measures to be adopted, it is not easy to come to any determination, for the evil exhibits itself in a vast variety of forms, and in a countless number of individual cases.   *   * In the Ceded and Conquered Provinces, our separate despatches relative to the settlement will show that we design, as far as practicable, to adjust, through the agency of the collectors, the rights and interests of every ryot in every village as it may be settled, and specifically to define the rights of the zemindars, with reference to the mofussil jummabundy so made. The existence of the permanent settlement in the Lower Provinces does not, in our judgment, oppose any legal bar to the adoption of a similar course there, if we can command sufficiency of fit instruments and the scheme be generally deemed expedient; for Government, in limiting its demand, specifically reserved the option of such interference; and if the zemindars have themselves failed to assess their ryots and to issue pottahs on equitable terms as provided, such an interference would require no other justification than the proof that it could be expediently exercised.

Revenue Selections, Vol. III, pages 441-442.

(*b*). As soon, therefore, as the regulation relative to the settlement of the Ceded and Conquered Provinces is published, we propose consulting the Revenue Boards on the expediency of enacting such rules as may enable the Revenue authorities in the Lower Provinces, under proper restriction, to make a mofussil settlement with the cultivators of estates held subject to a fixed jumma, or free of assessment, on behalf of the sudder malguzars or lakhirajdars.

(*c*). The subject, however, is so difficult and important, and the magnitude of the work to be performed is so strongly in contrast with the extent of the machinery we can apply to its accomplishment, that we must entreat your indulgence if we shall appear unnecessarily to postpone our final determination.

App. IV.   V.—Select Committee, *1831-32*—

REMEDIES.
Para. 10, contd.

(After the passage quoted in paragraph 9, section III). So long as the zemindar pays his fixed assessment, the Government have not interfered to regulate the cultivators' rates; but where arrears accrue, and a public sale of the zemindary revenue, as prescribed by the regulations, takes place (except the sacrifice on account of purchase money is very great), the authorities at home have directed every zemindary tenure "to be purchased on the part of the Government, and then settled with the ryots on the ryotwar principle." This order, it appears, has as yet had little practical effect in the Bengal Presidency, where it was at first opposed by the local authorities.

(*b*). Although such purchase and resumption of the right to manage the land revenue is the best mode for the Government to acquire the power of effectual interference on behalf of the ryots, the sacrifice of money requisite for the purpose would be so great as to impede the working of the system, if the sales of zemindaries for default of payment were numerous and extensive; and unless the Government should, either by public or private purchase, acquire the zemindary tenure, it would, under the existing regulations, be deemed a breach of faith, without the consent of the zemindars, to interfere directly between the zemindars and the ryots for the purpose of fixing the amount of the land-tax demandable from the latter under the settlement of 1792-93.

11. Summing up the information in this Appendix, we find that—

I. (Paragraphs 1 and 2).—The permanent settlement was conceived by Mr. Francis in a self-sufficient ignorance, and was carried out with precipitancy. With indecent haste, a weak benevolence destroyed the rights of millions of real proprietors, and created a small class of artificial or fictitious proprietors who, however, very soon acquired the terrible reality which insatiable demands, exaction, and oppression could give them.

II. (Paragraphs 3 and 4).—This was done in furtherance, forsooth, of injunctions of Parliament, and instructions of the Court of Directors, which had no other object than to continue established usage and principle (as indeed Parliament had no right to ex-propriate without giving full compensation), to secure real proprietors in the enjoyment of their rights, and to permanently limit the Government demand, and that, too, in only such sense permanently, that it should not be alterable except by the Court of Directors, in some urgent and peculiar case.

III. (Paragraph 5).—Even the author of the scheme of a permanent settlement, Sir Philip Francis, did not propose anything more than a settlement of the Government demand (with temporary cesses for extraordinary expenses of the

State), whoever might be the proprietor; and he proposed that the zemindars, with whom the Government permanently settled its demand, should give the same security of a permanent rent to their under-tenants.

IV. (Paragraph 6).—The principal objects of a permanent settlement were thus variously described by divers authorities.

a. COURT OF DIRECTORS.—To give to the different orders of the community a security which they never before enjoyed, to protect the zemindars and *ryots* from harassment by increasing debts from an increase of the Government demand, and to relieve the proprietors of small estates from the tyranny of powerful zemindars.

b. LORD CORNWALLIS.—That the zemindars of Bengal, on whom His Lordship was bestowing, as a free gift, one-third to two-thirds of the culturable area of Bengal, then lying waste, should, with the help of that gift, guard against inundation and drought, " the two calamities to which this country must ever be liable;" that (the Government demand upon them being fixed, and their income increasing with the extended cultivation of waste) they should refrain from exactions, should assist the ryots with money, and do all other duties which " ought to be performed" by zemindars.

c. SIR JOHN SHORE.—We must give every possible security to the ryots, as well as, or not merely, to the zemindars. This is so essential a point that it ought not to be conceded to any plan.

d. In case of a foreign invasion (said Lord Cornwallis), the proprietors (whom His Lordship ex-propriated by millions) were to be attached to us from motives of self-interest, and from a feeling of security that their rent could not be raised in proportion to their improvement of their lands, and that they could not be dispossessed or imprisoned for arrears of rent, or for refusal to pay an unjustly enhanced rent.

V. (Paragraph 7).—These were noble ends, or silly ones (as of children crying for the moon), according as the authorities who conceived these aims, at a time when they were still serving their apprenticeship in the civil administration of an immense and strange country, set about their purpose circumspectly or in rash presumption and ignorance. We find that—

a. " Without much concern for the production of proof," Mr. Francis assumed that the property of the land belonged to the zemindars, and that the pottahs which the grateful zemindars would honestly grant to the ryots would protect the latter from exaction. (The forcing of pottahs upon ryots proved one of the most effectual means of the destruction of ryots' rights by the zemindars.)

b. The Court of Directors, having prohibited the Collectors from entering into detailed enquiries on essential points when the decennial settlement was ordered, Sir John Shore, in deprecating the perpetuation of that decennial settlement as the permanent settlement, objected that there was great uncertainty about ryots' rights, and ignorance on the part of the ryot himself of what he should pay. Lord Cornwallis replied that if the Collectors, who ought to have known (but who, till three years since, were ordered not to know), knew but little, the Government knew still less, and could not hope to know more; and was the Government calmly to sit down, without creating great zemindars? "I must declare that I am clearly of opinion that this Government will never be better qualified, at any given period whatever, to make an equitable settlement of the land revenue of these provinces." The question, said Lord Cornwallis, "that has been so much agitated in this country, whether the zemindars and talookdars are the actual proprietors of the soil, or only officers of Government, has always appeared to me to be very uninteresting to them." It did not occur to His Lordship that the question was of overwhelming interest to the ryots; that his benevolence, like the bloody oppression of Jezebel, was taking Naboth's field, or the poor man's inheritance from his fathers, by the million, for gifts to rapacious and unworthy zemindars; and so, in three years, or in not quite one-fifth of the time that, in the present day, the Government of the North-Western Provinces, with the full knowledge of rights, acquired in a past settlement, is taking to revise, for only thirty years, the last expired settlements, Lord Cornwallis turned a decennial into a permanent settlement, after an experience of three years, which had sufficed to show him how ignorant his Government was, and that it could learn nothing more.

c. The ignorance of Lord Cornwallis was so profound, that he placed the village accountants entirely under the zemindars;—that is, he transferred "this most useful check against the exactions of the more powerful from the more helpless classes to the exclusive charge of the zemindars; for they thus obtained the complete surrender of the great check against their own rapacity."

VI.—It is not surprising that good intentions should have turned into folly or worse, when pursued in a credulous optimism, with rash presumption, and in disregard of the Government's paramount duty to adapt its means to its most momentous ends, e. g.—

a.   It was expected that the zemindar would assist the ryots with money for the expenses of cultivation.   He lent them money on heavy interest.

b.   The zemindar would improve his estate by laying out money in agricultural improvements; not quite thirty years showed that he did nothing of the kind; and that the ryots had to combine among themselves to provide for small improvements.   The increase of cultivation which has taken place since the permanent settlement, and more particularly since 1848, is mainly due to the increase of population, and to a rise of prices, particularly of kinds of produce for which the soil and climate of Bengal are peculiarly fitted.

c. The zemindar having the benefit of all the revenue from waste lands, which an increase of population, and not his enterprise, brought into cultivation, was to obey the law which prohibited him from increasing the ryot's rent.   His cheerful compliance with law was shown by his appreciation of Huftum and Punjum, and by his multiplication of suits for the enhancement of rent.

d. The zemindar, with an income improved by the cultivation of extensive waste lands, was to provide against famine.   In 1874-75 the Government spent six and a half millions sterling for the famine in Behar, that is, added to the Imperial debt a yearly charge of £292,000 for interest, while the land revenue from Behar is only £970,000, and the increase of that revenue since 1793 has been only £440,000, from lands not included in the settlement of 1793.

e. The Government was to be compensated for the permanent limitation of the land revenue demand by inland transit duties, and an increase of customs duties.   The transit duties were abolished in 1836; the customs duties have been threatened with abolition.

f. The object of the permanent settlement was to give security and contentment to the " great body" of inhabitants (para. 6, section IIIa), that is, to the millions of cultivating proprietors; it is precisely that class which the settlement has destroyed.

VII.—The failure of the permanent settlement in its essential objects was apparent so early as 1812, on evidence of an earlier date tendered to the Select Committee whic[h] wrote the Fifth Report; it was abundantly clear to th[e] Indian authorities that administered the country in 1815 an[d] until 1831-32, when another Select Committee of Parliamen[t] formally recorded that, in the permanently settled district[s] in Bengal, nothing had been settled, and little was know[n] but the Government assessment. In other words, the des[-] truction of ryots' rights was known in less than twent[y] years after the permanent settlement, that is, before right[s] in wrongs had become vested rights, and when the goo[d] faith and honour of England were specially concerned i[n] redressing the wrong; but beyond a record in a "Resolu[-] tion" in 1822, that it was the "bounden duty of Govern[-] ment to maintain" ryots' rights, nothing was done.

VIII.—The precipitancy which caused the failure of th[e] permanent settlement was not unavoidable; the authoritie[s] that rashly hastened the settlement were still but serving a[n] apprenticeship in civil administration in India; had the[y] waited but awhile they would have acquired the knowledge which, a few years later, sufficed for condemning their error[s] and preventing a repetition of the mistakes in the North-Western Provinces.

IX.—Even this much of patience was not necessary. I[f] the authorities were incontinently bent on establishing th[e] permanent settlement, it behoved them simply to do as the Madras Government did, about the same time, when intro-ducing a permanent settlement into the Northern Circars viz., to fix, as the zemindar's maximum permanent deman[d] on the ryot, the actual rate which was being paid by the latter at the time of introduction of the settlement. Instead of that, there was fixed a pergunnah rate which, it has been ruled, has no finality, and which being undetermined to this day, is the one principal cause of injurious litigation, and of strained relations between zemindars and ryots, eighty years after a settlement which was designed to protect the ryot from harassment by exactions.

X.—The Indian Government, however, reserved power in the engagements with the zemindars, and the Court of Directors, in their despatch confirming the settlement, reserved the right inherent in the British Power as sovereigns of the country, of making, from time to time, such regulations as might be thought proper for the protection of the ryots and the inferior landholders, or other orders of the people concerned in the cultivation of the land.

App. IV.
―――
Para. 11, contd.

XI.—The bestowal of power on the zemindar to increase the ryot's rent is destructive of proprietary right in the latter. The authors of the permanent settlement contemplated, from the first, that the demand upon the ryot should be permanently fixed in the same way as the Government's demand upon the zemindar, *e. g.*—

>   *a.* Sir Philip Francis, para. 5, *d.*
>   Sir John Shore,   „   6, IV, *c, d.*
>   Court of Directors   „   6, VI, and 10, II.
>   Sir John Shore   „   7, IX, *a, b.*
>   Bengal Government „ 10, IV.
>   Lord Cornwallis, compare para. 6, III*a* and *d* with
>   „   10, I*a* and *b* and III.
>   Lord Cornwallis—*see* also Appendix VII, para. 2,
>   sections I to III, and paras. 3 and 4.

XII.—This intention of permanently fixing the zemindar's demand upon ryots under the permanent settlement was carried out in that day,—when the intentions of the framers of the settlement were fully understood,—in the permanent settlements of Benares and of the zemindary tracts in the Madras Presidency. Indecent haste, ignorance, and mistakes caused the failure in Bengal of the like intentions, without the complete execution of which the zemindary settlement in Bengal became an act of spoliation and confiscation of the property of millions, unless it be affirmed (and it may be truly affirmed) that Lord Cornwallis made the zemindars proprietors of but the alienated part of only the Government's permanently limited gross share of the produce of the soil, the rest of that produce remaining with the resident cultivator as proprietor of the land which he cultivated.

APPENDIX V.

GOVERNMENT AND RYOTS.

1.—THE RIGHT OF THE STATE IS IN THE PRODUCE, NOT I THE SOIL.

APP. V. I.—BAILLIE—

Baillie's Land Tax, pp. XXIII and XIX.

Para 1.

The *ooshr* and *khiraj* are taxes on the vegetative powers of the so The soil itself, with everything belonging to it, is the absolute proper of the owner. * * From the manner in which *ooshr* and *khiraj* was origi ally imposed on the land, it is evident that a Mahomedan sovereign h no possible pretension to be considered the proprietor of *ooshree khirajee* land. *Khiraj* in particular is due by a proprietor of land to t sovereign as representative of the community, and the sovereign cann be creditor and debtor at the same time.

II.—PHILLIPS—

Tagore Law Lectures.

The sovereign never claimed any right to the soil itself as part his share, nor ever exercised a right to anything beyond the natural accidental produce of the soil. * *

III.—BRIGGS—

Land Tax, page 27.

Abundant evidence has already been adduced to prove that neith the Hindu nor Mahomedan sovereigns ever claimed to be proprietors any part of the soil, but of the waste, or of the lands escheated default of legal successors; and they certainly never pretended to de the proprietary right of occupants. This fact must have struck t

Page 130.

reader in every step of my enquiry. * * The reply of Ghol Hoossein Khan, one of the most able and intelligent Mahomedans Bengal, to Mr. Shore, the present Lord Teignmouth, on this point, is f of value. The question is, " Why did the king purchase lands, since was lord of the country, and might, therefore, have taken by virtue that capacity ?"

Answer.—" The emperor is not so far lord of the soil as to be a to sell or otherwise dispose of it at his mere will and pleasure. Th are rights belonging only to such a proprietor of land as is mentioned the first and second answers (*i. e.*, proprietor by purchase with mutual consent of the parties; by gift from the proprietor; or inheritance). The emperor is *proprietor of the revenue*, but *he is not p prietor of the soil.* Hence it is, when he grants *aymas*, *altumgahs*, a *jageers*, he only transfers the revenue from himself to the grantee."

IV.—WILKS' MYSORE—

Page 13.

I shall conclude this branch of the subject with an extract from Mahomedan law authority, which shall be hereafter quoted at grea length,—"Inheritance is annexed to property, and he who has the tribute from the land, has no property in the land; hence it is known that the king has no right to grant the land which pays tribute, but that he may grant the tribute arising from it."

V.—HARINGTON'S ANALYSIS (*quoting authorities of Mahomedan law on landed property*)—

Tributary land is held in full property by its owner, and so is tithed (or decimated) land. A sale, or gift, or a charitable device of it is lawful, and it will be inherited like other property. *   * And in the book *Alkhaniyah* it is written,—"The sovereign has a right of property in the tribute or rent." Page 94.

VI.—LAW AND CONSTITUTION OF INDIA—

The *people*, by law, claim only a *portion* of the *produce of the soil* as their right; and as no trustee can have a stronger claim than his constituent, the right of the *sovereign* must also be limited to a *portion* of the *produce*, and a right in the produce is not a right in the soil. Page 30.

VII.—*Lord Moira's Revenue Minute, 21st September 1815*—

The right of Government is to a certain proportion of the produce of every cultivated beegah. Such has been the recognized right of the ruling power in this country from time immemorial (Reg. XIX, Bengal, 1793), and it has descended to us entire and unimpaired (paragraph 28). Parl. Papers, Session 1831-32, Vol. XI.

2.—STATE'S DEMAND FIXED (*with abwabs*).

I.—HALHED (*Hindu law*)—

Land under cultivation was liable to a tax to the State of a certain proportion of its produce, the amount of which was an eighth, sixth, or twelfth part, according to the capabilities of the soil and the expense of the cultivation; the demands of the Government were limited to this amount, except on occasions of great public emergency, such as dearth, war, or foreign invasion, when a fourth part might be levied (*Munnoo*). Page 2.

Assessment.

Abwab.

II.—HALHED (*Mahomedan rule*)—

The usual jumma was ascertained about the year 1582, under the orders of the Emperor Akbar, by Rajah Torull-Mull, his Minister of Finance, upon statements of the actual sums paid by the ryots, furnished by the kanoongoes. *   * The *abwabs* were not deemed legal taxes, but looked upon as unjust exactions, and were tolerated under a conviction that the evils or privations resulting from the payment of them were less in reality than those which would be superinduced by opposition or resistance. * * * In Behar and the Western Provinces there were but few instances of *abwabs* imposed as a permanent increase of the resources of the State; some temporary impositions or forced contributions are on record, but the people being of a more warlike and turbulent disposition, Pages 43-44.

the reason for their immunity is accounted for : some zemindari cesses have always been enforced and submitted to, which will be treated of presently.

III.—Sir J. Shore, *June 1789*.

The variation in the public demands from the standard of Tury-Mull, for a period of one hundred and twenty years, was very small (para. 381).

IV.—Colonel W. H. Sykes.

Under the Native Government in the Deccan, the land tax as such was a fixed tax, known as the sostee dur, and it still continues ; but in addition there were extra cesses levied upon each beegah, or other denomination of land, which rendered nugatory the permanent land-tax, or sostee dur. A cultivator paid, for instance, a rupee for a certain quantity of land of a particular denomination. This his ancestors had paid before him ; this his neighbours paid around him ; this his children would pay after him, because his land, being hereditary, would descend to them. So far as this continued, it was a permanent land-tax, and the same rate is traceable in village papers for 100 years ; but there came Governors requiring additional revenue, and they put on an additional cess, calling it by a certain name. This imposition upon the whole village was divided amongst the cultivators proportionably to the land held by each ; but it did not affect the land-tax. There came another cess after that, then another and another, each for some specific purpose. In this manner the taxes paid by the cultivator became burdensome, but the original land-tax remained the same.

V.—Mr. A. D. Campbell's "Able Paper on the Land Revenue."

It has already been explained by the Committee of the House of Commons in 1812, that long anterior to the Mahomedan conquest, "through every part of the empire which has come under British dominion, the produce of the land, whether taken in money or in kind, was understood to be shared, *in distinct proportions*, between the cultivator and the Government." This principle is clearly recognised in some of the first enactments of the Bengal Government, confirmed by more recent discussions at that Presidency ; and there may thus be distinctly traced only two parties originally connected with the land in India,—the cultivators who paid, and the Government, or its representatives, who received the public dues. These were universally limited by immemorial local usage ; but, from the want of correct records of the established rates payable by the cultivators, such usage formed too often an ill-defined, though always an acknowledged, standard.

VI.—Sir C. T. Metcalfe, *7th November 1830*.

(*a*). With respect to the right of property in the soil, I am inclined to believe, as before observed, that it is much the same generally throughout India, and that it existed in the Ceded Districts as elsewhere, but it is everywhere saddled with the payment of a large portion of the produce to Government, and all right ceases for the time if this be not paid. I speak of the acknowledged law or custom of India, not of any artificial distinctions that our Regulations may have created.

App. V.
——
STATE'S DEMAND FIXED, WITH ABWABS.
Para. 2, contd.

(*b*). Where, as is frequently, if not generally, the case, the mass of the only persons who can justly be called proprietors are the actual cultivators, and pay rent to no one, unless the share of the produce to which the Government is entitled be so termed,—what is the right of Government on that plan? Is it definite or indefinite? Is it a fixed portion of the supposed rents, or an arbitrary one at the discretion of the assessing officer? Any villager, in any village, throughout India I mean, of course, generally can tell what share of the produce of the land belongs to the Government. This is an acknowledged understood right, differing probably as to amount in different parts, and in the same parts differing according to circumstances, but well-known to all the cultivators as the right or share of the Government, whatever the local usage may be as to amount. If, on the other hand, the question were put as to what share of the rent paid to the proprietor is the right of Government as revenue, I do not believe that it could be answered by any one from the lowest cultivator to the senior member of the Board of Revenue, because such a mode of setting the demand of Government is unknown in the revenue system of India, and has not, as far as I am aware, been established by our Government.

Ibid. pages 329-30.

VII.—MR. PHILLIPS (QUOTING MR. J. S. MILL).

The mode in which an increased assessment (*abwab*) was obtained, leads Mr. John Stuart Mill to infer, and with reason, that the ryots had customary rights, which could not safely be infringed in any more direct way. * * The passage from Mr. Mill may be usefully quoted here :—

Tagore Law Lectures, pages 177-78.

"In India and other Asiatic communities similarly constituted, the ryots or peasant-farmers are not regarded as tenants-at-will, nor even as tenants by virtue of a lease. In most villages there are, indeed, some ryots on this precarious footing, consisting of those, or of the descendants of those, who have settled in the place at a known and comparatively recent period; but all who are looked upon as descendants or representatives of the original inhabitants, and even many more tenants of ancient date, are thought entitled to retain their land as long as they pay the customary rents. What these customary rents are, or ought to be, has indeed, in most cases, become a matter of obscurity;—usurpation, tyranny, and foreign conquest having, to a great degree, obliterated the evidences of them. But when an old and purely Hindu principality falls under the dominion of the British Government, or the management of its officers, and when the details of the revenue system come to be enquired into, it is usually found that though the demands of the great landholder, the State, have been swelled by rapacity until all limit is practically lost sight of, it has yet been thought necessary to have a distinct name and a separate pretext for each increase of exaction; so that the demand has sometimes come to consist of thirty or forty different items in addition to the nominal rent. This circuitous mode of increasing the payments assuredly would not have been resorted to if there had been an acknowledged right in the landlord to increase the rent. Its adoption is a proof that there was once an effective limitation—a real customary rent; and that the understood right of the ryot to the land, so long as he paid rent according to custom, was at some time or other more than nominal."

VIII.—Sir J. Shore, *June 1789.*

The principles of Mogul taxation, as far as we can collect from the institutes of Timoor and Akbar, from the ordinations of the emperors, and the conduct of their delegates, however limited in practice, were calculated to give the sovereign a proportion of the advantages arising from extended cultivation and increased population. As these were discovered, the Tumar or standard assessment was augmented; and whatever the justice or policy of the principle might be, the practice in detail has this merit, that it was founded upon a knowledge of real and existing resources. In conformity to these principles, inferior officers were stationed throughout the country to note and register all transactions relating to the soil, its rents and its produce; every augmentation of cultivation was required to be recorded, as well as every diminution of its quantity.

An increase of revenue exacted from a zemindar under these circumstances affected his profits, but made no alteration in the rates upon the ryots; he paid a portion of the rents arising from discovered improvements in his lands, but the cultivators of the soil were not by this demand exposed to an enhancement.

IX.—Minute by Mr. Stuart, *18th December 1820.*

In Native Governments, a levy on the lands has from time immemorial constituted the chief resource of the State, which has claimed, apparently more as a right of property than as a tax, a share of the whole growing produce of the soil. It is, however, to be understood that this claim of the State was not indefinite and arbitrary, but was exercised, at least in good times and under just rulers, upon fixed and regular principles.

The Government limited its demand to a specific proportion of the produce of the soil, either taken in kind or estimated in money, and varying according to the nature of the land and of the crop and other varying circumstances. Considered, therefore, with relation to any given species of produce and certain portion of the land, the public demand might be said to have been permanent. The invariableness of the rates assured the cultivators a certain reward of their industry, while the unlimited extension of the rates to new lands reclaimed to cultivation, and to the improved produce of lands before under tillage, kept the demand of the State progressive with the wealth and prosperity of the country.

X.—Resolution of Government, *1st August 1822.*

There is, indeed, reason to believe that, in the best times of the Mahomedan rule, the rate according to which the land revenue was paid and collected were specifically fixed by the Government, being liable to alteration only on its authority (and that rarely exercised); and that, consequently, in so far as related to a given extent of land under a given description of tillage, the demand of the State and of its officers was, in one sense at least, permanent. Under such a system, sedulously matured and rigidly controlled, the evils incident to the re-adjustment of the jumma assessed on the several mehals might in a considerable degree be obviated, since there was, at least, a fixed and recognized principle by which the amount to be demanded was settled.

APP. V.
——
STATE'S DEMAND INCLUDED THE ZEMINDAR'S SHARE.
Para. 3.

XI.—SIR J. SHORE, *8th December 1789.*

But the perpetuity of assessment is qualified by Mr. Law by the introduction of a clause, that the proprietors of mokurrary tenures shall be subject to a proportion of a general addition when required by the exigencies of Government. This qualification is, in fact, a subversion of the fundamental principle; for, the exigencies not being defined, a Government may interpret the conditions according to its own sense of them; and the same reasons which suggest an addition to the assessment may perpetuate the enhancement. The explanation given by Mr. Law to this objection is, that temporary extraordinaries must have temporary resources, and even the land at home is liable to a general tax during war, but the land-tax in England does not bear a proportion of 9-10ths to the income of the proprietor. Notwithstanding the explanation, I shall consider the qualifying clause as either nugatory or pernicious, and as standing in direct contradiction to the principle of a mokurrary settlement. The very term implies an unalterable assessment; and if the explanation be founded on necessity, it is decisive against the perpetuity of it.

Fifth report, paragraphs 29 and 30.

3.—STATE'S DEMAND UNDER THE LAW AND CONSTITUTION OF INDIA IN 1765, INCLUDED THE ZEMINDAR'S SHARE.

I.—PATTON'S PRINCIPLES OF ASIATIC MONARCHIES.

I have thought it necessary to transcribe these passages from the institutes both of Tamerlane and Akbar *verbatim*, that the reader may view the subject exactly as they represent it, from which I think it clearly appears that the *rent* of the land, in all the countries that have been mentioned, is engrossed by Government, and that the property of the land rests between the occupant, who is generally the husbandman or actual labourer of the soil, and the sovereign, all other persons who are mentioned as having any interference in these matters being officers of the Government; either collectors, overseers, or tax-gatherers (another name for collectors), who have the management of the revenues, or military officers of high rank, to whom they are assigned, from the motive, apparently, of combining two transactions into one, allotting the rents immediately for the payment of the troops.

II.—LAW AND CONSTITUTION OF INDIA.

The truth is, that between the sovereign and the rubb-ool-arz[1] (who is properly the cultivator) no one intervenes who is not a servant of the sovereign; and this servant recovers his hire, not out of the pro-

---

[1] *i. e.,* Lord of the land.

APP. V.

STATE'S DEMAND
INCLUDED THE
ZEMINDAR'S
SHARE.

Para. 3, contd.

Page 36.
Fifth Report.

duce of the lands over which he is placed, but from the public treasury, as is specially mentioned by every lawyer.

III.—Sir J. Shore, *June 1789 (para. 437)*.

The mode by which the demand of Government upon the zemindar was regulated, and that by which the rents of the ryots were collected, are different. Admitting that, in some instances, the ryots paid the taxes imposed by the nazims upon the zemindars, in the same proportions to the assul, and under the same denominations as the zemindars, this was by no means invariably the case : on the contrary, I hold the reverse generally to be true.

IV.—Mr. H. Colebrooke, *1808*.

Bengal Revenue
Selections,
Vol I.,
page 46.

Mr. Shore (now Lord Teignmouth) whose diligence of research and whose thorough knowledge of the revenues of Bengal are universally acknowledged and need not the tribute of praise, estimated no less than a third of the amount received from the cultivator for the charges of collection and intermediate profit between Government and the ryot. This estimate is quoted and confirmed as corresponding with the experience on the coast of Coromandel by the Board of Revenue at Fort Saint George, in the very able report of that Board, dated 2nd September 1799.

It was with the belief that a third part of the collections made from the cultivator were applicable to the charges of the collection, and the support of the zemindars, that the assessment in Bengal and on the coast of Coromandel was fixed for ever.

V.—Mr. Ravenscroft, *Collector of Cawnpore, 1st January 1816*.

Bengal Revenue
Selections,
Vol. III,
page 186.

It appears to be an established principle between the landlord and tenant of the present day, which has probably its origin in the exactions of former Governments, that the rents of land shall amount to half the estimated produce on an average of years, leaving the other half for the support of the husbandmen. The demand of the State, therefore, in rents, would seem to be fixed at this moiety, and is claimed from the landlord, after deducting fifteen per cent., which, from the rules of the territorial assessment, is conferred upon him as a remuneration for his risk and responsibility.

VI.—Mr. Phillips.

Tagore Law
Lectures,
pp. 185-6.

It now remains to ascertain the proportion of produce taken by the State as revenue in Muhammadan times. The Fifth Report puts the State proportion at three-fifths in fully settled land, leaving the cultivator two-fifths. Out of the three-fifths taken by the State, the zemindar and village officers had to be paid ; that is, the deduction had to be made for muzkoorat, including nankar, and amounting theoretically to one-tenth. These deductions, as already pointed out, were to meet the whole cost of collection.

4.—Proportion of the Government's share of the produce.

I.—Land-tax of the ancients—Briggs—

One-fifth.

(*a*)—Egypt.—The fact of the land-tax in Egypt being usually one-fifth of the produce is proved by the Romans finding it so when they occupied that country; and in this respect it differed from all other Roman provinces, which only paid one-tenth of the produce.

(*b*)—GREECE.—In this account we may perceive several important facts. First, that the cultivated land paid *one-tenth of the produce* to the State; secondly, that uncultivated lands were used in common as pasturage, but one-tenth of the grazing beasts were made over to the Government, which, in other words, was exacting *one-tenth of the produce* of common pasturages also.

(*c*)—ROMANS.—The portion of the crop demanded by the State was almost everywhere confined to *one-tenth of the produce*, and the grain was usually laid up in public magazines, and sold or distributed according to circumstances.

(*d*)—PERSIA.—At a period anterior to the Muhammadan conquest, the cultivator paid *one-tenth of his produce* to the State, and it will be subsequently shown that the *asherra* (or tenth) is the legitimate land-tax which exists in all Muhammadan countries at the present day.

(*e*)—CHINA.—The whole of the lands are measured, and not only the extent, but the average rate of produce of each field is inscribed on a public register. One-tenth of the crop is set aside for the State, and the remainder is divided between the cultivator and proprietor, according to agreement.

(*f*)—COCHIN-CHINA AND SIAM.—The amount of the land-tax is estimated at 4 per cent. of the gross produce, and it is paid by the cultivator, who shares equally with the landowner or proprietor the remainder of the crop. Crown lands, made over to be cultivated by villages, pay one-sixth, or about 17 per cent. of the gross produce, to Government.

(*g*)—BURMAN EMPIRE.—"The Government impost on cultivated land is only a *tenth part of the produce*, in consequence of which agriculture is carried on with great success, and in a very excellent style."

(*h*)—Hindus.—"Of grain an eighth part, a sixth, or a twelfth, according to the difference of the soil, and the labour necessary to cultivate it." * * The tax on the mercantile class, which in times of prosperity must only be a twelfth part of their crops, and a fiftieth part of their personal profits, may be an eighth of their crops in a time of distress, or a sixth, which is the medium; or even a fourth, in great public adversity.

In the time of Alexander "the cultivators in India contributed a fourth part of their crops to the sovereign; and as long as the husbandman continued to pay the Government dues, the land occupied by him descended from generation to generation like private property." The fourth part alluded to was the war tax, which Porus, and those Indian princes who opposed Alexander, had a right to levy according to the law.

Of the rate of taxation so general among the Hindus, it is curious to find a proof in the pages of a Mahomedan historian. One of the earliest acts of the first Mussulman King of Cashmere, in the year A. D. 1326, was " to confirm for ever the ancient land-tax, which amounted to seventeen per cent., or about one-sixth of the whole produce of the land."

APP. V.

GOVERNMENT'S
SHARE OF THE
PRODUCE.

Para. 4, contd.

One-tenth.

One-tenth.

Page 14.

One-tenth.

Pages 14-5.

One-tenth.

Pages 31, 32 & 34.

Pages 106-7.

II.—Hindu Government—

App. V.

GOVERNMENT'S
SHARE OF THE
PRODUCE-

Para. 4, contd.

Halhed, page
128.
Tagore Law
Lectures, page 5.
Ayeen Akbary,
page 299.

Harington's
Analysis, page 5.

a.—The Hindu system estimated the rates at a sixth or an eighth (or in times of prosperity one-twelfth) according to the quality of the soil and the expense and labour of tilling it; in extreme cases of urgent necessity a fourth might be demanded, but pending the existence of the necessity which legalises it.

b.—In former times, the monarchs of Hindustan exacted the sixth of the produce of the lands; in the Turkish Empire, the husbandman paid the fifth; in Turan, the sixth; and in Iran, the tenth. But at the same time there was levied a general poll-tax, which was called kheraj.

c.—The natives whom I have consulted on this point, affirm that the ancient rajahs exacted a sixth proportion of the produce of the lands, which the possessors were authorised to sell or alienate, subject to the sovereign's claim for rent (*Sir J. Shore, 2nd April 1788*).

III.—Mahomedan rule—

Law and
Constitution of
India.
Page 97.

Half produce
the maximum.
Page 98.

(*a*).—By the Mahomedan revenue laws, a distinction is made between the Moslem and the non-Moslem or *Zimmee*, to which it is necessary to attend. This distinction, however, is applicable only to the land of *Arabia Proper*, and to conquered provinces when the lands are divided among the conquerors. There the Moslem pays the *ooshr* or tithe of his crop; the *Zimmee* the heavier impost of *khurauj*, which by law may amount to, but cannot exceed, half the produce, *i. e.*, five tithes. But, on the other hand, the Moslem is liable to several annual and occasional taxes from which the *Zimmee* is exempt, amounting to about two or three per cent. of his property (not of his produce merely) under the name of *sudukah* and *zukaut*, or pious benevolences.

Ibid.

2. The whole land of India, however, is *khiraujee* land, and by law the *ooshr* and *khurauj* cannot both be exacted from the same land; consequently, in India the land revenue payable by a *Moslem* and a *Zimmee* by law would be the same, and so *de facto* it was.

Page 62.

By the institutes of Timour, "the *khurauj* is to be settled according to the produce of the *cultivated* land. The lands irrigated by water constantly flowing should pay one-third, if only by rain water, therefore uncertain, to pay one-third or one-fourth. The land should be measured and divided into three classes, an average taken, and to pay so much."

Page 100.

4. The *khurauj* was fixed in two ways: one on the principle of a share in the produce, as a half (the highest), or a third, or a fifth; the last considered as the lowest extreme. This settlement was termed

Mookausumah.

mookausumah, from *kismut*, division, *i. e.*, the cultivator dividing the produce with the State. The principle of this settlement, therefore, is similar to tithing, the rate only is higher; and in this settlement, if there was no cultivation, there was no collection.

Page 100-1.

5. The other mode of fixing the *khurauj* (which was the radical mode, so that if the word *khurauj* simply is used, it is held to mean this mode of settlement) had reference to the quantity of cultivated land possessed, and the kind of crop produced. The rate of khurauj was

Mookatuaah or
Wuzeefah.
(Baillie's land
tax.)

fixed for the different kinds of crop the land was capable of producing. The land was measured, and each *jureeb* (or, as it is called in India, beegah) of sixty squares of nearly yards, if it produced wheat, paid a measure of wheat and a dirhum in money. Other dry crops paid also in kind and in money per jureeb; but all green and perishable crops paid in money only. This mode of settlement was called *mookautuah* from *kutoa* to cut or settle definitely. Thus certain lands produce a certain crop. The quantity of the land is known by measurement; the rate is fixed; consequently the quantum of revenue is fixed. By the former, or *mookasumeh* settlement, the quantity of revenue was not fixed, but depended on the harvest and on the cultivation. The *khurauj* was leviable under the *mookautuah* settlement, whether the owner cultivated or not; provided he was not prevented from doing so by some inevitable calamity as inundation, blast, blight; or if he was deprived of his field by force, he was not liable.

6. It appears that before the time of Shere Khan, the *mookausumah* settlement prevailed in Hindustan. The *Ayeen Akbari* says: "Sher Khan and Selim Khan, who abolished the custom of dividing the crop and measurement of the cultivated lands, used this *guz*" of thirty-two fingers. And Akbar seems to have restored the *mookhausumah* settlement, with conversion into money of the Government share, in some of the provinces. Of the fifteen soubahs which composed his empire, *ten* were measured. The remaining *five* soubahs were not measured; but the revenue was settled by *nussuk* or computation, and valuation of the crop before the harvest, and was paid in money. This was the custom in Bengal.

7. The soubahs not measured were Cashmere or Cabul, Tatta, Berar, Khandeish, and Bengal; those measured were Behar (part at least), Allahabad, Oudh, Agra, Malwah, Guzerat, Ajmeer, Delhi, Lahore, and Mooltan. The measurement of the cultivated lands thus made, and the ascertainment of the average produce of a beegah, were the data on which the assessment was formed. One-third of the average produce was fixed as the revenue, but in case of inundation, or other unavoidable calamity, the impost was less for the first four years following it. On the above basis, taking the average of ten years, Akbar made a decennial *mookatuah*, or permanent rate settlement, which is stated to have given great satisfaction to the people. It was done under the superintendence of Rajah Tudar Mull and Muzaffur Khan. It is the settlement so often alluded to by writers on this question, and the amount is known by the name of the *ussul toomar jummah*, established A. D. 1582.

8. The Mahomedan law, as I have observed, allows the khurauj to be levied as high as one-half. Some lawyers say, as much shall be left to the husbandman as will maintain his family, servants, and cattle till next crop, and all the remainder shall go to the crown; but one-fifth of the produce is deemed the equitable and commendable portion, being double the *oosher* or double tithe. The *Ayeen Akbaree* says, "former rulers of Hindustan took one-sixth, but then they imposed a variety of other imposts, equal to the whole quit-rent of Hindustan, which Akbar abolished; among these, the capitation tax."

(b). BAILLIE ON THE LAND-TAX OF INDIA—

1. The khiraj imposed by the Khaleef Omar on the Sowad of Irak, Page xv. (that is, the *wazeefah khiraj*, in all countries of *khirajee* land, such as

APP. V.
———
GOVERNMENT'S
SHARE OF THE
PRODUCE.
———
Para. 4, III,
contd.

India) seems to have been founded on an assumed equality in the capabilities of the soil, and to have been regulated solely by the degree of labour required for obtaining its measure, of which the different kinds of produce were taken as the tests or criteria, thus (1) on a *jureeb* or area of 60 by 60 jiras of grain, the rate imposed being partly in kind and partly in money, was a *kufeez* and a *dirhem*. (2) On the same extent of vegetables or plants whose roots remain in the ground for several years, the rate imposed was five *dirhems* in money: and on a similar quantity of land planted with vine and date trees, which are calculated to endure for many years, the rate imposed was ten *dirhems*. It does not appear that at the time when Omar made his assessment there were any other kinds of produce than the three descriptions above mentioned. But (4) saffron is particularly specified in the *Hidayat* and other authorities as not being included; and gardens or pleasure grounds, where the fruit trees are too widely dispersed to allow of their being classed with vineyards or date orchards, are also noticed as being different from any of the descriptions mentioned. In cases of this kind, which may be considered as omissions from the *wazeefa* of Omar, and beyond the authority of his example, a *khiraj*, which is some proportionate share of the produce, as a fourth or a fifth, was imposed. This, as seems, was the origin of the *mookassimah khiraj*.

Prge XVI.

2. The rate of the *mookassimah* is left within a certain limit to the discretion of the Imam, and may be any part of the produce that the land will bear, not exceeding the half, which is considered the extreme capability. The *wazeefa* is restricted to the rates established by Omar. No higher rate could lawfully be imposed, in the first instance, by any of his successors, on whom it appears that his example was imperative. Nor can a rate once imposed be afterwards lawfully increased without the consent of the people, except perhaps in one case, which seems to be of rather doubtful authority; nor a *wazeefa* changed to a *mookassimah* nor a *mookassimah* to a *wazeefa* without their consent.

Page XVII.

3. The *wazeefa* was calculated in three rates, which, according to the *Inayah*, were a maximum or *minimum*, and something intermediate. If we suppose, as seems probable, that the last was a geometric mean between the two others, the *minimum* would be $2\frac{1}{2}$ *dirhems* as the value of a *kufeez* and *dirhem*, or the *wuzeefa* on a *jureeb* of arable land. Ten *dirhems* in the time of Aurungzebe were equivalent to $2\frac{3}{4}$ rupees; and, on the authority of the *Ayeen Akbery*, a *jureeb* is the Indian beegah, of which about three are equal to an English acre. So that the *wuzeefa* on arable land, assuming it at $2\frac{1}{2}$ *dirhems*, would be about 11 annas the beegah, or taking the sicca rupee at 2*s.* 6*d.*, which is the highest exchange it has borne for any length of time, and is probably a good deal more than its intrinsic value, about 5*s.* the English acre.

Pages XVI and XVII.

4. The *wuzeefa*, as already observed, was calculated on an assumed equality of soils. But this can be assumed only under equal facilities in relation to water. In many countries of the East rain seldom falls, and little dependence can be placed on a constant supply of water where land is beyond the influence of the great rivers, or canals connected with them. In such circumstances, a *wuzeefa* after the rates of Omar, or any *wuzeefa*, that is, any fixed rate calculated on the capability of the soil, would be impossible. If imposed, it could not be borne, and the people,

App. V.
———
GOVERNMENT'S
SHARE OF THE
PRODUCE.
Para. 4, III,
contd.

rather than submit to it, would abandon their lands. For such circum-stances the *mookassima* is well adapted, as its rate admits of adjustment to the varying fertility of the soil, and is due only out of actual produce. For these reasons it is probable that in extensive countries, like Persia and India, where there are great varieties of soil, a *khiraj* of the *mookassima* kind was largely imposed on all but the alluvial lands within the influence of the large rivers. On these the *khiraj* would more properly be the *wuzeefa*. The *wuzeefa* was at first no doubt more onerous in its amount, as well as in other respects, than the *mookassima*, but its amount being fixed, while that of the *mookassima* was liable to increase up to a half of the produce, improvements in agriculture and a diminution in the value of money would gradually alter the relations of each to the other, until at length the *wuzeefa* would become less burden-some than the *mookassima*. The *wuzeefa* would thus admit of the gradual rise of a class of proprietors between the Government and the mere culti-vators. Under the *mookassima*, the proprietors would more likely be kept down by successive increases of the rate of *khiraj* to the condition of cultivators.

5. The greatest difference between the systems of Omar and Akbar was in the rate; but here the difference was more apparent than real; for though the rate of Omar varied according to three different kinds of produce, and the rate fixed by Akbar was the same for all produce, yet the different kinds specified by Akbar, though so many as eleven are mentioned for the spring harvest, and nineteen for the autumn, are all comprised within the first class of Omar; his other two classes, *viz.*, *rootbut* and *kirm* (or vegetables and vineyards) being entirely omitted by Akbar, probably because they were not required in the state of agricul-ture in India. The rate fixed by Omar on all articles falling within his first class was a *kufeez*, by measure, of the article itself, whatever it might be, and a *dirhem* in money; but it may be presumed that this rate was not fixed arbitrarily, but bore some ratio to the average produce of the land. The rate fixed by Akbar was a third part of the average produce of each article on land of average quality; and he took great pains to ascertain this average correctly. This rate may have been somewhat higher that that of Omar, for it is probable that it comprehended some compensa-tion for the *jizyut*, or poll tax, which, with many other vexatious exactions, were remitted by Akbar. The rate being thus fixed was commuted into money at the average prices of nineteen years; and it was left to the option of the cultivator to pay in kind or in money, that is, the fixed average third of the particular produce or its fixed average price. In all this there is not a trace of the *mookassima*; the *khiraj* was wholly *wuzeefa*. The settlement was made for ten years. Whether it was con-tinued beyond this period, or how far it entered into the arrangements of his successors, I am unable to say. As the *jizyut* was soon reverted to (though not by Akbar), it would probably be found too high.

(c). MR. PHILLIPS—*Tagore Law Lectures, 1874-75.*

The *wuzeefa khiraj* depending upon the capability of the soil, and Page 46. being independent of its actual cultivation, closely resembled in these respects the tax paid by the khodkhasts under the Hindu system.

App. V.

GOVERNMENT'S
SHARE OF THE
PRODUCE.

Para. 4, III,
contd.

Page 16.

(a). FIFTH REPORT, COMMITTEE.

The rule for fixing the Government share of the crop is traceable, as a general principle, through every part of the empire which has yet come under the British dominion, and undoubtedly had its origin in times anterior to the entry of the Mahomedans into India. By this rule, the produce of the land, whether taken in kind or estimated in money, was understood to be shared in distinct proportions between the cultivator and the Government. The shares varied when the land was recently cleared and required extraordinary labour; but when it was fully settled and productive, the cultivator had about two-fifths, and the Government the remainder. The Government share was again divided with the zemindars and village officers, &c.

(e). FIFTH REPORT, APPENDICES.

(1). As the rights of sovereignty were originally established at one-fourth of the gross produce of the land shared with the ryots; did from the beginning, do actually, and must ever, from necessity or policy, continue to be rated formally at the same equitable standard, it appears highly expedient for Government to realize its pretensions virtually, to such proportion (*Grant's Analysis of the finances of Bengal*).

2. SIR J. SHORE, *June 1789.*

I assume as facts, the ryots to pay in a proportion of one-half of the gross produce of their lands : the charges of collection, *viz.*, those only paid by the zemindars, farmers and other gradations of landholders and renters, to be 15 per cent. on this amount: and the intermediate profits between the Government and the ryots to be 35 per cent. more (paragraph 109).

3. IBID (*Same Minute*).

I believe that the ryots in Bengal are generally taxed in a proportion of one-half [1] the produce of their labour; and we must therefore admit that the assessment with respect to them is fully as much as it ought to be supposing it to be even one-third (paragraph 145).

4. *Same Minute.*

By the institutes of Akbar, we are informed that when, from motives of justice and humanity, the emperor ordered a settlement of the country to be made for ten years, he began by directing a measurement of the lands, and by fixing the rates of them, according to their qualities and produce. The proportion which he claimed for the State was one-third of the medium produce (paragraph 217).

Eventually, however, Akbar abandoned an assessment based on a fixed proportion of the produce, and substituted a revised assessment, based on actual collections: see this section, III*k*.

---

[1] *i. e.*, including the 15 per cent. for charges of collection, section 2, above.

App. V.

GOVERNMENT'S
SHARE OF THE
PRODUCE.

Para. 4, III,
contd.

5. Sir J. Shore, *Minute 8th December 1789.*

The proportion paid by the cultivators of the soil may be reckoned at a half, or it may be nearer perhaps to three-fifths of the gross produce. Taking this at 100 parts, the claims of the Government may be estimated at 45. The zemindars and under-renters may be supposed to have 15, and 40 remains with the cultivators of the soil. In the two last classes some enjoy considerably more than the assigned proportion : others, again, less.

Sir T. Munro, *15th August 1807.*

6. The assessment of Akbar is estimated by Abul Fazil at one-third, and by other authorities at one-fourth of the gross produce ; but it was undoubtedly higher than either of these rates, for had it not been so, enough would have remained to the ryot, after defraying all expenses, to render the land private property; and as this did not take place, we may be certain that the nominal one-third or one-fourth was nearly one-half. This seems to have been the opinion of Aurungzebe, for he directs that not more than one-half of the crop shall be taken from the ryot ; that where the crop has suffered injury, such remission shall be made as may leave him one-half of what the crop might have been ; and that when one ryot dies and another occupies his land, the rent should be reduced if more than one-half of the produce, and raised if less than a third. It is evident, therefore, that Aurungzebe thought that one-half was in general enough for the ryot, and that he ought in no case to have above two-thirds. The mode of assessment in the Ceded Districts and in the Deccan still limits the share of the ryots to those proportions, but makes it commonly much nearer to one-half than two-thirds of the produce. * * As, therefore, one-third of the produce is the highest point to which assessment can in general be carried without destroying private landed property, and as it is also the point to which it must be lowered before persons who are not cultivators can occupy circar land without loss, it is obvious that, unless the assessment is reduced to this rate, land can neither be occupied by all classes of the inhabitants, nor ever become private property. I am therefore of opinion that in a permanent settlement of the Ceded Districts, the rent of Government should be about one-third of the gross produce. The present assessment is about 45 per cent.

(*f*). *Tagore Law Lectures, 1874-75.*

Pages 195-96.

Sir George Campbell says, the State, before British rule, took from one-fourth to one-half of the gross produce, one-third and two-fifths being the most common proportions. The Fifth Report puts the State proportion at three-fifths in fully settled land, leaving the cultivator two-fifths. Out of the three-fifths taken by the State, the zemindar and village officers had to be paid, that is, the deduction had to be made for muzkoorat, including nankar, and amounting theoretically to one-tenth. These deductions, as already pointed out, were to meet the whole cost of collection. Mr. Shore gives two different opinions : his earlier opinion is that Government took one-third ; but his later opinion puts the Government share at from one-half to three-fifths.

App. V.
———
GOVERNMENT'S
SHARE OF THE
PRODUCE.

Para. 4, III,
contd.
Revenue
Selections,
1826,.
Volume III,
page 216.

Mr. Elphinstone says that one-third is a moderate assessment, and that the full share is one-half. Mr. Grant says the proportion taken was one-fourth, which he considers moderate.

(*g*). According to the rules of the territorial assessment decreed by Akbar, the two kinds of land called *poolj* (cultivated) and *parowly* (fallow) were thrown into three classes, *viz.*, best, middling, and bad. The produce of a beegah of each sort was added together, and a third of the aggregate sum taken as the medium produce of a beegah of cultivated or *poolj* land, one-third part of which was the revenue settled by that emperor. Previously to this period, Noorsherwan, who, for the purpose of ascertaining an equitable fixed revenue, made a measurement of all the arable land in his empire, determined that the third of the produce of a land measure of sixty square kissery guz or yards should be the proportion of revenue.

(*h*). MR. STUART'S MINUTE, *18th December 1830.*

Ibid., page 217.

I apprehend that the principle of levying upon the gross produce is often corrected by varying the rate according to the descriptions of land and cultivation, and that it does not extend to the more artificial and costly kinds of culture, a fixed monied payment upon which almost invariably obtains.

(*i*). MR. J. MILL, *9th August 1831.*

3rd Report,
Select Com-
mittee, 1831.

Q. 3438.—Is it not the fact that throughout that part of India where the land revenue is variable, it is commonly assumed that one-half of the gross produce is taken from the ryot, and that the greater proportion of that, namely, about 35 per cent. of it, is assumed as the share of Government?—Certainly not.

Q. 3439.—Is it not so under the Madras Presidency?—At Madras the sort of rule assumed by Sir Thomas Munro, and I should say erroneously, was, that one-third of the produce might generally be demanded by Government.

Q. 3440.—Was not that upon a very high assessment?—He overestimated the productive power of the soil, and upon a revision, directed that 25 per cent. should be diminished from it.

Q. 3441.—Was his original estimate in any case realised?—I should not say that it was in no case realised; I believe it was realised to a considerable degree for some years, but with a deterioration of the country.

Q. 3442.—Was the reduction made that he proposed?—It was; and even additional reductions in many cases have been found necessary, and have been directed.

(*j*). MR. H. STARK (*Chief of the Revenue Department in the India Board, 14th February 1832*).

Sessions,
1831-32, Vol. XI.

Q. 225.—The Committee have been informed that at the original settlement in 1793, it was regulated that the value of one-half the gross produce of the land should be reserved to the Government, and the other half reserved to the ryot, a portion of one-tenth only for the zemindar; if that distribution was correctly made at the time of the original settlement taking place, in what way can so large an increase of value have arisen as to enable those intermediate holders to grow up? —I am of opinion that the calculations that the Committee have received of the divisions of crops, as between the Government and the cultivators before 1793, are mere estimates. There was never, I believe, in Bengal, any actual division of crops between the ryots and Government; but the supposed quantity belonging to Government was thrown into money, and that was the assessment upon the village. The cultivators were decidedly interested in keeping the Government share as low as they possibly could ; and if the village officer and the cultivators succeeded in deceiving the European and native collectors employed in settling the revenue, the money-payment would not amount probably to a third of the produce. In some districts of the Madras territories, where they realise the revenue very much in that way still, by what is termed an *amauny* division of the crops, the complaint of the collectors is, that they are deceived by their native officers, who combine with the ryots in deceiving the Government. Of course, if a ryot gains 20 per cent. by bribing the *amauny* officers, he may reserve a clear gain of 15 per cent. to himself.

Q. 226.—Is it your opinion that those were very much undervalued ? —Yes.

Q. 227.—And that the amount reserved to the zemindar was never so much as it ought to have been?—It could not have amounted to half the crop as a general rate.

(*k*). Briggs.

(1). When his majesty (Akbar) had settled the length of the *guz* (standard rod), and the *tincul* (the chain), and the dimensions of the *beegah* (superficies), he classed the lands, and fixed a different tax on each, viz.,—

> *Pooluj* is that land which never lies fallow for a whole season.
> *Pirowty* is that land which is allowed to lie fallow to recover itself after exhaustion.
> *Chechur* is that land which has lain fallow for two or three years.
> *Bunjar* is land that has been left uncultivated for five or more years.
> *Pooluj* and *pirowty* lands are of three sorts, *viz.*, best, middling, and worst. They add together a beegah of each sort, and a third of that aggregate is assumed as the average produce, one-third part of which is the revenue settled by his majesty. *Pirowty* land, when cultivated, pays the same revenue as *pooluj*.

The estimate is made in kind, and Akbar particularly enjoins his revenue officers to receive the produce itself, if the husbandman objects to the commutation price.

(2). At a very early period, after Akbar's decennial settlement, his scheme to assess fields was discovered, in practice, to be full of embarrassment ; and, before his measurements even were completed, he was reduced to the necessity of assessing whole villages, and leaving it to the people themselves to distribute the portion payable by individuals.

This is one of the most instructive lessons we could have of the extreme difficulty of assessing land in any portion which approaches to the full profit of the landlord. The actual measurement, and the

App. V.

Government's share of the produce.

Para. 4, III, contd.

Page 126-7.

App. V.
————
Government's
share of the
produce.

Para. 4, III,
contd.
Page 122-3.

nominal assessments of Akbar, exist at the present day in the village records of those countries wherein they were introduced; but they may be deemed rather objects of curiosity than of utility. The village assessment of Akbar was adopted by his son Jehangier, and his grandson Shahjehan; and the European travellers who visited India in those days speak of the extraordinary prosperity and wealth of the country.

Aurungzebe abandoned the plan of Akbar, and reverted to that system, which has been before explained, in the times of Alla-oodden Khiljy, where the king claimed an equal division of the crop with the cultivator, as is related by Khafia Khan, a contemporary historian. This practice, however, was by no means universal; the proportion varied according to the nature of the land and of the crops. Thus, sugarcane, opium, ginger, and whatsoever produce required the extra labour of watering from wells, only paid one-fourth, if paid in specie; and one-third, if received in kind;—more expensive crops than these paid only one-eighth of the produce.

(3). Mr. Grant, in his history of the Northern Circars, "distinctly states that in the reign of Akbar there was a definite limit to the land-tax imposed in Delhi, Agra, Guzerat, Malwa and Behar, which he asserts was one-third of the produce payable in kind, but if converted into money, was to be received at one-fourth of the average market price. This law was instituted, as we have seen, in the latter end of the sixteenth century, and we perceive it is exactly double that which the Hindu law (according to the Ayeen Akbarry) and the institutes of Menu authorised to be taken."

(*l*). COLEBROOKE : HUSBANDRY OF BENGAL.

(1). In the rule for dividing the crop, whether under special engagements, or by custom, three proportions are known :—

Half for the landlord.	Half for the tenant.
One-third ditto.	Two-thirds ditto.
Two-fifths ditto.	Three-fifths ditto.

These rates, and others less common, are all subject to taxes and deductions similar to those of other tenures; and, in consequence, another proportion, engrafted on equal partition, has in some places been fixed by Government in lieu of all taxes, such, for example, as nine-sixteenths for the landlord and seven-sixteenths for the husbandman.

(2). Under Akbar, the revenue was settled at a third of the produce of lands cultivated for every harvest, or opened after allowing a short lay, in order that the soil might recover its strength; but for older fallows, much less was required. For example, if the land had been untilled during three or four years and was greatly injured, the payment in the first year was two-fifths of the standard, or two-fifteenths of the produce; in the second year three fifths of the standard; in the third and fourth years four-fifths; and in the fifth year the same rate as for land regularly cultivated. The rent of ground which had been waste was in the first and second years inconsiderable; in the third year, a sixth of the produce; in the fourth year a quarter of it; and, after that period, the same as for the land which had been regularly cultivated. These rates were applicable to corn only. Indigo, poppy, &c., were paid for in ready money, at proportionate rates. *Vide* Ayeen Akbarry, vol. I, pages 356, 361 and 364.

APP. V.
————
GOVERNMENT'S
SHARE OF THE
PRODUCE.

(*m*). MR. R. D. MANGLES, *31st March 1848.*

Para. 5.
Sessions,
1847-8, Vol. 9.

In the provinces not permanently settled, the Government takes from 65 to 75 per cent. of the rental which the landlord gets from his tenants (Q 3331-2).

(*n*). SESSIONS, 1857, VOL. 29.

The rate of land tax in Bengal cannot be given, but it is believed to amount on the average to about half the rental. In the North-Western Provinces, the tax is half the average net assets, *i. e.*, of the surplus, after deducting the expenses of cultivation, including the profits of stock and wages of labour.

5. The Government's fixed proportion is a maximum, and is nominal.

I. HARINGTON'S ANALYSIS OF THE REGULATIONS.

It may, however, be proper to advert to a custom subsisting in Jessore, *viz.*, that the nominal rate of land is three rupees per beegah, but that the real rate is only one, as the ryots possess fifteen beegahs where their pottahs state five only, and upon the last quantity, the assessment of three rupees for each is made.

II. MR. J. MILL, *9th August 1831.*

Q. 3444.—Can you point out the part of India in which, in your apprehension, a larger amount is taken from the cultivator than that which he is able, with comfort, to pay? It is not easy to answer that question in regard to any large portions of the country; in the same district, and under the same collector, more than the rent may be taken in one case, and less in another, anything like accuracy on the point we have no means of attaining, and one source of deception, and that a very natural one, to the collectors, in estimating the lands, is this, that in many villages they found the lands rated at a certain amount, that in those cases it was paid, and without difficulty or complaints. This was assumed for the different classes of land as a species of standard, and all the land was rated at this standard; but in reality it was too high, and the ryots had been enabled to pay so high a rate only by having a considerable portion of land, in addition to what they paid for, concealed, and never brought to account. Our vigilance being much greater than that of the government which went before us, a much smaller quantity of this concealed land was allowed to remain unassessed, and by this operation of detecting the unassessed land, and going upon the old rates, the assessment, it was found after a certain time, was too high; but the moment it was so discovered, a remission took place.

Q. 3445.—Of what part of the country are you now speaking? This has happened in all parts of the country not permanently settled.

6. In England a proprietor of land who farms it out to another is generally supposed to receive as rent a value equal to about one-third of the gross produce; this proportion will vary in different countries according to circumstances.—(*Wilks' Mysore, page 109.*)

6. Summing up the salient points brought out in this Appendix, it appears that—

Under the law and constitution of India the right of the sovereign was limited to a share of the produce of the soil. The sovereign—that is, the State—was not the proprietor of the land.

II. Among the ancients, the State's demand on the land was fixed, and its share of the gross produce varied from one-tenth to one-fifth. In India, after the Mahomedan conquest, the State's share was in a higher proportion, but still the ordinary demand was fixed.

III. It was fixed at a certain proportion of the produce, varying with the kind of produce; and it was greater when the State's share was taken in kind than when it was taken in money. Its incidence was further moderated by the cultivator's occupancy of more land than the area on which assessment was paid.

IV. The proportion forming the State's share included the zemindar's allowance from the State, and it was a maximum, below which it varied in different districts according to custom, but on principles which were so well understood, that the cultivators could readily tell the proper assessment for a particular field.

V. The State's share (which included the zemindar's share) of the produce of the land being thus fixed, even under native rule, the remainder of the produce did not belong to Government, who, accordingly, had not the power to give it away to the zemindar. The amiable and benevolent authors of the permanent settlement did not contemplate spoliation of the property of millions of ryots, but merely the giving away of what belonged to the Government; on the contrary, they contemplated the fixing of the demand upon the ryot as permanently as the Government's demand upon the zemindar (para. 2, sections VIII and XI). Accordingly, the transfer by the Government to the zemindar of property in its share of the produce did not confer on the zemindar any property in the ryot's share, which was outside the Government's fixed proportion of the produce.

VI. Besides the fixed ordinary demand thus ascertained, the cultivators were subject to payment of *abwabs*, or temporary cesses, which, in theory, were leviable only on the pretext of extraordinary expenses or emergencies of the State. These *abwabs*, thus, were of the nature of State taxes,

not of cesses, such as a private landed proprietor might exact
on a strained interpretation of rights, or by an arbitrary
exercise of power. Accordingly the Government, in transferring to the zemindar its fixed share of the produce, prohibited, in the proclamation of the permanent settlement, the
levy of fresh *abwabs* by the zemindar.

VII. The original assessment of Akbar broke down
because he had based it on a fixed proportion of the produce.
His revised assessment, or that of Toodur Mull, was based on
actual collections, which were distributed, downwards, to
pergunnahs, villages, and holdings, thus furnishing a fixed
amount of assessment in money, which was not liable to
increase from a rise of prices. In the subsequent revision
of assessment the increase on the previous demand was from
an increase of cultivation, not of rates of rent (para. 2,
sections VIII and IX).

APPENDIX VI.

ZEMINDARS BEFORE THE PERMANENT SETTLEMENT.

I.—LAW AND CONSTITUTION OF INDIA.

The word *zemindar*, generally rendered *landholder*, is a relative and indefinite term; and does no more necessarily signify an owner of land than the word *poddar* signifies an owner of money under his charge; or an *aubdar*, the proprietor of the water he serves up to his master; or a *soobadar*, the owner of the province he governs, or, in military language, the owner of the company of sepoys he belongs to; or *kellaadar*, the proprietor of the fort he defends; or *thanodar*, the owner of the police post he has charge of. On the contrary, I might venture to assert that the affix *dar*, according to the idiom of the Persian language, has more of a *temporary* meaning; it imports more an official or professional connexion between the person and thing connected, than a real right in the former to the latter; as *foujdar*, though the *fouj*, or troops, are the king's; *tehseeldar*, though the rents collected belong to the Government; *amildar*, though he acts for Government; *beldar*, *tubldar*, though the *spade* or *axe* is the property of the master. I say the word *zemindar* imports nothing more, *necessarily*, than that a relation exists between the *person* and the *zumeen*, or land. What that relation is, forms part of the subject to be discussed.

II.—SELECT COMMITTEE, *1812.*

(*a*). The duty of the zemindar, as declared in his sunnud of appointment, was to superintend that portion of country committed to his charge, to do justice to the ryots or peasants, to furnish them with the necessary advances for cultivation, and to collect the rent of Government; and, as a compensation for the discharge of this duty, he enjoyed, as did the zemindars of Bengal, certain allotments of land rent-free, termed *saverum*, which were conveniently dispersed [1] through the district, so as to make his presence necessary everywhere, in order to give the greater effect to his superintendence.

(*b*). He was also entitled to receive certain *russooms*, or fees on the crops, and other perquisites, drawn from the sayer or customs, and from the quit-rents of houses. These personal or rather official lands and perquisites, amounted altogether to about ten per cent. on the collections he made in his district or zemindary.

---

[1] This convenient dispersion of the zemindary lands through the district denotes the encroachment by the zemindar on, or his appropriation of, the lands of the village headmen or mocuddums.

App. VI.

THE ZEMINDAR WAS AN OFFICE.

Para. 2.

(*c*). The office itself was to be traced as far back as the time of the Hindu rajahs. It originally went by the name of *chowdrie*, which was changed by the Mahomedans for that of *crorie*, in consequence of an arrangement by which the land was so divided among the collectors, that each had the charge of a portion of country yielding about a crore of *dams*, or two and a half lakhs of rupees. It was not until a late period of the Mahomedan Government that the term *crorie* was superseded by that of *zemindar*, which, literally signifying a possessor[1] of land, gave a colour to that misconstruction of their tenure which assigned to them an hereditary right to the soil.

2. That the zemindar's was an office, and not a property in all the land in the zemindary, is illustrated by various incidents of the title, or in the treatment, of the zemindars. Thus—

I.—LIABILITY TO DISMISSAL.

Colebrooke's Supplement, page 190.

(*a*). In the *proclamation, dated 11th May 1772*, by which the Court of Directors—

" divested the Nabob Mahomed Rezah Khan of his station of Naib Dewan, and determined to stand forth publicly themselves in the character of Dewan,"

a list was published—

" of the several branches of business appertaining to the Dewance,"

and the seventh item in the list was—

" the constitution and dismissing of zemindars, with the concurrence of the Nazim."

(*b*). PATTON'S ASIATIC MONARCHIES.

Pages 167 and 54.

The removal of the whole of the zemindars in Bengal from their offices, by JAFFIR KHAN, the subadar, under the government of *Aurungzebe*, when all the powers of the empire were in their vigour, and when, of course, the sanction of Government attended the measure, is at once the most ample confirmation. That this removal was conformable to the rules laid down by that Emperor, appears from another firmaun which he issued, preserved in the *Remayat Aleemgeri*, which is considered as authentic. (Here follows an extract enjoining that if an " *aumeen, aumil, chowdry* (the same as *zemindar*), or *canoongoe* " be guilty of exactions, " and should not be restrained by punishment and coercive measures, write an account hereof to our presence, that he may be *dismissed from his office, and another* appointed in his room;" and again in the 12th article, " if any *ameen, crory* or *pottadar* * * acts contrariwise, intimate the particulars to our presence, that he may be discharged from his office, called to an account, and meet with the punishment due to his merits."

---

[1] Holder; the holder, unlike an owner, can hold for another.

APP. VI. II.—EXCLUSION OF INCOMPETENT ZEMINDARS—

THE ZEMINDARY
WAS AN OFFICE.

Para. 2, contd.
Fifth Report,
page 200, paras.
315 and 319.

(a). SIR J. SHORE, *June 1789.*

It was observed at the time of this reference that the orders of the Court
of Directors prescribed that the settlement should in all practicable instances
be made with the zemindars; but that as many of them are disqualified
from any real interference in the management of the collections, from
incapacity on account of *age, sex,* minority, lunacy, *contumacy,* or *notorious*
profligacy of character, there should, in such cases, be appointed a near
and respectable relative by way of guardian or dewan, before any temporary farmer or servant of Government.

III.—DISQUALIFIED TO TRANSFER OR SELL WITHOUT THE SANCTION OF GOVERNMENT.

(a). COURT OF DIRECTORS, *12th April 1786, para. 33.*

Select Commit-
tee, 1810, Appen-
dix No. 12.

Besides, if the policy of all nations has circumscribed within cautious limits the transfer of all landed property, it is far more necessary
to do so in Bengal, where so large a proportion of the land rents has
always appertained to the sovereign, and where, under the most liberal
construction of a zemindary title, no alienation could be valid unless
it were recognised and ratified by a new grant of the sovereign or his
viceroy.

(b). LORD CORNWALLIS, *3rd February 1820.*

Fifth Report,
page 485.

To keep them in a state of tutelage, and to prohibit them from
borrowing money, or disposing of their lands, without the knowledge
of Government, as we do at present, with a view to prevent them from
suffering the consequences of their profligacy and incapacity, will perpetuate these defects.

IV.—THE LARGENESS OF ZEMINDARIES WAS A DISPROOF OF PROPRIETARY RIGHT.

(a). COURT OF DIRECTORS, *19th September 1792, para. 26.*

Select Commit-
tee, 1810,'Appen-
dix No. 12.

Indeed, the facility with which annexations appear to have been made
to zemindaries, and the magnitude to which some of these have been
swelled, even by the originating acts of the Native Government itself,
must be admitted to furnish some presumptive argument against the
notion of strict proprietary title. In those annexations there seems to
have been always implied the existence of a despotic principle, which
left everything subject to new modification at its pleasure; and on
this account the circumstance, which probably gave rise to these extensive possessions, made them less an object of jealousy to Government.
But under the Company's Government the case has been different. The
impolicy of these extensive territorial possessions and jurisdictions, even
in the loose form in which they have hitherto been held, has not passed
unnoticed.

(b). WARREN HASTINGS' REVIEW OF THE STATE OF BENGAL, 1786. APP. VI.

The public in England have of late years adopted very high ideas of THE ZEMINDARY WAS AN OFFICE.
the rights of zemindars in Hindustan; and the prevailing prejudice
has considered every occasional dispossession of a zemindar from the Para. 2, contd.
management of his lands as an act of oppression. I mean not here to
enter into any discussion of their rights, or to distinguish between right,
fact, and form as applied to their situation. Our Government, on
grounds which more minute scrutiny may, perhaps, find at variance with
facts, has admitted the opinion of their rightful proprietorship of the
lands. I do not mean to contest their right of inheritance to the lands,
whilst I assert the right of Government to the produce thereof. The
Mahomedan rulers continually exercised, with a severity unknown
to the British administration in Bengal, the power of dispossessing
the zemindars on any failure in the payment of their rents, not only
pro tempore, but in perpetuity. The fact is notorious; but lest proof
of it should be required, I shall select one instance out of many that
might be produced; and only mention that the zemindary of Rajshahye,
the second in rank in Bengal, and yielding an annual revenue of about
25 lakhs of rupees, has risen to its present magnitude during the course
of the last eighty years, by accumulating the property of a great number
of dispossessed zemindars; although the ancestors of the present possessor had not, by inheritance, a right to the property of a single village
within the whole zemindary.

(c). LAW AND CONSTITUTION OF INDIA, 1825.

(1). It is beyond doubt a fact, and a matter of undoubted history, Pages 51 to 53.
that, at a comparatively late period, there was no such thing as a great
zemindar, either in Bengal or Behar. " It is not," says the author
of the *Ayeen Akbaree*, " customary, in the soobah of Bengal, for the
husbandman and Government to divide the crop. The produce of the
lands is determined by *nussuk*; that is, by estimate of the crop. The
ryots (husbandmen) in the soobah of Bengal are very obedient to
Government, and pay their annual rents in eight months, by instalments, themselves bringing mohurs and rupees to the places appointed
for the receipt of the revenue." And of Behar the same author says:
" It is not customary in Behar to divide the crop. The husbandman
brings the rent himself, and when he makes his first payment, comes
dressed in his best attire."

(2). The date of this authentic record is little more than two hundred years ago. How has, or by whom has, the right of property in
the soil been totally subverted throughout a country containing twenty-
five to thirty millions of people in so short a period? If these, the
great zemindars, have acquired lawful right to the soil, it must have
been subsequent to this. Let them show the deeds by which they hold;
for, except by inheritance, a regular instrument is required to establish
their title. Sunnuds from the *king*, as late *as the middle of the
eighteenth century*, are quoted by Lord Teignmouth as establishing
undoubted right in the soil. One in favour of the zemindary of
Rajshahye was granted, he tells us, " in consequence of the neglect of

the former zemindar to discharge his revenue." This may be good as a sunnud of zemindary; but this was not a grant of the soil;—not more than a commission—after superseding one collector of land-tax—by the king of England, would be a grant of the estates within the districts specified. So also the "zemindary of Dinagepore was confirmed by a firman of Shah Jehan about 1650." So the origin of the Burdwan zemindary may be traced to the year 1680, when a *very small portion* of it was given to a person named Aboo." Nuddea and Lushkurpore zemindaries are of later date, about 1719. See Mr. Shore's minute.

(3). We have seen above that at the very end of the seventeenth century, the "husbandmen paid their rents to the Crown." This goes to prove that, whatever be the antiquity of the families of the zemindars just mentioned, they were, at the date of the Ayeen Akbaree, considered "husbandmen;" and we know that the viceroy of Bengal, Jafur Khan, "dispossessed almost all the zemindars." I would again ask how this vast accumulation of property has arisen? Some of the zemindars pay half a million sterling of public revenue. Did they purchase the lands? The value, at ten years' purchase, would be five millions! The malikana of ten per cent., at ten years' purchase, would amount to four millions four crores of rupees. Where was the capital to purchase this? It is evident no purchase ever took place; that, consequently, no transfer of the soil was ever made; and that, therefore, those zemindars are not owners of it.

(*d*). SIR J. SHORE, *2nd April 1788.*

Most of the considerable zemindars in Bengal may be traced to an origin within the last century and a half. The extent of their jurisdiction has been considerably augmented during the time of Jafur Khan and since (1) by purchase from the original proprietors, (2) by acquisitions in default of legal heirs, or (3) in consequence of the confiscation of the lands of other zemindaries, (4) instances are even related in which zemindaries have been forced upon the incumbents.

As escheats appertain to the State, acquisitions in the 2nd, 3rd and 4th of the preceding methods denote official transfers, that is, an official relation to the lands transferred.

V. Hereditary succession to the office of zemindar has been regarded by the advocates of a zemindary settlement as conclusive proof of the zemindar's proprietary rights, but in reality it only marked his official title; thus—

(*a*). REVENUE LETTER FROM BENGAL, *6th March 1793* (*para.* 8).

The same principles which induced us to resolve upon the separation of the talooks, prompted us to recommend to you, on the 30th March 1792, the abolition of a custom introduced under the Native Governments, by which most[1] of the principal zemindaries in the country are made to descend entire to the eldest son, or next heir of the last incumbent, in opposition both to the Hindu and Mahomedan laws, which admit of no exclusive right of inheritance in favor of primogeniture, but require that the property of a deceased person shall be divided amongst his sons or heirs, in certain specified proportions. Finding, however, upon a reference to your former orders, that you had frequently expressed a wish that the large zemindaries should be dismembered, if it could be effected consistently with the principles of justice, we did not hesitate to adopt the measure without waiting for your sanction. (See also Francis' *Revenues of Bengal*, page 59.)

App. VI.

——

The zemindary was an office.

——

Para. 2, contd.

(*b*). Halhed's Memoir on the land tenure and principles of taxation in the Bengal Presidency.

(1). The mokudums are, in some pergunnahs, considered as executing their office of purdhan or mokudum under an original hereditary right, co-equal with that which sanctions the succession to patrimonial property in the soil ; in some instances, the purdhanee is included in the zemindary claims advanced by individuals, and its existence is acknowledged by the other proprietors : instances of the office being sold by the incumbent are on record ; in general, however, the purdhan's continuance in office depends upon the degree of consideration he enjoys in the eyes of those of his fellow parishioners who are landowners, and who will, by direct or indirect means, secure his dismissal if he neglects their interests. On the office falling vacant, the eldest son of the late incumbent, or a near relation, generally succeeds. But in some places the zemindar malgoozar is considered to have the privilege of nominating a successor ;—without the consent of the other landowners, however, his nomination would have little weight ; the difficulty of selecting a person who would attend to the interests of the zemindar malgoozar, and at the same time prove acceptable to the ryots, appears to have originated the preference now given to the son, or nearest relation, of the deceased purdhan, who, as a matter of course, inherits no inconsiderable portion of the local and personal authority possessed by his predecessors, and would be equally open to the influence of that species of corruption by which the greater malgoozars retain their power.

(2). The original office of a purdhan or mokudum appears to have been very similar to that of the gram adhiput of the Hindu system ; he is a public officer ; arranges all the revenue details of his parish ;[2]

---

[1] This adjective "most" is significant : the Native Governments perforce applied the official rule to zemindaries which had been officially created, such as the numerous creations of Jafur Khan : other zemindars, *viz.*, several minor zemindars, who were proprietors of the whole estates for which they paid revenue direct to the treasury, would be exempt from the official rule.

Here we see a close correspondence, an exact parallel, between the zemindar and the mokudum, in respect of succession to either office, under a law of primogeniture which departed from the Hindu and Mahomedan laws of succession to real property. Hence, and as the mokudum's privileges and lands eventually merged in the zemindar's, the several extracts in Appendix , No. , paragraph , which show the official character of the mokudum's status, equally illustrate the official character of the zemindar.

[2] These were precisely the functions also of the official zemindar over a larger tract than a village.

App. VI.

THE ZEMINDARY
WAS AN OFFICE.

Para. 2, contd.

Sess. 1831-32,
Vol. XI. Ques-
tions 2648 and
2649.

is the magistrate of the village, and, with the assistance of the chowkeedars or night watchmen, superintends the police of it.

(c). Mr. Holt Mackenzie.

Was this mode of sub-dividing zemindaries known in India previous
to the permanent settlement? I believe that there was no such system of
regular separation previously to the permanent settlement. In some
cases a zemindaree seems to have been regarded as an office generally
of little value. In others there appears to have prevailed a special
custom of primogeniture; and although the general system was to
recognize the property as hereditary and divisible, yet under short
leases divisions could scarcely be made pending a settlement.

Are there many districts in which the right of primogeniture is supposed to prevail? I believe it prevailed in regard to some estates in all
the provinces, but is now confined to certain extensive zemindaries on
the western frontier of Bengal and Behar, where the zemindars are
the descendants of old rajahs, who were never wholly subdued by the
governments that preceded us. In cases in which it had been adopted
from considerations merely of financial convenience, the custom was
abolished by the rules of 1793.

VI. The zemindar's was an office, inasmuch as other
officials would not have been employed as a check upon his
collections, and against his exaction from the ryots, if they
had been mere tenants on an estate of which he was the
proprietor.

(a). Patton's Asiatic Monarchies.

1. The office of regulation and control, in respect to the sources and
quantum of the rent, or revenue, so necessary for protecting the respective rights of the hereditary tenant and the proprietary sovereign,
and for checking imposition on the part of the *official* collector, was
filled by officers who have been denominated *canongoes* and *putwaries*.
The *canongoe* was the principal and the *putwary* the subsidiary officer
in the department of control. * * The relative duties of the *canongoe*
and the *putwary* are thus expressed in the *Ayeen Akbary*—"The *putwary*
is employed on the part of the husbandman to keep an account of
his receipts and his disbursements, and no village is without one of
these. The *canongoe* is the protector of the husbandman; and there is
one in every *pergunnah*. They were paid by Government for these benevolent purposes, and were essential to the encouragement of agriculture, and the consequent augmentation of the revenue, forming the
most marked feature in the financial system of Tudur Mull.

2. It is somewhat extraordinary that these officers are hardly
mentioned in the text of Sir Charles Broughton Rouse's *Dissertation* concerning Bengal. The truth is, their official existence was incompatible
with the proprietary claim which he assigns to the zemindars; and,
accordingly, since the *perpetual settlement* was adopted, their control over
the official conduct of the zemindars has entirely ceased.

VII.—The great difficulty and expense of obtaining the usual zemindary sunnud on hereditary succession to the office of zemindar, implies that the succession was to an office, no such difficulty and expense having been incurred by proprietors of land, not being zemindars, on hereditary succession to their property. App. VI.
THE ZEMINDARY WAS AN OFFICE.
Para. 2, contd.

(a). PATTON'S ASIATIC MONARCHIES.

The necessity for the sunnud or commission will appear by the following Pages 177-78. extract from an article in the Appendix to the *Dissertation*, showing the great difficulty and expense incurred in obtaining the *sunnud* from the court of the sovereign. This article, we are informed, was drawn out by BODE MULL, one of the ablest and best informed of the native exchequer officers. * * " The zemindars succeeded to their zemindaries by right of inheritance; but until they consented to the payment of the *peshkash*, or fine of investiture, to the Emperor, and a proportional *nuzzeranah*, or present to the *Nazim*" (Provincial Governor) " neither the imperial *firman* of confirmation was granted them, nor were they permitted to substitute their own signature *to the public accounts* in lieu of their predecessor's. It often happened that several years elapsed before the demand of Government could be adjusted. The officers of the *dewanny*" (the revenue department), " in addition to the *peshkash* and *nuzzeranah*, swelled the account with claims of arrears due from the deceased zemindar, and from which they seldom receded, till they had exacted from his successor all that it was in his power to pay." Strange! that such difficulties should attend the succession to a *patrimonial estate.*

VIII. The small proportion of the zemindar's share of the produce shows that he was an official, and not the proprietor of the zemindary.

(a). WILKS ON MYSORE.

Under the only doctrine which was recognised in this discussion Pages 191-29. about the permanent settlement, the proof—and it is abundantly satisfactory—that the land is not the king's, leaves no alternative but to consign it to the zemindar. The author of *The Principles of Asiatic Monarchies* argues, with great force, that the claim of the zemindar being limited to one-tenth of the sum collected for the king, it is absurd to distinguish, as proprietor, the person entitled to one-tenth, while the remaining nine-tenths are called a duty, a tax, a quit-rent. The argument is conclusive; but the ingenious author has not unfolded the whole of the absurdity. Under the utmost limit of exaction recorded in the modern history of India, the sovereign has received one-half of the crop. The real share of the crop which, even under such exaction, would go to this redoubtable proprietor would be one-twentieth, or five per cent.; according to the laws of Menu and the other Shasters, his share would be one-sixtieth, or 1⅔ per cent; and this is the thing which a British Government has named *proprietor of the land.* In the controversy to determine whether the sovereign or the zemindar were the

App. VI.
———
The zemindary
was an office.
———
Para. 2, contd.
proprietor, each party appears to me to have reciprocally refuted the proposition of his adversary, without establishing his own : they have severally proved that neither the king nor the zemindar is the proprietor.

b). Mr. H. Colebrooke, 1813.

Revenue Selec-
tions, Vol. I,
page 199.
But in that view
it was the occu-
pant and cultiva-
tor with whom
the assessment
should be ad-
justed, and on
his tenure the
revenue secured.
If the occupants and cultivators were the real proprietors, according to notions which have been entertained of the ryottee tenure, and the zemindars were merely public officers collecting the dues of Government, the tithe might have been a sufficient allowance as the recompense of an official duty. A proprietor surely should have more than the tithe, or twice the tithe of the net revenue of his estate.

IX.—The levy of transit duties by zemindars proved that the power exercised was that of an office, not of a landed proprietor.

(a). Patton's Asiatic Monarchies.

Page 132.
It is material to observe that the *zemindar* is collector of the *customs* and the *excise*, as well as of the *land rent*. These do not appear to be the necessary adjuncts of a great *land-proprietor* in Europe ! The zemindar appears to be the collector or farmer of the whole. This circumstance occasioned a minute to be delivered into Council by the great and dignified character (Cornwallis), who acted a part, of which he seems to have been unconscious, when he revolutionized India by establishing what has been called the *permanent settlement* Yes; Minute,
3rd February
1790; Fifth
Report, page
491. with the zemindars. The following extract, which I believe to be authentic, manifests the deception which misled him, and which was so strong as to prevent him from detecting an absurdity at the very time he was stating it. After admitting that zemindars " had hitherto held the *collection of* internal *duties*," he observes :—" It is, I believe, generally allowed that no individual in a State can possess an inherent right to levy a duty on goods or merchandise purchased or sold within the limit of his *estate*, and much less upon goods passing along the public roads which lead through it. This is a privilege which the *sovereign power* alone is entitled to exercise; and nowhere else can it be lodged with safety"—which circumstance ought to have informed the noble lord, that the *zemindary* was not an *estate*, but a *district ;* and that the *zemindar* was not a great *land-proprietor*, but an *officer of Government.*

(Instead of drawing this obvious inference, Lord Cornwallis resumed for Government the power of levying taxes of any kind upon commerce, and gave compensation for their illegal exactions to the zemindars; who, nevertheless, down to the present day, continue to levy some of these taxes.)

3. To the presumption raised by the nine groups of App. VI. extracts in paragraph 2, that the zemindary was an official THE ZEMINDARY WAS AN OFFICE. appointment, not a right of property in the whole landed Para. 5. estate for which the zemindar paid the land revenue to Government, the advocates of the zemindary settlement oppose the sole fact that the revenue was paid to Government by the zemindars. But—

RESOLUTION OF GOVERNMENT, *22nd December 1820.*

(1). Even where the tehsildar had no direct interest to mislead, the Payment of revenue to Government did not imply proprietary rights. convenience and despatch of public business would naturally suggest the expediency of limiting the number of persons with whom the business of the collections was to be conducted, and a preference would naturally be given to those who had heretofore paid the revenue under the Native Governments; but by these, as the distinction between farming and proprietary engagement was not always clearly observed, so the mere circumstance of a party's being the sudder malgoozar, appears to have been held as affording little or no ground for a conclusive judgment in regard to the nature and extent of his proprietary rights. Their system, therefore, did not require a minute enquiry into the point at the time of interchanging engagements, even if minute interference with the interior details of the villages, with a view to the adjustment of private rights, had been more a part of their practice (*para. 125*).

(2). Under our system, however, the record of the settlement is taken as a *primâ facie* evidence of property. * *

(3). Hence the great defectiveness of the records in which persons were entered as proprietors without a reference to mofussil possession, and a definition of the nature and character of the tenure held by the engager (*paragraph 127*).

(4). His Lordship in Council is indeed at a loss to conceive whence the opinion, that the party admitted to engage for the Government revenue acquired thereby any new rights of property adverse to those possessed by other individuals, can have so generally arisen (*para. 149*).

4. Perhaps these extracts are superfluous; since the one fact that the revenue was farmed throughout the provinces before the permanent settlement is conclusive that the engagers for the revenue were not the proprietors, for the farmers of the revenue were clearly not the proprietors of all the lands for the revenue of which they contracted with the Government.

5. Ideas on this subject were confused by the circumstance of the person who engaged for the revenue—whether zemindar, in the modern sense of the term in Lower Bengal, or farmer,—being responsible in his person, and in his actual landed property, for realising from all the lands for the revenue of which he engaged. (Colebrooke's Supplement, page 269; and paragraph 2, section IIa of this Appendix.)

6. The foregoing extracts corroborate the following accounts of the *status*, position, and rights of the zemindars. Mr. Grant's type of zemindar, as set forth in section I, will be recognized also in some of the other extracts, and in the account of *mocuddums* or heads of villages :—

I.—Mr. J. Grant, *Serishtadar of Bengal.*

Fifth Report, page 251.

Analysis of Finances of Bengal.

(*a*). It is incontrovertible that the zemindars or other classes of natives, hitherto considered the rightful proprietors of the lands, are actually no more than annual contracting farmers or receivers of the public rents, with stated allowances in the nature of a commission on the receipts, and a small estate, or portion of their territorial jurisdictions, set apart for constant family subsistence, whether in or out of office, but never exceeding on the whole, by a universal prescriptive law of the empire, 10 per cent. on the mofussil collections.

Ibid, page 276.

(*b*). The tenth part of the *rebba chouth* (or Government's one-fourth share of the gross produce of the land) was liable to defray the charge of intermediate agency of the whole body of the zemindars, acting permanently in one or all of the following official capacities, by virtue of *sunnuds* or letters patent from the high dewany delegate of Government, *viz.*, as—

1.—Annual contracting farmers-general of the public rents.

2.—Formal representatives of the peasantry.

3.—Collectors of the royal proprietary revenue, entitled to a russoom or commission of 5 per cent. on the net receipts of the mofussil or subordinate treasuries.

4.—Financial superintendents of a described local jurisdiction, periodically variable in extent, and denominated *cahtiman*, trust or tenure of zemindary, talookdary, or territorial servile holding in tenancy. Within this, however, is appropriated a certain small portion of land called *nankar*, partaking of the nature of a freehold, serving as a family subsistence to the superior landholder, to give him an attachment for the soil and make[1] up the remainder of his yearly stated tythe for personal management in behalf of the State.

(*c*). See also paragraph 1, section II, *a* and *b*, where the account given, though that of the Select Committee of 1812, is a concise abstract of the long involved sentences of the Serishtadar of Bengal.

II.—Sir J. Shore, *18th September 1789.*

Fifth Report, page 454.

(*a*). In his letter of the 23rd July 1789, the Collector details many objections, which I shall hereafter state, to a settlement with the immediate proprietors of the soil; recommends in preference the employment of farmers, contends for the propriety of this system, and proposes the plan of a ten years' settlement with fourteen farmers for Sarun, and four

---

[1] i.e.—5 per cent. russoom, and 5 per cent. nancar, equal to 10 per cent.

for Chumparun; and he gives the following definition of a zemindary
in Sarun :—

"That it is a portion of land consisting of sundry farms paying revenue to Government, belonging to numberless proprietors managing their lands, either by themselves or their agents, but acting in general under a nominal proprietor, called the zemindar (with whom they engage for their revenue) having a real property perhaps of a fiftieth part of the zemindary."

(*b*). I cannot reconcile the Collector's definition of a zemindar, or the fact of a zemindary settlement as made in September last with 74 proprietors, with the declared refusal[1] of the zemindars to rent[1] each other's lands, combined with the number of zemindars in Sarun (*paragraphs 18 and 19*).

III.—PATTON'S ASIATIC MONARCHIES.

(*a*). There can be no question that the appointment of a zemindar is an *office*. To deny this appears to me like denying that a man has a nose upon his face. The refutation is effected in the same manner; we point to the *nose ;* we point to the *zemindary sunnud*. Of the two, the evidence in the last case seems to be the strongest ; for, upon the feature in question, the word *nose* is not written ; but in the *sunnud*, the word *office* is expressly written, and the appointment declared to be an office.

(*b*). It seems, therefore, to be clearly established, that the *zemindars* could not possibly be the *proprietors* of the lands, the rents of which they were required, as the *aumils* of Government, to collect from the proprietors. But there was another description of land within the districts of the zemindars, of which they were the undoubted proprietors, which was distinguished by the name of *nankar* land, and which paid no rent at all to Government. The zemindar had it in absolute property in lieu or in part of salary of office ; for which reason it might be styled with propriety his official land. It was distinguished from the khalsah, or exchequer lands, whose rents were paid into the royal treasury, and also from the jagheer lands, the rents of which were assigned by the sovereign to an individual during pleasure.* *

(*c*). In the glossary annexed to the *Dissertation*, the explanation given to the word *comar lands* which are *khalsah* lands (or land whose rent is paid to Government) out of lease, or not possessed by pottah tenure, seems rather applicable to *nankar* lands ; they are called a *zemindar's demesne lands ;* upon what pretence, I cannot conceive. The *nankar* lands might be so denominated, because they are the zemindar's absolute property, which the others are not : for he must account for the rent of the *comar* lands to Government. * * It is somewhat extraordinary that this description of land, which really was *property*, and belonged absolutely and entirely to the zemindar, should have altogether escaped the notice of the author of the *Dissertation* (Sir Broughton Rouse). Was

---

[1] The zemindars willingly paid their shares of the Government revenue through a nominal proprietor or representative zemindar, while they refused to pay rent, in addition, to the latter.

THE ZEMINDARY WAS AN OFFICE.

Para. 6, contd.

it because of the difficulty to explain, where the *whole district* was said to belong to the *zemindar,* how a part of it should be so differently circumstanced from the rest.

IV.—Mr. Holt Mackenzie, *1832.*

Sess. 1831-32,
Vol. XI, page
306.

I shall only remark that the zemindars of Bengal, though many of them held originally a mere office, must be considered as having been vested by our settlement with the property of everything within their zemindaries, which belonged to the Government, and was not reserved by it.

V.—Mr. Fortescue, *12th April 1832.*

Ibid,
Questions 2276,
2278, 2282 to 84,
2287.

Generally speaking, the zemindars were not what the operation of the regulations afterwards made them. The term "zemindar" is a very indefinite expression; it does not imply any right in itself; it is merely a relative term, "zameen" meaning land, and "dar" a person having that relation; but in itself it expresses no precise relation; and we see consequently that the term zemindar is at times applied to a person who neither himself claims, nor is supposed by others to have, the proprietary right in the soil over which he is zemindar. A person who possessed property, obtained from other sources, might be a zemindar, but he had not that property, because he was a zemindar. It was, and is, the usual course for the son of a zemindar to inherit; but though that did obtain, it did not yield to him, necessarily, any proprietary right beyond what he had of his own and family; his was a right (to which he succeeded, perhaps) of arranging for the revenues of the extensive holding. It was a hereditary right to perform a given duty : but it did not affect the right of the ryots. * * What I wish is particularly to guard against any expression which should lead the Committee to suppose that the zemindar possessed property in the zemindary beyond that which was accidental.

VI.—Mr. A. D. Campbell's "able paper," *1832.*

(*a*). The zemindar, as such, was originally the mere steward, representative or officer of the Government, or rather the contractor for their land revenue, often hereditary; and the difference between the land revenue of the State which he received from the cultivators, and the lower jumma or contract price, compounding for it, which he paid in lieu of it into the Government treasury, constituted, after deducting his own actual charges in its collection, the value of his zemindary contract or tenure, generally estimated by Government from ten to fifteen per cent. above his jumma payable to them, and called *malikana,* or the peculiar property of which, alone, he is the owner (*malik*). * * He therefore possessed a valuable and often hereditary contract interest in the *land revenue* of the State, the collection of which, alone, was thus transferred to him; but as zemindar he possessed no right whatever *in the soil itself,* which, subject to the payment of that revenue, was held in fields exclusively by the cultivators on the various tenures described above.

(*b*). This view of the subject is by no means opposed to the fact, that nearly all the zemindars, from the highest to the lowest, were also themselves cultivators to a greater or less extent. The petty head of the village, besides being a zemindar, was also, perhaps, the greatest cultivator in his own neighbourhood; and each of the higher grades of zemindars, even to the tributary sovereign of the hills, had his private lands (*neez, kummattum*), whence he drew grain and other supplies for domestic purposes of his, perhaps, numerous household. But unless the public revenue on these lands had been remitted to him by Government, as *nankar* (food, subsistence), and thus constituted an addition to the *malikana*, granted by the State on account of his hereditary contract duties, he would have been required to account for the land revenue of his own fields, in common with that which he collected from those occupied by other cultivators, and his *malikana*, in that case, would have been confined to the mere established deduction from the joint aggregate. The fields which he held in his distinct capacity as a cultivator, were never, in the slightest degree, confounded by the native governments with his official contract or zemindary tenure.

(*c.*) The distinction between the right of the cultivator to the soil itself, subject to the payment of the public revenue, immemorially limited by local, though ill-defined usage, and the right of the zemindar to the receipt of that land revenue from the cultivator, subject to his own payment to Government of a separate lower or reduced composition in lieu of it, called *jumma*, periodically adjusted between the zemindar and the state, which was never subjected to limitation by those who preceded us in the sovereignty of India, is of the greatest importance. For, simple as this distinction now appears to be, to all who have waded through the vast mass of information now procurable, it is the want of a clear perception of these two very distinct rights which has given rise to the chief errors, committed at the period of the permanent zemindary settlement.

(*d*). At that period this distinction was unknown. In the discussions preceding the permanent zemindary settlement, however, it had been fully admitted that the cultivator possessed a right to the soil so long as he paid the public revenue demandable on his fields, which was held to have been limited by an act of the sovereign power, beyond the arbitrary determination of the zemindar. Indeed, this cannot be more broadly stated, nor in more distinct language. It was also maintained that the zemindar had no claim to an absolute property in the land itself; neither was there any proof " of the existence of such right discernible in his relative situation under the Mogul government in its best form;" yet the zemindar's undeniable, and often hereditary, property in the *land revenue* of his *entire zemindary* was confounded with the separate property in the land itself, which, as a cultivator, he possessed in some of its *fields* alone; and as he in general happened to occupy, in the ranks of society in India, the place held by the gentry or aristocracy in Europe, this fortuitous circumstance tended to confirm the error, and seems to have rendered it a matter even of policy, to acknowledge him in the new light of the landed proprietor, not only of his own few fields, but of every field even belonging to other cultivators situated within his entire zemindary or hereditary revenue jurisdiction.

VII.—Lord Cornwallis, *3rd February 1790.*

(*a*). The question that has been so much agitated in this country, whether the zemindars and talookdars are the actual proprietors of the soil, or only officers of Government, has always appeared to me to be very uninteresting to them; whilst their claim to a certain percentage upon the rents of their lands has been admitted, and the right of Government to fix the amount of those rents at its own discretion has never been denied or disputed.

(*b*). Under the former practice of annual settlements, zemindars who have either refused to agree to pay the rents that have been required, or who have been thought unworthy of being entrusted with the management, have, since our acquisition of the Dewanee, been dispossessed in numberless instances, and their land held khas, or let to a farmer; and when it is recollected that pecuniary allowances have not always been given to dispossessed zemindars in Bengal, I conceive that a more nugatory or delusive species of property could hardly exist.* *

(*c*). To those who have adopted the idea that the zemindars have no property in the soil, and that Government is the actual landlord, and that the zemindars are officers of Government, removable at pleasure, the questions regarding the right of the zemindars to collect the internal duties on commerce would appear unnecessary.[1] These are not the grounds on which I have recommended the withdrawal from the zemindars of the collection of internal duties.

(*d*). I admit the proprietary rights of the zemindars.

7. There were three parties, one or other of whom could have had proprietary right in the land, *viz.,* the Government, the zemindar, and the cultivator. In clause (*b*) the noble author of the zemindary settlement conceived that a more nugatory or delusive species of property than that of zemindars could not exist; he and the advocates of that settlement maintained further, that the State was not the proprietor of the soil: yet, far from admitting the proprietary right of the remaining or third party, the cultivator was put aside *sub silentio* (just as his rights passed away, in consequence, *sub silentio*) and the illogical conclusion (clause *d*) was affirmed that the zemindar was the proprietor; and so the rights of millions of the real proprietors were destroyed by the amiable and benevolent representatives of a nation which desires to do justice to India, which is rich enough to make the amends honestly due for even well-meant injustice, and which, in one of the famine problems of the present day, is confronted with the consequences of its unparalleled confiscation of rights in 1793.

8. Law and Constitution of India.

(1). The zemindars may purchase property like individuals; but that the name of zemindar is an official designation there can be no doubt. The

---

[1] This amounts to a strong assertion of the official *status* of the zemindar.

commission, or sunnud of zemindary granted to Cheytun Sing, of the zemindary of Bishenpore, which office was held by his grandfather, to whom he was appointed in succession, is well known. As a common work, I refer the reader for it to Patton's Asiatic Monarchies, Appendix No. 1. The sunnud is addressed to the mutsudees, chowdries, canoongoes, talookdars, ryots and husbandmen of Bishenpore, setting forth " that the *office of zemindar* has been bestowed on Cheytun Sing, " and certain conditions are specified. He is to pay a peshcush of one hundred and eighty-six mohurs, to be conciliatory to the ryots, so as to increase cultivation and improve the country, *to pay the revenue of Government into the treasury at stated periods ;* to keep the high roads in repair and safe for travellers, to be answerable for the property of travellers if robbed ; *to render and transmit the accounts required of him to the presence every year, under his own and the canoongoe's signature.* *   * We are then given the muchulcah, or written obligation given in by the nominee. He promises to be diligent in the discharge of his *office,* to be mild and conciliatory to the ryots, to increase the cultivation, to pay the revenne to Government regularly into the treasury at the stated periods, to transmit the accounts signed by himself and the canoongoe regularly. We have finally the security for his person of the canoongoe of Bengal " that the *office* of zemindar having been bestowed upon Cheytun Sing, I will be security for his person", &c.

2. So far, therefore, as the holders of large zemindaries, such as many of the zemindars of the province of Bengal are, it will probably not admit of dispute that their tenure was *official,* and that the *bonâ fide milkeeut* (ownership) of the soil did not rest in them.

9. The foregoing extracts, which affirm the official status of the zemindar, take account of his *malikana* or percentage on the collection of the Government land revenue from the cultivating proprietors, and of only those his *neej* lands, which were *nankar* lands, or the lands allotted as part of his remuneration as zemindar. With one exception, (Mr. Fortescue, section V), the lands other than *nankar,* of which the zemindar could be the proprietor, on the same footing as the other cultivating proprietors, are not mentioned. Notices of them will be found in the following extracts which, in other respects, confirm the preceding accounts of the official *status* of the zemindar.

I.—ROUSE's DISSERTATION CONCERNING LANDED PROPERTY IN BENGAL, *1791.*

Page 45.

To one in particular, a man of small but independent fortune, possessed of extensive learning, and a magistrate of unimpeached integrity, Mirza Mohsen, I formerly proposed several questions in writing, without communication with any person whatsoever, upon the subject of zemindars. The answers he gave me were the result of his reading and enquiry.

App. VI.

THE ZEMINDARY
WAS AN OFFICE.

Para. 9, contd.

Page 52.

Page 53.

Page 51.

Page 54.

Question (3).—In the Dewany sunnuds a zemindary is styled an office (khidmut), and an office is dependent upon the pleasure of the employer. But at present the children of the zemindar take possession of the land enjoyed by their father and grandfather, as an inheritance. How long has this rule of inheritance in zemindaries prevailed? and by what means has it been established?

Answer (a).—" The reason for calling the zemindary an *office* in the Dewany sunnud, is this,—The zemindars are commissioned on the part of the sovereign for three duties: First, the preservation and defence of their respective boundaries from traitors and insurgents. Secondly, the tranquillity of the subjects, the abundance of cultivators, and increase of his revenue. Thirdly, the punishment of thieves and robbers, the prevention of crimes, and the destruction of highwaymen. The accomplishment of these objects is considered, in the royal grant, as the discharge of office to the sovereign, and on that account the word office (khidmut) is employed in the Dewany sunnud for a zemindary.

(*b*). The zemindaries of the present period are of three sorts: (1) Jungulboory, (2) Intekaly, and (3) Ahekamy.

1. *Jungulboory* (clearing of waste) is a tract of land which having gone to decay, and become incapable of producing the amount of the royal revenue (jumma padshahy) has been restored to prosperity by the diligence and industry of another person, who has thereby re-established the revenue of the crown (kheraji). Such is the zemindary of Serayal, &c.

2. *Intekaly* (transfer) is land in a good state of cultivation and productive to the amount of the revenue, yet on account of the neglect of the incumbent, or for want of heirs to the land, another person has, with the permission of the emperor, or of the government delegated by him, obtained a sunnud for the office in his own name. Such is the zemindary of the Pergunnah Buldakhal, &c.

3. *Ahekamy* (by order or authority) is, when, notwithstanding the diligence of the zemindar in the duties of his station, the officers about the person of the prince, who are employed in the affairs of the zemindars, have, upon interested motives, obtained orders for zemindaries to be granted to them in their own names. Such is the zemindary of Rajah Luckinarain, and this mode has taken place in latter times.

(*c*). (Going back to *a*). It was a rule in the time of the ancient emperors, that when any of the zemindars died, their effects and property were sequestered[1] by the Government. After which, in consideration of the rights of long service, which is incumbent on sovereigns, and elevates the dignity of the employer, *sunnuds* for the office of zemindary were granted to the children of the deceased zemindar, and no other person was accepted, because the inhabitants could never feel for any stranger the attachment and affection which they naturally entertain for the family of the zemindar, and would have been afflicted if any other had been put over them.

(*d*). At present, the children of a zemindar take to the land possessed by their fathers and grandfathers as an inheritance; it is done upon the strength of the ancient customs and institutions, according to which the zemindary of the father was transferred by sunnud to the son.

---

[1] Evidence of official status.

If the office of zemindary, in the nature of their officers, were limited App. **VI.** to the life of the incumbents, they would never have exerted themselves to promote the improvement and prosperity of the country. Nor would the population and revenue have been advanced, as they are now, from what they were in former times. But when the emperors thought it politic, upon the decease of a zemindar, to continue the office of zemindary to his children, the zemindars on their part felt a confidence and satisfaction in discharging the duties of their situation, and always employed their strenuous endeavours to promote the prosperity of their districts.

App. **VI.**
—
THE ZEMINDARY WAS AN OFFICE.
Para 10.

(*e*). Such has been the progression of the general rule of inheritance in zemindaries. With regard to one species, indeed, the jungulboory, it is conformable to the holy law, and to common practice, that persons should gain an hereditary zemindary in land which they have cleared from waste, under the encouragement of the prince, and brought into state of cultivation, so as to produce the full revenue of Government, and the children of such persons have a decided right to hereditary possession, which both ancient and modern sovereigns have recognised. But as to the other zemindaries, styled *Intekaly* and *Ahekamy*, before explained in the second[1] article, which the possessors have received in a sate of perfect cultivation, effected by the industry of others, although their children also have claimed a hereditary right in these zemindaries like those of the sort called jungulboory, and upon the strength of ancient practice, have possessed the zemindaries of their ancestors upon a similar footing, yet the holy law does not of itself annex to these any hereditary title. The renewal of the sunnud from person to person is a argument against the inheritance by right. This must, therefore, depend upon the prince and the actual government of the country.

10. Perhaps it is hardly necessary now to add in the following extracts a statement that hereditary succession to the office of zemindar did not imply a proprietary title in the whole of the estates which formed the zemindary.

—PATTON'S ASIATIC MONARCHIES—

(*a*). The prejudices of Europe confirm hereditary establishments wherever they are to be found, and, if it be possible, convert them into tenures of *land*, because, among the English in particular, the law of primogeniture and hereditary succession applies peculiarly to *landed property;* nor can they suppose the hereditary rule to be followed in the disposal of a trust, or an office, which has a reference to land, without annexing to it the whole property of the official district, however extensive may be its boundaries: the argument is, that *hereditary succession* infers *property of land*. If a man had succeeded to his father, and his grandfather, and his great-grandfather, as the superior

Pages 195-96.

---

[1] To land, of which the proprietary right was not official, including reclaimed waste, inheritance was independent of a sunnud; but to the official part of the zemindary, including lands brought into cultivation by the industry of others, the succession was by sunnud, that is, only to one-tenth over the Government's share of the produce.

or steward of an estate, and they had all in succession enjoyed a farm
rent-free, for their trouble,—has this man a right to claim the property
of the whole estate? This appears to me to be precisely the situation
of the Indian zemindar. Now, stewardships, it has been observed, were
really hereditary among the Hindus; and on this account they appear
to have been conferred pretty generally, according to the same rule
by the Mahomedans. But to the Mahomedan succeeds the English
man, with his head full of the hereditary claims of *great landed proprie
tors*, derived from the feudal institutions of the north; and he insists
upon converting the humble *steward* into the princely *proprietor*, and
talks of *right* and *justice*, while he robs millions of their property, and
sacrifices to his prejudices all the proprietary prerogatives of government.

(*b*). (After quoting from Menu and the *Code of Gentoo
Laws* published by Mr. Halhed)—

Page 170.
     It therefore appears that if the *zemindary* had been a *landed estate*
continuing by hereditary descent in the same family, it would not, by
the Hindu law (which alone could be applicable), have descended to
one son, where there were many, nor to *one relative*, where there were
others of *equal kindred;* but it would have been equally divided among
all the equal relatives of the last occupant, which, not having been the
case, demonstrates, I think, that it could not be esteemed *landed
property*. So that the circumstance upon which the European idea
of landed property is founded actually infers an opposite conclusion
and establishes with certainty that the zemindary appointment must
have been an *office*, which, not admitting of division, could only be
continued (when given to persons of the same family) in the manner
that has been followed. But even if the application of the *law of
England*, in direct opposition to the *Hindu law*, could be admitted,
it would only apply to the *nankar land* of the zemindar, which was
officially his actual property, as it paid no rent; but it could not be
applied to the *khalsa*, or *exchequer* lands, the rents of which wholly
belonged to Government; and the overplus, whatever it might be, was
expressly declared to be the property of the cultivator or ryot.

     11. Under the ancient system, village boundaries were
defined; a certain proportion of waste land was included with
in this boundary; and co-sharers in the headship of village
(meerassdars), heads of villages, heads of groups of village
and zemindars, had, more or less generally, a property in the
waste to the extent of receiving rent from cultivators of it
subject to the payment of the Government revenue; some of
the extracts in the following sections relate to these offici
zemindars; the others illustrate generally that the rights of
the minor officials merged in those of the zemindar.

I.—Patton's Asiatic Monarchies.

Page 156.
     In a glossary which accompanies Sir Broughton Rouse's *Dissertatio
I find the word '*aumil*' explained *native collector or manager of a distr*

App. VI.

THE ZEMINDARY
WAS AN OFFICE.

Para. 11, contd.

on the part of Government. This definition seems applicable to a *zemindar.* But not being entirely satisfied upon this head, I applied to a gentleman, whose knowledge of the Persian language, and whose avocations in India, I understood, would give authority to his judgment, stating my questions in writing, without assigning any particular cause for the inquiry. To my question respecting an *aumil,* his answer was: "An *aumil* is an *agent.*" To my question—"A *choudry,* or a *zemindar,* collects immediately from the ryots?" Answer—"Doubtless." "How are these persons relatively situated?" Answer—"The zemindary officers are termed his *amila;* they act on his behalf, and under his authority; the *zemindars* themselves may be considered as the *amila* of Government. It was a general term, *comprehending all those employed in the collection of the revenue,* though now confined to the subordinate agents." The reader will observe that at the time, a hundred and thirty-two years since, when *Aurungzebe* issued this edict (firman of rules for the collection of revenue), the general term *amil* or *amila,* "comprehending all those employed in the collection of the revenues," must have included *zemindars;* but at any rate, even as the word is now understood, it must be applied to the *agents of zemindars,* in which case it is imposible that the cultivators, who are mentioned in the firamin as the *proprietors* of the land, could be the zemindars; because the *zemindars,* or their agents (under the designation of *aumils*), are the persons here instructed how to conduct themselves towards those very *proprietors.* Would the Emperor enjoin them how to behave towards *themselves?* or would he instruct the agents of the zemindars to *admonish the zemindars* to cultivate their land? The firamin says,—"The proprietor being present, and capable of cultivating it, let them (the *aumils*) admonish him" (the *zemindar!*). This cannot be. * * The second article in the firamin states: "But if, upon examination, it should be found that some" (husbandmen) "who have the ability, and are assisted with water, nevertheless have neglected to cultivate their lands, they" (the *aumils*) "shall admonish, and threaten, and use force and stripes."

In *kheraj mowezzeff* (rent paid in money) they (the *aumils*) shall acquire information of the conduct of the *proprietors of land,* from whom this tribute is to be collected, whether they cultivate or not; and if they (the *aumils*) learn that the *husbandmen* are unable to provide the implements of husbandry, they shall advance them money from Government, in the way of *tekavy,* and take security. In the same sentence, *proprietors of land* and *husbandmen* are here mentioned; do they mean the same persons? This seems to be answered in the affirmative, by the succeeding article. "Third. In *kheraj-mowezzeff,* if the *proprietor of the land, for want of means of providing the implements of husbandry,* has been unable to cultivate it, or has deserted, leaving the land uncultivated, they (the *aumils*) shall either give the land in farm, or allow another to cultivate it" (on account of the *proprietor*), "or they shall appoint a person to succeed the proprietor, who shall cultivate the land; and after paying the tribute, whatever remains, he" (the substituted farmer) "shall apply to his own use; when the *proprietors of the lands* shall again have the ability to cultivate them, they shall be restored to them." This article seems to establish that the *proprietor of the land,* and the *husbandman,* is the same person, and that it is impossible for the *zemindar,* who is the *aumil,* or whose agent is the *aumil,* to be the proprietor. The fourth and fifth articles contain other instructions to *aumils* respecting their duties towards *proprietors* or *husbandmen.* It seems, therefore, to be clearly established, that the *zemindars* could not possibly be the *proprietors* of the lands, the rents of which they were required, as the *aumils* of Government, to collect from the *proprietors.*

II.—SIR BROUGHTON ROUSE.

Page 25.

(*a*). I have examined from attested copies now in my own possession the sunnuds of a zemindar, talookdar, and chowderry, which latter, if I recollect right, is considered in the modern practice of Bengal as the head of several talookdars united under one name, and I find the tenor of them exactly the same.

(*b*). MIRZA MOHSEN, *a learned authority, quoted by Sir B. Rouse.*

Page 46.

(1). In times prior to the irruptions of the Mahomedans, the Rajahs who held their residence at Delhi, and possessed the sovereignty of Hindustan, deputed officers to collect their revenues (*kheraji*) who were called in the Indian language Choudheries. The word zemindar is Persian.

Ibid,
page 47.

(2). On the Mahomedan conquest, the lands in Hindustan were allotted to Omrah Jaghirdars for the maintenance of the troops distributed throughout the country. Several of these Omrahs having rebelled, the emperors thought it would be more politic to commit the management of the country to the native Hindus who had most distinguished themselves by the readiness and constancy of their obedience to the sovereign power. In pursuance of this plan, districts were allotted to numbers of them under a reasonable revenue (jummah monasib) which they were required to pay in money to the governors of the provinces, deputed from the emperor.

Page 48.

(3). The zemindar has a pre-eminence over a chowdhery in three respects which will be specified in another article. The chowdhery, under the sovereignty of the Rajahs, had no concern in the administration of the country, which has become the custom under the Imperial Government. Their business was simply to collect the established revenue (Zer mokerery).

III.—GHOLAM HOSEIN KHAN, *son of Fukheen-ool Dowlat, formerly Nazim of Behar (Appendix to Minute of Sir J. Shore, 2nd April 1788).*

Harington's
Analysis of
Regulations,
page 113 *et seq.*
Q. 1st.

(*a*). The literal meaning of the word *zemindar* is *possessor,* or proprietor of *land,* but in its general or accepted meaning it implies a proprietor of land who pays rent to the emperor or any other ruler, and is equally applicable to every landholder, whether possessing a greater or a less number of villages, or only a portion of a village. Land being a species of that property which is deemed transferable in all countries the proprietorship of it may be obtained in the same manner as that of any other property of a similar nature, *viz.*, (1) by gift, (2) by purchase, with the mutual consent of the parties, (3) by inheritance.

(b). The principal zemindars received titles and jageers according to APP. VI. their rank, whilst those of an inferior degree, in the event of their being THE ZEMINDARY WAS AN OFFICE. obedient to the orders cf Government, attentive to the improvement of their lands, and punctual in the payment of their revenues, received Para. 11, contd. *nankar* proportionate to their exigencies, besides which they had no Q. 13th. other allowances. The nankar was deducted from the revenue payable to Government. Afterwards, on the decline of the empire, villages were granted for nankar in lieu of money.

(c). What is a chowdry, and what is the difference between a chowdry Q. 26th. and a zemindar? Many of the principal landholders of Behar were denominated chowdries, as, for instance, Bishen Sing, the grandfather of Narain Sing, the zemindar of Seris Cotumba. In the time of Akbar and his successors, the crories, in obedience to the orders of the emperor, went to court. Such among the zemindar's relations as possessed abilities, the emperor, after satisfying himself on that point, nominated to the management of particular districts; and by conducting the business to his satisfaction, they obtained an allowance of nankar and received the appellation of chowdry, signifying chief, or director. Thus the superintendents of the customs are denominated chowdries, because it is their duty to superintend the business of this department. In later times, those zemindars who particularly distinguished themselves by their attention to the ruler, and by the good management of their district, obtained by common consent the title of chowdry. There is no other difference between a chowdry and a zemindar than what is here stated. A chowdry has no rights or privileges beyond nankar and malikanah; the former depending on his retaining the management of his district, and the latter on his losing it.

(d). What is a talookdary, and what is the difference between a Q. 27th. talookdary and a zemindary? The proprietor of 10 or 15 villages, or even of a less number, is called a talookdar. The word *zemindar* is a general term applied to all landholders, whether possessing an entire pergunnah or not, or only 10 beegahs of land. In this respect they are all equally zemindars. The only point in which there is a diifference among them is in regard to rank and authority.

(e). ROY ROYAN'S ANSWER.—The zemindars of a middle and inferior Q. 7th. rank, and the talookdars and muzkoories at large, hold their lands to this day solely by virtue of inheritance; whereas the superior zemindars (chowdries) (c), such as those of Burdwan, Nuddea, Dinagepore, &c., after succeeding to their zemindaries on the ground of inheritance, are accustomed to receive, on the payment of a nuzzeranah, paiskush, &c., a dewanny sunnud from Government. In former times the zemindars of Bishenpore, Pachete, Beerbhoom and Roshmabad, used to succeed, in the first instance, by the right of inheritance, and to solicit afterwards, as a matter of course,[1] a confirmation from the ruling power.

IV.—TAGORE LAW LECTURES.

(a). It appears to be pretty certain that the Mahomedan system of Page 42. government was throughout a non-hereditary system; while the Hindu

---

[1] The confirmation was not accorded, however, as a matter of course, but only after difficulty and delay, and the exaction of heavy fees, see para. 2, section VII.

system was essentially hereditary. * * And so we find that while the Hindu officers succeeded to their office simply by descent, or by the mixture of descent and election which sometimes prevailed, yet this established hereditary right was not sufficient in Mahomedan times without some recognition by the State. * * A system of government, which was opposed to hereditary offices, would naturally tend to become, if it was not originally, a highly centralised government; in this again presenting a marked contrast to the Hindu system, with its village communities. In this respect, also, there seems to have been a struggle between the two opposite principles, and the village communities ceased to develop and tended to decay under Mahomedan rule. * *

Page 60.
(b). The tendency of the Mahomedan rule would therefore be, as it seems to me, to depress, at any rate at first, the village community, and to make it shrink within itself, and to recognize very slightly any one below the chief collector of the revenue, whether headman or rajah; and the tendency would further be to enhance at first the rights and powers of the revenue collectors as agent against all below them, and thus give them the means of carrying on with success a struggle with the Mahomedan ideas, and of encroaching on the rights claimed by the State. * *

Page 61.
(c). Whether the causes be as I have suggested, or not, we find that zemindars did arise and become powerful in Mahomedan times, displacing to a great extent the village headman; and that the village fiscal organization fell into decay, and its growth and development were arrested.

Page 61.
(d). The Mahomedan rulers continued the same revenue machinery and collected the revenue through the Hindu chowdries, and, where these had existed, zemindars, as the established representatives of the cultivators, and as collectors of the revenue of a fiscal division or pergunnah. The chowdry afterwards became the Mahomedan *crory* administering a *chucklah*, or a district yielding a crore of dams, or $2\frac{1}{2}$ lakhs of rupees, and he was one of the officers from whom zemindars sprung.

Page 62.
(e). The headman generally continued to distribute the assessment amongst the villagers, as he did even down to British times; and he realised the revenues from the cultivators, which he paid into the treasury, or to the superior revenue authority. In later times the headman generally sank into the position of a subordinate revenue payer, or of a muzkooree, intead of a pujooree malguzar, paying revenue, not direct to the treasury or the superior revenue officer as such, but paying through a zemindar or talookdar. The village community appears to have gradually sunk, and to have lost its importance as a fiscal unit, although it may have retained and, perhaps, intensified its social influence.

Pages 63-64.
(f). In those parts of the country where the village communities were in vigour, the headmen seem to have retained their position to some extent, and to have dealt with the State direct as pujooree malguzars under the old Hindu titles of mokuddums, munduls, and bhunnias (or zemindars). But in other places the ancient rajahs and revenue collectors became talookdars and zemindars, and collected the revenue as such;

* * These zemindars and talookdars, as we have seen, generally contrived to absorb the functions, or at least the chief emoluments, of the
headman, and to displace him to a great extent. Thus the Rajah of
Benares is said to have attained his position by this means.

(*g*). Thus arose zemindars and talookdars. Many of the superior
zemindars descend by primogeniture, a fact which perhaps points to
their having been derived from the ancient rajahs, as a raj undoubtedly
descended mainly in this mode. The inferior zemindars grew out of
collectors, farmers, and other officers of revenue, headmen, and even
robber chiefs.

(*h*). At the Mahommedan conquest, those who claimed to collect the
revenue did not claim the ownership of the land; they claimed a right
to collect, and sometimes a kind of property in the collections, but
nothing more. But in course of time, the zemindars who had grown
out of these elements began to encroach upon the rights of both the
State and the cultivator; and by the time of Ala-ood-deen, who died
in A. D. 1316, they were thought to require curbing. The superintendents of the revenue department were accordingly required "to take
care that the zemindars demand no more from the cultivators than the
estimates the zemindars themselves had made," thus bringing them back
to their original position, to some extent, and forbidding what were
known as abwabs and cesses. But in spite of this check, the power of
the zemindars was not crushed, but they regained their position, and ultimately became almost independent.

12. Mr. James Grant, Sheristadar of Bengal, in a
pamphlet entitled "An inquiry into the nature of zemindaree
tenures," explained how there was brought about the dis-
cordance between truth, right and fact on the one part, and the
conclusion on which the Government acted in declaring the
zemindars to be the proprietors of the lands in their zemindaries. The substance of Mr. Grant's account is given by
Mr. Halhed in his "Memoir on the land tenure and principles of taxation: Calcutta, 1832."

I.—Mr. C. N. Halhed—

(*a*). The zemindars, who it is abundantly shown in the evidence laid
before a Committee of the House of Commons in 1772, were merely the
agents through whom the revenues were realised, and not the proprietors
of the soil, had been in the habit of borrowing money from individuals
at a high rate of interest, on their personal security, or on mortgage of
the ensuing crops.

(*b*). The creditors pressed the zemindars for their claims, but were,
for a time, content to obtain rewewed bonds, with accumulated
interest added to the principal, till at length these private claims
against the zemindars exceeded three millions sterling, and the revenues
were endangered. In the meantime, the Supreme Court of Calcutta,
viewing the zemindars as the servants of Government, deemed them, in
this capacity, amenable to the jurisdiction in the terms of their charter,

App. VI.
—
Usurpation by
zemindars.
—
Para. 12, concld.
Appendix A,
page 11.

Zemindars
recognised as
proprietors to
evade jurisdic-
tion of Supreme
Court.

Page V.

Page VI.

Page VI.

and entertained the suits which the holders of the bonds entered against them to recover the amount of their claims, seized their persons by mesne process and issued extents against their movable property.

(*b*). The Government feared that " a judicial enquiry into the zemindars' rights and tenures, whenever it shall happen, is likely to have important consequences on the Government of this country; should it be determined that a zemindar is an hereditary officer, who collects the revenue in trust for Government, whose jumma is fixed only to prevent embezzlement, and who is liable to be removed at will, it will be argued, and on plausible grounds, that every zemindar is a servant of the Company, an officer of Government, and, therefore, subject to the jurisdiction of the Court; should it, on the other hand, be decided that a zemindar is an absolute proprietor of his zemindary, in every instance where he is dispossessed he may reclaim his right thus established by a process in the Supreme Court against the Company, contest the grounds on which he is excluded from possession, or on which his land is assessed; in short, in whatever way the question may be decided it is likely to open a wide field for litigation, and serve to involve this Government in suits brought either directly against the Company, or which can be defended only by them and their officers.

(*c*). The course adopted to obviate the natural consequences of the interference of the Supreme Court with the agents of the revenue department, was perhaps the most injudicious which could have been taken; the Advocate General (Sir John Day), taking the Persian words in their literal sense, declared the zemindars to be landholders, and therefore not amenable to the jurisdiction of the Supreme Court; on this the Government acted, and induced the zemindars to plead against the jurisdiction.

(*d*). On this verbal translation of the term ' zemindar,' a new doctrine was founded and very generally embraced: " the Governor General and his Council were committed in their opinions to vindicate the plea set up against the jurisdiction of the Supreme Court, by admitting that the zemindars were landholders, and held their lands and right by inheritance; and opinions so well calculated to suit the prejudices of the people of England, who were generally unacquainted with the principles of Eastern governments, had a powerful influence in establishing a belief in the new doctrine, and finally overruling the disputed jurisdictions of the Court."

(*e*). But unfortunately the just claims of the *raeeuts* were altogether forgotten in settling the question of proprietary right; and, strange to say, without evidence, without proof, without investigation, the British legislature have delivered over, as tenants-at-will, millions of free proprietors to the tender mercies of a race of tax-gatherers and speculators, who, though not possessing a foot of land, have been, by a stroke of the pen, converted into exclusive proprietors and seignorial lords of the Bengal provinces.

13. But though the recognition of the zemindars as landed proprietors was a deliberate act of the Government, yet it was not competent for the Government by that act to transfer or convey to the zemindar any proprietary right

other than what the Government may have possessed. On
this subject the author of "Observations on the Law and
Constitution of India," &c., wrote as follows :—

(*a*). I shall conclude these remarks on the zemindary tenure by quoting the authority of an intelligent native, questioned by Mr. Shore (the present Lord Teignmouth), on the received opinion and custom of India with respect to the right of a zemindar in the soil, and of the sovereign to confer such right. This intelligent person was the son of the former Nazim of Behar. *Q.*—" How is a zemindar appointed ? " *A.*—According to the strict right, no person can become the proprie- tor of land, but by one of the three above-mentioned modes, *viz.*, by *purchase*, by *gift* from the proprietor, or by *inheritance* ; though by usage, the emperor or his representative may displace him (a zemindar) for contumacy and refractory behaviour, and appoint another by sunnud in his room. The person so appointed is by usage considered as zemindar and proprietor of the soil, though, according to strict right, he be not so. " *Q.*—" Is a zemindary hereditary ? " *A.*—" Whatever land a zemindar may have become the *proprietor of by any one of the three abovementioned modes* (*viz.*, purchase, gift, inheritance), descends in the line of inheritance ; but whatever is not *actual property*, is con- sequently not of an hereditary nature" (alluding to his official capacity of zemindar which is not " actual property " doubtless). " If a zemin- dary be the *actual property* of any person, his heir has an undoubted right to succeed without the sanction of the ruler."

Government recognition of land could not convey any proprietary right which Government did not possess.

(*b*). Now here it is evident a distinction is intimated between lands the " *actual property*," which may be called the " hereditary" estate, and lands belonging to the zemindary, not " *actual property*." For example, by sunnud from the king, the zemindar might be vested with the management of the revenue of his own hereditary lands, and other lands adjacent, and the charge of the police, &c. (for that was an essential part of a zemindar's duty) ; also the care of extending the cultivation of waste land, &c. ; and it is worthy of remark that, through- out the whole series of answers to Mr. Shore's queries, Gholam Hoseyn invariably keeps this essential distinction in view ; though from the questions that great distinction seems to be entirely overlooked by Mr. Shore, who appears to take it for granted that an imperial sunnud is a full title to the actual property of the soil, as it is to the official rights of zemindary.

(*c*). But a sunnud, firman, or by whatever name a grant from the crown may be called, can convey no right, but what is vested in the sovereign ; and that is, the collection of the public revenue : I mean over lands held by cultivators, such as I have defined. And let it be observed that this distinction is marked by the names given to the allowances which Government granted to zemindars, *malikana* and *nankar*, the former meaning the dues belonging to a " *malik*," or real owner of land ; the latter to a *manager*. " *Malikana*," says Gholam Hoseyn, " is the unalienable right of ownership ; but *nankar* depends upon fidelity, and a due discharge of the public revenue. *Nankar* is expressly the reward of *service*. If a zemindar is displaced, it would be undoubtedly taken from him. But *malikana* is the *right* of the *proprietor* of land, who receives it (*malikana*) under the rules; and therefore if he receives it (malikana) under the rules, how can an altumghadar, jageerdar, &c., withhold it from him?

(*d*). There are instances of a sovereign purchasing land from a zemindar. On this point Gholam Hoseyn is asked: *Q.*—"Why did the king purchase lands, since he was lord of the country, and might therefore have taken by virtue of that capacity?" *A.*—"The emperor is not so far lord of the soil as to be able, consistently with right and equity, to sell or otherwise dispose of it at his mere will and pleasure. These are rights appertaining only to such a proprietor of land as is mentioned in the first and second answers. The emperor is *proprietor of the revenue,* but *he is not proprietor of the soil.* Hence it is, when he grants *aymas, altumgahs,* and *jageers,* he only *transfers the revenue* from himself to the grantee."

14. Hence there was but too much truth in the remark of the Select Committee of 1812 in the Fifth Report, that—

"the conclusion of the decennial settlement has led to one of the most important measures ever adopted by the East India Company, both in reference to themselves, by fixing the amount of their land revenue in perpetuity, and to the landholders, in establishing and conveying to them rights hitherto unknown and unenjoyed in that country."

15. There is cold comfort in regarding the character and qualifications of those zemindars in whose favour these unheard-of rights were created.

I.—(*a*). Idiots, or of weak understanding.

Warren Hastings.—Mr. Francis seems to suppose that there is no necessity for the interposition of Government between the zemindar and the ryot. He observes "that if they are left to themselves, they will soon come to an agreement in which each party will find his advantage." This would be a just conclusion if the zemindars were all capable of distinguishing what was for their advantage. But it is a fact, which will with difficulty obtain credit in England, though the notoriety will justify me in asserting it here, that much the greatest part of the zemindars, both of Bengal and Behar, are incapable of judging or acting for themselves, being either minors, or men of weak understandings, or absolute idiots.—(Warren Hastings in *Francis' Revenues of Bengal, page 153*).

(*b*). Without this article, we should not think a settlement with the zemindar advisable, especially with the great zemindars. They are for the most part ignorant of, or inattentive to, business, and trust to their servants, who defraud or impose upon them.—*Ibid., page 12 (Messrs. Hastings and Barwell).*

II.—Ignorant and rapacious; ignorance baneful to ryots.

(*a*). Sir J. Shore, *8th December 1789.*

It is allowed that the zemindars are, generally speaking, grossly ignorant of their true interests, and of all that relates to their estates;

that the detail of business with their tenants is irregular and confused, exhibiting an intricate scene of collusion, opposed to exaction, and of unlicensed demand substituted for methodised claims; that the rules by which the rents are demanded from the ryots are numerous, arbitrary, and indefinite; that the officers of the Government, possessing local control, are imperfectly acquainted with them, whilst their superiors, further removed from them, have still less information; that the rights of the talookdars, dependent on the zemindars, as well as of the ryots, are imperfectly understood and defined. * * To the truth of this detail there will be no dissenting voice; and it follows from it, that until the variable rules adopted in adjusting the rent of the ryots are simplified and rendered more definite,[1] no solid improvement can be expected from their labours, upon which the prosperity of the country depends (*paragraphs 10 and 11*).

APP. V.

WORTHLESS
CHARACTER OF
THE ORIGINAL
ZEMINDARS.

Para. 15, contd.

If a review of the zemindars of Bengal were made, it would be found that very few are duly qualified for the management of their hereditary lands, and that in general they are ill-educated for this task, ignorant of the common forms of business, and of the modes of transacting it; inattentive of the conduct of it, even when their own interests are immediately at stake, and indisposed to undertake it. Let a zemindar be asked the simplest questions having any reference to the internal business and state of his zemindary, his replies would probably be the same as if he had never entered it, or he would refer to his dewan or some officer for information (*paragraph 170*).

(*b*). SIR J. SHORE, *June 1789.*

The ignorance of the zemindars, and their great inattention to the management of the concerns for which they are responsible, is as deplorable as it is universal. * * But the most serious consequences of the ignorance and incapacity of the zemindars are those which affect their ryots. Let the situation of a man in this predicament, at the head of a large zemindary, the management of which is intricate to a degree, be considered. Nothing can be more evident than that he must be exposed to endless frauds and impositions. His head farmers can obtain leases at an under-value, for private considerations paid to the managing officer; or, by the same means, remissions at the close of them. Impositions prevail through all the gradations of renters to the ryots; hence proceed alienations of land, unknown to the zemindar or his officers; deductions in the rents of some tenants made up by augmentations on those of others; fabrications and mutilation of accounts, at the end of a lease; fraudulent concealment for temporary stipulations; the perpetual introduction of new taxes; conciliatory remissions at the commencement of a lease; and arbitrary impositions at the expiration of it, with the endless catalogue of abuses which perplex mofussil accounts, and render a remedy difficult. * * I have assigned to incapacity and want of application in the zemindars, what has been attributed to worse motives; but this I believe is certain, that whatever their follies or vices may be, they are themselves the principal sufferers. It is not from profusion, or from the

Worthless char-
acter of the
original zemin-
dars.

---

[1] Not done to this day.

APP. VI.

WORTHLESS
CHARACTER OF
THE ORIGINAL
ZEMINDARS.

Para. 15, contd.

exorbitancy of the demands of Government that they are generally at
this time poor and in debt; ignorance and inactivity have loaded them
with the responsibility of discharging obligations which they might,
perhaps, with moderate abilities and attention have avoided. * * To
those who have been used to consider the zemindars as versed in all the
functions of their situation and trusts; as possessing an intimate
knowledge of their tenants and an immediate connection with them,
as animated with a regard for the prosperity of their estates[1], and as
faithful executors of the public duties, these remarks will appear extraordinary. They are the result of my own experience, combined with
that of others; and I fear no refutation of them, where they are examined with candour, and can be ascertained by local reference and information (*paragraphs 173, 178, and 192*).

III.—POOR CREATURES SUNK IN SLOTH AND DEBAUCHERY.

MR. R. D. MANGLES, *31st Mrach 1848.*

The Committee no doubt know that a great many of the permanently
settled estates changed hands shortly after the permanent settlement
from sale. I do not believe that that resulted in a majority of instances
from over-assessment, but from incapacity on the part of the land-
owners; and it must be admitted that we made regulations for the
protection of the ryots which prevented the zemindars very often from
collecting the rent from them. (*Question*)—You mean incapacity to
manage a landed estate? Yes: the landholders in general were a
miserable imbecile set; the Rajah of Burdwan is almost the only
instance of a great family who have kept their estates—enormous
estates—together; the majority of the great landholders were not men
of business, fit for the management of their own affairs, but poor
creatures brought up in the women's apartments, and sunk in sloth
and debauchery.

IV.—EXTRAVAGANT.

(a). MR. J. MILL, *9th August 1831.*

To a very great degree the original possessors in Bengal have, from
their own improvidence and other causes lost their estates. Few of the
old zemindars now exist. The men who now hold the property are not
resident; they are capitalists who reside in the towns, and manage by
their agents.

Q.—Are not these evils owing to the circumstance of the zemindars
being defective in their personal character, and not the best qualified?
or are they part of the system? They are not saving men, and I think
that may be predicated generally of the persons that live upon rent. I
know no country in which the class of men whose income is derived from

---

[1] These were natural inferences from the assumption of the proprietary right of the
zemindars. The facts and experience of Sir John Shore having discredited the inferences, the
assumption of the zemindar's proprietary right was equally discredited and destroyed.

rent can be considered as accumulators; they are men who spend their incomes, with a very moderate portion of exceptions. * * I think, in general, the persons who own rent and live upon rent consume it all : that is the rule almost universally with them in India, and very generally, I believe, elsewhere.

App. VI.

WORTHLESS CHARACTER OF THE ORIGINAL ZEMINDARS.

Para. 15, contd.

V.—NECESSITOUS ZEMINDARS.

(a). LORD CORNWALLIS, *3rd February 1790.*

I am sorry to be obliged to acknowledge, but it is a truth too evident to deny, that the land proprietors, throughout the whole of the Company's provinces, are in a general state of poverty and depression.

Fifth Report, page 493.

(b). MR. J. MILL, *19th August 1831.*

Supposing a zemindar to be involved in necessities, will he not be tempted thereby to endeavour to relieve those necessities by extracting the largest possible payment from the ryots? I believe he almost invariably does so : there are exceptions of benevolent zemindars, but I believe they are very rare.

Third Report, Select Committee, 1831-32. Q. 3946.

VI.—MORE PLAGUE THAN PROFIT.

(a). MR. J. MILL, *4th August 1831.*

Q. 3211.—Are the greater proportion of the zemindars resident upon their zemindaries? I believe a very considerable proportion of them are non-resident; they are rich natives who live about Calcutta.

Q. 3212.—Therefore the experiment of creating a landed gentry in India by means of the zemindary settlement may be considered to have entirely failed? I so consider it.

Q. 3213.—Have the zemindars been in any way useful in the administration of justice or police? In general quite the contrary : it has been found in cases in which the police of their districts was assigned to them that it was a source of perpetual abuse, and in almost all cases it was taken away.

(b). MR. HOLT MACKENZIE, *18th April 1832.*

Q. 2631.—The only difference is, that if there had been a ryotwar instead of a zemindary settlement in Bengal, the persons now living upon profit-rent would not have existed. Do they exercise a beneficial influence in Bengal, or otherwise? I think very little. Indeed, I am not aware of their being of any use; and although it is of use there should be persons in all countries who accumulate money, I am disposed to think that the aggregate accumulation might have been greater than it is, and that the mass of the people would have been happier.

Sess. 1831-32, Vol XI, Qs. 2630-31.

VII.—Obstructive zemindars.

Worthless
character of
the original
zemindars.

Para. 15, concld.
Sess. 1831-32,
Vol. XI.
Q., 2632-34.

Mr. Holt Mackenzie, *18th April 1832.*

Q.—Are the zemindars a class of persons who assist to uphold the Government, or do they embarrass the Government? I am not aware of their doing anything directly to uphold the Government; the indirect effect of a large body interested in maintaining the existing state of things may be considerable. But they still generally, I fear, dislike and fear us; and they certainly embarrass the Government whenever they think their own interests are likely to be affected by its acts. Thus they are very much averse to any inquisitions into their collections from their tenants, and set themselves to baffle the Government in all attempts made to discover the actual condition and rights of the great body of the people, though such attempts be professedly and actually directed to the better administration of justice. They appear to have been very successful in their resistance to all such measures, and so far have been, I think, very mischievous. *Q.* They stand between the Government and the people, so as to prevent the Government coming in actual contact with the real cultivators of the land? Yes. *Q.* And that to the disadvantage of the community at large? Yes, I think so; and even to their own disadvantage.

16. Respecting the fitness of zemindars for the exercise of police powers, Mr. Mill wrote in his History of India, Book VI, chapter 6, as follows :—

(*a*). One thing recommended for correcting the defective provision by Lord Cornwallis for the administration of penal justice was to re-invest the zemindars with powers of police; and among the interrogatories circulated by Government in 1801, the opinion of the Judges was asked on "the expediency of granting to zemindars, farmers, and other persons of character, commissions empowering them to act as justices of the peace." Among the most intelligent of the Company's servants, one opinion on this subject seems alone to exist. "I am persuaded," says the Magistrate of Burdwan, "that to vest the zemindars and farmers of this district with the powers proposed, would not only prove nugatory for the objects intended, but be highly detrimental to the country, and destructive of the peace of the inhabitants. Few of the zemindars and farmers of any respectability reside on their estates and farms. Allow them to exercise a power equal to the purposes, and to vest with it by delegation, their agents or under-farmers, the worst and most mischievous consequences are to be apprehended from their abuse of it." On this occasion the Magistrates of the 24-Pergunnahs say—"From the general character of the zemindars, farmers, and other inhabitants of the districts, we do not think that it would be advisable to vest any of them with the powers of justices of the peace. On the contrary, we are of opinion that such a measure, so far from being in any way beneficial to the police of the district, would be a source of great oppression to the lower class of the inhabitants, and of innumerable complaints to the magistrate."

(*b*). They add—"We have reason to believe, though it is difficult to establish proof against them, that the zemindars, not only in many instances, encourage and harbour dacoits, but frequently partake of the property plundered by them. The *choukidars* and *pikes* employed by them are concerned in almost every dacoity committed in the districts subject to our jurisdiction."

(c). To the same purport, the Judge of Circuit in the Rajshahye Division says, in 1808: "My informants attributed the success of the dacoits to the same cause that every body else does, namely, the protection given them by the zemindars and police officers, and other people of power and influence in the country. Every thing I see, and hear, and read on this subject, serves to convince me of the truth of this statement." * *

(d). The Judge of Circuit in the Benares Division in 1808, discants with great warmth upon the same topic, the extreme difficulty of maintaining order in any country without the assistance of a superior class of inhabitants incorporated with the people, and possessing that influence which superior property and education confer, over others deprived of those advantages : " In maintaining this opinion, I may " says he, " unless I greatly deceive myself, appeal to the general practice of almost all nations, originating doubtless, in circumstances and feelings common to all mankind. The natural mode of managing men is to employ the agency of those whom, from the relation in which they stand to them, they regard with respect and confidence. Accordingly, all governments seem to have made the authority of these native leaders the basis of their police ; and any hired police establishment which they maintain are not intended to supersede the native police, but to superintend, and watch its efforts. To take an example with which we are all familiar. In our own country we all know what services society contributes to its own protection. We know how much vigour is conferred on its police by the support which it receives from native gentry, from respectable landholers, from the corporations in towns, and from substantial persons of the middle class in the villages. We can form some conception of the mischief which would ensue if that support should be withdrawn, and an attempt made to compensate it by positive laws and artificial institutions."

VIII.— GENERAL CHARACTER OF THE WHOLE BODY.

SIR J. SHORE, *June 1789*.

If the real capacity of the zemindars were taken as a rule for determining the selection of them for employment, it is evident that they must be in general excluded.

17. The zemindars give as little help to the police in the present day, as they rendered to it in 1808 ; and the only resemblance which Lord Cornwallis succeeded in establishing between the zemindars of his creation and the landed proprietors in England is in the large incomes which a few of the former have acquired.

18. Summing up the information in this Appendix, it appears that the zemindary was an office for the revenue,

APP. VI.

WORTHLESS
CHARACTER OF
THE ORIGINAL
ZEMINDARS.

Para. 18.

App. VI.

WORTHLESS
CHARACTOR OF
THE ORIGINAL
ZEMINDARS.

Para. 18, contd.

police, and general administration of the area comprised in the zemindary. This is evident from various incidents which attached to the office. Thus—

(*a*). The zemindar's liability to dismissal.

(*b*). The exclusion of incompetent zemindars.

(*c*). The disqualification of a zemindar to transfer or sell the zemindary without the sanction of Government.

(*d*). The exceeding largeness of several zemindaries, and the history of their growth, showed that they were not acquired by purchase or inheritance.

(*e*). The hereditary succession to a zemindary showed that it was an office, for, by Hindu and Mohamedan law alike, real property is equally divided among children.

(*f*). And even hereditary succession was not effectual without great difficulty and expense to the heir; and while the tenth of the Government revenue thus acquired represented adequately the zemindar's remuneration, it fell far short of a proprietor's income from his own lands.

(*g*). Two other circumstances attested in a marked manner the purely official character of a zemindar, *viz.*, the appointment of canoongoes and putwarries to check the zemindars' proceedings and collections, as a protection to the ryots, and the levy of transit dues by zemindars, dues which were leviable in only their official character.

II.—In addition to these considerations, the zemindars' sunnud, the instructions of Aurungzebe to collectors of revenue, and the testimony of various authorities, attest the purely official character of the zemindars, who used their influence and authority to encroach on the rights and the property of the village communities and their headmen.

III.—The recognition by Government of proprietary rights in official zemindars, as such, was prompted by a desire to evade a jurisdiction which the Supreme Court in Calcutta asserted over the zemindars as officers of Government. But as the Government were not the proprietors of the soil, their recognition of the zemindars as proprietors could extend no farther than to a property in the revenue which belonged to Government. Even had the rights of the Government been those of conquerors, this, according to universal law and usage, would have been the extent and limit of transfer of proprietary rights to the zemindars; but the Government were not acting then as conquerors, but simply as dewans for the management of the revenues of Bengal, Behar, and Orissa. Not the Local Government, nor the East India

Company, nor Parliament, had the right, in law, to transfer proprietary right to zemindars, from the millions of cultivating proprietors to whom the right really belonged. Accordingly, in Regulation I of 1793, the term 'proprietor' is used in this restricted sense, inasmuch as only those who paid revenue direct to Government were recognised in that Regulation as proprietors; but, in practice, this meaning, like the cruelly good intentions of the authors of the permanent settlement, was forgotten.

IV.—The Select Committee of 1812 were constrained to record in their Fifth Report that the East India Company had conveyed to zemindars "rights hitherto unknown and unenjoyed in" Bengal; and they placed on record unimpeachable testimony that the persons in whose favour the proprietary rights of millions had been confiscated were worthless characters, as being—

a. (Many of them), idiots, or of weak understanding.

b. (Another large number), poor creatures sunk in sloth and debauchery.

c. Extravagant, necessitous, and therefore exacting.

d. (Including managers of the estates of *a, b* and *c*) ignorant and rapacious; harbourers of dacoits.

e. Obstructive zemindars, more plague than profit.

V.—Parliament knew these things, but did not correct them, though vested interests in abuses, oppression and wrong, which somehow are supposed to be hallowed by time, had not had time to establish themselves.

App. VI.

———

WORTHLESS CHARACTER OF ORIGINAL ZEMINDARS.

Para. 18, contd.

APPENDIX VII.

App. VII.
——
Classes of
Zemindars.

Sess. 1831-32,
Vol. XI, pages
305 to 307.

Zemindars after the Permanent Settlement.

1. Classes of Zemindars.

Mr. Holt Mackenzie 1832.

I. The only two classes that have a permanent title of property independently of grant from, or engagement with, the Government, are—

a.—The fixed occupants of fields, *i. e.*, those by whom, or at whose risk and charge, land is tilled, and its fruits gathered, and who cannot b justly ousted so long as they pay the amount or value demandable from them within a limit determined on certain fixed principles.

b.—Communities of cultivating zemindars (commonly called biswa dars or coparcenary occupants of villages) who assert, as colonists o conquerors, a property, several or common, in the lands lying withi defined boundaries, whether cultivated or waste, subject in certain case to the rights of the preceding class. From these they are distinguishe chiefly by this, that, besides a fixed title of occupancy in the fields actuall cultivated by them, they have a right, corporate or several, in all land lying within a specific division of territory, not appropriated to the use o others, and in the actual or reversionary advantages derivable from occu pied land, not taken by Government to itself, nor specifically admitted t belong to others; *in other words, a right in all waste lands within the vi lage boundary, and in all land cultivated by pykasht ryots or other tha fixed occupancy ryots.*

II. There are several others who have obtained a valuable property i the produce of the land, either as contractors for or assignees of th Government or revenue, through grants, concessions or engagements o our own and former Governments, but I need not specify them.

a.—I shall only remark that the zemindars of Bengal, though man of them originally held a mere office, must be considered as having bee vested by our settlement with the property of everything within the zemindaries which belonged to the Government, and was not reserved b it ; and inasmuch as the coparcenary rights, which I have above endeavoure to describe, do not seem to have belonged to any among the villag communities in Lower Bengal, where, as in the Northern Circars, th unoccupied lands and reversionary interests appear to have belonged the Government, they may now, in point of right to those lands, classed with the biswadars.

b.—It may be useful to explain that though I consider the zeminda as the assignees of Government, to have possessed the right of disposi of unoccupied land, yet if the khodkhast ryots have, without sp cial agreement, occupied such land, I would by no means infer that th are, even with regard to such lands, mere tenants-at-will. And I am n sure whether we are quite justified in denying to the village communiti

of Bengal Proper, the biswa right (*to waste*) asserted and maintained by
the sturdier men of the west.

c.—The rights of the zemindars, as collectors of the Government rent
or revenue chargeable upon land occupied by others, stand of course upon
a different footing. These must be interpreted with reference to the
claims of others, since Government cannot be understood tacitly to have
transferred to its contractors properties belonging to third parties; and
its declarations, as far as they go, are all directed to the point of maintaining these properties, however insufficient they have proved for the
full attainment of that object.

d.—Even in unsettled countries, it would be held tyrannical to
disregard long-established usage; and it is, I think, quite clear that in
the permanently settled districts, the Government engagees were bound
by their contract to maintain, with certain specified exceptions, the rules
and usages existing at the time the settlement was made. Hence, in
defining their interests in the produce of lands owned by others, we must,
of course, look minutely to local circumstances, which cannot be explained
in any general treatise.

III. (*a*).—The above explanation of the character of the several
classes of occupants, enables one to arrange the contractors also in three
great divisions:

1st, persons who possess the full biswa right in the part of which
they collect the revenue;

2nd, persons possessing a share in the biswa right, and acting in the
collection of the revenue as the representatives of other co-proprietors.

3rd, persons collecting the revenue of villages of which the biswa
right belongs wholly to others or to Government.

b.—Under the first division we may now place most of the zemindars
of Bengal, deriving their biswa interest from the act of our Government.
And there are also to be found in other provinces, cases in which the
biswadars of villages, or other parts, holding by succession or purchase
from the original settlers, colonists, or conquerors, are single; or, if many,
are all admitted to share equally in the advantage and responsibility of
the engagement with Government, and equally to see the function of
collection. To this class, most of the persons who have purchased
villages sold for the recovery of arrears of revenue, and several of the
great talookdars or hereditary revenue farmers, claim to belong.

c.—Under the second division come the managing or headmen of
village communities, prevalent in Behar, Benares, and the Western Provinces, of whom, though some claim an hereditary title in the post, all
may apparently be held to fall under the designation of representatives.
The freedom and mode of election is a separate thing.

d.—The third division includes many rajahs, talookdars, and zemindars, collecting the revenue of extensive parts, of which the villages are
occupied by other persons possessed of the biswa right. And although
such contractors may be the biswadars of some villages, the circumstance
does not (supposing a settlement by villages with defined limits) require
or justify a further sub-division of the class in question.

IV. If the distinction between the rights that attach to occupancy
of land (as I have defined it) and those which are incident to the collection, or assignment, of the Government revenue, be steadily kept in view,

APP. VII.

CLASSES OF ZE-
MINDARS.

Para. 1, contd.

with advertence to the classification I have above endeavoured to sketch, it seems to me that there cannot be much difficulty in determining accurately the general nature of the interests belonging to all classes, in so far as they can be determined without the ascertainment, village by village, and field by field, of the claims of individuals.

V. Where any one shall have established by prescription, under preceding Governments, or gained by stipulation from ours, the right of collecting the public dues, with a beneficial interest, immediate or contingent, of which it would be unjust to divest him except for sufficient cause, or without adequate compensation, such claims will, of course, require to be considered before we proceed to collect from all the occupants or from those who are also biswadars. But when once the character of such claims is defined, they will not hinder the adoption of any arrangement that may be best for the public good, if it be found in the compulsory surrender of such intermediate titles, a measure not lightly to be resolved upon.

VI. On the other hand, when any class, whether biswadars or not, are maintained in the practical exercise of a right of hereditary management over lands occupied by others, such right, its nature being distinctly ascertained, may easily be rendered consistent with the just claims of all other classes. The mischief hitherto done has arisen from the practice of employing the term proprietor, without defining the nature of the property : and from overlooking the fact that several distinct properties may very well attach to a single subject-matter.

2. The statement in the last three sections in the preceding paragraph, that the rights which the Government bestowed upon zemindars in the zemindary settlement in no way affected or derogated from the rights which ryots possessed independently of official sanction, is borne out by the reservation of ryots' rights in the sanction accorded by the Court of Directors to the Permanent Settlement, and by the following extracts.

I. LORD CORNWALLIS, *3rd February 1790.*

Fifth Report,
page 486.

a.—I agree with Mr. Shore, that some interference on the part of Government is undoubtedly necessary for effecting an adjustment of the demands of the zemindars upon the ryots; nor do I conceive that the former will take alarm at the reservation of this right of interference, when convinced that Government can have no interest in exercising it, but for the purposes of public justice. Were the Government itself to be a party in the cause, they might have some grounds for apprehending the result of its decisions.

b.—Mr. Shore observes that this interference is inconsistent with proprietary right : that it is an encroachment upon it to prohibit a landlord from imposing taxes on his tenant ; for it is saying to him that he shall not raise the rents of his estates ; and that if the land is the zemindar's, it will be only partially his property, whilst we prescribe the quantum which he is to collect, or the mode by which the adjustment is to take place between the parties concerned.

c.—If Mr. Shore means that after having declared the zemindar proprietor of the soil, in order to be consistent we have no right to prevent his imposing new abwabs or taxes on the lands in cultivation, I must differ with him in opinion, unless we suppose the ryots to be absolute slaves of the zemindars : every beegha of land possessed by them must have been cultivated under an expressed or implied agreement that a certain sum should be paid for each beegha of produce and no more. Every abwab, or tax, imposed by the zemindar over and above that sum is not only a breach of that agreement, but a direct violation of the established laws of the country. The cultivator, therefore, has in such case an undoubted right to apply to Government for the protection of his property ; and Government is at all times bound to afford him redress. I do not hesitate, therefore, to give it as my opinion, that the zemindars, neither now nor ever, could possess a right to impose taxes or abwabs upon the ryots; and if from the confusion which prevailed towards the close of the Mogul Government, or neglect, or want of information, since we have had the possession of the country, new abwabs have been imposed by the zemindars or farmers, the Government has an undoubted right to abolish such as are oppressive, and have never been confirmed by a competent authority ; and to establish such regulations as may prevent the practice of like abuses in future.

d.—Neither is the privilege which the ryots in many parts of Bengal enjoy of holding possession of the spots of land which they cultivate, so long as they pay the revenue assessed upon them, by any means incompatible with the proprietary rights of the zemindars. Whoever cultivates the land, the zemindars can receive no more[1] than the established rent which in most cases is fully equal to what the cultivator can afford to pay. To permit him to dispossess one cultivator for the sole purpose of giving the land to another, would be vesting him with a power to commit a wanton act of oppression from which he could derive no benefit. The practice that prevailed under the Mogul Government, of uniting many districts into one zemindary, and thereby subjecting a large body of people to the control of one principal zemindar, rendered some restriction of this nature absolutely necessary. The zemindar, however, may sell the land, and the cultivator must pay the rent to the purchaser.

Page 487.

II. LORD CORNWALLIS, 18th September 1789.

a.—I am also convinced that failing the claim of right of the zemindars (as against the Government), it would be necessary for the public good to grant a right of property in the soil to them, or to persons of other descriptions. I think it unnecessary[2] to enter into any discussion of the grounds upon which their right appears to have been founded.

Fifth Report.
Page 473.

---

[1] Here the author of the permanent settlement either ignored the distinction between khodkhast and pykhast, or relied upon what was fact at the time, viz., that the pergunnah rates, or those paid by khodkhast ryots, were higher than the rates paid by pykhasts. The facts are now all the other way, and Lord Cornwallis' benevolent conclusions have been all upset and are topsy-turvy.

[2] Where the Government was prepared to surrender its own right to the zemindar, discussion of his right was unnecessary ; but where the surrender of ryots' rights was involved, discussion of the zemindar's rights was imperative.

b.—I understand the word permanency to extend only to the jumma, and not to the details of the settlement; for many regulations will certainly be hereafter necessary for the further security of the ryots in particular, and even of those talookdars who, to my concern, must still remain in some degree of dependence on the zemindars. *   *   I cannot, however, admit that such regulations can, in any degree, affect the rights which it is now proposed to confirm to the zemindars, for I never will allow that in any country Government can be said to invade the rights of a subject, when they only require, for the benefit of the State, that he shall accept of a reasonable equivalent for the surrender of a real or supposed right, which in his hands is detrimental to the general interest of the public; or when they prevent his committing cruel oppressions upon his neighbours or upon his own dependents.

III. Mr. Hodgson, Member of the Board of Revenue, Madras, *28th March 1808.*

When a zemindary settlement in Dindigal was discussed in 1800, it was not known, and, I regret to say, is not now generally admitted, that two rights could, under the words "proprietary right" in the Regulations, exist; that the cultivators could possess one right, and the zemindars another; yet both be distinct rights. It was argued that the words "proprietary right" so frequently used in the regulations, and so formally confirmed by Sunnud Milkeeut Istemrar on all zemindars, hereditary or by purchase, was an unlimited right; that is, an undefined power, or a power to be exercised according to the discretion of the proprietor, over all the land of the zemindary or estate. It is declared to be inconsistent with "proprietary right" that the proprietor should be guided by any other rule than his own will, in demanding his rent; and emigration, under this interpretation, is admitted to be the only relief from an excessive rent. This mode of reasoning would not, perhaps, have gained so much ground if it had been within the means of all to have obtained the perusal of the interesting discussions on the subject between the Right Honourable Marquis Cornwallis and Sir John Shore, the Bengal Regulations, and the proceedings of the Board at Madras, on proposing the introduction of the permanent system. It could have been distinctly seen from those documents that the first principle of the per-manent settlement was to confirm and secure the rights of the cultivators of the soil. *To confirm and secure* are the terms which must be used, because no new rights were granted, or any doubt entertained upon the following leading features of their right, *viz.* :—

1st.—That no zemindar, proprietor (or whatever name be given to those persons), was entitled by law, custom, or usage, to make his demands for rent according to his convenience; or in other words;

2nd.—That the cultivators of the soil had the solid right, from time immemorial, of paying a defined rent and no more, for the land they cultivated. This right is inherent in all the cultivators from the most northern parts of India to Cape Comorin.

3rd.—The "proprietary right" of zemindars, in the Regulations is therefore no more than the right to collect from the cultivators that rent which custom has established as the right of Government; and the benefit arising from this right is confined, *first*, to an extension of the amount, not of the rate, of the customary rent by an increase of cultivation; *secondly*, to a profit in dealings in grain, where the rent may be rendered in kind; *thirdly*, to a change from an inferior to a superior kind of culture, arising out of a mutual understanding of their interest between the cultivator and proprietor.

APP. VII.
——
ONLY THE REVE-
NUE WAS PER-
MANENTLY SET-
TLED.

Para. 2, contd.

IV. Mr. N. J. Halhed, *1832.*

In the discussions which eventually led to the permanent settlement of the revenue in Bengal, Behar, Orissa, and Benares, the interests of the agriculturists were entirely forgotten; it appears from the minutes of Council that the point mooted was simply, whether the property in the soil vested in the sovereign or in the zemindar, or contractor for the revenue; and the question was set at rest by declaring the proprietary rights in the *estates*, or jurisdictions for the revenue of which they had contracted to pay, to belong to the latter.

Page 91.

V. Tagore Law Lectures, *1874-75.*

These extracts show in what light the zemindars were regarded before the decennial settlement, and that the question was considered mainly with reference to the matter then in hand—a more or less permanent settlement of the revenue. The conclusion arrived at was that the zemindars in Bengal were the proper persons to be settled with, inasmuch as they had long enjoyed the right to such settlement; and had acquired, if they did not originally possess, a proprietary right in the land, the extent of which it was unnecessary to discuss further than to ascertain that it justified a permanent settlement with them as the nearest approach to an English holder in fee-simple, and as the most likely class to develop into the English landlord (*see* next two extracts).

Page 282.

VI. Harington's Analysis of the Regulations.

If by the terms *proprietor of land,* and *actual proprietor of the soil,* be meant a landholder possessing the full rights of an English landlord, or freeholder in fee-simple, with equal liberty to dispose of all the lands forming part of his estate as he may think most for his own advantage, to oust his tenants, whether for life or for a term of years, on the termination of their respective leaseholds, and to advance their rents on the expiration of leases at his discretion; such a designation, it may be admitted, is not strictly and correctly applicable to a Bengal *zemindar*, who does not possess so unlimited a power over the *khodkhast* ryots, and other descriptions of under-tenants possessing, as well as himself, certain rights and interests in the lands which constitute his zemindary.

Page 222.

10

App. VII.

Sess. 1831-32,
Vol. XI.

Para. 2, contd.

VII. Mr. Fortescue, Civil Commissioner of Delhi, formerly in high Revenue Offices in Lower Bengal, *12th April 1832.*

a.—*Q. 2290.*—Do not you understand that the effect of the permanent settlement has been to vest in the zemindar a nominal property in the soil? Neither the spirit of the Regulations, nor the minutes recorded anterior to them, meant to convey any right which should injure the subordinate holders.

Question 2303.

b.—Neither the intention of the Government, nor the spirit of the Regulations, went to give any right to the zemindar that was to interfere with subordinate rights; next I would say, that had the rates by which the ryots were formerly liable to be assessed been recorded at the permanent settlement, and fixed, the value of the rights of the ryots would ere this day have been very considerable, and would have rendered them secure and comfortable. Such rates, in some instances, were recorded, and have been appealed to; and, if my recollection is correct, are to be found inserted in some of the ryots' pottahs.

c.—*Q. 2312.*—The Committee have been informed that whatever the theory and principle may be, practically the rights of the ryots have pretty much ceased in the Lower Provinces; is that so? Yes; but not, however, by formal act of the Legislature. An unrestrained practice, convenient indeed, perhaps, has grown up at variance with principle; but that is no reason for perpetuating the injustice.

Q. 2313.—Does it not appear to be an inevitable consequence of the Regulations? I do not see that it should have been, or continue to be; it was certainly not their principle. A person fairly studying the sense and spirit of the Regulations, and knowing their objects, could not say that it was competent for the Courts to deny that the ryots had rights.

Q. 2314.—Supposing that you make the zemindar responsible to Government, assuming a power of compulsion over him, and find it necessary also to communicate the same power of compulsion to him, over the actual cultivator of the land, does it not constitute him, to all intents and purposes, their landholder? No, I think not; the Government itself could give no more than it had, that is, its entire interest as far as it went, but no further; and the practice of all the preceding Governments, whether under settlements by Akbar, Turee Mul, or others, was that the arrangements for the revenue were formed with reference to ryots' rights. The term is constantly made use of, "*huq e reyaea,*" or "rights of the ryots." In the grants of former Governments, declarations and stipulations are made to secure that "*huq*" or right; therefore if such terms are made use of, they must have had reference to some right.

3. It has been seen (paragraph 2, section II *b*) that Lord Cornwallis disallowed the zemindar's right, under the contemplated permanent settlement, to increase the rate of rent for the ryot's usual cultivation. The sources from which the zemindar's income was to increase, despite this limitation of

the demand upon the ryot, were thus indicated in his Lordship's minute dated 3rd February 1790 :—

Sources of in-
crease of
zemindar's in-
come.
———
Para. 4.
Fifth Report.
Page 487.

I. Neither is prohibiting the landholder to impose new *abwabs* or taxes on the lands in cultivation tantamount to saying to him that he shall not raise the rents of his estates. The rents of an estate are not to be raised by the imposition of new abwabs or taxes on every beegah of land in cultivation. * * No zemindar claims a right to impose new taxes on the land in cultivation ; although it is obvious that they have clandestinely levied them when pressed to answer demands upon them-selves ; and that these taxes have, from various causes, been perpetuated to the ultimate detriment of the proprietor who imposed them.

II. The rents of an estate can only be raised—

a—by inducing the ryots to cultivate the more valuable articles of produce ;

b—by inducing them to clear the extensive tracts of waste land which are to be found in almost every zemindary in Bengal.

4. It appears from the preceding section I, that, in the opinion of Lord Cornwallis, no zemindar was entitled to enhance the rent of old lands in cultivation beyond the per-gunnah rate. All *abwabs* in excess of that rate were illegal and oppressive : and in allowing the consolidation of existing abwabs with the pergunnah rate, he was justified in prohib-iting fresh *abwabs*. Lord Cornwallis did not overlook that existing *abwabs* were partly extra cesses imposed on account of a rise of prices ; but as he exemptedzemindars from in-crease of assessment on account of a rise of prices, that con-tingency was disregarded in prohibiting fresh *abwabs*. It further appears from *a* and *b* of the preceding section II, that the only contemplated sources of increased collections from ryots were from new lands, and from a better kind of produce from lands already under cultivation. Thus an increase of the ryots' rent from a general rise of prices of the old kinds of produce was not contemplated. The exclusion of this from the possible sources of increased revenue was not inadvertent—it was intentional ; for the noble Lord had, in a previous paragraph of his minute, protected the zemindar from any increase of the rent payable by him to Government, on account of any such rise in prices—

Thus " equally favourable to the contributors is the probable altera-tion in the value of silver ; for there is little doubt but that it will continue to fall, as it has done for centuries past, in proportion as the quantity drawn from the mines and thrown into general circulation increases. If this be admitted, the assessment will become gradually lighter, because, as the value of silver diminishes, the landholder will be able, upon an average, to procure the quantity which he may engage to pay annually to Government, with a proportionably smaller part of the produce of his lands than he can at present."

Here the intention clearly was that the cultivating proprietor of land should benefit by a rise of prices of the produce of his land. But the Regulations of 1793 having restricted the term proprietor to those who engaged with the Government for the Government revenue from land, the right in the unearned increment was erroneously transferred to the latter, as regards all except khodkasht ryots, under a rule of assessment which was introduced for the first time by Act X of 1859. Sir J. Shore actually proposed that not only the rate, but the amount of the ryots' rent, should be fixed, and such a fixing of the amount was incompatible with any subsequent increase of rent from a rise of prices.

5. Nor was ryots' rent to be increased by *abwabs*.

I. SIR J. SHORE, *June 1789*.

a.—The *abwab subahdary*, or viceroyal imposts, which constitute the increase since 1728, enhanced the rates upon the ryots. They were in general levied upon the standard assessment in certain proportions to its amount, and the zemindars who paid them were authorised to collect them from their ryots in the same proportions to their respective quotas of rent. * * Jaffier Khan was the author of this innovation, the consequences of which he did not foresee. The tax imposed by him, which established the precedent, was trifling in its amount, and apparently intended as a fee to the king's officers (*paragraphs 33 and 34*).

b.—Long before the time of Jaffier Khan, impositions under various denominations, and to a very considerable amount, had been levied from the ryots beyond the tumar, or standard assessment. In many places they had been consolidated into the assul, and a new standard had been assumed as the basis of succeeding impositions (*paragraph 37*).

c.—The imposition of these cesses is generally discretional (with the subahdar); they differ in names, number, and amount throughout the country; their rates are variously regulated, at so much per rupee, or according to the number of months, and by other distinctions. The proportion of each is not calculated upon the assul only, but generally upon the aggregate of that and the preceding cesses, and so on progressively (*paragraph 223*).

d.—In every district throughout Bengal, where the license of exaction has not superseded all rule, the rents of the land are regulated by known rates called *Nirk*, and in some districts each village has its own; these rates are formed, with respect to the produce of the land, at so much per beegah; some soil produces two crops in a year of different species, some three; the more profitable articles, such as the mulberry plant, betel leaf, tobacco, sugarcane, and others, render the value of the land proportionably great. These rates must have been fixed upon a measurement of the land, and the settlement of Turee Mull may have furnished the basis of them. In the course of time, cesses were superadded to the standard, and became included in a subsequent valuation, the rates varying with every succeeding measurement. At present, there are many *abwabs* or cesses collected distinct from the *nerrik* and not included in it, although they are levied in certain proportions to it (*paragraphs 391 and 392*).

e.—The leading principles upon which I shall ground my propositions are two : *first,* the security of Government with respect to its revenues ; *second,* the security and protection of its subjects. The former will be best established by concluding a permanent settlement with the zemindars or proprietors of the soil ; the land, their property, is the security to Government. The second must be ensured by carrying into practice, as far as possible, an acknowledged maxim of taxation, *viz.,* that the tax which each individual is bound to pay ought to be certain, and not arbitrary.[1] The time of payment, the manner of payment, the quantity to be paid, ought all to be clear and plain to the contributor and every other person (*paragraphs 456 to 460*).

II. Sir J. Shore, *8th December 1789.*

a.—Notwithstanding repeated prohibitions against the introduction of new taxes, we still found that many have been established of late years. The idea of the imposition of taxes by a landlord upon his tenant implies an inconsistency ; and the prohibition in spirit is an encroachment upon proprietary right ; for it is saying to the landlord, you shall not raise the rents of your estate.[2] But without expatiating on this part of the argument, I shall only here observe, that with an exception of arbitrary limitation in favour of the khodkhast ryots, the Regulations for the new settlement virtually confirm all these taxes, without our possessing any records of them, and without knowing how far they are burthensome or otherwise. * * At present they are in many places so numerous and complicated, that after having obtained an enumeration of the whole, the amount of the assul, with the proportionate rates of the several *abwabs,* it requires an accountant of some ability to calculate what a ryot is to pay, and the calculation may be presumed to be beyond the ability of most tenants. The pottah rarely expresses the sum total of the rents ; and it is difficult to determine what is extortion (*paragraph 16*).

b.—The necessity of prescribing regulations for simplifying the complicated rentals of the ryots (which ought, if possible, to be reduced to one sum for a given quantity of land of a determinate quality and produce),[3] of defining and establishing the rights of the ryots and talookdars with precision, together with the expediency of procuring clear data for the transfer by sale of public and private property, are admitted (*paragraph 19*).

---

[1] This was a clear intimation that the ryot's rent was to be certain, that is, definitely fixed. The amount being fixed, it could not be increased from a rise of price.

[2] This inconsistency, which attaches only to the theory that the zemindar was proprietor, and not an official collector, should have shown Sir. J. Shore that the zemindar was not the proprietor.

[3] The amount of a rent fixed on these data would not be liable to reduction with a fall, or to increase with a rise, of prices.

APP. VII. III. LORD CORNWALLIS, *3rd February 1790.*

RYOTS' RENTS
NOT TO BE
ENHANCED.

Para. 5, contd.

Fifth Report,
page 486.
This is a distinct
affirmation that
the *amount*
payable by the
ryot was to be
fixed ; in other
words, it could
not be enhanced
from a rise of
prices.

Sess. 1831-32,
Vol. XI page
20, of App.
No. 6.

Mr. Shore's proposition that the rents of the ryots, by whatever rule or custom they may be demanded, shall be specific as to their amount ; that the landholders shall be obliged, within a certain time, to grant pottahs or writings to their ryots, in which the amount shall be inserted, and that no ryot shall be liable to pay more than the sum actually specified in his pottah—if duly enforced by the collectors—will soon obviate the objection to a fixed assessment, founded upon the undefined state of the demands of the landholders upon the ryots.

IV. MR. A. D. CAMPBELL.

It had been proposed by Lord Teignmouth, in Bengal, to fix the maximum rates of the public revenue payable by the cultivators to the zemindar at those actually assessed when the permanent settlement was introduced, which, though confirming existing illegal cesses, would, at any rate, have placed a bar against further abuse, and given a precise limitation to the zemindar's demand. The local or pergunnah rates, left undefined, were however preferred in Bengal.

(It can hardly be said that they were *preferred* in Bengal : both Sir John Shore and Lord Cornwallis distinctly advocated specification in the pottahs of the *amounts* payable by the ryots ; the omission to exact this security was only another of the numerous serious mistakes of benevolence in 1793 which must have made angels weep.)

6. It is clear that among the rights made over by Government to the zemindars in 1793, that of imposing *abwabs* was not transferred ; nor was the right transferable, because *abwabs* imposed by the subahdar were imposed for some alleged public exigency, and no such exigency can be pleaded by a zemindar of the present day for his *abwabs* (see paragraph 11). Indeed, Sir John Shore distinctly denied (paragraph 30 of his minute dated 8th December 1789) the title of even the Government to impose a war tax upon the zemindars as an *abwab*, after the declaration of the permanent settlement.

7. The progressive increase of the income of zemindaries may be discerned in the following extracts :—

I. MR. G. DOWDESWELL, *16th October 1811.*

Revenue
Selections, Vol.
I, page 172.

Eighteen years have now elapsed since the permanent settlement. It is computed that the population of a country doubles itself in twenty years. If, then, the cultivation of the country had not kept pace with the increase of its population, its produce would, at the present day, be totally insufficient for the support of its inhabitants. Exclusively of this consideration, almost every person's observation leads him to remark the extension of cultivation in one part of the country or another ; and we

have every reason to suppose that estates which before yielded to the
proprietors a surplus produce of ten or twelve per cent. on the jumma,
now yield them a surplus produce of thirty, forty, or fifty per cent.

II. Mr. H. Colebrooke, *1813.*

The extent and value of the general improvement may be judged
from the particular instances which come under the notice of the revenue
and judicial authorities, when occasions arise for ascertaining the proprietors' income by regular inquiry, or when it is incidentally made known,
or is deducible from other circumstances, such as the price which lands
fetch at public or at private sale. From such sources of information
there are grounds for reckoning the
net income of zemindars, upon an
average, at an amount equal to half
the assessment payable to Government. This indicates* an improvement in the proportion of one-third
of the former produce of the land.
* * The present landholders are
opulent and prosperous.

			Rs.	Rs.
* Sudder jumma	...	...	10	
Proprietor's present income	...	5		
		—		15
Sudder jumma	...	...	10	
Proprietor's former income	...	1		
		—		11
Difference	...	4		

III. Mr. J. Mill, *2nd August 1831.*

By the practice of preceding governments, one-tenth of what was
collected by the zemindar (I speak of Bengal) was allowed to him as his
remuneration; he had other sources of profit; but it was upon the
principle of this division that the permanent settlement was made: the
understanding was that nine-tenths of the rent, or of the net produce of
the land collected from the ryots, was paid to Government, and one-
tenth was reserved for the zemindars. The progress of circumstances has
very much altered those proportions.

IV. Mr. H. St. Geo. Tucker, *9th April 1832.*

The zemindar, most assuredly, has obtained under the permanent settlement much larger rents now than he could ever have done, perhaps,
under the former system: he has also had very great advantages from
bringing into cultivation waste lands, which have formed a new source of
rent to him.

V. Mr. A. D. Campbell, *1832.*

a.—The zemindars may be divided into three distinct classess: first,
the village zemindars, or cultivators in the provinces of Bengal and Behar
raised to this rank on the introduction of the permanent settlement
there; secondly, the purchasers of this right by public auction; and
thirdly, the ancient zemindars whom we found, as such, on our acquisition
of the country. A vast benefit has been conferred on the whole of these

classes, but on them alone, by limiting in perpetuity the demand of Government upon them. What proportion their present ill-defined receipts, from the cultivators, bears to the fixed payment they make to Government, cannot now be ascertained, except in such zemindaries as, from minority, lunacy, or other causes, have accidentally fallen, temporarily, under the charge of the Court of Wards at the two Presidencies. In Bengal it appears that, in a number of such zemindaries taken indiscriminately, the zemindars' receipts were more than double the jumma payable by them to Government. Thus, although the hereditary interest in the land revenue, confirmed to them when the permanent settlement took place, was at that time calculated not to exceed the permanent jumma reserved by Government to the extent of more than ten to fifteen per cent., it has risen to one hundred per cent., so that, in the land revenue of Government, now actually drawn from the cultivators of the provinces settled on the permanent zemindary system, the hereditary interest of the zemindar has frequently, at the present day, become greater even than that which the State reserved to itself.

Ibid.   *b.*—This has arisen from three distinct causes. It is owing (1st) to the general ignorance of the Government respecting the real amount of the land revenue payable by the cultivators, when the permanent settlement was introduced, which frequently, in the Bengal provinces especially, led to their fixing the zemindars' jumma at sums quite inadequate; (2ndly) to the want of due limitation of the zemindars' demand upon the cultivators in Bengal, which, as before explained, has placed them entirely at the zemindars' mercy; and (3rdly) to the new revenue derived from the further occupation of land, since the permanent settlement was introduced, the result of increased population, and of the gradual extension of agriculture to the lands then waste, which were, perhaps imprudently, relinquished to the zemindars at the period of the permanent settlement, by including them within the bounds of their respective zemindaries. But the benefits accruing to the zemindars from these causes have been felt only by those whose estates remain in the possession of themselves or their descendants, or by such as have happened to purchase at auction zemindaries favourably assessed.

VI. Mr. R. D. Mangles, *31st March 1848.*

On the average, for every 100 rupees that the zemindars in the permanently-settled provinces pay to the Government, they get 200 from their estates.

VII. Indigo Planters' Association, *10th June 1856.*

As the law at present is, the Collector is prohibited from receiving putnee rents. Most zemindaries yield at least 75 per cent. in excess of Government revenue; the Collector could, therefore, easily carry the amount due for Government revenue to credit, and hand the balance to the zemindar to do what he thought fit.

VIII. Protestant Missionaries, *April 1857*. Reverend A. Duff and Others.

It is notorious that the rental of zemindaries is ordinarily more than double their total land tax or sudder jumma.

8. These estimates relate to a period anterior to the rise of prices after 1854: and to the subsequent great increase of suits for the enhancement of rents, which for many years have now greatly strained the revenue courts, and latterly the civil courts in the Lower Provinces of Bengal. This enhancement of rent, or the second of the causes of increase of zemindars' income, which are mentioned in section V, clause *b*, of the preceding paragraph, has greatly augmented that income far beyond the amount reached in 1832.

9. One of the earliest methods adopted by zemindars of increasing their income without personally or directly enhancing the rents of the cultivators in their zemindaries, was that of sub-infeudation.

I. Mr. Hugh Stark, Chief of the Revenue Department, India Board, *14th February 1832*.

The Rajah of Burdwan illegally created sub-tenures which the Government passed a Regulation in 1819 to confirm. He holds lands for which he pays Government a jumma of 30 lakhs of rupees a year, and he has introduced a settlement within his lands, by which the cultivators are three or four degrees removed from the zemindar. The Rajah created putneedars: these in their turn divided their tenures into durputnees; and these latter into seputnees, each class reserving a profit: all the profits of these middlemen are squeezed out of the unfortunate cultivators.

Question 223.—If the rights and privileges of the ryots, as they existed in the year 1793, had been maintained, would it have been possible to create such a sub-tenancy as you have described? Not without actual rebellion in the country, because those people would have resisted: if Government had defined the land tax, and issued pottahs to every man, specifying the extent of his lands and the amount of the tax, the lands would have acquired value which they do not now possess.

II. Mr. Holt Mackenzie, *18th April 1832*.

I ought to mention a tenure which now prevails, especially in the estates of the Burdwan Rajah, and is denominated a putnee talook: it is a perpetual heritable and transferable lease, granted at a fixed rent, subject to conditions nearly similar to those under which the zemindar holds of Government, the reserved rent being, however, considerably in excess of the Government revenue. Under this tenure the Rajah is understood to have disposed of almost his entire estate, and the lessees, who are

APP. VII.   called putneedars, have sub-let to others called durputneedars, who hold
——   parcels of the original talook with an advance of rent, but otherwise on
RYOTS HARASSED   the same conditions; these, again, similarly sub-let the lands held by them,
BY SUB-
INFEUDATION.   or rather the rent thereof; and so, through several gradations, to the
——   renter of a single village or less.   The same system has extended to other
Para. 9, contd.   zemindaries, and has been made the subject of a distinct Regulation, *viz.*,
VIII of 1819.

Question 2619.—Do those persons who successively derive a profit-rent
reside on the land, or do they reside in the towns, or in Calcutta?   The
lowest class, who actually collect from the cultivators, generally, I believe,
reside upon the land: the superior tenures are held by various classes;
some I have known living in Calcutta and in other towns.

III. Mr. A. D. Campbell, *1832.*

Ibid., App.   (After a description of the sub-tenures similar to that in the two pre-
No. 6, pages   ceding extracts.)
16-17.
a.—The tenures of each of the three new orders of sub-zemindars are
perpetually entailed on their heirs and assigns so long as those fixed
augmented sums are paid to their respective superiors.

b.—If the zemindary system itself has failed to define the public
revenue payable by the cultivator, or to fix it on the fields he occupies,
still less can this most desirable end be accomplished when the cultivator
is driven to a fifth remove from the Government, his original and natural
protector: the intermediate ranks being filled by the zemindar and his
three successive hereditary sub-contractors, each constrained to realize
more than he pays, and each paying an augmented sum fixed in perpetuity.   The cultivator, indeed, from whom the whole has to be wrung,
whose payment was the only one limited by the despotic sovereigns who
preceded us in the government of India, is also now the only individual
whose payment, in these permanently-settled districts, the British Government have left undefined.

c.—Independently of the bad effect on the interests of the cultivators of these sub-tenures, their immediate tendency is not to transfer,
as the zemindar was previously competent to do, to another, any portion
of his zemindary, along with the duties annexed to it, but to separate
the property from the duties of the zemindary tenure, and thus to crum-
ble down, by successive alienations, the property in the land revenue
which the Government granted to the original zemindar; and to enable
him to divest himself entirely of the hereditary duties, which the inheritance of that property, and the perpetual confirmation of it, at the permanent settlement, evidently impose on the holder of each zemindary.

IV. Sir George Campbell.

Bengal Adminis-   The practice of granting such under-tenures has steadily continued
tration Report,   since 1819, until at the present day, with the putnee and subordinate
1872-73.
tenures in Bengal Proper, and the farming system of Behar, but a small
proportion of the whole permanently-settled area remains in the direct
possession of the zemindars.

V. Mr. H. Colebrooke, Husbandry of Bengal, *1806*.

The under-tenants, depressed by an excessive rent in kind, and by usurious returns for the cattle, seed, and subsistence advanced to them, can never extricate themselves from debt. In so abject a state, they cannot labour with spirit, while they earn a scanty subsistence without hope of bettering their situation. Wherever the system of an intermediary tenantry subsists, the peasant is indigent, the husbandry ill-managed.

10. It was observed by Sir John Shore (minute June 1789) :—

" If we admit the property of the soil to be vested in the zemindars, we must exclude any acknowledgment of such right in favour of the ryots, except when they may acquire it from the proprietor."

But he also stated the converse, *viz.*, that the rights of the resident occupancy ryot limited those of the zemindar; and similarly, the exactions or oppressions of the zemindars, which the Government of 1793 admitted their obligation to provide against, imply a proper limit to the demands upon the ryot, that is, the possession by him of some kind of right.

Harington's Analysis of Regulations, page 267.

11. Abwabs.

Abwabs and exactions are not a pleasant subject; what little of amusement could be found in the former was got by Sir Broughton Rouse, when he facetiously described *abwabs* as " little contributions spontaneously given to supply any extraordinary expense."

Pages 176-7 of his Dissertation.

I. Mr. J. Grant.

a.—When the number and amount of *abwabs* were increased, and were levied in the gross, according to the variable and gradually undefined extent of zemindary jurisdictions, leaving it to the interested landholders themselves to apportion the additional assessment throughout their subordinate lesser districts, instead of the State distributing the *abwabs* rateably according to the standard assessment, then it was that the constitution of India might be said first to have been violated, the rights of Government as well as of the peasantry infringed, and a system of fraud, peculation, or oppression, alike injurious to the commonalty at large, substituted in the room of the regular equitable mode of Mogul administration.

Fifth Report, pages 266 and 275.

II. Sir J. Shore, *June 1789*.

My objections to the principal of the subahdarry imposts have a reference to the circumstances under which they were established. If the rates in the tukseem of Turee Mull with respect to the ryots had not been previously augmented by impositions separate and distinct from those of the soubahs, perhaps the best possible mode of obtaining an increase would have been by demanding it in certain proportions to that

Ibid., page 175.

APP. VII.

———

ABWABS.

Para. 11, contd.

standard, with a due regard to the degree of improvement in the country. But the fact was otherwise; and these demands upon the zemindars confirmed and perpetuated their impositions upon the ryots, antecedently levied for their own subsistence and emolument, whilst it opened a door for future unbounded exactions (*paragraph 64*).

III. TAGORE LAW LECTURES, *1874-75.*

Pages 329-30.

Provision is made, both in the Decennial Settlement and under the regulations for the Permanent Settlement, for a penalty of double the amount in the case of exactions by the zemindars from these dependent talookdars. It is further provided that no new *abwab* or *mathoot* shall be imposed upon the ryots under any pretence whatever, and a penalty of three times the amount exacted is to be paid in case of such imposition. It is further provided that the cess called *najay* is not to be exacted: this, it will be remembered, was an exaction from the remaining ryots to make up the rents of those who had absconded or died. We have seen that exactions of all kinds are still levied.

IV. See also para. 5.

12. But while the zemindars were increasing their income by *abwabs*, and by sub-infeudations which enabled them to discount the unearned increment from enhancement of rents, the laws of inheritance were gradually working out a disintegration of zemindaries, which are only adding to the ryot's burdens by subjecting him to many masters, and to a class of small zemindars whose necessitous circumstances make them rapacious. The sub-division of permanent subtenures into fractional parts is also increasing the confusion.

I. SIR F. J. HALLIDAY, *2nd September 1856.*

a.—There is, however, a question whether there are not some post settlement under-tenures which, far from encouraging agricultural improvement, are by their nature so destructive and ruinous to the public weal, as to render it highly desirable to discourage them by all means in our power, and even to get rid of them as far as possible, instead of doing anything to encourage and perpetuate them. I mean those tenures which are extremely common in Bengal and Behar, and more particularly in Bengal, which convey a right of collecting a half, or a fourth, or any other share of the rents of a mehal, or a division of a mehal, or a village. There are numerous cases in which one khodkasht ryot has to pay his little rent in shares to three or four or more talookdars, or other under-tenants of the zemindar; every sharer trying to get the most he can, and to over-reach his co-sharer, and the ryot being ground to powder between them all. This is notoriously one of the curses of the country, carrying with it the most bitter and ruinous consequences.

b.—There are a great many districts under the Government of Bengal, including all the districts of the Behar Province, in which the

sub-division of shares is carried to a great extent.   I walked into a small
village a few days ago, in the Patna district, which I was told on the spot
was divided among, or held jointly by, seventy sharers; and at Chupra
I was visited by certain zemindars of old family, whose zemindary, never
large, is now held in seventy-five shares, of which each separate share is
owned by three or four different persons.   These were spoken of as
quite ordinary cases, and it seems obvious that the number of the
sharers will go on increasing under the Hindu law up to the limit of
starvation, especially if encouraged and fostered by unlimited separate
accounts at the Collectorate.   The question cannot but occur to me—is
it wise and politic to encourage this?

II. COMMISSIONER, PATNA DIVISION, *24th August 1858*.

One hundred and fifty sharers in a single undivided village is by no
means an unusual number in this division.   Is each ryot to be liable to
one hundred and fifty suits, and how is the Court to ascertain what the
precise share of each shareholder is?

III. PROTESTANT MISSIONARIES (REVEREND A. DUFF AND OTHERS, 1852).

Many estates are the joint property of a number of zemindars, of
whom one may be entitled to one-half, another to a quarter, a third to
the twelfth or sixteenth part of the proceeds.   In such cases it is the
usual practice for each shareholder to maintain a separate agency, and to
keep separate accounts, so that every ryot has transactions with a number of landlords.

IV. MR. B. J. COLVIN, *4th April 1857*.

The next proposed amendment has for its object to enable a sharer
in a joint estate to open a separate account for the revenue due upon
his share.   I doubt the policy of this rule; it will foster and encourage disputes, from the knowledge that separation is an easy thing.   At
present the necessity of preserving an estate makes people harmonize;
and I venture to predict that estates will soon by its operation be broken
up into infinitesimal portions.   I have witnessed such a result in attached
estates in the Pooree District, where the village co-parceners were
recorded separately in the zemindar's sheristah even to shares of a pie
or gundah each.   Some check should be put to such indiscriminate sub-
divisions.

13. EXACTIONS AND OPPRESSION.

I. On this subject Sir John Shore expressed himself with
a modest hesitancy, arising out of the ignorance of Government, which Lord Cornwallis set aside with his airy confidence in the all-saving efficacy of his benevolent Zemindary
Settlement.

SIR JOHN SHORE (*September 1789*).

a.—We are not fully informed of all the abuses which are practised   Fifth Report,
by zemindars, farmers, and their officers, in the detail of the collection, or   page 458.

fully prepared to correct in every instance such as we know or presume to exist, by specific Regulations : much may however be done, and many rules may be established, for remedying existing evils (*paragraph 67*).

LORD CORNWALLIS (*3rd February 1790*).

b.—We have found that the numerous prohibitory orders against the levying of new taxes, accompanied with threats of fine and punishment for the disobedience of them, have proved ineffectual ; and, indeed, how could it be expected, that whilst the Government were increasing their demands upon the zemindars, that they in their turn would not oppress the ryots ; or that a farmer, whose interest extended little further than to the crops upon the ground, would not endeavour to exact, by every means in his power, as large a sum as possible, over and above the amount of his engagements with the public ?

II. MR. H. COLEBROOKE—HUSBANDRY OF BENGAL.

The measurement is made by a beegah which contains twenty biswas. It is a square measure on a side of twenty cathas : but this varies from three and a half to nine cubits. A pole of the established length ought to be deposited in the public offices of the district, sealed at both extremities with the official seal of the province : and the measurement should be made with a pole of that length, or with a rope equal to twenty such poles. In either mode the tenant has been commonly defrauded by keeping the middle of the pole elevated, or by withholding a part of the rope. So great has been the customary fraud, that ryots have been known to consent to the doubling of their rates upon a stipulation for a fair measurement.

III. MR. J. MILL (*9th August 1831*).

There can be no doubt that the circumstances in which Bengal has been placed, independently of the zemindary system, have for a number of years been unusually favourable to the population generally, because they have been exempted from wars ; they have been exempted from the ravages of an enemy of any description ; they have enjoyed perfect tranquillity, and, to a certain degree, the protection of law. One evil which ought to be mentioned, a great proportion of which I think can hardly be ascribed to any other cause than the operation of the zemindary system, was the dacoity, or gang robbery, which prevailed to a frightful degree in Bengal a number of years ago, notwithstanding the general timidity and passiveness of the people. The evidence affords rather the means of inference than direct proof of the point ; but I cannot help believing that the degree in which the ryots were exasperated by being deprived of their rights, when the operation of the zemindary system began to be felt by them, was one great cause of these enormities.

Q. 3366.—Did not they exist prior to that period ? Not in any so alarming a degree.

Q. 3367.—Of what class of persons did the dacoits consist ? Chiefly of the agricultural population in all parts of Bengal—the ryots.

Q. 3368.—What is the state of dacoity at present? Exceedingly reduced; it is not altogether extinguished, but it now does not exist in a degree to be any very remarkable evil.

Q. 3369.—Do you think the people are taking more to agricultural habits? Great exertions, no doubt, were made to put down the practice; there were severe examples made, and everything was done to render the police effective, and those exertions no doubt had their effect; but I believe that the disposition of the people to acquiesce in what they found was remediless has also had its effect.

Q. 3370.—Might it not be possible that there has been less oppression on the part of the landlords? We have not any evidence to that effect; and I conceive that the ground of the exasperation was, in the first instance, when the men, who considered that they had a right to hereditary occupancy, were either turned out of their possession, or had the rates increased upon them to such a degree that they could not retain them; then it was that they became desperate, and had recourse to those extremities.

IV. Mr. N. J. Halhed.

Page 100

a.—To enable the proprietors to fulfil their engagements with the Government, it was likewise deemed expedient to vest them with certain extra-judicial powers of great extent over their under-farmers and tenants (for the *raeeuts*, under the operation of the Code, can be considered in no other light than as tenants-at-will), by which they were authorised to attach their crop and all personal property (tools and materials of manufacture, cattle, seed-corn, and implements of husbandry excepted) without reference to the courts of law, and to cause the same to be sold by the "Kazee," or other person appointed for the purpose, in liquidation of the arrears. It was supposed that no undue or improper exercise of those powers would be resorted to, in consequence of the severity of the penalties provided; but as these penalties could be enforced only on proof being given in a judicial court, an injured *raeeut*, with neither time nor money to spare, is ill able to bear the expense of both, which the institution of a suit, and the necessary attendance, involve. The chances of impunity are very much in favour of the oppressor, and those chances are enhanced by the denunciation of punishment for unfounded complaints, while the Code itself opposed an almost insuperable obstacle to the production of proof, by rendering it difficult, if not impossible, for the *raeeut* to summon the zemindary amlah to substantiate his plaint. On the other hand, the severity of the penalties for resistance of attachment, and for the removal or fraudulent transfer of the property, with intent to evade it, together with the certainty of their being enforced by summary process, rendered opposition hopeless. The *raeeuts* were subsequently subjected to further severities, and were rendered liable to personal arrest and imprisonment before trial, and in default of bail, by summary process for arrears;—their doors to be forced by the police, and their houses entered in search of distrainable property. In the event of their being endamaged by the decision passed after the issue of summary process, they could obtain redress only by instituting a civil action, the expense and delays attendant on which (arising out of the latitude of appeals in a great measure) opposed obstacles which, to a poor man, may be viewed as insurmountable. If a sale of the proprietor's estate in satisfaction of arrears of revenue took place, the sale cancelled all previous obligations between him and the *raeeut*, and the zemindars took frequent advantage of this claim, by forcing a sale, solely to enable them to repurchase, under a fictitious name, and to raise the rents fixed under former stipulations at a lower rate.

b.—The necessity for these harsh measures is said to have been indicated by defalcations of the revenue payable by the zemindars and other newly created exclusive proprietors, which they ascribed to the extreme difficulty alleged to have been experienced by them in realizing their rents from their under-farmers and tenantry. The preambles to the Regulations would induce the belief that their complaints were well-grounded : there are, however, strong reasons for supposing that much of the mischief arose from their own oppressive conduct and mismanagement. For instance, the newly-created proprietors are known to have taken every advantage of the privilege conferred upon them of letting out their estates: their farmers re-let their farms in small portions to others; and as the object of all parties was to make the best of their bargains, and as the gains of each were drawn from the cultivating classes, the means of these last became insufficient to answer the heavy demands made upon them: they fell in arrears to the middlemen, these again to the farmers, who could not fulfil their engagements with the zemindars, and a defalcation of the Government revenue was the necessary result.

c.—In many instances, also, the zemindars gave large portions of land, at a quit-rent, to their immediate relations, and raised the rates upon the other ryots to cover the deficiency—a piece of oppression they were authorised to inflict, as the latter were, in a great measure, placed out of the protection of the law, in consequence of their being unwilling to accept the leases which the zemindars were directed to grant to them (with the usual jumma and arbitrary cesses consolidated into one sum), under the well-founded conviction that in subscribing such engagements they would be resigning rights which they had hitherto deemed, and on the most substantial grounds, to be strictly allodial.

14. Having ascertained the facts, we may now consider their accordance with theory.

I. Sir J. Shore, *June 1789.*

a.—The situation of a zemindar combines two relations : one which originates in the property of the land, a portion of the rents of which he pays to the State; and the other, in his capacity of an officer of Government, for *protecting the peace of the country*, and for *securing the subjects of the State from oppression.*

(Para. 166.)

b.—To enlarge upon this subject (the management of zemindaries by women) is unnecessary. Nothing can be more absurd than to assign a trust of the utmost importance to Government and to its subjects, whose property and security depend upon the faithful discharge of it, to an agent precluded from all knowledge of its obligations, as well as from all interference in the execution of them: in short, to require the performance of acts of the first consequence to the State and its subjects, from a person incapable of any exertion.

App. VII.
Ryots' rights
destroyed.
Para. 14, contd.

II.—Firman of Aurungzebe to the Collectors of Revenue.

a. First.—They must show the ryots every kind of favour and -indulgence, enquire into their circumstances, and endeavour, by wholesome regulations and wise administration, to engage them with hearty good-will to labour towards the increase of agriculture, so that no lands may be neglected that are capable of cultivation.

Patton's Asiatic Monarchies, page 340.
Ibid., page 350.

b.—You will not give the *choudries* and *aumils* admission to you in private; but make it a rule for them to attend publicly at the cutcherry, and when the lowest ryots shall come to represent their case to you, you will make them your friend, by showing them notice, and treating them with kindness, that they may not have occasion for the patronage of another to express their wants.

III.—Proceedings of Government, *16th August 1869.*

It ought to be remembered that the welfare and good of the whole was never intended to be sacrificed to the enriching of a few who can show no pretence to these peculiar advantages.

Colebrooke's Supplement to the Regulations.

IV.—Mr. Fortescue, *1831-32.*

The engagements between the Government and the landholders based on those of the Native Governments, all contemplate and direct protection and justice towards the ryots. All jaghire, istimrar, enam, maafee and other grants from the native rulers go specifically to this point; and the fact of petition against and redress of grievance in former times, is no less notorious, than matter of historical record.* * The grants of the ancient Government recognize qualified rights in the ryots, and the fact of their having maintained them is established. Further, neither the permanent settlement, nor any subsequent Regulation, has cancelled those rights.

Parl. paper, Sess. 1831-32, Vol. XI, page 288.

V. Yet where are those rights? Mr. Stuart's minute, dated 18th December 1820, answered the question.

a.—From the disposition to view the subject according to European notions and principles, the chief engagers with the Government are often assumed to be like European landed proprietors, who have full power over their estates to lease them at their will, while the immediate occupants of the soil are their tenants. The payments of those occupants are held to be the landlords' rents, and the demand of Government to be a tax on rent. Viewing the subject in this light, it is the chief engagers alone who suffer from the tax, or can benefit from the remuneration of increase; and the measure carries the popular and captivating appearance of a voluntary limitation by Government of an invidious power on behalf of a favoured and respected class.

b.—But I need not remark how different is the real state of the case: that the payments of the ryots are the ancient and inherent dues of the State; and that any classes intervening between them and the ruler can claim only a defined and limited proportion of the produce of the soil, or some other limited remuneration.

Revenue Selections, Vol. III, page 221.

c.—Hence has been started the important question—might not any sacrifice of the fiscal interests of the State, which it may be in the power of the Government to make, be more beneficially made for the Government and the people in favour of the great body of the agricultural community, in preference to the higher classes connected with the land?

d.—But a settlement upon the principles of the permanent settlement in the Lower Provinces, is, as I have stated already, an assignment for ever of the dues of Government in favour of the chief revenue engagers; and such a measure obviously opposes a perpetual bar against the Government extending to the inferior classes of the agricultural community any relief from the burthen of their present payments.

e.—If, then, there be any force in the consideration, the Government may, by the adoption of the measure, forego for ever very noble means of promoting the welfare of the most numerous and most meritorious body of its subjects.

f.—But I have hinted at another light in which the matter may be regarded. The payments of the immediate occupants of the soil are a tax upon its produce; and, as I have stated above, names of high authority in the science of political economy have recently maintained that such an impost falls, not upon the cultivator, but the consumer.

g.—In this view, the necessary operation of a perpetual settlement would be to perpetuate a heavy tax upon the whole produce of the soil, and to leave the Government powerless to afford any relief to the community under any possible change of circumstances.

VI.—Mill's History of British India, Volume V, Book VI, Chapter 6.

a.—We have thus seen the effects of the new system upon the zemindars. Let us next endeavour to trace its effects upon a much more important class of men, the ryots. Unfortunately for this more interesting part of the enquiry, we have much more scanty materials. In the documents which have been exhibited, the situation of the ryots is in a great measure overlooked. And it is from incidental circumstances and collateral confessions that we are entitled to form a judgment of their condition. This result itself is, perhaps, a ground for a pretty decisive inference; for if the situation of the ryots had been prosperous, we should have had it celebrated in the loftiest terms as a decisive proof, which surely it would have been, of the wisdom and virtues of our Indian Government.

b.—When it was urged upon Lord Cornwallis by Mr. Shore and others, that the ryots were left in a great measure at the mercy of the zemindars, who had always been oppressors, he replied that the permanency of the landed property would cure all those defects; because " where the landlord has a permanent property in the soil, it will be worth his while to encourage his tenants, who hold his farm on lease, to improve that property." It has already been shown how inapplicable this reasoning was to the case which it regarded. It now appears that the permanency from which Lord Cornwallis so fondly expected beneficial results, had no existence; that the plan which he had established for giving permanency to the property of the zemindars, had rendered it less permanent than under any former system—had, in fact, destroyed it. The ryots, left without any efficient protection, were entrusted to the operation of certain motives, which were expected to arise out of the idea of permanent property; and, practically, that permanence had no existence. The ryots were by consequence left altogether without protection.

" Fifty means," says a very intelligent and experienced servant of the Company, " might be mentioned in which the ryots are liable to oppression by the zemindars, even when pottahs have been given. The zemindars will make collusive engagements, and get ryots to do so. *Bajehkherch* and village expenditure will go on at a terrible rate, as it does in the Circars, and where I have no doubt but there are farmers, and under-farmers and securities, and all the confusion that arises from them; that pottahs are not given, and that village charges are assessed on the ryot as formerly." [1].

c.—It is wonderful that neither Lord Cornwallis, nor his advisers, nor his masters, either in the East India House or the Treasury, saw that between one part of his Regulations, and the effects which he expected from another, there was an irreconcilable contradiction. He required that fixed unalterable pottahs should be given to the ryots; that is, that they should pay a rent which could never be increased, and occupy a possession from which, paying that rent, they could never be displaced. Is it not evident that, in these circumstances, the zemindars had no interest whatsoever in the improvement of the soil? It is evident, as Mr. Thackeray has well remarked, that in a situation of this description, it may be " the zemindar's interest not to assist, but ruin the ryot; that he may eject him from his right of occupancy, and put in some one else, on a raised rent; which will often be his interest, as the country thrives, and labour gets cheap."

d.—It is by the judges remarked, that numerous suits are instituted by the ryots for alleged extortions. The zemindar lets his district in farm to one great middleman, and he to under-farmers, to whose exactions upon the ryots it appears that there is really no restriction. In one of the reports in answer to the queries of 1802, we are informed that " the interchange of engagements between the parties, with few exceptions, extends no further than the zemindar's farmer, who is here called the sudder (or head) farmer, and to those among whom he sub-divides his farm in portions. An engagement between the latter and the cultivator, or heads of a village, is scarcely known, except the general one, to receive and pay agreeably to past and preceding years; and for ascertaining this, the accounts of the farm are no guide. The zemindar himself, seeing that no confidence is to be placed in the accounts rendered him of the rent-roll of the farm, from the practice which has so long prevailed of fabrication and false accounts, never attempts to call for them at the end of the lease; and, instead of applying a correction to the evil, increases it by farming out the lands literally by auction; and the same mode is adopted in almost every sub-division of the farm." [2] This is the security which is afforded to the cultivators by the boasted permanency of the property of the zemindars. That any prosperity can accrue to this class

---

[1] Mr. Thackeray's Memoir, April 1806, fifth Report, page 914.
[2] Answer of Mr. Thompson, Judge and Magistrate of Burdwan, fifth Report page 544.

of people, or encouragement to agriculture from such an order of things, is not likely to be alleged.

e.—The relation established by Lord Cornwallis between the ryot and the zemindar was remarkable. The zemindar had it in his power to pillage the ryot; but the ryot had it in his power to distress the zemindar. He might force him to have recourse to law for procuring payment of his rent, and the delay and expense of the courts were sufficient to accomplish his ruin. It is the habit of the people of India to pay nothing until they are compelled. A knowledge that they might always ward off the day of payment to a considerable distance, by waiting for a prosecution, was a sufficient motive to a great proportion of the ryots to pursue that unhappy course which, in the long run, was not less ruinous to themselves than to the zemindars.

f.—The following picture of these two great classes of the population is presented by a high authority (Sir H. Strachey in 1802). "By us, all is silently changed. The ryot, and the zemindar, and the gomastah, are, by the levelling power of the Regulations, very much reduced to an equality. The protecting, but often oppressive and tyrannical, power of the zemindar, and the servitude of the ryot, are at an end. All the lower classes—the poorest, I fear, often in vain—now look to the Regulations only for preserving them against extortion and rapacity. The operation of our system has gradually loosened that intimate connexion between the ryots and the zemindars which subsisted heretofore. The ryots were once the vassals of their zemindars. Their dependence on the zemindar and their attachment to him have ceased. They are now often at open variance with him; and, though they cannot contend with him on equal terms, they not unfrequently engage in lawsuits with him, and set him at defiance. The zemindar formerly, like his ancestors, resided on his estate. He was regarded as the chief and the father of his tenants, from whom all expected protection, but against whose oppressions there was no redress. At present the estates are often possessed by Calcutta purchasers, who never see them, and whose agents have little intercourse with the tenants, except to collect the rents."

Report by Sir
H. Strachey in
1802; fifth Re-
port, page 564.

"The ryots," says the same excellent Magistrate, "are not, in my opinion, well protected by the revenue laws; nor can they often obtain effectual redress by prosecuting, particularly for exaction and dispossession;" and these are the very injuries to which they are most exposed. The reason Sir Henry immediately subjoins: "The delay and expense attending a lawsuit are intolerable, in cases where the suitor complains, which almost invariably happens, that he has been deprived of all his property. The cancelling of leases, after the sale of an estate for arrears, must frequently operate with extreme harshness and cruelty to the under-tenants."[1] *Sir H. Strachey's answer to interrogatories, fifth Report ut supra, page 528.*

15. The Indian Government, in their observations addressed to the Court of Directors, "appeared," say the Select Committee of the House of Commons, "unwilling to admit that the evils and grievances complained of arose from any defects

---

[1] Report by Sir H. Strachey in 1802; fifth Report, page 564.

in the Regulations.   The very grounds of the complaints, the
Government observed, namely, those whereby the tenantry
were enabled to withhold payment of their rents, evinced
that the great body of the people employed in the cultivation
of the land, experienced ample protection from the laws, and
were no longer subject to arbitrary exactions;"—that the
great body of the people enjoyed protection, because they could
force the zemindars to go to law for their rent, is an inference
which it would be very unwise to trust; which appears to be,
as there is no wonder that it should be found to be, contrary
to the fact.   But suppose the fact had been otherwise, and
that the ryots received protection, was it no evil, upon the
principle of the Regulations, that the zemindars were ruined?
Yet so it is, that the organ of Government in India found
this ruin, when it happened, a good thing; affording, they
said, the satisfactory reflection, that the great estates were
divided into small ones; and that, by change of proprietors,
the land was transferred to better managers.

16. Summing up the information in this appendix, it appears that—

I. (*Para. 1*). The only two classes of proprietors holding
independently of the State, were the fixed occupants of fields,
by whom, or at whose risk and charge, land is tilled; and
the members of village communities. The title of these
included a right of occupying waste lands in the village, for
their sons and descendants, at the customary rates of rent
paid by khodkasht ryots. The rest derive their title from
the State, which could not confer any right to the prejudice
of the other two classes.

II. (*Para. 2*). Ryots' rights were reserved; and in reserving, Lord Cornwallis stated that he understood the word
permanency to extend only to the jumma, and not to bar
future regulation of ryots' rights, which his Lordship defined
to be the exemption from increase of the ryots' rent by
abwabs. Such increase, Lord Cornwallis held, could be
justified only by supposing "the ryots to be the absolute
slaves of the zemindars; every beegah of land possessed by
them must have been cultivated under an expressed or
implied agreement that a certain sum should be paid for
each beegah, and no more. Every *abwab*, or tax, imposed
by the zemindar over and above that sum, is not only a
breach of that agreement, but a direct violation of the estab-

APP. VII.

Para. 16, contd.

lished laws of the country. The cultivator, therefore, has in such cases an undoubted right to apply to Government for the protection of his property; and Government is at all times bound to afford him redress." In this passage Lord Cornwallis made no distinction between khodkasht ryots and other ryots. Including all in the general term cultivators, he stated that the cultivator had an undoubted title to fixity of rent, not subject to increase at any time thereafter, and that it was the Government's bounden duty, not then only, but at all times, to protect him in that right. In applying the principles of the Permanent Settlement in the Madras Presidency, the ryot's right was understood in this sense (paragraph 2, section III), and was secured by the Madras Government in this sense. The extracts in paragraph 5, sections I to III, show that this permanent limitation of the rent of "ryots," without distinction of classes of ryots, was discussed, and was affirmed in the course of the discussion, by both Sir John Shore and Lord Cornwallis. The Permanent Settlement was understood in this sense in Mill's History of British India, Vol. V, Book VI, Chapter 6 (paragraph 13, section V of this Appendix).

III. (*Paras. 3 to 6*). The zemindar's right to increase the ryot's rent was distinctly denied by Lord Cornwallis; and in enumerating the sources from which the income of zemindars was to increase, he did not include an enhancement of the rents of ryots from rise of prices, or from other cause than the cultivation of some better kind of produce. The amount, including old *abwabs*, to be paid by each ryot, was to be fixed, and fresh *abwabs* were prohibited: the fixing of the amount thus precluded its increase from a rise of prices or from *abwabs*.

IV. Yet so great was the extent of waste land which Government bestowed in free gift on zemindars, that, as population increased, the income of the zemindars, though fixed at one-tenth of the Government revenue, came to equal or exceed that revenue by 1848.

V. Shortly after the introduction of the Permanent Settlement, zemindars freed themselves from their landlords' duties towards their tenants by sub-infeudations, which greatly harassed the ryots, whose condition is impoverished by enhancement of rents wherever sub-infeudation prevails.

VI. *Abwabs*, or illegal cesses, exactions, and oppression of ryots, became rife after zemindars had been armed with special powers for recovering rent from ryots.

VII. The benevolent intention of the Government was
to confirm and secure the ryots' rights:—in the actual result
they were destroyed. Under the old Native rule, the only
assessment which was fixed was the ryot's; but under the
British Government, in the permanently settled districts in
Bengal, he is now the only individual whose payment has
been left undefined.

APPENDIX VIII.

VILLAGE PROPRIETORS AND RYOTS.

1.—CULTIVATOR OR RYOT.

I.—ROUSE.

If I have been able to ascertain rightly the title of the Indian land-holders in ancient times, they were called in Bengal *Buyan* or *Bhowmy*; in the northern parts of India, *Kirsan*.

The term *Kirsan* denotes ryots or cultivators.

II.—SIR T. MUNRO.

By the *occupier* I here mean not so much the person who performs the work, as him who procures the labour and directs the management; and I consider the whole profit as *received* by the occupier when the occupier is benefited by the whole value of what is produced; which is the case with the tenant, who pays a fixed rent for the use of land, no less than with the proprietor who holds it as his own. The one has the same interest in the produce, and in the advantage of every improvement, as the other. Likewise the proprietor, though he grant out his estate to farm, may be considered as the occupier, inasmuch as he regulates the occupation by the choice, superintendence, and encouragement of his tenants; by the disposition of his lands, by erecting buildings, providing accommodations, by prescribing conditions, or supplying implements and materials of improvement, and is entitled, by the rule of public expediency above mentioned, to receive in the advance of his rent a share of the benefit which arises from the increased produce of his estate. The violation of this fundamental maxim of agrarian policy constitutes the chief objection to the holding of lands by the State, by the King, by corporate bodies, by private persons, in right of their offices or benefices. The inconvenience to the public arises, not so much from the unalienable quality of lands, thus holden to perpetuity, as from hence—that proprietors of this description seldom contribute much, either of attention or expense, to the cultivation of their estates, yet claim, by rent, a share in the profit of every improvement that is made upon them. This complaint can only be obviated by long leases at a fixed rent, which convey a large portion of the interest to those who actually conduct the cultivation. The same objection is applicable to the holding of land by foreign proprietors, and in some degree to estates of too great extent being placed in the same hands.

III.—MR. HOLT MACKENZIE, *18th April 1832.*

It seems necessary, as the foundation of all discussions on the subject, to define the different tenures, as far as they are known, by which land is held, commencing with the lowest class of occupants (meaning by that term those by whom, or at whose risk and charge, the land is cultivated), and proceeding upwards to the persons who stand upon the Government records as responsible for the Government demand (*Q. 2568*).

IV.—LAW AND CONSTITUTION OF INDIA.

(*a*). "The land of the *Suwaud* of Erauk is the property of its inhabitants *(ahl)*. They may alienate it by sale, and dispose of it as they please; for when the Imaum conquers a country by force of arms, if he permit the inhabitants (*ahl*) to remain on it, imposing the *Khirauj* on their lands and the *Jizeeah* on their heads, the land is the property of the inhabitants; and since it is their property, it is lawful for them to sell it, or to dispose of it as they choose." *Surauj-ol-Vúhaúj.*

(*b*). The word in the above quotation translated " property " is, in the Page 33. original, *milk*, which in law signifies indefeasible right of property; and the word rendered " inhabitants " is in the original *ahl*, the import of which is simply that of dwelling, residing on the lands; as they say, *ahl-ool-busrah*, the inhabitants of Busrah.

(*c*). From this we see that if the inhabitants of India were suffered *Ibid.* to remain on their lands on paying the above impost, the right of property in the sovereign is gone at once; and if it was partitioned among the conquerors, the alienation is equally complete. The question at issue, therefore, is shortened by one claim at least of the three, *viz.*, the *sovereign*, the *zemindar*, the *cultivator*. But in order to determine the other two claims, we must see what persons are meant by the *ahl*, who are thus vested with indefeasible right of property, for it may be said that these were the *former proprietors* of the soil, and that by this settlement is meant merely a confirmation of *former rights*. But that this is not the case, it is only necessary to know that, by the Mahomedan law, when a Mahomedan army conquers a province by force of arms, every *right* and interest which the conquered inhabitants before possessed ceases and determines by the very act of conquest; that the sovereign has, by law, the power even of carrying the conquered inhabitants into captivity, &c. &c. By suffering the *ahl*, the inhabitants, however, to remain *under the conditions required by law*, viz., as *zimmees*, and to pay the *khirauj* and capitation tax, the property of the soil is *established* in them—not *continued*.

(*d*). But who are the *ahl* here spoken of? This is the only question Page 34. now remaining; and I answer, it will appear that they are those who cultivate the land. They, the *cultivators*, pay the *khurauj* and are termed *rubb-ool-arz*, or masters of the soil.

(*e*). The great Huneefeeah lawyer, Shuns-ool-Aymah-oor Sumhshee, Page 34. in speaking of *khurauj*, on the question what is the *utmost* extent of khurauj which land can bear? says " Imaum Moohummud hath said regard shall be had to the cultivator, *to him who cultivates*. There shall be left *for every one who cultivates his land* as much as he requires for *his own support* till the next crop be reaped, *and that of his family, and for seed*. This much shall be left him; what remains is *khurauj* and shall go to the public treasury." Here there is no provision made for, no regard paid to, a *zemindar* who contributes nothing to the pro-

APP. VIII.
——
Para. 1, contd.

duce of the soil. We have no ten per cent. *malikana* to recusant zemindars.

V.—REVENUE LETTER TO BENGAL, *9th May 1821.*

Parl. Paper,
Sess. 1831-33,
Vol. XI, page
103, para. 57.

The words of the Board of Revenue are these: "With respect to the observations of the Collector, that the talookdars have expended large sums of money in bringing the lands into a productive state, we are induced to think he is misinformed on that point. The ryots generally clear and cultivate the lands at their own expense. The period of exemption from rent may, in some instances, exceed that specified in the talookdar's grant, but the burthen of expense, generally speaking, falls on the ryot."

2.—MOOZARAUT UNDER MAHOMEDAN LAW.

I.—BAILLIE ON THE LAND TAX OF INDIA.

Page XVIII.

(*a*). The peculiar contract called Moozaraut was the most common way of cultivating lands through the agency of tenants in Mahomedan countries. The landlord's interest under it is a share of the actual produce: and the Government interest in the *mookassimah khiraj* is also a share of the actual produce. The only difference between them is that, under the *mookassimah*, the Government share is restricted to a half of the produce, which it never can exceed, while under *moozaraut* it may be anything that the land will yield above a bare subsistence to the cultivator. So long as the *mookassimah khiraj* is actually below a half of the produce, this distinction is practically of no consequence.

(*b*). But it may be thought that there is another difference which will always serve to distinguish the *mookassimah* proprietor from the *moozaraut* tenant. The former cannot be ejected so long as he pays the *khiraj*, while the latter may be ejected at any time after the expiration of his legal term. It will be seen, however, that in some circumstances, *moozaraut* tenants acquire a right of occupancy, so that after the lapse of time all distinction between them and proprietors under *mookassimah khiraj* may be entirely obliterated.

Page XXVI.

(*c*). The hiring of land was more commonly regulated by the contract already alluded to, called *moozaraut*. The name signifies *mutual sowing*, and the contract is essentially a co-partnership between two parties,[1] one of whom supplies the land, the other the labour.** There are indications of the existence of this contract in Persia in ancient times, before the Mahomedan conquest. The Khoosroes are alluded to as speaking of the *moozareas* as their partners in the produce of the soil. It was still common in that country in the time of Aboo Huneefa and his two leading disciples (that is, the eighth century of our era), and several centuries after it was in full vigour in the countries about the Oxus, where the principal writers lived, whose works on the subject are quoted in the following pages. The cultivators, as already observed, are described as living in *mouzahs*, or villages, which have peculiar customs of their own. In some the relation between landlord and tenant was constituted and kept up by express contracts, renewed from year to year, and varied with special conditions. In others the contracts were tacitly

---

[1] One of these parties could be the State.

continued from year to year, on the same terms, without any express renewal, and in some instances for so long a period, that at length the respective shares of the landlord and tenant in the produce of the soil became fixed by custom.

(d). There are only three legal kinds of *moozaraut*. Corresponding to these are three different conditions of the cultivator. In the first he supplies the labour only, and his condition is little better than that of a hired labourer; in the second he supplies the cattle also, and must therefore be in possession of ploughs and cattle of his own, ready to undertake the cultivation of any land with which he may be entrusted; in the third, he supplies seed as well as the labour and cattle, and is advanced to the condition of a small farmer, having some capital of his own. It is only in this last condition, when he may be said to sow for himself, that he can ever acquire a right of occupancy; for it is only by long possession, and repeated sowings of the land, with the tacit consent of the owner, that this right could ever be acquired. In Bengal there are three different kinds of land, and three descriptions of ryots or cultivators. These are called *theeka, paykasht,* and *khoodkasht. Theeka* is a Hindustani word which signifies hire, or hireling, and *theeka* land is land cultivated by labourers hired for the occasion. *Paykasht* is derived from two Persian words, the first of which signifies "after" or "on account of," and the second is a contraction for *kashta,* sown. *Paykasht* land is land cultivated by ryots who have no permanent interest in it, but live in other villages than those to which the land belongs. *Khoodkasht* is similarly derived from the Persian word *khood,* self, and *kashtee,* sown, and means literally *self-sown,* or sown for one's self. *Khoodkasht* land is land cultivated by ryots who have some sort of permanent interest in it, and reside in the village to which it belongs. The interest is rather vague and undefined, and it is difficult to say precisely which it is; but it seems to be no more than a right of occupancy so long as the *ryot* continues to pay a certain rate of rent which has been long established by custom, for the quantity of land in his possession.** It seems admitted that the ryot's right to possession descends, at his death, to his children; but it is very doubtful whether it can be transferred to another by the ryot in his life-time.

(e). There is thus a great similarity between the three descriptions of ryot or cultivator in Bengal, and the three different grades of *moozareea* under the Mahomedan law. The name *moozareea,* as already observed, applies to all classes alike. The *khoodkasht* ryot corresponds to the *moozareea* of the highest degree, who supplied the seed, and might be said to sow for himself; and who, in some cases, acquired special custom, or right of occupancy in his land. In like manner, the *paykasht* ryot corresponds to the *moozareea* of the next degree, who does not supply the seed, but sows what he obtains from another, and may therefore be said to sow on account of another. And the *theeka* ryot corresponds to the *moozareea* of the lowest degree, whose condition, as already observed, differed little from that of a common labourer or hireling.

(f). In some instances, and indeed frequently in the present times, (1853) the *paykasht* and *theeka* ryots are employed by, or work under, the *khoodkasht* ryot. There was a phase of the contract of *moozareut* that meets this case also. All *moozareeas* have the power of working

APP. VIII.

CULTIVATORS
UNDER MAHO-
MEDAN LAW.

Para. 2, contd.

through the agency of hired servants, unless there is an express condition in their contracts that they shall labour on the land themselves. The highest degree of *moozareea*, or the self-sown, had a further right, even without the consent of his landlord, of entering into a *sub-moozareeut* with another cultivator. In this secondary contract he would be in the position of a *rub-ool-arz* (owner of the land, or landlord), and it was probably this circumstance that has led some writers to look upon the *khoodkasht* ryot as the true *rub-ool-arz*, or proprietor of the land.

Page XXXII.
Glossary.

(*g*). In Southern India there are two classes of cultivators that seem to correspond very closely with the *khoodkasht* and *paykasht* ryot of Bengal. These are the *meerassdar* and the *paracoody* or *paragoody*. *Meeras* is an Arabic word that signifies inheritance, " but is used chiefly in Southern India to designate a variety of rights differing in nature and value, but all more or less connected with proprietory possession, or usufruct of the soil, or of its produce, as (among others) the right of the permanent cultivator to the hereditary usufruct of the land." *Dar* is a Persian word, signifying holder; *meerassdar* is the holder of a *meerass* right. "The paracoody or paragoody is a temporary tenant from another village, who cultivates the land of a *meerassdar*, and is the same as *pyagurry*, *pyacust*, and *pyacoody*." *Pyacust* is evidently the same as *paykasht*, which, by the same authority[1], signifies " farmers, who by contract cultivate lands to which they themselves do not belong." And *paycury* is the relative noun, from *paykur*, which differs from *paykasht* only as the adjective, or the active participle, does from the past, or as sowing from sown.

Page XXIV.

(*h*). In Persia, and the countries about the *Oxus*, the cultivators are represented as living pretty much in the same way as they are found in India, that is, congregated in *mouzahs*, or villages, to which the lands that they cultivate are in some manner attached, and which, in some instances, appear to have peculiar customs of their own. So that the system of village communities, which is usually considered an institution peculiarly Hindu, was either introduced into India by the Mahomedans, or is a phase of society common to India with the countries which adjoin it on the north-west.

3.—MEERASSDARS AND RESIDENT CULTIVATORS IN THE MADRAS PRESIDENCY.

I.—SELECT COMMITTEE, 1812.

Fifth Report,
page 136.

(*a*). Though the *meerassdars* appear for some years to have been regarded in the light of fixed cultivators only, with an hereditary right of occupancy so long as they paid the dues of Government, more particular enquiry seems to have established the fact that they possess a real property in the land, having the right of mortgaging, selling, and otherwise disposing of it; and that this right they have always exercised, and do still exercise. The lands held under this tenure are, of course, of greater or less extent, sometimes comprehending a whole village or more, but generally, part of a village only. A *meerassee* portion of land would, under the operation of the Hindu law (by which property descends equally to all the male children of a family,

---

[1] Glossary.

App. VIII.

MEERASSDARS
AND CULTI-
VATORS, MADRAS
PRESIDENCY.

Para. 3, contd.

and by which the adoption of children is admitted) be reduced by the divisions and sub-divisions of it, that would constantly take place, to estates, or rather scraps of land, of so small and minute a kind, were each individual to assume the part of it which under that law he succeeded to, as to be of little or no value to the owners of them, and quite insufficient to afford them a subsistence were they to cultivate them on their own account, unless they happened to possess other land in the vicinity. For the purpose of avoiding the inconvenience, it is the general practice throughout the peninsula to preserve the original property in its *entirety* as long as possible, by letting it stand in the names of those who have the principal shares in it, to whom it is left to manage it, for the common benefit of all interested; each person receiving his proportion of whatever it yields of grain, and in like manner bearing his proportion of loss, according to the extent of his interest in the *meerassee*, thus preserving a union and co-partnery which continues through several generations; a part of the proprietors attending to and cultivating their inheritance, and the rest of them being at liberty to seek and follow other occupations. The principal sharers, who nominally appear in the village accounts as the owners, are answerable for the payment of the public demand on the whole land. When an entire village is held under the *meerassee* tenure, it is common for a new distribution of lands to take place at stated periods, by the drawing of lots; and this custom appears to obtain where the *meerassee* constitutes but part of a village. In these cases, no part of the *meerassee* is the permanent property of any particular individual; the land belonging to the whole body of *meerassdars* connected with it. Before, therefore, a *meerassdar* can mortgage, sell, or bequeath his interest in this common property to another, the consent of the other *meerassdars* is necessary to the validity of the transaction.

(*b*). The term *meerassee*, by which this species of property is distinguished, was introduced by the Mahomedans; and since the establishment of their authority, the word has become familiar to all ranks. Among the Bramins it generally goes by the Sanskrit term of *sivastrum*, and by that of *caniatchy* among those shudras, or cultivating classes of inhabitants, who may not have adopted the general term *meerassee*.

(*c*). In the poorest kind of soil producing dry grain culture, the ryots appear to have little more interest in it than that of being hereditary cultivators. It is in the paddy or wet lands called *nunjah*, that the right of *meerassee* is found to obtain in a more or less perfect form. Where the demand of Government was so high as to have absorbed nearly the whole of the landlord's rent, that is, the whole produce, after deducting the expenses of cultivation, and what was necessary as subsistence to the owner, the land naturally ceased to be either a mortgageable or saleable commodity; but even in this case, if the *meerassdar* did not cultivate the land himself, but permitted another to do so, he was entitled to receive from the cultivator a *russoom*, or quit-rent, in acknowledgment of his proprietory right termed *sawmy boçum*.

(*d*.) In the Southern Provinces of the Peninsula, which are situated below the ghauts, the tenures which have been described were found to exist in a less impaired state than elsewhere. In these regions there was also a considerable quantity of dry grain land, the provinces of Coimbatore and Dindigal being principally composed of such; and although

APP. VIII.

——

MEERASSDARS
AND RESIDENT
CULTIVATORS,
MADRAS PRESI-
DENCY.

Para. 3, contd.

of the fields of that description, those only appear to be saleable that had the advantage of wells, or, from particular circumstances of local situation, were rendered particularly desirable, yet, to deprive an individual of any field he had long cultivated, while he continued to pay the rent, had always been considered an act of injustice. The same inhabitants are represented to have peopled the same villages, ploughed the same fields, from time immemorial. The oppressions of Hyder Ally, of Tippoo Saheb, and of the Nabob of the Carnatic, may have produced a temporary emigration ; but those who thus deserted their lands, returned to them from time to time.

(*e*). It also appears that neither the Hindu nor Mussulman Government, supposing their rights in the soil as proprietors to be undisputable, ever exercised such a right; that what was a fair assessment, and what was exaction, was known to the governing authority, and to those governed.

(*f*). Of the *pyacarries* or *paracoodies*, there are two descriptions. The *ool paracoody* is the fixed and permanent tenant of the *meerassdar*, who resides in the village in which the land is situated. The common *paracoody* is the temporary tenant, who is invited by the *meerassdar* from a district or a neighbouring village to cultivate his *meerassee*, under an engagement for a given period, at the expiration of which, his connection with the land determines, unless renewed by the formation of a new contract. It often happens from various causes that a *meerassdar* is unable or unwilling to cultivate his fields. In this case, it has been the practice for the Government or its managers to assign the culture of such land to *paracoodies* of their own nomination; but the right of the *meerassdar* in the soil is not impeached by this act arising from his inability ; he is still considered as the proprietor, and entitled to his *sawmy bogum*, or rent, from the *paraeoody* in possession, and may return again to the cultivation of his *meerassee* lands whenever he may be able or willing to occupy it.

(*g*). In those lands where there are no *meerassdars* to claim, the ryots may be considered as *ool paracoodies*, holding of the Circar, enjoying, as they do, an hereditary right of occupancy, subject to the condition of paying the rents demanded of them.

(*h*). This right, it has never been the practice, either of the Hindu or of the Mussulman Government, to take from the poorest cultivator, so long as he remained in obedience to the general authority of the Circar, and duly yielded the public share. Indeed, it is not to be discovered, in the history of the Hindus, from the reign of their first princes until the final downfal of the Hindu authority, that any of the landed rights to which your Committee have thus briefly adverted were ever impeached or destroyed ; on the contrary, their uninterrupted existence is proved by numberless records, and by none more distinctly than by the ordinary form of a deed of sale.

II.—COMMITTEE AT TANJORE, *22nd February 1807.*

The Committee will here remark that very extensive property in land is held by the *meerassdars*. Many possess from three to four

thousand acres, *not always a separate and distinct property in whole* APP. VIII.
villages, but in various proportions of the meerassee of different villages.

But the property of a much greater number is very small; *many of*
those whose property is extensive were formerly *puttuckdars ("a species of*
zemindar or collector in Tanjore, who had the charge of a greater or less
number of villages, and resembling the *Nantwars* on the Jaghir"), and
are said to *have acquired the property by means not always justifiable.*

Para. 3, contd.

This description,
particularly in
the passages in
italics, exactly
applies to the
zemindars of
Bengal, and to
their usurpation
of the rights and
property of the
headmen of
villages.

Sess. 1831-32,
Vol. XI.

III.—MR. A. D. CAMPBELL (*an able paper on the Land Revenue which*
has been furnished to your Committee by Mr. A. D. Campbell,
late a Collector under the Madras Presidency).

(*a*). Subject to local exceptions,[1] the cultivators in India, in general,
may be considered as divided into two great classes, *viz.,* those who are
vested with hereditary rights of occupancy, and those who are not.

(*b*). The last-mentioned, or lowest, class consists of what, in Bengal,
are termed the *paee khusht,* and at Madras, the *paracoody pyacarry,*
or stranger cultivators. These persons have their original domicile in
some village at a distance from that in which they cultivate or temporarily dwell, and thence are called *migratory* ryots. Their right is
never hereditary, nor transferable by sale or otherwise; and unless
special agreements are entered into, it expires with the cultivation of each year. But, unless otherwise expressly stipulated, the
annual demand, even upon them, is limited by local usage. When
employed by the higher classes of hereditary cultivators upon the
fields which those higher classes occupy, they are to be viewed either as
annual tenants, or as holding under special agreements. But it has
been usual for the Government, or its representatives, to call in the aid
of the lower class of people to occupy the inferior fields, which the hereditary classes subsequently described have left unoccupied. In this
case, they stand in direct relation to the Government, or its representatives, as the temporary substitutes for the higher classes of hereditary
cultivators; and the rates leviable from them by the Government
are occasionally lower than those leviable from the higher classes, on
account, evidently, of the inferiority of the fields occupied by this lower
class. It will be obvious, however, from the description here given,
that the occupation of a field by any of the higher hereditary classes
totally excludes its occupation by this class, except as the tenants of
the superior occupant.

(*c*). But as this class of migratory ryots usually obtain a bare subsistence from the land, they find it preferable to relinquish the inferior
fields they hold directly from Government, even at rates unusually low,
for those of a superior and more fertile nature cultivated by the higher
classes, or by themselves as the tenants of these higher classes; and
whenever such become vacant, they will gladly offer to hold them
directly from Government, or its representatives, at rates much higher
than they pay for their own inferior fields, or than can be paid, for
even the finer soils, by the hereditary cultivators, entitled by their
tenure to derive more than a bare subsistence from the land. This
body are, therefore, ever on the watch, by the offer of higher terms, to

---

[1] Chiefly in the western coasts of the Peninsula of India, Canara, and Malabar, where
the non-existence of village communities and other peculiarities, distinguish the people
entirely from all other Hindus.

APP. VIII.
——
TENURES IN
BENGAL AND
MADRAS PRE-
SIDENCIES.
——
Para. 3, contd.
tempt the Government, or its representatives, to oust the hereditary cultivator from his fields; but so long as the latter is willing to pay his established rates, this is universally considered an act of the greatest injustice.

(*d*). There exists, under the Madras Presidency, and perhaps elsewhere, a peculiar class of cultivators termed *oolcoody pyacarry*, holding an intermediate place between the foregoing and those who are subsequently described. Their tenure, originally, was precisely of the temporary kind above mentioned, and they continue frequently to hold of the higher class of cultivators; but in general they hold directly from Government. Having been allowed to occupy, from father to son, for several generations, chiefly the unirrigated fields in the Southern Peninsula, neglected by the highest class, whose stock is concentrated on the more fertile, artificially irrigated lands, they have gradually, but successfully, converted their temporary into an hereditary tenure; and ceasing to hold annually, or by special contract, their occupation of particular fields now excludes both their brethren possessing that more temporary right, and their superiors holding one, which, like their own, is based on prescription. Their right, however, continues untransferable by sale or otherwise, and in other respects corresponds with that before described, liable only to the payment of the public dues, as limited by local usage.

(*e*). The third, most numerous and most important class of all, termed under the Supreme Government the *khoodkasht* ryots (cultivating their own) to the northward of Madras, as well as in some of the western provinces of Bengal denominated *kudeems* (or ancients), and to the southward of the Madras Presidency, as well as in the Deccan, and in some parts of Bengal, called holders of *meerassee*, are distinguished from both the foregoing by being universally considered the descendants of the aboriginal settlers of the village, or of those who restored it, if it ever fell into decay. They, therefore, invariably hold directly either of the Government, or of its representatives, never, like those above described, of any other individual; and their tenure, being quite independent of any contract whatever, originates in the mere act of settlement, confirmed by hereditary succession. On condition of paying the public revenue defined by local usage, the holders of this tenure are vested with a perpetual hereditary right to the fields occupied by them, or at their risk and charge; and so long as that is paid, neither they nor their descendants can be justly ousted from their lands.

(*f*). It appears that the present village zemindars of Behar and Benares originally belonged to this important class of cultivators. In some villages, the whole of this tenure centres in a single individual, but in general it is vested in many. It is then held in one of two modes, either on what is called the "joint or common tenure," or on what has obtained the name of "tenure of severalty." Under the former, the village is divided into a certain number of fixed shares, supposed to have been determined when it was originally settled: and every holder possesses one or more of these shares, or fractional parts of a share, casting lots periodically for the actual occupation of fields in proportion to the share held by each; in this case no particular field belongs to any individual, but a certain share only in the whole

App. VIII.

Tenures in
Bengal and
Madras Pre-
sidencies.

Para. 3, contd.

village, which is itself kept entire. Under the latter system, on the other
hand, each holder has fixed possession of his own particular fields, which
descend to his heirs.

(*g*). This hereditary tenure is distinguished, in the provinces to the
southward of the Madras Presidency, by a remarkable peculiarity, connected, however, rather with its value than with its intrinsic quality or
character. In the provinces under the Bengal or Bombay Government,
it appears not to have been generally saleable, though the Regulations
of the former Presidency occasionally allude to it as transferable. In
the northern provinces, under the Madras Government, the sale or transfer of land held on this tenure appears to be quite unknown; but in
the districts to the southward of that Presidency, the tenure to which
the Mahomedans give the name of *meerassee* (an Arabic derivation
denoting landed property in general, better known to its usual holders,
the Hindu Soodras, as *cauniatchi, dominium ex jure hereditatis*, and to
the Bramins as *swastium*, one's own) has, from time immemorial, been
transferable by sale, gift, or otherwise.

(*h*). In addition to the rights above described, the Native Governments granted to the holders of *meerassee*, in the provinces of Arcot and
Chingleput, and indeed very generally throughout India, to the principal or leading men amongst this important class of hereditary cultivators, a remission of the public revenue on certain of their own or
other lands in their village. But this was in lieu of a money payment
for services to be performed by them as village collectors and as officers
of police, and has no connection, though it has occasionally been confounded, with their tenure as cultivators.

IV.—Mr. J. Mill (*11th August 1831*).

Third Report,
Select Com-
mittee, 1831-32.

Q. 3510.—Under the ryotwar system, if the ryot is divested of his land,
is it not in his power to return to the possession of it at any subsequent
period? That claim is maintained by a class of persons under the
Madras Presidency who are called *meerassadars*; even should they have
abandoned their fields, as they do when an assessment is demanded
which they think beyond what they can pay, and on other occasions, at
any period when they return, they claim the unlimited right of re-
occupancy.

Q. 3511.—Is that common to the ryotwar system in all parts of the
country? I should say, from my present recollection, that this claim is
peculiar to the *meerassadars*.

Q. 3512.—Is it a claim allowed by our Government? It has in some
degree been limited by our Government. It was found, where the lands
of the *meerassadars* were abandoned in this manner, that there was no
possibility of having them occupied without great disadvantage, because
the intermediate occupant was wholly uncertain with regard to the
period of his occupancy, if he was liable to be dismissed by the *meerassadar* whenever he returned; and accordingly Government have assumed
the power of assigning by pottah these lands of the *meerassadars* to
intermediate tenants for a period of years; and it has been under consideration, though I do not recollect whether or not the suggestion has

APP. VIII.
——
TENURES IN
BENGAL AND
MADRAS PRE-
SIDENCIES.
——
Para. 3, contd.

become law, to name a period beyond which the claim of the *meerassadars* should not be sustained.

Q. 3513.—Wherein does the situation of the *meerassadar* in Madras differ from the *khoodkasht* ryot in Bengal? According to my conception of the matter, the right of the *khoodkasht* ryot and that of the *meerassadar* are not essentially different. The difference consists, I think, in certain peculiarities. Over a great part of the Madras territory where those *meerassee* rights are claimed, the rights of the *khoodkasht* ryots generally have become extinct. The greater portion of the inhabitants of the village do not claim the hereditary right; the *meerassadars* are the only parties that continue to claim that right, and they commonly claim something more. There are certain fees, dues, and other privileges in the villages to which, in general, they advance claims; and they appear to me in those cases to be the descendants of the principal families who had borne office in the villages, and to whom, in that capacity, those dues belonged. Those two circumstances taken together, the hereditary occupancy of the *khoodkasht* ryots, and the claim to certain dues and distinctions in the village, which also had been enjoyed hereditarily, appear to me to account for the whole of the *meerassee* rights.

Q. 3514. Do you conceive that *meerassee* rights, or something very like them, existed throughout India till disturbed by the various modes of settlement which have been made? The *khoodkasht* ryots I considered to have been universal in India, and the land to have been held by them, with few exceptions; I also conceive that the principal offices in the villages were hereditary in certain families, to whom belong advantages similar to those now claimed by the *meerassadars* at Madras; that is, certain dues and privileges beyond the perpetual occupancy.

V.—REVENUE LETTER TO FORT ST. GEORGE (*12th April 1815*).

From the peculiar constitution of Hindu society, and the natural tendency of their laws of inheritance, we conceive that landed property in India, wherever it has existed, must have been more sub-divided than in any other country. If, in consequence of the immoderate exactions of the native Governments, you have found that species of private property, in many districts, either annihilated or nearly so; and if you are actuated, as you profess to be, by a sincere desire to restore it, the parties who should benefit from this intention are surely those, or the descendants of those, who have been reduced from the situation of proprietors to that of occupants of the soil; they are the great body of *oolcoody* or resident ryots, as distinguished from the *pyacarries* or migratory cultivators; and where it could have been done without injury to the great claims of the former, it would, in our judgment, have been an exercise of sound policy to have extended similar benefits to the latter, and thereby induced them to settle and concentrate their labours and industry in one spot (*para. 146*).

VI.—MINUTE OF BOARD OF REVENUE (*5th January 1818*).

(*a*). In every Tamil village, the exclusive right to the hereditary possession and usufruct of the several descriptions of land situated within its

boundaries was originally vested in the Vellalees, one of the principal
Soodra castes of that nation, by whom it is termed *Cawnyatche*, or free
hereditary property in the land. It would now be of little utility, were
it possible, to attempt to trace the different gradations by which, in the
course of time, this right has been partially transferred from the members of
this caste to the various other tribes in whose possession it is now to be
found. It is sufficient to know that in all parts of the Tamil country it is
still retained principally by the Vellalees, but is now frequently held by
the Bramins also, who distinguish it by the Sanscrit term *swastium*, signifying anything peculiarly one's own, and partly by other Hindu tribes,
by Mussulmans, and sometimes by Native Christians, among whom, as
well as among Europeans, it is now generally known by the name of
meerassee, a word of Asiatic derivation, denoting hereditary property in
general. * * *

(*b*). On the establishment of every Tamil village, as now constituted, *Ibid.*, page 903.
the rights above explained were vested in all the original Vellalee settlers
as a collective body—not in each individually ; every one of them, therefore, possessed a separate equal share in the whole *meerassee*, and have,
in each village, to the present day ; the number of equal shares into
which the *meerassee* was at first divided remains the same as when the
village was originally settled. In some villages there are a hundred
shares, in others of the same extent, fifty or ten only ; but whatever may
be now the number of *meerassadars*, the number of shares invariably
remains the same as at first determined. From the number of *meerassadars* having decreased since the settlement of the village, some of them
may now hold two, three, four, or fifty shares. From their number
having increased since that period, the shares may have been split into
fourths, sixteenths, thirty-seconds, or other fractional parts, and many
may therefore hold a part only of a share ; but the number of original
equal shares in each village has continued unaltered for ages. Supposing
a village to have been at first divided among thirty-two original settlers
into thirty-two equal shares, and its *meerassadars* to be now a hundred
in number, if any one of them is asked how many shares there are in a
village, he will immediately answer thirty-two, but when asked how
many of these belong to himself, or to any other particular *meerassadar*,
he will answer two, three, or four shares, or perhaps the half, the fourth,
or the sixteenth part of a share, as the case happens to be. * *

(*c*). Where land for a certain period, which varies in different places, *Ibid.*, page 905.
has for several generations been farmed by the same family, the tenant
is termed an *oolcoody pyacarry*, and by prescription becomes possessed
of an hereditary right to hold his farm in perpetuity, on condition
of the regular payment of the *mammool*, or customary waurum or
teerwa. The *oolcoody pyacarry* and his descendants never can be ousted
from their farm so long as this is paid, nor can the waurum or teerwa
be raised by the *meerassadar* ; but though they can mortgage, they can
never sell, these their hereditary privileges.

4.—MEERASSADARS IN THE DECCAN.

I.—BRIGGS *on the Land Tax in India.*

(*a*). The Collector of Poonah states the general divisions of husbandmen are two : " *tulkaries*, men who cultivate their own fields ; and

oopries, or tenants who cultivate lands not their own. A third class exists, called *wawandkury*, a temporary tenant, who, residing in one village, comes for a season to take land in another."

(*b*). The *tulkary* is a *meerassadar*. *Tul* signifies a field, and *tulkary*, the owner of land; he is considered, and invariably acknowledged by the Government, to have the property of the lands he cultivates. * * The *tulkary* pays a land-rent to Government, according to the extent and quality of his lands. This land-rent is supposed to admit of no increase.

II.—COLONEL W. H. SYKES *on Land Tenures in the Deccan (Decr. 1830).*

(*a*). My earliest enquiries led me to believe that the lands of villages were divided into hereditary family estates, called *thals*, bearing the names of ancient Mahratta families, the descendants of which were then in possession of them, or bearing the names of extinct families, of whose ancient possessions tradition bore testimony. The results of six years' research were confirmatory of these points. The lands of extinct families were, and still are, called gat-kul, from the Sanscrit *guta*, gone, passed away, and *kula*, a race, family. Under all changes of Government and new proprietary, the family names by which they were originally distinguished have rarely been disturbed, and it is probable that they are handed down from very remote times.

(*b*). The existence of hereditary estates being established, the tenures on which they were held will be best illustrated by an account of the relation on which the proprietors of portions of them stood, and still stand, to the Government. Persons so holding land are called *mirasadars*, a term of Arabic origin, from *miras*, heritage, patrimony. They are of two kinds, those who are descendants of the original proprietors of *thals*, and those who have purchased lands from the descendants of the original proprietors, or from the village authorities, who had at their disposal the lands of extinct families. In no instance that I am aware of, have the former documentary proof of their rights. With the latter, documentary proof is not uncommon, in the shape of a paper called a *miras patta*, o letter of inheritance, which is witnessed not only by the authorities of the ville where the letter is granted, but by those of neighbouring villages, and by the deshmook and despand of the district, and the privity of Government is consequently implied.

(*c*). *Mirasadars* of the present day claim a right to the personal occupancy of their land so long as they pay the Government assessment on it; and in case of failure in the payment of the Government dues, and the consequent forfeiture of the right of occupancy, they claim the right to resume it whenever they can pay their arrears, and also to mortgage or sell it at pleasure. The land-tax is asserted to have been fixed, and there is no reason to doubt it, as all *miras* land still continues to pay the *sosthi-dar*, or what is deemed the permanent tax; but Government at pleasure could put extra cesses on it, and thus neutralise the advantage of a permanent tax, and render the *miras* tenures valueless.

(*d*). Although *miras*, or hereditary land, was assessed permanently, yet it was at a higher rate than any other land, at least if we judge from the difficulty discoverable in village papers for the last half century of letting waste land at the *miras* rate. This permanent assessment on

the *miras* land was called, as I before stated, the *sorshi-dar;* there was App. VIII.
an extra tax also payable every three years, called *miraspatti*, or a
specific tax upon the hereditary land, being a kind of smart money for the Deccan
Tenures.
distinction which the term *mirasadar* conferred.

(*e*). From the extinction of numerous Mahratta families who were in Para. 4, contd.
possession of *thals*, or hereditary estates, great part of the land in the
country is without proprietors; in consequence, a very numerous class of
occupiers is the Upari. The proper meaning of this term is a stranger,
or one who cultivates land in a village in which he has not any corporate
rights. In practice he holds land on the *ukti* tenure, which is a land
lease by a verbal agreement for one year. In this tenure the rates are
not fixed; the parties make the best terms they can; but the *sosthi*, or
permanent rates, are insisted on as far as practicable. Persons in authority no doubt take advantage of the *ukti* tenure. * * *Mirasadars* are not
interdicted from holding lands on the *ukti* tenure, which carry a reduced
rent, from the depreciated value of land, and the difficulty of letting it.

III.—Mr. Hugh Stark, *Chief of the Revenue Department in the India Board* (*14th February* 1832).

In a great portion of the Poonah territories the *meerass* tenure was
found existing, but it is always combined with village institutions and
privileges. The *meerassadars* are the acknowledged proprietors of the
lands held by them. No person can acquire a *meerass* tenure without
the consent of the brotherhood. The villages were so much attached to
their tenures, that it enabled the Poonah Government to exact, in the
form of revenue, much more from the *meerass* lands than they could
procure from the same description of lands in the immediate neighbourhood not belonging to the *meerassadars*. * * There can be no question
of the right of the *meerassadars* to hold at fixed rates; and should the
Government be in a situation to reduce the tax, the country would
rapidly improve (*Q. 427, 428, 440*).

5.—Meerassadars in Cuttack.

Revenue letter to Bengal (*10th December 1822*).

I. The opinion varying from that of Mr. Melville, which Mr. Stirling
describes as held by Mr. Ker, that the ryots had the means of protecting
themselves against the zemindars, by making their own bargains as tenants
against their own landlords in England, is an old theory, which you have
unhappily had experience more than sufficient to disprove. Notwithstanding this opinion, Mr. Ker found a class of persons who are called
Mourousee Mocuddims, and whom he recognised as possessing a right in
the soil, and subject only to an ascertained rate of jumma. The name suggests the idea of a similarity with the class of *meerassadars* in some of the
more southern provinces of India. That the foundation of the rights of
these *meerassadars* was laid in those of the proprietary class of ryots,
known in your provinces by the name of *khoodkasht* ryots, seems to be
sufficiently ascertained. Where rights and prerogatives, beyond those of
proprietary ryots, are claimed on the part of *meerassadars*, they seem in

all cases to have been those annexed to the head ryots, the managers of the village, and in many cases, where ages of exaction had destroyed the rights and obliterated the claims of the general class of the *khoodkasht* ryots, the claims of the descendants of those headmen, under the title of *meerassadars,* seem to be all that are recognised in existence of the rights of the proprietary ryots.

II. We are not informed what numbers Mr. Ker discovered of the Mourousee Mocuddims. The words employed lead us to infer that they are but few; and the natural inference appears to be that their rights are all that are now asserted of the rights of a general class of *khood-kasht* ryots, a class which the measures you are pursuing for protecting the interest of the cultivating ryots may happily have the effect of reviving.

6.—REVENUE SYSTEM AND VILLAGE ORGANISATION.

I.—REVENUE ORGANISATION OR SYSTEM.

1.—SELECT COMMITTEE OF 1812.

Bengal:—Appendix II, paragraph 1, section VIII, and para. 2.
Northern Circars, Madras Presidency:—Appendix II, paragraph 1, section VII.

MADRAS PRESIDENCY.

Nearly the same system as in the Northern Circars prevailed in the modern possessions of the Company, which were not in the hands of poligars; for it was much the practice of the native Mahomedan Governments, and quite general under that of Mahomed Ally, the Nabob of the Carnatic, and his son, to farm out the lands in extensive tracts, often whole provinces, for a certain number of years, to individuals, who sub-rented them, by villages, to the potails or headmen, who were left to collect from the other cultivators as they pleased. The oppression of the under-renters principally consisted, as they did in the Northern Circars, in levying private contributions on frivolous and unwarrantable pretences; in under-assessing the lands in the occupation of themselves, their relations, and friends, making up the difference by an over-assessment of the other village cultivators, more especially on those who were the poorest, and therefore the least able to protect themselves; in forcing the inferior ryots to cultivate their lands, and perform for them, free of charge, various other services; in monopolising the produce of the several villages, which they afterwards disposed of at an advanced price, and in applying to their own use, the allowances and perquisites of the pagodas and village servants, by which the parties were deprived of their rights, or the inhabitants, as was often the case, were obliged to make good the loss. One of the greatest abuses which was found to exist, as more immediately affecting the interests of Government, was the undue and irregular alienations of land.

II.—WILKS' MYSORE.

Every Indian village is, and appears always to have been, in fact, a separate community or republic, and exhibits a living picture of that state of things which theorists have imagined in the earlier stages of civilisation, when men have assembled in communities for the purpose of reciprocally administering to each other's wants. [Here follows a description of village officials similar to that in Appendix II, paragraph 12, section III.] In some instances the lands of a village are cultivated in common, and the crop divided in the proportions of the labour contributed; but generally each occupant tills his own field; the waste land is a common pasture for the cattle of the village; its external boundaries are as carefully marked as those of the richest field, and they are maintained as a common right of the village, or rather the *township* (a term which more correctly describes the thing in our contemplation) to the exclusion of others, with as much jealousy and rancour as the frontiers of the most potent kingdoms. Such are the premature component parts of all the kingdoms of India. Their technical combination to compose districts, provinces, or principalities, of from ten to a hundred thousand villages, has been infinitely diversified at different periods by the wisdom or caprice of the chief ruler, or by the vigour and resistance of those who in every age, country, and condition, have coveted independence for themselves, and the power to govern the greatest possible number of their fellow-creatures. Menu's arrangement places a lord over one town with its district (which is precisely the township above described); a lord of ten, of twenty, of a hundred, and of a thousand, in a scale of regular subordination, reporting and receiving commands successively from the next in gradation, and fixes with precision the salaries and perquisites of each. His scheme of government recognises none of those persons who, in these days, are known by the several designations of wadeyars, poligars, zemindars, deshayes, &c. (all in their respective jurisdictions assuming, when they dare, the title of Rajah, or King). All the officers enumerated by Menu have, in their several circles, at different periods, simply acted as agents of the Sovereign.

III.—BOMBAY PRESIDENCY (DECCAN).

(a).—BRIGGS *on the Land Tax in India.*

In the administration of the office of Magistrate, the patel, or chief of the landed corporation, was here, as in other parts of India, the head of the village, and the representative of the people as well as of the Government. The existence of the local officers in the Mahratta Country is thus described: "A turuf is composed (Elphinstone) of an indefinite number of villages; it is under no particular officer.[1] Several turufs make a pergunna, which is under a Desmook, who performs the same functions towards the pergunna as the *Patel* towards the village. He is assisted by a Des Pandra, who answers to the Kulcurny, or Village registrar. It is universally believed in the Mahratta Country that the Desmooks, Des Pandras, &c., were all officers appointed by some former Government, and it seems probable that they were the revenue officers of the Hindu Government. These officers still hold the land and fees that were originally assigned them as wages, and are considered as servants of the Government; but the only duty they perform is to produce their old records when required to settle disputes about land by a reference to

---

[1] A Naek.

those records, and to keep a register of all new grants and transfers of property, either by Government or by individuals." Mr. Elphinstone rates the Desmook's profits at 5 per cent. of the collections, together with as much more in rent-free land; and half of those perquisites to the Des Pandra, or District registrar.

(b).—Colonel W. H. Sykes: Land Tenures of the Deccan (*December 1830*).

All lands were classed within some village boundary or other. Villages had a constitution for their internal Government, consisting of the *Patel*, or chief, assisted by a *Changala*, the *Kulkarni*, or village accountant, and the well known village officers, the *baraballo;* the numbers of the latter were complete or not, according to the population of the village, and the consequent means of supporting them. A few villages constituted a *naikwari*, over which was an officer with the designation of Naik. Eighty-four villages constituted a *Desmukh*, equivalent to a pergunna or county. Over this number was placed a *Desmukh*, as governor, assisted by a *Deschangla;* and for the branch of accounts there was a *Despand*, or district accountant and registrar. The links connecting the *Desmukhs* with the prince were the *Sar Desmukhs*, or heads of the *Desmukhs;* they were few in number. It is said there were also *Sar Despands.* The *Sar Desmukhs, Desmukhs, Naiks, Patels,* and *Changalas,* in short all persons in authority, were Mahrattas; the writers and accountants were mostly Brahmins.

(1). *Desmukhs* of such and such districts. Their rights were hereditary and saleable, wholly or in part. The concurring testimony of the people proves the hereditary right; and the proof of the power to sell is found[1] in Brahmins and other castes, and some few Mussulmans, being now sharers in the dignities, rights, and emoluments of *Desmukh.* * * The *Desmukhs* were no doubt originally appointed by Government, and they possessed all the above advantages, on the tenure of collecting and being responsible for the revenue, for superintending the cultivation and police of their districts, and carrying into effect all orders of Government. They were, in fact, to a district what a *Patel* is to a village; in short, were charged with its whole Government.

(2). *Despandahs* are contemporary in their institution with the *Desmukhs;* they are the writers and accountants of the latter, and are always Brahmins; they are to districts what *Kulkarnis* are to villages. Like the *Desmukhs*, they have a percentage on the revenue, but in a diminished ratio of from 25 to 50 per cent. below that of the *Desmukhs*. Their duties are to keep detailed accounts of the revenue of their districts, and to furnish Government with copies; they were also writers, accountants, and registrars within their own limits.

(3). *Patels*, usually called *Potails*,[2] or headmen of towns and villages. This office, together with the village accountant, is no doubt coeval with those of the *Desmukh* and *Despandah.* The Sanskrit term *Gramadikari,* I am told by Brahmins, would be descriptive of the lord or master of the

---

[1] Non-sequitur.　　　　[2] Or Mokuddum.

village, equivalent to the present term Sawa Inamdar, rather than that of *Patel ; gram,* in Sanskrit, meaning village ; *adikar,* the bearing of royal insignia, being pre-eminent. Originally the *Patels* were Mahrattas only ; but sale, gift, or other causes have extended the right to many other castes. A very great majority of *Patels,* however, are still Mahrattas ; their offices were hereditary and saleable, and many documentary proofs are extant of such sales. I made a translation of one of these documents, dated 104 years ago ; it was executed in the face of the country, and with the knowledge of the Government. This paper fully illustrates all the rights, dignities, and emoluments of the office of *Patel.* He was personally responsible for the Government revenue ; he superintended the police of the village, regulated its internal economy, and presided in all village councils.

(4). *Kulkarni.*—The next village tenure is that of *Kulkarni ;* the office is of very great importance, for the *Kulkarni* is not only the accountant of the Government revenue, but he keeps the private accounts of each individual in the village, and is the general amanuensis; few of the cultivators, the *Patels* frequently included, being able to write or cypher for themselves. In no instance have I found this office held by any other caste than the Brahminical.

(5). *Mokuddum.*—The term is applied to the *Patel's* office. It is an Arabic term, and meaning " chief, " " head, " " leader," and is properly applicable to an individual only. The equal right of inheritance in Hindu children to the emoluments and advantages of hereditary offices, the functions of which could be exercised only by the senior of the family, rendered a distinctive appellation necessary for this person, and he was called *Mokuddum.* The sale of parts of the office of *Patel,* however, to other families, the heads of which would also be " *Mokuddum,*" rendered the qualifying adjective necessary in all writings of half-*Mokuddum,* quarter-*Mokuddum,* &c., according to the share each family held in the office. Thus, His Highness Seendeh (Scindiah) is six-sevenths-*Mokuddum* at Jamgaon, the other Mahratta sharer one-seventh, and the like in other instances.

7.—HEADMEN OF VILLAGES.

BENGAL, *including N. W. Provinces and Behar.*

(a).—TAGORE LAW LECTURES (*1874-75*).

(1). I come now to consider the position of the village headman ; Page 26. and in considering his functions, we shall arrive at some understanding of the revenue system of the Hindu Governments, and of the relations between the king and the community. The headman bore various titles in different parts of the country. In Bengal, he was known by the name of *mokuddim* or *mundul,* at least in Mahomedan times, and seems to have corresponded with the *gram adheput,* or superintendent of a village, referred to in Menu ; other names were *gond* or *ganda, potail,* and *purdhan.* He was a partly elective, partly hereditary officer, and combined the functions of head of the municipality with those of an officer and representative of the Government. He was supposed to derive his right to the office through his descent from the founder of the village.

Whether the office was at first wholly elective, is uncertain; but considering the strong tendency of all Hindu offices to become hereditary, the office of headman probably had an hereditary element in very early times. The village might elect, but if it did not, the office generally went to the fittest member of the headman's family, usually with some preference to seniority. Sometimes, however, at least in modern times, the members of the family discharged its functions in rotation, the head of the family receiving, nevertheless, a larger share of the emoluments; thus there were sometimes found to be several *munduls* in a village. There are instances of the sale of the office by the occupants and also by the Government, on the dismissal or failure of heirs of the headman; but in general, the office could not be sold. The headman's tenure of office originally depended upon the approval of the village community, but later the zemindar sometimes nominated the headman. The State had probably always had a veto upon his appointment, since he was an officer of the State as well as the representative of the village, and the

The State could dismiss.   State could dismiss him at pleasure. In this way, the zemindar would come in some cases to assume the right of nominating as a superior representative of the Government; and in the decline of these communities, the villagers could have no choice but to acquiesce. The hereditary element nevertheless continued persistently to assert itself, even down to modern times, and in declining or decayed communities, and in most of the large talooks, descendants of the headman continued to claim the right to exercise the office on a vacancy.

Page 28.   (2). The headman's most important functions, as far as we are concerned, were those of adjuster of the revenue on the village, and of collector of the revenue. He arranged all the details of the assessment, ascertained the extent of each holding in the village, estimated the growing crop, and saw the threshed corn heaps weighed, and apportioned the revenue accordingly, either by estimate or by the actual outturn. He also received the share which represented the revenue, and delivered it in kind to the superior revenue collector, or at a later period to the *malgoozar*, or contractor for the revenue, or else handed it over for sale to the village weighman or the *muhajun* (or village merchant), who bought the grain of the village and advanced the amount of the revenue for payment in money. * * He settled the share to be paid by each ryot towards *deh khurcha* (or village expenses), and each ryot's share of the cost of watching the crops, and in Mahomedan times the amount of *abwab*, or extra assessment, that fell to each cultivator's share. He was bound to see that the *putwaree*, or village accountant, made the proper entries in his books. He was, besides, the village magistrate, and superintended the village police or *chowkeedars*.

Page 29.   (3). The headman's duties were numerous and responsible, and his emoluments were in consequence considerable. He had a few beegahs of land free of revenue for a garden, and paid a lower rate for the rest of his lands than ordinary ryots. He was allowed the services of one or more of the servile labourers of the village and of their families; and $\frac{1}{7}$th or $\frac{1}{8}$th of his grain crop was set apart for their maintenance before his crop was assessed. Or if he did not require their labour, he was sometimes allowed the deduction instead. * * *

(4). Although the headman had the strength of hereditary claims to support him, his office was not a freehold. He could be dismissed by the State, and then his services to the village being rendered useless, his emoluments ceased; but of course he retained his own lands, paying the ordinary revenue for them. He could not, however, be dismissed by the State, except for failure to make good the revenue assessed upon the village, and for the due payment of which he was responsible. In fact, he was in something like the same position as the zemindars subsequently, except that he was in some sort elected by the village, subject to the sanction of the State, and not appointed by the State.

(5). He might, however, have advanced claims to be considered the absolute proprietor upon almost as good grounds as have been advanced by, or rather for, the zemindars; but in truth he was a mere official originally, having nevertheless land which he cultivated himself within the limits of his jurisdiction, just as the zemindars afterwards had. The position and emoluments of the zemindars seem to have been an extension of those of the headmen; many of the headmen became zemindars, and their rights as headmen were combined with, and merged in, their claims as zemindars.

(6). We have seen that the assessment of revenue was upon the individual cultivator; but the headman and the entire village were responsible for its payment. The cultivator was dealt with individually, but as a member of the village, and through the headman; and so strong was the custom of having the assessment settled with reference to the village usages, and to the position of the individual as a member of the village, that in the Madras Presidency some villages were found where the individual cultivators had been assessed direct by the Government for half a century, but had always re-distributed the assessment amongst themselves according to their own usages.

(7). The headman was not generally a farmer of the revenue, or a contractor for it, like the Mahomedan zemindars. In settling the amount to be charged to the village, he acted chiefly in the interest of the village; and when the amount was settled, he collected that amount in money or kind from the villages, chiefly in his capacity of revenue officer. He was responsible for its collection, but does not appear to have been so otherwise than as a representative at once of the Government and the village. The assessment, as I have said, was upon the cultivator individually; but the whole village, and the headman as its representative, was responsible for the collection.

(b).—GLOSSARY.—FIFTH REPORT.

Mocuddim.— Placed before, antecedent, prior, foremost. Head *ryot*, or principal man in a village, who superintends the affairs of it, and among other duties collects the rents of Government within his jurisdiction. The same officer is in Bengal called also *Mundul,* and in the Peninsula, *Gond* and *Potail.*

N. W. PROVINCES.

(c).—MINUTE OF GOVERNOR GENERAL (LORD HASTINGS),—*31st December 1819.*

When an individual is deputed by his neighbours to bargain on their common behalf with Government, there is no change of relations; he is

APP. VIII.
———
VILLAGE HEAD-
MEN.

Para. 7, contd.
Page 31.

Ibid.

Page 31.

Page 33.

Sess. 1831-32,
Vol. XI, App. 78.

APP. VIII.
———
VILLAGE HEAD-
MEN.
———
Para. 7, contd.

only the spokesman of the community. * *   But a new capacity is conferred on him, if Government appoint him to be the person with whom, year after year, it is to settle the account.   When the character of a zemindar is assigned to him, and responsibility for the payment of the aggregate rent is attached to him, Government virtually constitutes him a public officer.   It necessarily invests him with the power of compelling, from the several families of the village, the payment of their respective portions of the general contribution, and our acquaintance with the propensities of the natives must make us sensible that such a power is likely to be misapplied in arbitrary and unjust demands.

(d).—RESOLUTION OF GOVERNMENT (*22nd December 1820*).

Revenue Selec-
tions, Vol. III,
page 240.

The persons who have been admitted to enter into engagements for the payment of the Government revenue, though ordinarily denominated in the Regulations zemindars, talookdars, and other proprietors of land, belong to various classes possessing very different rights and interests.

Paras. 74-5.

(1). In some cases, the sudder malgoozar is a person enjoying the full heritable and transferable property of the whole of the land for which he has engaged ; such a malgoozar may properly be considered proprietor or malik of the land, whether cultivating the land himself, or leasing it to cultivators or farmers.

Para. 77.

(2). In other cases, the occupants and cultivators of the land consist of hereditary cultivators, mouroosee ryots (usually denominated khoodkasht or chuppabund) or some kinds of dependant talookdars, enjoying a permanent, hereditary, and in some cases transferable, right of occupancy, subject to the payment of a fixed rent, or of a rent adjusted by certain fixed rules ; that is to say, the quantum of such rent and the mode of payment being regulated, not by the demand of the sudder malgoozar, but (in the absence of engagements contracted between the parties or their ancestors) by ancient usage and the rates of the pergunnah, mouzah, or other local division.

Para. 78.

In such cases, the sudder malgoozar, though admitted to possess a heritable and transferable property in the rents demandable from the inferior tenantry and ryots, is entitled, during the continuance of these tenures, to exercise only a restricted right of ownership, to be defined in each case by the nature and amount of the payments demandable from each ryot or dependant talookdar, and the other conditions of the tenure.

Para. 79.

The estate or interest, therefore, possessed by such a malgoozar consists, during the continuance of the under-tenant's tenure, rather in the profit derivable from the rent after discharging the stipulated revenue of Government, than in the property of the soil.   He ought, consequently, to be recognised rather as a rent-holder than as the *malik*, or proprietor, of the land occupied by under-tenants of the above description.

Para. 81.

(3). In other cases, the sudder malgoozar appears to possess merely the right of collecting the Sircar's share of the produce, or the revenue demandable by the Sircar in lieu of it ; the whole of the land being occupied by other persons having a full heritable and transferable property in the soil, subject to the payment of the Sircar's dues through

the sudder malgoozar, until regularly admitted to separate engagements,
and the profits of the malgoozar properly consisting only in the difference
between the amount which he is entitled to levy as revenue, or khiraj,
from those proprietors, and the rent which he has contracted to pay to
Government in perpetuity or for a term.

In such case, the sudder malgoozar may be considered as the mere
representative of Government; and though allowed a right of property
in the incidence of his management, yet he possesses no property in the
soil, nor any interest in the mehal, beyond the collection of the Sircar's
revenue or khiraj.

(4). In other cases, the sudder malgoozar possesses a portion of the
lands for which he has engaged in full proprietary right, while the rest is
occupied by other persons enjoying an equal right of property, subject,
until regular separation, to the payment, through the sudder malgoozar,
of the Sircar's khiraj, or by ryots or under-tenants possessing a hereditary
right of occupancy. Of such malgoozars, who occur in village communities, there are several descriptions.

(5). With this variety in the classes of zemindars, it can be a matter
of no surprise that very injurious consequences have followed from a
system of management under which all persons coming under engagements with Government, and entered in the Government books as
proprietors, have often been confounded as if belonging to one class,
and have frequently been considered as the absolute proprietors of the
lands comprised in the mehals for which they had engaged.

(e).—RESOLUTION OF GOVERNMENT (1st August 1822).

The zemindars, talookdars, and mocuddums would appear to have
differed in the extent, not in the nature, of the interests possessed by
them. If any distinction can be drawn, the last mentioned class may
be considered to have had a closer lien on the villages under their
management, resembling, nearly, the potails of the villages in the
territory recently acquired on the other side of India, who are indeed,
it would seem, likewise denominated mocuddums. In Cuttack, too,
as in the territory in question, the moccuddumy of waste or deserted
villages would appear to have been sold by the superior officers of
Government ; but the purchasers in such cases would seem to have
stood precisely on a footing with the hereditary mocuddums, who had
derived their office from their ancestors. So also the nature of the
tenure of the mocuddums and talookdars would appear to have been in
all respects the same, whether they paid their revenue directly to the
aumil, or through an intermediate and hereditary officer.

(f).—CIVIL COMMISSIONER AT DELHI (28th April 1820).

(1). Amongst the crowd of proprietors, the managers and leaders of
the villagers are the mocuddums. These have been from time immemorial the persons through whom the rents of the villages have been
settled and collected, and who have adjusted the quota of each sharer.

App. VIII.

VILLAGE HEAD-
MEN.

Para. 7, contd.

They are supposed to have been originally either selected by the proprietors, or to have raised and elevated themselves to the office from their superior knowledge and address in making terms for the villages with the officers of Government. The office is not necessarily hereditary, though usually descending to one of the sons of the family, from the superior opportunity which they have of inheriting the information of the parent ; nor is the number fixed or limited, though seldom exceeding eight or ten.

Para. 46.

(2). The mocuddums were rewarded either by the other sharers granting them a certain proportion of their own grain, by rating their cultivation less than their own, or by allowing them the produce of one plough untaxed. Besides this, the mocuddums used occasionally, if opportunity offered, to impose upon the other sharers by stating the jumma required by the ruling power at a sum beyond that really fixed, and then dividing the surplus amongst themselves, and they would similarly, in concordance with the Putwarry, enhance the statement of the village expenses and pocket the difference. * * *

Para. 195.

(3). The authority of the mocuddums was also at times very oppressive in other respects, and they became a little aristocracy ; but in general, they were the safeguards of the community, and had its welfare at heart. They were necessary to the people as the only individuals who attended to their interests, and without them the Government could in general effect nothing.

(g).—Bengal Government (1825 or 1825).

Sess. 1831-32,
Vol. XI,
App. 74,
page 189.

There was evidence to show that the term mocuddum is equally applicable to the headman and representative of a body of zemindars, possessing a clear heritable and transferable right of property in the soil, and subject only to the payment of their quota of the Government assessment, and of the village expenses, as to the headman and representative of a body of cultivators claiming no transferable property, and paying, along with the Government revenue, *a clear rent or zemindary russoom to one or more proprietors.* In the former case, it was obvious that the mocuddummee tenure might be regarded as superior in degree, at least where the mocuddum was able to preserve among his fellows the superiority which appeared to have belonged by custom of the country to the managing malgoozar, and to have secured any special emoluments of office. The mocuddummee tenure, in the above case, stands to the zemindary tenure in the relation of a director to any general body of proprietors, whose affairs he may be chosen to represent, such director being himself also a proprietor and, as such, drawing an income from his property distinct from the emoluments of his office, but eligible for that office in virtue of his proprietary character.

(h).—Sir C. T. Metcalfe (7th November 1830).

Sess. 1831-32,
Vol. XI,
App. 84,
page 331.

(1). There is no point on which we ought to be more careful than as to the acknowledgment of pretended proprietors in the Western Provinces, other than the real members of the village communities.

There is reason to suppose that in many a village, where the real proprietors were once numerous, some upstart fellow has acquired, without
right or by fraud, an ostensible pre-eminence, and now pretends to be
the sub-proprietor. In any settlement more precise and determinate
than those heretofore made, it will be necessary to be most cautious not
to sacrifice the proprietary rights, such as they are, of the numerous
proprietors of villages, to the pretensions of one or a few who may have
brought themselves more into notice, and obtained predominance,
whether by fair means or by foul. Investigation must be made in
each village ; for the names recorded in the Collector's books may be
either those of persons who are not proprietors, or those of persons
who being part proprietors are not exclusively so, but representatives of
the body of village proprietors. * *

(2). By far the most numerous class of settlements to be made will, Page 333.
I conclude, be those with village communities. In such settlements
the mocuddums, or headmen, by whatever designation known, come
forward to conclude the settlement as the representatives of the village
community. I believe that it is not an uncommon practice to consider
those who sign the engagements as exclusively responsible, in their
own persons, for the payment of the revenue. In my opinion, although
undoubtedly responsible as part owners of the village lands, and addi-
tionally responsible as collectors of the revenue, and managers of the
village, in which capacities they usually receive a percentage on the
revenue, which allowance is termed mocuddummee, they are not exclusively responsible, nor as landowners more responsible than the other
landowners of the village which they represent. Out of this practice of
considering the mocuddums as the contractors for the revenue, instead
of regarding them as the headmen and representatives of the village
communities, has arisen, I fear, the more serious evil of considering
them as the only land owners of the village, and thus annihilating the
rights of the rest of the village community.

(i).—COURT OF DIRECTORS.

The Hon'ble Court have at the same time stated a decided
opinion that (Resolution, 22nd December 1820, paragraph 191)
a proprietary right should be no further acknowledged in the
mocuddums than as concerns the lands on which they have a possessory
claim, and that the same right should, on the same principle, be admitted in the case of the other occupant cultivators.

BENGAL.

(k).—SIR J. SHORE (June 1789).

(1). In almost every village, according to its extent, there is one or more Page 31.
head ryot, known by a variety of names in different parts of the country, who has in some measure the direction and superintendence of the
rest. For distinction, I shall confine myself to the term *Mundul* ; he
assists in fixing the rent, in directing the cultivation, and in making the

APP. VIII.

VILLAGE PRO-
PERTY AND
VILLAGE ZEMIN-
DARS.

Para. 8.
Para. 244.

collections. This class of men, so apparently useful, seem greatly to have contributed to the growth of the various abuses now existing, and to have secured their own advantages, both at the expense of the zemindar, landlord, renter, and inferior ryots.

(2). Their power and influence over the inferior ryots is great and extensive; they compromise with the farmers at their expense, and procure their own rents to be lowered, without any diminution in what he is to receive, by throwing the difference upon the lower ryots, from whom it is exacted by taxes of various denominations. They make a traffic in pottahs, lowering the rates of them for private stipulations, and connive at the separation and secretion of lands. * *

8.—VILLAGE PROPERTY AND VILLAGE ZEMINDARS.

I.—BRIGGS *on the Land Tax in India.*

The revenue claimed by the Hindu sovereign in ancient times was not regulated by the superficies cultivated, but by the quantity of the produce. The sovereign's share rose and sunk with the prosperity or adversity of the husbandman. As regarded the latter, the sovereign's portion was fixed and definite; it varied not with the metallic value of the grain, nor was it affected by any other circumstance; the proportion was ever the same. In the country extending from Nellore, on the north, as far south as the Coleroòn river, the ancient cultivators of villages held a certain quantity of land rent-free, denominated *gramamaniam*, the township liberties, which enabled them to give a larger proportion for those lands paying tax to the sovereign. Besides this advantage, each of the original proprietors belonging to the corporation received certain fees from the tenants paying tax to Government. These the Board of Revenue particularly define not to be the fees paid to the village officers; they must be viewed as the remains of what were once land rents, but which, owing to the oppression of modern governments, have sunk into a mere peppercorn rental.

From this description, selected from the report alluded to of the Madras Board of Revenue, I conclude that the whole of the land in the tract of country described, belonged originally to village communities, as real property, either held in common or divided in severalty.

II.—LORD MOIRA'S REVENUE MINUTE (*21st September 1815*).

The Board of Commissioners have sought to uphold the village zemindars; and in the Upper Provinces, as well as in Behar and Benares, no doubt can be entertained that these have the only hereditary possession, and are the only persons fundamentally connected with the soil.

Your Hon'ble Board is well acquainted with the theory of the property and economy of villages in the possession of the indigenous proprietors or cultivating zemindars. The rights of all are well ascertained and defined, and though the divisions and sub-divisions appear intricate to a distant observer, they are productive of no confusion amongst them-

selves, it being only when disturbed by the operation of external causes App. VIII.
that the general harmony suffers interruption.

This system of village property was yet in being in the Upper Provinces when they fell under our dominion; for the farmers and officers
of former Governments, though arbitrary and unmerciful in their
exactions, seldom had the hardihood to attempt to interfere with this
state of real property. The village community was thus complete; and
though there was usually one amongst the sharers whose name was entered
in the public accounts as the person who collected and paid the revenue,
he was merely a malgoozar, in the same manner as a farmer or officer of
Government, and the circumstance of his name being so entered was
never held to convey any special privileges or exclusive rights.

III.—Revenue Letter to Bengal, Ceded and Conquered Provinces (15th January 1819).

The Board of Revenue, in another passage of their letter, with an
express reference to these village zemindars, state that "the mistake of
making the perpetual settlement with rajahs *as the proprietors of the
whole of the lands composing their rajes,* has chiefly affected an intermediate class, the village zemindars, to whom no compensation can now be
made for the injustice done to them by the transfer of their property to
the rajahs. Indeed, the whole of this valuable class of landholders may
be considered to be extinct in the *Lower Provinces,* with the exception
of a few fortunate individuals who have preserved their estates under
the names of independent and dependent talookdars, by the precaution
of their ancestors in providing themselves with written acknowledgments of the general zemindar, *who, in consequence of the interpretation
put on that title, was considered by the terms of the perpetual settlement
as the universal proprietor of the soil, and the fountain from which alone
any other person could derive a property.*"

These *village* zemindars were no other than those ryots of the
villages who are distinctly described by the Board of Commissioners in
their official correspondence, and by Lord Hastings in his minute, as the
real proprietors of the land in their respective occupations.

IV.—Select Committee (1812).

(1). *Benares.*—On the relinquishment by the Rajah of Benares of his
functions as zemindar, and in the course of the president's investigation
of the affairs of the province, the landholders, with whom the settlement
was to be made, appeared to be on a footing somewhat different from the
zemindars of the Lower Provinces. They are officially designated "for
the most part as *village zemindars,* paying the revenue of their lands to
Government jointly with one or more *putteedars,* or partners, descended
from the same common stock:" the designation adds that "some of these
putteedars have had their interior puttees or shares rendered distinct,
whilst those of the major part still continue annexed to, and blended or
in common with, the share or shares of the principal of the family, or
of the headman among the brethren, being either one or more, whose
names have been usually inserted in the pottahs, cabooleeats, and other

APP. VIII.

———

VILLAGE PRO-
PRIETORS.

———

Para. 8, contd.
engagements for the public revenue." There are others denominated "talookdars, who have depending on them a greater or less number of village zemindars, many of whom retain the right of disposing by sale of their own estates, subject of course to the payment of the usual jumma by the talookdar." These talookdars, by the terms of the perpetual settlement, "are left to assess their village zemindars, either in proportion to their own sudder jumma, with some addition for the charges of management, or according to the extent and value of the produce, as local custom or the good will of the parties may direct." It should appear from this that more distinct traces of the Hindu revenue system remained in Benares than existed in Bengal, during the enquiries which were prosecuted, preparatory to the permanent settlement of the land revenue in that province.

Fifth Report.
Ibid., page 50.
(2). *Ceded and Conquered Provinces.*—The landholders were chiefly of the class which has been described in Benares as village zemindars; but there were others of higher rank, who bore the title of rajah, and appear rather in the condition of tributaries than of subjects. While these persons discharged their assessment of revenue, they were left to the exercise of absolute dominion within their limits.

V.—BOARD OF COMMISSIONERS (*20th May 1815*).

Revenue Selec-
tions, Vol. I,
page 371, para.
6.
These village zemindars (*viz.*, those mentioned in Section III,) are, however, still numerous in Behar, and more so in Benares; and they will be found in the large estates of Behar to maintain their individual property against the general right created by the perpetual settlement, by the possession of the phulker and bunker, and in some instances the julker also.

VI.—RESOLUTION OF GOVERNMENT (*22nd December 1820*).

Ibid., Vol. III,
page 260, para.
218.
Although, as already observed, the rules of 1803 contain no specific provision for determining the mode in which the settlement of putteedary estates should be made, such as that contained in Regulation II, 1795, yet there are several specific enactments whence it may be inferred that the inferior putteedars (that is, the non-engaging proprietors in the Western Provinces) were designed to be regarded as a species of under-tenant, holding, until separated, under the selected malgoozar or recorded proprietor, in a manner analogous to the holding of an ancient talookdar in one of the Bengal zemindaries, and that, consequently, their tenures were to be maintained notwithstanding a sale in default by the engaging putteedars.

9.—KINDS OF VILLAGE PROPRIETORS AND CULTIVATORS IN THE NORTH-WESTERN PROVINCES.

DELHI TERRITORY (*Mr. Fortescue, Civil Commissioner, 28th April 1820*).

Ibid., Vol. III,
page 403, *et seq.*
para. 13.
I. (*a*). *Proprietary right in villages.*—In all villages of old standing, that is, those prior to the introduction of the British power into the

territory (for a period of one hundred or one hundred and fifty years, say), the right of property in the land is unequivocally recognised in the present agricultural inhabitants, by descent, purchase, or gift.

(*b*). Each village is imagined to have belonged to one caste or clan of persons, as Jauts or Goojars, &c. The smaller villages have more generally preserved their integrity in this respect than the larger, which incorporated other sects, and in this way often derived their numerical superiority and strength.

(*c*). In deserted villages which have been re-peopled since the introduction of the British Government, though the proprietary right has not been distinctly stated to be in the parties inhabiting them, it is yet pretty well understood to belong to them.

II. *Nominal division of the villages*.—The villages are usually divided into an indeterminate number of superior divisions, called *panes*, seldom exceeding four or five, which are again sub-divided into *tholas* of no fixed number, and these are again subject to still smaller separations. The grand division into *panes* and the sub-division of *tholas* are those which are reported to have happened early after the first establishment of the village, and they are supposed to have been generally maintained undisturbed.

(*b*). This primary distribution is conceived to have been accidental, and resulting from the number or the interest of the persons originally entitled to share. The divisions by *panes* and *tholas* are now more nominal than practical, with respect to the definition either of the extent of the proprietary right in the lands, or to the proportion of the public demand; although occasionally those terms do denote specific shares to particular families, clans, or classes, and regulate the quota of the aggregate jumma or public demand chargeable.

III. (*a*). *Proprietary division of the village land*.—The lands appertaining to the village are almost universally divided amongst the descendants of the original stock, or those holding in right of them, as above described. Some adjustments have taken place long prior to the memory of those living, and thus separated families or clans. Others have recently happened, and further division might again occur. These divisions of the lands depend upon the pleasure or convenience of the parties interested.

(*b*). The divisions are effected either by integral allotments of the land to be divided, or by fractional parts of the aggregate quantity of each description of land according to its quality. By the former method the shares are compact; by the latter they consist of many particular spots situated in different quarters, and a proprietor will thus possess a share consisting of a few beegahs, or perhaps but a small fractional part of one, made up of the rubbee, of khureef, of pasturage, and firewood, &c.

(*c*). The possession by the sharer of the land thus divided off is determined either by agreement or by a kind of lottery, as putting billets with the names or descriptions of the lots and of the sharers into two separate jars, from each of which a paper is drawn, uniting the sharer and his share.

App. VIII.
——
VILLAGE PRO-
PRIETORS.

Para. 9, contd.

Para. 14.

Para. 15.

Para. 16.

Ibid., para. 17.

Ibid., para. 18.

Para. 19.

Ibid., para. 20.

APP. VIII.

VILLAGE PRO-
PRIETORS.

Para. 9, contd.
Para. 23.

Para. 25.

Ibid., para. 28.

Para. 30.

IV. *Inheritance, Sale, &c.* (*a*).—If a sharer dies without heirs, his lands are at the disposal of the rest of the sharers of his division, whether *pane* or *thola*.

(*b*). A sharer cannot dispose of his landed property by bequest or gift, nor introduce a stranger without the general acquiescence of the *pane* or *thola*, or other division to which he belongs; nor sell it, until the sharers thereof in succession, up from each superior division, have rejected it on the terms proposed and to themselves meet. In farming, mortgaging, placing in trust, deposit, or management, and the like, the tacit will of the brotherhood is sufficient; but neither these modes of temporary relinquishment, nor the absolute estrangement of it for ever by sale, are prevalent. Every effort by the first-mentioned methods of temporary relinquishment, as well as dishonesty even, has been tried to meet necessity or misfortune, before the sharer could be brought to abandon his connection, home, and inheritance.

(*c*). No circumstance, however, nor any other short of an actual or implied demonstration of the will of the party to abandon his land, is sufficient to divest him of his property in it. No length of occupancy by another, nor of absence by the inheritable owner, is a defeasance; mortgages are ever open to equitable redemption, and the mortgagee, has no power to foreclose.

(*d*). But it may so happen that an outlaw, or one forced to quit the village for some offence, or a disorderly and troublesome person (either to the ruling power or to the other sharers), is deprived of his property; or, on the other hand, that an occupant of long residence, under circumstances in his favour, such as an understanding that the lands were deserted, that they would become his by residence, or that he had laid out money on them, and the like consideration, may gain the right of property. Questions of this kind were, as all others connected with land and rents, settled by the village assemblies in what they held to be, and I believe to have been, an equitable manner.

V.—DESIGNATIONS AND RIGHTS OF CULTIVATORS, OTHER THAN ORIGINAL PROPRIETORS.

(*a*). *Four classes of such cultivators, viz.*, the old residents (or ryot), the itinerants (pahee), the hired (kumera), and the partial cultivators (kumeen), though these appellations, particularly the first and third, do not exclusively apply to land-tilling, either in this territory or in other parts of the Company's provinces.

(*b*). *Old residents.*—They attain to the highest rights of the village subordinate to those of the proprietors. They are usually ancient family residents of the village, and have cultivated the same lands. They have come thither from various causes, as for security, from connection with some of the inhabitants, by invitation, or other inducement of profit or convenience. So long as they continue to discharge their proportion of the public assessment due from the extent of land that they occupy, they are not liable to ejectment, nor are their descendants who inherit from them. But if they fail in this, or abandon the land, and no individual sharer should have an exclusive right, it reverts to the division

or *thola*, or *pane*, as the case may be. These cultivators are little APP. VIII.
distinguishable from the proprietors in other respects, except that they
do not necessarily acquire rights of ownership; though even this point CULTIVATORS.
is scarcely questioned in respect to residents of very lengthened occupa- Para. 9, contd.
tion, and under the circumstances stated in paragraph 30 (Section IV—*c*,
above).

(*c*). The condition of these persons, however, is much affected by *Ibid*, par. 34.
the state of the village. Should the extent of land therein be limited,
compared with the number and means of the proprietors, and these should
wish to possess themselves of the lands, they will force the resident
cultivator to contribute, at least as fully on all scores as themselves,
towards the liquidation of the public jumma, or else to abandon the soil.
If, on the contrary, there is more land than the zemindars can make
use of, they will continue to allow the resident terms equal, or nearly
so, to those granted to itinerant or *pahee* cultivators; the advantage of
the proprietors, in this case, being the same as in that by perfect *pahee*
cultivation in their village, *viz.*, the proportion of the public jumma
which they can discharge from the contributions of these new proprietors, and the surplus from their own that may be thus saved to them.

(*d*). *Itinerant or pahee cultivators* are always residents of a different Para. 35.
village. The scarcity of good uncultivated land in their own village,
and the abundance of it in the one to which they proceed, is generally
the cause of these species of cultivation. There are, however, at other
times, more interested reasons, as the desire to avoid in their own village
contributing as zemindars, while they reap as *pahees* in the neighbouring villages. In this way they secure a larger surplus to themselves
from the land they cultivate, while they abandon their own to the profits
of pasturage and cattle.

(*e*). These cultivators can relinquish, and the owners of the land can Para. 36.
prohibit the *pahee* cultivators, at pleasure, mutually, though from their
desire to profit by the cultivation of the superabundant lands, the proprietors generally favour these people, and they usually get terms equal
to a contribution of a fourth less of their produce than established
cultivators.

(*f*). *Hired cultivators or kumeras* are of all castes and classes, being Para. 37.
mostly of the description of daily labourers, whom we have in India
under the denomination of coolies or the like. They are employed
chiefly by those who are above actual labour themselves, and in good
circumstances. They are permanently or temporarily engaged. In the
former case they earn from 3 to 4 rupees per month; or they agree to
receive one-sixth or so of the produce of the land, with half a seer of
grain per day, and at each harvest, clothing. In the latter case they
get their clothes and food per day, with a rupee or two at the end of the
month.

(*g*). *Partial cultivators or kumeens* are those whose occasional leisure
from their primary occupations permits them to cultivate a few beegahs
of land. They are either the professional men of the villages, as car-
penters, blacksmiths, &c., or the servants of it, as the sweepers, messengers, &c. The term *kumeen* denotes inferiority, and is applied to this
part of the community by the land owners, who conceive themselves to
be of the first rank, and the others of low condition. * * The kumeens

are almost always paid for their professional assistance by the proprietors, at a stated allowance of grain from each plough, generally 10 seers, with 20 seers each for the blacksmith, the carpenter, the water-carrier, and the tailor, 5 seers for the messenger, and 1 maund for the shoe-maker, cobbler, and leather-dresser, as the lowest allowance in all these cases.

10. It is evident from the preceding extracts that the rights of the *khoodkosht* ryots were the same as those of the village zemindars, or proprietors of land in village communities, and that in these communities, as in the Lower Provinces of Bengal, where the organisation of those communities had been impaired by the usurpations or encroachments of zemindars, the cultivators, other than *khoodkasht* ryots in a village, consisted of two classes, *viz.*, those who by long residence in a village, though belonging to another village, had rights of occupancy, and others who were tenants under mutual agreements with the proprietors of land, or tenants at will. Extracts illustrative of the rights and obligations of these classes of ryots might accordingly be continued in this appendix; but it will be convenient to devote to them a separate, or the next, appendix.

11. The salient points in this appendix are that—

I. The cultivating proprietor is the one at whose risk or charge the land is cultivated.

II. Under native rule the land was the property of the cultivator, to whom was left at least enough for seed, and for support of his family till the next crop, thus keeping him out of debt.

III. The classes of cultivators recognised in Mahomedan law, including cultivating proprietors, corresponded to those in village communities under the Hindu system.

IV. Though the separate properties in each village were sub-divided, under the Hindu laws of inheritance, among the descendants of the original sharer in each property, yet the original property was preserved in its entirety under the management of so many only of the sharers as were required to cultivate it, the rest of the sharers taking to other occupations or lands.

V. The Select Committee of 1812 considered it to be established "by numberless records, and by none more distinctly than by ordinary form of a deed of sale," that cultivating proprietors were undisturbed in their property so long

as they paid the Government rent as fixed at what was a
fair assessment defined by local usage.

VI. The resident cultivators had a hereditary right in
their lands; not so the temporary or stranger cultivators.
The rent paid by the former was higher than that paid by
the latter.

VII. From the sparseness of population, and the great
extent of culturable waste land, necessarily the class of
khoodkasht ryots or resident cultivators preponderated. Mr.
A. D. Campbell, in his able summary of the evidence given
before the Select Committees of 1831-32 and previous years,
described them as " the most numerous and most important
class of all" (para. 3, III*d*); and Mr. J. S. Mill stated in
his evidence in 1831 " the *khoodkasht* ryots I consider to have
been universal in India, and the land to have been held by
them with few exceptions" (para. 3, IV, Question 3514).
The rates paid by these *khoodkasht* ryots, who were the bulk
of the ryots, formed necessarily the pergunnah rates; and as
the rates paid by the *khoodkashts* were rates fixed and long
established by custom, and as they were higher than the rates
paid by temporary cultivators, it followed that the Government declared permanent rates of rent for all classes of ryots
when by law they limited the enhancement of the rents of
the unprotected classes of ryots to the pergunnah rates.

VIII. The village organisation included officers for revenue and police duties corresponding to the functions of
zemindars in Bengal, and remunerated in the same way, *viz.*,
by assignment of land in the village. The village official,
who more especially resembled the zemindar, was the village
headman, who was an officer of the State, as well as representative of the village. He held on the same tenure as the
zemindar in Bengal, *viz.*, under a liability to dismissal, though
his office was hereditary; and he encroached on the rights of
other cultivating proprietors in precisely the same way, and
by the same means, as the zemindars in the Lower Provinces
of Bengal; and by no other means more effectually than
those which were placed within his reach when he became
the engager with Government for the Government revenue
on behalf of his co-proprietors in the village. The mistake
committed by Government in describing, as proprietors, the
engagers with it for the Government revenue, was a fruitful
and the most potent cause of the confusion and destruction of
the proprietary rights of the other cultivating proprietors;—

APP. VIII.

VILLAGE
PROPRIETORS.

Para. 11, contd. (para. 7, *a*, *c*, and *d* 5). In the permanent settlement of Benares, the rights of cultivating proprietors, as distinguished from those of the zemindars who engaged with Government for the revenue, were ascertained and recorded (para. 8, sections II and IV), and the difficulties arising from enhancement of rents in Behar and in the other provinces under the Bengal Government are not experienced in Benares; nor are they experienced in the permanently-settled zemindaries in the Madras Presidency, the pergunnah rate of rent payable by the ryots, at the time of introduction of the permanent settlement, having been recorded by the Collectors.

APPENDIX IX.

RYOTS.

1.—Definition of a Ryot.

The cultivator who, whether by borrowing or in any other way, provides seed, cattle, implements, and labour for the land which he cultivates. See Appendix VIII, paragraph 1, sections II, III, and V, and paragraph 2, section I, *e* and *g*.

2.—The country's prosperity dependent on the ryot's.

I.—Sir J. Shore (*8th December 1789*).

Our measures have a view to permanency; but before we declare it, prudence dictates that we should have some certainty that the Government will not suffer by its liberality, and that the benefits of it will extend to that class whose labours are the riches of the State (*para. 26*).

Fifth Report page 481.

II.—Lord Cornwallis (*18th September 1789*).

It is for the interest of the State that the landed property should fall into the hands of the most frugal and thrifty class of people, who will improve their lands and protect the ryots, and thereby promote the general prosperity of the country.

Page 473.

III.—Mr. Stuart's Minute (*18th December 1820*).

It has always been regarded as one great advantage of the system of dividing the actual produce of the soil between the Government and the cultivator, that it gives the sovereign an immediate and powerful concern in the welfare of the agricultural community. We find accordingly that the protection of those classes, of the inferior orders more especially, is a permanent object in the institutions of native governments; we also see that it is celebrated in their histories and public acts and popular sayings as the chief virtue of a government.

Revenue Selections, Vol. III, page 216.

IV.—Court of Directors (*9th May 1821*).

We are certainly most desirous not only to see the ryots duly protected in their rights, but also to see them thrive and prosper; for upon this, more than upon anything else, depends the welfare and improvement of the country (*para. 60*).

Ibid, page 440.

App. IX. V.—Mr. J. Mill (*4th August 1831*).

COUNTRY CAN-
NOT PROSPER
UNLESS THE
RYOT PROSPERS.

Para. 2, contd.
I have no doubt that it is through the ryots, and by giving a proper protection to their property, and to themselves in the exercise of their industry, and through that mainly, that the improvement of India must take place (*Question 3299*).

Third Report,
Select Com-
mittee, 1831.
VI.—Select Committee, 1831-32 (*6th December 1831, 16th August 1832*).

Sess. 1831-32,
Vol. XI,
page 7.
(1). The proper ascertainment and recognition and security of the several tenures and rights within the villages are objects of the highest importance to the tranquillity of the provinces, and will greatly tend to the repression of crime. The natives of India have a deep-rooted attachment to hereditary rights and offices, and animosities originating from disputes regarding lands descend through generations.

(2). In the general opinion of the agricultural population, the right of the ryot is considered as the greatest right in the country; but it is an untransferable right. It seems questionable whether the ryot himself can transfer it, or whether the Government can transfer it.

(3). The ryot may, if harassed by our assessment, leave his lands, quit the neighbourhood, and return when he chooses and re-claim the lands, and ryots holding them will always resign them to him. The right never seems to die.

(4). This part of the evidence before your Committee has been particularly adverted to, as it is of so much importance, that the Government cannot be too active in the protection of the cultivating classes; for the vital question to the ryot is the amount of assessment which he pays. In corroboration of this remark, your Committee refer to a letter from the Court of Directors to the Governor General in Council at Bengal, dated as far back as 19th September 1792, in which they say: "In giving our opinion on the amount of the settlement, we have been not a little influenced by the conviction that true policy requires us to hold this remote dependency under as moderate a taxation as will consist with the ends of our government."

VII.—Mr. Newenham (*7th May 1832*).

Ibid., 2269 and
2738.
Looking at the old-established and populous villages, one finds men who have come down, by general acknowledgment and their own, from time immemorial, generation after generation, who have stood in times of difficulty firm to the village, whilst the zemindars have been in a state of perpetual change; and their being so constantly resident, their digging wells and water-courses, planting trees and cultivating the same fields from father to son, shows that they have a claim upon the soil stronger probably than any other claim that exists in the country; and as far as I know, from the general opinion of the agricultural population, I believe that the right of the ryot is the greatest right in the country, * * and that security of the ryot is indispensable to the general prosperity of the country.

VIII.—Mr. James Mill (*11th February 1833*).

Excess of exaction, by which I understand any encroachment upon the full remuneration of the cultivator, impedes agricultural improvement by impeding the accumulation of capital in the hands of the cultivator, and that equally whether the exaction is made by Government or by an intermediate party.

Khoodkasht
Ryots.
———
Para. 3.

Sess. 1831-32,
Vol. XI, page
278.

3.—Khoodkasht Ryots and hereditary occupancy.

I.—Mr. Halhed (*1832*).

(1). Hereditary ryots claim as the descendants of an original proprietor, whose privileges of administering the revenue affairs of the parish have been lost or forfeited in some former age; sometimes they do not advance such high pretensions, but claim a right to hold by long prescription; they can scarcely be said to be independent of the zemindar malgoozar (mocuddum), who has the power, and generally the will, to inflict many annoyances on those who act counter to his wishes; and under the regulations this power is unlimited, but under the ancient regimé, so long as they paid the prescribed amount of the tax leviable upon the crop they might raise upon the land, they could not be ousted from it.

Page 79.
The demand
upon the heredi-
tary ryot was a
fixed demand.

(2). In some parts of the country (Lower Provinces), after the permanent settlement, the *raeeuts* were so fortunate as to obtain a recognition of their rights; in the 24-Pergunnahs, for instance, they cannot be ousted from their lands; and in some other districts (Chittagong, Dinagepore, part of Tipperah, and Sylhet) the providence and foresight of the revenue officers secured to them their privileges, by requiring the malgoozars, on the promulgation of the code, to grant pottahs, in which the pergunnah rates were distinctly specified, and the quota of tax, in kind or money, leviable from the cultivator expressly limited.

II.—Sir J. Shore (*June 1789*).

(*a*). I suppose that the rents in Bengal may be collected according to ascertained rates throughout two-thirds of the country; and notwithstanding the various abuses which I have detailed, it is evident that some standard must exist; for, without it, the revenues could never be collected from year to year as they have been. Exactions on one side are opposed by collusions on the other; but we may with certainty conclude that the ryots are as heavily assessed as ever they were.

Fifth Report,
page 206,
para. 406.

(*b*). The land is divided into ryotty and khamar; the rents of the former are paid in money, and of the latter in kind. The usual division is half to the zemindar and half to the cultivator; but some part of the expenses generally fall upon the latter, in addition to the stipulated proportion.

Ibid., para. 405.

(*c*). Pottahs to the *khoodkasht* ryots, or those who cultivate the land of the village where they reside, are generally given without any limitation of period, and express that they are to hold the lands, paying the rents from year to year. Hence the right of occupancy originates; and

Ibid., paras. 388
and 406.

App. IX.
———
Khoodkasht
Ryots.
———
Para. 3, contd.

Fifth Report,
para. 407.

it is equally understood as a prescriptive law that the ryots who hold by this tenure cannot relinquish any part of the lands in their possession, or change the species of cultivation, without a forfeiture of the right of occupancy, which is rarely insisted upon ; and the zemindars demand and exact the difference. I understand also that this right of occupancy is admitted to extend even to the heirs of those who enjoy it.* * But though his title is hereditary, yet the ryot cannot sell or mortgage his land.

(*d*). *Pykasht* ryots, or those who cultivate the lands of villages where they do not reside, hold their lands upon a more indefinite tenure. The pottahs to them are generally granted with a limitation in point of time ; where they deem the terms unfavourable, they repair to some other spot.

When Sir John Shore wrote, there was superabundance of waste lands, and the competition was for ryots, not for land. Hence, probably the khoodkasht ryot could not sell his land. But when land acquired a market value, the khoodkasht did sell. In a petition, dated 27th September 1851, bearing, among others, the signatures of Babus Sumbhunath Pundit, Unnodaprosad Banerjea, Govindpersad Bose, and Hurris-chunder Mookerjea, all well known authorities, and of whom the last mentioned was Editor of the *Hindoo Patriot*, and afterwards Assistant Secretary to the Bengal British Indian Association, the following passage occurs :—

(*a*). It has, we believe, not yet been denied that the interest of a khoodkasht tenant is transmissible by sale, gift, and succession, and that his right of occupancy does not terminate by any of those acts or omissions which determine the rights of leaseholders generally. In certain points of view, a khoodkasht tenancy constitutes the highest title to real property known to the laws of this country ; in every respect, the rights of a khoodkasht tenant are among the most valuable that form the subject-matter of judicial inquiry.

(*b*). *N. W. P. Board of Revenue Circular, 26th September 1856.*— Although the rights of permanent cultivators are, in the Notification of Government, and in the present Circular, spoken of as implying solely a fixed and heritable possession, it is not to be inferred that cultivators can possess no other rights. The power of transferring his holding to another occupant—the original cultivator remaining responsible to the landlord—has long been admitted by the Government. The practice of permitting the cultivator to mortgage his fields is reported to exist in various parts of the country. And wherever transfers of rights of occupancy, subject to the regular payment of rent to the proprietor, are acknowledged in the practice of the people, they must be recognised by the Government and its officers.

III.—Indian Government (*October 1790*).

Distinct from these claims are the rights and privileges of the cultivating ryots, who, though they have no positive property in the soil, have a right of occupancy as long as they cultivate to the extent of their usual means, and give to the sircar or proprietor, whether in money or in kind, the accustomed portion of the produce.

App. IX.

Khoodkasht
Ryots.

IV.—Ceded and conquered Provinces (5th January 1819) (Board of Commissioners).

Although in pykaust tenures the landholder is stated to be bound by no fixed rules, but to make the best terms he can, these terms will of course be governed by the mutual interest of the parties, and not by his own discretion, while the pykaust tenants hold the lands from only year to year (paragraph 7).

Revenue Selec-
tions, Vol. III,
page 171.

These remarks apply, of course, only to the labouring tenants, or assamees, who are unconnected with the property in the soil. The numerous class of putteedars, and all the ramifications from the original stock, hold their lands at a fixed rate, and any attempt of the ostensible zemindar, or the person under engagements with Government, to innovate thereon, would be resisted by open force (*para. 8*).

V.—Mr. H. Colebrooke (1815).

At the period of the decennial settlement, subsequently declared permanent, the rights of zemindars and ryots, as well in relation to Government as to each other, underwent much discussion, of which a great portion is to be found recorded on the proceedings of this Board. Among many important points, one, which was then distinctly admitted, was that certain classes of subordinate tenants, and chiefly those denominated dependent talookdars, or khodkast or chupperbund ryots, possessed certain rights and immunities which it was just and expedient to uphold.

Revenue Selec-
tions, Vol. I,
page 378.

VI.—Mr. James Mill (2nd August 1831).

The great peculiarity, as it appears to me, in the state of the land in India, arises from the situation of the great mass of cultivators, who hold the land generally in small portions, in a way different from what is known in Europe, and to a considerable degree different from what obtains in other parts of Asia. The peculiarity consists in the mass of subordinate cultivators being landholders, having a right to the perpetual hereditary occupancy of the soil so long as they continue to pay the revenue demanded by Government, the demand of Government being unlimited, although practice, long continued, was understood in a certain vague way to fix a limit. The land of India, originally I imagine (generally speaking), was distributed in this way among a class of men who cultivated the land with their own hands and with their own means, having the right of perpetual occupancy, and subject to the demand of Government, which in general was limited according to established practice, but according to the declared right of the sovereign was unlimited, and, according to all I can gather from the practice of former governments, never was less than the full rent, probably in many instances more, not unfrequently as much more as could be raised with-

Select Com-
mittee, 1831-32.
Third Report
Q. 3114,'3282.
Khoodkasht
Ryots.

out diminishing the number of inhabitants and desolating the country.

Sir John Shore's information was different. In his Minute of June 1789 he observed : "The policy of the Mogul administration assumed the right of taxing improvement in proportion to its advance; but it is, I conceive, proved that, from the time of Akbar to that of Farockseer, they exercised it with moderation." Moreover, Mr. Mill admitted that the khoodkasht ryots, who, he supposed, paid more than the rent, did, generally, sub-let their lands to others who paid less than the khoodkasht rates—that is, less than the rent. The inconsistency should have made him reconsider his opinion, that the Government exaction was of the full rent : where it was so nominally, the pressure was lightened by cultivation of land in excess of that for which the ryot paid rent :—

Q. 3285.—Would it have been allowed under that system, where the ryot has none of the rent, and in cases where the ryot was in communication with the Government without the intervention of a middle-man, that the ryot should lease his right of cultivation to any one beneath him ? Yes, that is frequently done, and that constitutes the distinction between khoodkasht and the pykasht ryots; such a ryot had undoubtedly the power of employing other ryots, who had no right to the land, under him, on any terms he thought proper.

Q. 3268.—When he had placed his land in this situation, was not he to all intents and purposes in the situation of the proprietor of the soil, paying a tax to Government ? Only that he had a very limited interest.

Q. 3287[1].—Did not he receive a rent? It was very rarely that he received a rent; those people were commonly his servants or labourers, and when he assigned a particular portion to them (it was a sort of tenure that existed in Europe formerly), he had in general to advance the capital with which those people cultivated.

Q. 3288.—The question did not go to the practical operation of the system, but to the theory of it? I think it is rather a question about the meaning of a term, whether you would call this holding of the ryot an absolute property in the land. I think, according to the usual meaning of the word in England, where the ownership of the rent is in reality the beneficial interest of the owner of the land, you can hardly call the ryot, in the same sense, the owner of the land, seeing he is not the owner of the rent at all; *and there is a peculiarity worthy of remark in the cases in which the casual and perpetual occupants hold under the Government, that the perpetual occupant pays the larger rent of the two, his lands are more highly assessed.*[2]

Khoodkasht
ryots paid higher
rent than py-
kasht.

---

[1] Here Mr. Mill maintained that the khoodkasht ryot, who pays rent for all the land he holds, including the portion cultivated for him by the pykasht ryot, obtains from the latter, for that portion, less rent than he pays for it to the Government. The inconsistency can only be accounted for by his knowledge that the khoodkasht ryot held more land than had been assessed by Government, or consequently was assessable by the zemindar.

[2] This was the general practice even when the pykasht held from the village proprietors.

Q. 3514.—The khoodkasht ryots I consider to have been universal in India, and the land to have been held by them with few exceptions. I also concur that the principal officers in the villages were hereditary in certain families, to whom belong advantages similar to those now claimed by the meerassadars at Madras, that is, certain dues and privileges beyond the perpetual occupancy.

APP. IX.

KHOODKASHT RYOTS.

Para. 3, contd.

VII.—MR. HOLT MACKENZIE (*18th April 1832*).

(1). The persons whom I should call proprietors may be generally described as cultivators possessing a fixed hereditary right of occupancy in the fields cultivated by them, or at their risk and charge; their tenure being independent of any known contract, originating probably in the mere act of settlement and tillage, and the engagements between them and the zemindar, or (in the absence of a middle-man) the Government officer, serving, when any formal engagements are interchanged, not to create the holding, but to define the amount to be paid on account of it. They cannot justly be ousted so long as they pay the amount or value demandable from them: that is determined according to local usage, sometimes by fixed money rates varying with the quality of the land or the nature of the crop grown; sometimes by the actual delivery of a fixed share of the grain produce; sometimes by an estimate and valuation of the same; sometimes by other rules; and what they so pay is in all cases distinctly regarded as the Government revenue or rent, whether assigned to an individual or not, in none depending on the mere will or pleasure of another. There are varieties of right and obligation which one could fully explain only by a reference to individual cases; but this is my general conviction of the rights of the class whom I should consider the proprietors of the fields they occupy. In Bengal Proper they are usually called khoodkasht ryots (*i. e.*, ryots cultivating their own), and by this class of persons I believe the greatest part of the lands in that province is occupied.

Sess. 1831-32, Vol. XI, Q. 2575.

Khoodkasht ryot held without pottahs.

(2). The most general tenure in the Lower Provinces is that of cultivators possessing a fixed right of occupancy (I use the word occupancy to designate the tenure by him, by whom, or at whose risk and charge, land is tilled, and its fruits gathered) independently of any known contract, but limited to specific fields, who cannot be justly ousted so long as they pay the amount or value justly demandable from them, on fixed principles, as Government revenue, and in no case depending on the mere pleasure and will of another individual. The tenure appears to be generally recognized as hereditary and divisible among heirs, though commonly forfeited by relinquishment of possession, not compulsive, and the non-payment of revenue. To this class I consider the khoodkasht ryots of Bengal to belong, having no doubt that they are the proprietors of the fields they occupy though, as I shall explain below, doubtful of the extent of their rights in the uncultivated land attached to their villages.

Ibid., page 305.

VIII.—MR. T. FORTESCUE, *formerly Civil Commissioner of Delhi, and before that employed in Bengal* (*29th February 1832*).

(1). Opportunities of no inconsiderable local experience, directed with much solicitude to this topic, have satisfied my mind that the ryots are

Sess. 1831-32, Vol. XI, page 289, para. 12.

APP. IX.
———
KHOODKASHT
RYOTS.
———
Para. 3, contd.
not without their rights. I do not find that the ryots have perfect or absolute rights, without which many would consider that they have practically none; but I maintain that they possess certain qualified rights, or interests, if they should be rather so termed.

(2). Such qualified rights or interests are those of occupation and regulated share of the produce, according to local custom, which from very remote time determines what is the ryot's and what the zemindar's, or Government's, or jageerdar's fee, &c., for it matters not which of these receive; they are, as to the ryot, one and the same.

Ibid., para. 14.
(3). The various elements, and the practice too, for adjusting these qualified rights, exist; and though continually disregarded and violated, from there being no power in the present system of things to uphold and confirm them, they still erect a tangible, respected, and clear interest to the ryots on very many occasions.   *   *   *

Ibid., para. 18.
(4). I will only add on this head, by way of summing up, that the grants of the ancient governments recognize qualified rights in the ryot; and that the fact of their having maintained them is established. Further, that neither the permanent settlement, nor any subsequent regulation, has cancelled those rights.

IX.—REVENUE LETTER FROM BENGAL (CEDED AND CONQUERED PROVINCES) (*7th October 1815*).

Sess. 1831-32,
Vol. XI, App. 10,
page 91.
(1). Although we have but too strong grounds to believe that the ryots are frequently subjected to exactions by the zemindars and others, and although we unreservedly admit that the existing institutions of the country are very imperfectly calculated to afford to them, in practice, that protection to which, on every ground, they are so fully entitled, yet their rights, considering the question abstractly, do not appear to us by any means enveloped in that obscurity which might be supposed, from the elaborate discussions which the subject has occasionally undergone.

(2). We consider it as a principle equally applicable to all the provinces immediately dependent on this Presidency, and, we believe, we might safely add, to the whole of India, that the resident ryots have an established permanent hereditary right in the soil which they cultivate, so long as they continue to pay the rent justly demandable from them with punctuality. We consider it equally a principle interwoven with the constitution of the different governments of India, *i. e.*, of the country itself, that the quantum of rent is not to be determined by the arbitrary will of the zemindar, but that it is to be regulated by specific engagements between the parties or their ancestors, or, in the absence of such engagements, by the established rates of the pergunnahs or other local divisions.

X.—MR. WELBY JACKSON (*21st November 1849*).

(*a*). It is erroneous (though a common error) to speak of the relative rights of the zemindars and ryots of Bengal as those of landlord and tenant. These terms being inseparably connected with the ideas assigned to them in England, originating in the feudal system, their use is calculated to mislead. Nothing can be more different from the zemindar, who, in fact, only contracts to collect the government land tax, and to pay it into the treasury, reserving his own share, than the feudal lord, who held his lands liable only to certain military services. Nothing can differ more from the tenant in England, whose right originates in an assignment from the feudal lord, either for a time specified, or from year to year, than the ryot of Bengal, whose family has resided in one spot, in one village, from time out of mind, whose right of occupancy was established when the zemindars were actually mere collectors on the part of government, receiving a percentage on their collections and liable to removal at pleasure.

(*b*). There are but two parties having a right in the soil in India—the State and the cultivator. Each has a fixed share in the produce. Under the terms of the permanent settlement, the zemindar has an assignment of the government share, and summary right of distraint is vested in him to realize punctually that share from the cultivator. He cannot, however, raise the rent on a cultivator, without going through a prescribed form of notice under Regulation V, 1812, and without bringing a regular suit to establish his right to raise the rent.

(*c*). .The rights of the resident cultivators are generally reserved by express condition in the Regulations of 1793, and others, under a variety of terms—khoodkasht, chupperbund, mookuddum, &c., &c.; and it is left open to the courts to decide upon any other claim to hold upon fixed rents, or upon rents ascertainable by fixed rules.

(*d*). Generally, the ryots have a prescriptive right of occupancy. The exception is when a ryot living in one village cultivates a portion of another. These are called paheekasht, and have not the same rights as the resident cultivators. It is the resident cultivators who have brought the country into cultivation. It is to them that the improvement and extension of the tillage is to be ascribed.

XI.—Mr. Welby Jackson (*27th August 1852*).

The tenants are chiefly comprised under two denominations—khoodkasht or chupperbund, or resident ryots, cultivating land in the villages in which they reside, and paheekasht, or ryots cultivating in villages where they do not reside. The terms used to express these tenures in different parts of the country are different, but in effect the distinction is resident or non-resident ryots.

The resident ryots hold by prescription, and cannot legally be turned out as long as they pay the rent; their right has arisen by prescription and long hereditary occupation, and their right to occupy is acknowledged in the Regulation of 1793, which effected the settlement of the country: they have no leases or papers, indeed, they will not accept leases from the zemindars, their rights being anterior and independent of the zemindars.

Paheekasht or non-resident ryots can have no right to occupy except by lease, written documents, or agreement; with these the zemindar has full power, except in so far as he has bound himself. The engagements of a former zemindar, even, do not bind the present zemindar, if the latter has purchased at a revenue sale, which voids all engagements of the former zemindars. These non-resident ryots can give no trouble to the zemindar; they may be called in to show their leases, and, if they have none, they may be evicted.

But with the resident ryots the case is different; their title, though the best, most just, and most unquestionable in the country, has arisen from occupancy and prescription; and these are points which are not so easily proved in a court of justice. If they have any documents admitting their rights, they must be of date previous to the decennial settlement, to be of any use, and thus scarcely legible; and if oral evidence be offered, it is often rejected, because no oral evidence can reach back more than fifty or sixty years to the decennial settlement; and occupancy or residence since that date is not considered a proof of right. In the settlement of the Western Provinces, hereditary occupancy for two generations is admitted by the Government officers to give a claim to hold as a resident cultivator; but there is no such limit in Bengal; and in fact it is very difficult for a resident ryot in Bengal to establish his right in court under the present practice.

The resident ryots form the most valuable and by far the largest portion of the peasantry; but as their rights are independent of the zemindar's, and they have a weight and influence owing to their very respectability, the zemindars prefer the non-residents, whom they may treat as they please, and subject to a racked rent, without fear of opposition. * * If anything is likely to produce a popular disturbance, it is giving the zemindars the summary power to eject the old resident cultivators, the yeomen of the country, though the people of Bengal will bear almost anything.

Besides the peasantry above mentioned, there are mocururreedars, holders under written documents of various descriptions, at fixed rents, at rents ascertainable by certain fixed rules, with limited and limitable rights, some with rent payable in kind, some in money, the amount to be fixed at the value of the half share of the produce, and this to be fixed by a special rule.

XII.—TAGORE LAW LECTURES (1874-75).

There were three classes of cultivators having an interest in the soil—*1st*, the original settlers and their descendants; *2nd*, the immigrants who had permanently settled in the village; *3rd*, the mere sojourners in the village, or those who, without living in the village, cultivated land of the village. I shall proceed to consider the position of these classes more fully.

(*a*). The original settlers in the village, with their descendants, and those cultivators who had been admitted to share the same privileges, formed the class of *khoodkasht* (own cultivating) ryots, and they had an hereditary right to cultivate the lands of the village in which they resided. They were also called *chupperbund* (house-tied), *mooroossee* (hereditary), and *thani* (stationary). Their rights were regulated by custom, probably he custom of many centuries, and having at least as much force as any written law. These customs were no doubt in some cases violated by the hand of power; but that is only what happened with all rights, whether depending upon express and written law, or upon the unwritten law of custom; and these violations were doubtless more frequent in Mahomedan times. But it is to these customs we must look to ascertain the rights of almost all the parties having interests in the land.

APP. IX.
——
KHOODKASHT
RYOTS.
—·—
Para. 4.

(*b*). The khoodkasht class of ryots appears to have been the same as the class of *meerassadars* in Southern India (called also *ulcudies* in Tanjore), who existed in very early times, and were anciently called *caniatchy* ryots in Malabar. Page 13.

(*c*). They could not be ousted while they continued to cultivate their holdings and pay the customary revenue; but, on the other hand, they could not originally transfer their holdings without the consent of the community. Page 17.

* * We may therefore conclude that these cultivators held a permanent hereditary, and although originally an unalienable, yet probably subsequently a transferable, interest in the land.

(*d*). They paid the customary rate, which could not be raised; and in some parts, when the assessment was once fixed, custom prohibited a measurement of the land with a view to surcharging the khoodkashts.

* * * * * *

(*e*). From the description I have given of the position of this class of ryots, I think it clearly appears that they had proprietary rights of a very complete kind; but they do not seem to have been of that unlimited kind which we understand by a fee simple.

4.—PYKASHT RYOTS.

I.—LAW LECTURES.

The next class of ryots very nearly approach the position of the khoodkashts, and are sometimes ranked with them. There are, however, some differences which mark the distinction between the original settlers and those afterwards admitted to form part of the permanent village community. Page 19.

(*a*). (1). The cultivators of this class are generally included in the class called *pykasht* (cultivating in another village than their own); but sometimes the term *pykasht* is restricted to those strictly so, the mere sojourners in the village, or those who, living in another village, cultivate land in the village with respect to which they are reckoned *pykashts*. This second class of cultivators was also called *chupperbund* or *judeed*, names specially applied to immigrants who have permanently settled in the village to which they have emigrated. Pykasht of nearly khoodkasht *status, viz.,* chupperbund, or *pyacarries*, or *ool paracoodies.*

(2). Their right to a permanent interest in the soil, which nearly approaches that of the khoodkashts, depends upon their having settled as permanent inhabitants in the village, building and clearing and establishing themselves as members of the village community, ready to undertake a share in the responsibilities attaching to that position. It does not depend on the length of time they have occupied, except that the disposition to become permanent settlers could hardly be satisfactorily proved without some length of possession. Accordingly, those who had settled in the village for more than one generation, were generally considered to have sufficiently shown their intention, and such settlers became recognized as chupperbund cultivators. They appear to have come in originally to cultivate land abandoned by the khoodkashts, to whom they paid *russooms*, or fees, and to whom they were bound to surrender their holdings when required; but they were entitled to a proper compensation for the loss of them. They were called *pyacarries* and *ool paracoodies* in the Northern Circars and the South of India generally. Uninterrupted occupation and succession gave them a prescriptive right to occupy; but there is no instance of sale of their holdings; they were, in fact, conditional occupants, and had not so complete a right as khoodkashts.

(3). They could be dispossessed for default in payment of the assessment, or for not keeping up the full extent of cultivation; but they could not reclaim their holdings, as the khoodkashts could. They had no share in the management of the village or in the privilege of the khoodkashts. The right of the *pyacarries* in the Northern Circars is said to be a sort of life-estate; but the right of this class appears to have grown to an hereditary, though inalienable, right to occupy, paying the fixed assessment.

(4). That assessment was slightly lower in former times than that of the khoodkashts, but higher than that of the mere pykashts. They received 45 per cent. of the crops as their share, instead of 50 per cent., which was the proportion the ordinary pykashts received. Out of their share they had to pay fees to the khoodkashts.

(5). It is clear that this class of cultivators had a less complete proprietary right than the first class, or khoodkashts, but still they had a permanent hereditary proprietary right. This, however, was inalienable, and was otherwise subject to limitations and burdens from which the khoodkhasts were exempt, and did not so completly incorporate them with the khoodkashts as to entitle them to the same position in the village.

Pykasht Ryots.
Page 22.

(b). The third class is that of the strict pykashts, who came from another village, usually a neighbouring one, to cultivate the lands of the village which the khoodkashts were unable to cultivate. They were called *pyacarries*, common *paracoodies*, and *oopudies* in different parts of India. They were mere tenants-at-will, or more usually from year to year, but sometimes for fixed periods. They had to be attracted by favourable terms, since the competition formerly was for cultivators, and hence they got half the produce. They paid fees to the khoodkashts. They were mere sojourners in the village, or cultivated while living in neighbouring villages. This class of cultivators, although they had no proprietary right, could not be ousted between sowing and harvest. Their interest was of an uncertain and precarious description. Such rights were left to be settled by contract, and were hardly allowed to come under the higher protection of custom, which regulated all the more important and permanent interests.

II.—REPORT OF MR. PLACE (*6th June 1799*).

A pyacarry accordingly means a husbandman who cultivates the land of another, either for one or more years, by agreement, but mostly for one only, as leases do not seem formerly to have been in use; and having only a contingent interest in it, as an encouragement to induce him to bring part of his labours from his own village, or as an incitement to exertion, he receives one-half of the produce, which is, generally speaking, a greater share than a meerassadar receives. If the meerassadars are capable of cultivating all their lands, a pyacarry will not be admitted, nor can he on any account, in that case, have a preference, from any competent authority, without a palpable injustice to others.

Fifth Report, [pa]ge 715. Pykasht paid less rent than khoodkashts.

[Here follows a description of the special or superior pykasht or chupperbund tenure (approaching to that of khoodkasht), which is almost identical with the quotation in section I from the Tagore Law Lectures.]

III.—COURT OF DIRECTORS (*15th January 1819*) (*Revenue letter to Bengal*).

We do not clearly understand whether, in speaking of " resident ryots," you do, or do not, contemplate only the khoodkasht ryots, who have a permanent hereditary interest in the soil; and whether, in adverting to "those lands upon which no resident ryots are established," you do, or do not, intend all lands cultivated by pykahst or migratory ryots, whose tenure is temporary.

Revenue Selections, Vol. I, page 351. Pykashts entitled to protection equally with khoodkashts—a protection which they have not received.

Does this permanent hereditary interest in the soil constitute the only distinction between the khoodkasht and pykasht ryot? Or, if that be not the only distinction, are the payments to be made by the pykasht, equally with that of the khoodkasht, to be regulated according to the custom of the pergunnah?

Whatever may be the distinction between them as to their rights, it is clear that, in every respect, the two classes of ryots are equally entitled to the protection of Government; and we observe that you concur with us in the opinion that, however well intended for this purpose, our regulations under the permanent settlement have not been effectual to it.

5.—KHOODKASHT RYOTS PAID HIGHER RENT THAN PYKASHT.

I.—SIR J. SHORE (*June 1789*).

(1). Those who cultivate the lands of the village to which they belong (resident ryots), either from length of occupancy or other cause, have a stronger right than others, and may, in some measure, be considered

Fifth Report, page 152.

App. IX.

Pykasht paid
less rent than
Khoodkasht.

Para. 5 contd.

Page 193.

as hereditary tenants, and they generally pay the highest rents. The other class cultivate lands belonging to a village where they do not reside; they are considered as tenants-at-will; and, having only a temporary accidental interest in the soil which they cultivate, will not submit to the payment of so large a rent as the preceding class, and when oppressed, easily abandon the land to which they have no attachment.

(2). On the other hand, the (khoodkasht) ryots derive advantages even from abuses. The want of engagements, or of precision in the terms of them, affords them opportunities of imposing upon the landlords; artifice is opposed to exaction, and often with success. They cultivate lands of which there is no account, and hold them in greater quantities than they engage for; hence they are enabled to pay rents and cesses which appear extortionate; they hold lands at reduced rates by collusion; obtain grants of land fit for immediate cultivation on the reduced terms of waste land; and by management with a renter at the close of a lease, procure fictitious pottahs and accounts to be made out with a view to defraud his successor.

(3). It has been found that the ryots of a district have shown an aversion to receive pottahs, which ought to secure them against exaction, and this disinclination has been accounted for in their apprehensions, that the rates of their payments being reduced to a fixed amount, this would become a basis of future imposition; but admitting this to have its weight, the objection may be also traced to other sources, in the preceding explanations. The Collector of Rajshahye informs us "that he fears the ryots would hear of the introduction of new pottahs with an apprehension that no explanation could remove."

II.—Mr. H. Colebrooke—*Husbandry of Bengal* (*1806*).

Besides the variety of tenures which we have noticed, a difference arises from other circumstances. A tenant who cultivates the lands of a distant village, cannot be placed on the same footing with one who uses land in the village wherein he resides. Indulgence in regard to his rent is allowed for the purpose of enticing the distant cultivator; and the inconvenience of remote cultivation makes it necessary that he should be at liberty to relinquish at any time the land which he uses; and, consequently, his own continuance being precarious, he cannot have a title of occupancy which shall preclude the landlord from transferring the farm to a resident husbandman desirous of undertaking it.

III.—Mr. J. Mill (*4th August 1831*).

There is a peculiarity worthy of remark in the cases in which the casual and perpetual occupants hold under the Government, that the perpetual occupant pays the larger rent of the two, his lands are more highly assessed (*Q. 3286*).

IV.—Mr. W. M. Fleming (*30th March 1832*). App. IX.

(1). The common practice in Behar is for each of the sharers (who are generally Brahmins or Rajpoots, and work very little) to appropriate a portion of the land (for which they pay no rent) equal to what they suppose to be the profit of their respective shares; this they cultivate on their own account; the remainder of the land is let to the more industrious and hard-working classes of resident or non-resident ryots, who pay a rent equal to at least half the produce of the land cultivated by them, and from this fund the revenue and other charges are to be paid. In favourable years no difficulty is experienced, and there is sometimes a surplus to be divided amongst the sharers. * *

Pykasht paid less rent than Khoodkasht.

Para. 5, contd.

Third Report, Select Committee, 1831-32.

Sess. 1831-32, Vol. XI, page 284.

(2). There are also *pykasht*, or ryots who reside in villages and take a portion of land to cultivate from year to year, and generally pay a less rent than the lower class of resident ryots (chupperbunds) who have certain advantages, such as the choice of the land, and paying nothing for that occupied by their houses.

V.—Warren Hastings (*12th November 1776*).

There are two kinds of rieats; the more valuable are those who reside in one fixed spot, where they have built themselves substantial houses, or derived them by inheritance from their fathers. These men will suffer much before they abandon their habitations, and therefore they are made to suffer much; but when once forced to quit them, they become vagrant rieats. The vagrant rieats, as Mr. Francis observes, have it in their power in some measure to make their own terms with the zemindars. They take land at an under-rent, hold it for one season; the zemindar then increases their rent, or exacts more from them than their agreement, and the rieats either desert, or, if they continue, they hold their land at a rent lower than the established rent of the country. Thus the ancient and industrious tenants are obliged to submit to undue exactions, while the vagrant rieats enjoy lands at half price, which operates as an encouragement to desertion, and to the depopulation of the country.

Francis' Revenues of Bengal, page 154.

VI.—Resolution (*1st August 1822*).

The khoodkasht ryots in Cuttack would seem to have been so heavily taxed, that their tenures were without exchangeable value, and sales consequently were unknown. Their situation, indeed, is represented as having been, and as still being, inferior in comfort to that of the pykasht ryots, or contract cultivators, who claimed no permanent tenure in the lands occupied by them. In this respect Cuttack would appear to resemble the adjoining provinces of the Madras Presidency, in which it is stated that throughout the country from Nellore to Ganjam, the occupant cultivators, though enjoying the right of holding their lands from generation to generation, subject to the payment of the public dues, derived from it no rent, and have never been known to dispose of their tenures by sale. Such, indeed, would appear to have been generally the case of the khoodkasht ryots of Bengal. But, as

(Revenue Selections, Vol. III, page 337).

App. IX.
———
Pykasht paid
less rent and
was better off
than Khood-
kasht.

will hereafter be more particularly observed, there would appear to have existed in Cuttack no one to contest the right of the resident ryots to be regarded as the proprietors of the land they tilled (*paras. 136 to 138*).

VII.—Tagore Law Lectures (*1874-75*).

The khoodkashts paid a higher rate of revenue than other cultivators in former times; but from the changed state of these things under British rule, this is reversed. There is now some competition by the cultivators for land, and not, as formerly, merely a competition for cultivators. I shall have occasion to refer to this very significant fact again, when I come to discuss the nature of the proprietary rights of the holders of the various interests in the land. The khoodkashts, then, in consequence of the change referred to, came in later times to pay lower rates than the other cultivators, but in the Hindu period they paid higher rates.

VIII.—*See also para. 4, sections I and II.*

6.— Pergunnah Rates.

I.—Ayeen Akbery.

(*a*). Let the amelguzar see that his demands do not exceed his agreements. If in the same place some want to engage by measurement, and others desire to pay their proportion of the revenues from an estimate of the crops, such contrary proposals shall not be accepted. As soon as the agreements are concluded and executed, let them be sent to the presence. Let him not be covetous of receiving money only, but likewise take grain. The manner of receiving grain is after four ways :—

1st, kunkoot.—Kun, in the Hindovee language, signifies grain; and the meaning of *koot* is conjecture or estimate. The way is this—the land is measured with the crops standing, and which are estimated by inspection. Those who are conversant in the business say that the calculation can be made with the greatest exactness. If any doubt arise, they weigh the produce of a given quantity of land, consisting of equal proportions of good, middling, and bad, and form a comparative estimate therefrom. * * Let him not entrust the principal men of the village with making the estimates of kunkoot, for such a measure, by giving room for oppression, would create disgust, and consequently occasion indolence and neglect. But, on the contrary, let him transact his business with each husbandman separately, and see that the revenues are demanded and received with affability and complacency.

2nd, buttiey, and which is also called *bhaweley*, is after the following manner :—They reap the harvest, and, collecting the grain into barns, then divide it according to agreement. But both these methods are liable to imposition if the crops are not carefully watched.

3rd, kheyt buttiey, when they divide the field as soon as it is sown.

4th, lang buttiey—they form the grain into heaps, of which they make a division. Whenever it will not be oppressive to the subject, let the value of the grain be taken in ready money at the market price.

(*b*). The husbandman may always pay his revenue in money or in kind, as he may find most convenient. * * The husbandman has his choice to pay the revenue either in ready money, or by *kunkoot*, or by *bhaweley*.

APP. IX.
——
PERGUNNAH
RATES.

Para. 6, contd.
Ibid., page 314.

II.—BOARD OF COMMISSIONERS, CEDED AND CONQUERED PROVINCES (*5th January 1819*).

(*a*). From these reports of the collectors it will appear that for the more valuable articles of culture in all the districts, and for every sort of produce in some districts, money rents obtain universally; and that the tenures in kind, under the several demonstrations of *ulmlee bhowlee*, and *bhretlye*, prevail only for the inferior sorts of grain, and in those districts, or in those particular pergunnahs, where, from the nature of the soil, the want of means for artificial irrigation, and the consequent dependence on the uncertainty of seasons, the tenants are not disposed to subject themselves to a certain payment.

Revenue
Selections,
Vol. III,
page 170.

(*b*). In tenures of this description, the proportion of the crop, whether taken by the landholders in kind, or commuted for its value in money, is regulated by custom, which varies, according to the nature of the soil, from one-fourth and less in lands newly reclaimed, to one-half in lands under full cultivation; and the commutation in money is similarly governed by fixed custom, conformably to which the tenant purchases the landholder's share at a certain rate above the market price, after the produce of the field has been estimated by a regular appraisement on survey.

The Resolution of Government dated 1st August 1822 corrected the erroneous impression conveyed in this extract, that the *buttai* system prevailed extensively; see *post*, III *b* and *c*.

III.—TAGORE LAW LECTURES (*1874-75*).

(*a*). (1). The great object of Toodur Mull's settlement appears to have been to substitute a fixed money rate for the beegah, instead of the various rates which had prevailed under the complicated system of Hindu times. And accordingly, either at the original settlement, or very shortly afterwards, the revenue was fixed at a certain sum for the beegah, whatever might be the crop actually grown. This was called the *jumma-bundy neckdy*, or money settlement. The assessment was arrived at, as before described, by an average then made of the several kinds of crop which the land was capable of producing during ten years, and one-fourth of the gross produce was the rebba or State share.

Page 71.

(2). But although one of the main features of the settlement was the change in the mode of rendering the revenue, this mode was not obligatory, and the old methods might still be continued at the option of the

Page 72.

APP. IX. cultivator. The cultivator might choose to pay either in kind or in

PERGUNNAH RATES. money, but he was bound to make his choice of the two methods, and

to adhere to one of them.

Para. 6, contd.   (3). The two methods of ascertaining the Government share when paid

in kind, *viz., kunkoot,* or grain estimate, and *bhawley* or *bhaolee,* called

Page 73. also *buttiej* or *buttai* (division), have continued in use, with various modi-

fications, up to the present time. But the actual division of the crops

had, even at this period, begun in some parts to fall into disuse, the

cultivators having probably come to agree with the State in regarding

this mode of assessment as burdensome to the revenue-payer. And

where the *buttai* system still prevailed, and the cultivators did not feel

disposed to accept the new system, Toodur Mull endeavoured to supersede

the necessity for an actual division and sale by prescribing that the value

of the Government share of grain might be taken in money at the

market price of the day, whenever it would not be oppressive to the

ryots to do so.

Page 73.   (4). The *buttai* system continued in use in many parts of the country

in spite of the advantages supposed to be offered by the other system : and

a settlement under this system was known in the south of India in later

times as an *aumanee* settlement; but it was chiefly in Bengal that it

retained its hold; and it seems that the new settlement was less com-

pletely applied there, at least for a time, than in some other parts.

The information respecting the extensive prevalence of

the *buttai* system in Bengal is incorrect; the testimony of

high authorities, like the Select Committee of 1812 (the Fifth

Report), Sir John Shore, and Mr. Holt Mackenzie, is to the

contrary effect.

(*b*).—GOVERNMENT RESOLUTION (*1st August 1822*).

But though the Board for the Ceded and Conquered Provinces con-

sider the principle of actual division of the produce to be indisputable,

his Lordship in Council is not aware on what evidence they have admit-

ted the allegation. In Bengal, from the most ancient times of which

we have any clear accounts, the system of money rates would appear to

have prevailed; and in none of the provinces would the system of divi-

sion seem to have been universal. To what period the Board design to

refer by the terms 'ancient times' and the 'later periods of the Mahomedan

power,' does not appear; but his Lordship in Council apprehends that

the endeavour to go back to times when any general or systematic rule

of division existed, would lead us far beyond the limits with reference

to which the existing rights of the people will have to be settled.

(*c*).—*See also* post, *section VIII, b and c.*

IV.—BAILLIE'S LAND TAX IN INDIA.

Page XXXIII.   (1). It is worthy of remark that the Hindu-tax, being a share of the

produce, was in reality a *mookassimah,* and may therefore be confounded

with one kind of the *khiraj.* The account in the Ayeen Akbery further

states that Shere Khan and Selim Khan were the first who abolished the

custom of dividing the crops. Down to this period, then, it seems that the tax was *mookassimah;* but it is probable that it was the *mookassimah* of the Hindu, and not that of the Mahomedan Law, which, as already observed, was not applicable to infidels to the Moslim faith. The movement of Shere Khan and Selim Khan was probably the first step taken by any Mahomedan sovereign of India for the imposition of the true *khiraj* upon the land of that country. The system afterwards adopted by Akbar was only that of Shere Khan carried into effect with greater precision and correctness.   *   *

App. IX.

Pergunnah rates.

Para. 6, contd.

(2). In the interval between Akbar and Aurungzebe, some change must have taken place in regard to a part of the land, inasmuch as it had become *mookassimah,* on which rent is " due out of actual produce only;"—for under Akbar's settlement it was all *wuzeefah.* Many writers have noticed the preference given by the cultivators of India to the *mookassimah* or *buttai* method of taking the *khiraj,* as it is now called. The reasons assigned for this preference are the facilities which it affords for keeping back a portion of the crops. * * A *wuzeefah* (on which rent is due on the extent of land occupied, with reference to the capability of the soil, whether there be any produce or not) may be lawfully changed to a *mookassimah* with the consent of the people. This is recognized in Aurungzebe's firman. The transition, too, from Akbar's *wuzeefah* to a *mookassimah* was very easy. The peasant, who had the option of paying in money or in kind, would naturally pay in kind when his crops were abundant, and prices generally were below the Government average; but when the crops were scanty, he would, as a matter of course, reject the average on the ground of inability. When the Government officer collects direct from the cultivator, it will be found very difficult to hold him to the average, except when it happens to be for his advantage.

Page XXXVI.

(3). A period of great anarchy followed after the death of Aurungzebe, and continued more or less to our own times. During this interval considerable changes seem to have taken place in the state of the *khiraj.* A great deal of the land fell back from *wuzeefah* to *mookassimah,* or became the property of the State, and either sunk into *moojaraut,* or was granted to private individuals exempt from *khiraj,* &c.

Page XXXVII.

V.—Board of Revenue on deputation (*25th May 1831*).

(1). The revenue administration of Native rulers, we believe, has never recognized—nor does it now, where that form of government still exists — a right in cultivators to occupy lands at fixed money rates, though we are inclined to think that the permanent cultivating tenures have always been admitted and maintained by Native governments, subject to the contribution of a known proportion of the produce in kind, regulated according to local usage, either by qualities of soil, or description of crops, and commutable, at the pleasure of the parties interested, into money payment.

Sess., 1831-32, Vol. XI, page 315.

(2). We are satisfied a single instance would not be found, from the western extremity of Saharunpore to the eastern boundary of the Goruckpore district, including, perhaps, the dominions of the King of Oudh, and not omitting the reserved Delhi territory, of a zemindary, jageerdaree, mokurraree, or of any other description of estate held by a superior,

Ibid., para. 24.

in which the rent payers, of whatever name or character, claim a right to hold land at fixed money rates in perpetuity, or rates limited in the aggregate for a village, and fixed in detail on the *bach-h-burar* principle. The rule of *buttye* is, we believe, the only rule of limitation known; and that ought, of course, in every case to be ascertained and recorded. If that rule of division, instead of undefined and unknown pergunnah rates, had been assumed as the limit to the demand of zemindars in the permanently-settled provinces, on ryots who had rights of occupancy in particular lands, the injury to individuals would, perhaps, never have been heard of which has partially resulted from that great and beneficent measure, the permanent settlement.

VI.—Mr. Fortescue, Civil Commissioner, Delhi (*28th April 1820*).

Revenue Selec-
tions, Vol. III,
page 414,
para. 29.
Revenue Selec-
tions, Vol. III,
page 4145.

(1). Previously to the British rule, *nukdee* or ready money settlements were scarcely known anywhere; *buttee* (or division of the crops) was the plan of regulating the receipts from the zemindars;[1] and this method they infinitely prefer to money settlement for two reasons—that they can plunder most in this way, and that they are secure against extreme distress.

(2). In forming the assessment of this territory, a primary difficulty has been, and continues to be, obviated by measurements. The subsequent details do not differ from those in other parts of the country, and they are too well known to need notice here. In pergunnahs where order and any system of revenue or government has prevailed, the former pergunnah rates have continued; yet these are always subject to variation. As a common mode of gross calculation, they are applicable, but they are lowered or raised perpetually according to circumstances.[2]

(3). The prevalent impression is that these rates are ordinarily too high, because under our system of applying them, more of the produce is rated or brought to account than when those rates were promulgated and practised.

(4). The conviction for many years on my mind, from inquiry and practice, is that neither the usual pergunnah rates, nor the nominal one-half produce (borrowed, too, from the Native government) is tenable.

(5). No such minute and exact scrutiny took place formerly as at present. The revenue of our time always exceeds that of the late government, and amongst the sharers[3] of those territorial assets which did not formerly reach the public treasury, the zemindar was a principal one. He would still be happy, and ask nothing further than one-half of his produce by *buttae*, according to the former system, yet the result would soon establish to our government that we did not acquire the other half. * *

(6). Whether in measurement or in estimates, we must always throw in something in favour of the ryot (zemindar), giving a step or two in each beegah, or five or ten maunds in each hundred.

---

[1] Cultivating zemindars or ryots.

[2] According to this account, the pergunnah rates were fixed rates as regards proportion of produce demandable as rent, but were of variable amounts, according as the market price for valuing the fixed proportion of produce varied.

[3] *Sic.*

(7). The pergunnah rates when they have existed, or those which are assumed, must necessarily press hard or be easy upon the zemindar according to the price of grain in the market. He is, however, seldom or never a capitalist, and although the bunnea, or dealer, may profit by storing, delaying, and marketing, the proprietor is scarcely ever but a loser from the fluctuations of price. Although he may occasionally gain, yet his profit is never found to be a counterpoise in any degree to his sufferings when he loses.

APP. IX.
——
PERGUNNAH
RATES.
——
Para. 6, contd.

VII.—MR. H. COLEBROOKE (*1812*).

But if it be thought expedient, in place of abrogating the laws which were enacted for the protection of the tenantry, and especially of the khoodkasht ryot, or resident cultivator, that the right of occupancy, which those laws were intended to uphold, should be still maintained, and that the ryot should be supported in his ancient and undoubted privilege of retaining the ground occupied by him, so long as he pays the rent justly demandable for it, measures should be adopted, late as it now is, to reduce to writing a clear declaration and distinct record of the usages and rates according to which the ryots of each pergunnah or district will be entitled to demand the renewal of their pottahs upon any occasion of a general or partial cancelling of leases.

Revenue Selec-
tions, Vol. I,
page 263.

VIII.—SIR J. SHORE (*June 1789 and September 1789*).

(*a*). Tury Mull is supposed to have formed his settlement of Bengal, called the *Tumar Jumma*, by collecting, through the medium of the canoongoes and other inferior officers, the amounts of the rents paid by the ryots, which served as the basis of it. The constituent parts of the assessment were called *tukseem,* and comprehended not only the quota of the greater territorial divisions, but of the villages, and, as it is generally believed, of the individual ryots. The *Tumar Jumma* is quoted as the standard assessment.

Fifth Report,
page 170,
para. 11.

(*b*). In general, throughout Bengal, the rents are paid by the ryots in money, but in some places the produce is divided, in different proportions, between the cultivator and zemindar. This custom chiefly respects lands under the denomination of *khamar.*

Ibid., para. 226.

(*c*). The custom of dividing the produce of the land in certain proportions between the cultivator and the Government, or the collector who stands in its place, is general, but not universal, throughout Behar. In Bengal the custom is very partial and limited.

(*d*). In every district throughout Bengal, where the license of exaction has not superseded all rule, the rents of land are regulated by known rates called *nirk,* and in some districts each village has its own; these rates are formed, with respect to the produce of the land, at so much per beegah. Some soil produces two crops in a year of different species, some three. The more profitable articles, such as the mulberry plant, betel-leaf, tobacco, sugarcane, and others, render the value of the land proportionably great.

APP. IX.
———
PERGUNNAH
RATES.
———
Para. 6, contd.

(*e*). When the five years' settlement was concluded by the Committee of Circuit, several conditions were inserted in the agreements of the farmers and zemindars, calculated for the security of the Government, and the benefit of their tenants. * * They were directed to collect from the cultivated lands of the ryots in the mofussil the original jumma of the last and foregoing year, and abwat established in the present, and on no account to demand more. Where the lands were cultivated without pottahs by the ryots, they were to collect according to the rates of the pergunnah.

(*f*). In Sir J. Shore's draft of Regulations, eventually passed as Regulations for the Decennial Settlement.

In every mofussil cutcherry, the *nirkbundy*, or rates of land, shall be publicly recorded; and the zemindar is answerable for enforcing this regulation, under a penalty of fine for neglect, at the discretion of government.

This last extract (*f*) was omitted from the Decennial Regulations as finally passed; but that which Sir John Shore thus proposed should be enacted as law, did, however, in practice, guide the zemindars, so long as there was a competition for ryots. Intending cultivators used to refer to the recorded pergunnah rate before taking up land, for which they paid at that rate, unless they obtained a lower rate by special agreement.—*See Appendix X, para. 8, Section VIb.*

IX.—Mr. Stuart (*18th December 1820*).

Revenue Selections, Vol. III, page 221.

I believe that those most conversant with the subject consider the pergunnah rates as the maximum of the ryot's payments; that in ordinary seasons they can pay according to that standard, but must be allowed a remission in unfavourable harvests. Any estimate of the public revenue, therefore, formed upon these rates, should be corrected by accounts of the actual payments of the ryots for a series of years; and when this information can be obtained, there can be little danger of over-assessment.

X.—Collector of Cawnpore (*1st January 1816*).

Ibid., page 186, para. 29.

Money tenures being for the most part prevalent in this district, the rents are governed by mutual agreement of the parties, founded upon known and established pergunnah rates, with respect to all denominations of land.

XI.—MR. J. MILL (*4th August 1831*).

It seems to be at last agreed that there are no means in Bengal of ascertaining with any accuracy what are called the pergunnah rates, that is, certain payments which custom had established, and which were looked to, both by the Government and by the ryots, as a species of standard; not that the standard was of much advantage to the ryots, for though it was always appealed to, the zemindars and other collectors exercised the privilege of adding cesses (abwabs) over and above what was considered the standard cesses, which were arbitrary, and in general went to such an amount as to leave the ryot just enough to carry on his cultivation (*Q. 3202*).

PERGUNNAH
RATES.

Para. 7.

Third Report,
Select Com-
mittee, 1831-32.

XII.—TAGORE LAW LECTURES (*1874-75*).

(1.) The zemindar was, however, to some extent controlled in his assessment by custom, which required that the rates usually paid by the village should be adhered to, at least in form. Those rates were well known, and registers of them were kept by the putwaries and canoongoes in records called village and pergunnah *reybundees*. Nevertheless, the zemindar ultimately contrived to extract the main portion of his profit from the surplus of his receipts beyond the jumma he paid. And in this he was still further assisted when he settled with Government for a term of years, and when, consequently, his yearly settlements with the ryots could not at all be expected to be at the same rates as he paid to government. The rates were settled with the cultivators through the headman of the village in many cases; but there appear to have been cultivators who did not form part of any village organization, and with these, probably, the zemindar could deal untrammelled, at least by the village *reybundees*. * *

Page 112.

(2.) The ryots' payments were, however, regulated ostensibly by the customary rates, which were known and registered in the putwary's records, and which were called the *nirk* (or *nirik*). These rates sometimes extended to the whole pergunnah, and sometimes only to the village. The records of these rates were known as the village and pergunnah *reybundees*. If such rates did not exist for any particular village, a reference was made to the rates of the neighbourhood. These rates corresponded to, and were originally derived from, the assul jumma, and in like manner, as in the case of the assul jumma, *abwabs* and cesses were assessed beyond those rates, and from time to time consolidated with them.

Page 171.

7.—GENERAL OBSERVATIONS ON RYOTS' RIGHTS.

I.—PATTON'S ASIATIC MONARCHIES.

(*a*). In this way I account for the two-fold existence of landed property in Hindustan, which I have distinguished by the term *absolute property*, entitling to the rent and existing in the sovereign, who may

Page 75.

transfer or assign it,[1] and *possessory property,* liable for the rent and existing in the husbandman, ryot, or occupant, under the obligation of cultivating it, so as to produce rent or revenue to the State or its substitute, which being continuously hereditary, and also transferable, is to all intents and purposes property, but always subservient to, and dependent upon, the person who is *absolute* proprietor of the same subject.

(*b*). The firman of Aurungzebe, A. D. 1668, recognizes the right of the proprietor in mowezzeff to give his own ground in farm, to lend it to another, to mortgage or sell it (articles twelfth and thirteenth).

II.—SIR J. SHORE (*June 1789*).

(*a*). It is however generally understood that the ryots by long occupancy acquire a right of possession in the soil, and are not subject to be removed; but this right does not authorise them to sell or mortgage it, and it is so far distinct from a right of property. * * Pottahs to the *khoodkasht* ryots, or those who cultivate the land of the village where they reside, are generally given without any limitation of period, and express that they are to hold the lands, paying the rents from year to year. Hence the right of occupancy originates; and it is equally understood as a prescriptive law, that the ryots who hold by this tenure cannot relinquish any part of the lands in their possession, or change the species of cultivation without a forfeiture of the right of occupancy, which is rarely insisted upon, and the zemindars exact the difference. I understand also that this right of occupancy is admitted to extend even to the heirs of those who enjoy it.

(*b*). Pykasht ryots, or those who cultivate the lands of villages where they do not reside, hold their lands upon a more indefinite tenure. The pottahs to them are generally granted with a limitation in point of time; where they deem the terms unfavourable, they repair to some other spot (*paras. 406 and 407*).

(*c*). In some parts of the country, I understand, the zemindars are precluded from measuring the lands of the ryots, whilst they pay the rents according to the pottah and jummabundy (*para. 408*).

III.—WILKS' MYSORE.

At a very early period of the Company's government in Bengal, Mr. Verelst, when charged with the collections of the province of Chittagong, looking at the condition of the people with that sound, plain, common sense which distinguished his character, and not through the medium of Mahomedan institutions, confirmed the rights which he found the people actually to possess, of transmitting and alienating their landed property by inheritance, mortgage, sale, or gift. The recognition of that right (in the words of the judge and magistrate of that province in 1801) "has fixed a value on real property here which is not attached to it in other parts of Bengal, and has given existence to a

---

[1] The sovereign could only assign the revenue under conditions limited by the Mahomedan law; the possessor could alone assign the property in the soil.

numerous body of landholders unknown elsewhere," who are afterwards stated to consider themselves, and to be recognized by the Court, as "the actual proprietors of the soil." In a subsequent passage we find these remarkable words : " If comfortable habitations and a numerous and healthy progeny be proofs of a happy condition, the estates in this division have contributed to increase population, and to rear a temperate and robust species of men fit for every sort of labour."

IV.—TAGORE LAW LECTURES (1874-75).

(a). It is remarked by Sir Henry Maine that the distinction between proprietary rights and rights which are not proprietary, is that the latter have their origin in a contract of some kind with the holder of the former. We have seen that Lord Cornwallis was under the impression that the rights of the ryots might be treated as derived in this way ; but the regulations themselves save the rights of the ryots as they actually existed ; and it is now the opinion of most authorities on the subject that the actual rights of the ryots were proprietary rights. They were not derived from, or carved out of, an original theoretically complete proprietary right in the zemindar, in the way that all interests in land in England are theoretically derived or carved out of the fee simple.

Page 218.

(b). The Hindu law recognizes rights in the cultivators and in the sovereign, but does not appear to contemplate any ordinary use of the land, except for the purpose of cultivation, and contemplates an obligation to cultivate, corresponding to the right to cultivate, in the same way as it contemplates an obligation on the part of the king to protect the cultivator, corresponding with the right to receive revenue from him.* *

In Mahomedan law, again, we find no greater light thrown upon the question of the extent of the proprietary rights. The sale of land is contemplated, and the purchase of land for purposes of trade is spoken of, but no indication is given of the extent of the right which was transferred. We may, however, infer that it was at least a right to occupy and cultivate.

(c). If, then, express law is silent upon this point, we must look to the state of ideas, and to the practice of the various parties embodying these ideas. Such a practice is the foundation of what we knew as a custom ; as Sir Henry Maine observes, " the foundation of a custom is habitual practice, a series of facts, a succession of instances, from whose constant recurrence a rule is inferred." The practice here referred to need not, I conceive, be an undisturbed practice ; but it must be one constantly recurring, and, if disturbed, again resumed as a right. And for this reason it is necessary to take into consideration the ideas of those who reverted to the practice when disturbed. If we find that some cultivators were considered to have a right to go on cultivating so long as they paid the revenue, and that in practice they did continue permanent, and that when disturbed by the hand of power it was thought an unwarrantable act, we may, I think, fairly infer, with respect to such cultivators, that habitual practice and constant recurrence required by Sir Henry Maine's criterion as the foundation of a custom. And there can be little doubt that, as regards the interests in land, there was scarcely any other law but custom. * *

(*d*). Again, the period for the growth of custom was not closed, and hence we must not expect to find a custom so full-grown as our English customs. And the main law on the present point must be deduced from such customs as existed, customs in process of growth. As Sir George Campbell says, custom was and is " the only ever-surviving law of the East." Acts which are now prohibited by law were then prohibited by custom, in the same way as some acts are now prohibited by public opinion. Such acts as were against custom were, when possible, resisted and were condemned as violations of right, and not merely as an unjust use of undoubted rights. It is almost impossible for us at this late period to discover whether any particular act was condemned as a clear violation of right, or merely as a wrong and unjust act done in exercise of a right. And therefore we can get little assistance, except from the actual practice and from general considerations as to the state of opinions.

8. The salient points in this appendix are as follow :—

I. A ryot is a cultivator who, whether by borrowing or in any other way, provides seed, cattle, implements, and labour for the land which he cultivates.

II. The authorities in India, including Sir John Shore and the Court of Directors, recorded emphatic testimony that more than upon anything else, the prosperity of the country depends upon the prosperity of the ryots, whose labours are the riches of the State. The Select Committee of the House of Commons, in 1831-32, recorded that the ryots' right is the greatest right in the country.

III. The most perfect form of ryots' title is that of the dependent talukdar, khoodkasht ryot, resident cultivator, or member of a village community. Even so late as 1832 (para. 3, section VII) " the most general tenure in the Lower Provinces is that of cultivating proprietors having a fixed right of occupancy, independently of any known contract limited to specific fields, and subject to payment of an amount determinable on fixed principles, demandable as Government revenue, and in no case depending on the mere will and pleasure of another individual."

IV. The prevailing testimony is to the effect that this title was nothing more than a hereditary right of occupancy subject to payment of Government rent ; though the ryot might quit the land for years, yet he or his descendants could return and claim it, ousting any possessor who may have cultivated it in the interval. On the other hand, according to the testimony which thus restricts the right of occupancy the ryot could not sell his land ; but in the early period when this restriction is said to have prevailed, the khoodkasht ryots' land was practically not saleable, from the abundance of waste land and scarcity of population, and from the circumstance that the khoodkasht ryot's fixed rent was higher than the pykasht's variable rent. When, from the rise of prices, the khoodkasht's rent fell below the pykasht's, and his land became saleable, he did sell, according to some of the testimony in this Appendix, including the testimony in September 1851 of well known Hindu authorities, such as Babus Sumbhunath Pundit, Unodaprosad Banerjea, Govindprosad Bose, and Hurrischunder Mookerjea, Editor of the *Hindoo Patriot*, and afterwards Assistant Secretary to the Bengal British Indian Association.

V. So long as the khoodkasht ryot paid the customary rent to the Government, not to a zemindar as landlord, he was not disturbed in the enjoyment of his property.

VI. The amount payable to Government was a definite proportion of the produce, demandable on fixed principles determined by local custom dating from remote time, and not dependent on the mere will or pleasure of any man.

VII. The Government share or proportion of the produce may have varied in different districts, according to local peculiarities, but in each district or village it was a fixed proportion, well recognized from immemorial or remote custom, and thus it formed a permanent settlement with the ryot.

VIII. Under the earlier native rule, the Government share was taken in kind, with an option to the cultivator to pay its value, instead, at the market price of the new crop, the Collectors being at the same time requested not to require a money-payment if it would distress the cultivator, who thus had the benefit of a permanent settlement, with the advantage of sharing with the Government his loss in a bad season equally with his gain in a good season, for he paid only on the actual produce of his land.

IX. In Toodur Mull's settlement, however, under Akbar, the collections for each village, on an average for some years, were ascertained, and the yearly average for each holding in the village was assessed upon it at a fixed amount per beegah. This, too, formed a permanent settlement with the cultivator, but with the disadvantage of his paying on the extent of his holding, and not on the actual produce of the season, that is, without the benefit of remissions. He had the option, however, of paying, instead, on the buttye system (section VIII).

X. The assessment under Toodur Mull's settlement was not on the system of a division of produce;—it was payable in money, and the amount having been fixed per beegah, it was not liable to increase on account of any subsequent rise of prices. The assessment was virtually a permanent settlement with the ryot. At any rate, it was not altered during more than 100 years.

XI. The Government's fixed share or proportion of the produce was a maximum proportion, out of which remissions or reductions were allowed ; the khoodkasht ryot, moreover, had extra land, not assessed, the profit from which helped him to pay the maximum share of Government on the produce of his assessed land. Hence the pergunnah rates of 1793, if simply continued at the same amounts to this day, but without the abatements for unfavourable seasons and for unassessed lands, would have been tantamount to enhanced rates. The actual facts are that, not only have those two moderating circumstances ceased, but the gross amounts of the old pergunnah rates have been greatly enhanced.

XII. The chupperbund ryots, or those strangers whom village communities received into their brotherhood as permanent resident cultivators, had nearly the same privileges as khoodkasht ryots.

XIII. The pykasht ryots were of inferior status : as tenants on temporary lease, or at will, the rates they paid were specially adjusted with the owners of their land ; and at a time when there was competition for tenants, rather than for land, their rents were lower than those of the khoodkasht ryots.

XIV. The framers of the permanent settlement intended that the pergunnah rates then existing for ryots should be permanent, and through the care and painstaking work of the Collectors in the 24-Pergunnahs, Chittagong, Dinagepore, part of Tipperah, and Sylhet (para. 3, section I), the exemption of ryots in those districts from enhancement of rent was secured ;—but, because the Collectors in other districts did not exercise like foresight and judgment, one essential part of the permanent settlement, without which the remaining provisions of that settlement entailed confiscation of rights, proved nugatory, and thereby millions of ryots have been subjected to enhancement of rents.

XV. The Select Committee of the House of Commons in 1831-32 reported that " the proper ascertainment, recognition, and security of the several tenures and rights within the villages, are objects of the highest importance to the tranquillity of the provinces, and will greatly tend to the repression of crime. The natives of India have a deep-rooted attachment to hereditary rights and offices; and animosities originating from disputes regarding lands descend through generations. The vital question to the ryot is the amount of assessment which he pays."

XVI. The Court of Directors, in reviewing the position in 1819, considered that, whatever might be the distinction between khoodkasht and pykasht ryots "as to their rights, it is clear that, in every respect, the two classes of ryots are equally entitled to the protection of Government; and we observe that you concur with us in the opinion that, however well intended for this purpose, our regulations under the permanent settlement have not been effectual to it."

APPENDIX X.

THE RYOT SINCE THE PERMANENT SETTLEMENT, AND GOVERNMENT'S OBLIGATIONS TOWARDS HIM.

1.—GOVERNMENT'S OBLIGATIONS TOWARDS RYOTS.

I.—PRESIDENT AND SELECT COMMITTEE—*16th August 1769 (Bengal Government).*

(*a*). The ryot, too, should be impressed in the most forcible and convincing manner that the tendency of your measures is to his ease and relief; that every opposition to them is riveting his own chain, and confirming his servitude and dependence on his oppressors; that our object is not increase of rents, or the accumulation of demands, but solely by fixing such as are legal, explaining and abolishing such as are fraudulent and unauthorised, not only to redress his present grievance, but to secure him from all further invasions of his property.

(*b*). Among the chief effects which are hoped for from your residence in that province, and which ought to employ and never wander from your attention, are to convince the ryot that you will stand between him and the hand of oppression; that you will be his refuge, and the redresser of his wrongs; that the calamities he has already suffered have sprung from an intermediate cause, and were neither known nor permitted by us; that honest and direct applications to you will never fail of producing speedy and equitable decisions; that after supplying the legal due of the Government, he may be secure in the enjoyment of the remainder; and finally, to teach [1] him a veneration and affection for the humane maxims of our Government.

II.—WARREN HASTINGS—*1st November 1776 (not half so benevolent as Lord Cornwallis).*

(*a*). **Many** other points of enquiry will be also useful to secure to the ryots the perpetual and undisturbed possession of their lands, and to guard them against arbitrary exactions. This is not to be done by proclamation and edicts, nor by indulgences to the zemindars and farmers. The former will not be obeyed, unless enforced by regulations so framed as to produce their own effect, without requiring the hand of Government to interpose its support; and the latter, though it may feed the luxury of the zemindars, or the rapacity of the farmers, will prove no relief to the cultivator, whose welfare ought to be the immediate and primary care of Government.

---

[1] And a terribly benevolent and well-meaning teacher the Government of those days proved.

(*b*). The design of establishing new pottahs for the ryots, the failure of which has been objected to as a reproach on the late administration, has been tried with equal ill success by the present, in their late settlement of Burdwan, when, notwithstanding the solemn engagement of the zemindar and the peremptory injunctions of Government, not a pottah has yet been granted (if my information is true, and it may be easily proved), nor will be granted, of a different tenure from those which have been customary for some years past, unless more regular means are taken to produce them. It is the interest of the zemindar to exact the greatest rent he can from the ryots, and it is as much against his interest to fix, in deeds, by which the ryots hold their lands and pay their rents, certain bounds and defences against his own authority.

APP. X.
GOVERNMENT'S OBLIGATIONS TOWARDS RYOTS.
Para. 1, contd.

III.—COURT OF DIRECTORS (*19th September 1792*).

Mr. Shore contends that we should advance to a perpetual settlement only by gradual measures. He infers this, among other considerations, especially from the extreme difficulty of forming and executing such regulations as shall secure to the great body of the ryots the same equity and certainty as to the amount of their rents, and the same undisturbed enjoyment of the fruits of their industry, which we mean to give to the zemindars themselves (*paras. 36 and 37*).

Report from Select Committee, 1810, App. 12 A, page 172.

IV.—COURT OF DIRECTORS (*9th May 1821*).

(*a*). The purport of the report from the Board of Commissioners in Behar and Benares you correctly describe in the following words : " The doctrine which it is the chief object of the report in question to support, is that the prosperity of the country will best be obtained by the annulment of all the prescriptive rights possessed by the resident ryots." This is the more remarkable on the part of these Commissioners, as in the third paragraph of that very report of theirs they say : " It is almost superfluous to observe that in the discussions prior to the decennial settlement, it was allowed that the ryots had vested rights in the lands, and the revenue authorities were especially enjoined to secure them in them." The annulment of all those rights, therefore, is or would be the most extensive act of confiscation that ever was perpetrated in any country. This is a subject of immense importance, and we are happy to see that you have not passed it over lightly. * * So long as the rights of the inferior classes of the agricultural population shall remain unprotected, the British Government must be considered *to have fulfilled very imperfectly the obligations which it owes to its subjects* (*paras. 49, 50, and 58*).

Sess. 1831-32, Vol. XI, page 101.

(*b*). But though we must agree with the Commissioners that where the zemindar is left to settle as he pleases with the ryot, all rights in the land on the part of the ryot are actually for the time extinguished, yet we do most fully agree with you that Government did not by that enactment bind itself to sacrifice for ever the rights of that numerous and valuable class of its subjects, or even to abstain from retracing that very step, if it should find upon consideration and experience that it was a false one. This enactment[1] was no part or condition of the permanent settlement; it is therefore revocable, and ought not to be maintained if found to be inconsistent with that protection of the ryots in their rights, and that security from arbitrary exactions, which did form, in principle at least, a part of the permanent settlement, and is the foundation as it were on which your revenue and judicial system professed to be built (*para.* 54).

V.—COURT OF DIRECTORS (*15th January 1819*).

It is well known (and even if it were questionable, the practice of the provinces which have lately fallen under our dominion would set the doubt at rest) that the cultivating zemindars (ryots) were, by a custom more ancient than all law, entitled to a certain share of the produce of their lands, and that the rest, whether collected by pergunnah zemindars or by officers of Government, was collected as the *huck* of the Circar (*para.* 28).

The paramount importance, on every ground of justice and expediency, as connected with the welfare and prosperity of the British empire in India, of adopting all practicable means for ascertaining and protecting the rights of the ryots, has, in our former correspondence, been made the topic of frequent and serious representation; nor can it be otherwise than most satisfactory to us to find that the members of your Government, and those acting under its authority in the internal administration of the country, are now so earnestly occupied in the furtherance of this most important and essential work (*para.* 29).

We fully subscribe to the truth of Mr. Sisson's declaration that "the faith of the State is to the full as solemnly pledged to uphold the cultivator of the soil in the unmolested enjoyment of his long-established rights, as it is to maintain the zemindar in the possession of his estate, or to abstain from increasing the public revenue permanently assessed upon him" (*para.* 30).

It is also a circumstance which is not to be overlooked, that, although so many years have elapsed since the conclusion of the permanent settlement, yet no resort has been had to the exercise of the power we then expressly reserved, of interfering for the purpose of defining and adjusting the rights of the ryots. We conclude that the supposed difficulty or impracticability of the operation was the cause of this non-interference. We find, however, that, antecedently to the permanent settlement, this power was successfully exercised in several parts of the territory under your Government; and that the advantages of this policy are still felt in those districts, although the general system of your revenue and judicial administration has been unfavourable to the preservation and improvement of the advantages thus obtained. We particularly allude to the 24-Perguunahs and to part of Dinagepore (*para.* 39).

---

[1] Regulation V of 1812.

VI.—RIGHT HON'BLE JOHN SULLIVAN.

APP. X.
___
GOVERNMENT'S
RIGHT TO INTER-
FERE FOR THE
RYOT RESERVED.

(*a*). The advocates for a permanent settlement could not more highly venerate the memory of the founder of that measure in Bengal, more estimate the value of proprietary right in the soil, or the advantages that attach upon perpetuity of tenure, than Lord Buckinghamshire, President of the Board of Control, and his colleagues, did, and endeavoured to support. The difference between those advocates and the Board turned upon a question as to the party in whom that right did and should continue to vest. It is hoped, from what has appeared in the preceding pages, that the question, not only of right, but the principle in policy, has been made apparent by the admission of the Supreme Government, after a long and laborious discussion in favour of the cultivating occupants of the soil.

Para. 2.
Sess. 1831-32,
Vol. XI, page 65.

(*b*). The door may, therefore, be said to have been kept open for the restoration of that right to those who may have been unduly deprived of it, and for extending it to those migratory ryots who under encouragement may become stationary, thereby laying the best and surest foundation for the public prosperity.

VII.—COURT OF DIRECTORS (*10th November 1824*).

We regard this subject of the means of protecting the rights of the ryots by ascertaining and defining them, as of paramount importance, and the means of obtaining the end which is here proposed as affecting the character and prosperity of your Government more deeply than almost anything else to which your attention can be directed (*para. 30*).

Revenue
Selections, Vol.
III, page 443.

2.—THE GOVERNMENT'S OBLIGATION BEING RECOGNISED, THE GOVERNMENT'S RIGHT TO INTERFERE FOR SECURING THE RYOT'S RIGHTS WAS EXPRESSLY RESERVED IN THE PERMANENT SETTLEMENT.

1.—COURT OF DIRECTORS (*19th September 1792*).

(*a*). But as so great a change in habits and situation can only be gradual, the interference of Government may, for a considerable period, be necessary to prevent the landholders from making use of their own permanent possession for the purposes of exaction and oppression; we therefore wish to have it distinctly understood that, while we confirm to the landholders the possession of the districts which they now hold, and subject only to the rent now settled, and while we disclaim any interference with respect to the situation of the ryots, or the sums paid to them, with any view to any addition of revenue to ourselves, we expressly reserve the right which clearly belongs to us as sovereigns, of interposing our authority in making from time to time all such regulations as may be necessary to prevent the ryots being improperly disturbed in their possessions or loaded with unwarrantable exactions. A power exercised for the purposes we have mentioned, and which has no view to our own interests, except as they are connected with the general industry and prosperity of the country, can be no object of jealousy to the landholders,

Report of Select
Committee, 1870,
App. 2-a,
pages 174-75.

APP. X.
———
GOVERNMENT'S
RIGHT TO INTER-
FERE FOR THE
RYOT RESERVED.

Para. 2, contd.

and instead of diminishing will enhance the value of their proprietary rights. Our interposition where necessary seems also to be clearly consistent with the practice of the Mogul Government, under which it appeared to be a general maxim that the immediate cultivator of the soil, duly paying his rent, should not be dispossessed of the land he occupied. This necessarily supposes that there were some measures and limits by which the rent could be defined, and that it was not left to the arbitrary determination of the zemindar, for otherwise such a rule would be nugatory. *   *

(b). * * You will, in a particular manner, be cautious so to express yourselves as to leave no ambiguity as to our right to interfere from time to time, as it may be necessary, for the protection of the ryots and subordinate landholders, it being our intention in the whole of this measure effectually to limit our own demand, but not to depart from our inherent right as sovereigns of being the guardians and protectors of every class of persons living under our Government (*paras. 46 and 48*).

[The foregoing was embodied in section 8, Regulation I, of 1793 and a clause to the above effect is also inserted in the engagements with the landholders.]

II.—COURT OF DIRECTORS (*15th January 1819*).

(a). Although the zemindars with whom the permanent settlement was made are, in the regulations respecting that arrangement, declared to be " the actual proprietors of the soil;" although their zemindaries are called landed estates, and all other holders of land are denominated their " under-tenants;" and although, as we shall have occasion more particularly to observe in the course of this despatch, the use of these terms, which has ever since continued current, has, in practice, contributed, with other causes, to perplex the subject of landed tenures, and thereby to impair, and in many cases to destroy, the rights of individuals yet it is clear that the rights which were actually conferred upon the zemindars, or which were actually recognized to exist in that class by the enactments of the permanent settlements, were not intended to trench upon the rights which were possessed by the ryots. Lord Cornwallis explicitly recognized the ryot's title to be protected by Government in his rights," and the right to accord this protection was reserved in section 8 of Regulation I of 1793 (*paras. 13 and 15*).

III.—MR. HOLT MACKENZIE (*1832*).

(a). It was not, I think, until after 1813, in so far at least as concerns the Bengal Presidency, that much thought was given in the management of the main item of revenue (the land rent) to the rights and interests of the great body of the people. The principle of the zemindari or contract settlements (using the term zemindar as employed in Bengal proper) was non-interference; the men who engaged to pay the Government demand, and those from whom they collected it, being left to settle the disputes necessarily arising out of the relation in the best way they could, under laws passed for the guidance of the Courts of Judicature. The right of interfering was indeed reserved to Government (it could not have been relinquished without an abandonment of its highest functions), and rules were passed against the arbitrary enhancement of demands upon the cultivators, which seemed to show the intention of the legislature to regard the zemindar as possessing in many cases merely the right of collecting a fair assessment, and as being assessors of the public demand—not rent-holders.

(b). The right of interference is clear, and has indeed been specifically reserved; and in many cases, I doubt not the rules against arbitrary enhancement of rent would enable us, in making a settlement with the ryots, unquestionably to restrict the zemindar's demand within such bounds as would leave the former a property of value in these fields. But in other cases the question will arise how far (the Government having assigned to the zemindars a right which, if strictly [1] enforced, will swallow up the property of the inferior tenantry) we can now come and proceed on general principles to limit that right. If done without their consent, we must, I apprehend, interfere by a new law, and be prepared to allow the zemindars compensation, or allow a reduction of revenue.

IV.—Mr. A. D. Campbell (*1832*).

The pledge, reserving the right to protect the ryots, indeed still stands forth on the front of the Bengal Regulations; but the Government, having once shut themselves out from all direct communication with the village landholders, by permanently interposing the zemindars between themselves and the cultivators, have hitherto entirely neglected to redeem it. In 1786, the Court of Directors of the East India Company observed : " In ordering the settlement (or revenue contract) to be made in every practicable instance with the zemindar, we conceive that we adopt the true spirit of the 30th section of the Act of the 24th of Geo. 3rd." In 1792 they proceed to state that "in order to simplify and regulate the demands of the zemindars upon the cultivators, the first step is to fix the demand of the Government itself" upon the zemindar; and justly treating this as the mere preliminary to a far more important ultimate end, they add, " we are led to believe that the situation of the ryot varies in different districts, according to local manners, customs, or particular agreements, and it appears as if in some instances the rights of ryots of different descriptions, though in the same district, are considered more or less permanent and secure. The application, therefore, of any general principles must be guided by minute local investigation, and we shall expect particular regulations, adapted

App. X.
____
Government's
right to inter-
fere for the
ryot reserved.
____
Para. 2, contd.
____
Masterly inac-
tivity.

Ibid., question
2673.

Ibid., App. 6,
page 14.

---

[1] Mr. Mackenzie was referring here to the conventional 50 per cent., or half-produce, as the Government's share, which he considered would generally swallow up " all the rent" (question 2671) ; but he overlooked the considerations that the 50 per cent. was maximum rate, and that the ryots had concealed cultivation on which they paid no rent, and for which consequently the Government was taking nothing from the zemindar, and that the zemindar was precluded from measuring the ryot's lands so long as he paid the customary rent on his assessed lands.

APP. X.
———
GOVERNMENT'S
RIGHT TO INTER-.
FERE FOR THE
RYOT RESERVED.

Para. 2, concld.

to all the different circumstances, to be prepared and finally submitted to our consideration." In 1793, Lord Cornwallis, in reply, without allusion to any such particular rules, merely refers to his general enactment (Regulation I of 1793, section 8), as reserving to Government the power of hereafter framing such regulations as they may occasionally think proper "for the protection of the ryots and inferior landholders, or other orders of people concerned in the cultivation of the lands." It is true that the Committee of the House of Commons in 1812 (Fifth Report) reported that " with respect to the cultivators or ryots, their rights and customs varied so much in different parts of the country, and appeared to the Government to involve so much intricacy, that the regulation (VIII of 1793) only provides generally for engagements being entered into, and pottahs or leases being granted by the zemindar, leaving the terms to be such as shall have been customary, or as shall be particularly adjusted between the parties; and in this it is probable that the expectations of Government have been fulfilled, as no new regulation yet appears, altering or rescinding the one alluded to." But the very reverse has been the actual result.

3.—DESTRUCTION OF RYOTS' RIGHTS.

I.—COURT OF DIRECTORS (*15th January 1819*).

Sess. 1831-32,
Vol. XI,
App. 11.

(*a*). Such (paragraphs 1 and 2 above) having been the sentiments of Lord Cornwallis and the ruling authorities in England, and such having been the acts of the Local Government on the first introduction of the permanent settlement, the question naturally occurs, whence it has arisen (to use your own words) "that our institutions are so imperfectly calculated to afford the ryots, in practice, that protection to which on every ground they are so fully entitled," so that it too often happens that the quantum of rent which they pay is regulated neither by specific engagements, nor by the established rates of the pergunnahs or other local divisions in which they reside, but by the arbitrary will of the zemindars.

(*b*). We have of late years taken frequent occasion to call the attention of your Government to the state of insecurity and oppression in which the great mass of cultivators were placed; but we must confess that, anxiously and fully as this subject had engaged our thoughts, we had not formed an adequate idea of the state of things under your Government, in this respect, until we met, in its proceedings, with the correspondence between the judicial functionaries and the Court of Sudder Adawlut, which was referred by you in 1809 and 1810 to the consideration of the Board of Revenue, the answers which were returned by the Collectors of districts to the circular letter of that Board, dated 7th June 1811, and the minute of Mr. Colebrooke thereon.

(*c*). Among the most important documents upon this interesting subject which have lately reached us, are the report of Mr. Cornish, Fourth Judge of the Patna Court of Circuit, dated the 26th July 1814; the letter of the Board of Commissioners, and the minutes of Messrs. Roche and Colebrooke, of the Board of Revenue, recorded on your Revenue Consultations of the 12th August 1815; the letter addressed by Mr. Thomas Sisson, under date the 2nd April 1815, on the relative state of the landlord and tenant in the district of Rungpore; and the Governor General's minutes of the 21st September and 2nd October 1815, on the revenue and judicial administration of the territories dependent on your Presidency, together with the reports of the local officers which accompanied them.

(*d*). The documents here enumerated unequivocally confirm the truth of all the information of which we were previously possessed, respecting the absolute subjection of the cultivators of the soil to the discretion of the zemindars, while they exhibit to us a view of things, with reference to the landed tenures and rights of that valuable body of the people, which satisfies us that a decisive course of measures for remedying evils of such magnitude must be undertaken without delay.

(1). MR. CORNISH states on this subject: "The ryots conceive they have a right to hold their lands so long as they pay the rent which they and their forefathers have always done. The zemindars, though afraid openly to avow, as being contrary to immemorial custom, that they have a right to demand any rent they choose to exact, yet go on compelling them to give an increase; and the power of distraint, vested in them by the regulations, soon causes the utter ruin of the resisting ryot."

(2). MR. COLEBROOKE asserts, from his own experience, that disputes between zemindars and ryots, in the Lower Provinces, were less frequent and more easily determined anterior to 1793 than they now are; and he further states that "the provisions contained in the general regulations for the permanent settlement, designed for the protection of ryots or tenants, are rendered wholly nugatory," and that "the courts of justice, for want of definite information respecting their rights, are unable effectually to support them. I am disposed, therefore," he adds, "to recommend that, late as it now is, measures should be taken for the re-establishment of fixed rates, as nearly conformable to the anciently established ones as may be yet practicable, to regulate distinctly and definitely the relative rights of the landlord and tenantry."

(3). MR. SISSON, in his letter on the relative state of landlord and tenant in Rungpore, describes the "arbitrary oppression under which the cultivator of the soil groans, as having at length attained a height so alarming as to have become by far the most extensively injurious of all the evils under which that district labours;" and expresses an apprehension "that until by a steady adherence to the most decisive and vigorous measures the bulk of the community shall have been restored from their present state of abject wretchedness to the full enjoyment of their legitimate rights, it will be in vain to expect solid and substantial improvement." The sentiments of many other of the local authorities employed in the internal administration of the country, whose reports are now before us, are equally strong upon this subject.

(4). THE MARQUIS OF HASTINGS describes the situation of the village zemindars to be such as to call loudly for the support of some legislative provision. "This," observes his Lordship, "is a question which has not merely reference to the Upper Provinces" (of which he had previously been speaking), "for, within the circle of the perpetual settlement, the situation of this unfortunate class is yet more desperate. In Burdwan, in Behar, in Cawnpore, and indeed wherever there may have existed extensive landed property at the mercy of individuals, whether in farm or jagheer, in talook or in zemindary, of the higher class, complaints of the village zemindars have crowded in upon me without number; and I had only the mortification of finding that the existing system established by the Legislature left me without the means of pointing out to the complainants any mode in which they might hope to obtain redress. In all these tenures, from what I could observe, the class of village proprietors appeared to be in a train of annihilation, and unless a remedy is speedily applied, the class will soon be extinct."

(*e*). In the consideration of this subject it is impossible for us not to remark that consequences the most injurious to the rights and interests of individuals, have arisen from describing those with whom the permanent settlement was concluded, as the *actual proprietors of the land*. This mistake (for such it is now admitted to have been), and the habit which has grown out of it, of considering the payments of the ryots as rent instead of revenue, have produced all the evils that might have been expected to flow from them. They have introduced much confusion into the whole subject of landed tenures, and have given a specious colour to the pretensions of the zemindars, in acting towards persons of the other classes as if they, the zemindars, really were, in the ordinary sense of the words, the proprietors of the land, and as if the ryots had no permanent interest but what they derived from them. * * There can be no doubt that a misapplication of terms, and the use of the word " rent," as applied to the demands on the ryots, instead of the appropriate one of " revenue," have introduced much confusion into the whole subject of landed tenures, and have tended to the injury and destruction of the rights of the ryots (*paras. 54 and 63*).

II.—LAW AND CONSTITUTION OF INDIA.

When the Emperor Akbar approved the settlement submitted to him by his able Financial Minister Rajah Todur Mull, * * the law of the land was not altered by the minister, and by his able Mahomedan colleague, Mujuffur Khan, but a settlement was made, having the law for its basis, and the detail was ably projected and superintended by those valuable servants of the State, who neither did, nor would have dared to depart, in anything essential, from the law and the usage of the country.

In modern times, conquering [1] statesmen have greater confidence. They do not hold themselves hampered by custom, however sacred, ancient, or universal! There is not in the history of the world a more extraordinary instance of disregard of the usages of a people, than is to be found in the conduct of those who swayed the councils of India when the great financial innovation of 1793 swept away the ancient landholders of Bengal, and limited its territorial revenue for ever.

4. The authors of the permanent settlement with zemindars saw clearly enough that the dangers attending it were a

---

[1] The permanent settlement was concluded in virtue of dewanny rights acquired under treaty.

possible loss of revenue (or, as the authorities a few years
later perceived, a stationary revenue with a growing expenditure), and the destruction of the ryots' rights. The former
was regarded with horror and shrinking fear, the latter with
an airy confidence that all would come right by the zemindars
giving pottahs to the ryots. Respecting the financial results
of the settlement it was observed—

I.—COURT OF DIRECTORS (*19th September 1792*).

No consequences more formidable could be presented to us from
the proposed system than a diminution in perpetuity of the Company's
revenue, with the still continued subsistence of all or any of those
disorders in the mode of imposing and levying it from the great body
of the people, which have already done such essential injury to the
country, and must ever prove a bar to its prosperity. Very clear and
solid arguments were requisite to dispel the diffidence which this view
of the subject, from such an authority as Mr. Shore, had a tendency
to create, and to encourage us to persevere in our original idea of
giving a fixed constitution to the finance and land tenure of the country.
But this satisfaction Lord Cornwallis has afforded us in his minutes of
the 18th September 1789 and 3rd February 1790.

II.—COURT OF DIRECTORS (*16th December 1812*).

(*a*). In the permanent settlement of the Bengal Provinces, the protection of the ryots against the oppressions and exactions of the zemindars,
was justly held to be the main spring from which the improvement of
the country and of its internal resources was to be expected; and an
express provision was accordingly made in the regulations that were
passed when that settlement was formed, and the principles of it promulgated, requiring that pottahs should be given by the zemindars
to the ryots. There are, however, but too strong proofs on the records
of the Supreme Government that this Regulation has almost become
a dead letter (*para. 10*).   *   *

(*b*). We applaud the principle which first suggested the introduction
of Lord Cornwallis' judicial system into the British possessions in India,
and we venerate the character from which it emanated; but the
experience of nearly twenty years in Bengal has furnished unequivocal
evidence that it has not been possible, by every practicable extension
of the judicial establishment, to render it adequate to the great end for
which it was instituted, namely, the speedy as well as the impartial
administration of justice; but that, while the expenditure has been
augmented from the sum of 220,000*l.*, at which the annual charge
for the provinces of Bengal, Behar, and Orissa, not including the charge
of police and the diet of prisoners, was calculated by Lord Cornwallis,
to the sum of 306,000*l.*, at which the correspondent expenditure had
arrived in those provinces by the accounts for 1809-10, and which, by its
extension to the ceded and conquered territories under that presidency

APP. X.

FINANCIAL CON-
SEQUENCES OF
THE PERMANENT
SETTLEMENT.

alone, amounted, in that year, to the alarming expenditure of 870,000*l.*, still the arrear of causes has gone on increasing, until it has attained a height that calls imperiously for the application of some effectual remedy.

Para. 4, concld.

And so the Court of Directors would have none of the permanent settlement for the temporarily settled provinces. A fixed income and a growing expenditure of the Government were regarded as intolerable; but the prevention of growing demands of zemindars and diminishing incomes of millions of cultivators was matter in 1793 for a hopeful, airy confidence in the all-saving efficacy of a zemindary settlement.

5. Pottahs from zemindars to ryots will keep everything straight.

I.—COURT OF DIRECTORS (*19th September 1792*).

Select Com-
mittee, 1810,
page 175.

In the meantime it must be the duty of our servants to watch incessantly over the progress of the change introduced by the permanent zemindary settlement, to see that the landholders observe punctually their agreements with Government and with the ryots; that they neither pass invented claims on the eve of a permanent settlement, nor fraudulently shift the burthen of revenue by collusive transfers, nor by any other sinister practices diminish the payment of their stipulated assessments; that they likewise give to the ryots written specific agreements, as also receipts for all payments, and that those agreements be on the one side and the other fairly fulfilled. In this way and in this only can the system be expected to flourish (*para. 49*).

II.—COURT OF DIRECTORS (*6th January 1815*).

Revenue
Selections,
Vol. I, page 284.

We cannot with too much earnestness direct your attention to the enforcement of the pottah regulation, a measure which was contemporaneous with the permanent settlement, was then considered as an essentially necessary branch of the system, and upon the observance of which the security of the ryots, and consequently the general prosperity of the country, were stated mainly to depend. • Had that regulation been duly enforced, and had the penalties attached to the breach of it been regularly imposed, a degree of confidence might[1] have been established between the zemindars and ryots, which would gradually have spread its influence into our other provinces. * * But it has unfortunately happened, and we must say much to the discredit of the executive authorities abroad, that the pottah regulation has been suffered to become a dead letter. The only immediate security for the ryots against undue exaction is that regulation, and if measures are not speedily adopted to enforce compliance with its salutary provisions, the ryots must continue entirely at the mercy of the zemindars or renters (*paras. 46 to 48*).

On the contrary, the pottah regulation, wh. h the Government vainly hoped would curb the zemindar, was used by him as an engine of oppression.

III.—COURT OF DIRECTORS (*15th January 1819*).

With respect to the original pottah, Regulation VIII of 1793, we have to observe that more seems to have been expected from its enactments in favour of the ryots than they were calculated to effect unsupported by other institutions, and that it was in fact almost wholly nugatory (*para. 45*).

APP. X.

POTTAHS FROM
ZEMINDARS WILL
KEEP EVERY
THING STRAIGHT.

Para. 6.

Sess. 1831-32,
Vol. XI, page 97.

IV.—GOVERNMENT RESOLUTION (*1st August 1822*).

Ibid., page 221.

The example of Bengal has shown that further securities than those provided in the existing Code are indispensable, and his Lordship in Council is strongly inclined to the opinion that no real security can be given to the ryots, unless we distinctly act upon the principle of minutely ascertaining and recording the rents payable by individual ryots, of granting pottahs, or, at least registering the ryots' holdings, and of maintaining the rates established at the settlement during the term of such settlement, as an essential part of the assessment. The adoption of this course will apparently be entirely consistent with everything we know of fixed principle in the system of preceding Governments (*para. 25*).

6. This reliance on the sufficiency of pottahs to secure the ryots evinced an astonishing credulity, and was accompanied by a curious ignorance of the main facts, on the part of the authors of the permanent settlement.

I.—CREDULITY.

(*a*).—LORD CORNWALLIS.

Mr. Shore's proposition that the rents of the ryots, by whatever rule or custom they may be demanded, shall be specific as to their amount; that the landholders shall be obliged within a certain time to grant pottahs or writings to their ryots, in which this amount shall be inserted, and that no ryot shall be liable to pay more than the sum actually specified in his pottah, if duly enforced by the collectors, will soon obviate the objection to a fixed assessment founded upon the undefined state of the demands of the landholders upon the ryots.

Fifth Report,
page 486.

When a spirit of improvement is diffused throughout the country, the ryots will find a further security in the competition of the landholders to add to the number of their tenants.

(*b*).—LORD MOIRA (*21st September 1815*).

It has been urged, however, that though the rights of the former cultivating proprietors have passed away *sub silentio*, still, as the zemindar and his tenants have reciprocal wants, their mutual necessities must drive them to an amicable adjustment. The reciprocity is not, however, so clear. The zemindar certainly cannot do without tenants, but he wants them upon his own terms, and he knows that if he can get rid of the

Sess. 1831-32,
Vol. XI, page 84,
App. 9.

App. X.

Government's
credulity and
ignorance.

Para. 6, contd.

hereditary proprietors who claim a right to terms independent of what he may vouchsafe to give, he will obtain the means of substituting men of his own; and such is the redundancy of the cultivating class, that there will never be a difficulty of procuring ryots ready to engage on terms only just sufficient to secure bare maintenance to the engager (*paras. 146 and 147*).

II.—Ignorance.

Lord Cornwallis' Government reporting the Permanent Settlement in letter to Court of Directors (*6th March 1793*).

From the proceedings which we shall forward to you by the next despatch, you will find that we have anticipated your wishes respecting the pottahs to be granted by the landholders to the ryots. It is with pleasure we acquaint you that throughout the greater part of the country specific agreements have been exchanged between the landholders and the ryots, and that where these writings have not been entered into, the landholders have bound themselves to prepare and deliver them by fixed periods. We shall here only observe that under the new arrangements to which we shall presently advert, the ryots will always have it in their power to compel an adherence to these agreements by an appeal to the Courts of Justice whenever the landholders may attempt to infringe them (*para. 20*).

7.—The Pottah Regulation scorned by the Zemindar.

I.—Collector of Rajshahye (*16th August 1811*).

Revenue
Selections,
Vol. I, page 241.

The regulations have now been printed and published since 1793, a period of eighteen years; and I am convinced, notwithstanding the wish of Government that pottahs should be granted and kabuliuts taken, there are as few now as ever there were. It will naturally be asked—how does this happen? The only explanation I can offer is, that the rights of the ryots have never been determined, or if determined not well understood. The consequence is, the zemindar, who pretends to consider his ryot a tenant-at-will, tenders a pottah at an exorbitant rate; the ryot, who considers himself (from the circumstance of having held his lands for a very long period) a species of mokururidar, conceives that he is entitled to hold his lands at a fixed rent, and therefore refuses the pottah; the zemindar distrains, and the ryot is ruined.

II.—Sir Edward Colebrooke (*5th January 1819*).

Revenue
Selections,
Vol. III, pages
171-72.

No particular measures appear to have been adopted for enforcing the delivery of pottahs, and we may observe that documents of this description are only applicable to the labouring tenants. A person connected with the property in the soil will never accept a pottah from the nominal zemindar, or person under engagements with Government; he holds his land and regulates his payments by a much more solid tenure, and would

consider himself as departing from his rights, by the acceptance of a
document tending to convert him from a Malik to an Assamee. It will
accordingly be found in the correspondence already submitted to your
Lordship, relative to the byacharry tenures in Bundelcund, that the
enforcement of the delivery of pottahs has been the instrument through
which the purchasers of estates in that district have attempted to annihilate the putteedary rights. Pottahs, however, appear to be general in
some districts, but where the putwary accounts are regularly kept, they
are, to both landlord and tenant, a sufficient substitute for pottah and
cabooleut (*para. 12*).

App. X.

FOTTAH REGULA-
TION MOCKED
BY THE ZEMIN-
DAR.

Para. 7, contd.

III.—MR. SISSON'S REPORT (*2nd April 1815*).

(*a*). It had been enacted by section 2, Regulation XLIV, 1793, that
no lease whatever, except for erection of houses and for gardens, could be
made for a longer period than ten years. This regulation had been
modified in favour of the ryot the following year ; but not by exempt-
ing him from the operation of that regulation, but by entitling him to
a renewal of his lease after the expiration of the period which had been
limited by the rule above cited (*para. 17*).

(*b*). Regulation V of 1812 annuls the provisions of Regulation
XLIV of 1793, and provides that the renewal of pottahs as prescribed
by Regulation IV, 1794, is no longer necessary, and that the landlord and
tenant are at liberty to come to such agreement as may mutually appear
to them conducive to their respective interests.

(*c*). It will be allowed that the illiterate ryot could never, under the
old rules, have felt his right to perpetual possession confirmed by a deed
which expressly limited his lease to ten years. On the contrary, it is
well known to those who have been at the pains to enquire into the
opinions of the lower orders, that the ryots, in general, have always felt
a solicitude to avoid taking such pottahs, under the impression that
they would, thereby, be compromising their right to unlimited occupancy.

(*d*). They see nothing of the law but what, in the limitation of the
pottahs under Regulation XLIV, 1793, to ten years, militates against
the existence of such a right, and therefore they can have no opportunity
of reconciling the circumstance of limitation with the preservation of
it. Let them go to the Mundul or Pramanick ; he is equally ignorant
with themselves ; or if he has casually heard vague mention of the
favourable clause, being in nine cases out of ten bribed to the interest of
the zemindar, it is not likely that he will be communicative. Let them
go to their putwarry ; he is in the regular pay of the zemindar, and is
removable from office at his pleasure ; from him, therefore, they will
collect nothing favourable. Let them go to the moonsiff ; here they not
unfrequently find as much ignorance as before, and always as much
collusion in favour of the opposite party.

(*e*). Under these circumstances, it may easily be imagined that a ryot
whose lease, granted in pursuance of Regulation XLIV, 1793, for a
period of ten years, had expired in 1803, considering his right to unlimited occupancy to have been destroyed by his having taken a pottah for a

APP. X.
——
POTTAH REGU-
LATION MOCKED
BY THE ZEMIN-
DAR.
——
Para. 7, contd.

limited period, would feel himself, at the end of that period, altogether dependent upon the caprice of his landlord for a renewal of his lease upon any terms. This I know to have been a very general effect of the limitation noticed. Is it to be wondered at that the zemindar should convert this ignorance on the part of the ryot into a means of self-emolument? After the expiration of the decennial pottah, where such pottahs have been granted, the zemindar has, if he found the condition of the land admitted it, very generally enhanced the rate of the former lease, and given the new pottah for a much shorter term than ten years.

IV.—LORD MOIRA (*21st September 1815*).

(*a*). In all these tenures, from what I could observe, the class of village proprietors appeared to be in a train of annihilation; and, unless a remedy is speedily applied, the class will become extinct. Indeed, I fear that any remedy which could be proposed would, even now, come too late to be of any effect in the several estates of Bengal; for the license of twenty years which has been left to the zemindars of that province will have given them the power, and they have never wanted the inclination, to extinguish the rights of this class, so that no remnants of them will soon be discoverable.

(*b*). The cause of this is to be traced to the incorrectness of the principle assumed at the time of the perpetual settlement, when those with whom the Government entered into engagements were declared the sole proprietors of the soil. The under-proprietors were considered to have no rights, except such as might be conferred by pottah; and there was no security for their obtaining these on reasonable terms, except an obviously empty injunction on the zemindar amicably to adjust and consolidate the amount of his claims.

(*c*). The indefeasible right of the cultivating proprietors to a fixed share of the produce was annihilated by our directing that pottahs should be executed for a money payment, in which all the claims of the zemindars should be consolidated. The under-proprietor was thus left to the mercy of the zemindar, to whose demands there were no prescribed limits. The zemindar offered a pottah on his own terms. If the under-proprietor refused it, he was ejected, and the courts supported the ejectment. If the under-proprietor conceived that he could contest at law the procedure, a regular suit, under all the disadvantages to which he is known to be exposed, was his only resource; but when, after years of anxiety and of expense, the case was at last brought to a hearing, he lost his action, because it was proved that the pottah was offered and refused, and there was no criterion to which he could refer as a means of proving that the rate was exorbitant.

(*d*). The omission of the framers of the perpetual settlement to fix any criterion for the adjustment of these disputes, has not been supplied to this day. The consequence of the omission, in the first instance, was a perpetual litigation between the zemindars and the under-proprietors, the former offering pottahs on their own terms, the latter not having forgotten that they possessed rights independent of all pottahs, and

refusing demands they conceived unconscionable. When, at last, the
revenue of Government was affected by the confusion which ensued,
without inquiring into the root of the evil, the Legislature contented
itself with arming those who were under engagements to the Government with additional powers, so as to enable them to realise their
demands in the first instance, whether right or wrong—a procedure
which unavoidably led to extensive and grievous oppression.

(*e.*) On the large estates, I believe, it will be found that the system of
pottah and kabuliut has not yet been fully established between the
zemindars and the cultivating proprietors. The zemindar takes engagements from the farmers and officers he employs to collect his rents, and in
the event of their failure, makes the lands and the crops answerable for
the amount. The zemindar feels none of the evils of insecurity; for, as
far as the whole produce of the soil will go, he is armed by the VIIth
Regulation of 1799 with the power of enforcing his demand; and considering the constitution of our civil courts, it seems unanimously agreed
that the ryot or under-proprietor, unless he be a puttidar, is debarred
any adequate means of redress for the most manifest extortions.

8.—POTTAHS DECLINED BY KHOODKHAST RYOTS.

I.—SIR J. SHORE (*June 1789*).

(*a*). Pottahs to the khoodkasht ryots, or those who cultivate the land
of the village where they reside, are generally given without any limitation of period; and express that they are to hold the lands, paying the
rents for them from year to year. Hence the right of occupancy
originates.

* * The pottahs to *pykhast* ryots are generally granted with a limitation in point of time (*paras. 406-7*).

(*b*). *Chittagong*.[1]—It has never been the custom to grant pottahs to
the fixed jummabundy ryots, who would refuse them on an idea that the
zemindars might then grant pottahs to whom they pleased (and
generally the reports of other collectors testified that pottahs were not
in use).

(*c*). No order of Government should ever be issued unless it can be
enforced; to compel the ryots to take out pottahs where they are already
satisfied with the forms of their tenure, and the usages by which rents
are received, would occasion useless confusion; and to compel the zemindar to grant them under such circumstances, or where the rules of
assessment are not previously ascertained, would in my opinion be
nugatory (*para. 432*).

II.—COLLECTOR OF SAHARUNPORE (*9th January 1816*).

Where established rates exist, they are so far considered binding
upon the good faith of the landholder that pottahs are seldom or never
required or granted.

---

[1] Collector of Chittagong, quoted by Sir John Shore.

App. X. III.—Mr. Sisson (*2nd April 1815*).—*See paragraph 7, section IIc.*

POTTAHS RE-
FUSED BY RYOTS.
Para. 8, contd.
Ibid., page 258.

IV.—Resolution of Government (*22nd December 1820*).

(*a*). The cultivating proprietors naturally resist what they consider an attempt to reduce them from being the co-sharers, to the situation of the under-tenants of their engaging brethren, and to convert a tenure of independent property derived from their ancestors by immemorial succession, into one of modern creation and uncertain stability (*para. 200*). * *

(*b*). Thus, however desirable in itself that all engagements should stipulate the payment of a specific sum of money for a certain quantity or defined tract of land, yet both zemindars and ryots, and more especially the latter, will, in a multitude of cases, strongly object to such a scheme; and former attempts to effect the distribution of pottahs seem very generally to have owed their failure to the endeavour at giving to those instruments a precision inconsistent with the usages of the country, and repugnant to the habits and prejudices of the people. In many cases, too, the objections to fixed money-payments appear to be well founded, the precariousness of the produce and the poverty of the cultivator rendering it necessary that the rent should either be paid in a proportion of the crop, or that the ryots should adopt the less advantageous mode of trusting to an undefined understanding that a part of the stipulated rent will eventually be relinquished (*para. 201*).

V.—Resolution of Government (*1st August 1822*).

In all practicable cases, pottahs shall be granted to each ryot, or at least a distinct register should be prepared, specifying lands held by each, and the conditions attaching to the tenure. The collectors will, of course, understand that, however desirable it is to render the engagement of the cultivator specific, both as to land and rent, it is not intended to force things unnaturally to this issue. In many cases the objections of the ryots themselves to engage permanently to cultivate a given extent of land will probably be found insuperable, and in such cases it may not be practicable to do more than to prepare a general schedule specifying the rates and conditions on which the land is to be cultivated (*paras. 214 to 216*).

VI.—Sir J. Shore (*28th June 1789*) (*quoting the Collector of Behar*).

Harington's
Analysis of the
Regulations,
pages 256-57.

(*a*). My difficulties have originated with the ryots, who, in this part of the country, have an insuperable aversion to receive pottahs or execute cabuliuts, for specific quantities of land. The origin of this aversion is two-fold, *viz.*, partly an apprehension lest, from the disease or loss of their cattle, kinsmen or servants (by which term I mean particularly to allude to *cummeas* or ploughmen), they should be unable to bring the

whole specified quantity into cultivation; and partly a dread lest, after
having brought it into cultivation, the expected crop should be damaged
or destroyed by drought, storms, or inundation. Of the 45 pergunnahs
(including the jageers) which compose this district, there is not one in
which I have not spoken with the ryots of several villages on this
subject, and heard the same objection from all. It is not therefore from
report, but from personal knowledge, that I state their sentiments. I
well remember that, on my observing to a head ryot belonging to a
village not far from the jageer of the Nawab Delawur Jung "that the
ryots refusing to enter into counter engagements was hard upon the
zemindars, as it prevented these last from estimating with precision the
value of their lands; the man replied: "We ryots are sensible of this;
but as we are poor and the maliks rich, and as they have many other
advantages over us; it is but just that in this respect they should be
bound, while we in some measure remain free;" adding, "if you will
examine into the state of the Nawab's jageer, you will see the bad effects
of endeavouring to oblige the ryots to receive pottahs specifying the
quantity of ground they are to pay rent for." As the reply fixed my
attention, I immediately made further enquiry, and found that the assertion was literally true, a number of ryots having actually left the jageer
in consequence of the Nawab's manager having strongly urged them to
receive pottahs specifying the quantity of ground to be rented by them.
Yet Hajee Jakoot Khan, the Nawab's manager, is a very liberal and
enlightened man, and appears to have had no object in view but the prevention of chicane and the further security both of the landholders and
the ryots.

(*b*). In consequence of this reluctance on the part of the ryots to
enter into specific engagements, the following mode is pretty generally
adopted in this part of the country. The zemindar signs and deposits
in each village a voucher (which is, though somewhat improperly, called
a pottah) specifying the rates and terms on which ryots may cultivate
land in that village. This voucher serves the ryots as a guide. If they
approve of the rates, they take attested copies of the instrument and
cultivate as much ground as they can, though, for the reasons above
specified, they will not engage for a certain number of beegahs. When
the crop is ripe, the land is measured, and the ryot or tenant pays the rent
thereof to the zemindar, according to the rates specified in the general
village pottah. But in adjusting the accounts it is always understood,
though not, indeed, expressed in writing, that the ryot is only to pay
in proportion to the produce; and that in the event of his crop having
failed or being damaged, he is to receive a proportional deduction according to the rates expressed in the village pottah; and this indulgence it is
which chiefly renders the ryots so unwilling to engage to pay rent for
specific quantities of ground, lest, if they did, they should be considered
as obliged to pay rent for the whole, even though they might not have
been able to bring it into cultivation. It is also understood that the
ryot has a sort of prescriptive right to continue in the ground thus
occupied by him, while he adheres to the rates expressed in the village
pottahs, insomuch that I do not recollect an instance of a zemindar's
having attempted to remove a ryot who has not been guilty of a breach
thereof.

APP. X.

POTTAHS
REFUSED BY
RYOTS.

Para. 8, contd.
3rd Report,
Select Com-
mittee, 1831-32,
Questions 3924
to 3926.

VII.—MR. J. MILL (*19th August 1831*).

In the permanent settlement by Lord Cornwallis, it was one of the essential points that the ryots should all have leases or pottahs; but it was considered to be impracticable, and the regulation has remained a dead letter. Pottahs were directed to be given, and some attempts were made to have the thing done; but it never was done, except partially, and in very few instances. Difficulties and objections were alleged; both the zemindars and the ryots disliked them.

VIII.—MR. T. FORTESCUE (*12th April 1832*).

Sess. 1831-32,
Vol. XI,
Question 2304.

Attempts have been made to force the zemindars to grant leases or pottahs, but they have not generally succeeded. The ryot as well as the zemindar has objections; the former have always opposed themselves to recognise any person in the character of proprietor, which they consider themselves to be: besides, by binding themselves by such a deed, they might be ruined by untoward events beyond their reach, although they do not object to pay the demand of Government.

IX.—MR. A. D. CAMPBELL (*1832*).

Ibid., App. 6,
page 15.

In merely prescribing the interchange of written engagements between the zemindars and the cultivators, the Government required the whole body of the latter to enter into engagements previously confined only to the lowest class amongst them, or to such as possessed no hereditary right of occupancy in the soil; and great repugnance to this arrangement has naturally been evinced by the hereditary or great mass of the cultivators under both the Presidencies. But when such engagements were required to be exchanged in Bengal, according to local rates and usages, which have been left undefined, without any measures being taken by Government for ascertaining or recording them, for the mutual guidance of both the hereditary payers and hereditary receivers of the land revenue, the enactment became a mere nullity.

X.—BENGAL BRITISH INDIA ASSOCIATION (*14th February 1859*).

Fifteen-sixteenths of the tenures in Bengal are at present held without the interchange of pottahs and kabuliuts.

9. Thus the safeguard of pottahs, in ignorant, credulous reliance on which the permanent settlement was concluded in hot haste, proved nugatory.

I.—LAW AND CONSTITUTION OF INDIA.

Page 166.

(*a*). Neither the zemindar nor the ryot is willing to grant or receive pottahs; the former, that he may exact the utmost; and the latter, that he may not be bound beyond what he may be able to perform; both

proceeding from the same cause, that want of good faith which is
universal, and seemingly the legitimate offspring of the ill-defined
situation in which the parties are unhappily placed.

(*b*). The inconsistency, however, of an enactment not to increase the
rents of an estate with a declaration of a proprietary right, is obvious
enough.   But having bestowed the absolute property of the soil, absolute
power over it naturally followed, if it did not accompany, the grant ;
and to attempt to control the effects of this by a legislative order,
displayed in no small degree a want of knowledge of the science of
government and of mankind, which the best of men are often most
void of.   Thus, with every desire to do good, did Lord Cornwallis
humanely commit the most manifest injustice.

(*c*). An intelligent person, speaking of the zillah of Juanpore in 1819
on this subject, writes as follows :   " The fact is, that though the settlement which Government made with the zemindars is unchangeable, and
though these persons have no right to raise the rents upon tenants who
live on the soil, or to oust them while they pay their rents regularly ;
and although there is, *at the very least,* one-third more land in cultivation
now than at the time of the permanent settlement, the rent of land
has risen *three-fold,* and no zemindar will accept of rent in kind (that
is, half the produce) who can by any means, fair and unfair, get his
rent in cash.   The zemindar has various means of evading the right
of the resident tenant to hold his land at a fixed rate, independent of
his power, by the regulations, to oust on failure of regular payment of
rent, of which they seldom fail to avail themselves.   Should a zemindary be sold by Government for arrears of revenue, all leases become
void (by the regulations) ; and a very improvable estate is frequently
thrown in arrears to Government that it may be sold to void the leases,
and purchased by the owner.   Except for this purpose, from disputes
among joint proprietors, and from intrigues in various departments,
I believe estates are seldom sold.

" Now from three to four rupees are given per beegah for land to
cultivate indigo ; formerly, one rupee ten annas to two rupees eight annas
was the usual value.   On an average, it may be fairly stated that, of the
land held by resident tenants on lease, by Brahmins and Rajpoots, seven-
tenths have risen from ten annas per beegah to one rupee eight annas,
and of the lands held by the lower class of cultivators, half has risen
from one rupee to two rupees eight annas, one-fourth from one rupee
eight annas to four rupees, and one-fourth from two to five rupees.
With such an inducement to oust the ancient tenants, it is not to be
wondered at, though every landholder should exert himself to do so," &c.

II.—MR. J. N. HALHED.

(*a*). As the proportion of produce (or the amount in money for which
it was commutable) which each individual was liable to be called on to
contribute, through the malguzar, as land tax to the State, was, in all
well cultivated districts, defined and understood, under the native
regimé, the amount of land and species of crop cultivated being ascertained, the assessment upon each *raeeut* was easily made by the malguzars ; and the only points upon which the parties were likely to be at

APP. X.

SAFEGUARD OF
POTTAHS NUGA-
TORY.

Para. 9, contd.

issue were a failure on the part of the *raeeut* to cultivate in due proportion those crops which paid the highest rates to the malguzar, and the levy of the *abwabs;* but as such demands were unsanctioned by the then existing law, and could not consequently be enforced through its means, the consolidation of these items with the *ussul*, or legal prescriptive assessment, and the specification of the amount in the pottahs, was, in the opinion of the *raeeuts*, equivalent to an enhancement of the ancient rates, and their acceptance of such pottahs would have been an acquiescence in the right of the malguzars to levy further impositions, and to raise the rents at pleasure—a right which they were not prepared to admit, and the direct enforcement of which they would, in all probability, have resisted. As it was, for some time, optional with the ryots to accept or decline the new pottahs, they availed themselves of the latter alternative, in order to evade the concession of their privileges, which humiliation the Code demanded of them as the price of its protection.

Page 113.

(*b*). The *raeeuts* opposed the pottah system, because they considered that by acceding to it, they would have become accessories to their own ruin; as in so doing they would record their concession of their allodal rights, whereas, under a contrary course, by declining to accept these leases they evaded the claims of the new proprietors to revenue; for (section 6, Regulation VIII, 1793) "they were not cognizable under the Code, unless a lease, and its counterpart, had been *interchanged*." This was met by an enactment (section 5, Regulation IV, 1794) declaring "a public notification by the proprietor, that pottahs at the established rates were ready for delivery, to be a sufficient and legal tender to the *raeeuts*, authorising the former to receive from the latter, by process or distraint, or by action at law, the rents at the rates specified in the said pottah." The *raeeuts*, from henceforward, were by the law degraded from the rank of actual proprietors to that of tenants on sufferance.

Page 102.

(*c*). It had been in the first instance declared that regulations for the protection and welfare of the *raeeuts* and other cultivators would be enacted; but none have ever been effectually passed, restoring them to any of their rights; even the single stipulation (VIII, 1793, cl. 2, section 60,—LI, 1795, section 10) most in their favour, which was intended to prevent the zemindars from raising the rents of khoodkasht ryots, was so worded that it gave every zemindar the means of enhancing his demands at pleasure; since, to entitle the *raeeut* to the benefits of the provision set forth in the clause in question, it was necessary, in the first place, that he should have accepted a lease or pottah, and as in so doing he would have acknowledged a feudal over-lord in the person of the zemindar, he was naturally averse to become a party to the annihilation of his rights.

10. The uncertainty in which the authors of the permanent settlement were content to leave the liabilities of the ryot, ended in the destruction of his rights. This result was brought about, although Sir John Shore and Lord Cornwallis had distinctly laid down that the amount payable by the ryot should be recorded. The former observed (3rd Decem-

APP. X.

OTHER MORE
EFFECTUAL
MEANS OF PRO-
TECTING THE
RYOTS WERE
NEGLECTED OR
DESTROYED BY
GOVERNMENT.

Para. 11.

ber 1789, paragraph 19) : " On the other hand, the necessity of prescribing regulations for simplifying the complicated rentals of the ryots (which ought, if possible, to be reduced to one sum for a given quantity of land, of a determinate quality and produce), of defining and establishing the rights of the ryots and talukdars with precision, together with the expediency of procuring clear data for the transfer by sale of public and private property, are admitted." Lord Cornwallis' determination that the amount of the ryots' rent should be clearly expressed, was even more explicitly stated (paragraph 6, section I of this Appendix). Even this provision for stating the amount payable by the resident cultivator, derogated from his rights, because they included his privilege of paying assessment on only the actual produce of the year, and his option of paying the established proportion of the produce in kind instead of in money. Still, a statement of the amount of the ryot's rent, even though it would have set aside this privilege and this option, would have afforded a substantial protection to the ryot; it would at least have secured him from an increase of his rent consequent on a rise of prices since 1793.

11. The Court of Directors, in their Revenue letter to Bengal, dated 15th January 1819, paragraphs 44 to 46, summed up as follows :—

I. We are on this occasion naturally led to notice what is stated by you on the subject of the regulations passed in 1793 concerning pottahs, and of those subsequently enacted.

II. With respect to Regulation VIII of 1793, we have to observe that more seems to have been expected from its enactments in favour of the ryots than they were calculated to effect, unsupported by other institutions, and that it was in fact almost wholly nugatory. By section 2, Regulation XLIV of 1793, it was enacted that no lease should be granted for a period of more than 10 years, and that no lease should be renewed except in the last year of its term ; and every lease granted in opposition to that prohibition was declared null and void. By another section of the same Regulation it was provided that whenever lands are sold by public sale for arrears of the public revenue, all engagements with under-farmers and ryots, as well as with dependent talukdars, should stand cancelled from the day of sale, the purchasers being left at liberty to collect from the talukdars, ryots, or cultivators, according to the rates and usages of the pergunnah (which rates and usages were left unascertained) as if the engagements so cancelled had never existed; and the operation of the foregoing rule was extended, by Regulation III of 1796, to the entire annulment of leases of lands, of which a part only might be sold for the recovery of arrears of revenue. The primary and, indeed, sole object of Regulation XLIV of 1793 evidently was to guard against a permanent diminution of the public revenue under the settlements that had been concluded

APP. X.
——
OTHER MORE
EFFECTUAL
MEANS OF PRO-
TECTING THE
RYOTS WERE
NEGLECTED OR
DESTROYED BY
GOVERNMENT.
——
Para. 11, contd.

with the zemindars, by which a permanent limitation had been set to the demands of Government upon them; and it was still further to guard against such a consequence that the modifications it underwent by Regulation III of 1796 were adopted. When we bear in mind the fact stated by Mr. Roche in his minute recorded on your Revenue Consultations of the 12th August 1815, that subsequently to the period of the permanent settlement "probably one-third, or rather one-half, of the landed property in the province of Bengal may have been transferred by public sale *on account of arrears of revenue*," we can readily perceive how prodigiously numerous must have been the instances in which engagements between zemindars and ryots were annulled.

III. The original Pottah Regulation (VIII of 1793) was also very materially defective, in making no sufficient provision for the ascertainment of the rights in which it professed to secure the ryots by their pottahs. It was of much more importance, for the security of the ryot, to establish what the legitimate rates of the pergunnah were, according to the customs of the country, or at all events to have ascertained the rates actually existing, and to have caused a record of them, in either case, to be carefully preserved, than merely to enjoin the exchange of engagements between them and the zemindars, leaving in total uncertainty the rules by which those engagements were to be formed. It is true that to have taken the rates at which the ryots were actually assessed by the zemindars, at the period of the permanent settlement, as the maximum of future demands, would have had the effect, as Mr. Shore observed in one of his minutes, of confirming subsisting abuses and oppressions; but it would, at least, have fixed a limit to them. The necessary information respecting these rates might, in a great measure, have been found in the registers of the canoongoes, had that office been maintained in its original state of efficiency. But the canoongoes' office had been most unfortunately abolished in the Lower Provinces when the permanent settlement was introduced, instead of being reformed and brought back to the purposes of its institution; and the putwarries, whose accounts were of the utmost importance in all cases of disputed claims between zemindars and their tenants, and between renters and ryots, having, at the same time, been virtually made the servants of the zemindars, naturally became averse to produce any documentary proof of exactions levied by their employers, and little credit was due to their accounts when produced. The consequence was, that the only safeguards left for the ryots were the pottah regulation and the courts of justice. That regulation must have been very inadequate to protect their interest against further encroachments, even had it been generally acted upon; but its originally imperfect construction, together with the modifications and restrictions which it afterwards underwent, indisposed the ryots to comply with its provisions; and the courts of justice could not avail much in cases of dispute where there were no data on which to decide, even if they had in other respects been competent to settle questions of that nature.

IV. But what appears to have had a more sensible operation in the depression of the ryots than perhaps any other cause, was the power vested by Regulation VII of 1799 in zemindars, talookdars, and other landholders and farmers of land, of distraining for rent.

APP. X.
——
OTHER MORE
EFFECTUAL
MEANS OF PRO-
TECTING THE
RYOTS WERE
NEGLECTED OR
DESTROYED BY
GOVERNMENT.

Para. 11, contd.

V. The representations which were made by some of the most intelligent of the judicial and revenue functionaries, within a very few years after the passing of that regulation, and which were generally made in the course of 1809 and the two following years, of the enormous exactions and oppressions which were practised under the last mentioned Regulation, led, in 1812, to a revision of the existing rules respecting pottahs and other engagements between landholders and their tenants, as well as respecting distress and other summary modes allowed to the zemindars for enforcing payment of their demands ; and Regulation V of 1812, which was subsequently explained by Regulation XVIII of that year, was passed for amending some of the rules then in force for the collection of the land revenue.

VI. Mr. Colebrooke, on whose suggestions Regulation V of 1812 appears chiefly to have been framed, after stating that " there is actually no sufficient evidence of the rates and usages of pergunnahs which can now be appealed to for the decision of the questions between landholder and ryot," and consequently no definite rules for the guidance of courts of justice, expressed himself in the following terms :—

(*a*). " In this state of matters, it would be better to abrogate most of the laws in favour of the ryot, and leave him for a certain period, to be specified, under no other protection for his tenure than the specific terms of the lease which he may then hold, than to uphold the illusory expectation of protection under laws which are nearly ineffectual.

(*b*). " The parties would be thus compelled to come to an understanding, and the result would on every consideration be preferable to the present state of uncertainty, which naturally leads to oppression, fraud, and endless litigation." It was avowedly with much reluctance that Mr. Colebrooke suggested the adoption of this alternative, for he immediately added : " If it be thought expedient, in place of abrogating the laws which were enacted for the protection of the tenantry, and especially of the khoodkasht ryot, or resident cultivator, that the right of occupancy which these laws were intended to uphold, should be still maintained, and that the ryot should be supported in his ancient and undoubted privilege of retaining the ground occupied by him so long as he pays the rent justly demandable from it, measures should be adopted, late as it now is, to reduce to writing a clear declaration and distinct record of the usages and rates according to which the ryots of each pergunnah or district will be entitled to demand the renewal of their pottahs, upon any occasion of general or partial cancelling of leases."

(*c*). He added : " I had it at one time under consideration to propose a plan for the preparation of such records, under the superintendence of the revenue officers, assisted by the canoongoe office, to be re-established for that and for other purposes, and in communication and concert with the zemindars and principal ryots of each pergunnah, and I had made a considerable progress towards maturing the plan of this great undertaking, but after much consultation with the Acting President of the Board of Revenue (Mr. Crisp), and with other experienced and well informed officers of the Revenue Department, I have been diverted from this project by the apprehension that the intelligence and activity requisite for the due superintendence of its execution within each zillah are not to

App. X.

Other more
effectual
means of pro-
tecting the
ryots were
neglected or
destroyed by
Government.

Para. 11, contd.

be universally and generally expected, and that if it were ill-performed, it might, not improbably add to the subsisting evils instead of remedying them."

VII. The same considerations which had induced Mr. Colebrooke to abandon the measure alluded to in the passage last quoted (which measure, nevertheless, he afterwards, as appears from his minute of the 30th April 1815, felt the great expediency of pursuing), probably influenced the decision of the late Government, and Regulation V of 1812 was framed in consonance with Mr. Colebrooke's first suggestion.

VIII. It had been urged, at the time of passing that regulation, that although the rights of the cultivating classes had been most materially violated, yet as the zemindars and the ryots had reciprocal wants, their mutual necessities must drive them to an amicable adjustment. Upon this doctrine it is well observed by Lord Hastings that "this reciprocity is not, however, so clear," &c. &c.[1]

IX. It always appeared to us that the provisions of Regulation V of 1812 would operate as a very imperfect correction of the evils which it was intended to remedy, and this we expressed in our despatches of 28th October and 9th November 1814 and 6th January 1815. Subsequent information has not only confirmed us in the opinions which we from the first entertained, but has satisfied us that, in practice, the regulation has been the very reverse of beneficial. In Mr. Sisson's letter of the 2nd April 1815, to which we have already referred, it is stated to have produced the *most injurious consequences.* The zemindars of Rungpore are represented by him as *perverting its provisions to the entailment in perpetuity upon their wretched victims, the peasantry* (by which he means he actual occupants of the land), *of a long series of exactions,* of which he gives some most striking specimens. Section 2, Regulation XVIII of 1812, runs thus : "Doubts having arisen on the construction of section 2, Regulation XVIII of 1812, it is hereby explained, that the true intent of the said section was to declare proprietors of land *competent* to grant leases for any period, even to perpetuity, and at any rent which they might deem conducive to their interests," &c. This provision has been construed to give to zemindars the power of demanding from the ryots *any rent* they might think proper, without regard to the customary rates of assessment in the pergunnah. The inference seems unavoidable that the persons with whom the permanent settlement was made, and those who, by inheritance or purchase, may succeed them, are authorised by the existing law to oust even the hereditary ryots from possession of their lands, when the latter refuse to accede to any terms of rent which may be demanded of them, however exorbitant.

X. In the consideration of this subject it is impossible for us not to remark that consequences the most injurious to the rights and interests of individuals, have arisen from describing those with whom the permanent settlement was concluded as the *actual proprietors of the land.* This mistake (for such it is now admitted to have been), and the habit which has grown out of it, of considering the payments of the ryots as rent instead of revenue, have produced all the evils that might be expected to flow from them. They have introduced much confusion into the whole subject of landed tenures, and have given a specious colour to the pretensions of the zemindars, in acting towards persons of the other classes

---

[1] See the passage as quoted in paragraph 6. section I.

as if they, the zemindars, really were, in the ordinary sense of the words, the proprietors of the land, and as if the ryots had no permanent interest but what they derived from them.

APP. X.

———

OTHER MORE
EFFECTUAL
MEANS OF PRO-
TECTING THE
RYOTS WERE
NEGLECTED OR
DESTROYED BY
GOVERNMENT.

———

Para. 12.

12. The review was continued as follows :—

I.—BENGAL GOVERNMENT'S REVENUE LETTER (*1st August 1822*).

(*a*). We have derived much satisfaction from the full explanation which you have afforded us in these paragraphs of the sentiments entertained by you on the important subject of the adjustment of the rates of rent payable by the ryots. In general, those sentiments concur entirely in the views by which we have ourselves been guided. As to the partial operation of the laws applicable to the Lower Provinces, it must, we imagine, be generally admitted that they have been unfavourable to the interests of the inferior classes of the tenantry. But it is, nevertheless, important to observe that the uniform design of the Legislature has been very different, and that there is nothing in the laws, when duly considered, calculated in the slightest degree to bar the Government from the adoption of such measures as it may see fit to adopt, with the view of securing the ryots.

(*b*). [Here followed a paragraph respecting the right of Government, even in 1822, to order a settlement for the adjudication and record of ryots' rights, which rights, by a custom more ancient than law, limited the rights of Government. The paragraph is quoted in Appendix IV, para. 10, section IV *a*.]

(*c*). We freely, indeed, admit that, even though the ryots of Bengal had possessed no right of holding their lands at determinate rates, considered in their relation to the sovereign, it was unquestionably competent to the Government, in fixing its own demands, to fix also the rates at which the malguzar was to make his collections; and it was, we think, clearly intended to render perpetual the rates existing at the time of the perpetual settlement. The intention being declared, the rule is of course obligatory on the zemindars. * *

(*d*). We are not insensible to the disadvantages of fixing rates, though the perpetual adjustment of them might still of course leave rents to vary; but our conviction certainly is, that the custom of the country gives to the ryots rights limiting the right of Government, and that the rights so possessed could not be set aside by the supreme authority without the imputation of injustice. * *

II.—REVENUE LETTER TO BENGAL—*10th November 1824* (COURT'S REPLY TO PRECEDING).

(*a*). You consider that there is nothing in the law, that is, in any rights which you may have exerted in favour of the zemindars, "to bar the Government from such measures as it may see fit to adopt with the view of securing the ryots." * *

(*b*). It is in the highest degree important that your design of adjusting the rights and interests of the ryots in the villages, as perfectly in the

APP. X.

OTHER MORE
EFFECTUAL
MEANS OF PRO-
TECTING THE
RYOTS WERE
NEGLECTED OR
DESTROYED BY
GOVERNMENT.

Para. 12, contd.

Lower as in the Upper Provinces, should be carried into effect. The doubts which we have expressed with respect to the sufficiency of the collector's agency will receive from you a due degree of attention. * * Should you succeed in securing to the ryots those rights which it was assuredly the intention of the permanent settlement arrangements to preserve and maintain ; and should you, in all cases where the nature and extent of those rights cannot now be satisfactorily ascertained and fixed, provide such a limit to the demand upon the ryots as fully to leave them the cultivators' profits, under leases of considerable length, we should hope the interests of that great body of the agricultural community may be satisfactorily secured.

13. It appears from this appendix that—

I. In 1769 the Bengal Government made an earnest appeal to the ryot to confide in his Collector, who would stand between him and the hand of oppression, be his refuge and the redresser of his wrongs, secure him from further invasions of his property, and teach him a veneration and affection for the humane maxims of the Government.

II. Later, the Government, at various times, repeated assurances like the following :—

(*a*). The welfare of the ryot ought to be the immediate and primary care of Government (*Warren Hastings, 1776*).

(*b*). Under the permanent settlement, the great body of the ryots were to be secured the same equity and certainty as to the amount of their rents, and the same undisturbed enjoyment of the fruits of their industry, as were to be given by that settlement to the zemindars (*Sir John Shore*).

(*c*). The ryots had vested rights in the land, and the annulment of those rights would be the most extensive act of confiscation that ever was perpetrated in any country. "So long as the rights of the inferior classes of the agricultural population shall remain unprotected, the British Government must be considered *to have fulfilled very imperfectly the obligations* which it owes to its subjects" (*Court of Directors, 9th May 1821*).

(*d*). The State's share of the produce, out of which was provided the zemindar's, was fixed by a custom more ancient than law, and all the rest of the produce belongs to the ryot. "The faith of the State is to the full as solemnly pledged to uphold the cultivator of the soil in the unmolested enjoyment of his long-established rights, as it is to maintain the zemindar in the possession of his estate, or to abstain from increasing the public revenue permanently assessed upon him" (*Court of Directors, 15th January 1819*).

(*e*). Protection of the ryots in their rights, and security from arbitrary exactions, formed, in principle at least, a part of the permanent settlement, and they are " the foundation, as it were, on which your revenue and judicial system professed to be built" (*Court of Directors, 9th May 1821*).

III. With these convictions of the Government's obligations and duty towards the ryots, the Court of Directors reserved their right as sovereigns to intervene from time to time, as may be necessary, for saving the ryot from exactions, and from being dispossessed of the land he occupied.

IV. But these professions and convictions of the Government were unavailing, because the Government declared a policy of non-intervention, in pursuing which it destroyed some effectual means of protecting the ryots, and in conceiving which it relied in credulity and ignorance, on the efficacy of pottahs which it was persuaded that the zemindars would grant, and which, indeed, the Government soon persuaded itself that the zemindars had granted, to the ryots, whereas, the zemindars turned their obligation to grant pottahs into an engine of oppression, while the ryots refused pottahs as the instrument of their subjection, in bondage, to zemindars.

V. As a natural consequence, the ryot's rights were destroyed; they passed away *sub silentio;* and, then, the Court of Directors, in viewing the wreck, recorded (as if exclaiming " Alas! poor Yorick!") that the ryots, and not the zemindars, were the *actual proprietors of the land ;* the Court passed no orders upon a suggestion by Mr. Colebrooke in 1815, that even at that late hour, " measures should be taken for the re-establishment of fixed rates, as nearly conformable to the anciently established ones as may be yet practicable, to regulate distinctly and definitely the relative rights of the landlord and tenantry." But later, in 1824, they approved of one of the numerous infructuous good intentions which Governments of former days devoted to the ryots in return for a confiscation of their proprietary rights, *viz.*, that by a detailed survey and settlement, similar to that in the North-Western Provinces, the rights of ryots should be recorded, and their rates of assessment permanently fixed. Had that order been carried out, ryots' rents would have been permanently settled before the great rise of prices which has issued in constant enhancements of rent.

VI. It was intended that, as a part of the permanent settlement, the pottahs which the zemindars were to give to the " great body of the ryots" should show " in one sum, for a given quantity of land, of determinate quality and produce,"

17

App. X.
——
Summary.
——
Para. 13, contd.
the amount which each ryot was to pay, " and that no ryot shall be liable to pay more than the sum actually specified in his pottah." This was tantamount to fixing a permanent assessment for each ryot, which was not liable to be increased from any subsequent rise of prices; and hence it may be assumed, even did pottahs not exist, that the rates of rent in the present day, for the class of ryots whom pottahs should have protected, ought to be fixed irrespective of the great rise of prices since 1848.

APPENDIX XI.

ZEMINDARS AND RYOTS FROM 1793 TO 1859.

1. Evidence of the failure of the permanent settlement in one of its principal objects, *viz.*, the protection and security of cultivators, has been set forth in Appendix IV under the two divisions of the oppressive rule of the old race of zemindars down to 1858, and of the consequent wretched condition of the ryots. The exactions and oppressions by the earlier zemindars have been noticed more minutely in Appendix VII, and the destruction of ryots' rights in Appendix X. Further detail will now be supplied of the ways in which the ryot's right was destroyed. The highest authorities declared that right to be the greatest right in the country, and its preservation to be the bounden duty and paramount obligation of Government, if the zemindary settlement, which was to redound to the glory and honour of England, was not to be branded as an unparalleled confiscation of the rights of millions of proprietors.

2. The history of that settlement is a sad record of the confusion and discord between right, law, and fact;—of the confusion between right and law, from the almost exclusive concern of the latter for the Government's right to revenue, and its too general forgetfulness of the ryot's right to the soil, and (where right and law harmonised) of the discord between them and fact; the zemindars of past generations, and many of them to this day, turning into fresh instruments of oppression laws which from time to time have been designed for the protection of the ryots.

3. It is a strange spectacle!—the most law-abiding people on the earth are the British conquerors of India. The greatest contemners of the law, and deriders of its equities, have been a comparatively few, and, among them, mostly half-educated men belonging to the subject race, in a province which for centuries has accepted foreign domination, and which, were English rule to be withdrawn, would accept some other, as it accepted the Mahomedan before the British rule. As yet, the zemindary settlement has only pointed this curious satire on national independence; where a few, and those not generally the worthiest of the conquered, bend to their

App. XI.

—

THE WAYS IN
WHICH RYOTS'
RIGHTS HAVE
BEEN DE-
STROYED.

—

Para. 3, contd.

own uses the laws, and so stultify the purposes of the conquerors; enjoying, thus, a greater liberty of license than they could dream of, or dare to indulge in, if they were not of a conquered race.

4. As in the discussions before 1793, relating to the permanent settlement, and in the Regulations of that year, so in the subsequent correspondence between the Court of Directors and the authorities in Bengal, the literature of those legislators and administrators is replete with admirable sentiments of justice, veneration of right, philanthropy, benevolence, and mercy to the poor. These, however, furnished only the embellishments of the history of the zemindary settlement from 1793 to 1857; the actual history was made, and its repulsive facts were supplied, by the lawlessness of zemindars, who corrupted and controlled the police, corrupted the underlings in civil and criminal courts, in days when, judges being few, evidence was recorded, not by the presiding officer, but by mohurirs in corners of a crowded court-room, and in a country where the suitor needs, or needed, to bestow on the execution of a decree as much anxiety and careful watching as during the progress of his suit.

5. The history is exciting, with its incidents of crime, dacoity, violence, forgery, and perjury; but its tragedy is revolting, for those incidents brought ryots into predial bondage to zemindars; and ryots could not help themselves when required, at the zemindar's bidding, to pay enhanced rents, with or without agreement, and, so, to destroy their ancient rights, even if by a miracle they had preserved proofs of those rights. After sixty years of this disorder,—this tyranny of might over right,—Act X of 1859 laid down rules for the enhancement of rent, as if that period had been one of peaceful calm in which the zemindars had abstained from increasing rents, except in accordance with established custom, and as if the ryots had carefully preserved documentary proofs of privileges, and been free to refuse more than the customary rents.

6. Custom and law may have been ever so clear about the ryot's right, but their testimony was useless so long as a weak, corrupt police could not prevent his ejectment from his land by a powerful zemindar. This power of the zemindar would deter the ryot from even the semblance of resistance, and make him sign anything, agree to anything. If the police was known to be in the zemindar's pay; if dacoits were harboured or protected by him; if the village chowkidars, who were known to be dacoits, were

those who collected the zemindar's rents ; if the zemindar kept bands of clubmen ; and if violent or fraudulent evictions of some ryots, with destruction of their property, and with worse treatment of them, were practised with impunity, the thousands of other ryots who witnessed these things, and who felt the hopelessness of kicking against the pricks, were, perforce, cowed into subjection. We may give precedence, therefore, to evidence respecting the state of the police.

.7.—POLICE.

I.—MINUTE OF THE GOVERNOR-GENERAL, *7th December 1792.*

(*a*). With respect to the landholders, some of the principal of them in Bengal (the zemindars of Burdwan, Nuddea, and others) have been allowed considerable deductions in the adjustments of their jumma for the maintenance of thannadars and pykes, for the express purpose of enabling them to perform the condition of keeping the peace, annexed to their tenures. This condition may appear, at first sight, to promise general security ; but experience has proved the fallacy of delegating to individuals one of the most important duties of Government.

(*b*). Of the zemindars who have been allowed the above-mentioned deductions, some keep up no establishments whatever, whilst others, instead of entertaining creditable persons, and allowing them an adequate salary, dispose of the employments for pecuniary considerations. As the offices afford no source of emolument but such as are derived from the most iniquitous practices, it can answer to none but professed robbers to purchase them ; most of the thannadars appointed by the zemindars are, accordingly, persons of this description. The annexed proceedings of the late Acting Magistrate of Burdwan (the principal zemindary in Bengal) will show that the police appointments were sold by the zemindars' officers to the most notorious robbers, who plundered the country which it was their duty to protect. The same abuses prevail, in a greater or less degree, in every zemindary the proprietor of which is allowed to keep up a similar establishment.

(*c*). In some parts of the country, particularly in the eastern and the southern districts of Bengal, many of the petty landholders, encouraged by the great distance of the magistrate's place of residence, and by there being no officers stationed on the spot, on the part of Government, for the protection of the country, have, from time immemorial, been in the habit of perpetrating robberies themselves, or conniving at them in others. It is, indeed, notorious that most of the principal gangs of robbers are in league with some of the zemindars, and generally with those in whose districts they leave their families and deposit their plunder.

(*d*). To exonerate the zemindars from all responsibility would be improper. The condition annexed to their tenure may be converted to the most beneficial purposes in aid of an established police, by limiting the operation of it to cases in which they may be proved to have connived at robberies, harboured robbers, aided their escape, received any part of property stolen, or omitted to give effectual aid to the officers of Government in the apprehension of offenders.

II.—GOVERNOR-GENERAL, TO GOVERNOR IN COUNCIL, MADRAS—*31st December 1799 (respecting a permanent zemindary settlement of the Madras Presidency).*

(*a*). Independent of these important considerations, to abandon the charge of the police of the country to the landholders must always give rise to the most flagrant abuses. In the inquiries which preceded the resumption of this charge from the landholders in Bengal, it was established that the offices of police were held chiefly by the most notorious robbers, who paid large sums of money to the zemindars or to their officers and dependants for these situations, the possession of which enabled them to carry on their depredations with impunity.

(*b*). The arrangement suggested will not prevent your Lordship in Council from deriving every assistance from the landholders in maintaining the peace of the country, in their individual capacity of proprietors of estates; on the contrary, a clause should be inserted in their engagements, binding them to convey to the magistrates or to their officers the earliest information of every circumstance affecting the good order of the country; and they should be subjected to punishment, extending in certain cases of enormity to the forfeiture of their estates, if it should appear that they had connived at robberies, or protected robbers or other disturbers of the public peace.

(*c*). The magistrates, and the officers acting under them, should possess the most absolute control over all the village watchmen of every description. At the same time, these village watchmen should be carefully secured in the lands, fees, and allowances of which they are stated, in the 571st paragraph of the Report of the Board of Revenue, to be in the enjoyment, so as to render their services efficient to the original purposes of their institution.

III.—MR. W. B. BAYLEY, *Secretary to the Government of Bengal* (*16th April 1832*).

Parl Papers,
Sess. 1831-32,
Vol. 12.

(*a*). The police jurisdictions under darogahs were originally intended to include spaces of about 20 square miles, but they are of greater or less extent, as circumstances require. There are from 15 to 20 thannas or darogahs' stations in a zillah, the total number being in the Lower Provinces near 500, and in the western near 400. At each station under the darogah are a mohurir, or writer, and a jemadar, with from 20 to 50 burkundazes, peons, or irregular soldiers.

(*b*). It is not to be understood that the whole business of the police is performed by these establishments. The zemindars or their agents, or other local officers under them, are required to give immediate information at principal police stations of all crimes committed within their limits; and the duty of tracing and apprehending criminals is chiefly performed by the village officers or servants, under the occasional direction or supervision of some person from the thanna.

(c). The darogahs report their proceedings regularly to the magistrate, and receive orders from him. Their principal duties are to receive criminal charges, to hold inquests, to forward accused persons, with their prosecutors and witnesses, to the magistrate, and, generally, to perform such acts as the regulations prescribe with a view to the discovery, apprehension, and ultimate trial of offenders.

These extracts show that the poorly-paid darogahs were sufficiently few to be kept in the secret pay of zemindars; also that their duty was not to stir until crime was reported to them; and that the duty of reporting crime appertained to the village chowkidars, who collected revenue for zemindars. The following extracts from the report of the Police Committee[1] of 1837 show the character of the village police and of police darogahs :—

IV. (a). We now come to the most important subject connected with the police of Bengal, namely, the state of the chowkidari establishments. In some districts, their numerical strength appears to be very great; yet they are utterly inefficient, and have been described in the most unfavourable terms. Mr. W. T. Holborn, Judge of Zillah Cuttack, in his letter already referred to, observes: "That, from the total absence of any supervision over the village police for a series of years, it may be said that at present such a body does not exist. The race of people denominated chowkidars retain the name, apparently to blind the people as to their real character. They are employed during the day to assist the zemindar in collecting his rents, and at night they act as the agents of notorious characters, to point out where property is to be found! This is easily accounted for. The office is held by the very lowest caste of natives, and they are allowed by the zemindars to realise what they can from the villagers for their maintenance. They have, in a measure, held us at defiance heretofore. If a chowkidar be accidentally detected at conniving at any offence, and the magistrate orders his dismissal, directing the darogah, through the zemindar, to appoint another in his stead, his son or his nephew's name is handed up for approval, and, in ignorance, he is appointed. The chowkidars in Bengal and Behar are, for the most part, of the following castes :—Harrees, Bagdhees, Banees, Dusads, and Domes. In Orissa Pans, Kindeahs, and Mehters. These castes are deemed so inferior, that they are employed as scavengers, and in such like degrading offices. No Hindu native of a higher caste would even touch them : to do so, or to take anything from them, is held to be forfeiture of caste. They seldom realise by honest means above one or two rupees per mensem at the utmost, and are, therefore, always ready to connive at offences, on the promise of getting a share of the stolen property. It is not an uncommon trick amongst the chowkidars to apply for leave of absence before a burglary or a dacoity takes place, to quiet suspicion against them, after having informed where property is to be found, and the time and manner in which the theft can be accomplished with the least chance of detection to the parties concerned."

---

[1] Comprised of Messrs. W. W. Bird, W. Braddon, F. C. Smith, J. R. Herschell, J. Lowis, F. J. Halliday, D. C. Smyth, and T. C. Scott.

(*b*). Mr. W. A. Pringle, in his letter dated the 7th February 1837, gives similar testimony : " At present the village watchmen are badly and irregularly paid ; and though nominally under one master only, the darogah, they are bullied and oppressed by almost every man in the village. The zemindars and farmers, and their amlah, too often employ them in collecting rent and in oppressing the ryots." *   *

(*c*). Mr. T. R. Davidson, also, in his letter dated the 10th June 1837, remarks : " At the lowest computation, this branch of the police (chowkidars) in he four districts Sarun, Shahabad, Patna, and Behar, exceeds 15,000 men ; yet it is so utterly worthless, that I am not sure the country would be in a worse position in point of police were every chowkidar dismissed. They comprise the most debased class of the inhabitants, and are, I fear, usually, rather engaged in robbery and theft, than in guarding the property of their employers. In the district of Sarun they are said to be the leaders of gangs ; and they are notoriously the medium by which stolen property is restored throughout the division." *   *

(*d*). The papers submitted for our consideration abound with evidence to the same effect ; but the above will be sufficient to show that nothing can be in a worse state than these establishments, and that the most urgent necessity exists for a thorough revision, not in one or two districts merely, but throughout the country, in order to place them in a state of efficiency. In some districts the allowances for watchmen are very great. In Purneah, for instance, they are stated by Mr. Pringle to amount to no less than sicca Rs. 1,96,132 per annum—a sum which, at the rate of 4 rupees per mensem, would admit, under a well-regulated system, of the employment for that district alone of 4,000 men ; and yet the establishment is described, not only as utterly useless for police purposes, but as a curse, instead of a blessing, to the community. It is the same almost everywhere else ; and it is even a question whether an order issued throughout the country to apprehend and confine them would not do more to put a stop to theft and robbery, than any other measure that could be adopted. *   *

(*e*). The magistrates are overwhelmed ; the darogahs and their subordinate officers are corrupt ; the village watchmen are poor, degraded, and often worse than useless ; and the community at large, oppressed and inconvenienced in various ways, are not only disinclined to afford aid to the police, but, in most cases, had rather submit quietly to be robbed, than apply to the police officers for assistance to apprehend the thieves, or recover the stolen property.

(*f*). The defect which we have next to bring to notice is one that has been already referred to, namely, the corruption and utter worthlessness of the thannadars. All concur in thinking that this class of functionaries are on the worst possible footing, and that it would be better to dispense with them altogether, unless inducements can be held out sufficiently strong to dispose persons of character and respectability to offer themselves for the appointment. In proof of what is above stated, we beg leave to refer to the evidence given before us by Babu Dwarkanath Tagore, on the 8th November last, from which the following is an extract :—

" *Q. 263.*—You had, then, many opportunities of observing the condition of the police ; state what you think of it ? I think that, from the darogah to the lowest peon, the whole of them are a corrupt set of people—a single case could not be got out of their hands without paying money : the wealthy always get advantage over the poor. In quarrels between the zemindars and indigo-planters, large sums are expended to bribe these people. When any report is called for by the magistrate from the darogahs, even in a true case, that report could not be obtained without paying a large sum of money; and should the case be between two rich parties, the richest, or he who pays the highest, would get the report in his favour. If a jemadar or peon is sent to a village for any inquiry, there is immediately a tax levied by them from all the ryots of the village, through the gomashta of the zemindar; and this mode of extortion has so long prevailed as almost to give it the character of a just demand—so much so, that not a single ryot would even make an objection to pay it. Indeed, they look upon it as an authorised tax. If a dacoity takes place in any neighbourhood, the darogah and all his people will go about the villages and indiscriminately seize the inhabitants, innocent or culpable; and it often happens that persons so taken, although of the most suspicious character, in the particular transaction are released on some money inducement being given to the officers. * * In short, nothing can be done without paying for it whenever they are called upon to interfere."

V.—MINISTERS AND MISSIONARIES RESIDENT IN CALCUTTA (1852-53).

(a). Your petitioners greatly fear that it will be found on enquiry that in many districts of Bengal neither life nor property is secure; that gang-robberies of the most daring character are perpetrated annually in great numbers with impunity; and that there are constant scenes of violence in contentions respecting disputed boundaries between the owners of landed estates.

Sess. 1852-53,
Vol. 27,
App. 7.

(b). The radical cause of both these evils is the inefficiency of the police and the judicial system. Your petitioners find that the sole protection of the public peace in many places is a body of policemen (called village chowkidars), who are, in fact, the ministers of the most powerful of their neighbours, rather than the protectors of the people. The body of peace officers appointed and paid directly by the State will, on inquiry, be found to be entirely insufficient for the great districts for which they are provided; but, few as they are, they will be found to be the oppressors of the people. The records of the criminal courts, and the experience of every resident in the districts of Bengal, will bear testimony to the fact that no confidence can be placed in the police force (either the regular force or the village chowkidars); that it is their practice to extort confessions by torture; and that, while they are powerless to resist the gangs of organised burglars or dacoits, they are corrupt enough to connive at their atrocities.

(c.) Your petitioners believe that a strict and searching inquiry into the state of the rural population of Bengal, would lead your Hon'ble House to the conclusion that they commonly live in a state of poverty and wretchedness, produced chiefly by the present system of landed tenures, and the extortion of the zemindars, aggravated by the inefficiency and the cruelties of the peace officers, who are paid by the chowkidari tax or by the Government.

VI.—MR. W. THEOBALD, MR. THEODORE DICKENS, AND BRITISH AND OTHER INHABITANTS OF CALCUTTA AND THE NEIGHBOURING PARTS IN LOWER BENGAL, 1852.

Para. 7, contd.

(a). The police of the Lower Provinces totally fails as respects its proper purposes—the prevention of crime, apprehension of offenders, and protection of life and property; and it is become an engine of oppression and a great cause of the corruption of the people. Your petitioners desire to state a few facts in connexion with these propositions. The Lower Provinces, concerning whose police your petitioners are now speaking, are divided into 32 counties (zillahs), and contain an estimated population of 30 millions, and compose an area larger than France. The proper police force in these counties consists of superintendents (darogahs), sergeants (jemadars), and constables (burkundazes), amounting, on the whole, to 10,000 [1] or 11,000 persons; and to these have to be added the village watchmen, who are paid by the villagers, and not by the Government, and are so rarely known to prevent a theft or other crime, or to apprehend the criminal, that they must count for very little in an honest appreciation of the general system. These numbers are insufficient with reference to the existing state of the population; and in the present state of crime, an exclusively native police, however numerous, can hardly be made sufficient.

(b). Effective superintendence over the native police there is, and can be, none under the existing institutions, owing to the paucity of magistrates, their heavy judicial duties, which being alone sufficient to occupy their time, are incompatible with the activity and locomotion required for superintendence, and the large size of districts, the zillah being perhaps as large as Yorkshire, or an area of 6,000 or 7,000 square miles, and containing a population of one million, with one magistrate, an "assistant" or pupil of the civil service, and a deputy magistrate for the whole zillah.

(c). Your petitioners will make a brief statement in illustration of the practical bearing of the existing system on the condition of the people. In case of the apprehension of an offender, and in order to prosecute him, it is necessary for the injured party and his witnesses to go before the magistrate; but this may be a journey of from 15 or less to 50 miles or more, in consequence of the extent of his district; and when arrived at the magistrate's office, he may be detained days or weeks from a variety of causes. In fact, a magistrate's compound in the Lower Provinces often presents the spectacle of hundreds of persons thus kept in detention for weeks; and if the offence is of a gross character, or beyond the jurisdiction of a magistrate, he and his witnesses may be required to take a second journey of the same distance to the sessions, and be there detained for days or weeks waiting for a trial. At the sessions, also, hundreds of persons are constantly detained, at great distances from their homes. To avoid these inconveniences, the population render little or no aid to the police for the enforcement of the law, but on the contrary they are generally averse to do so; and hence ha

---

[1] Corroborated by Mr. Marshman's evidence, Q. 3590.

ZEMINDARS AND RYOTS FROM 1793 TO 1859.   267

APP. XI.

A WEAK,
CORRUPT
POLICE.

Para. 7, contd.

arisen a practice which is a great reproach to the police system, namely, that witnesses generally, and prosecutors often, are made prisoners, kept under arrest, and sent to the magistrate, and afterwards to the sessions, in actual custody.   From this state of the law and the police result the following, among other evils : persons robbed deny the fact of a robbery ; or if they complain, the persons who could be witnesses deny all knowledge of it, the immediate interests of these classes being arrayed, by reason of the state of the law and jurisdictions, against the objects of law and justice.   Often under these circumstances the native policeman, to do his duty, employs the means of terror ; and torture is believed to be extensively practised on persons under accusation, and the injured party for not assisting him becomes an offender.   All the evil passions are thus brought into play, and ingenuities of all kinds, both by people and police, are resorted to.   Another result is the constant device of proving a true case by witnesses who know nothing about the matter. Justice is supposed to be thus satisfied ; but convenient perjury becomes familiar, and perjury loses its criminal character among the people. Thus, and in a thousand other ways, the law and police operate to corrupt the people, and spread corruption ; moreover, the very circumstances which repel the honest, attract those who have revenge to gratify, rivals to injure, enemies to destroy ; and for these and other dishonest purposes the police and criminal courts are resorted to, and police and law under the present system are terrible evils.

(*d*). A further aggravation of evil results from some powers possessed by the native police, which, practically, are magisterial—such as the power of receiving confessions, and in all cases of taking (though not on oath) the deposition of witnesses, which powers are exercised by the sergeant (jemadar), in the absence of his immediate superior (the darogah) ; and thereby, practically, the course of criminal justice takes its direction from them, and thus the police control the magistrate's functions, instead of his superintending and controlling the police.   * *

(*e*). The legislation respecting crime is equally unsatisfactory.   By reason of the state of the police, every landholder, planter, banker, considerable trader, and storekeeper, is obliged to keep men, often in very considerable numbers, armed according to the custom of the country, to defend his property against midnight-gangs, called dacoits, and other robbers.   Such irregular forces, though necessary for self-protection, are of course liable to be employed by neighbours at enmity against one another, and by circumstances to become aggressive ; and hence the frequency of affrays, which are to be deplored.   But the primary evil, in the whole set of circumstances, is the state of the police ; and its reform is the proper and essential remedy.   Instead of which, mere[1] legislation against crime is resorted to ; ingenuities are exerted to bring the propertied classes within the criminal categories ; the laws on paper are made more severe ; increased judiciary powers are given to the magistracy ;— but the real evil remains unabated.   It is obvious that legislation of this kind is only acceleration on the road to ruin.

---

[1] Just in the same way as the Government in 1793 were content to secure the ryots by legislating about pottahs.

App. XI.

INEFFICIENT
POLICE.

Para. 7, contd.

Sess. 1852-53,
Vol. 27, App. 7.

VII.—BENGAL BRITISH INDIAN ASSOCIATION AND OTHER NATIVE IN-
HABITANTS OF THE BENGAL PRESIDENCY.

(*a*). The Association thank the British Government for having ensured to them freedom from foreign incursions and intestinedissen sions, and (speaking doubtless on behalf of the ryots) security from spoliation by lawless power.

(*b*). The Company's courts are not so constituted as to render substantial justice to the natives, or afford them a just confidence as to security of life and property.

(*c*). The police of the country has always been in a state not at all creditable to an enlightened Government, and has, indeed, been acknowledged by the servants of Government to be "as bad as it can be." The Court of Directors have, it is true, expressed themselves solicitous of the improvement of the police at any cost; but their solicitude has been without any effect. The Government, on appointing a Police Committee in 1837 to hold inquiries on the subject, strictly prohibited the suggestion of any reforms which should involve any great increase of expenditure. From that day to this no reforms have been attempted beyond the appointment of a few deputy magistrates, and, very recently, of a commissioner for the suppression of dacoity, who has not yet entered upon the duties of his office. Hence, the utmost insecurity of life and property prevails in every district, and even in the immediate vicinity of the metropolis of British India.

(*d*). The insufficiency of the police arises, not only from the small establishments maintained by the Government, but from the extensive jurisdiction of the magistrates, and the practice of appointing very young men to that office, and removing them to higher posts as soon as they begin to acquire experience. The extent of country which is to be travelled over to arrive at the station of the magistrate, the difficulty of obtaining access to that functionary, except through the medium of the ministerial officers, the necessity of presenting every petition in writing, and on stamped paper of the value of half a rupee (about four times the value of a labourer's daily wages), combine to render it a matter of impossibility to the poorer classes to obtain justice from the criminal courts. The large powers vested in the darogahs are liable to abuse, owing to the insufficient remuneration they receive, and the difficulty of exercising proper control over them. Their entrances into villages to trace out the perpetrators of heinous offences, or discover property alleged to be stolen, are regarded by the people as visitations. The fact is so notorious, that the Government have found it necessary to pass a law, Regulation II of 1832, to prevent the darogahs from investigating any cases of burglary, unless expressly desired by the party injured, or directed by the magistrate. Hence, it is difficult adequately to represent to your Hon'ble House the actual situation of the poor in the interior, in consequence of the badness of the police system, since those who are most exposed to the attacks of the powerful and the lawless have most to dread the exactions of the officers of the police, many of whom are actually in the pay of the rich, while some have been convicted of practising torture to obtain their ends.

Zemindar's
opportunity of
securing these
offices against
the ryots.

Zemindar's
opportunity.

(e). To remedy such a state of things, it is urgently required that a
suitable augmentation of the police be made for the repression of dacoity
and other crimes attended with violence, as well as that a sufficient number of magisterial officers, unencumbered with extraneous duties, be
attached to every district.

App. XI.
───
INEFFICIENT
POLICE.
───
Para. 7, contd.

VIII.—Sir Frederick Halliday (*14th March 1853*).

Q. 1896.—Here, again, I must limit my answer by saying that I
speak with reference to the police in the Lower Provinces of Bengal, with
which I am more familiar than any other. I cannot give it a good
character; at the same time I must say that, in the hands of a good
magistrate, even now the police are capable of being made more efficient,
and that they are more efficient than you would suppose to be the case,
judging from the complaints to which allusion has been made. Much
of the fault attributed to it, and the want of success which has been
complained of, is almost insuperable, in consequence of the character of
the people with whom you have to deal. You have a cowardly and
untruthful people, not in the smallest degree disposed to aid the police,
but rather the contrary; you have persons of power and influence, connected with the land, who, so far from assisting you, are charged by
their countrymen with assisting thieves and robbers, and participating
in their spoil; you have, at the very foundation of the police, a system—
a thoroughly ill-paid and demoralised set of village watchmen, with respect to whom the zemindars resist most strongly any attempt made to
put them upon a better footing, because it will cause them, they think,
additional expense; and you have to work through native agents, and
through a class generally whom you cannot afford to pay sufficiently,
and who, therefore, are exceedingly untrustworthy; you had a system
which, in fact, was rotten when you found it, and which will take
many years to put into a proper state; at the same time I am far from
saying that much might not be done, and far from hoping that much
will not be done.

Q. 1906.—Do you believe that the class of men by whom the police
is now carried on are open to bribery, and to all kinds of corruption?
To an immense extent.

Sess. 1852-53,
Vol. 27.

IX.—Mr. J. C. Marshman (*28th April 1853*).

The state of the police in Bengal is unfortunately very unsatisfactory; it is perhaps the worst part of our administration; there is very
little security to property, and those who commit depredations are very
seldom apprehended and punished. * * The people never can be roused
to protect themselves; they submit to the exactions and to the oppressions of dacoits and public officers almost without a complaint.

Sess. 1852-53,
Vol. 27,

X.—Indigo Commission's Report (*27th August 1860*).

As regards the conduct of the police, it is not denied that up to this
time, as a body, they are liable to the charge of venality and corruption,
and there can be no question that indigo, like every agricultural or
mercantile pursuit, may suffer from the want of a really good police.
* * The cases in which the assistance of the police is most sought for,

are when lands are said to be sown or occupied forcibly. And when this interference is asked for, there can be little doubt with which party the advantage will ordinarily be. The frankest admissions have been made before us by planters as to the way in which money is given to officers of the police to ensure their doing their duty, or to prevent them acting or reporting unfairly. When matters come to this, that the assistance or support of the police can be purchased like any other article, it is quite clear that the advantage will remain with the party who has the freest hand and the fullest purse.

8. The two principal means by which zemindars, after 1793, sought to destroy the occupancy rights of the ryot, were to dispossess or to ruin him. The prevalence and impunity of violent crime were favourable to either method; and of such crime, dacoity was the most effectual to the zemindar's end, as it was most under his control. The zemindars began, before 1800, by appointing robbers to superintend the police; the evictions of ryots turned them into dacoits (App. VII, para. 13, section III); and the ball was then kept rolling down to near the period of the rent and sale laws in 1859, which put the ryots on proof of their rights, seventy years after the decennial settlement—that is, after a seventy-years' reign of spoliation, oppression, and lawlessness. The story of dacoity, down to 1831, is given by Mr. Mill in Appendix VI, (above); it is continued in the following extracts :—

I.—COURT OF DIRECTORS, TO BENGAL GOVERNMENT (*30th March 1831*).

In 1812, the evil of dacoity in Bengal was particularly noticed in the Fifth Report of the Committee of the House of Commons. The Committee referred to a despatch from Bengal dated in 1810, in which it was stated that the commission of robberies and murders, and the most atrocious deliberate cruelties, was established; that these offences were not of rare occurrence, or confined to particular districts—they were committed with few exceptions, and with slight modifications of atrocity, in every part of Bengal. The Committee adverted to the endeavours of the Government from 1801 to 1807 to suppress dacoity; and they remarked : " But, notwithstanding these measures, the disorders which they were intended to subdue still increased, and towards the end of 1807 had acquired such a degree of strength, as to oblige the Government to resort to measures much more forcible than had hitherto been tried for the deliverance of the country from this growing and intolerable evil." But since 1812 the reported offences of dacoity had fallen from 1813 to 1817 to a yearly average of 339, and in 1828 to 167, against a yearly average from 1803 to 1807 of 1,481, and from 1808 to 1812 of 927.

II.—MR. J. C. MARSHMAN (*28th April 1853*).

Dacoities are very frequent in Bengal, more especially in the districts immediately round the presidency. * * * Dacoity is the normal crime of Bengal, especially of the Lower Provinces. As far as we have any knowledge, it has always existed.   It fluctuates with the vigorous efforts of the Government to put it down.   About forty years ago, the system of dacoity had reached such a state of perfection, that the Government were obliged to employ Mr. Elliot and the well known Dr. Leyden to go into the disturbed districts; and the most stringent measures were adopted, and the district of Kishnaghur in particular was almost cleared from dacoits; but the crime has now revived.

III.—Sir F. J. Halliday (*14th March 1853*).

Q. 1920.—In four or five districts in the immediate neighbourhood of Calcutta, so far from a diminution, there has been an increase of dacoity of late years; in other districts there has been a diminution; but all over Bengal there has been a great diminution during the last few years in the atrocity of the nature of those gang-robberies; dacoities are more numerous, but they are more insignificant in character.

Q. 1921.—Do you mean to say that there has been an increase in the number of gang-robberies of late years, as compared with the period when gang-robberies were so rife in Kishnaghur and Burdwan in former years? I am not prepared to say whether it is so or not; but as regards the periods with which I am better acquainted, there has been a great increase.

IV.—Mr. Welby Jackson—*October 1853 (report of an official tour of inspection of Bengal).*

(*a*). So far from the zemindars supporting the police to the utmost of their power, as they are by law bound to do, there is reason to believe that the crimes attended with violence which are committed, and which have been most troublesome to check, have been fostered and connived at by the zemindars. The dacoities now so common, and the affrays, both of them often attended with bloodshed, are known to be usually committed by the hired servants of the zemindars, commonly known by the name of *latyals*, or clubmen. The present Dacoity Commissioner informs me that, from the information he receives from his approvers (I believe the best information to be had), this fact is quite clear.   It is to be held in mind that these *latyals* (clubmen) are not usually natives of Bengal, but hired ruffians from the North-West or Behar, bold and powerful men, who subsist by a life of plunder, receiving pay from the zemindars, to whom they attach themselves for protection only on the occasion of special service done him.

(*b*). *Zemindars oppose, instead of supporting police.*—It is notorious that many zemindars keep up large bodies of these fighting men to terrify their neighbours, and defend themselves. They do not deny it; and plead, in excuse, that the practice is so general, as to render it impossible for any individual to discontinue it with due regard for his protection. These men, or rather bodies of men, are more than a match for our police; and as long as the practice of retaining them is kept up, so long will dacoity and affray be prevalent. * * The zemindars and landholders must be brought under the power of the police, and must be made to support it; so long as they withhold their help, and even oppose it, and are allowed to do so with impunity, the police cannot be rendered efficient.

V.—COMMISSIONER OF DACOITY (*20th April 1862*).

The Magistrates of Shahabad and Ghazipore, and the Dacoity Commissioner of Behar, have been endeavouring to arrest the persons who compose this formidable gang. But the dacoits are protected by the landholders in those districts; and unless a stringent order is passed on these confederates of dacoits, it will be difficult to apprehend them. The existence of the gang was known to the late Superintendent of Police, who, I find, issued a circular to all magistrates on the 19th January 1857 to watch these dacoits. It will not be easy to exterminate the gang until the zemindars who protect them are compelled to give them up. The Dacoity Commissioner of Behar informs me that he is baffled in all his attempts by the zemindars. The evidence collected in this office against the dacoits is sufficient to ensure their conviction; and it is to be regretted that the influence of the zemindars should be used to aid these persons in their endeavours to escape punishment. It appears to me very clear that the zemindars share in the profits of dacoity.

9. The zemindar's power of summoning ryots to his cutcherry, and the law of distraint (Huftum and Punjum, or Regulations VII, 1799, and V, 1812) were powerful instruments of oppression of the ryots. They were only repealed by Act X of 1859. The advantage which Huftum and Punjum gave to the zemindar has been described as a knock-down blow to the ryot by way of a beginning (Appendix XII, para. 9, sections II and III). Through the corruption and dishonesty of distrainers and sale ameens, the blow was always effectual.

I.—BOARD OF COMMISSIONERS, FURRUCKABAD (*6th August 1811*).

In securing the landlords from these difficulties and embarrassments, which opposed even the most moderate use of this summary proceeding, the modifications introduced by Regulation VII of 1799 have, without intending it, furnished them with an engine of oppression and extortion as irresistible as their original powers were ineffectual. The penalties annexed to any unfounded complaints against the distrainer have operated as a denunciation against all complaint whatever on the part of the tenant, whose mistrust of the result of a long litigation with a powerful and opulent antagonist is increased by the present danger attaching to a failure; and he is, therefore, induced to submit patiently to every injustice, rather than attempt to seek redress at the expense of an immediate interruption of the labour on which his family depend for support, and with a prospect of total ruin in the end.

II.—MR. WELBY JACKSON (*October 1853*).

(*a*). The state of the law for the decision of suits between landlord and tenant requires alteration. Every one concurs in condemning it, and declares that Regulations VII, 1799, and V, 1812, are mere instruments of oppression in the hands of the landlords. By the help of these instruments, a zemindar by simply stating an untruth can either consign a man to prison, or sell off his property by distress as a preliminary, without any previous inquiry into the validity of his claim by a court or public officer. This power is not only in the hands of the zemindars, but also in the hands of their agents, gomashtas, petty farmers—in fact, of any one who pleases to assert falsely, whether in part or entirely, that a cultivator is in balance of rent due to him. How totally regardless the Bengalis are of speaking the truth, and how perfectly ready they are to make use of any fraudulent trick to serve their purposes, is too notorious to need mention. Fraud and falsehood from the highest to the lowest are the rule in Bengal, and, when successful, are not in the least disreputable; it may easily be inferred what a terrible engine of oppression these laws form in such hands.

(*b*). *The tenants have no effectual remedy.*—It may be said the ryots have a remedy in giving security and bringing their suit to remove the attachment of their goods, or prevent the incarceration of their persons; but what a difficult, almost impossible, matter it is for a poor man to find security; and further, it must be security to the satisfaction of the ferosh ameen or the nazir, both of whom are probably bribed by the more powerful party to reject it if tendered; and, again, the party arrested must go under arrest to the sudder station, sometimes from 50 to 100 miles off, before his tender of security can be considered, leaving his wife and children starving in his absence; and after reaching the sudder station, he is of course distant from the assistance of all who might be disposed to be his security. The fact is, security cannot be given by a poor man; and the remedy assigned him by the law, the preliminary of which is security for the amount claimed, is useless. The result is, that his property and his person are completely in the hands of his landlord.

(*c*). Again, though the ryot might in very gross cases be able to give security, he seldom has the opportunity. If the object is oppression, and the claim a false one, the zemindar who issues the notice of claim, either himself or through the collector's nazir, takes good care that it shall not be served; but a return of service is made without. True, he is liable to punishment for this on suit; but it is impossible to prove it against him, so that, in effect, he acts with perfect impunity. These legal remedies are available only in the hands of the rich; the poor are without the means of profiting by them.

(*d*). *The zemindar has, in effect, arbitrary power.*—Such must be the case where the zemindar acts spontaneously on his own legal responsibility, and the ryot is left to enforce that responsibility by process of law. There is but one remedy—that the zemindar shall no longer be allowed to be judge in his own case, subject merely to unreal and ineffective restrictions; no ryot or other persons should be liable to be imprisoned, or to have his goods sold by distraint, without some previous enquiry by an impartial person into the validity of the claim against him. The enquiry, too, must not be formal, but fair and real. It is too much the practice in Bengal, even for the courts of justice, to say, "The witnesses say so and so; I have no reason to disbelieve them," when it is well known that the witnesses can be purchased for a few annas a piece; and that, unless there is something more than their assertion to establish a fact, no one is convinced of the truth of it. I would urge that the previous inquiry should be careful and effective, as well as speedy, that a poor labouring man, whose daily bread depends upon his daily labour, may not be starved into compliance by legal delays.

(e). It is scarcely to be conceived how enormous is the extent of tyranny and oppression carried on under the present law; so much so, that zemindars and men of respectability have assured me that almost all the claims enforced by those means are false; the ryots so well know the power of the zemindars that, if they are really in balance, they never think of contesting the point.

III.—EDITOR OF THE "HINDOO PATRIOT" (BABOO HURISH CHUNDER MOOKERJEE), BABOO SUMBHUNATH PUNDIT, AND OTHERS (27th September 1857).

The number of summary processes available by landholders against their tenants for various purposes is already large; and it is a notorious fact that they are frequently abused for the purposes of oppression and extortion. Tenants are compellable by force, used at the discretion of private individuals, to attend at the cutcherry of their zemindars to adjust the accounts of rent; their personal and moveable property and crops are liable to distraint and sale after a mere reference to the local revenue authorities; they are liable to be arrested with or without previous notice by a process issued on the application of the landlord or his servants without any previous enquiry as to the necessity thereof; they are liable to be amerced in sundry penalties on a summary investigation of complaints preferred against them. These remedies, devised originally for the better realisation of the land revenue of the country, public and private, are, it is well known, now a terror to the well-disposed part of the tenantry of the country, and have practically reduced an immense majority of the nation to a condition considerably below that of freemen. The proposed law, "to facilitate the ejectment of occupiers of land whose title has ceased," will, we have ample reason to fear, complete the misery of their cottierism.

IV.—BILL TO AMEND LAW FOR RECOVERY OF RENT—10th October 1857 (STATEMENT OF OBJECTS AND REASONS).

(a). MR. E. CURRIE.—I have made considerable alterations in the law of distraint, in the interest of the tenant, with the view of preventing as much as possible the abuses which have been so generally complained of; * * and I have made alterations in the mode of procedure, mainly with the object of preventing the abuses, now said to be very general, of selling property on a mere nominal distress, without any opportunity allowed to the tenant to replevy.

(b). JOINT MAGISTRATE AND DEPUTY COLLECTOR, CHUMPARUN, 5th March 1855 (his letter having been selected as an annex to Mr. Currie's statement of objects and reasons, because "it contains a forcible statement of some of the evils which the Bill seeks to remedy"). The whole system of distraint, however, is radically bad; and I should be very glad to see the power of distraint, as it at present exists, entirely taken away from the landholders. I have seen many instances since my arrival in this district of oppression under this Regulation. One I remember in particular, where a teekadar had distrained property to the amount of two hundred rupees, alleged deficit of rent on fifty beegahs of land. I happened to be encamped shortly afterwards at the village in which the land was said to be; and on going to the fields (at the request of the defendant), and calling in the putwaree and others to show the 50 beegahs said to be cultivated by the man whose property had been distrained, the whole affair came out. The *assamee* in reality cultivated four and a half beegahs only; all the rest was a fictitious claim got up *merely to drive the man into paying enhanced rents*. This, I fear, is only one of a very numerous class of cases. Had I not been on the spot, the other party would have provided such strong evidence as it would have been impossible, even if the man could have got anybody to speak for him, to rebut; kabuliuts would have been forged, and a decree in all likelihood given for the value of fifty beegahs instead of four. The unlimited power of distraint possessed by the zemindar is not sufficiently checked by the provisions of Regulation V of 1812, and becomes a tremendous engine of oppression against the ryot.

V.—Mr. F. A. Glover, Officiating Judge, Rungpore (*1858*).

I would allow no landlord to distrain without first appearing before the Collector or other constituted authority, and making oath as to the truth of the arrear. More oppression is committed under the power of distraint than is conceivable by any one who has not had a long and personal acquaintance with the way in which distraint for rent is managed in the Mofussil. I venture to say that in nine cases out of ten, the arrear is fictitious. No ryot, if really in arrears, would refuse to enter into arrangements with his landlord. A ryot can have no security, either in person or property, so long as it is in his (zemindar's) power to distrain his goods, or arrest him, merely because he, the zemindar, chooses to allege that a balance is due. The privilege of having the distraint withdrawn on giving security to bring a suit against the distrainer, is worthless to a man who lives from hand to mouth, and would rather put up with the first loss, if it spared him from absolute ruin, than go to law with a man who possesses so many ways of oppressing him, and who would be sure, in the end, to be victorious. * * I have seen too much of the tyranny and rascality exercised under the guise of law in this matter of distraint, even to approve of a Regulation that continues such powers in the hands of people so utterly unworthy of possessing them.

VI.—Mr. W. Tayler, Judge, Mymensing (*1858*).

I must confess, however, that I would like to see the zemindar's powers of distraint either wholly abrogated, or placed under still more stringent restrictions. I know not to what extent the power may be abused in Bengal; but in Behar it is seldom resorted to, except for purposes of injury and oppression.

VII.—Mr. H. C. Halkett, Officiating Judge, Hooghly (*1858*).

Where the zemindar is disposed to behave tyrannically, nothing whatsoever that I can see interposes to prevent his attaching property for pretended arrears, where, when, and from whatever tenant he pleases to make his victim.

VIII.—MR. H. C. METCALFE, JUDGE OF TIPPERAH (*1858*).

The power granted by the old law to distrain movable property is thus taken away, and very justly too, as much oppression is committed by distrainers under the existing law, who may, and do, plunder a ryot of all he may be possessed of, and then, to save themselves from the criminal courts, give in a list of a few of the articles to the sale carriage as attached by them for rent. * * A creature of the distrainer is often made a co-defaulter with the real owner of the attached property, and the attachment is fraudulently made in their joint names, and the property given up to the creature of the distrainer, who is a mere man of straw, under the pretext of security being furnished by him.

10. Regulation VII of 1799, section XV, clause 8, recognised the power of zemindars and other landholders "to summon, and if necessary compel, the attendance of their tenants for the adjustment of their rents, or for any other just purpose." This law was only repealed by Act X of 1859—that is, after it had operated for sixty years with the following results:—

I.—REVD. A. DUFF AND 20 OTHER MISSIONARIES *April* (*1857*).

(*a*). The power of the zemindars to compel the personal attendance of their tenants, for the adjustment of rent and other purposes, is, practically, in many parts of the country a substitute for the regular and ordinary processes of the law, and is virtually the subjection of the tenants to a state of slavery. And, further, this evil is in many instances greatly aggravated by the estates being held in co-tenancy, so that several shareholders, who are often in a state of conflict, equally exercise an arbitrary and unrestrained authority.

(*b*). While the law thus presses severely on the tenants, the zemindars, who were primarily regarded simply as collectors of the land-tax, or farmers of the revenue, now derive, from the increased cultivation of the soil, and the greatly increased value of its produce, a revenue greatly in excess of the revenue which they pay to Government. Thus, while the zemindar has been rising in wealth and power, the tenant has been sinking into penury and dependence, subject to illegal and exhausting exactions, harassed by contending proprietors, and oppressed by the exercise of extra-judicial powers. * * These zemindars have, since the perpetual settlement, not only acquired by law the power of enforcing their demands by *ex-parte* proceedings, commencing with the arrest and imprisonment of the tenants, but have also received the sanction of the law, as already stated, to their custom of enforcing the personal attendance of their tenants at their pleasure; and both these powers, especially the latter, your petitioners believe they often greatly and shamefully abuse.

II.—SIR FREDERICK J. HALLIDAY (*20th November 1858*).

There is some variation of opinion among the officers consulted as to the restriction put upon zemindars by section VIII of the Bill, in respect to compelling the personal attendance of their ryots. Upon this I agree fully with Mr. Samuells that, although the withdrawal of this power

will be severely felt by some small zemindars, whose ryots have easy
means of escape from their power, yet the present system leads to such
grave abuses, and allows of such intolerable oppression, that it ought,
without doubt, to be amended in the manner proposed by this Bill.

App. XI.

———

RYOTS
ATTENDING AT
ZEMINDARS'
CUTCHERRIES.

Para. 10, contd.

III.—Mr. F. A. Glover.

The oppression practised by the landholders in this particular is
enormous; they can bring to the verge of ruin any one whom they may
have a spite[1] against, by summoning him to their cutcherries on the
pretence that he is in balance, and keeping him in what is actual duress,
away from his employment. No private individual should hold such
irresponsible powers.

IV.—Board of Revenue (*1st December 1858*).

The Board heartily approve of the abolition of the power of the
zemindars to compel the presence of their under-tenants for the settlement of their rents. They consider this power to be a fruitful source
of oppression, and its existence to be quite unnecessary for the protection
of the zemindars.

V.—Mr. E. Steer, Commissioner of Revenue (*27th August 1858*).

There is no denying that, under the power possessed by landlords of
compelling the attendance of their tenants, the greatest oppression has
prevailed throughout the length and breadth of the land. But the
authorities have been always severe in dealing with such cases when
they have been brought to light; and my own belief is, that there is
not now anything like the tyranny exercised over the ryots by their
landlords that there used to be.

VI.—Mr. A. Grote (*2nd October 1858*).

The power, and with it the temptation, to harass and detain, is all
that is taken away; and one of the gratifying consequences of this
provision will be the discharge of numerous *nugdees* and *latyals* who
have hitherto fed upon the tenantry.

VII.—Mr. W. H. Elliot, Commissioner of Burdwan (*1858*).

The Officiating Collector of Beerbhoom protests against the withdrawal of the zemindar's power to compel the ryot's attendance, as utterly
ruinous to the landholder. I rejoice in it, and think it will be generally
approved as a long-needed boon, and just delivery from fearful tyranny.

The foregoing accusers of the law which, by compelling
ryots to go to the zemindar's cutcherry, fostered tyranny and
oppression throughout the length and breadth of the land,
were, however, mere devil's advocates; the following saint-
like pleading in its favour was based on the eternal principles
of the zemindary settlement.

---

[1] Or whose rent they may have wished to enhance.

VIII.—BENGAL BRITISH INDIAN ASSOCIATION (*14th February 1859*).

Your petitioners regard this provision as highly objectionable, believing, as they do, in the utility, and even necessity, of the existing rule. The power of summoning the ryot to the zemindar's cutchery on necessary occasions is so essential to the management of an estate, that every one, with a practical knowledge of its working, will allow that its abolition will bring the machine of the zemindary system to a stand-still. It is from this belief and conviction, your petitioners sincerely believe, that the legislature legalised a power which the zemindars had enjoyed from time immemorial, and in the exercise of which they had met with vexatious interference from the magistrates of the time. Indeed, the rights of the zemindars could not be exercised, and the duties to the State, which are imposed on them under heavy penalties, could not be performed, were the power to be withheld from them. * * It is said that the abuse of this power suggests the withdrawal of it as proper. But those who urge this, not merely forget all the reasons for which it was granted, and which render the continuance of it indispensable, but they overlook the injustice of punishing the many for the crimes of the few.

11. This reasoning was ineffectual, but it ought to have prevailed; for its perception of the spirit of the zemindary settlement was exquisite; the spirit, that is, of a weak benevolence which loaded the zemindars with benefits at the expense, not of itself, but of the ryots, which carved out estates for zemindars by confiscating the rights of millions of ryots, and which released a few zemindars from liability to confinement by subjecting millions of ryots to actual confinement in their turn in zemindars' cutcherries. Until the zemindary settlement, zemindars used to be imprisoned if they failed to pay the revenue. With a benevolence "worthy the soul of Cornwallis," zemindars (a very small body compared to the ryots) were exempted, in 1793, from this liability; and in 1799 the *Huftum* Regulation armed them with power, over millions of cultivating proprietors, to procure the imprisonment of ryots by the Collector on false *ex-parte* statements of balances due; and further, to save the zemindars the trouble of a false statement before the Collector, they were armed by this Regulation, VII, section XV, clause 8, of 1799, with power to cause ryots to be dragged to zemindars' cutcherries, with the obvious natural consequences, *viz.*, unlawful imprisonment, and ruin if the ryots did not submit to the exactions of the zemindars. The benevolence of Government shrank from imprisoning a few zemindars for non-payment of a moderate perpetual rent; accordingly, exemption from that liability was conceded to those few by the vicarious imprisonment from time to time,

during sixty years, of millions of ryots, so that they might
be the better forced to pay rack-rents to lightly assessed zemindars. Sixty years having hallowed, into vested rights, these
huge enormities of benevolence—this vicarious imprisonment
of myriads for the benefit of a few—the British Indian
Association urged, with much truth and seriousness, that the
withdrawal of the vested rights involved "the injustice of
punishing the many for the crimes of a few."

12. Perhaps there is a slight inaccuracy in this statement.
For it may be that we should distinguish between 1793 and
1799. In the earlier year, benevolence was active; in the later
year it slumbered, and its place was taken by that in whose
name meanness and wrong have been conscientiously and
self-complacently done in all ages, viz., principle—the principle, in this case, of securing, no matter at what hazards to
helpless millions, the Government revenue, which the Government had benevolently fixed for a few zemindars at
a light assessment for ever. All the tyranny and oppression under the Regulation of 1799 were allowed for sixty
years, on the " principle " that they were necessary for the
punctual realisation of the public revenue. And, in due time,
" principle " reaped its reward. Under the Regulations of
1799 and 1812, the ryots in Orissa and Behar, more markedly than in other parts of the Lower Provinces, were ground
down to a wretched poverty by the tyranny and exactions of
zemindars; and in 1866 and in 1874 " principle " had the
rare satisfaction of stepping aside, while benevolence took
its place, and spent in the relief of famine some seven millions sterling—that is, more than " principle " need have lost,
in arrears of revenue, if it had spared the ryots the tyranny,
exactions, and rascality (paragraph 9, section iv), which
were tolerated for the sake of " principle " in the sixty years
from 1799 to 1859.

13. The chains of the ryot were riveted, further, by fraud,
perjury, and forgeries,—by incomplete or worthless pottahs
or leases to ryots,—by forged kabuliuts or agreements pur-
porting to have been given by ryots to zemindars,—by the
withholding of receipts, and by like frauds. These were the
additional weapons with which zemindars strove for possession
of Naboth's field, or to raise his rent.

I.—INCOMPLETE POTTAHS AND KABULIUTS.

(a).—MR. P. TAYLOR, JUDGE, WEST BURDWAN (1858).

In Zillah Behar, when I was Collector, it was customary in bhowli
cases, or those of ryots paying commutation for rent in kind, for the

zemindars to evade giving any *pottahs* at all, and, instead of *kabuliuts*, to exhibit with their summary plaints mere *hissab baquees*, drawn up without the apparent knowledge of the ryots at the close of the year. By this dishonest and oppressive system, they entirely evaded the rule of the decennial settlement, which directed that, " in cases where the rate can be specified, such as where the rents are adjusted upon a measurement of the lands, after cultivation, or on a survey of the crop, or where they are made payable in kind, *the rate and terms of payment*, and proportion of the crop to be delivered, with every condition (including the length of the rod used in measurement), should be clearly specified." At the same time, by the above expedient, the zemindars contravened another rule, which enjoined calculation and ascertainment of all instalments, with reference to the time of reaping and selling produce; moreover, by fixing the *hakim's hissab* at the end of the year, when grain was dearest, they obtained a much larger money value for it than was equitable to the cultivator.

(b).—Mr. E. A. Samuells, Commissioner of Patna (*1858*).

The first interpolation is necessary, in order to protect the ryot against the fraudulent suits, so common in Behar, in which he is sued for the rent of land which he never occupied; the frequent changes in the quantity of land cultivated by the ryot rendering this fraud more difficult of detection in Behar than elsewhere. In pottahs for lands held under a butaee or bhowli tenure, it is impossible to specify any money rent. The section, therefore, provides that such pottahs shall state the proportion of produce which the ryot is to deliver; but it is evident that, unless the area is also given, this provision is useless. The same pottah or its counterpart may form the basis of a suit for five hundred rupees, or for five rupees, as the landlord pleases.

(c).—Mr. W. H. Elliott, Commissioner of Burdwan (*1858*).

I think it most important that the pottah and kabuliut should invariably contain a very clear specification of the tenant's land. Many will be found merely to mention " about   bigahs of land in the village of   , at an annual rental of Rs.   "; and a poor ryot is frequently made to pay for " *other* land" declared to be in his possession, and so proved by witnesses, when the fact of his having paid for what is named in his pottah cannot be denied.

II.—Forged Kabuliuts.

(a).—Mr. H. Atherton, Officiating Judge, Tirhoot (*1858*).

An excellent provision, if the ryot can register his pottah in the Collector's office; but, unless the pottah be registered, the kabuliut will be fabricated, when needed, by the zemindar, and the denial of the poor ryot will rarely protect him.

(b).—Mr. E. Lautour, Judge, 24-Pergunnahs (*1858*).

The great evil at present is the general resort to forged instruments—forged kabuliuts on the one hand, forged receipts on the other.

(c).—Mr. W. S. Seton-Karr, Officiating Judge, Jessore (*1858*).

(2).—Does this mean that any person producing a *kabuliut* of any kind as given by a cultivator may distrain the produce of the land? If this be intended, I fear that the ryot will be much less protected than was hoped for. To make a *kabuliut*[1] costs nothing; and few talukdars, zemindars, or others will have the slightest hesitation in procuring a forged document of this sort, if its production will enable them to sell produce off-hand.

(d).—Bengal British Indian Association (*14th February 1859*).

The consequence to be dreaded from such a state of things is, either that the courts will be swamped with suits for the enforcement of *kabuliuts*, which, with the present machinery, it will be next to an impossibility to get through within any reasonable period, or that the zemindar will betake himself to fabricating *kabuliuts* to enable him, under the proposed law, to realise his just dues by process of distraint, which, in the generality of cases, is his only remedy.

(e).—Revd. A. Duff and 20 other Missionaries.

Your Hon'ble Court, for instance, may, in the Rent Bill, provide that no distress shall issue, save on the production of a *kabuliuts;* but there exists no security that forged *kabuliuts* will not be produced with impunity, the only remedy of the cultivator being a hopeless litigation in a civil court, in which the expense or the delay would alone effect his ruin.

(f).—Mr. H. C. Metcalfe, Judge of Tipperah.

The zemindar, to protect himself, will no doubt resort to two subterfuges, for which a loophole is allowed him by sections IV and V. He will either declare that "the land is khamar, nij-jote, or seer land," belonging to the proprietor of the estate or tenure, and leased for a term, or year by year, to a resident cultivator; or will produce a false written contract or *kabuliut* for the payment of specific rates of rent, which he will prove by perjured witnesses; and thus, in both cases, the rule will fail to secure the land to the ryot at the pergunnah rate. A great deal of litigation and perjury will be the consequence.

III.—Receipts for rent evaded by Zemindars.

(a).—Mr. H. Atherton, Officiating Judge, Tirhoot (*1858*).

If this rule be allowed, it will be absolutely necessary to allow the ryot to deposit his yearly rent in the Collector's hands, for receipts for payments are constantly refused; and if the ryot cannot be allowed to deposit his rent, his only course will be to refuse payment altogether, until he has had a decree given against him, which is a common practice

---

[1] The agreement which the ryot signs and gives to the zemindar.

now, simply from the impossibility of getting receipts from the zemindar or his agent.

(b).—Mr. E. Lautour, Judge, 24-Pergunnahs (*1858*).

So of receipts. What are the rubbishy bits of paper as evidential exhibits, which the zemindar may repudiate or his ryot forge, and either of which is done daily? * * Again, the law should provide for tender of payment into court whenever a zemindar refuses to receive the rent. I have cases where that is systematically going on, partly to harass the under-tenant and oppress him with law expenses, and partly to get a decree upon which to found proceedings on eviction. In Shahabad this was the method taken invariably by the Dumraon Rajah to evict his mokurridars for value. Here it goes on in the Sunderbunds, where a grantee is systematically adopting these same tactics to eject his ganty-dar; and his method is to refuse rents and institute oppressive Act VII suits in the collectorate, setting on foot the usual consequent civil suits. Numerous cases are always occurring in which the greatest boon would be conceded if parties were allowed to pay into deposit, to the credit of the zemindar, any sums the zemindar refused to receive.

(c).—Mr. G. L. Martin, Judge, Sarun (*1858*).

During my residence in this zillah and Tirhoot, I have frequently observed that the mode of granting receipts to ryots is not on separate pieces of paper in the usual form of an acknowledgment, but on a single slip, which is headed with the ryot's name, and below that the several payments made in the year are entered with the dates; but the signature of the receiver is seldom, if ever, affixed, and the result of this practice, which extensively prevails, is, that when tendered as exhibits in suits, they are easily repudiated, and extremely difficult to prove. Of course it is optional with the ryots to accept an acknowledgment which can so easily be denied; but, in the main, they are so entirely at the mercy of the landlord, farmer, or agent, and often so ignorant, they cannot help themselves. The practice referred to appears to me to proceed from much the same sort of feeling which is often shown by proprietors and farmers, in their reluctance to grant " farugs," or acquittances.

IV.—Frauds, Perjuries, and Forgeries.

(a).—Collector of Rajshahye (*16th August 1811*).

The alarming and distressing height to which perjury has risen in this country is, I firmly believe, in a great degree to be attributed to the power of distraint at present vested in the zemindars; and I think I may venture to assert that there are but few gentlemen in the judicial line who do not coincide with me in the opinion.

(b).—Indigo Planters' Association (*1856*).

This procedure is regarded by different members with various degrees of apprehension, as a probable source of frauds, forgeries, and perjuries—the usual instrumentality of mofussil litigation.

(*c*).—Mr. H. Atherton, Officiating Judge, Tirhoot (*1858*).

Section VII supposes that the ryot is capable of contesting the demand of his zemindar. He cannot, generally speaking, do so from his poverty, and from the fact of the zemindar or his agent, when inclined to be unjust, being able to secure any amount of evidence against the ryot. Nothing, in my opinion, can protect the ryot against oppression, but the registration of his pottah in the collector's office, with permission to pay the rent of the year in one sum into the collector's hands.

(*d*).—Bengal British Indian Association (*14th February 1859*).

Your petitioners would respectfully beg to be understood that it is not from a captious spirit of opposing a beneficial measure that they have been induced to offer these remarks, but from a sincere conviction of the unnecessary hardship, not to say injustice, which the proposed law is calculated *to entail upon the landholders, and the encouragement it offers to perjury and forgery*, which your petitioners conceive will be effectually checked if the exchange of pottahs and *kabuliuts* were directed to be made with the knowledge of the collector of the district, in the manner suggested by your petitioners.

(The Association hinted thus mildly that perjury and forgery were ordinary weapons of offence and defence in the litigation between ryots and zemindars.)

(*e*).—Rev. A. Duff and 9 other Missionaries (*9th March 1858*).

Perjury has almost ceased to be regarded as morally wrong; it constitutes the stock-in-trade by which numerous witnesses for hire subsist. The impunity and success with which systematic perjury and the forgery of documents are commonly practised, tend to encourage the already too prevalent habits of falsehood and deception among the great body of the people; and, as a necessary consequence, justice is now constantly mocked and defeated, or the powers of the law are used, without remorse, as engines of oppression and extortion, through the infamous arts of the traders in corruption.

14.—Summary.

Rev. A. Duff and 20 other Missionaries (*April 1857*).

Year after year the condition of the tenants appears more and more pitiable and hopeless. Your petitioners are compelled to add that other evils increase the wretchedness of the condition to which a tenant is thus reduced. The village chowkidars are the servants of his landlord; the Government police are corrupt, and he cannot vie with his landlord in purchasing their favour. * * Superadded to the evils the cultivating classes endure from a corrupt and inefficient police, and an administration of civil and criminal justice which confessedly requires extensive improvement, they are liable to be constantly harassed by the conflicting and unsettled claims, either of contending shareholders of joint estates, or of contending neighbouring proprietors; by the severe laws of distraint and arrest; by the power of their superior landholders, whether

†

zemindars or middlemen, to compel personal attendance at their pleasure; by illegal exactions; by the unfixed nature of their tenures; and by the prevalent custom of refusing both leases and receipts.

15. It appears from this Appendix that the period from 1793 until near 1859 may be characterised as a period of lawlessness of zemindars, who corrupted, kept in their pay, or controlled the police; harboured dacoits and employed club-men who kept ryots in terror; abused the *Huftum* and *Punjum* Regulations, and the zemindar's power of summoning ryots to their cutcherries; gave incomplete pottahs and receipts for rent; used forged *kabulyuts;* had recourse to frauds, perjuries, and forgeries. All this was not done personally by the zemindar; the greater part was done by middlemen and subordinates; but the result was the reduction of the ryots into absolute subjection to zemindars. Act X of 1859 was then passed with the view of protecting the ryot; but it required from him proofs of right which could have survived this period of lawlessness only by a miracle.

APPENDIX XII.

App. XII.

LAND REVENUE
AT THE PERMA-
NENT SETTLE-
MENT.
___
Para. 3.
Administration
Report, 1872-73,
Part II, page 71.

ZEMINDARS AND RYOTS, IN THEIR RELATIONS AS LAND-
LORDS AND TENANTS, ACCORDING TO REPORTS FROM 1871
TO 1876.

1. The land revenue, as fixed at the decennial settlement for Bengal, Behar, and Orissa (excluding the Cuttack
division), was as follows :—

			Bengal. Rs.	Behar. Rs.	Total. Rs.	Sicca. Rs.
1790-91	...	...	2,32,78,541	53,09,181	2,85,87,722	2,68,00,989
1871-72	...	...	2,55,04,775	97,04,021	3,52,08,866	
Increase	...		22,26,234	43,94,910	66,21,144	

2. The settlement embraced, roughly speaking, the tracts
of country now comprised in the divisions of Burdwan, the
Presidency, Rajshahye, Dacca, Chittagong, Patna, and Bhau-
gulpore. It also comprised part of the Hazareebaugh and
Maunbhoom districts in the Chota Nagpore division, as well
as Julpigoree, Goalpara, and Cooch Behar, which are now in
the Cooch Behar division, but which then formed part of the
Rungpore Collectorate. The revenue of the districts in the
Assam and Cuttack divisions, and of the districts of Lohar-
dugga, Singbhoom, Darjeeling, and the Bhutan Dooars, for
1871-72, has been excluded, as none of these districts were
covered by the settlement of 1789 to 1791.

3. Some additions were made to the revenue demand
when the zemindars were relieved of police charges, and otherwise; and in 1824-25 the demand had risen to Company's
Rs. 2,98,62,021, being an increase of Rs. 12,74,299. After
that period the revenue expanded as resumptions of invalid
revenue-free tenures proceeded under Regulation II of 1819.
In 1828-29 the current demand was Company's Rs. 3,04,27,770.
Eighteen years later (in 1846-47) it had risen to Rs. 3,12,52,676;
and after this period a fresh and very marked enhancement
occurred, bringing the demand in 1848-49 up to Rs. 3,40,96,605.

APP. XII.
———
LAND REVENUE
AT THE PERMA-
NENT SETTLE-
MENT.
———
Para. 3, contd.

During the three years 1847, 1848, and 1849, no less than 6,198 estates were added to the revenue roll by resumption; and the revenue was otherwise swelled by escheats, the assessment of lands brought to light by the Survey, and resettlements of Government estates. After this the demand remained almost stationary up to 1856-57, in which year it appears at the slightly reduced amount of Rs. 3,37,38,783. In the following year it rose to Rs. 3,39,10,362; and from that time there has been a steady expansion, interrupted in the year 1866-67 only by the famine, up to Rs. 3,55,34,022, which represented the current demand for 1872-73.

4. The increase up to 1846-47, when the revenue amounted to Rs. 3,12,52,676, was Rs. 26,64,954. The expenditure in 1874-75-76 for the Bengal famine amounted to 6½ millions sterling, interest on which at 4½ per cent. amounts to £292,500; so that the whole of the increase down to 1846-77, and a portion of the subsequent increase, have been lost, leaving the increased charges of administration since 1793 to be met from the remaining revenues of the province. One object of the permanent settlement was to secure in a rich landed proprietary, a provision against famine; instead of that, the famine expenditure saved many zemindars, among a class that is enriched not only by all that can be extracted from ryots on the scale in other parts of Bengal, but by a great deal more than is extracted from China through Administration
Report, 1875-76,
Part I, page 39. the opium revenue. In the Administration Report for 1875-76 it was observed: " Without the relief afforded by Government to the famishing people, there must have been some serious failure in the land revenue, and (what would have been a very great evil) some extensive transfer of landed property and ruin of old families. One counterbalancing advantage, then, of the heavy relief expenditure incurred by Government, was this, that the great interests pertaining to the land revenue were preserved intact."

I. The land revenue assessed in the last century, when the conditions of the country, and the relative capabilities of different districts, were vastly different from what they now are, bears no sort of proportion to the present value of the land; while in some places the revenue may still amount to a tolerable assessment, in others it amounts to no more than a very small quit-rent. The total rental of each estate may be to the revenue in the proportion of 3, 10, 50, or 100 times. It is evident, then, that the land revenue could not be taken as any guide to an assessment upon landed property; on the contrary, the value of the property and the free income of the proprietor are in the inverse ratio to the amount of the assessment.

II. The Bengal Road Cess Act of 1871 is a measure which provides for the valuation of the lands and of the various rights to the land, and for the record of the holders of these various rights. It then establishes local bodies for determining the expenditure, and striking a rate for the year to meet the necessary expenditure on the whole immovable property of the district. This rate may in no case exceed one-half anna in each rupee of the net profits of the landholders and other owners, that is, about three per cent. The valuation is to last for five years, and to be subject to revision at the end of that period.

III. The zemindars are bound to render an account of all rents receivable by them from their under-tenants, it being provided throughout, in addition to penalties for false returns, that no rent not returned shall be recoverable by law. When the zemindar's returns are received, if, as generally happens, their immediate tenants are sub-holders, superior to the cultivating ryot, the same process is gone through with the sub-holders; they are required to file a statement of holdings under them, and so on, it may be through several gradations, till the actual ryot is reached.

IV. In regard to cultivating ryots paying less than Rs. 100 per annum, no attempt is made to distinguish between the different classes of ryots possessed of more or less beneficial interest in the soil. It is not sought to make an actual rack-rent valuation of the soil, but only an account of the rent actually paid.

V. The Road Cess Act proceeds on the principle that half the rate is to be paid by the occupiers, that is, by the ryots, and half by the rent-receivers, each according to his own share of the profit. On the superior holders is also imposed the duty of collecting the money due from those under them, and paying the whole in a lump for each estate. A valuation roll of each estate, and of the district, being completed, and the rate for the year being declared, half of that rate will be published as the rate payable by the ryots. The holder immediately above the ryots will collect from them the half-rate, and pay to his superiors the full rate for his holding, less half-rate on the rent or revenue receivable by the superior; and each superior holder will pay to his own superior in like manner, till the zemindar holding direct of Government pays the whole rate on the whole estate, less half-rate on the share of profits which goes to Government as land revenue. The effect is, that each holder passes on the ryot's half-rate, with a half-rate paid by himself on his own share of the profits.

VI (a). The provision which throws half the rate on the ryot is one which caused to the Lieutenant-Governor much doubt and hesitation at the time—he may say extreme doubt and hesitation; and he has been subject to a recurrence of doubt and qualms of conscience on the point ever since. Among other reasons to which he yielded (with recurring spasms of doubt) was the following :

(b). The law allows the proprietor to sue for enhancement whenever the productive powers of the land, or the value of the produce, have been increased by any means other than by the labour, or at the expense of the ryots. Now, if the roads and canals made by a local assessment on the proprietors open up the country, render it more easy to bring produce to market, and so increase the value of agricultural produce, it will

follow, in law and logic, that the proprietors will be entitled to an enhancement of rent on that ground. Either, then, the ryots will have to
submit to an increase of rent, or there will be given to the zemindar an
additional incentive to that process of general enhancement by litigation
which, in the Lieutenant-Governor's judgment, is of all things most to
be deprecated in the interest of all parties. The view which under these
circumstances he has taken is, that it is really better for the ryot that the
law should step in, and by a summary rule make that adjustment which
would otherwise follow by a long and difficult process. We now say to
him : " Improvements are about to be made by which you, the ryot, will
benefit as well as the proprietor, and on account of which, if they be
made by the proprietor, you would be liable to an enhancement of rent.
Instead of allowing that process to go on, we will impose on you a very
light rate, which we believe that you are able to pay ; the expense of the
improvements will be divided between you and the proprietor ; they will
not be improvements made otherwise than at your expense, but your own
improvements in the expense of which you have shared ; and thus by so
sharing now, you will avoid the liability to consequent enhancement
hereafter." It is thus that the Lieutenant-Governor justifies the
imposition of the half-rate on the ryots ; he may be right or he may
be wrong, but of this he is sure, that on the whole question he has been
actuated, and he believes that his Council have been actuated, by a regard
for the interests of the people at large.

5. The number of estates and tenures of all sorts, valued
for the road cess according to the latest returns in the
Administration Reports to the end of 1876-77, including
sub-tenures, but excluding ryots' holdings, is as follows :—

	Number of estates valued.		Number of tenures valued.		TOTAL OF		VALUATION MADE OF		Revenue of district.
	Paying revenue.		Paying rent.		Estates.	Tenures.	Estates.	Tenures.	
	Over Rs. 100.	Rs. 100 and under.	Over Rs. 100.	Rs. 100 and under.			Rs.	Rs.	Rs.
BENGAL—									
Eastern Districts (only Dacca Division)	4,870	1,03,259	21,926	5,31,573	1,08,129	5,53,504	2,55,48,750	2,09,46,131	51,02,916
Western Districts ...	4,573	13,596	10,059	1,43,201	18,169	1,53,260	1,84,90,625	1,20,84,901	77,33,517
Central Districts ...	6,187	17,403	20,476	1,70,910	23,590	1,91,386	2,96,35,353	1,77,03,581	98,96,840
	15,630	1,34,258	52,461	8,45,689	1,49,888	8,98,150	7,36,74,728	5,07,34,613	2,27,33,273
BEHAR	16,876	41,848	24,458	88,148	58,724	112,606	4,92,99,203	2,39,91,475	1,11,87,103
ORISSA	2,825	28,487	2,470	31,621	31,312	34,091	40,19,130	14,92,631	17,36,845
Lohardugga, Hazaree-baugh, Maunbhoom...	258	1,164	4,236	50,645	1,422	54,881	37,40,869	35,36,294	3,01,102
	35,589	2,05,757	33,625	1,016,103	2,41,346	1,099,728	13,07,33,930	7,97,55,013	3,59,58,323

The demand for the road cess on lands and mines amounted for 1876-77 to Rs. 28,65,506, and for the cess year 1877-78 to Rs. 30,63,845. Besides this, the demand for the Public Works road cess for 1877-78 amounted to Rs. 34,99,334. The number of estates in Bengal and Behar paying revenue to Government were classed as follows for 1872-73 :—

App. XII.

CONDITION OF
THE ZEMINDARS.

Para. 7

	Estates upwards of 500 acres.	Estates under 500 acres.	Total.
Sylhet	570	53,368	53,938
Tirhoot	980	12,452	13,432
	1,550	65,820	67,370
Behar (remainder) ...	7,281	21,057	28,338
Bengal (do.) ...	7,449	51,043	58,492
	16,280	137,920	154,200

In 1877-78 the total number of estates was 146,380, a number of estates in Calcutta having been merged in the books as one estate in 1876-77. Of these numbers of estates many belong to one proprietor, so that the number of proprietors is less than the number of estates.

6. I. With respect to the valuations thus obtained for the road cess, we must remember that, as has been said, we have not sought to press the screw as tight as might be possible, on this the first valuation. We have been content to get a good approximation to a full valuation, trusting to the second valuation five years hence to render the result more exactly complete. In addition to the general disposition to under-state rather than over-state values, and to the possible under-valuation of small estates summarily assessed, it must be understood that, actual rents only being rendered, all persons classed as ryots who hold at fixed rates, having occupancy rights, or being otherwise in any degree privileged or beneficial tenants, are assessed only on the rent they pay, not on the rack-value. So far, then, as any ryots pay short of rack-rents, the valuation is below the outside valuation.

Administration
Report, 1872-73,
pages 39-40.

II. Taking all things into consideration, we may say that probably the land which has given an assessable rent-roll of something more than three times the land revenue, is probably worth four or five times the revenue, especially if we take permanently-settled districts only. The few not permanently settled pay a higher revenue in proportion than the others.

7.—Mr. R. B. Chapman (3rd June 1868).

I. As a matter of fact, the State resources which were given up in 1793 are not now, and have not for many years been, accumulated in the hands of a few wealthy individuals, who pass their time in selfish and careless luxury, but are distributed among a very large number of persons.

Parl. Paper,
Sess. 1870,
Vol. 52.

II. From statements which I have seen made, not without authority, and in places where error and ignorance on such subjects are not to be expected or assumed, I incline to think that I shall cause some astonishment when I assert, as I do without fear of contradiction by any one who is really acquainted with the facts, that the zemindars of Bengal are not, as a body, wealthy men. There are *some* rich men among them, a few *very* rich men, but the bulk of the class are men of very limited income, and too many of them of embarrassed circumstances.

III. I think it very likely that not one-fourth of the primary payments of the cultivators reach the Government treasury, and that the proprietors of the land in Bengal divide among them a profit of at least £10,000,000 a year. But this is distributed over an immense variety of tenures, from the ryot with a right of occupancy, who, it is probable, ordinarily does in practice enjoy some beneficiary interest, to the Rajah of Burdwan, or the Rajah of Durbhunga.

IV. The settlement has, I repeat, so worked (not, I think, disadvantageously), that the accumulation of immense properties in the hands of individuals is not common. The vast majority of the estates for which revenue is paid direct to the Government are *petty* properties, and the larger ones are almost all so charged with subordinate tenures of a more or less permanent character, as often to leave the so-called owner with only a moderate annuity.

8. The illegal levies by the zemindars may be divided into two classes—illegal transit and market taxes levied from the general public, and illegal cesses levied from the agricultural ryots by their landlords, in addition to the legal rents. In the original settlement, certain items classed under the general name of "sayer" were included in the assets of the zemindars; dues levied on produce brought to market, tolls taken on boats passing along rivers, or on goods landed and shipped, and so on; but these practices having led to abuse, it was determined to abolish and prohibit them all, and to give compensation to the zemindars who had profited by them. A Regulation for this purpose was passed in 1797, and thenceforward all such collections were strictly prohibited. All dues on transit and purchase and sale were declared to be illegal, and forbidden under penalty of confiscation of the estates of those who contravened the law. It was specially enacted that no dues whatever were to be levied on markets, saving only regular monthly or annual rents for shops; and for the market dues, as well as for all other collections, full compensation was given. Yet it turns out that these enactments have been wholly set at defiance; dues on goods brought for sale are levied in almost every market in the country. One case has come to light near Calcutta, where the proprietor to this day draws from Government annual compensation for his abolished market dues, but has only moved his market to a short distance, and there levies the dues just the same.

I. The agricultural cesses consist of various dues and charges levied from the ryots, in addition to the regular rent, and generally in proportion to the rent. The permanent settlement regulations positively prohibited all such duties, strictly confining the zemindars to the customary rent proper; but in this, as in other things, these laws have been wholly set at defiance in modern times. The modern zemindar taxes his ryots for every extravagance or necessity that circumstances may suggest, as his predecessors taxed them in the past. He will tax them for the support of his agents of various kinds and degrees; for the pay- ment of his income tax and his postal cess; for the purchase of an elephant for his own use; for the cost of the stationery of his establishment; for the cost of printing the forms of his rent receipts; for the payment of his lawyers. The milkman gives his milk; the oilman his oil; the weaver his clothes; the confectioner his sweetmeats; the fisherman his fish. The zemindar levies benevolences from his ryots for a festival, for a religious ceremony, for a birth, for a marriage; he exacts fees from them on all change of their holdings, on the exchange of leases and agreements, and on all transfers and sales; he imposes a fine on them when he settles their petty disputes, and when the police or when the magistrate visits his estates; he levies blackmail on them when social scandals transpire, or when an offence or an affray is committed; he establishes his private pound near his cutcherry, and realises a fine for every head of cattle that is caught trespassing on the ryots' crops. The *abwabs*, as these illegal cesses are called, pervade the whole zemindari system. In every zemindari there is a naib; under the naib there are gomashtas; under the gomashta there are *piyadas*, or peons. The naib exacts a *hisabana*, or perquisite for adjusting accounts, annually. The naibs and gomashtas take their share in the regular *abwabs;* they have their little *abwabs* of their own. The naib occasionally indulges in an ominous raid in the mofussil; one rupee is exacted from every ryot who has a rental, as he comes to proffer his respects. Collecting peons, when they are sent to summon ryots to the landlord's cutcherry, exact from them daily four or five annas as summons fees.

II. In most districts there are cesses peculiar to the district; in all districts it must be said that these exactions largely prevail. It has been found that they are really almost quite universal, the only difference being that in some places and in some estates they are levied in greater numbers and amount, and in less numbers and amount in others.

III. In Nuddea there is a small hamlet of ten or fifteen householders, men neither of substance nor yet of exceptional poverty. The zemindari gomashtas proceeded with their peons to this village during the inundation of 1871, and, apportioning on an average their requirements at three annas to every rupee of rental, demanded a benevolence of Rs. 54-2 as the sum of various kinds of *abwabs*. This amount was actually realised; yet the ryots did not complain. They never would have complained in this case had the zemindars allowed matters to stop at this point. But the zemindars ventured, within three or four days after the realisation of this amount, to impose another cess of forty rupees upon this petty village, as its contribution towards the marriage expenses of the daughter of one of their own number. Yet even in these straits the ryots exhausted every means of complying with the additional exaction. They sowed indigo for the planter, and they applied to him for assistance, but in vain; they besought their mahajun for the money, but fruitlessly, and only as a last resource petitioned the magistrate for redress.

IV. This case was especially reported by the Board of Revenue to Government. The Board observed: "The case seems to prove the unmerciful manner in which unauthorised cesses are demanded; the fear of the oppressed royts, which induces them to comply with oppressive demands, of the illegality of which they may be aware, and the extreme difficulty of obtaining any adequate redress; and to show conclusively that some means should be afforded to the Government to check the rapacity of the zemindars and their agents, and to afford protection to their victims."

V. It has been the ryots' immemorial practice to pay these *abwabs*, and they pay accordingly; they pay because they have always paid, and because in the long run it involves less trouble to pay than to refuse. Upon a full review of the matter, the Lieutenant-Governor came to the conclusion that the system of these exactions was now in such universal vogue, was so deeply rooted, and so many social relations depended thereon, that it became a question whether it was desirable that Government should, by any general or very stringent measures, interfere to put a stop to them. It was at the same time made thoroughly clear that the Government, in hesitating to adopt severe or extreme measures, in no degree recognised or legalised those cesses. Illegal, irrecoverable by law, and prohibited by law, they must,' it was said, remain; but it was deemed that it would perhaps be better, under all the circumstances, not to interfere, except in extreme cases. As the people get better protected, better educated, and better able to understand and protect their own rights and position, things would, it was felt, no doubt to some extent, adjust themselves. At present the people certainly prefer to pay moderate cesses to an enhancement of rent.

VI. In Orissa, however, the case is in many respects different and worse than it is in Bengal. Not only has it been established that illegal exactions have there been carried to a monstrous point, but the inquiries on this question, and the separate inquiry regarding remissions of land revenue specifically granted by Government on account of the famine of 1866, on the express condition that the rents of the ryots should also be remitted, show conclusively that, as a rule, the zemindars did not give the benefit of either the remissions or the advances they received to the ryots, but continued to collect their rents. Further, in some parts of Orissa at any rate, the Government settlement made direct with the hereditary ryots has been utterly set at nought; the Government leases have been taken from the ryots; the rents fixed by the Government officers have been increased many fold; and the main object of the extension of the settlement for a fresh term of thirty years after the famine, *viz.*, permitting the ryots to hold on at the old settlement rates, has been utterly defeated.

VII. For the rest, the papers showed most conclusively, in the Lieutenant-Governor's opinion, the utter failure of the system adopted in Orissa of making a minute and careful settlement of the rights of all parties, and then leaving the settlement to itself without the supervision of Government, and the machinery of tehsildars, canoongoes, and village accountants, by which such settlements are worked and carried out in other provinces. Nowhere was the settlement more carefully made, or made in greater detail, than in Orissa; perhaps nowhere were the status and privileges of the ryots so well protected in theory as in Orissa; yet we find, after the expiry of a thirty-years' settlement, during which no annual or periodical papers were filed, and the settlement records were in no way carried out, that this whole system of record and protection have utterly collapsed, the records have become waste-paper, and the ryots, supposed to be so well protected, are among the most oppressed in India. The papers brought home to the Lieutenant-Governor most strongly that, so far at least, the settlement should be immediately revised, * * and that it should be revised at the expense of the zemindars, as the Commissioner proposed.

App. XII.
———
ZEMINDARS'
POWERS UNDER
THE LAW.

Para. 9.

9.—RENT LAWS AND ENHANCEMENT OF RENT.

I. Administration Report, 1872-73.—The general provisions of the Regulations of 1793 were in favour of the tenant. The theory of the permanent settlement was to give to all under-holders, down to the ryots, the same security of tenure as against the zemindars which the zemindar had against the Government. Sub-holders of talooks and other divisions under the zemindars were recognised and protected in their holding, subject to the payment of the established dues. As respects the ryots, the main provisions were these: all extra cesses and exactions were abolished, and the zemindars were required to specify in writing the original rent payable by each ryot at the pergunnah or established rates. If any dispute arose regarding the rates to be so entered, the question was to be "determined in the civil court of the zillah in which the lands were situated, according to the rates established in the pergunnah for lands of the same description and quality as those respecting which the dispute arose." It was further provided that no zemindar should have power to cancel the leases, except on the ground that they had been obtained by collusion at rates below the established rates, and that the resident ryots should always be entitled to renew pottahs at these rates. In fact the fixity of tenure and fixity of rent rates were secured to the ryots by law. It has already been pointed out that provision was made for canoongoes and putwaries, an object of whose appointment was declared to be "to prevent oppression of the persons paying rent." On behalf of the ryots it was a record of rights only that was wanting. The status that was designed for the tenantry was, however, much impaired, and in great part destroyed, by the great powers subsequently given to zemindars under the old *huftum* (seventh) and *punjum* (fifth) Regulations, with a view to enable them to realise their rents.

Administration Report, 1872-73.

Zemindars' powers under the law.

II. Mr. Buckland, Commissioner of Burdwan, 1872-73.—From the expressions as to public opinion which will be found in the district reports, I think that it is shown that the trial of rent suits in the civil courts is a mistake. I think that it was too great and sudden a transition from the other extreme of *huftum* and *punjum*, which, once household words, will soon have to be explained to the inquisitive rising generation of ryots. Under the *huftum* process (Regulation VII of 1799) the person of the ryot could be seized; under the *punjum* process (Regulation V of 1812) his property could be distrained; and in either case the proceedings commenced by a strong presumption, equivalent to a knock-down blow, against the ryot. It may not be generally known that the Regulation of 1799 was enacted in order to save the perpetual

Commissioners' Reports, 1872-73, page 80.

APP. XII.

ZEMINDARS'
POWERS UNDER
THE LAW.

Para. 9, contd.

settlement, the existence of which was then imperilled by the excessive independence which the ryots enjoyed; for, although it is now the custom to say that the rights of the ryots were not properly protected in the perpetual settlement, it turned out at the time that they could take such good care of their own rights, that the zemindars could not collect their rents from them until the Government came to the rescue of the zemindar, and made the ryots liable to arrest for default of payment of rent. It is, I fear, a mistake to have gone so far and so quickly in the opposite direction; and I have looked in vain in the published records of the Bengal Legislative Council debates for any sufficient cause there shown for the substitution of the ordinary form of suit for the old summary suit. From the very nature of the case, where almost every thing depends upon a ripening crop, a summary trial is necessary, or the only thing worth fighting for will have vanished.

Commissioners'
Reports, 1872-73,
page 4.

III. Lieutenant-Governor.—Mr. Buckland recites the history and present situation of the Rent Law. His Honor fears that it is the fact that the status designed for the ryot by the Regulation of 1793 was much impaired, and in great part destroyed, by the great powers subsequently given to the zemindars under the old *huftum* and *punjum* regulations, with a view to enable them to realise their rents. As Mr. Buckland truly describes the process under the law of 1799 and that of 1812, the proceedings began in both cases by a strong presumption, equivalent to a knock-down blow against the ryot. The law of 1859 reduced the powers exercised by the zemindars themselves, while it increased the grounds of enhancement, and afforded the remedy of a summary process before Deputy Collectors, who were, however, often very insufficiently qualified. Rent suits are now transferred to the civil courts; they are better tried, and the rights of the ryots are more respected than they were; but, on the other hand, there certainly seems now good ground of complaint that there is difficulty in quickly realising undisputed rents by legal process.

Report of Bengal Famine
Commission,
1866, Part III,
paras. 32-5.

Right of occupancy at a fixed
rent.

10. I. Last in the scale come the ryots. There can be no doubt that it was the intention of Lord Cornwallis and his advisers to give to this class also the benefit of his famous settlement. Although it was not found possible, as at first intended, to record all individual rights, the clearly expressed provisions, that the zemindars should not take more from the ryots than the established rates of each pergunnah, and should not eject them, seem distinctly to confer on the ryots permanency of tenure and general fixity of payment. For seventy years the only ground of enhancement recognised by the Courts was, that particular ryots were paying rates exceptionally low and under the established and legal rates. Even as respects such ryots, the courts had held that possession at the same rate of rent for twenty years before the settlement gave a right to hold at that rate for ever, however low it might be; and Act X of 1859 has so far extended this right, that all who have held at the same rate since the settlement are entitled so to hold for ever. In theory, therefore, the ryot of the time of the permanent settlement has by law as permanent and fixed a tenure as the zemindar; and the law has further protected him against the difficulty of proving his holding by providing that, if he can prove a holding at a uniform rate for twenty years, he shall be presumed to have held from the settlement, unless the

contrary be proved. But in practice there are several difficulties.
The knowledge of a right to hold at fixed rates, in a country where till
then no payments, superior or inferior, had been fixed beyond the reach
of despotic interference, but slowly reached the lower classes of the
people; the zemindars, themselves in those days highly assessed, as
peace and prosperity increased the resources of the ryots, irregularly
pressed either for increased rents or for various unauthorized extra cesses
and benevolences, such as in India constantly crystallize into fixed
payments, and many compromises were made under which they were
bought off by somewhat increased payments. The holder of the most
ancient tenure may any day find his fixity utterly destroyed by the
exhibition in his zemindar's books of some small unexplained varieties
in his actual payments in the time of his grandfather, fifty or sixty years
ago. The case is also frequent in which holdings are declared variable,
not because the rent is shown to have varied, but because the holder
cannot give that amount of proof of twenty years' unvaried holding, which
satisfies the local courts. So great is the unreliability of evidence, as
it is taken in this country, that many judges consider oral evidence
always worthless, and documentary evidence gradually worse. Except
in the case of those men who have already successfully run the
gauntlet of all the courts, it may be said that the most painful uncertainty exists, whether each man is proprietor of valuable land or a
mere tenant. In some districts there are many ancient and valuable
ryoti-tenures at fixed rates, but in other parts of the country all depends on
the tendency of the litigation, much of which is yet, we fear, to come.

II. The remaining class of rights is that of those ryots who have
right of occupancy, but not right of holding at a permanent fixed rent.
Till the passing of Act X of 1859, the only standard of enhancement
for these men was that of the pergunnah rates, which had become
extremely vague and ill-defined. By the last-mentioned enactment, the
principle was introduced that these ryots should be liable to enhancement of rent on account of enhancement in the value of the produce
of their lands, arising from causes other than their own industry and
improvements. It has been ruled by the highest court that this entitles the zemindar to enhance in proportion to the increase in the
market value of the staples of production; and the effect is, so far
to put the ryot somewhat on the footing of a permanent holder on a
fixed corn rent. If adequate machinery be provided for working out this
principle, it will admit of a tenure beneficial to a considerable degree;
and we think that such machinery should be provided something after
the fashion in which the "fiars" prices are struck in Scotland.

III. This, however, is not all. The old provision for enhancement
to the rates payable by the same class of ryots, for lands of the same
class, still remains as an additional instrument of enhancement, and the
pergunnah rates having much fallen into desuetude, there is still much
uncertainty, not yet fully dealt with judicially, on the question what
constitutes a *class of ryots;* while the provision to save improvements
effected by a man's own labour and money not being introduced into this
clause of the law, it is still doubtful whether a man who by his own
industry has converted barren land into first class garden land may be
charged first class rates.

APP. XII.

RIGHT OF OCCU-
PANCY AT
PERGUNNAH
RATES.

Para. 10, contd.

IV. All these uncertainties are rendered doubly harassing by the farming system, under which the profit of the farmer largely depends on successful enhancement.

V. On the whole question we can only here say that the great necessity of Bengal is to render certain and definite the rights in the land, and thus to enable a man with money in his hand to deal confidently with some one person as the absolute owner of at least the *dominium utile* over the field which he wishes to buy. At present there are so many various interests, and so much uncertainty regarding all, that most dealings in land are a species of gambling, and comparatively few have an interest so complete and secure as to enable them to improve with prudence, if otherwise willing to do so.

11. At the time of the permanent settlement, when the rights of the ryots were destroyed, the blow was mitigated by the scantiness of the population compared to the land, which circumstance made it the interest of zemindars to attract ryots to their estates. In the present day, circumstances are reversed. In the Administration Report for 1871-72 it was observed as follows :—

Administration
Report, 1871-72.
Part I, page 35. I. If we eliminate the exceptional tracts of hill, waste, marsh, and jungle, we shall find that the districts, and parts of districts in the plains which are without special drawback, cannot average less than about 650 souls per square mile—say one person per acre of gross area. In the best districts we can hardly allow less than 25 per cent. for rivers and marshes, roads and village sites, and other areas for any reason unculturable or uncultivated. Say we have 75 per cent. of cultivation, or three-fourths of an acre per head; we may allow one-third of that for products other than the food of the population—oil-seeds and fibres, indigo and opium, and commercial exports of all kinds, including a large export of rice, as well as the dress and luxuries of the people of the country. The result will be that we can hardly have more than half an acre per head devoted to raising the food of the population. If this be compared with the average given to raise food by agriculture and grazing in England, and the quantity of food imported there, it will probably be found that, deficient as may be the Indian agriculture, it supports more people from the same breadth of cultivated land than any European countries.

II. On the other hand, this scantiness of the land, compared to the population, suggested the great social difficulties which may arise if population much further increases. * * *

III. No statement of occupations has yet been received, but one thing is very plain, *viz.*, the extraordinary absence of large towns. The population beyond Calcutta and the suburbs seems to be almost wholly rural. Patna has 159,000 people, and there are a few second-rate towns in Behar. In Bengal proper, the largest town is Dacca, 69,000. The supposed great city of Moorshedabad, the seat of the Nawab Nazim and his numerous followers, even including some outlying places not properly in the city, has only 46,000 souls; and there is not another town above 31,000, and scarcely a dozen averaging 20,000 each.

Rungpore, the capital of the great district of Rungpore, contains 6,100 souls, and Jessore 6,152 ; each of these districts having a population over two millions.

Mr. Beverley, in his account of the census of Bengal, observed that outside Calcutta and its suburbs there are probably not more than half a [dozen towns with a population of 50,000 inhabitants; and even of these the boundaries sometimes include large rural tracts, and some of them might more justly be described as groups of villages formed into an union for municipal purposes, than as towns in the European sense of the word.

12. From these extracts it appears that population is pressing on the means of subsistence, with the necessary result of raising prices ; and that it is pressing on the means of occupying land, with the result of multiplying competitors for cultivators' holdings; and these results of the growth of population conspire to enhance rents.

13. Respecting enhancement of rents, the following notices are extracted from the Administration Reports of the Bengal Government, and from those of Commissioners of divisions :—

1871-72—

I. (*a*). The mutiny led to one of those strange oscillations of Indian opinions which seem to occur periodically like the tides. By a very unintelligible concatenation of ideas, because the North-Western Provinces had been the chief scene of the sepoy mutiny, it was held by many that the civil administration of these provinces and of the Punjab, previously believed to be remarkably successful, must be bad. Many people thought that the mere fact that an institution obtained in those provinces, was enough to condemn it. Settlements of the land with small holders were declared to be open to every possible objection, and there was a great revival of the school which maintained the advantage of great landlords and absolute rights of property. In 1859 a very important Act for the regulation of the relations between landlord and tenant, based upon old principles, with some modern additions, was passed quietly enough, but soon after there sprung up a storm of opposition ; it was denounced as confiscation of the rights of landlords; attempts were made to put upon it a construction which would have nullified all the protection it afforded to ryots ; and it was not till after years of hot and angry discussion and keen litigation, that the highest court gave to it an authoritative construction, and settled the action of the courts into a course not unfavourable to the ryots who have means enough, or combination enough, to litigate.

(*b*). In the south-eastern districts of the Delta, where, as in most districts of Bengal proper, the agricultural ryots are chiefly Mahomedans, it is the fashion, whenever a landlord quarrels with his tenants,

Administration Report, 1871-72, Part I, page 48.

Ibid.., Part I, page 22.

App. XII.
—
ENHANCEMENT
OF RENT.
—
Para. 13, contd.

to stigmatize the latter as "Ferazees," a sect professing reformed tenets and doctrines of equality, and to attribute to their conduct a political character. * * * There is, however, no doubt that the people of these tidal districts are hot-blooded and pugnacious more than other Bengalees, and more given to the use of arms, which they possess in abundance. At the same time there is, the Lieutenant-Governor believes, no serious element of disaffection in their religion *per se*, though the Ferazee doctrines, which so many of them hold, might, in the event of serious agrarian questions, form a bond and rallying cry among them; and this part of the country is thus not without some elements of political anxiety. The Lieutenant-Governor has expressed his satisfaction that many landlords of these parts have found it to be their best policy to take a bonus from the better ryots (who are often prosperous and well-to-do), and to give them perpetual leases at fixed rents. The registration records show a very large creation of such tenures in these districts; and the Lieutenant-Governor trusts to this distribution of the rights of property upon a wide oasis as the best conservative force, and the best security for peace and observance of the law.

Ibid., Part I, page 23.

(*c*). The enhancement of rents has been alluded to as a cause of excitement in particular cases; but it may be said that the rights of enhancement, conferred on landlords by Act X of 1859, have not been the occasion of much serious excitement, or great social disturbance in these provinces, generally, in the past year. Of late years the courts have shown a tendency to scrutinize thoroughly the grounds of enhancement, and to watch the cases affecting great classes of ryots, who are individually unable to contest particular cases with zemindars on equal terms in respect of money and legal aid. And the zemindars of Bengal have not generally been very pushing in this respect. It was principally in connection with the indigo question that the planters of Bengal proper fought and lost the battle of an unlimited enhancement of the rents of the ryots possessed of a right of occupancy. The zemindars are most frequently content if they can get extra cesses and benevolences—illegal, but which the ryots certainly prefer to enhancement of rent. In Behar, where the rights of ryots are, it is believed, less respected than in Bengal, the indigo system has rather tended to keep down rents, as it did in Bengal, till the ryots refused to grow indigo on the old terms. An ordinary farmer of a village or group of villages, under the fashion prevailing on most great estates, makes it his sole business to exploit the rents; whereas an indigo-planter farms the village for the sake of the indigo, and generally leaves the rents alone, so long as the prescribed tale of indigo cultivation is maintained.

1872-73—

Administration.

II. (1). (*a*). Meantime the unsettled questions between landholders and ryots have been brought into prominence by what are known as the Pubna rent disturbances. This district, at the confluence of the Ganges and Brahmaputra, is one in which the ryots have some independence of character, and have of late acquired some knowledge of their rights. It appears that the zemindars had been in the habit of levying very heavy illegal cesses. More recently, probably alarmed by the inquiry into these cesses, and foreseeing the effect of the obligation to return a statement of rents, by which they would be bound, in case the road cess (already in operation in the neighbouring districts, but not in Pubna) was extended to Pubna, the zemindars became anxious to consolidate the cesses with the rents, and to take the opportunity of obtaining at the same time a large increase of rent. But they had not served the legal notices of enhancement by which enhancement must be preceded, and legal means would be tedious, expensive, and difficult in these days, when the ryots of Eastern Bengal have learnt to unite for common action, and the courts have expounded the laws in a manner favourable to the ryots, for which the landholders were not prepared. In this dilemma they attempted to obtain their object by irregular and illegal pressure. Some of the more unscrupulous zemindars certainly put on much improper pressure of this kind, and attempted by this means to obtain very unfair, extortionate, and illegal documents, binding the ryots to pay largely increased rents, to pay all cesses imposed by Government, whether on the occupier or the owner, to surrender the right of occupancy in case of difference with the zemindar, and altogether to place themselves at the landlord's mercy. There can be no doubt that in this attempt to overrule the law, and obliterate the rights of the ryots, some of the zemindars acted very illegally, and that the first fault lay with them.

(*b*). But trade unions are an old institution in India, and local ryots' unions are common enough in Eastern Bengal. The ryots who were hard pressed by the worst zemindars, and who had nearly yielded, obtained the support of their fellows, who knew that their turn would come next, and a very extensive ryots' union was formed and rapidly spread. Then, as is so apt to happen in such cases, some of the men of the union committed themselves by breaking the peace and the law. There was a violent and threatening outbreak, of which of course many bad characters took advantage. The deeds of the rioters were enormously exaggerated; in reality, they did nothing of a very atrocious character, but there were serious breaches of the peace, a little plunder of property, and some old quarrels were worked off. There was no loss of life or very serious personal injury. But the landholder class was thoroughly alarmed, and terrible stories of the atrocities committed by an excited Jacqueire have been told all over Bengal, and partly believed in. * *

(*c*). The difficulties were enhanced by disputes as to measurement, which all over Bengal have always afforded a fertile source of quarrel between landlord and tenant, there being no uniform standard, and the local measuring rod varying from pergunnah to pergunnah and almost from village to village. In Pubna especially there is extreme diversity of measuring standards. All the zemindars were not equally bad, but there were undoubtedly some among them who resorted to illegal pressure, and strongly attempted illegal enhancement; in the cases where the shares were much sub-divided, also, especial oppression was practised, and the quarrels among the sharers themselves had not a little to do with the recent outbreaks. It is the practice for each sharer in an undivided estate to collect separately both rents and cesses, benevolences, &c., and in the estate in which the worst of the Pubna outbreaks occurred, one

Administration
Report, 1872-73,
Part III,
page 29.

shareholder had sublet his share to parties who were inimical to the other shareholder—a state of things which led to much dispute.

.(d). *Rajshahye Division.*—There are several very noteworthy indications referred to in this report, that there is a rising among the ryots of a more independent spirit than previously existed, and of a better knowledge of their rights. A general impression is spreading in the country, that the hitherto undefined relation between landlord and tenant must be replaced by something better. The Lieutenant-Governor fully recognizes that we are progressing, and that things must gradually be put on a more defined footing. His Honour, however, considers that it may be doubtful whether legal definitions, and facility of recourse to courts, where rich men and lawyers prevail, will be altogether to the advantage of ryots in this country; and he does not desire to go too fast in substituting legal definitions for customary adjustments, so long as the parties get on fairly well one with another. His Honour would hope that Government officers may avail much by their influence in effecting adjustments among the parties themselves.

(e). *Orissa.*—Since the last few years a sort of antipathy has sprung up between the zemindar and his ryot, the endeavour of the former being always to keep the latter under subjection, and that of the latter to shake off the subjection. The ryot is convinced that in a court of justice the zemindar has no better privilege than himself—a belief which, though it compels him to seek redress in the courts, tends ultimately to his material injury. Whether he gains or loses the lawsuits, his sufferings in both cases are certain. The zemindar has many things in his favour to proceed in his own way; he would deprive the ryot of his arable lands, and harass him with lawsuits.

(2). As the country is subjected to inundation, the character of its soil is liable to frequent changes; a ryot, therefore, dares not take a jote at a high rate of rent for a fixed period, lest it be covered with sand by the inundation, and lose its productiveness. He is consequently a tenant-at-will throughout his life. The zemindar, on the other hand, is quite reluctant to give a pottah to a ryot, knowing that it would secure the interests of the latter against his own; and if he at all grants a pottah, he would never note therein the number of the land in the *bhouria*, or make any other specification of it; so that, even where a ryot possesses a pottah, his right is not secured by its vague terms, and in case of dispute the pottah becomes of no use to him. He cannot identify his land and establish his right to it by the production of the pottah. Therefore, whenever he becomes an object of displeasure to the zemindar, the latter either dispossesses him of his jote, or waits till his crops become ripe and fit for cutting, when he demands an exorbitant rent from him, which if not complied with, he appropriates the crop by the easy and simple process of distraint and sale. So the poor ryot is obliged to give up the crop, the produce of his labour and the hope of his future maintenance. Every year the zemindar measures his land by the *paddika*, which by the skill of his underlings would make a man measure more than it really is; and unless the poor ryot can please the man making the measurement, he is compelled to pay a rent higher than what would have been justly due from him if the measurement had been made justly. The zemindar is also a ryot's mahajun.

He will not suffer a ryot to borrow money or paddy from anybody but himself; so in every case he binds the ryot hand and foot, and the latter has no alternative but to submit himself to the zemindar's unjust claims.

(3). Although the rise of prices and the increase of trade have become sources of means to the ryot, yet the continual endeavour of the zemindar to squeeze him, and, in case of opposition, to harass him with lawsuits, have become great bars to his progress. During my winter tour of inspection, I have learnt that, in addition to the rent due from the ryot, the zemindar exacts from him cesses and *abwabs* of various kinds. The ryot unwillingly submits to these exactions for fear of being harassed by Act X suits—the easy mode of binding a ryot to subjection; so his position with respect to his landlord is quite helpless and unpleasant.

(4). No zemindar makes any endeavour to improve his zemindari; and as the demand for arable land has increased, he, instead of endeavouring to improve the lands which lie uncultivated, and make them fit for cultivation, only increases the rate of rent, or deprives one ryot of his land and gives it to another, whenever such opportunity presents itself.

1874-75—

III. (*a*). The rent laws (Acts X of 1859 and VIII of 1869) are commonly called the charters of the ryot. These enactments, indeed, left unchanged the ryots of the superior classes, the tenure-holders, and the sub-proprietors on the one hand, and the ryots of the lowest class and tenants-at-will on the other; but they raised up, intermediate between these two classes, a class of men with an occupancy status—that is, a class of men who, having held for twelve years or more, would not be liable to ejectment while they paid the rent, nor to enhancement of rent, save by decree of a court of justice. The effect of this rule, which has operated now for fifteen years, has, according to all accounts, been very great. Many experienced natives believe that the great majority of cultivators have acquired this occupancy status, and that the mere tenants-at-will are comparatively few. At first the zemindars either acquiesced in, or took no pains to prevent, this gradual change. And although some zemindars do insert provisions in the leases to prevent this status accruing to the tenants, still the majority do not, either because they acquiesce, or because they cease to resist what they regard as inevitable. The general consequence is, that the bulk of the ryots or cultivators have become much raised in position.

Administration Report, 1874-75, Part I, page 8. Right of occupancy.

(*b*). On the other hand, the rent laws, while doing so much for the status of the cultivators, did something also for the landlord, inasmuch as they asserted the principle that even from occupancy ryots he should be entitled to increase of rent under certain conditions. Of these conditions the most important was this, that the value of the produce, or the productive powers of the land, must have been increased otherwise than by the agency or at the expense of the ryot. Around this condition are clustered various questions which excite more lively interest than any other questions in Bengal at the present time. The growth of the export

Administration Report, 1874-75, Part I, page 13.

APP. XII.

ENHANCEMENT
OF RENT.

Para. 13, contd.
trade in agricultural produce has greatly augmented the profits of cultivation to the cultivator. The zemindar considers himself entitled to a share in this improved income, and he founds his demand on the condition above cited. The ryot hesitates to comply altogether; he will pay something additional, but he will not accept the arbitrament of the zemindar, and he is disposed to join issue at law. He will withhold the payment of rent altogether, if he cannot come to terms with the landlord.

Ibid., Part I,
page 2.
(*c*). It is the fact that in some parts of Bengal, especially the eastern districts, the rent-paying powers of the land and the profits of the cultivation have much increased. The ryot is entitled to a large share in the benefit of this; the zemindar may also justly claim a share. The apportionment of the respective shares is the main cause of dispute.

(*d*). In many districts where these special circumstances of increase are not so readily demonstrable, it is reported that the zemindars would be unable to raise their rents if they were to try, as the ryots would contest the demands, and as the tendency of the decisions of the courts is thought to be adverse to such claims on the part of zemindars. This confirms the belief that the status of the ryot is improving, and that, whereas he was once the weaker, he is becoming the stronger party.

Ibid., Part I,
page 13.
(*e*). The zemindars see that the days of force and compulsion are passing away. Though they certainly regard themselves as something more than annuitants on the land, with fixed rents not to be enhanced as the profits of agriculture increase, and reasonably assert their right to a part of "the unearned increment," still they recognise the justice of allowing to the cultivator a good share in the increased produce of his toil, and the expediency of maintaining with their tenantry those friendly relations which ought to spring from community of interest in the soil. Though far from saying that they do anything like all that they ought, still they evince a growing disposition to help their tenantry in time of need. Such certainly is the inference to be drawn from the experience of the famine of 1874. In all parts of these provinces, signal instances of active and comprehensive beneficence and of munificent liberality for all sorts of useful objects on the part of the zemindar frequently occur, which would be deemed honourable to the landlord class in any country.

(*f*). It is true that more capital than at present ought to be laid out by the landlord class on the improvement of the land, &c.

1875-76—

Administration
Report, Part I,
1875-76, page 8.
IV. (*a*). The Act for the prevention of agrarian disturbances arms the Government with full power to prevent agrarian trouble, and the importance of this can hardly be over-estimated. Under the agrarian and rural circumstances of the country, moreover, the materials for such disputes are unfortunately so abundant, that many well-informed observers think that, notwithstanding the outward calm which now prevails, there are questions growing inwardly between landlords and tenants which must sooner or later burst forth in the shape of extensive quarrels,

unless some rules more definite than any which now exist shall be framed for the guidance of the authorities in the determination of rents.

Para. 13, contd.
——
Ibid., page 9.

(*b*). It is not possible, under the circumstances of Bengal, that rents should remain unchanged. If the value of land is to increase with the rise of prices and the improvement of produce, it follows that there must be a moderate and gradual augmentation of rent throughout the country from time to time, enough to satisfy the rights of the landlord, while leaving a clear and liberal margin of profit to the ryot. If the material resources of the nation are to grow and expand; if the culture of new staples is to flourish—the jute of yesterday, as it were, the tobacco of to-day, the flax of to-morrow; if the use of machinery is to spread, not only around capital cities, but also to the remote interiors; if, in short, agriculture is to advance, then concurrently some augmentation of rent is to be expected, equitable doubtless, and consistent with the maintenance of a stable and valuable occupancy status for the ryot, but still augmentation. The very law itself, by presenting the conditions under which rent may be enhanced, contemplates the possibility of such enhancement. It is too late now to recede from that position. Although the permanent settlement in Bengal did clearly imply protection for the tenantry, it did not promise[1] that their rents should never be enhanced. Such a promise would have involved a special and perpetual settlement with the ryots, which, in fact, was never attempted. Though the settlement virtually presented the established local rates (pergunnah rates) as guides, it yet did not stipulate that these rates should never be augmented as time went on. Nor were these local rates definitely ascertained and settled in the beginning; such an ascertainment would have amounted to an authoritative settlement of rents through the country—an operation which has not been, and doubtless will not be, undertaken.

Administration
Report, 1875-76,
Part I, page 10.

(*c*). On every ground, then, there is a case for interposing by legislation while it can be dispassionately considered, and before the angry feelings on both sides shall become so inflamed as to render settlement almost impossible.

Ibid., page 10.

(*d*.) Meanwhile, as the best rule that could be framed in the absence of any guidance from the law, the High Court devised what is known as the rule of proportion. According to that, the new rent should bear the same proportion to the old value of the produce as the old rent bore to the old value of the produce, at the time when the rent was last fixed, or at some subsequent period which may be taken as a starting-point. But although this rule may be the only one that could be put forth without resorting to legislation, still it is essentially defective and cannot be easily worked. The whole area of contest is opened out, as to what the value of the old produce of the land really was; and even as to what the old rent really was, inasmuch as there are no village records filed in any public office, and unless the ryot possesses the old receipts, there is no one who holds a record save the zemindar, and his record would be disputed by the ryot. Further, it by no means follows that the old

---

[1] So spake Sir Richard Temple: for the different utterance of Sir George Campbell, see para. 9, section I.

rent was right, merely because it was the old rent. In the disputes which now arise, it will be alleged that the old rent was faulty, and that a new rent ought to be determined on better principles. But the rule of proportion in a great degree stereotypes and perpetuates whatever faults existed in the old rent.

(e). If, then, some better rule is to be found, how is it to be attained? In order to solve this question, I have for some time past been gathering opinions from all quarters, whence the best information might be obtainable, European and native, official and non-official; propositions and counter-propositions have been laid before Government; a mass of valuable ideas and suggestions has been collected.

(f). It is admitted that our proposals need not go beyond the class of occupancy ryots, leaving the non-occupancy class to the operation of the economic law of supply and demand. Probably, however, the occupancy category comprises the vast majority of the ryots.

(g). Two alternatives have, after the fullest consideration, been put forward, namely—*firstly*, to take the ordinary rent rates paid by the occupancy ryots or tenants-at-will, which may be regarded as representing the competitive rent for which the land might be let in open market, and to assume that as a standard for the occupancy ryot, allowing to him a favourable difference of 20 to 25 per cent. less; in other words, the rent of the occupancy ryot being made so much less than that of the non-occupancy ryot; or *secondly*, to calculate the rent of the occupancy ryot at a certain proportion of the value of the gross produce, the said proportion to be taken at from 15 to 25 per cent. of the said value. It is necessary to propose some margin within which the discretion of the court of justices may be exercised—the difference, less in favour of the occupancy ryot, to be from 20 to 25 per cent.; the proportion to be from 15 to 25 per cent., because in different parts of the country the customary rates of rent vary proportionally to the value of the produce, being lower in Northern and Eastern Bengal, and higher in Central and Western. It is also proposed that no claim for the reduction or abatement of existing rents shall be entertained in consequence of the rules.

Administration
Report, 1875-76,
Part I, page 11.

(h). The adoption of the non-occupancy rent as a standard for the occupancy rent has been advocated by the British Indian Association, the most important society of landlords in the country. It is remarkable, then, that an objection has been urged to the effect that the occupancy ryots are in many places already paying as much as, or more than, the non-occupancy. Well, but then the effect would be that the occupancy ryot would be by this rule protected altogether from enhancement, which protection he would enjoy on the express recommendation of the landlord.

(i). The prevailing opinion, among the many persons who have been consulted, is in favour of the rent being adjusted according to a proportion of the value of the gross produce taken at 15 to 25 per cent. But objections are made, to the effect that in some places the actual rent levied amounts to much more than 25 per cent., and in some places to less than 15. The answer is, that where it exceeds 25 per cent., the ryot is protected from further enhancement; and where it is less than 15, it must in reason be raised gradually to that proportion, in the absence of specific agreement to the contrary; but the enhancement would be made, not necessarily at once, but by degrees, and from time to time.

(*k*). There is a question as to what should be regarded as the produce of the land for this purpose. By ordinary staples of our agriculture are of course meant rice, wheat, oil-seeds, jute-fibre. But besides these, there are certain products which require special tending and a certain outlay of capital on the part of the ryot, but which are, on the other hand, very valuable, such as sugarcane, mulberry, tobacco, and turmeric. It is thought most convenient to provide that these crops should be charged at rates double those of the ordinary staples.

(*l*). There are certain tenure-holders intermediate between the zemindar and the ryots, who are not protected (as most tenure-holders are) either by the old regulations or by particular agreements. It has been proposed that their rents shall be fixed at rates 20 per cent. less than those of occupancy ryots.

(*m*).—Such are the principal features of the proposals, to the principles of which the assent of the Government of India has been obtained, and which I have embodied in a draft Bill, which has been transmitted, under existing rules, for the previous consideration of the Secretary of State.

V. (*a*). The argument for defining a new rule of enhancement of rent may be summed up thus: If there is to be enhancement in any class of cases, it virtually cannot be without a decree of court, because, although the rent of a tenant-at-will can be enhanced without such decree, some persons say that there is no such class existing any longer; they have all, or nearly all, become occupancy ryots. Those classes, such as korfa, ootbundi, and the like, are said to be not tenants at all, and to be little more than farm labourers, though this view of their status may be open to dispute. Probably, however, the great majority of ryots are in such a position that their rents cannot be enhanced without a decree of court. The existing law, no doubt, does lay down the circumstances under which there may be cases for enhancement, which are mentioned in section 18 of Act VIII of 1869. There are three circumstances under which cases arise for enhancement in the case of a ryot having a right of occupancy: (1) that the rate of rent paid by such ryots is below the prevailing rate payable by the same class of ryots for land of a similar description and with similar advantages in the places adjacent; (2) that the value of the produce, or the productive powers of the land, have been increased otherwise than by the agency or at the expense of the ryot; (3) that the quantity of land held by the ryot has been proved by measurement to be greater than the quantity for which rent has been previously paid by him. But this law only lays down the circumstances under which enhancement of rent may be possible. Granted the three conditions which justify enhancement, still there is nothing in them whatever to show how the enhancement should be adjusted; there is nothing to show what are the data, what are the principles, on which the court should proceed in its adjudication. How is enhancement to be settled? As to that, there is positively nothing. The courts have elaborated what is called the rule of proportion—that rule which, in default of anything better, the highest tribunal has tried to frame as the best rule which could be made under the unsatisfactory

App. XII.
——
Enhancement
of rent.
——
Para. 13, contd.

Ibid., page 12.

Ibid., Part II,
page 10.

condition of the law. As above shown, the rule amounts to no rule whatever ; it positively bristles with difficulties from beginning to end.* * Then, of course, there is extreme difficulty in finding out what was the produce, and what was the rent, at some anterior period. It is not always easy to find these things out at the present day ; but it is infinitely more difficult to ascertain what these lands produced, and what was the rent, so many years ago, particularly, too, when the character of the cultivation of the land has changed. And it is this change of culture that so often causes disputes about rents ; it is perhaps the commonest ground for such disputes. Whereas the land grew common crops once, it bears superior staples now. But when and how the change began, whether it began since the time selected as a starting-point, can hardly be ascertained in the absence of any records filed in the collector's cutcherry. It is very well to take into consideration the produce of certain fields as they are now. But to ascertain whether each field grew this or some other crop so many years ago, is an unsatisfactory undertaking in the face of conflicting statements. The Lieutenant-Governor is constrained to say, with the greatest respect to all the eminent authorities who tried to frame this rule, that it is unworkable, and is apt to become a trap for unwary litigants. If, then, this rule cannot work, what is to happen ? At present no decisions are given, so that the subordinate courts are perfectly puzzled, and when in doubt what to do, they decide to do nothing, and the disputes remain. The inevitable consequence of economic changes causes disputes to arise, and they are left unsettled, to the great detriment of landlords and tenants.

1876-77—

VI. (a). The progress of the registration of perpetual leases has been watched by Government for some years with interest. Since 1871-72, when the number registered was only 47,181, it has rapidly extended without any check until the year which has just elapsed. Though the system appears to be gradually making its way in Central and Western Bengal, it can only be said to have taken deep root in Jessore and the south-eastern districts of Backergunge, Furreedpore, Noakhally, and Chittagong. During the past year there was a considerable increase in the 24-Pergunnahs, Nuddea, Moorshedabad, Maldah, and Furreedpore, and a very large increase in Jessore.

(b). *Dacca Division.*—The relationship between landlords and tenants has for some years past been such as to cause district authorities the gravest anxiety. The origin of this was of course the not unreasonable desire on the part of the zemindars that they should participate in the increased value of the produce of the land, which had been brought about by no special expenditure on the part of the ryots, either of labour or of capital. In this increased value, therefore, the zemindars had, in my (Commissioner's) opinion, a perfect right to share. No sooner, however, was the attempt made to enhance rents, than the ryots combined, not absolutely refusing to pay the enhanced rent claimed, but in many cases any rent at all.

14. We have seen that the income of the zemindars has increased from an increase of cultivation, from an enhancement of rents which is still in progress, and from the levy of illegal cesses and transit dues. Respecting the increased income from enhanced rents, Sir George Campbell observed in his Administration Report for 1871-72 :—

"Inquiries in the course of the year have since brought out cases wherein the rental of permanently-settled estates is now 10, 15, 60, and even 120 times the Government revenue as assessed at the permanent settlement, although the officers who made the settlement in 1793 intended at that time to reserve for Government ten-elevenths, and to leave for the zemindars one-eleventh of the rental of the country."

And again—

" The land revenue assessed in the last century, when the conditions of the country and the relative capabilities of different districts were vastly different from what they now are, bears no sort of proportion to the present value of the land. While in some places the revenue may still amount to a tolerable assessment, in others it amounts to no more than a very small quit-rent. The total rental of each estate may be to the revenue in the proportion of 3, 10, 50, or 100 times."

And of the illegal cesses, Sir George Campbell incidentally remarked as follows :—

" If, say, an average charge of one per cent. on the rental of the ryot were made in order to open out local roads and water-channels in every direction, such a charge would be a mere flea-bite compared to the cesses which so many zemindars now levy."

Whilst these enormous gains have accrued to the zemindars, the Board of Revenue, in 1873, in a memorandum on the Land Revenue of Bengal, asked the question—

" Who has reaped the benefit of the multiplied rental of the country ?"

And answered it thus :—

" But the position of the money-lenders is more clearly defined. It is not too much to say that, while the ancestral landholders have, by their apathy and shortsightedness, fallen out of the race and lost their share of the growing wealth of the country, the money-lenders have by thriftiness, care, and a rapacity that could never have been tolerated by a less patient and indolent race, amassed such riches and such influence as to have become the most powerful class in the community. The condition of the ryot all over Bengal is that of hopeless indebtedness to his mahajun. The cultivation of the country is carried on upon advances made by them, and the well-being and comfort of the lower classes, and of a large portion of the higher classes also, is in their hands. Fortunately for all parties they are wise in their generation, and though they exact usury at rates unknown in other parts of the world, they know how to adjust their demands to the immediate capacities of their debtors, and so avoid the catastrophe of a general bankruptcy, which would involve themselves. These men, it must be added, very commonly invest their accumulated gains in landed property, either by direct purchase, or by the foreclosure of mortgages, which are freely given by needy applicants for funds, as security for the repayment of loans. In this way the landholding class has been, and is being, largely supplied with new blood, a process of undoubted benefit to the country at large. These self-made men bring fresh energy and intelligence to bear upon the development of the resources of their properties, and are not addicted to the lazy and careless habits that lead to absenteeism and management by agents."

15. Summing up the information in this Appendix it appears that—

I. In the permanently-settled districts of Bengal and Behar the land revenue had increased since the permanent settlement, up to 1871-72, by 66 lakhs, including 44 lakhs in Behar, the famine in which province cost $6\frac{1}{2}$ millions sterling, which represents a yearly charge of 29 lakhs. The oppression of the ryots by the zemindars in Behar is not equalled in any other part of the territories under the Government of Bengal.

II. From the valuations, for the road cess, of the income of owners and occupiers of land, the Bengal Government considered that the income of the land in the permanently-settled districts is probably worth four or five times the revenue. This is exclusive of the illegal cesses and transit and market dues levied by the zemindars, who tax their "ryots for every extravagance and necessity that circumstances may suggest."

III. Yet the zemindars, as a body, are not wealthy men, though *some* of them are very rich. Too many of them are in embarrassed circumstances; and with all their illegal cesses, and considerable enhancement of rents, the bulk of the zemindars are in debt, and, in their stead, money-lenders have benefited by the vastly improved income of the zemindars.

IV. The mass of the ryots are impoverished or in debt (with large exceptions, chiefly, however, in Eastern Bengal); and while this is their state, the question of enhancement of rents has assumed importance in the relations between zemindars and ryots.

V. Besides the difficulties which beset enhancement of rents, there are illegal cesses, respecting which the Board of Revenue testify to the "unmerciful manner in which unauthorised cesses are demanded," and express their conviction that "some means should be afforded to the Govern-

App. XII.

——

Summary.

——

Para. 15, contd.

ment to check the rapacity of the zemindars and their agents, and to afford protection to their victims."

VI. Outside Orissa, the Local Government accepted this state of things as inevitable. " As the people get better protected, better educated, and better able to understand and protect their own rights and position, things would, it was felt, no doubt to some extent, adjust themselves." Ninety years ago, the Bengal Government, in hastily framing a zemindary settlement, had faith that the zemindar would give his ryots pottahs which would fix their rents for ever; ninety years later, the Bengal Government was driven to hope that ryots would in time learn to resist the oppression of zemindars.

VII. With regard to the ryots in Orissa, however, the Bengal Government refused to be comforted with this hope : " Nowhere was the settlement more carefully made, or made in greater detail, than in Orissa; perhaps nowhere were the status and privileges of the ryots so well protected in theory as in Orissa : yet we find after the expiry of a thirty years' settlement, during which no annual or periodical papers were filed, and the settlement records were in no way carried out, that the whole system of record and protection have utterly collapsed, the records have become waste paper, and the ryots, supposed to be well protected, are among the most oppressed in India."

VIII. And so, varying somewhat the Board's enquiry, the question arises, what earthly good has come of a permanent settlement with zemindars instead of with the millions of proprietors whose rights were confiscated—in fact, though not in law or intent—by the authors of that settlement ?

APPENDIX XIII.

ZEMINDARS AND RYOTS;—THEIR CONDITION ACCORDING TO REPORTS FROM 1871 TO 1876.

APP. XIII.
1. From the time of the permanent settlement until 1872-73, the district officers in Bengal had no means, such as those afforded by the tehsildaree establishments in the other provinces and presidencies, of acquiring information about the interior of their districts; from the same cause, and from an inefficient police, their control over the interior of their districts was weak; and when the police was enlarged on the introduction of a revised constabulary in 1861, its utility to the district officer was lessened by the formation of the police "under a separate departmental control, which made it, in a great degree, independent of the magistracy." The Administration Report for 1871-72 noticed these several points as follows:—

Part I, page 24.
I. When the Government of Lord Cornwallis, abandoning the attempt to manage the land revenues in a more direct fashion, made them over to the zemindars, who were bound to pay their quotas into the collector's treasury, under penalty of sale of the estates confided to them, it became unnecessary to maintain the tehsildars, or native collectors, and establishments subordinate to them, who, in all other parts of India, collect the revenue in sub-divisions of the districts presided over by the European collectors. These native collectors have since become much more than mere tax-collectors, being in part, in their degree, administrators for very many purposes, just as the district collector is an administrator in his superior degree. In some respects, indeed, the tehsil establishments are the very backbone of our administration in most provinces. But they are to this day entirely absent in Bengal, and the circumstance has much detracted from our knowledge and means, and causes the want of an important link in the connection between the Government and the people. Many things done by tehsildars in other parts of India are not done at all, and many things which we should know through them we do not know. For many things which must be done there is a constant deputation of temporary deputy collectors, surveyors, and other occasional establishments, under a system which is very inconvenient and unsatisfactory in many respects.

II. At first the superior police administration also was entrusted APP. XIII.
to the Bengal zemindars,. but it was soon found that they were unequal
to this duty, and they were relieved of it. The obligations in regard to
village police, keeping the peace, and the duties of watching and apprehending criminals, giving information, &c., attached to the holding of
land, were continued; but a superior Government police was established,
and the country was portioned out into police circles or thannas. This
police long remained the only permanent mark and instrument of our
rule in the interior of the Bengal districts, till, at a later period, subordinate judicial establishments were also pretty generally distributed.
For executive purposes, however, the police are to this day the only
permanent instruments available.

THE SECURITIES PROVIDED IN 1793 FOR RYOTS' PROTECTION SET AT NOUGHT BY ZEMINDAR.

Para. 2.

Part I, page 42.

2. This marked deficiency and weakness of the executive
disabled the Government from fulfilling the obligations which
it undertook at the permanent settlement to protect the
ryots from the zemindars, who, till then, had been administrators as well as collectors of revenue, and whom the
Government's acknowledgment in 1793 of its clear and distinct
obligations to protect the ryots had placed in antagonism to
the Government. On this point the Administration Report
for 1871-72 observed:—

(I). Although at the time of the permanent settlement the collection
of the land revenue was made over to the zemindars, and certain proprietary rights were assured to them, still, as the Lieutenant-Governor
has several times had occasion to point out, nothing was farther from
the intentions and acts of the governments of Lord Cornwallis and his
immediate successors than to bestow on the zemindars an absolute property in the English sense, or "to abstain from interference between
landlord and tenant," according to the phraseology of more modern days.
This much any one who will take the trouble to read the Regulations
of 1793 and the following years may see for himself. Those early
Regulations were most careful in their provisions for restraining the
zemindars and protecting the ryots.

All the securities provided in 1793 for the ryots' protection set at nought by the zemindar.

Ibid., pages 43-4.

(a). The zemindars were prohibited from ousting the ryots, or from
taking rents in excess of the rates established by custom for each local
division or pergunnah.

(b). They were bound to maintain the village accountant or putwaree,
and to file full accounts of their demands and collections, with the
canoongoes or superior accountants and record-keepers of sub-divisions
under the collector, who was thus to have complete information of all
revenue affairs, and easy means of reference in regard to all questions of
rent, rates, &c.

(c). A general power of interference on behalf of ryots was reserved
by express enactment, and a registry of all rights and obligations was
to have been compiled. This last great work, however, was never carried
out. Various attempts were made to organise a canoongoe establishment
in different parts of the country; but there was difficulty about funds,
and the arrangements were never completed, till, a generation later, a
time came when different ideas prevailed, when canoongoes were abolished,

App. XIII.

THE SECURITIES
PROVIDED IN
1793 FOR RYOTS'
PROTECTION SET
AT NOUGHT BY
ZEMINDAR.

Para. 2, contd.

putwarees discouraged—when zemindars were considered to be landlords in the English sense, and interference between landlord and tenant was said to be contrary to the laws of political economy.

(d). Meantime, it has also become, in most instances, quite impossible to use the zemindars as administrative instruments. Most of the original zemindars failed to pay, and their estates were sold and split up.

(e). By the operation of the Hindu and Mahomedan laws of inheritance, and a vast system of sub-infeudation, the rights in the land have come to be held by many sharers, and in many gradations of over and under holders; and, as mere property, those divided rights are held, in very many cases, by speculators, women, children, and others, from whom no administrative help could be expected.

(f). It may be said, too, that while there has been a general tendency to insist upon, and indeed exaggerate, the rights and privileges conferred on landholders by the permanent settlement, there has been, at the same time, an equal disposition to forget, evade, and ignore the terms, conditions, and obligations attached to those rights and privileges by the very Regulations which conferred or confirmed them. The idea of property has become stronger and stronger, and the idea of obligation attached to the functions of landholders has become weaker and weaker. It may be said that every point about which there could be any doubt has been allowed to settle itself in favour of the landholder and against the public.

(g). Thus, then, it has happened that in the provinces which we have held the longest of any in India, we have less knowledge of, and familiarity with, the people than in any other province; that British authority is less brought home to the people; that the rich and strong are less restrained, and the poor and weak less protected, than elsewhere; and that we have infinitely less knowledge of statistical, agricultural, and other facts.

Part I, page 46.

II. The events of the mutiny necessarily caused things to be a good deal thrown back; and there were in those days great domestic evils to be coped with. It has been said that, in Bengal, the rich and powerful have been less restrained, and the poor less protected, than in other provinces; and up to that time this was so, in the most literal sense of the word. There was, in the interior of Bengal, a lawlessness and high-handed defiance of authority by people who took the law into their own hands by open violence, which would not have been tolerated for a moment in any other part of India. It required all the energies of the first Lieutenant-Governor to deal with these and other potent evils; and it may be said that the government of the second Lieutenant-Governor was a continued struggle with questions arising out of past lawlessness, and affecting important interests which suffered by the transition from an old-fashioned state of things to a rule of law and order. He succeeded in this task, and achieved a very lasting improvement, but he was, it is believed, wearied by the struggle, and retired before completing the usual term of office.

Ibid., page 46.

III. One of the most important results of the measures taken by the two first Bengal Lieutenant-Governors was the establishment of sub-divisions of districts, in each of which an officer was placed with the powers of a magistrate and some other powers. The system has not

even yet been fully carried out in all districts, but in most districts it App. XIII.
has been so, with the effect of very greatly reforming the habits of open
lawlessness above mentioned. A Bengal sub-division is on the average
perhaps about twice the size of the tehsil of other parts of India; but
still the institution has sufficed to bring to the knowledge of the people
of Bengal that there are courts for the redress of flagrant and open
injuries, and so far, the hands of the district magistrates have been very
greatly strengthened.

THE REIGN OF MIGHT OVER RIGHT.

Para. 3.

IV. The Lieutenant-Governor ventures to think, however, that in Part I, page 47.
the sub-divisional and other arrangements hitherto subsisting, too great
prominence has been given to judicial, and too little to executive, considerations. The sub-divisional officers have no executive establishments
whatever, and no authority over the police; they have been little more
than local judges of petty criminal courts; and, latterly, they have been
so much tied down by treasury and sedentary duties of various kinds,
that it has been scarcely possible for them to make those inquiries on the
scene of crimes and other serious occurrences by which the benefit of a
local magistracy is chiefly felt.

V. Courts, both civil and criminal, are now pretty generally spread Ibid., page 47.
over the country (though, even now, there are but few, compared to the
greatness of the population); and if courts could do everything, the deficiency would not be so great. But the Lieutenant-Governor has had
too much experience of, and practice in, our courts, to be very confident
that what the people think justice is always secured. It is the fashion
among Englishmen to suppose that everything must be right which is
done under the forms of law; but it may be that our courts are sometimes
Juggernauths, crushing those who fall under their relentless wheels as they
follow the course traced out for them by law and rule. The appetite for
an excessive legal technicality grows rapidly in India; and it may be
that the rich man, with troops of lawyers at his back, still sometimes
oppresses the poor as much as when he operated with troops of clubmen.

VI. About the same time as the increase of sub-divisions after the Ibid., page 47.
mutiny, a change took place, which greatly detracted from the executive
authority of the district magistrates. Under Lord Canning's government it was determined to reform and re-organise the police all over India
and, under a new police law, the force still known as the new police was
organised with a good deal of military forms in its composition, and under a
departmental control, which made it to a great degree independent of the
magistracy. In other parts of India the magistrate-collector had still
revenue and executive establishments to fall back upon; but in Bengal,
where he had none such, loss of authority over the police meant loss of
almost all executive authority, or, at any rate, of all executive instruments.
As departments were multiplied, and more and more masters put over
him, the magistrate-collector of a district became more of a drudge and
less of a master than is desirable in a country where personal authority
must always go for much.

3. Thus, whereas, in 1793, the Government bound itself
to the ryots by pledges of protection as solemn as the engagements not to increase the rents of the zemindars, from that
year to 1856 a weak executive, with a police not worthy of

APP. XIII.

THE REIGN OF
MIGHT OVER
RIGHT.

Para. 3, contd.

the name, was powerless to afford that protection, and, in consequence, that period was one of lawlessness, in which the strong oppressed the weak—but with one cause less for oppression during that time than in the present day, *viz.*, an absence of the great rise of prices since 1856, which has created the subsequent difficulties that beset an enhancement of rents. Since 1856, the brute power of might over right has been curbed, but the reign of law, which has accompanied the restoration of order, has also enabled zemindars to substitute for brute force the power of the rich to oppress the poor through expensive litigation, which often is ruinous to the latter, even when they succeed in the courts.

Condition of
zemindars in
Bengal.

4. But among the visions which floated in the benevolent mind of Lord Cornwallis was that of rich landed proprietors, who would protect their tenants, help them in improvements, in their ordinary exigencies of cultivation, and in seasons of adversity. The testimony, in the Administration Reports, to the character and condition of the zemindars of Bengal is as follows :—

Part II, page 97.

Zemindars give
no help to the
police.

I. *1872-73.*—While the village watch is thus inefficient, the complaint is universal that the zemindars give the regular police no help. The Lieutenant-Governor has caused them all to be formally and fully warned of what the new Criminal Procedure Code requires of them ; and it will now rest chiefly with magistrates to see that the obligations imposed by the law are duly fulfilled.

Ibid., page 73.

Comparatively
few estates in
the immense
territories under
Bengal Government.

II. (*a*). *1872-73.*—In 38 districts of Bengal proper and Behar, out of a total number of 154,200 estates at present borne on the public books, 533, or 3·4 per cent., only are great properties, with an area of 20,000 acres and upwards ; 15,747, or 10·21 per cent., range from 500 to 20,000 acres in area ; while the number of estates which fell short of 500 acres is no less than 137,920, or 89·44 per cent. of the whole. In the district of Sylhet, with its 53,368 small estates, 556 medium, and 14 large estates, the original settlement was nearly ryotwari ; and in that of Chittagong, with its 1 large, 671 medium, and 3,577 small estates, special causes have produced the great disproportion observable between the number of large and small estates upon the roll ; but in other parts a large number of petty estates shown in the list owe their separate existence to the causes already mentioned. In the Behar districts, where, next to Sylhet and Chittagong, the disproportion under notice is most remarkable, a large proportion of the estates seem to have been from the first comparatively insignificant in size, while there were, and are, some extremely large estates in that province. Subsequent partitions have contributed greatly to crowd the revenue rolls of these districts with petty estates. It must be explained, however, that in all districts a large proportion of the petty estates are resumed rent-free tenures of a petty character settled with the holders.

Sub-division is
in progress.

(*b*). *1876-77.*—The effect of the laws of partition in multiplying estates in Behar is again very marked, the numbers on the rent-roll

having risen from 37,619 to 39,781 during the year.   In Tirhoot alone par- App. XIII.
tition added 1,438 estates to the rent-roll. Mr. Worsley explains that' —————
the indigo (ticcadar) system is largely to blame for this. A shareholder Condition of
zemindars in
leases his share to a factory; the factory endeavours to seize all the *zerat*, Bengal.
and the other shareholders are driven to partition in self-defence. In —————
1850 there were only 5,069 estates on the Tirhoot rent-roll; in 1860, Para. 4, contd.
only 6,342; but in 1875 there were 15,117. In Mozufferpore there are now
10,815, and 6,767 in Durbungah; 2,052 estates in the former district
paying only Rs. 4,504 Government revenue between them. In Part I, pages
Durbungah upwards of 50,000 owners have applied for registration under 14-15.
the new Act. These figures show the remarkable extent to which the Landlord class,
as a whole, is
sub-division of estates has been carried out, and there is every prospect of far from rich;
the process being continued. One effect of this separation of shares is ties believe
many authori-
to increase materially the work of the treasury establishments; the really poor.
that it is mostly
number of separate payments on account of land revenue, road cess, and
other dues being now something enormous.

III. (*a*). *1874-75.*—It is true that more capital than at present
ought to be laid out by the landlord class on the improvement of the land,
though notable instances have occurred, and may yet occur, of combined
action on the part of zemindars for the execution of drainage projects.
But it is also to be remembered that though many zemindars are wealthy,
still the landlord class, as a whole, is far from being rich, and by many
authorities is believed to be, for the most part, really poor. They have
numerous relations and retainers wholly dependent on them. The joint
undivided family system, and many social usages, compel them to incur
heavy expenses not obvious to ordinary European observers.

(*b*). *1874-75.*—The division of the title and ownership of the land,
if not of the land itself, equally among brothers by the Hindu law of
inheritance, constantly augments the number of small landlords without
means or resources. Indeed, from various causes, the sub-division of the
ownership of land throughout the country is becoming remarkably great.
Probably the original idea of Hindu legislators was this, that brethren
would dwell together, subsisting jointly on the undivided proceeds of the
ancestral estate; but as society advances, the tendency must be for each
member of the family to separate off his share, and to establish himself
independently. And although the Bengalees still evince a more than
ordinary capacity for the joint undivided family existence, which capacity
forms an interesting and amiable feature in their national character, still
the natural tendency towards partition of lands and rights according to
inherited shares has long asserted itself among them, and will probably
assert itself more and more. Hitherto the law of partition (*butwara*)
framed in early times (1814) has been, in many respects, cumbersome
and tedious. Its simplification (which, in justice to all concerned, is being
undertaken by the legislature) must have the effect of facilitating sub-
division.

(*c*). *1874-75.*—Again, there is the process known as ' sub-infeudation,'
which may be taken to comprise leases of all kinds, permanent and
temporary, and which in many districts has developed itself greatly, and
in some districts, such as Chittagong, to an extent so extraordinarily
great, as to cause a marked social change. The permanent leaseholders
do not, so far as the ryots are concerned, differ essentially from zemindars.

APP. XIII.

CONDITION OF
ZEMINDARS IN
BENGAL.

Para. 4, contd.

In such cases the zemindar becomes a nominal landlord, with a very limited income ; though there are instances of great zemindars, with estates of territorial size, who let out their lands on leases, and yet maintain the status and discharge the responsibility of landlords. The temporary leaseholders, however, are worse than zemindars from the ryots' point of view. Having no abiding interest in the land, they may be tempted to resort to extortion, and are often much complained of ; indeed, a portion of the agrarian troubles which have occurred at various times in Bengal is traceable and attributable to temporary leases.

(d). 1874-75.—It is not found that absenteeism is disadvantageously prevalent in Bengal. The great majority of zemindars live on, or near their estates ; clusters of well-built mansions are to be found in the interior of most districts, where cousinhoods or brotherhoods of zemindars reside.

Pages 38-9.

IV. 1875-76 (a).—In most parts of Eastern and North-Eastern Bengal, indeed, the land-revenue equals only a very small portion of the rental, and the prosperity of the landowning class would be quite extraordinary, were it not for the sub-infeudation, or, in other words, the division of the rent payable by the cultivator between the proprietor and several classes of sub-proprietors. In Central and Western Bengal the landlords are less prosperous.

In other words, the Government, by withholding the large famine relief outlay, could have broken the permanent settlement, without breaking faith with the zemindars.

(b).—The fiscal advantages of this settlement were most severely tested during the famine of 1874, when the revenue was collected without any postponement, or remission, or default, or any failure whatever. Without the relief afforded by Government to the famishing people, there must have been some serious failures in the land revenue, and (what would have been a very great evil) some extensive transfers of landed property, and ruin of old families. One counterbalancing advantage, then, of the heavy relief expenditure incurred by Government was this, that the great interests pertaining to the land revenue and to the land were preserved.

5. The account may be continued from the Annual Administration Reports of Commissioners of Divisions, which on their present plan were begun with those for 1872-73, and from the Government Resolutions passed on those Reports.

I.—PRESIDENCY DIVISION—

Page 149.

(a). 1872-73.—During the year the conduct of zemindars was, on the whole, good throughout the division ; though there were, of course, some instances of complicity in riots, neglect to give information of heinous cases to the police, &c. I cannot, however, say that, as a rule, they have any great sympathy with their ryots, except in so far as the collection of rents is concerned. Indeed, instances of landlords actively exerting themselves to effect improvements in the condition of the tenantry, or undertaking works of public utility within their estates, are rare. But this is scarcely to be wondered at, as the present reign of law and system has done much to destroy the friendly feeling that used to exist, even though the zemindars exercised somewhat feudal power, and to substitute for it continual lawsuits to try and establish the legal rights of

property. [The report closes with mention of two excellent landlords,
one a European, and of two others, of whom one built a pucka
house for a dispensary, and the other had kept up a dispensary for 20
years.]

(b). *Jessore. 1875-76.*—On every side there are the marks of moral and
material progress. It must be admitted, however, that the zemindars, taken
as a body, are not in a prosperous or flourishing state. A few of the distinguished houses have been utterly ruined, while others are in a state of
rapid decay. This sad state has resulted partly from their own acts, and
partly from other causes. The laws of inheritance lead to the rapid multiplication of shares in joint property. An imaginary estate which yielded a
handsome income to the original owner is but a moderate competence to his
six successors, and will be but a pittance to, say, 36 grandchildren. The
present management of the property, however, requires the consent of
the six owners, who are suspicious of each other, and can agree to nothing. Mismanagement results, and, sooner or later, ruin is inevitable.
It is generally accelerated by habits of extravagance. Family pride, bad
advisers, and priestly influence counsel the maintenance of a scale of
expenditure which, consistent enough with the means of the original
owner, is altogether beyond the competence of his successors.

(c). *1876-77.*—The conduct of the zemindars has, with few exceptions,
been worthy of praise. There were no serious quarrels with tenants in
any district. In Nuddea, the zemindars have shown great interest in
education and in the future of the Kishnaghur College. * * Messrs.
Sibbald, P. Smith, A. Hills, Macnaughten, Jones, and Sherriff are
specially noticed as good landlords. In Moorshedabad, Rao Jogendro
Narain Rai, of Lalgola, is distinguished for charity to the poor and kindness to his tenantry; while the name of Maharani Surnomoyee stands
foremost in Bengal for works of charity.

(d). *1876-77.*—In Nuddea it is stated that the people have been
generally quiet, and that there have been but few instances of violent
disputes either between zemindars amongst themselves or between
zemindars and ryots. Such disputes as occur among the zemindars
themselves have their origin, for the most part, in conflicting claims
regarding shares, or in connection with indigo-planting. The disputes
with ryots usually have reference to rents and *abwabs;* and these, it is
correctly noticed, will never cease till the pernicious practice is abandoned
of paying mere nominal salaries to zemindari servants. The larger
zemindars in the Bongong and Kooshtea sub-divisions are for the most
part non-residents, but in other parts of the district the zemindars
generally live on their estates. Many properties have become much
sub-divided, and it is said that their owners are on the highway to ruin,
since they cannot forget that they are zemindars, and postpone, so far as
they can, the evil day when they and their families must work for their
subsistence. The subject of education has generally received the greatest
support from the zemindars of the district.

II.—Burdwan Division—

(a). *The division generally. 1872-73.*—Among the native zemindars
who have been distinguished for active benevolence and liberality, the

Commissioner notices Baboo Joykisen Mookerjea in Hooghly, Baboo Nobin Chunder Nag in Midnapore, Baboo Radhabullub Singh of Kuncheakoli, Baboo Damoodur Singh of Maliara in Bancoorah, and Baboo Ramrunjunj Chuckerbutty of Hetimpore in Beerbhoom.

1875-76.—The Lieutenant-Governor observes with pleasure that amicable arrangements exist between landlords and tenants in the Bankoora district, and that Baboos Radhabullub Singh Deo, Damoodur Singh, and the Banerjeas of Ajudhya are specially commended among the resident landlords of the district for their liberality. The Maharanee of Burdwan and Rajah Jotindro Mohun Tagore are highly spoken of by the Collector of Midnapore as animated by a genuine desire to do their duty to their tenantry, and spend money on drainage and improvements. (In the report for 1876-77 the former is mentioned as the best proprietor in Midnapore.) Messrs. Watson and Co. are reported to be "strict and unsympathetic landlords, but able, and on the whole just."

1876-77.—The relations between landlord and tenant are described as amicable, except in the district of Midnapore, where the pressure of the rent question has made itself generally felt.

(*b*). *Bancoorah. 1872-73.*—The inhabitants of the district are, generally speaking, poor. The Collector attributes this very much to landlord absenteeism, and to the system of letting and sub-letting in putni tenure, which so generally prevails here. The large amount of jungle also tends to keep in existence a very poor class of people.

(*c*). *Midnapore. 1872-73.*—Allowing for the large area of jungle mehals, Midnapore may be reckoned a very heavily assessed district; but it is worthy of remark that the only portion of the district where the old families hold up their heads at all is where the land revenue is heaviest. Those where it is lightest, probably owing to the extravagant habits which pecuniary ease afforded, are most inextricably in debt.

(*d*). *Burdwan. 1875-76.*—The practice of employing budmashes as nugdees, and of screening these budmashes when they commit dacoities or thefts in the neighbourhood, is far too prevalent amongst the landholders of this district. The relations between landlord and tenant are on the whole good in this district, but recovery of rents is very difficult.

III.—RAJSHAHYE DIVISION—

(*a*). *General. 1872-73.*—The Lieutenant-Governor regrets that, upon the whole, he is not able to notice favourably the conduct of the zemindars of the division. One, however, was distinguished for a very liberal school endowment at Rampore Beauleah, and three others were mentioned as having been well spoken of by the Magistrates of their districts. "The Maharanee Surnomoyee is pre-eminent, as usual, for the efficient administration of her property."

(*b*). *Rajshahye. 1872-73.*—Although there has been an increase in the number of notices of enhancement issued to the extent of 50 per cent., the present number, 234, is very trifling when compared with the number of cultivators in the district. The number of notices of relinquishment of cultivation has risen from 180 to 431. I find that the ryots in question are principally those who are under new proprietors, especially new putnidars. New brooms sweep clean, and putnidars are especially likely to recoup themselves as soon as possible for the premium they have paid; in fact it may be said that in letting estates under this system in perpetuity, the landholder is really discounting future cesses, which he leaves the putnidar to realise. Beyond these cases, there are at present, happily, but few disputes between landlord and tenant.

I learn that illegal exactions are less resorted to than formerly, and that the measurement of holdings by the zemindars is on the increase. The amount of land at present held by the ryots on easy terms, the real area or productive power of the land being concealed by them, is very large; and the zemindars are likely to find this legal mode of enhancement as remunerative as the exaction of cesses, though more troublesome in the first instance.

1875-76.—The Collector writes: "The zemindars of this district are much above the average in intelligence, and, I think I may say, in integrity."

IV.—DACCA DIVISION—

(*a*). *General. 1872-73.*—For two districts so intimately connected with each other as Dacca and Furreedpore, the difference between the condition of the land tenure is very remarkable. In the former, it is an extreme case to find two middlemen between the zemindar and the cultivator; while in the other, five are common, and in some zemindaries the number reaches seven. Backergunge is also much broken up into petty holdings by the system of sub-infeudation. In this district they have under the zemindars the talookdars, oosut talookdars, howladar, neemhowladar, meras kursadars, kursadars, and the burgadar. The zemindars, again, often buy the rights of one of the under-tenure holders—say the howladar—and the multiplicity of the interests held makes partition cases exceedingly difficult in this district.

1875-76.—Many of the large landholders in the Dacca division are absentees from their estates. The conduct of several zemindars is, however, brought favourably to the notice of Government by the district officers. The names of Nawab Abdool Gunnee, C.S.I., of his son, Kajah Ahsanoollah, and of Rajah Kali Narain Roy Chowdry, all of Dacca, are conspicuous, as usual, for their liberality and good behaviour as landlords. Among other names mentioned are three in the Mymensingh district, three in Furreedpore, the Rajah of Tipperah, and one zemindar in the Tipperah district.

1876-77.—In Furreedpore, as in most other districts of the division, the majority of the zemindars are non-resident. As regards their dealings with their ryots, there is not much to be said in their favour, their main object being to get as much out of their tenants as possible with the least possible amount of trouble to themselves.

(*b*). *Mymensingh. 1872-73.*—(1). The incidence of the land-revenue having been extremely light in Mymensingh, the present zemindars are for the most part representatives of the families who entered into engagments with the Government at the time of the permanent settlement. Two or three points appear worthy of notice with regard to the district zemindars in general. *First,* that though so large a proportion of the population are

Mahomedans, only two or three of the large zemindars hold the Mahomedan faith ; *secondly*, that a very considerable number of the present zemindars are women ; *thirdly*, that though the existing zemindars mostly represent old families, a great many of them have attained their present position by adoption, and not by birth.

(2). As a body, the district zemindars are conservative, ignorant, and suspicious, trammelled by superstition and by social prejudices, and with much stronger ideas of their rights than of their duties. Under the circumstances of the case it was inevitable that this should be their general character. Living for the most part upon their own estates, and seldom enlarging their minds by travel, they have grown up within a narrow circle of ideas ; and it is only of late years that their tenants have attempted any opposition to their wishes. At the same time, they can only be made amenable to influence judiciously exercised ; and in one respect they contrast favourably with the zemindars of some districts, as they are not mere absentee annuitants upon the land, but live among their ryots, and generally take an active personal share in the management of their estates.

1875-76.—In Mymensingh the levy of the road cess since October last has brought to light the fact that the zemindars very generally levy a sum from their ryots in excess of what the law allows, probably with a view of partly recouping themselves for the loss of the cesses they used formerly to get, but which the ryots now refuse to pay. Even in an estate recently taken charge of by the Court of Wards, in which the owner was generally popular as not being in the habit of oppressing his ryots, the levy had been at *four times the legitimate demand.*

(*c*). *Dacca and Furreedpore.*—See above.

(*d*). *Backergunge. 1876-77.*—In Backergunge, with the exception of Nawab Ahsanoollah, Baboo Mohini Mohun Doss, Rajendro Chunder Roy of Bowal, and Doorga Mohun Doss, a Dukhinshabazpore zemindar, all of whom largely assisted their ryots after the cyclone, not a single zemindar is mentioned as having taken the smallest interest in his tenantry, or done anything material to assist them over the time of trouble they have been recently passing through. The example thus set by the zemindars has been followed by the talookdars and howladars in the storm-affected tracts. Few have done anything to assist the ryots, many of whom would, but for our assistance, have fared badly indeed. Speaking generally of the conduct of the zemindars, Mr. Burton repeats what he said last year, that anything like an enlightened desire to improve their estates or improve the condition of their tenantry is wanting—an opinion which, I am sorry to say, my own experience of them leads me to adopt.

V.—CHITTAGONG DIVISION—

(*a*). *General. 1872-73.*—From the scattered position of their estates, the zemindars of Chittagong do not exercise great local influence or authority. In the Tipperah district they are mostly absentees, and do nothing for the district. [Two zemindars in Chittagong and one in Tipperah were, however, mentioned " for their liberality and public spirit."]

(*b*). *Chittagong*. *1876-77.*—The conduct of the zemindars is negative, as most of them are in debt, and therefore incapable of exerting
an influence either for good or for evil.

(*c*). *Noakholly*. *1876-77.*—Except the zemindars of Bullooah, no other
did anything to help their ryots at the crisis succeeding the cyclone, and
none undertook any work of public utility. Considering, however, that
many of the zemindars of the district are not residents of the place, and
that, excepting the owners of the Bullooah estates, few are capable of
undertaking works of utility on a scale sufficiently large to attract public
notice, I am disposed to think that their shortcomings may have proceeded
rather from inability than from unwillingness. The Bullooah zemindars
did very kind and praiseworthy service by affording aid to their tenants
and others during the critical time which followed the cyclone, by giving
them medicine, clothes, and rice gratis. In Chittagong, where the talookdars and zemindars are all residents of the place, a good many tanks,
roads, and other petty works were constructed.

(*d*). *Estates paying revenue*—

		Chittagong.	Noakholly.
Estates paying revenue not exceeding Rs. 10 ...	...	25,989	482
Exceeding Rs. 10, not exceeding Rs. 50 ...	...	2,408	647
„ „ 50 „ „ 100 ...	...	768	244
„ „ 100	...	1,062	265
		30,227	1,638
Number of estates in the towjee ...	...	29,002	1,644
		Rs.	Rs.
Total amount of revenue ...	...	7,50,185	6,15,433
„ „ collected ...	...	5,72,718	4,29,184
		13,22,903	10,44,567

VI.—BHAGULPORE DIVISION—

(*a*). *General*. *1872-73.*—(1). A conspicuous fact connected with the
land system of the division is stated to be the absence of intermediate
permanent rights between those of the zemindars and the cultivating
ryot, and the general practice of farming estates on short leases. This is
a thorougly bad system, like that of the old Irish middlemen. "There
are very few, if any, zemindars," says the Commissioner, "who can be
brought to the notice of Government for anything done by them during
the year to improve the condition of their villages. As a rule, big
estates are let out in farms, and the condition of the ryots is not cared
for. The zemindars do not understand or care for improvement; in
many cases they are spendthrifts, and their estates are heavily encumbered." The Government is making every effort to rid every estate over
which it has influence from this farming system, and executive influence
has been brought to bear, with the most beneficial effect, in the case of the
estates of Rajah Leelanund Singh, the greatest zemindar of the division.

(2). The indebtedness and embarrassment of Leelanund Singh's estate is a lesson that ought not to be lost upon other zemindars who will resort to litigation. No man has been so systematic a litigant, and so successful, as Rajah Leelanund; he has got many great decrees against Government as well as against others, and yet the net result of it all is, that he is greatly involved in debt, and, until Government afforded its assistance, his people were mismanaged and discontented.

(3). The Lieutenant-Governor believes that nowhere have the rents of a peaceable, industrious, and submissive population been more screwed than in Bhagulpore. It was the same action of the zemindars that was leading to rebellion in the Sonthal Pergunnahs. As regards particular zemindari estates, however, where the tenantry belong chiefly to low castes, it is stated that they will leave an estate on the smallest provocation; and it is a comfort that the industrious poor are thus able to go off to another estate when exaction is carried to excess.

(4). *1875-76.*—The condition of landholders generally in the division is described as most unsettled. "Considerable changes," writes Mr. Barlow, "may be expected. The old houses are heavily involved; many of them have already been sold up, and others are gradually breaking up, owing to mortgages being foreclosed or sales being concluded; and new blood, chiefly of the mahajun class, is being infused into the zemindars. I have no doubt that, as time goes on, we shall see, except perhaps in the largest estates, a new set of zemindars comparatively free from indebtedness, and bestowing more personal attention upon the management of their estates than the old ones could do." * * The Commissioner reports that in some cases the landlords are reducing themselves to the position of annuitants on their estates, by giving leases to middlemen, who are not accustomed to show as much consideration towards their tenantry as would be shown by a resident proprietor.

(5). *1876-77.*—In his report for 1875-76, the Commissioner drew attention to the gradual break-up of many of the old zemindari families, owing to accumulated debts and mismanagement, and also to the mischievous effects of the farming system as worked in many parts of this division. In the present report a lamentable account is given by the sub-divisional officer of the state of things in the Barrh sub-division, two-thirds of which are leased out in farm to non-resident speculators, while in the remaining one-third at least half of the landlords are also non-resident. The farms run usually for seven years, and are only renewed on the payment of a heavy and increasing premium, which falls entirely on the ryots. The tenants are said to have no rights, to be subject to the exaction of forced labour, to illegal distraint, and to numerous illegal cesses, while the collections are made by an unscrupulous host of up-country *piadahs*. Rajah Leelanund's zemindari is said to be one of the worst. * * The Commissioner speaks well of many of the zemindars and native gentlemen of his division, but specially singles out Rajah Ramnarayan, of Monghyr, as a model landlord.

(b). *Maldah. 1876-77.*—The large zemindars here are non-residents. These seem mostly to let their estates to farmers and then to stop. Interest or care for their ryots they have not. This is not of so much

consideration here, as rents are low, and so much can be made by silk,
&c., that the ryots are generally well off.

VII.—Patna Division—

(a). *General.* *1872-73.*—(1). The conduct of the zemindars in the division, especially the smaller landholders, is unfavourably reported on. They are described as oppressive on their tenants, and indifferent and apathetic on subjects of public interest. All over the world, petty landlords are apt to exact more than very large and rich ones. That is the nature of things; and it probably would be the case in Behar, that great landholders might be made amenable to advice if they really managed their estates direct. The Lieutenant Governor, however, fears that the fact is much as described by the Deputy Collector of Nowada and the Collector of Sarun in the following passages :—

" The very system adopted in this division for land management renders a faithful discharge of the duties imposed under the regulations impracticable. The landed property is let out in farm, generally on *zuripeshgi ticca,* for a term of years, to speculators in land, who, during their short incumbency, do their best to squeeze as much out of the tenants as possible.

" The zemindars, whenever they have a substantial share in a village, are, as a rule, oppressive, and on the estates of many of the larger zemindars, perhaps, the least consideration for the tenantry is shown. The system of farming widely prevails, and were it not that the full rent-roll is not levied in villages leased out to indigo-planters, the stimulus to enhanced rent-rolls, afforded by indigo cultivation, would have occasioned even a greater rise in rents."

(2). Where the pettiest proprietors are also cultivators, they are thriving and prosperous, and there is no better condition; but His Honour is no admirer of very small proprietors, who have abandoned all cultivation, and live on the rents only. Sir George Campbell is, however, inclined to think that there are in Behar a good many who come within the class of peasant proprietors, as there are also in the North-Western Provinces, though no doubt they are not general, as they are in the Punjáb and elsewhere. The Lieutenant-Governor notices that in this district the average rent rate per acre is stated to be Rs. 5-3-3.

(3). *1876-77.*—* * The majority of the zemindars in Tirhoot are unfavourably mentioned, being described as grasping and oppressive to their tenantry. * * The relations between landlords and tenants in North Behar are described as being by no means cordial. The zemindars complain that the ryots do not pay their rents, and that they are unable to enforce decrees; while the ryots complain of illegal distraints, oppression, enhancements, and summary ejectments. There can be no doubt whatever that the combined influence of zemindars and *ticcadars* has ground the ryots of Behar down to a state of extreme depression and misery. The majority of them probably do, as a matter of fact, possess rights of occupancy, but, owing to change of plots, and the subjection of the putwarees to the zemindars, are unable to produce legal proof of this.

1877-78.—The low condition of the agricultural and labouring classes in Behar has formed the subject of much consideration of late years.

It is needless to repeat what has been often said before as to the ignorance, indebtedness, and general helplessness of the Behar ryot. No fresh touches are added in this year's report to the melancholy picture, but it may be fairly assumed that, as it was a year of short crops and high prices, there must have been even more than the usual pressure upon the masses. The division was unable to retain and pay for its own produce, and exportation carried away a large proportion of the crops and stocks. It is only apparently in the north-east of Shahabad and along the Soane that the ryots have anywhere got a position of comfort.

(4). *1872-73 (Commissioner).*—I have already dealt elsewhere with the conduct of zemindars in regard to the general condition of the ryots. I have nothing special to remark on their conduct as zemindars during the year. There have been no very serious affrays; the help given to the police is mostly half-hearted, and only given where the Magistrate insists on it; while in very many instances the petty maliks are the great supporters and protectors of bad characters. The traditional oppression ever used towards the ryots is really of the most grinding nature in many parts, though from the fact of its being customary, its real nature is perhaps unrecognised by either party; and I cannot say that the relations between zemindars and their ryots are other than amicable as amicableness is understood.

*   *   *   *   *

There have been some conspicuous instances of liberality on the part of individuals in subscribing to schools, in starting dispensaries, and in building bridges; but these are quite exceptional, and, as a rule, the zemindars of the division are indifferent and apathetic on all such subjects, and can, with great difficulty, be made to contribute anything for their support, though they themselves and those around them are to be benefited. I must say that, as a rule, I believe the ryots to be more oppressed under the rule of petty maliks, kyests, and babhuns, than under the large zemindars, or even the Mussulmans of old family.

(*b*). *Sarun.*—Considering how lightly the land revenue falls on the land at the present day, and the large profits which in consequence accrue to landed proprietors, it might be expected that at least the zemindars of the district would, as a body, be extremely well off, and so they undoubtedly would be, were it not for the influence of the Hindu law of division of property. As it is, owing to the constant sub-division of property into numerous and, for the most part, infinitesimal fractional shares, the profits of the land are divided among so large a number, that many of the so-called zemindars find it impossible to subsist on their proprietary income alone, and eke out an existence by means of cultivation or service, while still eager to retain the shadow of their zemindari status long after its substance has departed. There are still, however, a few considerable zemindars in the district, and these of course, where not involved in debt, are in prosperous and often wealthy circumstances.

VIII.—Orissa Division—

(*a*). (1). *1872-73.*—Considering how the zemindars of Orissa have been created by us, as is clearly shown in Mr. Toynbee's recent publication, and

how, notwithstanding their great increase in wealth, and the enlarged cul- APP. XIII.
tivation, the former thirty years' settlement has been extended for another
thirty years, the Lieutenant Governor thinks their grumbling and complaints of a breach of faith (paragraph 68), because they do not also get
constant remission of revenue besides, is most unreasonable and preposter-
ous. It shows that there are some people who are only spoilt by indulgence.
The conduct, too, of a large proportion of these men towards their tenantry
makes it clear that, far from doing as they have been done by, they
have sought to exact from those beneath them the uttermost farthing of
that which had been forgiven them by their lord. This, and a great deal
more besides, they have exacted. His Honour, however, is rejoiced to
see that even already, independently of the measures which may eventually
be adopted, much good has been effected by the exertions of Messrs.
Beames, Fiddian, and of the Commissioner himself; and the way in which
these officers have brought abuses to light, entitles them to the highest
credit.

(2). *1872-73.*—A few of the wealthier zemindars are fairly educated;
but the great majority can only read and write tolerably, with a fair
knowledge of arithmetic and accounts. Almost every appointment
above the lowest in public or in private service is held by members of
this class. The changes consequent upon succession by inheritance, and
upon the abandonment of occupancy or other secondary rights during
the famine, without any efficient record of rights, have led to endless
litigation, from which but few of the zemindar class can escape. The
richer zemindars also engage largely in money-lending, and the result of
litigation and usury is demoralising. These men are brought face to face
with Government by the settlement, and it is natural that they should
have complaints, and that when these are rejected, they should think
that Government has broken faith with them. The question of remissions is an endless source of complaints and dispute. There can be no
doubt that the interpretation put upon the settlement engagements by
Sir H. Ricketts and his contemporaries was more favourable to the
zemindars than that of the officials who succeeded him, and the zemindars are apt to think that they have been, at times, treated illiberally,
if not unfairly; hence there is no great confidence as to the future action
of Government in any matter.

IX.—CHOTA NAGPORE DIVISION—

(*a*). *General, 1872-73.*—(1). The progress of Christianity among the
people tends to make them independent. It may be hoped that the officers
of Government will be able to render their position tolerable, notwithstanding the wide rights improvidently given to chiefs in the early days,
when the only object was to protect the plains against the hill people,
and the revenue was alienated to those who were bound to guard the
passes, but have now become almost a sinecure.

(2). *1872-73.*—His Honour notices what is said of the landlords in
Maunbhoom, that they have served on their tenants notices of enhancement of rents at treble, quadruple, quintuple, and even higher rates.
The explanation of the talookdars—than which, as Colonel Dalton says,
a more unjust reason for enhancement could not have been given—is,

that having accepted their talooks with a spurious rent-roll, according to which the head proprietor himself never dreamt of realising, they were compelled to increase heavily to make some profit out of the transaction. Be that as it may, His Honour is certain that if justice is fairly done, such attempts cannot succeed.

(3). *1872-73.*—The condition of the people throughout the division is favourably reported on. The great landed proprietors were a few years ago much in debt ; but some of the largest estates have come under the Court of Wards, and, with one exception, all these are now in a very solvent position. There are others, the owners of which are hardly able to hold their heads above water; but this does not affect the people. The ryots, for the most part occupancy men, are not at all dependent on the wealth of their landlords, who, whether wealthy or indigent, do little or nothing to improve their estates, and the ryots have to improve their own holdings as best they can. This is one reason why they object so strongly to the enhancement of rents. Their own condition has no doubt been improved ; they have more movable property and more comforts than they had before ; but they declare, with truth, that if this be not entirely owing to their own exertions, it certainly does not arise from anything their landlords have done for them.

6. The condition of the ryots and of the people is noticed as follows in the Administration Reports :—

Part I, page 38.   I. *1871-72.*—(*a*). Large as the population is, and probably increasing, it has been common among Europeans and others to speak of the great increase of wages, and sometimes to assume that the labouring classes are better off than heretofore. Some increase of wages there has no doubt been everywhere, or almost everywhere, and in some places that rise has been large. In the districts of cheap labour which throw off a surplus population, as in Chota Nagpore and Behar, the wages of coolies employed by Europeans may have risen from three half-pence to two pence per day in the first-named province, and from two pence to two pence halfpenny, or even three pence, in that last mentioned In some districts day-labourers may even earn as much as six pence per day at busy seasons. Domestic servants, who formerly received five and six rupees per month, may have risen to six and seven or eight rupees.

(*b*). Still it may be doubted whether in the country generally wages have risen more than prices and the expenses of living, and whether those who work for hire are materially better off than they used to be. At the same time, there is perhaps more of regular work for regular wages, and there is probably less abject poverty than there once was. In fact, in times of fair crops and ordinary prosperity, there is not much appearance of want, and the people, even in hard times not amounting to downright famine, still maintain themselves, as they always have in a wonderful way, without dependence on charity or public relief of any kind.

(*c*). The agricultural ryots or small farmers are a more numerous class in most districts than the labourers for hire; and as they benefit by a rise in prices, it may be hoped that their condition is improving in districts in which enhancement of rent does not follow too rapidly and too severely. It has been said that in Bengal direct enhancement has not been generally pushed to an extreme; and it is the Lieutenant-Governor's hope that, more or less, the most important class in the agricultural system—the ryots—are beginning to share to some extent in the general prosperity of the country.

(*d*). (1). The ryots may be divided into three classes: those who, under the provisions of the permanent settlement in favour of ryots generally, or in virtue of subsequent contracts, are entitled to hold at fixed rents ; those who have a right of occupancy, subject to a regulated variation of rents ; and tenants from year to year, commonly called tenants-at-will. Owing to the difficulty of proving an actual or constructive possession from the time of the permanent settlement, and to a rule which makes every man who or whose ancestors have in fact at any time submitted to any increase of rent, just or unjust, liable to enhancement for ever, it is to be feared that the ryots safely established in the first-mentioned class, holding at fixed rents, are comparatively few in number.

(2). The line between tenants-at-will and occupancy ryots is not, Part I, page 179. in practice, very well defined; one class runs very much into the other, and in many parts of the country customary rents are regulated by the same customary rules in both cases. * * It may be said, however, that the mass of ryots are either occupancy ryots or ryots whose rent is similarly regulated by customary adjustments rather than by the strict law of supply and demand and the rent definitions of the economists. In considering this matter, then (the road cess), the occupancy ryot may be taken as the normal type of the ryot to be dealt with.

(3). Now, taking this normal ryot, it must be first said that there is reason to hope, as the Lieutenant-Governor believes, that his status has considerably improved of recent years. There has been a material improvement in the position and means of the Bengal agricultural community, owing to the increasing demand for the great staples of commerce. It is hoped that the rise in rents has not been so great as to absorb the whole of the ryot's share in the general improvement. It may even not improbably be that if the proprietors, instead of levying irregular cesses, were systematically to pursue in the courts a course of enhancement to the utmost limit that the law allows, they might still establish grounds for further enhancement in many cases, while the expenses of such a mode of proceeding would fall very heavily on the ryots, whatever the event of such suits.

II. *1872-73*—(*a*). (1). As a rule, the people in these provinces are comparatively better off in the east, and worse off in the west. They are better off in the former in two respects, which may be more or less interrelated as cause and consequence: (1), the rate of wages is higher in the east, at the same time that food is for the most part cheaper (Orissa in the west, perhaps, excepted with respect to cheapness of food) ; and (2), rents in the east are less screwed up to rack-rent pitch, and probably are lighter in comparison to the productiveness of the soil and remunerative character of such staples as jute, &c.

(2). It is indeed certain that if the practical working of the permanent settlement had accorded with the theory of the Regulations of 1793, if the ryots had fixity of rent as the zemindars have fixity of revenue, the condition of the people of Bengal would now be the easiest in India; but it is unfortunately far otherwise; and the degree to which rents have been racked in different districts is in a considerable degree the measure of the comfort or discomfort of the people.

(b).—EASTERN BENGAL—

(1). In the Dacca division the material condition of the people has certainly improved, as compared with what it was only a few years back. Immense sums of money now come into the country for payment or purchases of country produce; and though a share clings to the fingers of those through whom it passes on its way from the exporting merchant to the cultivators, still there is no doubt that a good proportion of it does reach the ryot. * * On the whole, it may fairly be said that the agricultural class of the inhabitants of Eastern Bengal are in a condition of increasing comfort and independence.

(2). Under the term Eastern Bengal may also be included the Chittagong division. The material condition of the people of Chittagong is said to be very prosperous. The residents are mostly agriculturists; and even day-labourers, domestic servants, &c., have their patch of land which is cultivated by themselves or their families. That they are well off is manifested by their independence, and the fact that it is sometimes difficult to get labourers, even at a fair rate of wages. * * The cost of living has increased, but the people are better off. Nearly every one has an acre or so of land in cultivation.

(c).—WESTERN DISTRICTS—

(1). In Orissa there is reason to believe that a change for the better is taking place. Vast sums of money have been spent in the country on irrigation works, and but a small proportion of this is carried away; much of it does, and must, sink in the country. Labour is abundant, and is paid for at remunerative rates. Trade has improved; exports and imports increased. A large number of people are better housed, clothed, and fed, and have more home comforts than formerly. The improvement has probably affected the mercantile classes more than the actual cultivators. Even, however, in remote villages a greater air of comfort may be observed—a better thatch to the houses; and this in Orissa is one of the best signs of improvement, as it is about the first thing an Ooriah ryot does when he gets a little above water. * * At the same time, the comparative well-doing of the people is somewhat alloyed by the extreme poverty of a large landless labouring class. The Collector of Balasore writes that he has known many cases where a family only ate food once in two days, and no member of the family has more than one garment. It is fortunate that there are now ample facilities of emigration.

App. XIII.

CONDITION OF
THE RYOTS.

Para. 6, contd.

Burdwan divi-
sion.

The extraordinary increase of passenger traffic between Calcutta and Orissa, and by sea, is a most gratifying sign that the population are more and more learning to help themselves.

(2). Of the Burdwan division it may be said that the people are, upon the whole, poorer than the average of the inhabitants in Bengal, and that wages are low, except in the vicinity of Calcutta and along the Hooghly river. Throughout the division the lower classes are a poor and improvident people ; and although their actual bodily wants are small and easily satisfied, there is but small approach to anything like an accumulation of capital among them at present. There is a good deal of emigration from the western borders of the division, but not apparently from the alluvial tracts, or from Beerbhoom.

(3). The census returns show the district of Hooghly and a few thannas of Midnapore (now invaded by the fever), with two or three thannas of Burdwan, to be the most populous tracts in these provinces— probably in India. The question arises whether any considerable proportion of the whole population are townspeople and non-agriculturists. In some parts of Hooghly this is, no doubt, the case. Allowance must be made for the towns and great villages, containing a large town, mercantile and fishing population, which fringe the river Hooghly in the Hooghly district, including Howrah in that term. But, apart from this, we find in the back-lying thannas of the low and marshy country in a purely rural tract an immense population. Similarly, in Midnapore, the most crowded thannas are those in the pit of the low land between the great rivers. These, with a population ranging from 939 to 1,093 per square mile, seem to form a low-lying water and watery tract, stretching from behind Howrah to near Midnapore, absolutely agricultural, without a single town, and still with an average population fully equal to, or exceeding, 1,000 per square mile of gross area. This population is enormous. On the other hand, living as rural Bengalees do in scattered villages, it is not certain that the country population is necessarily so thick as to affect health.

(d).—CENTRAL DISTRICTS—

(1). The condition of the people in the Presidency division is believed to be improving. All ryots have, now-a-days, become better off, owing to the increased price of agricultural produce. It is stated that some years ago it was not unusual to find even tolerably substantial ryots living on one meal a day ; now they have two, and sometimes more, many of them taking a small meal of cold rice, salt, and onions early in the morning. It is, however, not only in the way of a more plentiful supply of food that their condition has been improved—a change for the better is observable in their houses, which are better raised and better constructed. They have a larger supply of clothing, while a *tuktaposh* (bedstead) and a quilt stuffed with cotton have taken the place of the mats on which they lay, and of the rags with which they covered themselves. True, the ryots work hard all day to provide for themselves and their families, but the better class of them, as a rule, now enjoy something more than necessaries. "Well-to-do," in the sense of owning substantial property, the great mass of ryots certainly are not ; for they are, as a rule, indebted to the *mahajuns* from year to year. But, so far as provision for necessaries is concerned, the average ryots cannot be said to be badly off in a prosperous year. The mildness of the climate obviates the necessity for expensive houses and clothing. Their luxuries are few and simple, and their food inexpensive in comparison with the value of their labour.

24-Pergunnahs.

(2). It is certain at least that the people are fairly prosperous, by an Indian standard, in the 24-Pergunnahs district. The proximity of Calcutta affords a ready sale and a comparatively high rate of wages; while from the north, south, and west of the district rice is largely raised and exported, and quantities of timber and firewood and thatching leaves can be obtained from the Soonderbuns for the mere trouble of cutting. Immigration into this district is still steady, and there are no complaints of non-population.

Jessore and
Nuddea.

(3). It is to be regretted that the peasantry of Jessore and Nuddea are not so well off; but in Jessore, though the ryots may be poor, there are many *jotidars, gautidars,* and others, who, with their rice fields and date gardens, occupy something of the position of peasant proprietors. In Nuddea the people came wonderfully through the floods, and then and since have shown much self-reliance.

Rajshahye divi-
sion.

(4). In the large division of Rajshahye there is probably more wide variety. Moorshedabad partakes more of the character of the western districts, and its account is not very favourable. Labour seems to be cheaper and food dearer than elsewhere. On the other hand, as regards the north-eastern districts, there is no doubt that a more favourable account is correct. The marked improvement among all classes is denoted by the better clothing which is used, by the substitution of metal vessels for earthenware, by the increase in the rate paid for labour, the independence of servants, and by the freedom from debt of the majority of the cultivators. In Rungpore there can be no doubt that, with fine produce and favourable tenures, and a great demand for labour, the people are very well off; though they are suffering from a temporary discouragement, owing to the fall in the price of jute. Again, in Dinagepore, with a comparatively sparse population and very productive soil, the people are well off, and will no doubt become much more so when the railway is completed.

Cooch Behar.

(5). The condition of the people of Cooch Behar is good. The reis no overplus of population. The soil is everywhere fertile, and want is rare. The cultivator can count on three crops—jute, tobacco, and *dhan,* and often mustard; and the season which may be fatal to one is beneficial to the others.

(e).—CHOTA NAGPORE DIVISION—

The condition of the Hindu population of the Chota Nagpore division is said to be tolerable. * * The Koles of Singbhoom, who but a few years back were a savage and barbarous population, are now a prosperous people, and their villages are described as often perfect pictures of comfort and prettiness. The ryots, for the most part occupancy men, are not at all dependent on the wealth of their landlords, who do nothing to improve their estates, and leave the ryots to improve their own holdings as best they can. The ryots' condition has no doubt been improved; they have more movable property and more comforts than they had before; but they declare, with truth, that if there be improvement, it is entirely owing to their own exertions, and it certainly does not arise from anything their landlords have done for them. On the other hand, it must be admitted that, although labour is abundant, wages are perhaps lower in Chota Nagpore than almost in any other part of India, and have not risen in proportion to the increase in the price of the ordinary food staples. That the people are, on the whole, well off, is owing to their freedom from prejudice and local ties and their industrious disposition, which enables them to go forth from their own country to earn money by labour. The labourers of this division largely emigrate for employment. They pour into all parts of Bengal after their own harvest in December, and return with their modest earnings in May. The tea districts are also mainly recruited with coolies from Chota Nagpore.

1877-78.—Most of the zemindars in Chota Nagpore are so deeply involved in debt that they are unable to incur any expense for the benefit of their districts, or even to assist their own ryots when in distress. There are, however, some few exceptions to this.

App. XIII.
———
CONDITION OF
THE RYOTS.
———
Para. 6, contd.

(*f*).—BÉHAR (1872-73)—

BEHAR.

(1). The local officers all report strongly of the poverty of the ryots in the Patna division, and it is beyond doubt that the people are badly off. Late years have not been bad, and food has been comparatively cheap. But it is a good deal dearer than it formerly was, and the wages of labour are still very low. Except during the harvest and planting seasons, the rate of unskilled labour is only one and a half annas per diem. Although Gya and Shahabad have an apparently smaller population rate than elsewhere, they have so much of barren hill tracts, that in the well populated area they are practically no doubt just as overcrowded as those districts which show a larger rate. In Gya it is said that the agricultural labourer is worse off than anywhere else in the division. He is generally paid in grain, and lives really from hand to mouth. Two or three seers of some coarse grain, representing a money value perhaps of $1\frac{1}{4}$ annas, suffice him to support life, and enable him to work. With the Soane works, however, close at hand, and two annas a day to be earned there, there is a brighter side to the question. The zemindars of this division, especially the smaller landholders, are stated to be oppressive on their tenants. On the larger estates, the system of farming out villages widely prevails—a system of profit upon profits, under which the cultivators sadly suffer. Happily, emigration is a resource well known, and in some degree practised by the people. * * There is a periodic emigration of labourers from the Sarun district, who go to Purneah, Julpigorie, Rungpore, and Cooch Behar.

Patna division.

(2). There seems to be a good deal of difference of opinion regarding the general condition of the people of the Bhagulpore division. In the Bhagulpore and Monghyr districts, the population is large and rents are high. Wages, on the other hand, are low—certainly lower than in most districts in Bengal proper, and very much lower than in the eastern districts. Food also is dearer than in these latter. Wages have risen,

Bhagulpore
division.

APP. XIII.

CONDITION OF
THE RYOTS.

Para. 6, contd.

compared to former times; but so, it is stated, has the price of food. Still the people are, for the most part, a decidedly industrious people—quiet, simple, and careful. They seem to be content in their small humble way. There is little or no emigration, the small number of emigrants reported being in great part inhabitants of other districts. What emigration does take place is confined to the north-west corner of the division, adjoining Tirhoot. In the reports of the eastern districts, it is not often said that labourers from Bhagulpore come to seek for employment. The Magistrate of one district made inquiries during the past cold weather into the condition of the ryots on the frontier territory, and the result is discouraging, in that, after very fairly weighing the respective advantages and disadvantages of both, he comes to the conclusion that the condition of the Nepal ryot is, on the whole, better than that of the British ryot. Although the smaller rent taken from the former by the Nepalese Government is supplemented by forced labour and the purveyance system, on the other hand, the illegal cesses and exactions of zemindars, middlemen, &c., and other vexations, turn the scale against the British cultivator. In Purneah, however, where the population is much more sparse, it is probably a correct statement that the people are better off than elsewhere in the division. They suffer a good deal from fever and from the ravages of the river Koosee; but those who escape these evils are perhaps in their means above the average of the ryots of these provinces.

Sonthal Pergunnahs.

(3). The people of the Sonthal Pergunnahs are a simple and improvident race. They had in the past earned easily a poor living, and spent their little easily, so long as they had plenty of land, light rents, and little interference in their own jungly country. But since they have been invaded by grasping speculators and adventurers, and the zemindars by these instruments have begun to levy heavy rents and exactions, the Sonthals have felt distress.

Part I, page 16.

III. *1874-75.*—Special inquiries have been made regarding the indebtedness of the cultivators as a class. It is not so serious as it once was, but it still exists very largely. It is worst in Behar, somewhat considerable in Central and Western Bengal and in Orissa, less decidedly in Eastern and Northern Bengal, and altogether disappearing in parts of Eastern and Northern Bengal. In those districts where it exists, there is no class of cultivators—not even those with occupancy rights or sub-proprietary tenures—who are free from it. Indeed, the stronger a man's tenure, the better is his credit. The amount of debt is, for the most part, not excessively burdensome; and, upon a general average, the amount of debt may be estimated as being equal to about the cultivator's income for two years. The ordinary rates of interest are believed to be as high as two pice in the rupee per month for money lent, equal to 37½ per cent. per annum; and 50 per cent. is usually paid as interest on rice advances. The security, according to which the lender exactly measures the loans, is the standing crop. The creditors are generally the village bankers, but often they are the zemindars. The loans are contracted partly for purchase of cattle and implements of husbandry, to some extent for law expenses, and largely for marriages. It is remarkable that relatively extravagant ideas regarding marriage expenses should spread even to these humble classes.

App. XIII.

CONDITION OF
THE RYOTS.

Para 6, contd.

Part I,
pages 41-2.

IV. *1874-75.*—(1). It is difficult to generalise upon the prices of common food, because they differ so much at the central marts, and in the isolated tracts of the interior respectively, being tolerably uniform in the former, but being sometimes extraordinarily cheap in the latter. As might be expected, the increasing facilities of transport keep the prices within a moderate range of valuation at all the principal centres; a superabundant yield in one place, the Gangetic delta for instance, will not cause food-grains to be merely a drug in the market there, but will cheapen the prices throughout Bengal. Food-grains, which are quoted at high prices in central places, are obtainable most easily and cheaply, immediately after harvest time, by those who dwell at the places of production. But, according to the quotations at the central places, the prices are much higher than they used to be in former times. Now-a-days in Bengal and Behar a rupee will ordinarily purchase from 20 seers to 25 seers of common rice, and in Orissa 25 seers to 30 seers. During the last preceding generation, it would have purchased 40 seers, and in the generation before that, 60 seers and upwards. In Calcutta itself, the present prices are dearer; there a rupee will seldom purchase more than 16 seers of common rice. In Behar, however, maize and other cereals, besides rice, are consumed, and of these a rupee will purchase as much as 35 seers. The bearing of these large facts on the condition of the labouring classes cannot, however, be fully seen without advertence to the rates of wages and the modes of remunerating labour.

(2). The wages of labour may be generally stated at one to two annas a day in Behar; two annas in Orissa; three annas in Northern Bengal; four annas in Central Bengal; four annas in Eastern Bengal; and six annas in Calcutta. During the last generation, the rates ranged from one anna at the lowest to three annas at the highest, the lowest being the generally prevalent rate. On the whole, the wages of labour have risen almost coincidentally with the prices of common food. So far, then, we may hope that the lot of the labourer, which was always very hard, has not become harder of late. But we must sorrowfully admit that it is almost as hard as can be borne. A plain calculation will show that the wages will suffice for little more than the purchase of food, and leave but a slender margin for his simplest wants. In Behar, indeed, a comparison of prices with wages might indicate that his lot must be hard beyond endurance. It must be remembered, however, that wages are often paid in kind, especially for labour in the fields. The labourer and his family all work; the man, the woman, and the child receive each a dole of grain, enough to sustain life; they could hardly get less now, and probably they never got more: still, low as the condition of the labourer everywhere is, it is lowest in Behar. The industry and endurance, not only of the men, but of the women and children, in these classes are remarkable. One cause of the lowness of the wages is the comparative inefficiency of the labour; which, again, is caused by the low and weak physique of these poor people, by reason of the poverty of their nurture, one cause acting and re-acting upon another; while at the same time, despite the high rate of mortality, the high rate of births more than maintains the total number, which is probably increasing rather than decreasing.

V. *1875-76*—(*a*). The comparative low condition of the ryots and peasantry in those parts of the province of Behar which lie north of the Part I, pages 13-14.

Ganges, and especially in the upper half of the old district of Tirhoot, continues to cause regret and apprehension. * * The revised census and other enquiries instituted in consequence of the scarcity of 1876 showed that the power of distraint which the law gives to the landlord with certain well-defined limitations had in North Behar generally, from time immemorial, been exercised by the landlord to an unlimited extent, placing the crop of the tenant, from sowing time to harvest, virtually at the disposal and under the watchful control of the landowner. The practice, when carried thus far, is subversive of the status which the ryots ought to possess, and which the law meant them to have. * * *

(*b*). The material advancement of the sub-proprietors, the ryots, and the peasantry in Eastern Bengal, has been mentioned with satisfaction on former occasions. A remarkable illustration has been afforded by the detailed enquiries which are being made for the valuation of the land in the deltaic district of Backergunge. It appears from the road cess returns that the rent-roll payable to the intermediate tenure-holders is often ten, twenty, or fifty times the rent paid to the superior landlord. It seems probable that not less than a crore of rupees (assumed as equal to one million sterling) are annually paid in rent in this district, and that the value of the agricultural produce of the district can hardly be less than five millions sterling annually, and may be much more. The returns, moreover, while they show the prosperous condition of the tenure-holders and other middlemen, show also how the profits of the land are slipping out of the hands of the zemindars, who have permanently alienated their interests in the soil, and in many cases have fallen into the position of needy annuitants.

Part II, page 13. (*c*). It is unfortunately true that although the Durbungah estate may be better managed than any other in Tirhoot, this estate does not essentially differ from the rest of the province in respect of the inferior condition of the peasantry as compared with the surrounding provinces. Undoubtedly the condition of the peasantry is low in Behar, lower than that of any other peasantry with equal natural advantages, in any province which Sir Richard Temple has seen in India. In 1868 the inferior status of the peasantry and tenantry was the subject of much official correspondence. In 1872 and 1873 this matter caused some anxiety to Government. In 1874 the famine supervened; the immediate solicitude of Government was rather to save the lives of the people than to protect their legal rights. In 1875, after the famine storm and crisis, it was thought advisable to let the land have rest from all sorts of agitation. But during the past year a part of the very tracts which previously suffered was again threatened with scarcity, and the question of tenant-right once more forced itself upon the attention of Government.

7. This account of the condition of the ryots may be continued in detail of divisions from the Administration Reports of Commissioners of divisions, and (where so indicated) from the Administration Reports of the Bengal Government.

I.—EASTERN DISTRICT—

(*a*).—DACCA DIVISION—

(1). *1872-73.*—The Lieutenant-Governor observes that the general result of the information collected regarding the crops is to show exceeding readiness rather than backwardness on the part of cultivators to meet the demands of the market. Para. 7, contd.
Page 22.

(2). *Dacca District.*—The condition of the ryots is [1] excellent. The poorest class of persons now are petty landowners, whose ancestors have given out all, or nearly all, their lands as permanent under-tenures, and who have thus received no increase of income in proportion to the rise in price of all the necessaries of life. There are many of these people who despise any trade, and they must feel the rise in prices severely. Page 266 of
1872-73.

(3). Sub-infeudation is small in Dacca, excessive in *Furreedpore,* where the people are not quite so well off as in Dacca. 1872-73, pages 24
and 238-39,
1875-76.

(4). *Backergunge* is much broken up into petty holdings (1872-73, page 24). "It has long been, I believe, a recognised fact that the most prosperous ryots in all Bengal were those of Backergunge, and that, amongst them, the ryots of Dukhinshahbazpore were better off than the rest."

(5). *Sylhet,* a district of peasant proprietors. "The material condition of the people is prosperous to a degree unknown in a good many of the most prosperous districts in Bengal. Everywhere in this district, except the west of it, the ryots' houses present a well-to-do appearance. Nowhere else do the commonest ryots enjoy such luxuries as fish and fruits to the same extent as in Sylhet. * * The great object in life with the poorest Sylheti is to have a patch of land that he can call his own. When he goes out for work, he does so more to assist his brothers, from whom he hopes to get the same return, or from the hope of some unusually good wages. 1872-73, page 272.

(6). *Mymensingh.*—Many small estates in the district. Only one-third of the district is under cultivation, and land can be rented all over the district on very easy terms. The Lieutenant-Governor cannot pretend to state, even approximately, the annual money-value of the commercial transactions of the district; but there cannot be the least doubt that the value of the exports greatly exceeds that of the imports, and that a large balance is regularly paid in silver. It is pretty certain that, during the last three years, above a crore of rupees has been paid to Mymensingh growers and dealers for the single article of jute. The mass of the people are agriculturists of simple habits and inexpensive tastes, and their demand for imported goods is comparatively small. The consequence is, that a stream of silver is steadily flowing into the district; and it would at first sight appear remarkable that the rise in prices has not been greater than it has; but the solution of this problem lies in the fact that the silver is partly melted down into ornaments and partly hoarded, so that there is little, if any, increase in the circulating medium. It would not be safe even to hazard a conjecture as to the amount of money hoarded in the district; but it may be stated generally that almost every well-to-do ryot (and there are many thousands of them in the district) 1872-73, pages
248-51.

has a pot of money buried beneath the floor of his house, or a bag of rupees hidden away in a corner of the family chest.

(7). *Tipperah.*—Very well off (Government Resolution, 1875-76).

II.—CENTRAL DISTRICTS—

(a).—PRESIDENCY DIVISION—

(1). *24-Pergunnahs District.*—People tolerably well off (1872-73).

(2). *Jessore and Nuddea.*—People not so well off as in 24-Pergunnahs, but in 1875-76 there was a marked improvement in the material comfort and social position of the cultivating class in *Jessore*, who had benefited by a rise in the price of rice, their rents not having risen in proportion. The zemindars in Jessore, as a body, are, however, not prosperous, a few of the distinguished houses having been ruined, while others are in a state of rapid decay from the minute sub-division of zemindaries under the law of inheritance (1875-76). In *Nuddea* a wide-spread indebtedness prevails among the tenantry.

(3). *Moorshedabad.*—The prosperity of the people is far less marked than it is in the eastern and deltaic districts of Bengal. In Eastern Bengal the ryots are for the most part frugal and independent; but in Moorshedabad they appear to be improvident and poor and heavily indebted to *mahajuns*, like those in many of the Behar districts (1875-76 and 1876-77).

(b).—RAJSHAHYE DIVISION—

Throughout this division the demand is for labour and not for land. The cultivating classes are substantial and well-to-do, and great bodies of hired labourers annually come in from Behar and Nepal, seeking work, which they readily obtain. Neither local labourers nor skilled artisans are to be found, save at very high rates (1876-77).

(1). *Bograh* is under-populated (1876-77) : a marked improvement among all classes is denoted by the better clothing which is used, by the substitution of metal vessels for earthenware, by the increase in the rate paid for labour, the independence of servants, and by the freedom from debt of the majority of the cultivators (1872-73). " I (Collector) hear that some years ago the majority of cultivators were in debt, but that now most of them are free. I learn, however, that in the northern part of this district a small section of the population are the victims of the merciless system of usury known as *adhiari*, which, literally translated, means fifty percenting. A ryot borrows a maund of rice, undertaking to repay a maund and a half in the following year; he generally fails, and the maund and a half is treated as a debt bearing the same outrageous compound interest. In course of time the ryot assigns the produce of his holding to his creditor, and lives on such loans as it suits the latter to advance him, and thus becomes a mere serf of his creditor (1872-73) ; yet," the Collector adds," this district is so favoured, both in its soil and in its seasons, that emigration for agricultural purposes is unknown (1872-73)."

1872-73, page 194

(2). *Dinagepore.*—In this district, with a comparatively sparse population and very productive soil, the people are stated to be well off, and will

no doubt become much more so when the railway is completed. App. XIII.
Mr. Robinson, the Magistrate of Dinagepore, expresses the opinion that CONDITION OF
the people are better off than in other parts of India, and adduces the THE RYOTS.
testimony of a gentleman who had lately been travelling in Oudh, and Para. 7, contd.
who says nothing could be plainer than that the Bengal ryot, with a
permanent settlement,[1] is much better off than the peasantry of Oudh.
This comparison, however, can hardly be said to involve a high standard,
as the ryots of Oudh, besides forming a dense population, have had less
rights recognised than any peasantry in India.   When the Magistrate
can compare favourably with Bombay, the Punjab, and Madras, we shall
have more to pride ourselves upon (1872-73, page 13).

   The same merciless system of usury, known as *adhiari*, which has 1872-73, page
been described by the Collector of Bogra (above), is much more prevalent 19½.
(the Collector is told) in Dinagepore than in Bogra.

   (3). *Rungpore.*—In this district there can be no doubt that, with fine
produce and favourable tenures and a great demand for labour, the
people are very well off, although they are suffering from a temporary
discouragement owing to the fall in the price of jute (1872-73,
page 13).

   (4). (*a*). *Maldah.*—The ryots of the southern and central tracts of this
district are notably a well-to-do body.   Both mulberry-growing and
silk-rearing are the occupations of most of them and are extremely
lucrative, bringing in a substantial return for their time and labour.
To the north and east the ryots are apparently poorer and more primitive, but withal apparently contented, though in most instances
they are entirely under the will and control of their landlords on
whose treatment the welfare or otherwise of the tenantry chiefly
depends.

   (*b*). The greater portion of the cultivating classes in Maldah are said 1875-76.
to be hopelessly involved in debt to their *mahajuns*; so much so that
the registration proceedings of that district disclose instances of debtors
binding themselves to render personal service to their creditors for a
term of years, varying from three to ten, until the whole amount of the
debt has been worked out.   Not only do debtors bind themselves for
their own debts, but also for those of their fathers; and during last year
a deed was registered whereby three sons bound themselves to serve a
mahajun for seven years in lieu of money-payment of a debt to the
mahajun incurred by their father.   Such contracts as these, it is to be
hoped, are peculiar to this district.

III.—Western Districts.—

(*a*).—Orissa—

   There can be no doubt that there has been for some time past
an annually expanding trade between Orissa and the outside world
which will, the Lieutenant-Governor hopes, be the means of placing
the prosperity of the province on an assured basis (1876-77).

---

   [1] A permanent settlement is exactly what the Bengal ryot wants, but cannot get.

(1). *Balasore.*—It is evident that the public wealth and the expenditure of the people, both upon luxuries and necessities, are increasing (1875-76).

(2). *Cuttack.*—The Collector reports : " Wherever I went in my tour I met with prosperity. The Ooriah peasant does not display his wealth, being penurious by nature ; but the villagers' houses were in good repair, and at marriages and festivals brighter clothing and richer ornaments were observed. In my tour in the south I witnessed the novel spectacle, for Orissa, of foreign merchants settling in nearly every village, buying surplus produce from the peasantry, and paying for it in hard cash, as well as making advances for next year. One firm alone has one lakh and a half of advances out in the Juggutsingpore and Urtot thannas. A good harvest is more profitable to the peasant now than formerly ; now he can sell all his surplus produce at a good price, whereas formerly a good harvest sent down the prices, and his produce fetched him in comparatively little. The only persons who suffer are those residents of towns who live on fixed incomes, and shop-keepers who have no land. These were disappointed to find that so excellent a harvest did not result in greater cheapness of rice ; and perceiving that the cause lay in the briskness of export, bitterly complained against the merchants. The material condition of the people has strikingly improved, and this re-acts on the shop-keepers ; for the peasant can now afford to spend more money in the purchase of imported articles, and trade thereby improves. That this is the case is shown, among other things, by the rapid increase of the city of Cuttack, where the shop-keepers mostly deal in imported clothes, brassware, and ornaments. New and handsome shops are rising in all directions ; mud walls are giving place to masonry, and thatch to *pucka* roofs (1875-56).

(3). *Pooree* district has less trade than either Balasore or Cuttack, and although the past few years have afforded good crops and the people are for the most part well off, material improvement is less marked in Pooree than in other parts of Orissa (1875-76).

(b.)—BURDWAN DIVISION—

With regard to the material condition of the people, there is no perceptible change during the year. Mr. Harrison, in Midnapore, writes of the people as impoverished and unfitted for, and likely to be impatient of, direct taxation. In Burdwan the people are said to be poor, but resigned to their fate. In Hooghly it is to be feared that in some parts of the country in villages once most flourishing, there is now a grievous exhaustion of the people, especially of the labouring classes ; the adult having been consumed by the ravages of the epedemic fever during the last ten years, and the ordinary ratio in the production of children having been sensibly reduced, as is shown in the census returns. " I " (Commissioner) " fear that throughout the division the lower classes are a poor and improvident people, and although their actual bodily wants are small and easily satisfied, there is but a small tendency to anything like an accumulation of capital among them at present" (1872-73, page 74).

(1). *Hooghly.*—The district consists of a few very large estates, formerly portions of the Burdwan Raj, and held by rich, powerful, and, as a rule, well educated and well disposed zemindars, who, however, have, owing to the land being let in putni to a great extent, but little to do with the actual management; a few more moderately-sized estates generally of a very profitable nature, and some 3,000 estates of the most petty description, consisting of a few beegahs of land, and paying revenue varying from a few annas to a few rupees. These latter are almost all resumed lakhiraj holdings. Besides these there is an immense number of unresumed lakhiraj holdings.

The above, however, by no means comprise all the area of the Hooghly district. About one-half is occupied by talooks of great size belonging to the estate of the Maharajah of Burdwan, or land belonging to other estates on the Burdwan towjee. So many and so large are the talooks belonging to the estate of the Maharajah of Burdwan, that a special Regulation (VIII of 1819) was passed, under which the rents of these talooks (Rs. 4,61,626 a year) are paid into the Hooghly Collectorate, and from thence transferred to his credit.

The ryots' holdings are generally small, as much as a family can plough without assistance. The fever which has been so fatal for a period of ten years in this district, by diminishing the number of members in a family has tended to break up the holdings, and has forced on the ryots the employment of hired labour. A considerable portion of land is held as *khamar* land by the zemindar, and is cultivated by hired labour, or under a system of *bhagi jote*. It is to be feared that the condition of the cultivators is very unsatisfactory. They have to pay higher rents generally than formerly, and though they have greater facilities for obtaining employment and for sale of their produce, yet their wants have increased. However, many have acquired occupancy and fixed rent rights which they had not before; and possibly improvements in the communications of the district will do much to better their condition, by opening out markets for produce, which at present it is not worth while to grow, except in the immediate neighbourhood of the railway and river. But unquestionably the road cess will be a heavy burden to the poorest classes of ryots.

1875-76.—" I " (Collector, Sir J. Herschell) "see no general marks of material improvement, compared to the condition that people enjoyed twenty years ago; but the number of good houses and of pucka buildings has certainly increased, and more clothes are worn by all classes above the labourer or agriculturist. Well fed cattle are more common, but starved ones more scarce decidedly, than they used to be. Milk is now so valuable that calves have little chance of growing; grazing lands are few, and the cattle trespass law is strong."

The truth appears to be that Hooghly, more than the 24-Pergunnahs even, or any other district, has become, as it were, the suburban settlement of Calcutta; and that the densely populated villages all along the banks of the river, for more than twenty miles north of Howrah, are peopled with a well-to-do metropolitan population, who are increasing in comfort and prosperity, while farther in the interior the increase in population and in the demand for food has put pressure on the cultivators, who have been gradually compelled to place even the worst soil under the plough, and are, as was clearly shown in the recent enquiries that were made, far inferior, in material condition and prospect of improvement, to the ryots of the eastern and northern districts of these provinces (Government Resolution, 1875-76).

(2). *Nuddea and Jessore.*—In these districts, though the people are in a far better condition than has been represented more than once of late years, in sensational letters to Government and the Press, the peasantry are not yet independent of mahajuns and zemindars. It is always necessary to have recourse to the mahajuns in the course of the year, and this is expensive, as the next crop is hypothecated on terms that are unfavourable to the ryot. The position of the people in Jessore and Nuddea would, however, have been more favourable but for the recent floods, which entailed great loss on them.

(3). *Midnapore.*—As the district is being opened out by roads and canals, there can be no doubt that the classes that live by agriculture are improving in position. This improvement, however, is but very faintly perceived among the lowest classes, who, as long as they adhere to the existing custom of living for at least three-fourths of the year on the security of their ensuing crop, cannot be much benefited. It can be no exaggeration to say that half the actual cultivators of the soil borrow their sustenance for the latter portion of the year from either the local mahajun or the zemindar. The rate of interest is so high that it is quite impossible for them to clear off their debt, and they do not try to do so. Practically the creditor finds it his interest to support them at the lowest scale of maintenance which they will tolerate without rebellion, and hence he leaves them as much of the one crop, or advances them as much on the other, as he finds necessary : they work, they sow, they reap for his profit, and he takes as much for principal and interest as he thinks he safely can insist upon.

No state of things can be more absolutely destructive of all independence of spirit, as well as more detrimental to all attempts to better their condition. As in such a condition, paradoxical as it may seem, no taxes can touch them, so, on the other hand, no removal of taxation can benefit them. In the distribution of wealth they are able to get just as much as keeps them up to working efficiency; and however Government operates on this wealth, whether to increase or decrease its sum total, their share remains the same, and they neither suffer nor benefit. If a portion of their share falls under the tax-collector's clutch, the mahajun must release to them so much more, to enable them to live. If a cess they pay to the zemindar is put a stop to, the mahajun can screw them down to a similar extent. If the crop is a failure, he must still keep them alive, as his best chance of recouping himself the following year ; if a success, he leaves them the same residuum to live upon. Of course there is some fluctuation : in a good year the ryot is a little more leniently treated ; in a bad year a little more harshly. On the other hand, in a good year a few persons who are nearly clear, rescue themselves from debt, while in a bad year some who were nearly free and clear, get again deeply entangled ; but as regards the great bulk of the people, the only way their condition can be ameliorated is to raise their standard of living, so as to enable them, as a body, to stand out far more than they do at present.

1875-76.—At the commencement of the year both the cultivators and the weavers were in a very depressed condition, owing to the drought of 1873, the paralysing effects of the epidemic fever, and the destructive action of the cyclone of 1874; but the bumper harvest of 1875 relieved them a good deal. The ryots, however, were far from being in easy circumstances, as their whole crop had to go at the low prices prevailing, to satisfy the claims of their creditors; and by the end of April scarcely any of the year's crop remained in the possession of at least 75 per cent. of the cultivators; but their credit has been restored, and they anticipate no difficulty.

1876-77.—If the large destruction of the chief rice crop by inundations reduced the harvest reaped over the whole district to an average one, the *aus* and *boro*, amounting together to nearly one-eighth of the *amun*, were very good; while the mulberry was so good as to recall the golden season before 1873. In addition to this, prices ranged very high on account of the Madras famine, and a large surplus crop remained in store from 1875; and it may be stated that both the agricultural and trading classes were in a very prosperous condition. As a set-off against this, the Collector mentions that a large portion of the agricultural community were in debt to their mahajuns; and where this was the case, the benefit of a good year was considerably diminished, as is the misfortune of a bad one. Mr. Harrison explains that by paying up a large portion of his debt, the ryot obtains better credit, as he has to borrow more money or paddy, and on less favourable terms, in a bad year; but in either case, the chief gainer or loser is the mahajun, who cannot but support the ryot in a bad year, as the best hope of future payment, while in a good year he takes a larger portion of his earnings.

(4). *Midnapore (Irrigation Revenue Report), 1875-76.*—This year the ryots were, almost to a man, in debt to the mahajuns; they were in arrears to their zemindars, and in arrears for water-rate to the Deputy Revenue Superintendent for Irrigation. Hence all these pressed the ryot simultaneously. The Deputy Superintendent says that the zemindars were not more successful than the Government, and certain it is that they very much resented the water-rate collections; " and I " (Collector) " hear that certain of their number, even those who try to stand well with Government, have issued peremptory, but secret, instructions that they will bring their whole power to bear on any of their tenantry who lease in future.

" On the other hand, the mahajuns have been very successful in collecting their dues. The ryots know that it is a matter of life and death not to deprive themselves of future loans; and when they saw that they could not keep the crop themselves, they preferred their mahajuns to the other creditors.

" It seems to me worthy of special attention that it is this state of indebtedness of the ryots which makes it impossible for them to appreciate the benefit of the canal water, except in years in which almost the entire crop is due to it. In the present year our statistics show that the water was worth to the ryots more or less five maunds of rice per acre and twelve maunds of straw, which, even in this year of low prices, would bring them in Rs. 3 to Rs. 3-8 an acre, against Re. 1-8 payable as water-rate. On the other hand, it is quite certain that the ryots, almost to a man, think themselves losers by their leases last year (1875-76). The explanation of this is not far to find. The mahajuns take from the ryots interest at from 33 to 75 per cent., but they are quite satisfied with actually netting 15 to 20. The balance represents remissions of interest and bad debts. The effect of the better crops is to diminish their amount of bad debts, and enable them to collect a larger proportion of their outstandings; but they do not leave much more with the ryots than heretofore. Thus, a mahajun to whom the ryot owed in 1875 Rs. 40, has recovered Rs. 30, instead of (say) Rs. 24, because the ryot's land produced 21, instead of 16, maunds per acre; but he has left the ryot enough only to pay his rent and carry on three or four months until the next crop is sown.

"To a ryot in this position, the Government demand of Re. 1-8 per acre comes in the aspect of pure loss. That he has reduced his mahajun's debt to Rs. 10 instead of Rs. 16 is, to an improvident man, a matter of very little consequence; all he looks to is, that he has recovered his credit with the mahajun, and can rely on getting another advance in the approaching rains. On the other hand, the Government demand is obtrusive and urgent, and is a very definite and practical evil. No wonder, therefore, if they seem to themselves to be no better off at the end of the year than their non-irrigating neighbours, while they have the Government water dues to meet in addition to the rent, which is common to both."

1876-77.—The irrigation revenue demands were enforced mostly by process of law, the people resisting them to the last. Very little of the demand for the year was recovered during the year; but the recoveries of arrears of former years were so vigorously carried on, that the actual collections exceeded those of any previous year, except 1874-75.

It is impossible to record this result with any satisfaction, as it seems certain that the arrears, and the difficulty of enforcing payment, were mainly, if not solely, due to the extreme poverty of the people. It is melancholy to read of 12,714 certificates having been issued for the recovery of the arrears, after abandoning all claims for less than one rupee, and making remissions to a large extent on other grounds; and this in a district where the irrigators have, as a rule, dealt fairly with the Government, and have always been ready to pay, when they had the means. One can hardly read the description of the revenue operations of the year, and, it may be added, of previous years, without a wish that if the state of the cultivators is such as it is described to be by the Collector and his subordinates, irrigation, which, according to them, only enhances the difficulties of the people in ordinary years, had never been introduced at all. The Deputy Revenue Superintendent remarks: " The most potent cause about the gradual decline of the area leased is the indebtedness of the Midnapore ryots. They are involved over head-and-ears; and it is a matter of infinite regret that their debts are increasing as their connection with the Government irrigation is growing older. Excepting during the year under review, the canal irrigation as compared with the unirrigated crop has always increased the yield from three to five maunds in the acre; but the Government irrigators are not in a position to benefit by it; all that they obtain from the fields go punctually to fill the coffers of the mahajuns, and they have finally to borrow money for the payment of the water-rate. The increased yield of the crop, if reserved for the liquidation of the Government debt, is sure to prove more than enough for the purpose; but no notice is taken of it, and when the irrigator is forced to pay for the irrigation of his land, he blames the canal for the increase of his debt."

Again : " Attachments and sales of the debtors' property were very frequent, and where they had not the desired effect, the debtors were arrested for the realisation of the Government dues ; and it is now a very common saying within the irrigable area that the major portion of the Government irrigators have been deprived of their plough-cattle for the payment of the water-rates. This is not very untrue, as the most valuable saleable property in the possession of the cultivators are the bullocks ; and where we could catch hold of them, no other movable or immovable property belonging to them was attached or sold. The number of sale-notices and warrants for the arrest of the debtors issued during the year was unusually large ; yet, from the well known poverty of the Midnapore ryots, the result has not been as satisfactory as was anticipated.

" The zemindars, whose resistance to the spread of irrigation was hitherto passive, have now broken out in action, and many of them have openly prohibited their tenantry from using the canal water on the penalty of incurring their severe displeasure. They have done this with the view of securing realisation of their own dues, and of preventing their ryots from increasing their debts unnecessarily, as they call it. The mahajuns, also, have been telling the ryots not to resort to the canal any longer.

" It should be noted, in passing, that the year 1876-77, in which coercive measures on a large scale were found necessary for the realisation of the Government irrigation revenue, was one of exceptionally high prices, and, so far, peculiarly favourable to the ryots.

" The previous year having been a very favourable one for the unirrigated crops, the area leased for in 1876-77 fell from 55,995 acres to 32,681 ; and as the season advanced, and its real character developed, the lessees repented of their engagements, and endeavoured to evade them by every possible means—first, clamouring for a remission of the Government demand, on the ground that the water was of no value to them (which, as it has turned out, was true) ; and when this was refused, endeavouring to prove that water had not been properly supplied. The result has been disheartening for both Government and people."

IV.—BEHAR—

(a).—PATNA DIVISION—

(1). *General.* 1876-77.—The material condition of the mass of the population in this division is extremely low. The wages of the labouring class are barely sufficient to furnish them with the means of supporting life. They live from hand to mouth, are always underfed, and the slightest abnormal pressure brings them to the verge of acute distress. Mr. Worsley shows that in Tirhoot the money wages of field labourers have remained practically unchanged for the last sixty years. Although the prices of food-grains have risen, and are still apparently rising, one anna to one anna and a half per diem is still the usual wage of an able-bodied labourer. The apparent hardship of this is, however, somewhat mitigated by the fact that it is the custom of the district to pay the labourers in kind rather than in cash, and that, even when cash is paid, the labourer usually gets also his midday meal. At harvest time the labourers are remunerated by a percentage of the crop reaped—one sheaf of every sixteen is said to be the usual proportion. Under this arrangement, as Mr. Macdonnell points out, the labourer is worst off in a bad year; and bad years have in North Behar been very frequent of late.

The cultivating classes are generally involved in debt. "Even in time of plenty" (the Commissioner writes) "after paying the rent and the numerous cesses exacted by the landlords, very little is left to them for their support. When such is the condition of the people in the ordinary years, the failure of a single crop is sure to cause distress." This is felt most in the tracts where rice is the principal crop, as that is most susceptible to injury from drought. In the year of report, relief measures on a limited scale had to be organised on this account in parts of Mudhoobunnee, which is almost entirely a rice-producing tract, and which suffered from a failure of the autumn rains of 1875, while the other sub-divisions of Durbhunga were in comparatively good ease.

(2). *Chumparun.*—In this district 75 per cent. of the population are hopelessly in debt, exclusive of the labouring population, who live from hand to mouth. The great number of the ryots are described as insufficiently fed, and the labouring classes are said to be impoverished, and without the means of maintaining their families. The average holding is about five acres, insufficient to enable the tenant to repay to the mahajun the grain advances of former years at from 20 to 25 per cent., and to pay the rent and maintain his family as well. The indebted tenant lives on the verge of starvation, wholly dependent on his mahajun to tide him through all difficulties.

(3). *Durbhunga.*—As you advance from the Ganges towards the frontier, the material prosperity of the people varies. The farther northward you go, the less satisfactory is the people's condition. The district is purely agricultural, and on the character of the harvest depends the material condition of the great mass. The character of the harvest is determined by the rainfall, and the effect of unseasonable rainfall varies with each crop. * * It is obvious that in years when the rainfall fails, the rice-producing regions suffer more severely than others. The rubbee harvest depends to a large extent on the sufficiency of the rains in the preceding year. If those rains are markedly deficient, the soil will be devoid of moisture, and rubbee sowings will not prosper. Within those tracts near the Ganges inundation is never wanting, and consequently the riparian tracts always yield good crops.

The Tajpore sub-division is a bhadoi and rubbee-growing region. It has a large river frontage, annually fertilised by inundations of the Ganges. It is more or less independent of vicissitudes of season. Mudhoobunnee, on the other hand, is chiefly a rice plain; inundations there are more hurtful than beneficial, for they are inundations of mountain streams, often depositing noxious sand, not fertilising alluvium.

The main stand of the sub-division is the one crop (rice) most susceptible of injury from abnormal weather. * *

In the preceding pages I have endeavoured to point out the natural
causes to which may be attributed, in some way, the differences which
undoubtedly exist between the material prosperity of the inhabitants of
each sub-division. There are, in addition, causes of an artificial nature,
which combine with the natural causes to render unsatisfactory the
material condition of the people of Mudhoobunnee. These artificial
causes have been so thoroughly ventilated in Mr. Geddes' report (in
which I generally concurred), and in subsequent reports that have been
furnished to you, that it seems needless to go over the whole ground
again. It will suffice, then, for me to say here that not alone to a succession of bad years and adverse harvests is due the present unsatisfactory condition of the Mudhoobunnee ryots, especially in the eastern
portion of the sub-division. These causes, added to others, such as excessive enhancements, irregular realisations on their own account practised by zemindari amlahs, have helped to bring about the present
unsatisfactory condition of the people.

(4). *Tirhoot. 1872-73.*—Where there is a native landlord, the Tirhoot
ryot will not be allowed to enter into independent agreements with the
indigo-planter, unless the landlord sees his way to getting the lion's share
of the profits, and retaining his hold over the tenant; and the planter
has no means of counteracting those obstacles, save by taking leases at
rates which nothing but large indigo profits will cover.

1875-76.—The condition of the agriculturists varies in different
parts of the Mozufferpore district. In Seetamurhee, within this year,
in very many villages there has been great distress, and the villagers
have had to part with their movable property to procure the means of
purchasing food. Large numbers are indebted to mahajuns. There is
no variation in the condition of the labouring classes from year to year;
theirs is a hand-to-mouth existence, with no prospects of brighter
days.

Of the people of Mozufferpore the Collector states : " Most of the lower
classes are more or less indebted to their mahajuns, and the poorest and
lowest classes of all are visibly deteriorating in physique and strength,
&c.

"With the better class of cultivators, such as Koenes and Koormees,
life has more diversity. These men are usually well off, and are able to
cultivate paying crops, such as opium, tobacco, &c."

1876-77.—The marked contrast between the independent position of
ryots in Bengal and the slavish subjection of ryots in Tirhoot, suggest
that our code of laws and administrative system, though well suited to
Bengal, have been too advanced and refined for the backward people
of these parts. The great desideratum is an easy mode of proving
occupancy rights, and a larger number of revenue courts scattered
throughout the interior for the trial of rent suits.

(5). *Sarun.*—The zemindars of this district, wherever they have
a substantial share in a village, are, as a rule, oppressive, and
on the estates of many of the larger zemindars perhaps the least
consideration for their tenantry is shown. * * Nothing more
discreditable to large and influential zemindars could well have

APP. XIII.
————
CONDITION OF
THE RYOTS.

Para. 7, contd.

occurred than was brought out by the inquiry held in the villages along the Gunduk, which had suffered from inundation for several years past. Notwithstanding there being among them men of wealth and position, * * * the conduct of the zemindars was disgraceful in the extreme, as may be gathered from the mere circumstance that after four years, in which the crops had been periodically destroyed, the outstanding rents in all these villages only amounted to one-half their annual rental, while in no village was there as much as one year's rent in arrears. The Sub-deputy Magistrate reported that the ryots were constantly pressed for payments; that they were cruelly and heartlessly treated, and that in some instances an enhanced rental was demanded and realised from them, even at a time of such exceptional distress.

1872-73.—The district is remarkable for the high rate of rent of land prevailing therein. The average rate of rent prevailing throughout the district is as high as Rs. 5-3-3 per acre, this district average being obtained from averages prepared for each pergunnah. It may be interesting to note that so far back as 1788 ordinary grain lands paid Rs. 2 per beegah, and poppy lands from Rs. 5 to Rs. 10.

The holdings of the ryots are generally small, and the ryots are for the most part all more or less indebted. The high rates of interest also tell greatly against the ryots. In the old records I find it stated that in 1787 the usual rate of interest on loans to ryots was Rs. 3-2 per cent. per mensem, and at the rate of 50 per cent. per annum where the transaction was in grain. These rates are common enough still, and they are charged with compound interest. Nothing but a system of Government loans for the relief of debt-incumbered tenures, on the security of the tenure itself, can save the ryots from falling deeper and deeper into the clutches of the mahajuns. This would, of course, presuppose a general record of all ryots in connection with the land, and compulsory registration of all changes thereafter.

Wholesale
enhancement of
rent in a village
in one night.

(6). *Gya.*—A general understanding exists between the ryot and his landlord that he is not to be dispossessed so long as he pays his rent, which is not fixed, but regulated by the rates current in the village. The rates current in the village are varied at the will of the landholder. No one single individual ryot is subjected to an isolated invasion of the village usage, but a wholesale enhancement upon all brings all to a common level, and such enhancement may take place, as it were, in a single night. The letter of the rules is kept, for no exceptions are made; the new rates are as current as were the old. The penalty for non-payment of rent is as lightly incurred by the cultivator; but his possession is not disturbed on that account; upon the contrary, a cultivator not in debt is viewed with dislike and suspicion, and debt is their common burden. The village landholder or the village mahajun knows that his investment is a safe one, although his only security is the helplessness of the borrower and his attachment to the soil. So long as this continues, is it reasonable te expect the ryots to devote themselves to the business of cultivation with either zeal or assiduity? If they limit their exertions to evoking from the land as much as will maintain themselves and families, and meet if possible their obligations to the landlord, is it less than should be expected? Fifty per cent. of the cultivators are in debt for grain lent by their landlords, and forty per cent. are in debt to mahajuns for either grain or money. The latter section consists of men of some substance, who can command credit; but the former are the poorer class of cultivators, and the grasp of the landlord on them is firm and unrelaxing. He knows that they can do nothing else but cultivate; that they must cultivate their fields for food for themselves and their families; that they are wedded to the village to which they belong; and that for these reasons they will continue to stay and to endure.— (*Sub-division Sasseram*).

8.—*Bengal Government, No. 2122, 7th September 1878, to Commissioner, Patna Division.*

In Bengal the primary want is a ready means of recovering rents which are clearly due, and which are withheld either for the sake of delay, or in pursuance of some organized system of opposition to the zemindar. In Behar, what is most wanted is some ready means of enabling the ryot to resist illegal restraint, illegal enhancement, and illegal cesses, and to prove and maintain his occupancy rights.

Apart from the backwardness and poverty of the ryots, there are many points in the existing system of zemindari management in Behar which seem to call for speedy amendment. The loose system of zemindari accounts, the entire absence of leases and counterparts, the universal prevalence of illegal distraint, the oppression incident to the realization of rents in kind, the practice of amalgamating holdings so as to destroy evidence of continuous occupation, are evils which necessarily prevent any possible development of agricultural prosperity among the tenant class, and place them practically at the mercy of their landlords, or the *thikadars,* to whom ordinarily their landlords sublet from time to time.

* * * Nearly every local officer consulted is agreed that, while a system of summary and cheap rent-procedure is required in the interests of both zemindar and ryot, the most urgent requirement of Behar is an amelioration of the condition of the tenantry.

9. The principal suggestive matter in this Appendix is as follows :—

I. The provinces (Orissa and Behar) where the condition of the ryots was the worst, from the oppression of the zemindars, were those desolated by famine. The largest expenditure (*viz.*, 6½ millions sterling) was in Behar; and there the condition of the ryots and peasantry is worse to this day than in any other territory under the Bengal Government.

II. The 6½ millions sterling of famine relief to Bengal in 1874 was afforded at the expense of the general revenues of British India; but for that relief, and by pursuing a policy similar to that of Joseph in Egypt, the Government could have broken the permanent settlement over a very large part of Bengal.

III. From 1793 to 1859, the securities for the protection of ryots, provided by the Regulations of 1793, were set at nought by the zemindars. With a weak executive, and a police not worthy of the name, the Government, though solemnly pledged to the ryots, was powerless to afford protection (paras. 2 and 3).

IV. The country has profited nothing; the zemindars have benefited but little by the unrighteousness and wrong of their class: the bulk of the zemindars are poor and mostly in debt.

(a). Two collectors, too, have testified that still the zemindars in their districts, as of yore, harbour dacoits (bands of robbers) and bad characters.

(b). And of those (the majority of) zemindars who are in debt, it is inevitable but that their necessities compel them to rack-rent their tenants.

(c). While small zemindars who live upon rents are needy and rapacious, cultivating zemindars or proprietors are prosperous.

(d). The levy of irregular cesses has been mentioned in a previous Appendix. From the further testimony in this Appendix it appears that the servants of zemindars, from being underpaid, are forced to levy cesses on their own account; a circumstance evidencing the tremendous power of zemindars, under the shadow of which their underlings levy benevolences for their own behoof.

(e). This tremendous power is possessod by zemindars who, from 1793 to 1859, set at nought laws for the protection of ryots: new laws may not be of much greater avail against that power.

V. Wherever the conditions a to c, and in most cases d in section IV, prevail, the condition of the ryots is bad. They are prosperous in the 24-Pergunnahs or suburban district of the Presidency Division (and in Chittagong), where they enjoy fixed rents; in the eastern districts, where, through intelligence, strength of character, and force of circumstances, they have successfully asserted rights against undue enhancement of rent; in parts of the central districts, and in some northern districts where there is a demand for labour. But elsewhere the condition of the ryots is one of deep indebtedness and poverty.

VI. Wherever, through fixity of rents, as in the 24-Pergunnahs and Chittagong, or through exemption from undue enhancement and from rack-rents, the ryots are prosperous, wages are high and labour is efficient; in other parts of Bengal, where the ryots are oppressed, wages are low: they are lowest in Behar, next in Orissa (two annas a day), three annas in Northern Bengal, four annas in Central and Eastern Bengal, and six annas in Calcutta; and the intensity of ryots' indebtedness is distributed in the same order. Referring to the wages just mentioned, the Bengal Government observed in the report for 1874-75; " So far, then, we may hope that the lot of the labourer, which was always very hard, has not become harder of late. But we must sorrowfully admit that it is almost as hard as can be borne. A plain calculation will show that the wages will suffice for little more than the purchase of food, and leave but a slender margin for his simplest wants. In Behar, indeed, a comparison of prices with wages might indicate that his lot must be hard beyond endurance."

VII. We have seen that where the zemindar is the ryot's sole banker, the latter remains in the thraldom of a pure rack-rent. Where his indebtedness is to the village moneylender, the result is the same. " The creditor finds it his interest to support the ryots at the lowest scale of maintenance which they will tolerate without rebellion, and hence he leaves them as much of the one crop, or advances them as much on the other, as he finds necessary ; they work, they sow, they reap for his profit; and he takes as much for principal and interest as he thinks he safely can insist upon."

VIII. In a district in Bhagulpore Division, the Magistrate, in 1872-73, " made enquiries into the condition of the ryots on the frontier territory, and the result is discouraging, in that, after very fairly weighing the respective advantages and disadvantages of both, he comes to the conclusion that the condition of the Nepal ryot is, on the whole, better than that of the British ryot. Although the smaller rent taken from the former by the Nepalese Government is supplemented by forced labour and the purveyance system, on the other hand, the illegal cesses and exactions of zemindars, middlemen, &c., and other vexations, turn the scale against the British cultivator." Respecting another class in Orissa, the Bengal Government observed in its report for 1872-73: " At the same time, the comparative well-doing of the people is somewhat alloyed by the extreme poverty of a large landless labouring class. The Collector of Balasore writes that he has known many cases where a family only ate food once in two days, and no member of the family has more than one garment. It is fortunate that there are now ample facilities of emigration."

IX. On the whole, a ninety years' experience of the decennial, afterwards the permanent, settlement of Lord Cornwallis leaves the bulk of the millions of cultivating proprietors, whose rights were confiscated in that settlement, in a state of impoverishment and of rack-rent to the zemindar or to the village money-lender, notwithstanding the immense amount of "unearned increment" since 1789, which, yet, has not prevented the bulk of the zemindars from remaining impoverished or in debt, and which has not accrued to the Government.

X. As in the previous Appendix, we close this summary with the interrogatory—of what earthly good to any but the money-lender, and a very few zemindars, is the existing permanent zemindary settlement? Would not the small minority of ryots who are in tolerable or in good circumstances have been better off without it? While to the great majority, of both zemindars and ryots, it has brought nothing but indebtedness and impoverishment, notwithstanding an increase of the value of the produce of Bengal since 1789 manifold greater than the increase of population.

APPENDIX XIV.

MIDDLEMEN.

1. Lord Cornwallis's associations were of a country where property has its duties as well as its rights: that is, has rights in virtue of its exercising the duties of property. Imbued with this feeling he conceived a zemindary settlement, the theory of which was the maintenance of large landed estates under wealthy proprietors able and willing to guide their tenants in improving agriculture, and to assist them in effecting improvements and in carrying on cultivation without recourse to the money-lender. In the expectation that the zemindar would discharge these duties of property, he was clothed with rights of property previously unheard of in Bengal, and it was hoped that his execution of these duties would establish kindly relations between him and the ryots.

2. The progress of events has dispelled this, as it has dispelled all other illusions under which Lord Cornwallis confiscated the rights of millions of proprietors. The theory of large landed estates has been destroyed in two ways, viz., (1st) by the sub-division of zemindaries under the Hindoo laws of inheritance, which sub-division has already, to a great extent, impoverished the class of zemindars, and in two generations more may complete the work; (2ndly) by the creation of numerous classes of middlemen between the actual cultivators and the great zemindars who were to establish kindly relations with ryots by assisting the latter in effecting agricultural improvements. In place of this assistance, the zemindars have provided middlemen who chastise the ryots with scorpions.

3. There are two kinds of middlemen, viz., those—the great majority—who are mere farmers of rents, and others who take leases of parts of zemindaries for actual cultivation of the more valuable agricultural products. This latter class is small; in it we may include indigo-planters, who, though not generally cultivating their own lands with hired labour, yet are actively interested in the cultivation by ryots of the indigo which the planters manufacture for the market. Extracts showing the effect of the system of middlemen on

the condition of the country, will be presently given; it will be found that the preponderance of evidence is against the system, but it will be seen that this adverse testimony is practically directed against those middlemen who are mere farmers of rents; on the other hand, the evidence, here and there, in favour of the system, applies entirely to those middlemen who farm, not for rents, but for cultivation.

4. Sub-infeudation formed no part of the zemindary settlement established by Regulation I of 1793: it was not recognized until Regulation I of 1819, as follows:—

I. By the rules of the permanent settlement, proprietors of estates paying revenue to Government, that is, the individuals answerable to Government for the revenue then assessed on the different mehals, were declared to be entitled to make any arrangements for the leasing of their lands, in talook or otherwise, that they might deem most conducive to their interests. By the rules of Regulation XLIV of 1793, however, all such arrangements were subjected to two limitations: first, that the jumma, or rent, should not be fixed for a period exceeding ten years; and secondly, that in case of a sale for Government arrears, such leases or arrangements should stand cancelled from the day of sale. The provisions of section II, Regulation XLIV, 1793, by which the period of all fixed engagements for rent was limited to ten years, have been rescinded by section II, Regulation V, 1812; and in Regulation XVIII of the same year, it is more distinctly declared that zemindars are at liberty to grant talooks or other leases of their lands, fixing the rent in perpetuity at their discretion, subject, however, to the liability of being dissolved on the sale of the grantor's estate for the arrears of the Government revenue, in the same manner as heretofore.

II. In practice, the grant of talooks and other leases at a fixed rent in perpetuity had been common with the zemindars of Bengal for some time before the passing of the two regulations last mentioned; but notwithstanding the abrogation of the rule which declared such arrangements null and void, and the abandonment of all intention or desire to have it enforced as a security to the Government revenue in the manner originally contemplated, it was omitted to declare in the rules of Regulations V and XVIII of 1812, or in any other regulations, whether tenures at the time in existence, and held under covenants or engagements entered into by the parties in violation of the rule of section II, Regulation XLIV, 1793, should, if called in question, be deemed invalid and void as heretofore. This point it has been deemed necessary to set at rest by a general declaration of the validity of any tenures that may be now in existence, notwithstanding that they may have been granted at a rent fixed in perpetuity, or for a longer term than ten years, while the rule fixing this limitation to the term of all such engagements, and declaring null and void any granted in contravention thereof, was in force.

III. Furthermore, in the exercise of the privileges thus conceded to zemindars under direct engagements with Government, there has been created a tenure which had its origin on the estates of the Rajah of

Burdwan, but has since been extended to other zemindaries; the character of which tenure is, that it is a talook created by the zemindar to be held at a rent fixed in perpetuity by the lessee and his heirs for ever. The tenant is called upon to furnish collateral security for the rent, and for his conduct generally, or he is excused from this obligation at the zemindar's discretion; but even if the original tenant be excused, still, in case of sale for arrears, or other operation leading to the introduction of another tenant, such new incumbent has always in practice been liable to be so called upon at the option of the zemindar. **

IV. These tenures have usually been denominated putnee talooks, and it has been a common practice of the holders of them to underlet on precisely similar terms to other persons, who, on taking such leases, went by the name of durputnee talookdars: these, again, sometimes similarly underlet to seputneedars; and the conditions of all the title-deeds vary in nothing material from the original engagements executed by the first holder. * *

V. The tenures in question have extended through several zillahs of Bengal; and the mischiefs which have arisen from the want of a consistent rule of action for the guidance of the courts of civil judicature in regard to them have been productive of such confusion as to demand the interference of the legislature. It has accordingly been decreed necessary to regulate and define the nature of the property given and acquired on the creation of a putnee talook as above described; also to declare the legality of the practice of underleting in the manner in which it has been exercised by putneedars and others. * *

VI. It is hereby declared that any leases or engagements for the fixing of rent, now in existence, that may have been granted or concluded for a term of years, or in perpetuity, by a proprietor under engagements with Government, or other person competent to grant the same, shall be deemed good and valid tenures, according to the terms of the covenants or engagements interchanged, notwithstanding that the same may have been executed before the passing of Regulation V, 1812, and which the rule of section II, Regulation XLIV, 1793, which limited the period for which it was lawful to grant such engagement to ten years, was in full force and effect, &c., &c.

VII. (a). First.—The tenures known by the name of putnee talooks, as described in the preamble to this Regulation, shall be deemed to be valid tenures in perpetuity, according to the terms of the engagements under which they are held. They are heritable by their conditions; and it is hereby further declared that they are capable of being transferred by sale, gift, or otherwise, at the discretion of the holder, as well as answerable for his personal debts, and subject to the process of the courts of judicature, in the same manner as other real property.

(b). Second.—Putnee talookdars are hereby declared to possess the right of letting out the lands composing their talooks in any manner they may deem most conducive to their interest, and any engagements so entered into by such talookdars with others shall be legal and binding between the parties to the same, their heirs and assignees, &c., &c.

VIII. If the holder of a putnee talook shall have underlet in such manner as to have conveyed a similar interest to that enjoyed by himself, as explained in the preamble to this Regulation, the holder of such a tenure shall be deemed to have acquired all the rights and immunities declared in the preceding section to attach to putnee talooks, in so far as concerns the grantor of such undertenure. The same construction shall also apply in the case of putnee talooks of the third or fourth degree.

IX. The right of alienation having been declared to vest in the holder of a putnee talook, it shall not be competent to the zemindar or other superior to refuse to register, and otherwise to give effect to such alienations by discharging the party transferring his interest from personal responsibility, and by accepting the engagements of the transferee. In conformity, however, with established usage, the zemindar or other superior shall be entitled to exact a fee upon every such alienation; and the rate of the said fee is hereby fixed at two per cent. on the jumma or annual rent of the interest transferred, until the same shall amount to one hundred rupees, which sum shall be the maximum of any fee to be exacted on this account, &c., &c.

5. The Bengal Government, in Sir George Campbell's Administration Report for 1872-73, gave the following history of these sub-tenures :—

(a). At the permanent settlement, Government, by abdicating its position as exclusive possessor of the soil, and contenting itself with a permanent rent charge on the land, escaped thenceforward all the labour and risks attendant upon detailed mofussil management. The zemindars of Bengal Proper were not slow to follow the example set them, and immediately began to dispose of their zemindaries in a similar manner. Permanent undertenures, known as putnee tenures, were created in large numbers, and extensive tracts were leased out on long terms. By the year 1819 permanent alienations of the kind described had been so extensively effected, that they were formally legalised by Regulation VIII of that year, and means afforded to the zemindar of recovering arrears of rent from his putneedars, almost identical with those by which the demands of Government were enforced against himself. The practice of granting such undertenures has steadily continued until, at the present day, with the putnee and subordinate tenures in Bengal Proper and the farming system of Behar, but a small proportion of the whole permanently-settled area remains in the direct possession of the zemindars. In these alienations the zemindars have made far better terms for themselves than the Government was able to make for itself in 1793. It has rarely happened that a putnee, or even a lease for a term of years, has been given otherwise than on payment of a bonus, which has discounted the contingency of many years' increased rents. It is a system by which, in its adoption by the zemindars, their posterity suffers, because it is clear that, if the bonus were not exacted, a higher rental could be permanently obtained from the land. This consideration has not, however, had much practical weight with the land holders. And if a gradual accession to the wealth and influence of sub proprietors be a desirable thing in the interest of the community, the selfishness of the landholding class is not, in this instance of it, a subject for regret.

(*b*). The process of sub-infeudation described above has not terminated with the putneedars and ijardars ; however, gradations of sub-tenures under them called dur-pûtnees and dur-ijaras, and even further subordinate tenures, have been created in great numbers. And not unfrequently, especially where particular lands are required for the growth of special crops, such as indigo, superior holders have taken under-tenures from their own tenants. These tenures and under-tenures often comprise defined tracts of land ; but a common practice has been to sublet certain aliquot shares of the whole superior tenure, the consequence of which is that the tenants in any particular village of an estate now very usually pay their rents to two, or many more than two, different masters, so many annas in the rupee to each. It must be added that in many cases where an estate or tenure has been sublet, the lessor has reserved certain portions, generally those immediately contiguous to his residence, in his own possession. These he may cultivate by keeping ryots upon them, or especially, if he be a European indigo planter, by hired labour.

(*c*). All the under-tenures in Bengal have not, however, been created since the permanent settlement in the manner above described. Dependant taluks, ganties, howlas, and other similar fixed and transferable under-tenures existed before the settlement. Their permanent character was practically recognized at the time of the settlement, and has at any rate since been confirmed by lapse of time.

6. Respecting the general character of the middlemen that have sprung up under the laws for protecting under-tenures held between the zemindar and the ryot, there is the following testimony :—

1. BENGAL GOVERNMENT, No. 1263, DATED 5TH MARCH 1855, TO BOARD OF REVENUE.

Forwarding extracts from a memorandum on the District of Chumparun, submitted by the Joint Magistrate and Deputy Collector, on the occasion of the Lieutenant-Governor's recent visit to that district :—

(*a*.) The curse of this district is the insecure nature of the ryots' land tenure. The cultivator, though nominally protected by Regulations of all sorts, has, practically, no rights in the soil. His rent is continually raised ; he is oppressed and worried by every successive ticcadar, until he is actually forced out of his holding and driven to take shelter in the Nepaul Terai. A list of all the ryots who have abandoned their villages on account of the oppression of the ticcadars within the last ten years would be a suggestive document.

(*b*). Another great evil is the way in which villages are continually sublet. I have known an instance where there were five different ticcadars within eight years. Of course, all these five raised the rents of the village besides taking *salaamee*, and a hundred other oppressive *abwabs*, from the unfortunate cultivators. Within the Bettiah Rajah's zemindaree, villages are frequently given in the first instance to some durbar favourite, coachman, or a table-servant, for instance, who immediately sublets it at a profit. The original grantee never goes near the village, nor takes the slightest interest in it. His object is simply to make as much of it as possible within the shortest time. * *

(c). (After further extracts regarding the oppressive working of the laws for distraint and sale, the Lieutenant-Governor observed) : Everywhere during his march through this district, I am desired to say, the Lieutenant-Governor found the strongest evidence of the oppression which the tenants of the Rajah of Bettiah are here described as suffering. In every village and on every roadside the Lieutenant-Governor was beset by their complaints, and ample corroboration of all they stated was afforded by the indigo-planters and the authorities of the district.

II.—Petition of Protestant Missionaries residing in or near Calcutta (*1852*).

In many cases the zemindars themselves are not aware of all the misery which is inflicted in their name upon the ryots by the agents whom they employ in collecting the rent. These middlemen are, in truth, the greatest tyrants. And as such middlemen would have to be employed by Government in case the ryotwari system should be substituted for the zemindary system, it is clear that such a change would not be of any great advantage to the ryots, probably of none at all. It is well known that the middlemen employed by humane European indigo planters are in many cases as oppressive as those employed by native zemindars. What is wanted is that the ryot should have direct access to his landlord, and that the interests of both should be the same. And this object would probably be accomplished, in process of time, if, by legalizing the commutation of the land-tax, the prospect of becoming free landholders was open to capitalists. (*Alexander Duff and 20 other signatures*).

III.—Zemindars, 24-Pergunnahs (*February 1857*).

The immediate effect of the enactment of the proposed law will be the multiplication of these middle-tenures. That the multiplication of middle-tenures is an unmitigated evil, is a fact proved by the circumstance that rent is highest and the rights of the resident tenantry have suffered the most in those districts of Bengal in which middle-tenures abound, it being notorious that middlemen are the most oppressive and extortionate of landlords all over the world.

IV.—Bengal British Indian Association (*May 1857*).

The advocates of this Bill would seem scarcely to have enquired to what extent the new security given to middle-tenures is called for by experience or sound policy, as proved by actual facts, rather than theoretical clamour. Since the date of the settlement, it is notorious that these tenures have largely increased, both in number and in value, and do continue to increase. Then, the policy of increasing middle-holdings is unhesitatingly negatived by all practical men. Your petitioners affirm that, were evidence upon the point taken at the Bar of your Honourable

Council, it would soon be apparent, and conclusively proved, that rent is highest, and the interests of the cultivator have been most neglected or borne down, wherever middle-tenures abound, and that the worst of landlords are the middlemen, whom it is the object and necessary consequence of the proposed legislation to encourage and to multiply. Your petitioners say this, not in abuse or condemnation of the holders of such tenures (which are not sparingly shared among your petitioners themselves), but as showing the necessities of their position, and the impolicy of holding out a premium for an extension of the class.

V.—MR. A. SCONCE, COMMISSIONER OF CHITTAGONG (*19th February 1850*).

The bane of the landed interest in India, that is, of all those who are primarily interested in the land—the landholders on the one part, and the actual cultivators on the other—is the creation of sub-tenures for the benefit of those who seek to lease rents, not lands; who speculate upon the opportunity they may be enabled to command of realizing extortionate rents; and who, being neither landlords nor cultivators, are permitted to absorb such an amount of the profits of the land as is calculated to paralyze the efficient operations of those with whose prosperity the prosperity of the entire country is most nearly identified. We require no law to facilitate farming of rents; but, on the other hand, as it must always happen that ryots of land already in cultivation will be found located within the areas which intending farmers, whose object is either to clear waste land, or to cultivate more profitable products, may wish to lease, it is perfectly just to recognize, and it is perfectly easy to distinguish, such cases from others in which a permanent intermediate interest is sought to be alienated.

VI.—MR. A. FORBES (*13th February 1850*).

I consider it necessary to state my reasons in detail for not granting further protection to middlemen (persons between the cultivator and the zemindar) on the pretext of their being capitalists and making advances to the actual cultivator. It would obviously lead to frauds on the purchasers, and foster and perpetuate a most oppressive system, as the middlemen would practise every art to keep the cultivator in debt, that he may continue to receive the produce of the particular crops that the cultivator is compelled to grow.

VII.—MR. E. CURRIE, LEGISLATIVE COUNCIL (*17th May 1856*).

Even with respect to putnees, dur-putnees, se-putnees, and so on, he for one was not prepared to say that the conditions under which under-tenures had existed since their first creation, some 50 years ago, and which were recognized and confirmed by Regulation VIII of 1819, ought to be abrogated, or that the terms of the contracts under which they held should be set aside. He believed that the direct tendency of the putnee system of subletting was so to grind down the ryot, that every new link in the chain of under-tenure was an additional burden on his back.

VIII.—CAPTAIN W. H. CRAUFURD (*26th May 1856*).

The Honourable Member representing the Government of Bengal has gone so far as to declare, in his place in Council, that putnee and other tenures of that class are the scourge of the country, and that the legislation contemplated is peculiarly for their security, and calculated to tend to their multiplication. Any argument that I might urge to show that the creation of these tenures usually relieves the ryots from the exactions of an embarrassed landlord, and replaces him by one with whom the primary object is not the collection of rent, but the encouragement of agricultural operations, might be looked upon with suspicion. But the present head of the Government (Sir Frederick Halliday) has, fortunately for me, recorded his opinion on this point in the following words (see paragraph 7, section II).

7. The policy of discouraging or encouraging undertenures is discussed in the following extracts :—

I.—LORD DALHOUSIE (*21st October 1852*).

(*a*). I am still, however, inclined to think that *perpetual* leases ought not to be favourably recognized, except in the case of manufactories, tanks, or permanent buildings. I conceive that a perpetual lease for any agricultural purpose can hardly be advisable.

(*b*). I regard the protection of under-tenures from the effects of a sale for arrears of public revenue as of the highest value for giving that security to the property of the ordinary cultivator, or of the man of enterprise and capital, without which it is hopeless to expect any substantial improvement in Bengal, or any material increase of its resources.

II.—MR. F. J. HALLIDAY (*14th October 1839*).

If ever any great improvement is to happen to this country, it must come by means of the introduction, as *under-tenants* of zemindars, of men of skill, capital, and enterprise.

III.—MR. J. LOWIS (*19th June 1840*).

The agricultural resources of all countries are, I believe, developed best and fastest by the farmer—the man, that is, who subsists mostly upon the profits of capital applied to land. To afford this man adequate security, is to ensure the application of the largest portion possible of intelligence and capital to the land; thus enlarging to the utmost the true sources whence all revenue, whether settled permanently or not, is derived, and widening the marginal excess of rent over revenue, which the settlement of 1793 bestowed upon and endeavoured to secure to the zemindars of Bengal.

IV.—MR. WELBY JACKSON (*16th June 1840*).

The provision in favour of *bonâ fide* leases of 20 years appears to me objectionable in this respect: the zemindars have never had the right to create such a lien on the property, and it would be an alteration of the whole system to allow them to do so now. * * * If the zemindars or their farmers were in the habit of laying out capital on the improvement of their lands, it would be an object to retain them; such a zemindar would pay his revenue, and would not run a chance of being ousted: but how few zemindars lay out the smallest sum; in this manner, how few farmers? The farmers, and indeed the zemindars too, generally collect as much as they possibly can; they make a very high nonimal rent-roll, and then collect as near as they can to the amount; but it is almost always impossible to collect the whole, and their ryots are thus always in their debt, though the balances are nonimal. The only farmers who are really improvers are the European indigo and other manufacturers; by creating a demand and advancing the means of producing the raw material, they extend and improve the cultivation: these men it is desirable to support.

V.—Mr. H. T. Prinsep (*8th July 1841*).

In the first place, protection is given to the ijaradars, or mere tuhseel people, who took their lease with no speculation of cultivating and laying out money in improvements, but merely on a calculation of what they could grind from other under-tenants by skill in Regulation processes and chicanery, and perhaps even by violence.

VI.—Mr. A. Sconce (*4th April 1857*).

I would repeat what I said in 1850 (paragraph 6, section IV), that we need no new law to facilitate farms of rents. Yet the taluks and other intermediate tenures that press for permanent recognition are nothing else but farms or assignments of rents. Talukdars are not agriculturists; and when we are invoked to develope agriculture, let it never be forgotten that it is from the ryot—from the man who ploughs and sows, and not the talukdar—that the development is to come. It is time to part with the notion that agriculturists cannot distinguish between profitable and unprofitable crops, and that they will not adopt the former in preference to the latter. No men, according to their simple lights, incur greater sacrifices to secure their harvests; and as freely as any set of men will they change the course of their familiar agriculture if the change promises to pay them better. The most erroneous of all notions is to describe or limit the development of agricultural resources by the payment of advances, or to measure, for example, the advantage of advances by the manufacture and export of indigo. If upon that we build agricultural development, we build upon deception and delusion. Who that has seen has not admired the careful, almost triturated, cultivation of tobacco and wheat fields in the higher lands of rice countries? Who grow safflower? Who produce the immense crops that supply our greatest market with jute and oilseeds? From such facts are the objects of agricultural improvement most truly presented to us, and the means by which it may be attained most correctly indicated. Our greatest and never sleeping purpose, it seems to me, should be to secure to our agricultural population the utmost benefit of their labour, and to disencumber them—always within the bounds of reason and law—from an intending succession of middle-tenures ; this purpose was set forth in clause 1, section VIII, Regulation I, 1793 ; and instead of redeeming what I will call the pledge then undertaken to exact laws necessary for the protection and welfare of the ryots and other cultivators of the soil, the tendency of the present Bill will practically be to interpose a screen between our sight and theirs, by fostering the creation of middle-tenures, and perpetuating them against all contingencies.

8.   The extracts in this Appendix contain a general and unqualified condemnation of those middlemen, the bulk of the class, who are mere farmers of rents.

APPENDIX XV.

WASTE LANDS AND MISCELLANEOUS.

1.—WASTE LANDS.

I.—LAW AND CONSTITUTION OF INDIA.

(*a*). We see, therefore, that the practice of India corresponds with the written law in this; for in the reign of Akbar it was the cultivated land only that was measured; it was the cultivated land whose value was ascertained; and it was the cultivated land that afforded the datum for making the decennial settlement; and it was from the records established on that basis that the revenues of the Lower Provinces were limited for ever by what is called the permanent settlement. Consequently, by the law of India, all the uncultivated land (which is, according to Mr. Colebrooke, "one-half, and about half of which is capable of cultivation, the other half irreclaimable, or on rivers and lakes") of the whole of the three provinces still remains the property of Government; for, without an *express equivalent and specification of revenue*, there existed no power legally capable of giving them away, by any lawful deed of conveyance or any legal mode whatsoever.

(*b*). Nor, in equity, can these lands be deemed to have been given away, because no equitable value was put upon them by either party to the permanent settlement. It was the productive land, the rent-paying land, that was the subject-matter of settlement between the parties; and that rent-paying land consisted of "villages;" for all the land of the country resolves itself into the land of such or such a village. There are larger and smaller divisions; but this is the most definite and best known, and therefore I follow the native registers in adopting it.

(*c*). The quantity of land belonging to every village is stated in beegahs; the boundaries perhaps specified, but probably not well defined. One of the contracting parties at least (the zemindar) was, therefore, bargaining for a specific quantity of land. This quantity of land was the land in cultivation; and must have been so. The zemindar had no capital to enable him to offer a rent to Government for land that was not immediately productive; nor could Government have believed that he had, without entertaining the most extravagant fancy. I say, therefore, that not only the law, but even the equity of the case, is against the alienation of the uncultivated land. * * *

(*d*). The Act, under the authority of which the permanent settlement was made, gave no power to grant waste land. It is the 24th Geo. III, chap. 25, sec. 39. By this section, the Court of Directors were required to give orders for settling and establishing "upon principles of moderation and justice," *according to the laws and constitution of India*, the permanent rules " by which the tribute, rents, and services of the rajahs, zemindars, polygars, talukdars, and other native landholders, should be in future rendered and paid to the United Company."

(*e*). Here there is no authority to give away waste land, or uncultivated lands, or, indeed, land at all; nothing in the most remote sense authorizing the giving any *permanent right* to land of any kind. It is to "fix *permanent rules* for the payment of *rents*, tributes, and services due from native landholders," such as rajahs, zemindars, polygars, talukdars, to the Company; affording a presumption, indeed, in direct opposition to the idea of property in the soil existing in any of the classes of persons mentioned. And these "rules for paying rents" were ordered to be fixed "according to the law and constitution of India," which debars even the Emperor himself from giving away one inch of waste or any other land without an equivalent.

2. From the immense extent of waste land at the time, this stretch of authority, beyond even the power possessed by the Emperor, was unjustifiable: thus—

Law and Consti-
tution of India,
page 157, and
Revenue Selec-
tions, Vol. I,
page 46.

(*a*). Lord Cornwallis at the same time estimated no less than a third of the Company's territory to be a jungle; which Mr. Colebrooke confirms, and states that "the researches on which I (Mr. Colebrooke) was engaged at the time, furnish me with grounds for the opinion that the estimate may, with great approximation to accuracy, be understood as applicable to lands fit for cultivation, and totally exclusive of lands barren and irreclaimable." Here, then, we have confessedly one-third of the whole cultivable land (and one-third of the whole "gross collections from the cultivator, for charges of collection and intermediate profits between Government and the rental") avowedly relinquished by the Government; and we are told that this should be the basis of the permanent settlement.

3. The Emperor's power to give away waste land was restrained by the Mahomedan law, which limited, very precisely, the application of the revenue from land to specific objects: thus—

Page 60.

(*a*). The khurauj and the juzeeut or capitation tax, &c., shall be appropriated, says the Mahomedan law, to the use of troops, in building and maintaining fortifications, guarding the highways, in digging canals, in maintaining those who devote their lives to the good of the people (as kazees, mooftees, mooazzins, public teachers), in feeding the poor, paying collectors of the taxes, building and repairing mosques, bridges, &c. "Finally, every Moslem in want has a claim on the public treasury, according to his exigencies, for himself, wife, and children under age, for decent food and raiment; but holy men, and those learned in the law, the descendants of Aalee and the noble, have a claim to a greater share, because dignifying them, dignifies the sons of Islaum."

Page 61.

(*b*). "Four classes of men," says the *Ayeen Akbaree*, "have lived on pensions granted them for their subsistence: *1st*, the learned and their scholars; *2nd*, those who have retired from the world, holy men, and goohanusheen; *3rd*, the needy, who are not able to help themselves; *4th*, the descendants of great families (an error in the translation for descendants of Aalee), who from false shame will do nothing for themselves; besides the army, the pay of which amounted to Rs. 77,29,652."

Pages 65 & 68.

(*c*). The sovereign has the power of making a grant of waste land on condition that the grantee pay the assessment to which such land is liable for what he does cultivate. * * The sovereign cannot make a *donation* of the khurauj of the lands of an individual to the owner, unless the donee be of those to whom the law assigns a public maintenance (literally, "an object of, or one entitled to, a share of the khurauj"). But should the sovereign assign the khurauj to the owner, and leave it with him, the owner being of those who are entitled by law to share in the khurauj, it is legal, according to Aboo Yoosuf's opinion; and this is decided law, as Kazee Khan states. Imam Moohummud dissents. This, however, it is evident, can only be a personal grant, and must, at all events, cease with the existence of the individual to whom it is made, inasmuch as the qualities or circumstances which render one individual an *object* entitled to share in the khurauj, *viz.*, his being a soldier, kazee, mooftee, teacher, collector of revenue, a police officer, or other public functionary of Government, a learned or holy man, are altogether personal.

(*d*). By the Mahomedan law, the sovereign, as we have seen, has no power to give away public property of any kind without an equivalent. He cannot bestow a lakheerauj grant in any other way than that above mentioned, *viz.*, by an appropriation of the khurauj of one's own estate to the owner himself, with the condition attached of his being one of those classes of persons to whom the law assigns a public provision. An appropriation of this kind would be necessary to accompany even a religious endowment, if exemption from the revenue were designed; and this would be permanent, if the body or class endowed continued to exist as objects of benefice, but would cease to be so with the existence of the last incumbent, who might come under the description of persons entitled by law to the benefit of a public maintenance.

(*e*). So little power is by the Mahomedan law vested in the sovereign to give away the property of the public, that although, on the eve of a battle, he may hold out special rewards of an additional share of plunder in order to encourage the troops, yet, after the battle is over, he cannot give away an atom of prize property beyond the regular share; except, indeed, from the share of the crown, which is a fifth of the prize property.

4. Sir John Shore and the Court of Directors both considered that waste lands should not be included in zemindaries, but be reserved as a source of income in the future: thus—

I.—Sir J. Shore (*8th December 1789*).

Another proposition is, that the waste lands remain as crown lands for future allotment, as proposals for them may be tendered.

The first question that arises upon this is, to whom do the waste lands at present belong? Are there no zemindars proprietors of them? If there are, is Government, by usage or law, authorized to take them away, or have the proprietors consented to part with them? These are preliminaries which ought to be examined and decided.

But I shall consider the proposition in another point of view. The limits of the villages are left undetermined by any marked boundaries. The quantity of land in each, although stated in beegahs, is confessedly unascertained. The proprietors, therefore, may extend their possessions, and encroach upon the present waste lands gradually; and this mode, it is probable, they will attempt, instead of undertaking the cultivation of waste lands under any specific engagement to pay revenue for them. The proposition must, therefore, rely upon a new accession of inhabitants from foreign countries; and, in any other sense, it appears to me almost useless.

Para. 44.
Notwithstanding the objections stated by Mr. Law, to determining the extent of the villages by ascertained boundaries, I still think that this should be done, to guard against the consequences of litigated limits. * * To ascertain the limits of the land by boundaries, it will rarely, I conceive, be necessary to measure it. As they are now disposed of, there is no criterion for determining the quantity. * * I think the Government ought to know what it gives, and the proprietor what he receives; and, provided limits were marked out, the term "more or less" would be unimportant. The difficulties of the operation are by no means, in my opinion, so great as Mr. Law apprehends. He says that the boundaries of cultivated villages are well ascertained; if so, let them be marked and recorded.

Para. 45.
If the plan should, in its progress, be attended with the improvement expected from it, the limits of the estate will then become very important; and some time or other there will be a necessity for defining them. * * But if ever necessary to be done, the limits may certainly be marked with more facility at this time than they can be at any future period.

II.—Letter from Governor General to Court of Directors, *6th March 1793.*

(*See* Appendix IV, para. 6, II.)

III.—Select Committee (*1812*).

Fifth Report, page 21.
Referring to the estimated amount at which the Government demand might be fixed in the permanent settlement, the Court of Directors observed that they did not wish to expose their subjects to the hazard of oppressive practices by requiring more; yet, on consideration of the extent of land which lay waste throughout the provinces, and adverting to what had formerly been the practice of the native government, in participating in the resources derivable from its progressive cultivation, they would be induced to acquiesce in any arrangement which might be devised, with a view to secure to the East India Company a similar participation in the wealth derivable from such a source; provided it could be effected without counteracting the principal object of encouraging industry, and be reconciled with the principles of the system which was about to be introduced.

IV.—Court of Directors (*15th January 1819*).

Sess. 1831-32, Vol. XI, App. 11, page 100.
We have already enjoined you to reserve the waste lands in making any future settlement; but we have not been able to satisfy ourselves as to the nature of the interest possessed by the zemindar in the waste lands in those districts which have been permanently settled. Your

construction seems to be, that his power over them is absolute and unconditional, and that he is at liberty to contract for the occupation of them at whatever rates he can obtain. It is, however, the opinion of many considerable authorities, that on the leases of waste as well as of other lands, the pergunnah rates form a standard not to be exceeded (paragraph 67).

App. XV.
—
STATE'S RIGHT IN WASTE LANDS.
Para. 4, contd.

V.—REGULATION II, 1819.

(a). It is hereby declared and enacted that all lands which, at the period of the decennial settlement, were not included within the limits of any pergunnah, mouzah, or other division of estates for which a settlement was concluded with the owners, not being lands for which a distinct settlement may have been made since the period referred to, * * shall be considered liable to Government assessment in the same manner as other unsettled mehal.

(b). The foregoing principles shall be deemed applicable not only to tracts of land, such as are described to have been brought into cultivation in the Sunderbuns, but to all churs and islands formed since the period of the decennial settlement, and generally to all lands gained by alluvion or dereliction since that period, &c., &c.

VI.—RESOLUTION OF GOVERNMENT (1st August 1822).

His Lordship in Council considers it to be well established that the Native Governments, in the exercise of their prerogative, were in the habit of making grants of unappropriated waste land. * * Ordinarily, indeed, His Lordship in Council would be disposed to consider the assumption to be justly open to Government, that wastes unappropriated are the property of the State, unless the contrary can be clearly shown, the proof resting with the zemindar; and arguing from the analogy of extensive principalities, our revenue officers appear in several cases too easily to have admitted indefinite claims to waste, on the part of persons whose property ought to have been distinctly restricted to the limits assigned to them by the public records (paragraph 228).

Sess. 1831-32, Vol. XI, page 209.

VII.—MR. SISSON (2nd April 1815).

The additional profits which were to accrue to the zemindar from the permanent settlement of his estate were confined to but one source, i.e., extension of cultivation. He was vested with no power to enhance the rents of his tenants, with reference even to the waste lands which his exertions might bring into cultivation; he was peremptorily restricted from exacting a higher rent than that which lands of a similar quality might be rated at in the nirkhbundy of his estate. The profit that was to arise to him from bringing the waste lands into cultivation was the enjoyment of the Government's share of their produce, in addition to his own.

Revenue Selections, Vol. I, page 385.

App. XV.

STATE'S RIGHT
IN WASTE LANDS.

Para. 4. contd.

Third Report,
Select Com-
mittee, 1831-32.

Questions 3264
to 3267.

VIII.—Mr. J. Mill (*4th August 1831*).

Many of the zemindaries that were settled in 1793 contain a considerable portion of waste land which the zemindars have been permitted to cultivate without any further assessment. The consequence has been that the value of those estates where waste land susceptible of cultivation has been cultivated, has greatly increased, which is to a great degree the reason of the very great diversity in what appears to be the value of the estates, the number of years' purchase that one estate sells for beyond another.

There is a question whether the Government had any right to limit the cultivation of waste land by assessing a portion of it. What has been supposed to determine the point is the question—what was naturally, according to the just interpretation of the law of 1793, to be considered as included within the limits of an estate? If there is any portion of waste that by no proper construction, at the period of the permanent settlement, could be considered as within the limits of that estate, it is held to be the property of the Government; but the Government have compromised the question, and, as it appears to me, in a very liberal manner. They have come to a resolution that, even though the property in the waste might be considered as doubtful, if it is a moderate quantity lying between one estate and another, it shall be considered as the property of the zemindars, according to an equal distribution among themselves; but where there is any vast portion of waste, comprehending a considerable portion of country, which lies distinct by itself, and is only bordered upon by a zemindary, as it cannot, with any propriety, be considered as coming within the limits of any estate, it is held to be the property of Government; but even there they come to a further compromise with the zemindars, that as far as the zemindar has cultivated any portion of that waste, it shall be regarded as his own property, as much as any other part of his zemindary; and not only so, but that such a proportion of waste as is in general annexed to cultivated land, shall be considered as his in addition; but beyond this, that a line shall be drawn, and the rest shall remain the property of the Government, to be disposed of as they shall see best.

Q. 3268.—Was there not a considerable dispute, at various periods, with regard to the extent to which the zemindars had a right to take the waste? There were doubts in regard to those cases where there was a portion of waste surrounded by different estates. By a liberal construction of the permanent settlement, it might be considered that it belonged to the zemindars whose estates surrounded it; and so the Government have allowed it to be considered. The only case where they have now drawn a distinction is that of large tracts of waste country that stand by themselves—as the Sunderbunds, for example.

IX.—Mr. J. N. Halhed.

The code provided for the annexation of the neezjote or nankar lands held by the zemindars, free of revenue, to the khalsa or revenue land, on the formation of the decennial settlement, as also for the resumption of the *chakeraun* lands, or portions set apart in lieu of money-payments, for the support of the police and other establishments of local public officers; but as there were no means of ascertaining the correctness of the returns made by the zemindars of these lands, under a system which interdicted reference to measurements, and comparative detailed statements of cultivation and produce, the greatest portion of these neezjote and *chakeraun* lands merged in the jurisdictions acquired by the landed aristocracy, under the perpetual settlement, without being accounted for, and are held by them absolutely without payment, they having ejected the public servants who formerly held them, and who having no other means of subsistence, became robbers.

As the zemindars in the permanently assessed provinces have appropriated to themselves all the *chakeraun*, all records relating to which have now been lost or destroyed through their machinations, they should be required to keep up, at their own charges, an efficient establishment of subsidiary police in each village or estate.

X.—Sir George Campbell (*1st June 1864*).

There is very much in the custom of India to show that the ryots of each village have a prior claim to cultivate the waste of the village, and to take up land abandoned by other ryots; and, so cultivating or taking without special stipulation, to hold on the same terms as those on which they have their original holdings.

XI.—Mr. W. S. Seton-Karr (*2nd June 1864*).

Now, the mass of ryots who have not held from before the permanent settlement, or who cannot prove by irrefragable evidence that they have so held, who are neither mokurraridars, nor even khoodkasht ryots with rights dating from 1793, must be very considerable. There must, I say, be a very large class of respectable and substantial fotedars, resident on their own homesteads, and cultivating lands on the plain at no great distance therefrom, who have now held for two generations, but who have either held without pottahs, or with pottahs in which neither the term of years is fixed, nor are the rents declared unalterable, and who may, therefore, be any day liable to enhancement * *. I am not aware that the permanent settlement in any way altered the *common law of the country as to ryotty tenure in land,* or that there are good grounds, legal or political, for placing ryots whose tenures date, say since 1800, or who cannot show positively that their forefathers held their lands before 1793, in a much more disadvantageous position than others who are fortunate enough to be acknowledged as the lineal descendants of those concerning whom Shore and Hastings wrote copious minutes.

5. The limitation of the demand upon the ryot for waste land brought under cultivation to the general rates of the pergunnah, is affirmed in the preceding Sections, IV, VI, and X. As the pergunnah rates, or those paid by the khoodkasht ryots, were the highest or maximum rates in the pergunnah,

Margin notes: App. XV. State's right in waste lands. Para. 5. — Page 134. — Rent on reclaimed land.

APP. XV.

STATE'S RIGHT
IN WASTE LANDS.

Para. 5, contd.

the impossibility of the assessment upon waste lands exceed-ing those rates consistently with indispensable inducements to ryots to cultivate those lands, is self-evident. Nevertheless, as the point is of importance, further testimony on the subject may be cited.

I.—BAILLIE'S LAND TAX OF INDIA.

Page XIV.

(*a*). Waste land when brought into cultivation by a *zimmee* (infidel) is in all circumstances subject to *khiraj ;* when cultivated by a Mooslim, it is *ooshree* or *khirajee*, according to the character of the neighbouring[1] land.

Page XXIII.

(*b*). The law of India under the Mahomedans was the Hanneefa Code, according to which waste land is so absolutely in a state of nature, that it may be acquired by the first occupant who reclaims or brings it into a state of cultivation. What amounts to reclaiming is explained in the fifth chapter. According to Aboo Haneefa, the permission of the Imam is necessary, but according to the other two, it is not necessary ; and being the majority, it is presumed that their opinion constitutes the law upon the subject. When brought into cultivation, whether with or without the Imam's permission, there is no doubt that land which was waste is liable to the *wazeefa*, if reclaimed by a *zimmee ;* and to either *ooshr* or *khiraj*, according to the nature of the adjoining land, if cultivated by a Mooslim.

Page 3.

(*c*). When a person has brought waste land into cultivation, if it be contiguous to *khirajee* land it is *khirajee*, and if it be contiguous to *ooshree* land it is *ooshree*. But this only when the person who brought it into cultivation was a Mooslim ; for if he were a *zimmee*, the land would be *khirajee* even though it should be contiguous to *ooshree* land.

(*d*). Property in waste is established by reclaiming it with the permission of the Imam, according to Aboo Haneefa, and by the mere act of reclaiming, according to Aboo Yoosuf and Moohummud ; and a *zimmee* becomes the proprietor by reclaiming, in the same way as a Mooslim would acquire the property.

(*e*). Dead or waste land is land on the outside of a town for which there is no owner, nor any one who has a particular right in it. * * Qoodooree has said that what is Adee ("what has been long spoiled or desolate"), or has been long desolate, and is without a proprietor, or if it ever was appropriated within the time of *Islam*, its owner is unknown, and the land itself lies at such a distance from any village, that if a person were to stand on the nearest limit of cultivated land and cry out, his voice would not be heard in it, is waste ;—and *Kazee Fakhr-ood-deen* has said that what has been said is most correct, that when a man standing on the verge of the cultivated land of a village cries out at the pitch of his voice, whatever place his voice reaches to is to be considered as within the confines of the cultivated land, because the people of the village have need of so much for pasture to their cattle, and for other purposes ; and that what is beyond this is waste, when it has no known

---

[1] *i. e.*, the pergunnah rate.

owner. Aboo Yoosuf has made distance from a village to be determined, as aforesaid, a necessary condition; but, according to Moohummud, regard is to be had to the actual fact whether the people of the village derive any advantage from the land or not, though it should be near to the village; but Shums-ool-Aëmmah relies on what was approved by Aboo Yoosuf (*Kazee*).

This last extract (*e*) is suggestive. *Firstly*, it shows that Mahomedan law recognized village communities, by recognizing a village's proprietary right in a certain amount of waste land external to the actual cultivation of the village; *secondly*, the particular mode of determining what was waste land involved a continual advance of the village lands upon the waste; for, as the space beyond the confines of cultivated land over which the human voice could be heard, constituted the village common, every fresh cultivation of that common by the growth of village population caused the common to encroach upon the waste. In other words, we trace here, *1st*, the Poor Law Fund under Native rule, *viz.*, the reservation of waste land for the growth of population, subject to payment of the prescribed land tax; *2nd*, the direction in which khoodkasht rights multiplied outside the lands of—and irrespectively of hereditary rights derived from— the original settlers in the village. The new land reclaimed from waste by the descendants of those settlers became, for the former, their *own land* (khoodkasht), subject only to the payment, not of the lower rent paid by pykashts, but of the higher or maximum pergunnah rate, *i. e.*, a rate which was fixed by custom. Thus the two elements of a title by prescription, *viz.*, occupancy of what was *res nullius*, and a rate of rent determinable and known in each village by custom, were constantly present. The custom or prescription was not terminated by the permanent settlement; its continuance was explicitly recognised in the Huftum Regulation VII of 1799, which enacted that "the Courts of Justice will determine the rights of every description of landholder and tenant, when regularly brought before them; whether the same be ascertainable by written engagements, or defined by the laws and regulations, or depend upon general or local usage, which may be proved to have existed from time immemorial." And thus the real genuine right of occupancy, that which the Law and Constitution of India recognized, grew and extended with the increase of population, and through the encroachment of cultivation upon the waste.

II.—Sir John Shore (*18th September 1789*).

Whether the proportion of jungle is more or less than a third of the Company's territorial possessions in Hindostan, I know not, but with respect to the past, I am, from my own observation, as far as it has extended, authorised to affirm that since the year 1770, cultivation is progressively increased, under all the disadvantages of variable assessments and personal charges; and with respect to the future, I have no hesitation in declaring that those zemindars who, under confirmed engagements, would bring their waste lands into cultivation, will not be deterred by a ten years' assessment from attempting it. If at this moment the Government chose to confer grants of waste land in talookdary tenure, under conditions that no revenue should be paid for them during five years, and that at the end of ten, *the assessment should be fixed according to the general rates of land in the districts where the tenures are situated*, they would find no difficulty in procuring persons to engage, even upon less favourable terms. If I mistake not, *the grants in Ramghur were precisely on these principles, which are conformable to the usage of the country.*

The passages in italics place beyond doubt that waste lands brought into cultivation paid, in no case, any rent higher than the old established pergunnah rates.

III.—Regulation XLIV, 1793.

The dues of Government from lands consist of a certain proportion of the annual produce of every beegah of land, demandable, according to the local custom, in money or kind, unless Government has transferred its right to such proportion to individuals for a term or in perpetuity, or fixed the public demand upon the whole estate of a proprietor of land, leaving him to appropriate to his own use the difference between the value of such proportion of the produce and the sum payable to the public, so long as he continues to discharge the latter.

The same definition of the Government's due, and of what the Government made over to the zemindar in the perpetual settlement, occurs in the preamble of Regulation XIX of 1793. The transfer to the zemindar was of the proportion of the produce of the land, in money or in kind, according to local custom, which was payable by the ryot to the Government, less the Government land revenue. With regard to waste land, therefore, it was the whole of merely the proportion of produce demandable from the ryot according to custom. By custom, the proportion demandable was only the pergunnah rate, and in Bengal the pergunnah rate demandable, according to custom, was in money, and not in kind; that is to say, what the Government made over to the zemindar in respect of waste lands was the pergunnah rate as payable in money at the date of the permanent settlement. If, as shown in another Appendix, the pergunnah rate was not liable to increase beyond its amount in 1793, neither was the rate leviable on waste land brought into cultivation liable to increase beyond the amount of the pergunnah rate in 1793.

App. XV.
STATE'S RIGHT
IN WASTE LANDS.
Para. 5, contd.

IV.—Regulation XIV, 1793, Section VI.

In cases in which no engagement may exist between the defaulter and his dependent talookdars or ryots, the Ameen is to collect from them according to the established rates and usages of the pergunnah.

If, thus, only the established rate of the pergunnah was demandable, in the absence of an engagement, for lands long under cultivation, and presumably accessible to markets, and possessed of attractions or advantages which ensured their occupancy and cultivation, much more then must it have been impossible that, by any custom, rates higher than the established rates of the pergunnah could be leviable on waste land brought into cultivation by ryots who had to be attracted to it. And in Regulations XLIV of 1793 and XLIII of 1795, the waste lands allotted to invalided native officers and private soldiers were, on the death of the invalids, continued to their heirs at a perpetual rent which the collector, not the zemindar, assessed on fixed principles, though the amount was payable to the zemindar. His title to any future increase of rent for these reclaimed waste lands on account of a rise of prices was disallowed.

V.—Mr. H. Stark, Chief of the Revenue Department, India Board of Control (14th February 1832).

Q. 198.—If, subsequently to permanent settlement, jungle or waste lands should be brought into cultivation, would that land be taxed? It depends upon whether it was included within the boundary of the district permanently settled; if it was not included, of course the Government have a right to tax it; there have been many disputes upon it. I cannot give a better notion of the opinions of zemindars upon that than by saying that many of the zemindars whose lands border upon the Sunderbuns, claimed the sea as their boundary where it was 60 or 70 miles off. The Government resisted those claims; but in cases where the zemindar was allowed to include the improved estate within his boundary at a fixed rate of half a rupee per beegah, the right of the cultivators to hold the lands at a fixed rate was at the same time secured to them. The zemindar as proprietor can only demand for them one quarter rupee in excess of the Government jumma; so that the original clearer of the land holds it subject to a fixed rent of three quarters of a rupee, and if it yields him a profit of 100 or 150 per cent., that is his profit.

Parl. Papers,
Sess. 1831-32,
Vol. XI.

6. Property in waste land could not be acquired, except by cultivating it, and paying to the sovereign rent for it at the pergunnah rate. Hence, the zemindar, whose title as proprietor of land was created in the way shown in the following extract, had no inherent title to waste land; whilst, as has been seen, the gift of it to him in the permanent settlement was by a stretch of authority beyond what the law and constitution of India recognized in even the Emperor, under the Mogul rule.

Mr. H. Colebrooke, *Husbandry of Bengal* (1806).

(*a*). In examining this question, it was pre-supposed that a property in the soil, similar to that which is vested, of right or by fiction, in the sovereign, or in some class of his subjects, throughout every state of Europe, must vest in some class of the inhabitants of Hindustan, either sovereign or subject. If it were denied to the zemindar (a denomination which readily suggested the term of 'landholder' for its equivalent), the sovereign has been thought the only member of the State to whom that property could be attributed. Besides the presumption arising from the literal interpretation of the name, the hereditary succession of zemindars pointed out these for the real proprietors; and although the succession did not follow the rules of inheritance established by law for landed property, and admitted in practice for real estates of which the revenue had been granted away by Government; and although the hereditary succession to offices of account was as regular and as familiar as it was to zemindaries, the advocates for the rights of zemindars deemed the argument conclusive, or appealed to humanity in support of it. For, perceiving no competitor but the sovereign for the lordship of the soil, it escaped their observation that the rights of more numerous classes might be involved in the question, and that the appeal to humanity might well be retorted.

(*b*). These and other arguments were assisted by considerations of expediency, which decided the question; and accordingly the zemindars are now acknowledged as proprietors of the soil. Yet it has been admitted by a very high authority, that anciently the sovereign was the superior of the soil; that the zemindars were officers of revenue, justice, and police; that their office was frequently, but not necessarily, hereditary; that the cultivator of the soil, attached to his possession with the right to cultivate it, was subject to payments varying according to particular agreements and local customs; that, in general, he continued on the spot, but that the revenue to be paid by him to the State was to be determined by the zemindars;[1] that the riat certainly had a title by occupancy, in right of which he might retain the land, without reference to the will and approbation of a superior, but subject to contributions for the support of the State. To assess and collect these contributions, regulated as they were by local customs or particular agreements, but

---

[1] View of plans, &c.

varying at the same time with the necessities [1] of the State, was the
business of the zemindar, as a permanent, if not as a hereditary officer.

7. Thus it appears that the Law and Constitution of India
at the date of the permanent settlement were doubly violated
in the gift of waste lands to zemindars. In the *first* place,
title to waste land could only be acquired by reclaiming and
cultivating it, and this the zemindars of 1793 had not done.
Secondly, the law restricted the Emperor, and therefore it
restricted the East India Company, when they " stood forth as
dewan," from giving away waste land except on payment of
the prescribed tax or revenue to the State. While this was
the unsatisfactory title of the zemindar to the waste lands,
it did not give him an absolute property in those lands ; what
was transferred to him was merely the State's reversionary
interest in a fixed amount of revenue or rent whenever the
waste lands might be brought into cultivation ; those who
reclaimed the waste were, by the Law and Constitution of
India, regarded as making their " own," that is, khoodkasht,
what, till then, was no man's land, and as so making it
khoodkasht subject to payment of a rent not liable to increase
beyond the pergunnah rate, that is, of a fixed rent. The
immense waste lands in 1793 were the Poor Law Fund, and
the provision, for a growth of population, and their gift to
the zemindars has created one of the famine problems of the
present day.

8.—OUSTING BETWEEN CULTIVATION AND HARVEST.

(1).—J. N. HALHED, *page 83.*

Pahee kashtees and casual occupants may not be ousted from their
land in the interval between cultivation and harvest ; thus a person
laying out his land for sugarcane is entitled to hold for two years at
the least, and may not be ousted.

Between cultiva tion and harvest.

(2).—MR. H. COLEBROOKE (*Minute, 1812*).

In respect to the more extensive power of annulling all leases when
lands are sold for arrears of public revenue, and still more generally
with respect to the landholder's right, however vested in him, or from
whatever cause arising, of enhancing the rent payable by a ryot or
occupant, I am of opinion that further provision should be made for the
security of the tenant, in addition to, or amendment of, the existing rule,
that pottahs shall not be cancelled before the close of the year, in con-

Revenue Selec- tions, Vol. I, page 264.

---

[1] *Abwabs.*

sequence of a sale taking place subsequently to the second month of the year.

The principle on which the amendment I mean to propose will be founded is that of a tenant's not being liable to pay a quarter's rent more than he had reason to expect he should be subject to, when he entered on the cultivation of the land, for the crop of the current season. Whether his lease has even expired, or were on any account voidable, if he has been, nevertheless, allowed to commence the cultivation of the ground, at the expense of his money and of his labour, without notice of an enhanced rent, he cannot justly be chargeable with a higher rent than that borne by his former lease, or usually paid by him. More he could not expect would be demanded from him ; and if more be exacted, it is a surprise, little short of fraud, since he has been deluded into the expenditure of capital and the employment of labour in the confidence of being only subject to the former rent; and has not had the opportunity of choosing between the relinquishment of the land and the payment of the enhanced rent required of him.

It should therefore, in my opinion, be made a universal rule, that no cultivator or tenant of land shall be liable to pay an enhanced rent, though subject to enhancement under subsisting regulations, nor any landholder, or renter, or sequestrator, have power to demand it, unless written engagements for such enhanced rent have been entered into by the parties, or formal written notices have been served on such cultivator or tenant at the season of cultivation, *viz.*, in the month of Jeth (or earlier in districts where the cultivation for the year commences at an earlier period), notifying the specific rent under the landlord's right of enhancing it, to which he will be subject for the ensuing Fuslee, or for the current Bengal year. Unless the due service of such notification be proved, no greater rent should be exigible by process of distress or confinement of person, nor recoverable by suit in court, than the cultivator or tenant was bound to pay by his previous engagements; and if more be levied from him, he should be entitled to a refund of the excess with damages, on proof of the circumstances before a court of justice.

In the rules here proposed, I have assumed the month of Jeth as a season of cultivation, that being the period at which cultivation is reckoned. to commence in the districts which compute by the Fuslee era. It is, I believe, sufficiently early for the Bengal districts also ; and, in that case, the indefinite clause which has been inserted may be omitted, for the very desirable purpose of certainty and precision, which will be best attained by restricting the period of notice to the single month specified.

(3).—Mr. Holt Mackenzie (*18th April 1832*).

Q. Do you happen to know whether the non-occupancy ryot is generally entitled to hold by the year ?—I never heard of anything under a year.

Q. Have they a right similar to that which prevails in England, that they can only be called on to quit their farm at a known period of the year ?—It is generally understood that the interval between the setting in of the last crop of one year and the ploughing for the next is the time at which it is settled.

(4).—MR. H. NEWNHAM (*7th May 1832*).

The right of the absent occupancy ryot has been admitted by all ryots; they themselves maintain that, directly the heir of an absconded ryot, or the absconded ryot himself, returns, all he has to do is to come to a compromise for the crop on the ground, and the land is restored to him immediately.

9. The salient points in this Appendix are—

I. That zemindars had no inherent title in waste lands; and that the gift of extensive waste lands to them in the permanent settlement was bestowed by a stretch of authority beyond that allowed by the law and constitution of India.

II. That as the State had never been entitled to more than the established pergunnah rate of rent on lands reclaimed from waste, so the State's unconstitutional gift to zemindars was limited to that rent; it did not confer a property in the land; that appertained, according to immemorial custom, to him who reclaimed the land from waste.

III. That under the law and constitution of India, the waste lands provided for an extended and long continued growth of khoodkasht proprietors of land.

IV. That the resident cultivator of waste land in his own village becomes the proprietor of it, subject to payment to the State, or now, to the zemindar, of only the pergunnah rate; that the custom under which the resident cultivator acquired this waste by bringing it into cultivation subject only to payment of the established pergunnah rate, was not interrupted by the zemindary settlement, which gave no property to the zemindar in the waste lands of a village beyond a reversionary interest in the pergunnah rate of rent on those lands whenever they might be brought into cultivation; and that the Court of Directors informed the Government of Bengal that "it is the opinion of many considerable authorities that, on the leases of waste as well as of other lands the pergunnah rates form a standard not to be exceeded." This opinion of several high authorities accords with Mahomedan law, and it is not gainsaid by any authoritative opinion to the contrary.

V. Besides the levy by zemindars of rates exceeding his pergunnah rate, on new cultivation since the permanent settlement, they have benefited in Bengal by absorbing police lands, according to the extract from Mr. Halhed's memoir.

VI. According to universal custom in India at the date of the permanent settlement, which agreed with the custom in England, even a temporary cultivator could not have his rent raised over his head until after he had removed his crop from the ground, and before his sowing for the next crop.

APPENDIX XVI.

OBSCURITIES IN THE REGULATIONS OF 1793.

1. It is clearly established that, until 1793, the only original rights in the produce of the soil, namely, those independent of each other, which had originated in an ancient established custom of centuries, were the rights of the ryots or cultivators, and of the State. The zemindar of Lord Cornwallis' settlement had, unless by purchase—until 1793 at least—no rights, except those which he derived from Government; while the ryot's was an actual, veritable, heritable right (limiting the right of Government), which (derived from ancient custom) the breath of Lord Cornwallis did not make, and could not unmake; and which it was farthest from his Lordship's wish or thought to unmake. Hence, the enquiry now to be prosecuted should result in showing that the intention and meaning of the authors of the permanent settlement were not destructive of the rights of the ryot.

2. To understand in this matter the mind of the authors of the permanent settlement, we must, however, go farther back than 1793, to the predecessors of Lord Cornwallis, with whom the idea of a permanent settlement originated: the main difference between them and him was in their clearly-expressed resolve that the demand on the *ryot* should be fixed, and in his hot-haste that the demand on the *zemindar* should be fixed for ever; theirs was the merit of a permanent settlement to be concluded with the ryots, his the shame of a zemindary settlement—shame, that is, if Lord Cornwallis, in his settlement, intended to, and did advisedly, destroy the rights of millions of cultivators. But, as already observed, this was farthest from his Lordship's thoughts.

3. A remarkable event in the history of landed tenures in Bengal, *viz.*, the universal dispossession of zemindars by Jaffier Khan, was yet fresh in the minds of the British administrators of the province from 1765 to 1793. It showed unmistakably (what the law and constitution of India also established) that the only sharers, as principals, in the produce of the soil were the Government and the cultivator; and that, when a zemindar was interposed, he simply inter-

cepted part of the *Government's share*. Accordingly, in all the discussions of settlements of land revenue in Bengal, from the earliest down to the decennial settlement, we find, as the central idea, that what was due to the State by established custom constituted the gross demand on the ryot; and that exaction from him of anything beyond this, without the sanction of the Government, amounted to oppression.

I.—PRESIDENT AND SELECT COMMITTEE (*16th August 1769*).

Colebrooke's
Digest, pages
175-6.

Another grievance, which is equal to the former, is the variety of demands which the collectors, from the aumil and zemindar to the lowest pyke, impose, without any colour or license from the Government; some of which have been so long exacted and paid, that the ryots begin to imagine the oppression is sanctied by Government, and is not the mere fraud of the collectors. The multiplying of superfluous agents and inferior collectors may also be deemed a source of extortion.

II.—GOVERNOR-GENERAL IN COUNCIL (*19th July 1786*).

E. I. Revenue
Selections, Vol.
I, page 458.

(*a*). The simple and correct ancient revenue system of the country, by its useful checks from the accountant and assessor of the village through its several gradations upwards to the Accountant General of the Exchequer, was, we have reason to believe, no less calculated to protect the great body of the people from oppression than to secure the full and legal rights of the sovereign.

(*b*). * * More especially in the time of the later Nazims, and principally about the time and since our acquisition of the Dewanee, the ingenuity of the native collectors, in greater measure than previously, has endeavoured to confound the limits of different districts, to vitiate accounts, to increase old *abwabs* and superadd new ones, and, in short, to involve oppression in such mystery and difficulty as nearly to defeat and set at defiance all attempts at detection.

III.—SIR JOHN SHORE (*June 1789*).

Fifth Report.

(*a*). The gross jumma of any district is properly the amount paid by the ryots, which is liable to various deductions on account of the charges incidental to the collection of the revenues in its different stages.

(*b*). Where these variations of demand upon the ryots take place by any established rules founded on the quality of the soil, its produce, and the uses to which the land is applied, however perplexing they may be to the collector, or other officers of Government, I do not deem them of material inconvenience to the ryots, who from usage understand them, and can tell when they are opposed to exactions (para. 220).

(*c*). I shall here insert a remark of the Committee appointed to conduct the investigation in 1777, which is agreeable to my own information and belief:—

" It appears to have been an established measure in this country, that the accounts of the rents of every portion of land and other sources of revenue should be open to the inspection of the officers of Government; it was chiefly by the intimate knowledge, and the summary means of information which the Government thereby possessed, that the revenue was collected, and the zemindars were restrained from oppression and exactions. To the neglect of these ancient institutions, to the want of information in the government of the State and resources of the country, may perhaps be justly ascribed most of the evils and abuses which have crept into the revenue." (paras. 247-8).

(*d*). Where the rates of land are specific and known, a ryot has a considerable security against exaction, provided the officer of Government attends to his complaints and affords him .redress; and without this he can have none. *The additional sanction which he derives from a pottah*, supposing it to be properly drawn out, is this—that it specifies, without reference to any other account, the terms upon which he holds the land, *and the amount of the abwab or cesses*, which are not mentioned in the nerikbundy, nor always in the jummabundy (para. 401).

(*e*). I do not observe in the correspondence of the collector any specific rules for the security of the ryots. I well know the difficulty of making them; but some must be established. The great point required is, to determine what is and what is not oppression, that justice may be impartially administered according to fixed rules. In Behar the variations in the demands upon the ryots are not so great as in Bengal ; the system of dividing the produce affords a clear and definite rule, whenever that prevails; and the regulations need not be so minute as those which I proposed for Bengal (para. 145).

(*f*). When the five years' settlement was concluded by the Committee of Circuit, several conditions were inserted in the agreements of the farmers and zemindars, calculated for the security of the Government and benefit of their tenants. Thus, * * they were directed to collect from the cultivated lands of the ryots in the mofussil the original jumma of the last and foregoing years, and *abwab* established in the present, and on no account to demand more; where the lands were cultivated without pottah by the ryots, they were to collect according to *the established rates of the pergunnah* (para. 450).

It appears from these extracts that anything beyond the rates established by long usage, and the amounts sanctioned by Government, was not demandable from the ryots, and could be levied only by oppression, or as an exaction. It further appears from (*d*) that the ryot's customary security was the official record of the pergunnah rate in the local register. The mass of the khoodkasht ryots depended on this security, and held without any pottah. The pottah was devised by Sir John Shore as a necessary part of his settlement, simply as an additional security which would ensure to the ryot the further advantage of recording the amount of the *abwabs* or cesses, as well as the pergunnah rate. The pottah was a mere record of the ryot's independent right; not the document from which he derived his right.

APP. XVI.   4. The purpose or resolve of the Governments preceding
————   that of Lord Cornwallis, to fix, permanently, the demand
PERMANENT
SETTLEMENT FOR leviable from the ryots, is shown in the following extracts :—
RYOT.
————
Para. 4.

I.—PRESIDENT AND SELECT COMMITTEE (*16th August 1769*).

Colebrooke's   (*a*). For the ryot, being eased and secured from all burthens and
Digest, page 178. demands but what are imposed by the legal authority of Government
itself, and future pottahs being granted him specifying that demand, he
should be taught that he is to regard the same as a sacred and inviolable
pledge to him, that he is liable to no demands beyond their amount.
There can, therefore, be no pretence for suits on that account—no room
for inventive rapacity to practise its usual arts.

Colebrooke's   (*b*). The ryot, too, should be impressed in the most forcible and con-
Digest, page 180. vincing manner * * that our object is not the increase of rents, or
the accumulation of demands, but solely, by fixing such as are legal, explaining and abolishing such as are fraudulent and unauthorised, not
only to redress his present grievances, but to secure him from all further
invasions of his property.

II.—GOVERNOR-GENERAL (WARREN HASTINGS)—*1st November 1776*.

E. I. Revenue   Many other points of inquiry will be also useful, to secure to the
Selections, Vol. ryots the permanent and undisputed possession of their lands, and to
I, page 436. guard them against arbitrary exactions.   This is not to be done by pro-
clamations and edicts, nor by indulgences to the zemindars and farmers.
* * The foundation of the work of establishing new pottahs for the
ryots must be laid by Government itself.   All that I would here propose
is to collect the materials for it, by obtaining copies of the present pottahs, and of the nerikbundy, or rates of land, by which they are regulated in each district, and every other information which may throw a
light on this subject, and enable the Board hereafter to establish a more
permanent and regular mode of taxation.

III.—MR. P. FRANCIS (*1776*).

considered that the rate of assessment per beegah should be fixed for ever
upon the land, no matter who might be the occupant (Appendix IV,
para. 5, section d).

Here, again, we see in I and II, that the pottah was designed as a record, and the sole record, of the rights of ryots.
5. The bare amount demandable under established custom
had for two centuries been known as the *assul jumma*: to
these there had been added by the State *abwabs*, or cesses,
partly for alleged temporary exigencies of State, partly on
account of a rise of prices.   These State cesses and the *assul
jumma*, together, constituted the demand which was leviable
from the ryot with the sanction of Government; all else was

levied through the exaction or oppression practised by zemin-dars and farmers. The *assul jumma* was the fixed demand; its amount per zemindary was revised at distant intervals, so as to take in new lands brought into cultivation; but the revision was made so as not to alter the established or pergunnah rate of assessment per beegah, The *abwabs*, or cesses, however, were, to some extent, not wholly referable to a rise of prices. These statements are supported by the following extracts:—

I.—WARREN HASTINGS (*4th July 1786*).

E. I. Revenue
Selections, Vol. I,
page 455.

(*a*). The ryots will not venture to refuse to pay the *established due to the Circar* or Government. Custom is a law whose obligation operates in their own defence, nor have they any idea of disputing it; they consider it as a species of decree from fate. But as the value of money in proportion to its plenty must have decreased in India as well as in Europe, so it has been found that the ryots of a village and of a whole district could pay a greater revenue than that originally settled by custom. Hence arose the oppressive catalogue of *abwabs*, or special additional assessments, by Government. On this head Mr. Grant has given us much useful light. The abwabs, or successive additional taxes, make regular heads in the accounts of every village and district; nor are the *abwabs*, established openly by Government, of that oppressive nature which Mr. Francis in his ingenious Minutes has supposed.

(*b*). The sources of real oppression are in secret *abwabs*, or unavowed taxes, which the great farmer or zemindar imposes at will on the ryots, and of which we have such cruel examples in the investigation at Rungpore. Here, again, we see the great advantage of being able to examine the revenue system, and to trace back oppression to its source, according to the thread and light of established usage and ancient accounts.

(*c*). A *clear principle* is ascertained. It is, fortunately, the check against the oppression of the ryot or peasant, and the bulwark against corruption in the officers of Government. If, for example, an additional revenue is imposed upon the ryot, it cannot be imposed secretly; it must be by *abwab*, or additional tax, which must appear in the accounts in every village, pergunnah, or zemindary, and be recorded, in some shape, in various native accounts of the revenue for the year.

II.—SIR J. SHORE (*June 1789*).

Fifth report,
Paras. 30-1 of
Minute.

(*a*). The assul jumma, under the Mogul rule, was at long intervals increased in total amount for each zemindary, so as to give the sovereign the advantages arising from extended cultivation and increased population. This increase made no alteration in the rates upon the ryots.

Para. 33.

(*b*). But the *abwab* soubadary, or viceregal imposts, which constitute the increase since 1728, had a contrary tendency, for they enhanced the rates. They were in general levied upon the standard assessment in certain proportions to its amount, and the zemindars who paid them were

APP. XVI.

PERMANENT
SETTLEMENT FOR
THE RYOT.

Para. 5, contd.
Para. 35.
Para. 64.

authorised to collect them from the ryots in the same proportions to their respective quotas of rent.

(c). An enhancement in the rates of taxation may be defended on the grounds of the increase of commerce and increase of specie between the time of Tury Mull and the administration of Jaffier Khan.

(d). My objections to the principle of the soubadary imposts have a reference to the circumstances under which they were established. If the rates in the tukseem of Tury Mull with respect to the ryots had not been previously augmented by impositions separate and distinct from those of the soubahs, perhaps the best possible mode of obtaining an increase would be by demanding it in certain proportions to the standard, with a due regard to the degree of improvement in the country.

(e). See, also, Appendix VII, paragraph 5, sections I and II.

6. In extracts (c) and (d) Sir John Shore considered the contingency of an enhancement of rents on account of a rise of prices, and the particular mode of enhancement by the rule of proportion. In the following extracts from his minutes, both the future enhancement of rents and the particular form of it were advisedly precluded by the demand upon the ryot being permanently limited to the amount which was to be inserted in pottahs, which the zemindars, as a part of the permanent zemindary settlement, were to grant to the ryots as a record of their rights.

I. I do not observe in the correspondence of the collectors any specific rules for the security of the ryots. I well know the difficulty of making them, but some must be established. * * I have taken the liberty to prepare, for the consideration and determination of the Board, the propositions which result from the preceding considerations in the form of resolutions.

II.—PROVISIONAL RULES FOR THE SECURITY OF THE RYOTS.

That, whereas, from the ignorance, inattention, and oppressions of zemindars, the greatest abuses have been practised in the collection, and the ryots have been exposed to exactions, the following rules are now prescribed to all zemindars, talukdars, and persons entrusted with the revenues for their immediate direction and guidance:—

(a). That the rents to be paid by the ryots, by whatever rule or custom they may be demanded, shall be specific as to their amount. If by a pottah containing the *assul* and *abwab*, the amount of both shall be inserted in it, and the ryot shall not be bound to pay anything beyond the amount specified, on account of kurcha or any other article.

(b). If by a tikka pottah, the whole amount payable by the ryot is to be inserted in it. If by any rule or custom such as the payments of the last and preceding years, the rate of the village, pergunnah, or any other place, an account is to be drawn out in the beginning of the year, showing what the ryots are to pay by such rule or rate, and a copy of it is to be given to them.

(*c*). Where the rents are adjusted upon a measurement of the lands after cultivation, the rates and terms of payment shall be expressed in the pottah.

(*d*). If by any established and recorded jummabundy, that is to be the rule for demanding the rents. If the rents are paid in kind, the proportion which the ryot is to pay shall be specified in account or written agreement.

(*e*). That no zemindar, farmer, or person acting under their authority, shall be allowed to cancel the pottahs of the khoodkasht ryots, except upon proof that they have been obtained by collusion, or that the rents paid by them within the last three years have been reduced below the rates of the nerikbundy of the pergunnah, or that they have obtained collusive deductions, or upon a general measurement of the pergunnah for the purpose of equalizing and correcting the assessment.

(*f*). That when the jumma of a ryot has been ascertained and settled, he shall be authorised to demand a pottah from the zemindar, or person acting under his authority, whether farmer, gomashta, or other; and any refusal to deliver the pottah shall be punished by fine proportioned to the expense and trouble of the ryot in obtaining it.

(*g*). That the zemindar be not authorised to impose any new *abwab* or *muthote*, on any pretence whatever, upon the ryots; and every exaction of this nature to be punished by a penalty equal to three times the amount imposed. If, at any future period, it be discovered that new *abwab* or *muthote* have been imposed, the zemindars shall be made responsible for the penalty during the whole period of such impositions.

This last clause *b* was misplaced among the Provisional Regulations, for Lord Cornwallis and Sir John Shore distinctly laid down that the levy of fresh *abwabs* by the zemindars should be prohibited.

III.—PERMANENT PLAN FOR THE EASE AND SECURITY OF THE RYOTS.

(*h*). That as the impositions upon the ryots, from their number and uncertainty, have become intricate to adjust, and a source of oppression to the ryots, the zemindars shall be compelled to make a revision of the same, and to simplify them by a gradual and progressive operation, as follows:—

(*i*). They shall begin with those pergunnahs where the impositions are most numerous, and having obtained an account of them, shall, in concert with the ryots, consolidate the whole, as far as possible, into one specific sum; but so, that in no case the sums demanded from the ryots shall exceed three articles, viz., *assul*, *abwab*, and *kurcha*. Having prepared this account, they shall submit it to the collector for his inspection; after which it is to be enforced by the authority of Government, and any enhancement of the *abwab* or *kurcha* to be punished as extortion.

(*j*). That where, by mutual consent of the ryots and the zemindars, the *abwab* can be wholly reduced and consolidated, it be done accordingly; and the rates of the land, according to the nature of the soil and the produce, to be the rule for fixing the rent.

(*k*). That the rents of each pergunnah on the zemindary be annually adjusted in the same manner, until the whole be completed; and that the exact proportion which the *abwab* and *kurcha* bears to the *assul* jumma be precisely determined. The zemindar is to be positively enjoined to regulate a certain proportion of his zemindary annually, so that the whole be completely performed within *x* years from the date of his agreement.

7. The foregoing seven provisional and three permanent rules occur in the draft Propositions for Bengal appended to Sir John Shore's minute dated 18th June 1789. He had urged a provisional or experimental term (ten years) for the new settlement before declaring it permanent. The provisional regulations would have been carried out in that experimental period. The provisional rules, it will be observed, distinctly provided that the pottahs which were to fix future rents were to be issued to all classes of ryots, including those under temporary leases. The permanent rules provide for all ryots without distinction. Illustrating the permanent by the temporary rules, the intention of permanently fixing in the pottahs the rents of all classes of ryots was manifest.

8. In the proposed Resolutions for Behar, appended to the first of Sir John Shore's two minutes of 18th September 1789, only the first four of the provisional rules detailed in the preceding extract (*viz.*, para. 6, II, *a* to *d*.) are included, Sir John Shore having in his later minute of 18th September insisted more strenuously than in the first minute of 18th June on the experimental limitation of the settlement to ten years, and having relied on the consideration that "in Behar, the variations in the demands upon the ryots are not so great as in Bengal; the system of dividing the produce affording a clear and definite rule, whenever that prevails, and the regulations need not be so minute as those which I proposed for Bengal."

9. I. In a minute dated 8th December 1789 Sir John Shore, previous to his departure for Europe, recorded, among others, the following "doubts regarding the propriety of declaring the assessment now to be imposed upon the country, fixed and unalterable":—

(*a*). It is allowed that the zemindars are, generally speaking, grossly ignorant of their true interests, and of all that relates to their estates; that the detail of business with their tenants is irregular and confused, exhibiting an intricate scene of collusion opposed to exaction, and of unlicensed demand substituted for methodised claims; that the rules by which the rents are demanded from the ryots are numerous, arbitrary,

and indefinite; that the officers of Government possessing local control APP. XVI.
are imperfectly acquainted with them, whilst their superiors, further
removed from the detail, have still less information; that the rights PLAN OF THE
PERMANENT
of the talukdars, dependent on the zemindars, as well as of the ryots, SETTLEMENT.
are imperfectly understood and defined; that in common cases we Para. 9, contd.
often want sufficient data and experience to enable us to decide, with
justice and policy, upon claims to exemption from taxes; and that
a decision erroneously made may be followed by one or other of these
consequences—a diminution of the revenues of Government, or a confirmation of oppressive exaction.

(*b*). To the truth of this detail there will be no dissenting voice; and Para. 11.
it follows from it that, until the variable rules adopted in adjusting the
rent of the ryots are simplified and rendered more definite, no solid
improvement can be expected from their labours, upon which the prosperity of the country depends. * *

(*c*). No one, I believe, is so sanguine as to expect that the perpetuation
of the zemindary assessment will at once provide a remedy for these
evils. * * We know from experience what the zemindars are. * * The
necessity of some interposition between the zemindars and their tenants
is absolute; and Government interferes by establishing regulations for
the conduct of the zemindars, which they are to execute, and by delegating authority to the collectors to enforce their execution. If the
assessment of the zemindaries were unalterably fixed, and the proprietors
were left to make their own arrangements with the ryots, without any
restrictions, injunctions, or limitations—which, indeed, is a result of the
fundamental principle—the present confusion would never be adjusted.

(*d*). This interference, though so much modified, is in fact an invasion
of proprietary right, and an assumption of the character of landlord,
which belongs to the zemindar; for it is equally a contradiction in terms
to say that the property in the soil is vested in the zemindar, and that
we have a right to regulate the terms by which he is to let his lands
to the ryots, as it is to connect that avowal with discretionary and
arbitrary claims. If the land is the zemindar's, it will only be partially
his property, whilst we prescribe the quantity which he is to collect, or the
mode by which the adjustment of it is to take place between the parties
concerned.

Consistently with Sir John Shore's proposals for fixing
the rent of the ryots, and recording the amount of the rent
in a pottah, and with his arguments in the other preceding
extracts, which support those proposals, the drift of the hazy
argument in this extract seems to be that, to avoid the appearance of Government interfering with the zemindar's right by
"regulating the terms by which he is to let his lands to the
ryots," that is, by fixing the ryot's rent and recording his
right, though "the necessity of some interposition between
the zemindars and their tenants is absolute," an experimental
term should be allowed for the initial stage of the settlement,
during which the rent to be fixed for the ryot and to be
included in his pottah would be settled by mutual agreement

between the zemindar and ryot. The opportunity of seeing whether this would be done, was the main advantage to Government for which Sir John Shore contended in advocating an experimental introduction, at the outset, of the decennial settlement.

Para 16.

(e). Notwithstanding repeated prohibitions against the introduction of new taxes, we still find that many have been established of late years. The idea of the imposition of taxes by a landlord upon his tenant is an inconsistency, and the prohibition in spirit is an encroachment upon proprietary right; for it is saying to the landlord, you shall not raise the rents of your estate. But, without expatiating on this[1] part of the argument, I shall only here observe that, with an exception of an arbitrary limitation in favour of the khoodkasht ryots, the regulations for the new settlement virtually confirm[2] all these taxes, without our possessing any records of them, and without knowing how far they are burthensome or otherwise. In some cases, a knowledge of those impositions has been followed by the abolition of them; in others it may be equally necessary; wherever it takes place, there is a risk that the assessment will suffer diminution. At present they are in many places so numerous and complicated that, after having obtained an enumeration of the whole, the amount of the *assul* with the proportionate rates of the several *abwabs*, it requires an accountant of some ability to calculate what a ryot is to pay; and the calculation may be presumed beyond the ability of most tenants. The pottah rarely expresses the sum-total of the rents, and it is difficult to determine what is extortion. * *

Paras. 18 & 19.

(f). Amid this confusion, the necessity of prescribing regulations for simplifying the complicated rentals of the ryots (which ought, if possible, to be reduced to one sum for a given quantity of land of a determinate quality and produce), of *defining and establishing the rights of the ryots with precision*, together with the expediency of procuring clear data for the transfer by sale of public and private property, are admitted.

Para. 20.

(g). Under all these circumstances, is it not better to introduce a new principle by degrees, than establish it at once beyond the power of revocation? If we are convinced that any meditated arrangements are sufficient to correct present and future abuses, or that we can in the sequel establish regulations for this purpose without affording pleas that shall affect the permanency of the assessment; if the relative rights of the individuals concerned are not sufficiently determined, or can be determined, without the same consequence from any future decisions; if we are sufficiently informed, with respect to the present exactions, to declare that they may be continued, without establishing a rack-rent, or, if they are abolished, that the suppression of them will not diminish the assessment, no objections will remain to declare it permanent and unalterable. But upon these points I have my doubts, and they are justified by past experience. * * Those who contend for the permanency of the assessment, must maintain the affirmative of all the dubious propositions which I have stated.

---

[1] This blowing of hot and cold.
[2] That is, establish a permanent settlement for the ryot, though it be an oppressive one.

(*h*). I consider this as a period of experiment and improvement, during which, by a systematical conduct, regularly directed to one object, we are to give confidence to the zemindars, and procure a simplification of the present complicated rental of the ryots. The foundation of this improvement is to be laid in regulations to be established, and the proposed reform depends upon the execution of them, without which, I may venture to predict, no assessment can be permanent.[1] * * If, instead of presumptions arising from the supposed collections of the zemindars, we knew what the ryots paid, and whether that amount was burthensome or otherwise; and if the assessments of the land tax were regulated by a general standard, the arguments founded on equality would lose much of their weight; * * I hold it prudent in establishing great innovations in principle, under an acknowledgment of defective information, to take experience for our guide. Our measures have a view to permanency; but before we declare it, prudence dictates that we should have some certainty that the Government will not suffer by its liberality, and that the benefits of it will extend to that class (ryots) whose labours are the riches of the State.

App. XVI.

PLAN OF THE PERMANENT SETTLEMENT.

Para. 9, contd.

Para. 26.

These extracts (*e*) to (*h*) make it clear, as stated in the remarks on (*a*) to (*d*), that, owing to the difficulty of Government officers settling what, on the basis of existing rents and *abwabs*, were to be entered in the pottahs as the *established* rents, for the future, under the permanent settlement, the zemindars and ryots were to come to an agreement about the amounts which should be so entered in the pottahs. This done, the rates to be thus entered in the pottahs would be the permanent rates for the ryots, in like manner as the amounts entered in the zemindars' agreements with Government became the only revenue payable for ever to the Government, under that settlement.

II. Lord Cornwallis replied to Sir John Shore in a minute dated 3rd February 1790. His reply to those remarks of Sir John Shore which asserted the necessity of fully securing and establishing the rights of the ryots was as follows :—

(*a*). To the representations of Sir John Shore which are quoted in (*a*) and (*c*) of section I, Lord Cornwallis replied in passages which are set forth in Appendix IV, para. 7, section II.

(*b*). Mr. Shore observes that we have experience of what the zemindars are ; but the experience of what they are or have been, is by no means the proper criterion to determine what they would be under the influence of another, founded upon very different principles. We have no experience of what the zemindars would be under the system which I recommend to be adopted.

---

[1] In 1878-79 enhancement of rent remains as great a difficulty as though there had not been any permanent settlement in 1789-93.

Lord Cornwallis soon realized "what the zemindars would be." The decennial settlement was promulgated in 1789 and 1790; and his Lordship, in a minute dated 7th December 1792, recorded that—

"some of the principal zemindars in Bengal (the zemindars of Burdwan, Nuddea, and others), though allowed considerable abatements from their jumma for the maintenance of thannadars and pykes, either keep up no police establishments whatever, or sell the appointments in the police to the most notorious robbers and murderers, who plunder the country which it was their duty to protect. The same abuses prevail, in a greater or less degree, in every zemindary the proprietor of which is allowed to keep up a similar establishment."

Yet, without the slightest consciousness how these appalling evidences of the wolfish disposition of the zemindars of that day destroyed grounds of childish expectations, that miscreant zemindars, suffused with gratitude for the decennial settlement, would give pottahs to ryots at the customary rates, Lord Cornwallis, on 22nd March 1793, issued, without compunction or remorse, his proclamation of a permanent zemindary settlement. In his minute of 3rd February 1790 Lord Cornwallis continued :—

(c). With regard to the ignorance and incapacity of zemindars * * I must here observe, however, that the charge of incapacity can be applied only to the proprietors of the larger zemindaries. The proprietors of the smaller zemindaries and taluks in general conduct their own business, and, I make no doubt, would improve their lands were they exempted from the authority of the zemindars, and allowed to pay their revenue immediately to the public treasuries of the collectors.

But on 7th December 1792 Lord Cornwallis wrote: "In some parts of the country, particularly in the eastern and southern districts of Bengal, many of the petty landholders, encouraged by the great distance of the magistrate's place of residence, and by there being no officers stationed on the spot, on the part of Government, for the protection of the country, have, from time immemorial, been in the habit of perpetrating robberies themselves, or conniving at them in others. It is, indeed, notorious that most of the principal gangs of robbers are in league with some of the zemindars, and generally with those in whose districts they leave their families and deposit their plunder." But his Lordship's benevolent proclamation of 22nd March 1793, which placed millions of cultivating proprietors at the mercy of these zemindars, was issued notwithstanding.

III. The hazy arguments of Sir John Shore in the passages (*d*) and (*e*) of section I, elicited from Lord Cornwallis the reply set forth in Appendix VII, paragraph 2, section I, and paragraph 5, section III. In the same breath his Lordship denied the right of zemindars to enhance the ryot's rent beyond the amount at which it might be fixed, as a part of the permanent settlement, by Government, or under an arrangement (about pottahs) to be brought about by Government; and asserted that pottahs to be granted by wolfish zemindars were necessary to secure perpetual fixed rents for ryots; thus admitting that the permanent settlement could not be introduced without, at the same time, effectually establishing and securing the ryots' rights.

(*a*). With regard to the rates at which landed property transferred by public sale, in liquidation of arrears, and, it may be added, by private sale or gift, are to be assessed, I conceive that the new proprietor has a right to collect no more than what his predecessor was legally entitled to; for the act of transfer certainly gives no sanction to illegal impositions. I trust, however, that the due enforcement of the regulations for obliging the zemindars to grant pottahs to their ryots, as proposed by Mr. Shore, will soon remove this objection to a permanent settlement. For, whoever becomes a proprietor of land after these pottahs have been issued, will succeed to the tenure, under the condition and with the knowledge *that these pottahs are to be the rules by which the rents are to be collected from the ryots.*

(*b*). By granting perpetual leases of the lands at a fixed assessment, we shall render our subjects the happiest people in India; and we shall have reason to rejoice at the increase of their wealth and prosperity, as it will infallibly add to the strength and resources of the State.

Thus, Lord Cornwallis indicated, as distinctly as Sir John Shore, that the pottah to be issued in 1790 was to be the rule for collecting rents from the ryots, and that the rule was to be obligatory, not only on the zemindars of that day, but upon their successors;—"whoever becomes a proprietor after these pottahs have been issued" must be bound by them;—in other words, the rent specified in the pottah was to be the permanent rent; for the regulations did not provide for the alteration of the pottah in any case, except by *mutual consent* of ryot and zemindar, or with the view of conforming the pottah rate to the ancient established rate of the pergunnah.

IV. The only effective parts of Lord Cornwallis' reply were those which confirmed Sir John Shore's argument, that proper security should be provided for permanently fixing the zemindar's demand upon the ryots. His Lordship's remaining reasons for precipitating a zemindary settlement without providing this essential security, merely display the optimism of a weak benevolence; but, from 1790 to this day, the one who delivers the last word has been regarded as the incarnation of wisdom, and so his Lordship's views prevailed against even the appalling warnings from his own murderous and dacoitee zemindars.

V.—COURT OF DIRECTORS (REPLYING TO BENGAL GOVERNMENT'S REPORT OF PROCEEDINGS WHICH ESTABLISHED THE DECENNIAL SETTLEMENT —*19th September 1792.* ENT)

(*a*). Your enquiries were rightly directed to the past history and present state of the districts;—their changes; new impositions and peculiar customs; the ancient rights of the different orders of landholders and tenants; * * and the regulations which should be adopted for removing defects, and securing, especially to the inferior occupants and immediate cultivators of the soil, the enjoyment of their property, subject only to moderate and known demands from the principal landholders.

(*b*). The difference of opinion which has subsisted, we find not to relate so much to general principles as to the application of them. That the tax which the subject[1] is to pay to the State should not be arbitrary, but ascertained and fixed; that all besides which his industry can produce to him should, as far as possible, be secured to him; and that, in order to the prosperity of a country, property should be rendered definite and certain.

(*c*). It would be doing Mr. Shore injustice not to acknowledge that as his opinions in general against precipitating a permanent zemindary settlement are advanced with ability, so there are several of his objections which are very serious in themselves, and have considerably impressed our minds. These are drawn from the still imperfect knowledge of our Government respecting the real resources of the different divisions of the provinces, as well as of the respective rights of zemindars, talukdars, and ryots; from its inability to discriminate what parts of the taxes actually levied from the two classes by the zemindars ought[2] to be sanctioned by Government in a permanent settlement; from the uncertainty of accomplishing that settlement with a due regard to the rules prescribed for it; and especially from the extreme difficulty of forming and executing such regulations *as shall secure to the great body of the ryots the same equity and certainty as to the amount of their rents, and the same undisturbed enjoyment of the fruits of their industry, which we mean to give to the zemindars themselves.*

---

[1] The subject who pays the tax out of which the Government and zemindar's shares are provided is the ryot. The subject whose industry grows the produce out of which the tax is paid is the ryot.

[2] This was a clear intimation that the ryot's assessment at the date of the permanent settlement would become permanent, under that settlement, excepting any illegal cesses which might be expressly disallowed.

As matters have turned out in the nearly ninety years
since the Court wrote their beautiful sentiments, the ryots
have done everything, the zemindars nothing, for the
improvement and extension of agriculture; and, without
having put forth any of their own industry, the zemindars
are enjoying, and the ryots, in many parts of Bengal, are
denied, the fruits of the ryots' industry; and the great body
of the ryots are left in uncertainty as to the amount of those
rents which were to have been made certain in 1793.

(*d*). Upon these grounds it is contended that, as some districts of
the country will probably be over-rated, and others suffer from droughts
and inundations, the proprietors unable to make good their assessments
will, without anything blamable on their part, be deprived of their
lands by judicial sale; that the Company will from such causes as
these be exposed to a continual diminution of the stipulated revenue,
without a possibility of any augmentation to balance their losses.

(*e*). And that, after all, unless we succeed in introducing and establishing equitable regulations between the landholders and their tenants,
the great objects for which such sacrifices and a permanent settlement will
have been made, that is, the improvement and happiness of the country,
will be unattained, and, therefore, the evils of the old system will subsist.

(*f*). From all these considerations, and others of inferior weight
urged by Mr. Shore, he infers that we should attempt to advance to a
perpetual settlement only by gradual measures; that the first decennial
period should, therefore, be regarded as a period of experiment and
improvement, wherein the knowledge of our Government as to the state
and resources of the country, and the relative rights of the different
orders of the people, is to be improved;—wherein confidence is to be
given to them; the mode of collecting and fixing the rents from the
ryots to be simplified; due regulations of every kind established and
enforced; the people by degrees formed to the new system of certainty
and security, &c., &c.

(*g*). No consequences more formidable could be presented to us from
the proposed system than a diminution in perpetuity of the Company's
revenue, with the still continued subsistence of all or any of those
disorders in the mode of imposing and levying it from the great body
of the people which have already done such essential injury to the
country, and must ever prove a bar to its prosperity.

(*h*). Very clear and solid arguments were requisite to dispel the
diffidence which this view of the subject, from such an authority, had
a tendency to create, and to encourage us to persevere in our original
idea of giving a fixed constitution to the finance and land tenure of
the country. But this satisfaction Lord Cornwallis has afforded us
in his minutes of the 18th September 1789 and 3rd February 1790,
which we sincerely regard as two very valuable records, written with
enlarged and just views upon the soundest principles of policy, with
perfect fairness, great acquaintance with the subject, and the most conclusive reasoning in favour of a permanent assessment.

(*i*). As to the formidable consequence of a decrease in perpetuity of the Company's revenue, the Court were pleased to find that they would escape this danger, whatever might befal the ryots (*l* below). They observed:—

We find it convincingly urged that a permanent assessment, upon the scale of the present ability of the country, must contain in its nature a *productive principle;* that the possession of property, and the sure enjoyment of the benefits derivable from it, will awaken and stimulate industry, promote agriculture, extend improvement, establish credit, and augment the general wealth and prosperity. Hence arises the best security that no permanent diminution can be expected to take place, at least to any considerable amount.

(*k*). As to the great acquaintance with the subject manifested in Lord Cornwallis' minutes, the Court observed:—

To another class of objections formed upon our still defective knowledge of the resources of the country, the rates, and the amount of the collections actually made on it by the zemindars and farmers, Lord Cornwallis opposes the long series of time and investigations already past; the labors of the collectors for three successive years in his administration; the communication of all the knowledge they could obtain; their superior fitness for carrying into execution that system with a view to which they had been so long employed; the improbability of succeeding better with other collectors and fresh reports,—from all which his Lordship infers that there remained only the alternative of sitting down passive and despondent under the supposed existing difficulties and disorders, or of acting upon the information already acquired.

Admitting, as we do, the imperfect knowledge of our servants in the details of the revenue, and lamenting it, not without some mixture of mortification, on considering the long course of opportunities which our possession of the country has afforded, we must nevertheless concur with Lord Cornwallis in thinking that it would be too sanguine to expect any future general improvement in this respect.

(*l*). As to the formidable consequence of leaving the rights of the ryots in uncertainty and insecurity, the Court had not much faith in pottahs to be given to ryots by grateful, rapacious zemindars, but, reciprocating Lord Cornwallis' opinion, they thought that zemindars who had appointed robbers and murderers to offices in the police, and who harboured dacoits, would become as lambs, if Government, by permanently limiting its demand upon them, and not providing for the security of the ryots, would hold up the "unearned increment" to the zemindars as a constant temptation to wrong-doing. Thus:—

(1). With respect to the objections drawn from the disorder and confusion in the collections, the uncertainty of their amount, the variable

indefinite rules by which they are levied, the exactions and collusions App. XVI.
thence too prevalent, the intricacies in the details of the revenue business,
and the ignorance and incapacity of the zemindars, Lord Cornwallis Plan of the Permanent Settlement.
charges these evils, so far as they exist (and we think with great justice),
upon the old system, as a system defective in its principle, and carrying Para. 9, contd.
through all the gradations[1] of the people, with multiplied ill effects, Para. 47.
that character of uncertain arbitrary imposition which originated at the
head.   He therefore very properly contends that reform must begin[2]
there, and that, in order to simplify and regulate the demands of the
landholders upon their tenants, the first step is to fix the demand of
Government itself.

(2). The greatest obstacles to the execution of the new system being, Para. 44.
as already noticed, the difficulties of establishing an equitable adjustment
and collection of rents between the zemindars and the ryots, we are
happy to see that Lord Cornwallis is of opinion that the propositions which
Mr. Shore himself has made for this end, recommending written specific
agreements in all cases, would, if duly followed, be effectual.   On this important branch of the subject we do not feel ourselves sufficiently in possession of all the necessary details to form a final and positive determination.

(3). No conviction is stronger in our minds than that * * of all
the generated evils of unsettled principles of administration, none has
been more baneful than frequent variations in the assessment.   It has
reduced everything to temporary expedient and destroyed all enlarged
views of improvement.   Impolitic as such a principle must be at all
times, it is particularly so with respect to a dependent country, paying a
large annual tribute, and deprived of many of its ancient supports.
Such a country requires especially the aid of a productive principle of
management.   * *   Long leases, with a view to the gradual establishment of a permanent system, though recommended upon the ground of
safety, we must think, would still continue in a certain degree the evils of
the former practice; periodical corrections in the assessment would be, in
effect, of the nature of a general increase, and would destroy the hope of a
permanent system, with the confidence of exertion it is calculated to inspire.

In this passage the Court of Directors simply amplified
an argument of Lord Cornwallis.   What would they and he
now say to the results of their permanent settlement which,
in the present day, has issued in short leases of three or five
years, so as to afford frequent opportunities to landlords
or middlemen for raising the ryots' rents?   The permanent
settlement, which was to have given to the cultivator the
security of a perpetual lease, has subjected him to the
tyranny of short leases, which are incompatible with agricultural improvement and with the prosperity of the cultivating
classes.

---

[1] Thus the Court contemplated fixity of demand through all gradations down to the
ryot; but they stopped at the zemindars.
[2] But it also ended there; and his Lordship took no thought of preventing that termination of his reform.

(4). But as so great a change in habits and situation (*viz.*, to the state of things in which the zemindars will see that their own interests are permanently connected with the security and comfort of the cultivators of the soil) can only be gradual, the interference of Government may for a considerable period be necessary to prevent the landholders from making use of their own permanent possession for the purposes of exaction and oppression. [Here follows a passage which is set forth in Appendix IV, para. 10, section II]   *   *

(5). There remains but one subject to mention in this letter—that, however, is a subject of the last importance; it is the watching over, rearing, and maturing of this system; maintaining, under future administrations, the energy which has commenced it.   All the benefits hoped for from it to the country and the Company, all its success, must depend upon this vigilance and fostering care of our Government and our servants.   No mistake could be more fatal than that of supposing that it can be left to its own execution, and that all the effects it is fitted to produce will necessarily, and of course, flow from it.   If any conclusion is to be drawn from the descriptions given of the people, it is surely this— that the powerful are oppressive, and the weak fraudulent: having neither wisdom nor confidence to act for distant good, and being unrestrained by moral considerations, they are prone to avail themselves of present opportunity.   It is true that the new system reckons upon their self-interest—and this is an excellence in it; but it will take time to assure them that the system is solid, and to discover to them that their interest[1] is best promoted by following the dictates of justice and humanity.   *   *   It must be the duty of our servants to watch incessantly over the progress of the new institution; to see that the landholders observe punctually their agreements with Government and with the ryots; that they neither pass invented claims on the eve of a permanent settlement, nor fraudulently shift the burthen of revenue by collusive transfers, nor by any other sinister practices diminish the payment of their stipulated assessments; that they, likewise, uniformly give to the ryots written specific agreements, as also receipts for all payments, and that those agreements be on the one side and the other fairly fulfilled. In this way, and in this only, can the system be expected to flourish.

(6). It is a truth of great importance that the *neglect* of instituted regulations has, more than the imperfections of former plans, been noxious to our affairs.   We now establish the best system, and hence the most fitted for execution, but for which constant attention is requisite; and we wish, therefore, that all our servants may be constantly awake to this truth, and consider their own immediate interests and honour, as well as those of the Company and the nation, involved in the prosperity of the system of permanent taxation, and in the strenuous support and enforcement, according to their respective situations, of all the regulations framed for its success.

(*m*). With this glowing language, the Court of Directors confirmed the declaration of a permanent zemindary settlement, in full knowledge that its success depended on the good faith with which the zemindars of 1790, who were notorious

---

[1] The interest of harbourers of dacoits and murderers.

as oppressors, extortioners, harbourers of dacoits and murderers, and participators in the gains of these miscreants,
would grant pottahs to ryots fixing for ever the amount of
rent payable by the latter. Practically, the honour of the
nation was confided to the keeping of those worthless
zemindars of 1790, and the rights of the ryots passed away
sub silentio.

10. The provisional and permanent plans proposed by Sir
John Shore for securing the established rights of the ryots
are detailed in para. 6, sections II & III. In promulgating
the regulations, a portion of the provisional part was omitted,
in accordance with the decision to declare that the decennial
settlement would be made permanent; the rules corresponding to those proposed by John Shore, which were embodied
in the regulations of the decennial settlement, as finally
established in Regulation VIII of 1793, were as follows:—

(*a*). LIV.—The impositions upon the ryots under the denominations
of *abwab, mahtoot,* and other appellations, from their number and uncertainty, having become intricate to adjust, and a source of oppression
to the ryots, all proprietors of land and dependent talukdars shall revise
the same in concert with the ryots, and consolidate the whole with the
assul in one specific sum.

In large zemindaries or estates the proprietors are to commence this
simplification of the rents of their ryots in the pergunnahs where the
impositions are most numerous, and to proceed in it gradually till completed, but so that it be effected for the whole of their lands by the
end of the Bengal year 1198 in Bengal districts, and of the Fusli and
Willaity year 1198 in the Behar and Orissa districts, these being the
periods fixed for the delivery of pottahs, as hereafter specified.

(*b*). LV.—No actual proprietor of land or dependent talukdar, or
farmer of land of whatever description, shall impose any new *abwab*
or *mahtoot* upon the ryots, under any pretence whatever. Every exaction of this nature shall be punished by a penalty equal to three times
the amount imposed; and if, at any future period, it be discovered that
new *abwab* or *mahtoot* have been imposed, the person imposing the same
shall be liable to this penalty for the entire period of such impositions.

See Permanent
Rules in para. 6,
section III.

11. Here we see that the rate of rent being once fixed and
entered in a pottah, *abwabs* levied *at any future period* would
be illegal, and the zemindars would have to refund them with
full retrospective effect. This was a clear intimation that
the rent to be entered in the pottah was to be a permanent
rent. It should also be noticed that the period fixed for the
completion of the delivery of pottahs by zemindars to ryots
was the end of the Bengalee year 1198, *i. e.,* christian year
1792, or before the proclamation of the permanent settle-

ment. In other words, it was a part of the new zemindary settlement, with its bestowal of, till then, unheard of privileges on zemindars that the rent payable by ryots should, before the proclamation of the permanent settlement have been recorded in pottahs, without power to zemindars to increase the rent thereafter, under any regulation then contemplated.

12. The provisional rules proposed by Sir John Shore, (para. 6, section II) related to the delivery of pottahs, which work, as we have seen, was to have been completed by 1792. Sir John Shore quitted India in 1789, and the draughtsman of the decennial regulations, afterwards made permanent, embodied his provisional rules among the permanent without distinguishing those which were strictly temporary, and which were to have terminated in 1792, thus causing much of the obscurity in the Regulations of 1793.

(*a*). LVI—

(1). (It is expected that, *in time*, the proprietors of land, dependent talukdars, and farmers of land, and the ryots, will find it for their mutual advantage to enter into agreements, in every instance, for a specific sum for a certain quantity of land, leaving it to the option of the latter to cultivate whatever species of produce may appear to them likely to yield the larger profit.)

(2). Where, however, it is the established custom to vary the pottah for lands according to the articles produced thereon, and while the actual proprietors of land, dependent talukdars, or farmers of land, and the ryots, in such places shall prefer an adherence to this custom, the engagements entered into between them are to specify the quantity of land, species of produce, rate of rent, and amount thereof, with the term of the lease, and a stipulation that, in the event of the species of produce being changed, a new engagement shall be executed for the remaining term of the first lease, or for a longer period, if agreed on; and in the event of any new species being cultivated, a new engagement, with the like specification and clause, is to be executed accordingly.

The proper order of the first and second clauses of this extract is perhaps inverted; the immediate agreement was to be for the rate of rent payable for land which has a rotation of crops: *viz.*, a rate of rent varying with the kind of produce. The authors of the permanent settlement indulged a hope that, *in time*, ryots and zemindars might be found to agree for an average rate of established rents, irrespective of the kind of crop.

(*b*). LVII.—

See Provisional
Rules, para. 6,
section II.

(1). *First*.—The rents to be paid by the ryots, by whatever rule or custom they may be regulated, shall be specifically stated in the pottah, which, in every possible case, shall contain the exact sum to be paid by them.

(2). *Second.*—In cases where the rate only can be specified, such as where the rents are adjusted upon a measurement of the lands after cultivation or on a survey of the crop, or where they are made payable in kind, the rate and terms of payment and proportion of the crop to be delivered, with every condition, shall be specified.

(c). LX—

(1). *First.*—All leases to under-farmers and ryots, made previous to the conclusion of the settlement, and not contrary to any regulation, are to remain in force until the period of their expiration, unless proved to have been obtained by collusion, or from persons not authorised to grant them.

(2). *Second.*—No actual proprietor of land or farmer, or persons acting under their authority, shall cancel the pottahs of the khoodkasht ryots, except upon proof that they have been obtained by collusion; or that the rents paid by them within the last three years have been reduced below the rate of the nirkbundy of the pergunnah; or that they have obtained collusive deductions; or upon a general measurement of the pergunnah for the purpose of equalising and correcting the assessment. The rule contained in this clause is not to be considered applicable to Behar.

The foregoing were included by Sir John Shore among his Provisional Rules, that is to say, they were to be superseded by the delivery of pottahs prepared in accordance with those rules, and the pottahs once delivered were to determine, thereafter, the amount of rent recoverable from the ryot, without power to the zemindar of ever revising the amount in the pottah, without the ryot's consent, that is, without power to the zemindar of raising the ryot's rent as inserted in the pottah. It is further noticeable that the expression khoodkasht-*kudeemee* ryot is not used in section LX, the word used is simply "khoodkasht."

13. The Regulation VIII of 1793 was dated 1st May; on the same date were issued other Regulations, which contain the following provisions respecting rates of rent:—

(a).—REGULATION XIV, 1793 (*1st May*).

The ameen, deputed by a collector to collect the rents and revenues from the estate or farm of a defaulter, is to collect according to the engagements that may subsist between the defaulter and his dependent talukdars, under-farmers, and ryots, and shall not make any alterations whatever in such engagements, or exact more than the amount specified in them, whether they be conformable to Regulation XLIV, 1793, or not. *In cases in which no engagements may exist between the defaulter and his dependent talukdars or ryots, the ameen is to collect from them according to the established rates and usages of the pergunnah.*

APP. XVI. (*b*).—REGULATION XXVI, 1793 (*1st May*).

(1). By the original rules for the decennial settlement of the three provinces, minors were declared disqualified for the management of their estates; and, according to the rules for the establishment and guidance of the court of wards passed on the 15th July 1791, and re-enacted with modifications by Regulation X, 1793, the minority of proprietors of land is limited to the expiration of the fifteenth year. In fixing this period, Government were guided solely by legal considerations, the Mahomedan and Hindu laws, although they present no specific age for the termination of minority, indirectly pointing out the fifteenth year as the time when persons are to be considered competent to the management of their affairs.

(2). Instances, however, have recently occurred, that evince the inexpediency of vesting proprietors with the charge of their lands at this early period. * * At this early age, the proprietors must necessarily be unacquainted with the laws and regulations which they are bound[1] to observe in the management of their estates. * *

(3). But the pernicious consequences resulting from the incapacity of the proprietors are not confined to themselves. The cultivators of the soil, and the various orders of people residing upon their lands, suffer equally by the rapacity and mismanagement of their agents; the payment of the public revenue is withheld, and the improvement of the country retarded.

It appears from paragraph 3 that the levy of more than the authorised or customary rate of rent constituted rapacity in a zemindar.

(*c*).—REGULATION XLIV, 1793 (*1st May*).
　　　　　　 ,,　　 XIX,　 ,,　　 ,,

(1). Both these Regulations affirmed that the zemindar has only a part of the Government's share of the produce of land, as determined by ancient and established usages of the country; see Appendix XV, para. 5, section III. Regulation XLIV of 1793 added (para. 42, III, of this Appendix) that zemindars, to raise money or from other motives, often let lands at low rents. To check this practice without interfering with the letting of waste lands at temporary low rents, the regulation enacted as follows :—

It is, at the same time, essential that proprietors of land should have a discretionary power to fix the revenue payable by their dependent talukdars, and to grant leases or fix the rents of their lands for a term sufficient to induce their dependent talukdars, under-farmers, and ryots, to extend and improve the cultivation of their land :—upon the above grounds, &c. &c.; it is enacted as follows : * *

(2). No zemindars, independent talukdars, or other actual proprietors of land, nor any persons on their behalf, * * shall let any lands in farm, nor grant pottahs to ryots or other persons for the cultivation of lands,

---

[1] This, and the deviation from Hindu and Mahomedan law which this reason justifies, discredit the status of a zemindar as other than an official proprietor.

for a term exceeding ten years.   Nor shall it be lawful for any zemindar, &c., who may have granted pottahs for the cultivation of lands for a term not exceeding ten years, to renew such engagement, lease, or pottah, at any period before the expiration of it, excepting in the last year, at any time during which it shall be lawful for the parties to renew such engagement.   (Eleven months later, or in Regulation IV of 27th March 1794, it was enacted that the landlord, in granting the renewal, should not exact any rate higher than the established rates of the pergunnah; see *post*, section *d*, 3).

(3). Whenever the whole or a portion of the lands of any zemindar, independent talukdar, or other proprietor of land, shall be disposed of at a public sale for the discharge of arrears of the public assessment, all engagements which such proprietors shall have contracted with dependent talukdars whose taluks may be situated in the lands sold, as also all leases to under-farmers, and pottahs to ryots for the cultivation of the whole or any part of such lands (with the exception of the engagements, pottahs, and leases specified in sections VII,—privileged dependent taluk-dars,—and VIII,—ground for dwelling-houses, &c.) shall stand cancelled from the day of sale, and the purchaser or purchasers of the lands shall be at liberty to collect from such dependent talukdars, and from the ryots or cultivators of the lands let in farm, and the lands not farmed, whatever the former proprietor *would have been entitled to demand, according to the established usages and rates of the pergunnah or district in which such lands may be situated, had the engagements so cancelled never existed.*

(4.) By the law of 1793 the land, or the mass of the ryots, paid the pergunnah rate;—the practice against which Regulation XLIV of 1793 was directed, was the letting of land at less than the pergunnah rate, except for the purpose of reclaiming it from waste. The ten years' lease at reduced rates was permitted by the new law expressly to enable zemindars to hold out sufficient inducement to dependent talookdars and ryots " to extend and improve the cultivation of land." This was the sole purpose of the limitation :—but for this purpose, the new law would have simply declared null and void the letting of land at less than the pergunnah rate; yet the law has been twisted to the prejudice of the occupancy ryot's title.

(5.) According to the passage in italics in clause 3 of the extract, the auction purchaser of the defaulter's estate was entitled to cancel (with certain exceptions) all privileged rates of rent, that is, rates below the established pergunnah rates; but he was debarred from taking from cultivators of any class more than the amount demandable according to the established local usages and local rates. Hence, the discre-tionary power mentioned in clause 1 of the extract was discretionary, merely, as to the term or period (not more than ten years) for which a zemindar might grant a lease to a ryot at less than the pergunnah rate, and not as to raising the rate of rent at pleasure,—that being limited by established custom.

(*d*).—(1). REGULATION VIII, 1793, SECTION LIX.

A ryot, when his rent has been ascertained and settled, may demand a pottah from the actual proprietor of land, dependent talukdar, or farmer, of whom he holds his lands, or from the person acting for him; and any refusal to deliver the pottahs, upon being proved in the Court of Dewany Adawlut of the zillah, shall be punished by the Court by a fine proportioned to the expense and trouble of the ryot in consequence of such refusal. Actual proprietors of land, dependent talukdars, and farmers, are also required to cause a pottah for the adjusted rent to be prepared and tendered to the ryot, either granting the same themselves, or entrusting their agents to grant the same.

(2).—REGULATION IV, 1794, SECTION V.

The ryots in the different parts of the country frequently omitting or refusing to take out or receive pottahs, although the persons from whom they are entitled to demand them are ready to grant them in the form and on the terms prescribed by the regulations, it is declared that, if a proprietor or farmer of land or a dependent talukdar, after the approbation of the collector to the form of the pottah or pottahs for the lands in his estate or farm shall have been obtained, as prescribed in section LVIII, Regulation VIII, 1793, shall fix up in the principal cutcherry or cutcherries of his estate or farm a notification in writing under his seal and signature, specifying that pottahs according to the form approved, *and at the established rates*, will be immediately granted to all ryots who may apply for them, and stating where and when, and by whom, the pottahs will be delivered, the notification shall be considered as a legal tender of a pottah, and the proprietor of land, &c., shall be deemed to have complied with the orders in Regulation VIII, 1793, and the persons so tendering pottahs shall be entitled to recover the rents due to them from such ryots, either by the process of distraint laid down in Regulation XVII, 1793, or by suit in the Dewany Adawlut.

SECTION VI.

If a dispute shall arise between the ryots and persons from whom they may be entitled to demand pottahs, regarding the rates of pottahs (whether the rent be payable in money or in kind), it shall be determined in the Dewany Adawlut of the zillah in which the lands may be situated, according to the *rates established in the pergunnah for lands of the same description and quality as those respecting which the dispute may arise*.

(3.)—SECTION VII.

The rules in the preceding section are to be considered applicable, not only to the pottahs which the ryots are entitled to demand in the first instance under Regulation VIII, 1793 (*d*, 1 above), but also to the renewal of pottahs which may expire or become cancelled under Regulation XLIV, 1793 (*c*, 2 and 3 above); and to remove all doubt regarding

the rates at which the ryots shall be entitled to have such pottahs renewed,
it is declared that no proprietor or farmer of land, or any other person,
shall require ryots whose pottahs may expire or become cancelled under
the last-mentioned regulation, to take out new pottahs at higher rates
than the established rates of the pergunnah for lands of the same quality
and description; but that ryots shall be entitled to have such pottahs
renewed at the established rates, upon making application to the person
by whom their pottahs are to be granted, in the same manner as they are
entitled to demand pottahs in the first instance.

14. These extracts contain all that was said in the
Regulations of 1793 respecting the status and privileges of
ryots; they may be considered under the heads of (1) the
rate of assessment; (2) the tenure of the ryot; (3) the
record of his rights; (4) the permanency of the rate of assessment, or to whom belongs the unearned increment. As
to rates of assessment, we find that the following are mentioned in the several extracts, *viz.* :—

I.—UNDER-POTTAHS TO BE GRANTED BY THE ZEMINDAR AS PART OF THE
    PERMANENT SETTLEMENT.

(*a*). A fixed amount of rent;—in which existing customary rates and
abwabs were to be consolidated by the zemindars in concert with the ryots
"in one specific sum." (Para. 10, *a*.)

(*b*). Where it is the established custom to vary the rate according to
the produce, the special rate for the particular article of cultivation is to
be inserted in the pottah, which, in addition, should, in all practicable
cases, specify the exact amount of rent and the quantity of land.
Where the rent is levied in kind, the rate and terms of payment, and
proportion of the crop to be delivered, with every condition, were to be
specified. (Para. 12, (*a*) *1* and *2*, and (*b*) *1 and 2*).

(*c*). *In time*, zemindar and ryot may find it to their advantage to
enter into special agreement for a rate per beegah which, unlike (*b*), shall
not vary with the kind of produce, so as to leave it discretional with the
ryot to cultivate any kind of produce he likes. (Para. 12 (*a*) *1*).

II.—KHOODKASHT RYOTS.

The pergunnah rate;—unless they claim a lower rate under a pottah,
or on proof that they paid such lesser rate for more than three years
before the decennial settlement   (Para. 12, section (*c*) *2*).

III.—UNDER TEMPORARY LEASES.

The rate (specified in the lease) that was being paid at the time of
the decennial settlement; thereafter, *i. e.*, on expiration of lease, the
established pergunnah rate. (Para. 12 (*c*) *1*, and para. 13, (*d*) *2*).

IV.—WITHOUT ENGAGEMENTS, OR ON CANCELLATION OF ENGAGEMENTS ON
    SALE OF AN ESTATE FOR ARREARS OF REVENUE.

According to the established rates and usages of the pergunnah
(para. 13, (*a*), and (*c*) *3*).

26

V.—ON RENEWAL OF TEMPORARY LEASES (III), OR OF CANCELLED ENGAGE-
MENTS (IV).

RATE OF
ASSESSMENT
UNDER THE
PERMANENT
SETTLEMENT
OF 1793.

Para. 15.

According to the established rates and usages of the locality.

15. It appears from this summary that for all classes of ryots, whether under old titles or under new engagements after the decennial settlement, there was but one authorised rate. *viz.*, the customary established rate of the particular locality;—the exceptions being (*1st*) any khoodkasht ryots (the expression khoodkasht-*kudeemee* no where occurs) who, under special pottahs,· or under prescription of more than three years preceding the decennial settlement, paid less than the pergunnah rate that was customary for the great body of khoodkasht ryots; and (*2ndly*) pykasht ryots whose temporary leases remained unexpired at the date of the decennial settlement, but who, on expiration of those leases, had to conform to the established pergunnah rates.

16. In other words, the Regulations of 1793 prescribed as the general rule what is now, and has always been, the rule in ryotwari provinces, *viz.*, that the rate of assessment for the ryot should be fixed upon the land, irrespective of the persons who cultivate it. This general rate was fixed at the rate established by custom for each locality; and, as will be presently shown, the rate established by custom was immutable for the particular class of land and particular kind of special products of the soil. The exceptions from this general rate in favour of persons were only two—the one a permanent, the other a temporary exception. The permanent exception was in favour of those khoodkasht ryots (the minority of that body) who had held at rates lower than the pergunnah rates from three years before the decennial settlement, and the hereditary successors of those khoodkashts in those excepted holdings. The temporary exception was in favour of pykasht ryots (until the expiration of their leases), and the cultivators of newly-reclaimed waste lands (until the expiration of the term for which privileged rates may have been allowed them as an inducement to cultivate). Practically, the principle of assessment established by the Regulations of 1793 for ryots, old and new, tended to bring the whole body of cultivators under the ancient established pergunnah rates.

17. The extract in section (*a*) 1 of paragraph 12 seems on the surface to contravene, but on closer examination it will be found to harmonise with this conclusion. The rate which, according to that extract, the proprietors of land and

App. XVI.

RATE OF ASSESS-
MENT UNDER
THE PERMANENT
SETTLEMENT.

Para. 17, contd.

ryots might, *in time*, find it convenient to adopt, instead of the customary rate, was one non-existent at the date of the settlement, and was a mere speculative idea of the framers of the regulations. As such, it was mentioned as simply a permissive or optional rate, which, depending on *mutual agreement* between the zemindar and ryot, gave no right to the former to impose it on the ryot, or to set aside the customary rate. The ideal optional rate had reference to the cases of rotation of crops, and to any other cases in which the customary rate varied according to the produce. In cases of rotation of crops, the rate varied every year with the crop, but still it was the ancient customary rate for the special product for its own year. Reckoning the rate for the whole term of rotation, it was the immutable customary rate of the pergunnah. Similarly, with regard to lands cultivated without rotation of crops, the ancient established rate of the pergunnah, which was binding on both zemindar and ryot, implied adherence by the ryot to the particular articles of produce, *viz.*, the common staple products of the locality, for which the rate had been established. It was not open to him to vary the produce, without also changing his rate to the established or customary rate for the new product. Every such alteration of produce, whether in a rotation of crops or in the second class of cases, involved a corresponding alteration of the pottah, for insertion therein of the new customary rate. The extract in paragraph 12, section (*a*) 2, provides for these alterations of the pottah in conformity with established custom. But, inasmuch as under the regulations, and as the weak point of the permanent settlement, the pottah was the only record of the rights of the ryots, the framers of the regulations threw out, as a forlorn hope, the idea expressed in the extract in para. 12, section (*a*) 1, that the zemindar and ryot would agree for a rate per beegah, irrespective of the kind of produce, after which there would be no further alteration of the pottah. This rate, by special agreement once entered into, would be as perpetual as the zemindar's rent, and the conditions prescribed for the agreement respecting the rate were such, that the rate would conform to, and be based upon, the ancient established rates of the pergunnah; for the regulation made it optional with the ryot to agree to this special rate, irrespective of produce, if he preferred it to the established pergunnah rates for the several kinds of produce. Necessarily, the ryot's choice, if in favour of an invariable rate, would be for an amount about equal

App. XVI.

RATE OF ASSESS-
MENT UNDER
THE PERMANENT
SETTLEMENT.

Para. 17, contd.

to the average of the established local rates for varying kinds of produce. Thus, the extract in section (a) 1 did not empower the zemindar to put aside the established pergunnah rates, or to enhance them;—it merely provided a means by which zemindar and ryot could, by mutual agreement, simplify the statement in the pottah of the established pergunnah rates by which zemindar and ryot alike were bound.

18. It may be noted, further, that the Regulations of 1793 no where speak of "equitable or fair rates of rent" for ryots, as if the rent were matter of opinion or bargain; they speak of existent actual rates, or matters of fact, determined by custom as established pergunnah rates; and when, six years later, Regulation VII of 1799, section XV, clause 7, spoke of a "rent determinable on certain principles according to local rates and usages," the expression was restricted to the rents payable by certain holders intermediate between the zemindar and the ryot.

19. The next head in paragraph 14 is the tenure of the ryot, as exhibited in the extracts in paragraphs 12 and 13; see para. 14. Under native rule, the offices of kanungo and patwari were kept up independently of the zemindar; and the records of these officers showed the quantity of land held by each ryot, and the rate at which he held it. These entries in the official records constituted the title and security of the khoodkasht ryots, who accordingly, at the date of the permanent settlement, held their lands without leases or pottahs, except when they held at lower than the pergunnah rates; in which case they had pottahs which secured the favoured rates to them. Accordingly, at the date of the permanent settlement, there were the following classes of ryots :—

(1). Khoodkasht ryots at favoured rates, secured by pottahs.

(2). Khoodkashts who paid the maximum or pergunnah rates, and had no pottahs.

(3). Embryo khoodkashts, or the descendants of hereditary cultivators, who were occupying newly-reclaimed waste land with or without lease, with eventual liability to pay the pergunnah rate.

(4). Pykashts, or stranger cultivators from other villages, who held under temporary leases at favoured rates, and who, according to established usage, attained to the status of khoodkashts by long, that is, by permanent residence, on their paying the established pergunnah rate.

App. XVI.

Ryots' tenures
under the
Permanent
Settlement.

Para. 21.

20. The third and fourth classes in the preceding paragraph, who held at temporary rates less than the pergunnah rates, are included in the Regulations of 1793 in the extract para. 12 (e) 1; the minority of khoodkasht ryots who held at favourable rates (first class in preceding paragraph) are also mentioned; but the great body, the vast majority by far, of the cultivators in 1793, *viz.*, the khoodkasht ryots who held without pottahs and who paid the full pergunnah rates, are not specifically mentioned as khoodkashts in the Regulations of 1793, for the reason that, as they already paid the pergunnah rates, and as the zemindars were prohibited from exacting more than the pergunnah rates from any one, specific mention of these khoodkashts was not necessary. Inasmuch, however, as they had a substantial right of property in land, which they had derived from ancient custom, and as they constituted the mass of the cultivators, the mere omission to notice them, specifically, in a regulation which, as it did not touch their pergunnah rate of rent, did not concern them, had not the effect of disestablishing them. If it had been intended to disestablish them, the regulation would have said so, and would no doubt have provided for them the requisite compensation, without which it was no more competent for the Government, any more than it was the intention of the Government, to destroy their rights.

21. The khoodkashts who paid full pergunnah rates are, however, mentioned in the Regulation VIII of 1793, though not as khoodkashts. A comparison of the extract from that regulation in paragraph 13, section (d) 1, with the detail in paragraph 14, shows that the extract in (d) 1 refers mainly, though not exclusively, to the khoodkashts who paid the full pergunnah rates. Now, the structure of the regulation in that extract is such as to establish, rather than to destroy, the proprietary right of the khoodkasht ryot; it entitles him to demand a pottah at his full pergunnah rate of rent from the zemindar, and to enforce the demand in a civil suit, if necessary. In the absence of any other record of the rights of khoodkasht ryots, the pottah to be given by the zemindar was to constitute the record. This regulation, accordingly, was framed for the security of the ryot; though, like almost every other law passed in his favour, the zemindars have perverted it to his undoing; and the courts only too effectually helped them, by regarding the pottah not, as it was meant to be, a mere record, for the ryot's security, of rights independent of the pottah, but as the document from which

APP. XVI.
——
THE POTTAH
WAS A MERE
RECORD OF THE
RYOT'S SEPARATE
RIGHT.

Para. 21, contd.

(and therefore from the zemindary author of which) the ryot derived his rights. This error underlies Sir Barnes Peacock's reasoning in his judgment on the great Rent Case.

22. That the pottah was designed merely as an additional evidence of a ryot's right, which was otherwise derived and was independent of the pottah, is also evident from Section 62, Regulation VIII of 1793, or the rules respecting putwarees. Those rules would have been superfluous with tenants-at-will. They were framed for the security of ryots having rights of occupancy, who held without lease, on rents known as the customary pergunnah rates.

23. It may also be mentioned, as limiting the zemindar's and establishing the ryot's proprietary right, that the former was restrained from realising rent until after harvest; and he had no power to raise the rent beyond the established pergunnah rate for any class of ryots whatever; also he had but a limited power of restricting the occupation of land by ryots, *viz.*, that of simply fixing, for other than permanent hereditary occupants, *i.e.*, for non-residents from another village, the term of lease during which they might occupy on paying the established pergunnah rate. On the expiration of his temporary lease, the pykasht ryot was entitled to demand its renewal at the established pergunnah rate (paragraph 13, section *d* 2).

24. The remaining head in paragraph 14 is the permanency of the ryot's assessment, and whether the unearned increment belonged to him or to the zemindar under the Regulations of 1793. We have seen that the khoodkasht ryot could not be required to pay more than the pergunnah rate; that the pykasht ryot, at the end of his temporary lease, had to pay the pergunnah rate; and that the ryot who was employed on a beneficial rate of rent, in bringing waste land into cultivation, also paid, eventually, no more than the established local rate. In short, for old lands or new, for resident cultivators or non-resident, the established customary pergunnah rate was the eventual rate for both kinds of land and for all ryots alike, excepting the comparatively few who paid at favoured rates. If, therefore, the zemindar obeyed the law, the customary, established, prevailing pergunnah rate would be immutable. It follows that the unearned increment, which in process of time would accrue beyond the established rate, from a rise of prices, belonged to the ryot, unless, *firstly*, the established rate contained a germ of development through which the amount of rent would

increase, without express provision for the increase in the
Regulations of 1793.; or, *secondly*, unless those regulations
allowed, and we know that they did not allow, of an increase
of the established customary rate of the pergunnah.

25. As to the possibility of increase of the pergunnah rate
through a hidden germ of development, such germ could only
exist in a pergunnah rate of a kind which implied a yearly
division of the crop between the Government and the ryot,
according to the market value of produce each year. In
such case, necessarily, the Government's share of rent, or the
portion thereof transferred to the zemindar, would increase,
pari passu, with a rise of prices, without help from any
ingenious rule of proportion. This was, and is, the case in
Behar, where the condition of the ryots is wretched; but
there was no scope for such expansion of the pergunnah
rate in Bengal. As shown in Appendix IX, paragraph 6,
section VIII, and as observed by the Select Committee of
1812 in the Fifth Report, "the difficulty was increased by
a difference which had originally prevailed in the mode of
forming the assessment in Bengal from what has been
described as the practice in Behar. In Bengal, instead of a
division of the crop, or of the estimated value of it in the
current coin, the whole amount payable by the individual cultivator was consolidated into one sum called the
assul, or original rent." This fixed amount was irrespective of any particular price of produce; not varying with
such price, it was the ancient established maximum pergunnah rate, or that paid by the great body of cultivators,
namely, all the khoodkasht ryots who held without pottahs.
As these khoodkashts were protected from any increase of
this established rate, whilst others who paid less were protected from an increase beyond the same established rate,
which, as we have seen, was an amount fixed irrespective of
current prices, it follows that the established pergunnah rate
could not be legally increased beyond its amount in 1793.
The regulations of that year explicitly recognise the established rate as the maximum.

26. They could not have done otherwise; for if those regulations had asserted (and no where do they countenance)
the possibility of an increase of a maximum established rate
which was fixed in amount, the assertion would have involved a contradiction in terms, as just explained. Perforce it
is the practice of the majority which determines custom:
the vast majority of cultivators were the khoodkashts, who

paid the maximum pergunnah rates; it was not to their interest to vary the custom by consenting to new rates higher than the established pergunnah rate, which thus remained the rule for all new admissions to the privileges of resident cultivators. Hence, except by encroachments or high-handed proceedings of the zemindars, the Regulations of 1793 provided no way whatever of increasing the pergunnah rates of 1790,—an increase from rise of prices being barred as explained in paragraph 25.

27. Nor could the zemindars find any help outside the Regulations of 1793, in claiming the unearned increment from the ryots. Under native rule, the ancient established rate of *ryot's* rent was never increased; though the amount of land tax of the *zemindary* was increased periodically, or by arbitrary cesses. When the increase of the amount payable by the zemindary was periodical, it was obtained by taxing, at the old rates, the new cultivation in the zemindary since the last increase, the customary local rates of rent remaining unaffected;—when the increase was by an arbitrary impost or State *abwab*, the amount thus imposed on the zemindary was distributed among the ryots, in proportion to their previous rents, and was separately levied at a percentage thereon, without disturbing the established local rates. These arbitrary imposts were, in a measure, as observed by Warren Hastings and Sir John Shore, enhancements of rent from a rise of prices. But, with full knowledge of this fact, Sir John Shore proposed, Lord Cornwallis concurred, and accordingly the Regulations of 1793 prescribed, that then existing rates of rent of the ryots, with *abwabs*, should be consolidated in one amount, thus giving to the zemindars the benefit, through the old *abwabs* therein consolidated, of all enhancements up to 1793 from a rise of prices. But (fresh *abwabs* being prohibited) it was also enacted that the computed amount in which old *abwabs* and the established rate were consolidated should be entered in the pottah, which it was made imperative on the zemindar to grant, and which was to constitute the whole amount recoverable from the ryot by the zemindar or his successor. Thus the only ancient form for the enhancement of rents on account of a rise of prices, *viz.*, fresh *abwabs*, was deliberately withdrawn from the zemindar by the Regulation or Act which also fixed his own rent in perpetuity, free from any enhancement from a rise of prices.

28. Hence, neither explicitly nor by implication, did the Regulations of 1793 countenance any pretence, that the un-

earned increment could become due from the ryot to any body. The amount to be entered in the pottah, before the end of 1791, was to constitute the whole amount recoverable thereafter from the ryot. The regulations neither provided for, nor allowed of, the revision of the amount once entered in the pottah, except where the cultivator varied the produce of his land, when there was to be a corresponding alteration of the pottah, at the ancient established rates, and when the substituted rate was to become the pergunnah rate. With this sole exception, and that only a nominal exception (for the excepted alteration still conformed to the ancient customary rates for the altered produce), the pottah issued was the formal permanent record of the ryot's rights and obligations. As stated by Lord Cornwallis, the zemindar was not to recover from the ryot any amount in excess of that entered in his pottah; and the Regulations of 1793 were in harmony with this decision.

29. A tacit assumption that the pergunnah rates of 1790 were not susceptible of increase, occurs in two other Regulations of 1793—the Partition and the Sale Laws—though the Sale Laws have been strangely perverted to the enhancement of rent, and of pergunnah rates.

I.—PARTITION OF ESTATES.—Regulation XXV of 1793, section VIII, contained the following provisions :—

(a). The public revenue is to be assessed upon each estate into which the property may be ordered to be divided, in conformity to the rules prescribed in Regulation I, 1793; but in selecting the mehals or villages to be included in each separate estate, the advantages or disadvantages arising from situation, the vicinity of roads or navigable rivers, the nature and quality of the soil and produce, the quantity of waste land, the depth at which water may be procurable, &c., and every other local circumstance affecting the present, or likely to influence the future, value of the lands, are to be duly considered, and the mehals or villages to be included in each estate fairly and impartially selected accordingly.

(b). A strict adherence to the above rule is essential to rendering the division equitable. For if the mehals or villages containing a large proportion of waste land and situated in the vicinity of a navigable river, or possessing other local advantages, are included in one estate, and the mehals or villages liable to inundation, or comprising a small proportion of waste land, or situated at a greater distance from a navigable river, or subject to other local disadvantages, are included in another, it is obvious that the selection of the mehals and villages included in the two estates will not be fairly and impartially made, although the public revenue may be assessed upon each estate agreeably to the rules prescribed in Regulation I, 1793, as far as regards their immediate produce at the time of the division. The former estate will be more valuable than the latter, from being capable of improvement without being liable

APP. XVI.

SALE LAWS
IMPLIED
ADHERENCE
TO THE OLD
PERGUNNAH
RATE.

Para. 29, contd.

to be affected by the calamities of season; whilst the latter will be subject to those calamities without possessing the same advantages as the former.

Had zemindars possessed a right of generally enhancing rents, the circumstance of ryots paying low rents in one estate, and being rack-rented in the other, would have constituted such a signal superiority in the former, as could not have been omitted from the enumeration of possible advantages and disadvantages in the foregoing extract *b*. That no such mention occurs, is proof that no such power of enhancing rent existed in 1793.

II.—SALE LAWS.

(*a*). For the correct interpretation of these laws it should be constantly borne in mind that (1st) in 1793 one-third or more of the cultivable lands was waste, that is to say, the bulk of the ryots were resident cultivators or khoodkashts, for they had no need to quit their own village, unless to escape oppression; and not even then, in any considerable number, where oppression was general; (2nd) the khoodkashts being the preponderant class of cultivators, the rent which they paid (and which was higher than that of pykasht ryots) formed the pergunnah rate; (3rd) the khoodkashts on full pergunnah rates held without pottahs; and zemindars or farmers entered into written engagements with only those ryots who paid less than the pergunnah rates, *i.e.*, the classes which held written egagements were—

(1). Old khoodkashts, who possessed written engagements, entitling them and their descendants to hold at less than the pergunnah rates.

(2). Khoodkashts, on land newly reclaimed from waste, for which, in the first few years, less than the pergunnah rate could be paid only on written engagements.

(3). Pykashts who, until their residence in the village matured into occupancy right subject to payment of the full pergunnah rate, could hold on only temporary lease from the zemindars, practically at less than the pergunnah rate.

(4). Khoodkashts of other villages, attracted by the zemindar to a stranger village by the offer of low rents, such offer being necessarily secured by a written engagement.

(*b*). The principle of the Sale Laws may be gathered from the following regulations, *viz.*, (1st) as to transfers and sales

otherwise than for arrears of revenue; (2nd) as to sales for
arrears of revenue, *viz.* :—

—SALE LAWS
IMPLIED
ADHERENCE
TO THE OLD
PERGUNNAH
RATE.
———
Para. 29, contd.

TRANSFERS OR SALES OTHERWISE THAN FOR ARREARS OF REVENUE.

(1).—REGULATION XLIV OF 1793.

Where the division of a joint estate shall be made at the request of
the proprietors, or pursuant to a decree of a Court of Justice; or

If the whole or a portion of any estate shall be transferred by public
sale (excepting it be so disposed of for the discharge of the arrears
of the public revenue), or by private sale, gift or otherwise; or devolve
to any person by inheritance, under the Hindu or Mahomedan law :—
The sharers, in the first-mentioned case, of division of a joint estate,—or
the person or persons to whom the lands may be transferred, or on
whom they may devolve by inheritance, in the second-mentioned cases,—
shall not demand from their dependant talookdars, under-farmers, or
ryots, any sum beyond the amount specified in the *engagement, lease,* or
pottah, which *may have been entered into* between them and *the former
proprietor* previous to the partition, transfer, or devolution, but such
engagement (if not repugnant to section II of this Regulation, for limiting to ten years the term of leases, pottahs, &c., at favoured rates)
shall remain in full force until the term of it shall have expired.

(2).—REGULATION XX OF 1795 (for disposing of lands at public sale,
     pursuant to decrees of the Courts of Justice).

The rules in the preceding sections are to be considered applicable to
lands held exempt from the payment of revenue to Government, as far
as they may be applicable to the circumstances thereof, with this addition, that the purchaser of such exempted lands is to be considered as
having succeeded only to the rights of the former proprietor, and that the
transfer is not to bar any claims of Government for the recovery of the
public dues, under any existing regulation, or any other regulation
that may be hereafter enacted.

(3).—REGULATION VII OF 1799.

The purchaser under a decree of Court or by private sale is entitled,
by the terms of his purchase, only to the rights of the late incumbent
(except in the cases provided for by Regulation XLIV, 1793). Whatever
disputes may arise between him and the under-tenant, must be settled
between them, or by the usual course of law, in like manner as they
would have been between the under-tenants and the late incumbent, if
the sale had not taken place.

(4).—REGULATION VIII OF 1819 (PUTNEES, DURPUTNEES, &c.).

1st. Any talook or saleable tenure that may be disposed of at a
public sale, under the rules of this Regulation, for arrears of rent due on
account of it to the zemindar, is sold free of all incumbrances that may
have accrued upon it by act of the defaulting proprietor, his representatives, or assignees (unless the right of making such encumbrances shall
have been expressly vested in the holder by a stipulation to that effect on

APP. XVI.

SALE LAWS
IMPLIED
ADHERENCE
TO THE OLD
PERGUNNAH
RATE.

Para. 29, contd.

the written engagements under which the said talook may have been sold). No transfer by sale, gift, or otherwise, no mortgage or other limited assignment, shall be permitted to bar the indefeasible right of the zemindar to hold the tenure of his creation answerable, *in the state in which he created it*, for the rent, which is, in fact, his reserved property in the tenure (except the transfer or assignment should have been made with a condition to that effect, under express authority obtained from such zemindar).

2nd. In like manner, on sale of a talook for arrears, all leases originating with the holder of the former tenure, *or creative of a middle interest between the resident cultivators and the late proprietor*, must be considered to be cancelled, except the authority to grant them should have been specially transferred; the possessors of such interests must consequently lose the right to hold possession of the land, and to collect the rents of the ryots; this having been enjoyed merely in consequence of the defaulters' assignment *of a certain portion of his own interest the whole of which was liable for the rent.*

3rd. Provided, nevertheless, that nothing herein contained shall be construed to entitle the purchaser of a talook or other saleable tenure, intermediate between the zemindar and the actual cultivators, (1st) to eject a khoodkasht ryot, or resident and hereditary cultivator, (2nd) nor to cancel *bonâ fide* engagements made with such tenants by the late incumbent or his representative, except it be proved in a regular suit, to be brought by such purchaser, for the adjustment of his rent, that a higher rate would have been demandable at the time such engagements were contracted by his predecessor.

The import of the disjunctive " nor " is, that all resident cultivators who paid the full pergunnah rates were protected, and in addition, all similar cultivators who paid lower rates under such engagements entered into with the former proprietor as were in accordance with the law (para. 15 of this Appendix). In other words, the power of enhancing rents beyond the pergunnah rate was not recognised.

SALES OF LAND FOR ARREARS OF REVENUE.

(5).—REGULATION VII OF 1799.

Provided further, that whenever the land may have been sold to discharge an arrear of the public assessment upon such land, or upon the estate of which such land formed a part, no private claim thereto on the plea of sale, gift, or other transfer; or of pledge, mortgage, or other assignment; or any other private claim whatever, is to be admitted by any Court of justice in bar of the prior and indefeasible right of Government to hold the whole of the lands answerable in the first instance for the public revenue assessed thereupon, as immemorially known and acknowledged, and frequently declared in the regulations and otherwise.

(6).—REGULATION XI OF 1822, SECTION 30.

(*a*). In pursuance of the principle of holding the estate of a defaulter answerable for the punctual realisation of the Government revenue in the state in which it stood at the time the settlement was concluded (at

App. XVI.

SALE LAWS
IMPLIED
ADHERENCE
TO THE OLD
PERGUNNAH
RATE.

Para. 29, contd.

which time, by the dissolution of its previous engagements, Government must be considered to resume all rights possessed on the acquisition of the country, save where otherwise specially provided), all tenures which may have originated with the defaulter or his predecessors being representatives or assignees of the original engager, as well as all agreements with ryots or the like settled or credited by the first engager or his representatives, subsequently to the settlement, as well as all tenures which the first engager may, under the conditions of his settlement, have been competent to set aside, alter, or renew, shall be liable to be avoided and annulled by the purchaser of the estates, or mehal, at the sale for arrears due on account of it, subject only to such conditions of renewal as attached to the tenure at the time of settlement aforesaid, saving always and except *bonâ fide* leases of ground for the erection of dwelling houses or buildings, or for offices thereto belonging, &c.

III.—

(*a*). The sales of estates least injurious to sub-tenures are private sales; the purchaser, in these cases, acquiring the rights of merely the out-going proprietor. The negative form in which the rights of a purchaser of this class are stated is significant; he is restrained from raising the rents of those who may have entered into engagements with his predecessor, for the term of their engagements; there was no similar injunction against his raising the rents of other ryots who paid customary rates. The Legislature in 1793 to 1799 evidently took for granted that neither out-going zemindar nor incoming purchaser ever dreamt or could ever dream of enhancing these rates, and so raising the general pergunnah rates;—their power was limited to raising to the pergunnah rate, on expiration of temporary leases, any who held at favourable rates.

(*b*). Sub-tenures were injuriously affected most when an estate was sold by Government for arrears of revenue, or when a sub-tenure of later date than 1790 was sold at the instance of a zemindar for arrears of rent. In these cases the status of all the tenants on the estate, or within the sub-tenure, reverted to what it was at the date of the permanent settlement, as regards Government sales for arrears of revenue, or at the date of the creation of the sub-tenure by the zemindar, as regards sales, at his instance, for arrears of rent. In these latter cases the tenures annulled by the sale were (as explicitly stated) the middle interests between the zemindar, or his original creation of sub-tenancy, and the resident, cultivators. The resident cultivators themselves were protected from enhancement of rent. (II *b*, 4).

(*c*). (1). On the sale of an estate by Government for arrears of rent, all middle tenures (created since the decennial settle-

APP. XVI.

SALE LAWS
IMPLIED
ADHERENCE
TO THE OLD
PERGUNNAH
RATE.
___
Para. 29, contd.

ment) between the zemindar and the resident cultivator, were liable to be annulled, consequent on the estate reverting by the sale to its status in 1790. For ryots or cultivators, this reversion to the *status* of 1790 involved payment by them of the pergunnah rates, *plus abwabs, of that year*, unless any of them could prove a title, older than 1787, to pay a lower rate.

(2). The amount of the Government assessment on a permanently settled zemindary in 1878 is the same as it was in 1790; that assessment would therefore be amply secured if the ryots of such zemindary were to pay now the same pergunnah rate of rent as in 1790, and if all intermediate tenures between the zemindar and the resident cultivator, created since 1790, were to be annulled. Neither more nor less than this is involved in the theory that, for the security of the public revenue, all interests in an estate which is sold for arrears of revenue should revert to their *status* in 1790.

(3). There has indeed been a great increase of cultivation, and of cultivators who pay rent, in permanently settled zemindaries since 1790; but inasmuch as the Government assessment of that year is consequently recovered now from a much greater number of cultivators than in 1790, the increased cultivation negatives instead of strengthening the ryot's liability to pay more than the pergunnah rate of 1790, which sufficed to make up that assessment even when it was levied from a smaller area of cultivated land and from a smaller number of cultivators.

(4). Enhancement of the ryot's rent beyond the pergunnah rate of 1790, *plus abwabs* of that year, is repugnant therefore to the spirit and to the theory or principle of the Sale Laws of 1793 and 1799; and the letter of the laws harmonised with their spirit; what stood cancelled, or became liable to be annulled by the sale of an estate for arrears of revenue, were the *engagements entered into* by the zemindar, or his successors, since the settlement, with ryots, &c.; but we know that these written engagements were executed only when the ryots required favourable rates, *i.e.*, lower than the pergunnah rates; in the vast majority of cases in which ryots paid the pergunnah rates, they held without written engagements from the zemindar; moreover, the great body of the ryots, *viz.*, the khoodkashts, held independently of the zemindar, while they held without pottahs even until 1859, (Appendix XIX, para. 13, section III *a* 3). The Sale Laws which cancelled engagements since 1790, for specific rents

App. XVI.

THE UNEARNED
INCREMENT,
IS NOT THE
ZEMINDAR'S.

Para. 32.

lower than the pergunnah rate, did not affect the tenures of these resident cultivators who held at pergunnah rates.

(d). The different view of the Sale Laws which is accepted will be examined in the sequel; here it suffices to note, as the conclusions established in (a), (b), and (c), that the Sale Laws did not empower the zemindar to raise the rent of the ryots beyond the established pergunnah rate of 1790, and that any such enhancement was repugnant to the spirit, the principle, and the letter of those laws.

30. Thus, in the Regulations of 1793 and 1794 which form the deed of the permanent zemindary settlement, and even in later regulations the zemindar's power of enhancing ryot's rent beyond the established customary rate in 1790 was not recognised either in the Sale Laws or in any other of those regulations.

31. Before the permanent settlement, the right to the unearned increment belonged to Government: by that settlement, Government surrendered the right—not however to the zemindar, for it prohibited him from levying fresh *abwabs*, the only form in which the State had levied the increment in Bengal. Necessarily, the surrender was to the ryot; and need there was that it should be so left to him, as his only benefit from a permanent settlement which, in the words of its authors, was designed mainly for his welfare, "whose labours are the riches of the State," and for promoting cultivation by "securing to every man the fruits of his own industry." The ryot having done everything, the zemindar nothing, to improve and extend cultivation,—no more in equity, than under the Regulations of 1793, did the unearned increment belong to the zemindar.

32. Thus the Regulations of 1793 established a permanent rate of rent for the ryot; and this not inadvertently, but of set purpose—not as a new idea, but in accordance with the clear deliverance of Lord Cornwallis' predecessors in the government, in conformity with the explicit proposal of Sir Philip Francis, that, in the permanent settlement, the ryot's rent should be so fixed, and in harmony with the decision of the Court of Directors that the same security of permanency should be given to the ryot as to the zemindar. The spirit, intent, and express provisions of the Regulations of 1793, in this regard, were indeed defeated by the zemindars setting at nought the pottah regulation, and turning it into an engine of oppression. No man, however, is entitled to benefit by his own wrong; but for

APP. XVI.

THE UNEARNED
INCREMENT
IS NOT THE
ZEMINDAR'S.

Para. 32, contd.

that wrong the ryot's rent to this day would have remained permanently fixed at its amount in 1793; and in the degree that the rent is higher now than in 1793, by so much have the zemindars profited by their own wrong beyond the letter, spirit, and intent of the Regulations of 1793; so that, if further enhancement of ryots' rent were to be now prohibited, the ryot would secure but a small part of the justice and protection for which the faith and the honour of the nation were, in the words of the Court of Directors, as solemnly pledged to him as to the zemindar, in that perpetual settlement which, to this day, has left the ryot's rent unsettled,—though the secure enjoyment by the ryot of the fruits of his own industry was the beginning, the end, the key-note, of the arguments by which Lord Cornwallis justified the alienation of the State's revenue—not for the purpose of enriching the few, but for laying deep, in the well-being and happiness of the great body of cultivators, "the foundation of the prosperity of Bengal, and of the glory and honour of England!"

33. Given, what the Regulations of 1793 clearly imply, that the demand upon the ryot was permanently limited by the perpetual settlement, then the memory of Lord Cornwallis is rescued from the shame of his having by statute bestowed property on zemindars at the expense of millions of cultivating proprietors. The demand upon the ryot being permanently limited, the property then bestowed upon the zemindar was carved out of the Government's share in the produce of the soil, without legal power to the zemindar to encroach on the ryot's share. And from this it follows that the rights of ryots, which were thus reserved outside the Government and the zemindar's shares, were not, after the permanent settlement, derived from the zemindar.

34. Respecting the status of zemindars as proprietors of the soil, it may be noted as follows:—

I. By a custom dating from the origin and development of private property in land, the property in land in Bengal down to the permanent settlement, and later, belonged to the resident cultivators in the several villages, by a title which it was not competent for Government or for Parliament to annul without allowing a compensation which was never given (Appendix I).

II. The origin and various incidents of the zemindary tenure, down to the time of the permanent settlement, show that the zemindar's was an office the tenure of which did not constitute him proprietor of all the land in his zemindary (Appendix VI).

III. Some years before the permanent settlement, in 1789, the zemindar, who till then had been a mere superintendent of land and

APP. XVI.

———

ZEMINDAR A
PROPRIETOR OF
RENT, NOT OF
LAND.

———

Para 35.

collector of revenue, was styled landholder by the Government, in order thus to evade a jurisdiction over him which had been asserted by the Supreme Court, Calcutta- (Appendix VI, paras. 12 and 13).

35. The very limited sense in which the zemindar was proprietor of the soil, down to the time of the permanent settlement, is apparent also from the following extracts :—

I.—Select Committee of Secrecy, appointed by the House of Commons to inquire into the state of the East India Company in 1773.

(*a*). Your Committee having inspected the books and correspondence of the Company, and having examined Harry Verelst, Esquire, late President of Fort William in Bengal, who had been employed for several years in the collection of part of the said revenues, your Committee find that   *   *

(*b*). All the lands of the said provinces are considered as belonging to the *Crown*, or sovereign of the country, who claims a right to collect rents or revenues from all the said lands, except such as are appropriated to charitable and religious purposes; which, having been granted by different Princes, are understood, by the general tenor of such grants, to be exempted from payment of any rent to the sovereign.

Here the proprietary right spoken of was simply in the rent paid by the ryot, not in the soil; whether the land was held rent-free or not, the ryot paid all the same, in the one case to the State, in the other to the alienee of the State's share or rent.

(*c*). And Mr. Verelst informed your Committee that, by the ancient rule of Government, agreements with the ryots for lands, which they and their families have held, were considered as sacred, and that they were not to be removed from their possessions as long as they conformed to the terms of their original contracts; but that this rule had not always been duly observed.

(*d*). And your Committee having enquired whether the Raja, Zemindar, Farmer, or Collector, have a right to lay any duties, or augment the old ones by their own authority, they find that they have no such right,—though the books and correspondence of the Company afford many instances of the country having been exceedingly distressed by additional taxes levied by the Zemindar, Farmer, or Contractor, but not so much by the two former as by the latter. And Mr. Verelst informed your Committee that the Government *have a right to call upon them for everything so collected*, and that they have been called to an account, since the Company held the Dewannee, in several instances.

(*e*). Your Committee find that the *Rajas* and *Zemindars* have certain lands, perquisites, and allowances, which they hold in virtue of their *offices* for their support. And your Committee find that the *rents* arising from all the other lands of the said provinces, besides those held by grants in the manner above mentioned, are paid in such proportion as

27

APP. XVI.

ZEMINDAR A
PROPRIETOR OF
RENT, NOT OF
LAND.

Para. 35, contd.

is settled *annually* by the Dewan with the several zemindars, farmers, or collectors, who *rent* or hold the said lands.

(*f*). The Dewan collects the revenues by leasing them out to the Rajas or Zemindars, who are considered as having a *sort* of hereditary right, or at least a right of *preference* to the *lease* of the revenues of the province to which they respectively belong—or to other farmers under the name of izardars, and other appellations—or to officers appointed by Government, under the names of fouzdars, aumils, and tussildars, with all of whom the Government make, in general, annual engagements for the revenue of the several districts.

(*g*). And your Committee find by the correspondence of the Company, that the President and Council of Fort William are endeavouring to ascertain the amount of the Mofussil collections, or the revenues levied by the Raja, Zemindar, or Farmer, in the several districts of Bengal, in order to fix the profits of the said Raja, Zemindar, or Farmer at a stated and reasonable sum, to prevent in future undue charges in the collections, and to preserve the ryot from oppression by undue, additional, and arbitrary demands.

These extracts clearly assert that the State's property was in the rent recovered from the ryot, not in the soil, and that the zemindar was not entitled to collect more than this gross Government rent out of which, exclusively, his charges and remuneration were to be paid.

II.—Board of Revenue in Calcutta (*1786*).

J. Grant's
inquiry into the
nature of the
zemindary
tenure—App. I.

In conformity to an injunction of an Act of Parliament in 1784, and implied orders of the Court of Directors, the great question of zemindary pretensions to the property and inheritance of their territorial jurisdictions, was formally and deliberately agitated by the Board of Revenue in Calcutta, the members of which unanimously resolved, after the most mature consideration of sunnuds, records, practice, and local information, that the zemindars had neither proprietary nor heritable rights to the lands they held under the constitution of the Mogul Government; but that their tenures were merely temporary and official, in terms of their respective grants.

III.—Fifth Report, Select Committee (*1812*).

(*a*). In the progress and conclusion of this important transaction (the permanent zemindary settlement), the Government appeared willing to recognize the proprietary right of the zemindars in the land—not so much from any proof of the existence of such right, discernible in his relative situation under the Mogul Government in its best form, as from the desire of improving their condition under the British Government, as far as it might be done consistently with the permanency of the revenue and with the rights of the cultivators of the soil. The instructions from home had warned the Government against the danger of delusive theories; and the recent inquiries had disclosed a series of rights and privileges, and usages, admitted in the practice of the Native Govern-

ment, from the principal zemindar down to the actual labourer in hus- APP. XVI.
bandry, which it was necessary should be attended to before the ————
zemindar could be left to the uncontrolled management of his estate. PROPRIETOR OF
The *talukdar*, the *chowdry*, the *mundul*, the *mokuddum*, had each his RENT, NOT OF
distinct right admitted under the Native Government. LAND.

Para. 35, contd.

(*b*). The Court of Directors, in their reply (dated 29th September
1792) to the reference which was made to them on the progress of the
settlement, and to the proposal of rendering it perpetual, expressed
themselves in high terms of approbation of what had been done, and of
assent in regard to what was further proposed to be accomplished. They
seemed to consider a settlement of the rents in perpetuity, not as a claim
to which the landholders had any pretensions, founded on the principles
or practice of the Native Government, but a grace which it would be
good policy for the British Government to bestow upon them. In
regard to proprietary right to the land, the recent inquiries had not
established the zemindar on the footing of the owner of a landed estate in
Europe, who may lease out portions, and employ and dismiss labourers at
pleasure ; but, on the contrary, had exhibited from him down to the actual
cultivator, other inferior landholders, styled talukdars and cultivators of
different descriptions, whose claim to protection the Government readily
recognized, but whose rights were not, under the principles of the
present system, so easily reconcilable as to be at once susceptible of
reduction to the rules about to be established in perpetuity. These the
Directors particularly recommended to the consideration of the Government, who, in establishing permanent rules, were to leave an opening for
the introduction of any such in future as from time to time might be
found necessary to prevent the ryots being improperly disturbed in
their possessions, or subjected to unwarrantable exactions.

IV.—Sir John Shore (*June 1789*).

A property in the soil must not be understood to convey the same Para. 383.
rights in India as in England ; the difference is as great as between a
free constitution and arbitrary power. Nor are we to expect under a
despotic Government fixed principles, or clear definitions of the rights of
the subject; but the general practice of such a Government, when in
favour of its subjects, should be admitted as an acknowledgment of their
rights.

V.—Lord Cornwallis.

For His Lordship's opinion, that "a more nugatory
or delusive species of property could hardly exist" than the
zemindar's proprietary right, see Appendix VI, paragraph 6,
section VII; and yet, in the Regulations of 1793, he
styled the zemindars "proprietors of the soil." By this
Lord Cornwallis only meant that the zemindar was proprietor in that part of the Government's share of the produce
of the soil which the Government allowed him to keep.
This is evident from the curious perversion of views of pro-

APP. XVI.
———
ZEMINDAR A
PROPRIETOR OF
RENT, NOT OF
LAND.
———
Para. 35, contd.

prietary right which occurs in the following notice by his Lordship of the illegal levy of transit dues by zemindars :—

MINUTE (*18th September 1789*).

(*a*). As to the question of right, I cannot conceive that any Government in their senses would ever have delegated an authorised right to any of their subjects to impose arbitrary taxes on the internal commerce of the country. It certainly has been an abuse that has crept in, either through the negligence of the Mogul governors, who were careless or ignorant of all matters of trade, or, what is more probable, connivance of the Mussulamaun, who tolerated the extortion of the zemindar that he might again plunder him in his turn.

(*b*). But be that as it may, the right has been too long established or tolerated to allow a just Government to take it away without indemnifying the proprietor for any loss. And I never heard that in the most free State, if an individual possessed a right that was incompatible with the public welfare, the Legislature made any scruple of taking it from him, provided they gave him a fair equivalent. The case of the late Duke of Athol, who a few years ago parted very unwillingly with the sovereignty of the Isle of Man, appears to me to be exactly in point.

If his Lordship compensated zemindars for taking from them that to which they had no right, and which they held only by robbing the public, much more readily would he have compensated the millions of cultivating proprietors if by his zemindary settlement he had annulled their rights. Inasmuch as he did not compensate them, it follows that his Lordship did not by Regulation VIII of 1793 annul their rights.

36. Thus, down to the decennial settlement, the proprietary right of zemindars was of the weakest kind, and of mushroom growth, compared with the ancient custom of several centuries which sustained the rights of the cultivating proprietors. Lord Cornwallis and Sir John Shore, however, had set up a theory, that the alleged large proportion of the produce of the soil, which, under native rule, was appropriated as the Government's share, left to the ryot no real property in the soil; though Sir John Shore had himself pointed out, what was of course known to the native rule, that the seemingly heavy rate of assessment on the khoodkasht ryot was lightened to him by his concealed cultivation of other land for which he paid no rent. From this assumption they deduced that the real property in the soil was represented by the Government's share; and, in dividing it with the zemindar, they styled him, in virtue of his share, proprietor of the soil. In accordance with this theory, the Regulations of 1793 restricted

the term "actual proprietors of the soil" to those, whether
zemindars, independent talukdars, or other actual proprietors
of the soil (chowdries), who paid revenue direct to Government,
that is, paid the gross Government share of the produce of
the soil, as recovered from the ryots, less their own shares.

37. That this property in the soil (in a technical sense
only) was a new creation of the Government, is evident from
the language in Regulation II, 1793, *viz.* :—

(*a*). The property in the soil has been declared to be vested in the
landholders.   *   *   The property in the soil was never before formally
declared to be vested in the landholders :—

compared with the language in Regulation VIII of 1819,
when the similar proprietary right of putnee talookdars was
recognised for the first time ;—

(*b*). The right of alienation having been declared to vest in the holder
of a putnee talook, &c.

38. The suitableness of the fiction by which the payers
of land revenue into the Government treasury were declared
proprietors of the soil, is apparent from Appendix XVII, para.
14; and the reasons for it may be gathered from paragraphs
34 to 36 of this Appendix, while an additional reason is stated
in Sir John Shore's minute dated June 1789. In the 383rd
paragraph he affirmed, as we have seen, that "a property in
the soil must not be understood to convey the same rights in
India as in England." Yet a few minutes later, in his
389th paragraph, he added—"If we admit the property of
the soil to be solely *vested* in the zemindars, we must exclude
any acknowledgment of such rights in favour of the ryots,
except where they may acquire it from the zemindar."
Sir John Shore was, doubtless, familiar with the fictions by
which English law represented rights of property in land,
more or less limited, or the conveyance or transfer of such
rights ; and it was part of his plan that the same permanency of assessment which the Government bestowed on the
zemindar should be secured to the ryot, through a record of
his right in a pottah which the zemindar, a proprietor in a
very limited sense, was to be *compelled* to grant to the ryot,
in terms which would leave with the ryot the whole produce
of the soil, except the Government's permanently limited
gross share of that produce as determined by ancient custom.
Only in this way is the glaring inconsistency between Sir John
Shore's 383rd and 389th paragraphs intelligible : without this
explanation, that inconsistency—the logic with which he
coldly reasoned away proprietary rights, based on the custom

APP. XVI.

ZEMINDAR A
PROPRIETOR OF
RENT, NOT OF
LAND.

Para. 38, contd. of centuries, such as law has always held sacred, in favour of rights created by the breath of Government—would betray a levity in dealing with the proprietary rights of millions, who could not make themselves heard in the Council Chamber, such as would dishonour his memory.

39. Yet English lawyers, saturated with fictions of the English law of real property, but imbued, nevertheless, with its reverence for rights founded on custom, have, from this one patent legal fiction in the Regulations of 1793, gravely reasoned away the only real proprietary rights existent in Bengal before the decennial settlement, which are traceable to the common source where all countries in Europe and Asia find the origin of the rights of private property in land.

40. Referring, however, to paragraphs 35 to 38 in this Appendix, it may be affirmed, with due deference to those able lawyers, that the right of property which the Government of 1793 vested in the zemindars by the Regulations of that year, was the right simply in a portion of the Government's limited gross share in the produce of the soil, which was claimable only under such conditions of established custom as left intact and permanent the ryot's portion or share of that produce, and as left with him the whole of the unearned increment in Bengal, where specific money rents prevailed in 1793, and a portion of that increment in Behar, where the rents in 1793 were ascertained by yearly division of the produce, and where the condition of the ryots to this day is wretched in the extreme.

41. If the zemindar understands his true interest, he will insist on this interpretation of his limited proprietary right in Government's strictly limited gross share of the produce of the soil;—so limited, the zemindar's interest has a certain great assurance of permanency. If, however, forgetful that what a breath of the legislature has made, a breath of the legislature can unmake, he stretch farther the interpretation of his mere statutory right, so as to hold that the Regulations of 1793 destroyed, in favour of his worthless miscreant predecessors, the ancient customary rights of millions of cultivating proprietors, whose labours constitute, in the words of the authors of the permanent settlement, the riches of the State, he will turn the Regulations of 1793 into a mystery of iniquity, which must continue to bear evil fruit,—to keep the land in unrest,—the conscience of English rulers unquiet,—and their subject millions in a constant tendency to deteriorate

APP. XVI.

REGULATION
XLIV OF 1793
DID NOT VITIATE
RYOT'S TITLE.

Para. 42.

towards cottierism, through a growth of population, a consequent increase of competitive rents, and the baneful influence
of a landed system under which the so-called proprietors of land
appropriate the unearned increment, while they divest themselves of the duties of property, and of the burden of supporting the unemployed poor, which proprietors of land,
especially, should bear.

42. Regulation XLIV of 1793 must be noticed. With the
view of preventing zemindars from granting leases or pottahs
at a reduced rent, for a long term or in perpetuity, it restricted them (until the issue of Regulation V of 1812, section II) from granting either lease or pottah, but did not
debar them from letting waste land for a short term,
at a low but progressive rent, according to the custom of
the country (para. 13, section c), for a period exceeding
ten years. This regulation was directed against the under-
mentioned practices of the zemindars, but, as usual, it was
turned to their advantage, and to the destruction of ryots'
rights.

I. At the time of the permanent settlement, one-third
of the cultivable land was waste. Those zemindars who understood the position attracted ryots from other zemindaries by
low rents, increasing thereby their income without paying
additional revenue. But the zemindars whose ryots were
thus enticed away suffered, and their loss was great in the
degree that too many of them had exacted oppressive rents.
Necessarily, many became defaulters, and their zemindaries
were sold. This explains a large proportion of the sales for
arrears of revenue which occurred after the permanent
settlement.

II. When the permanent settlement was proclaimed,
the intention to resume invalid rent-free tenures was also
declared. Many of these had been created in favour of Brahmins; and on their creation being interdicted, perpetual
leases to Brahmins on low rents were, doubtless, substituted
from "ignorance or from other causes or motives," as stated
in the regulation.

III. Through the permanent limitation of the Government demand, and the gift of waste lands, zemindaries
improved in value. Some zemindars, "from improvidence, or
with a view to raise money," let parts of their estates at low
rents for present payment of a *bonus*, thus selling the unearned increment, as is now done—but only at current rates
of rent in the present day.

App. XVI.

Regulation
XLIV of 1793
did not vitiate
ryot's title.

Para. 43.

43. The recollection of the first two practices, which endangered the permanent settlement, was yet fresh in the minds of the authorities.　Thus—

I.—Sir J. Shore, *Fifth Report* (*June 1789*).

Lastly, the detection and resumption of alienated lands, particularly such as are possessed by Brahmins and others, who have obtained them in charity, are operations attended with great difficulty and peculiar embarrassment to the Government and its officers, and such as are not easily surmounted.　*　*　The Mahomedan Government certainly tolerated these alienations, though not perhaps to the extent to which they have now arisen (paras. 118 and 119).

II.—President and Select Committee (*16th August 1769*).

Colebrooke's
Digest, page 182.

(*a*). The increase in the number of taluks has been highly impolitic and detrimental to the general prosperity, and to the diffusion of population in the country.　The tenants of a taluk are possessed of so many indulgences, and taxed with such evident partiality and tenderness in proportion to the rest, that the taluks generally swarm with inhabitants, whilst other parts are deserted; and, in addition to the natural desire of changing from a worse to the better situation, enticements are frequently employed by the talukdars to augment the concourse to their lands.　*　*

Ibid., page 183.

(*b*). As the unequal diffusion of inhabitants has been the cause of this scarcity of cultivation in different parts, every expedient should be used to encourage people to settle on the comar and waste lands, that they may be converted into ryoty.　The great towns, whose populousness only serves to propagate poverty and idleness, might undoubtedly afford numbers of useful hands, who in their present situations are either a burthen or a pest to a community.　These should be sought out and taught to apply to culture, setting such prospects and expectations in their view as will engage their consent.　The taluks and jagirs will likewise be found to contain many idle and unserviceable hands, who may, in like manner, be induced to transplant themselves into these lands, and become farmers.

III.—Governor-General in Council, Revenue Department (*31st May 1782*).

Ibid., page 225.

That this practice of alienating lands affects the revenue of Government, is evident, first, by the actual alienation of the rents of lands included in the general rental; and secondly, by lessening the value of the revenue lands.　This is effected by withdrawing the ryots from the revenue lands and inducing them to settle on the bazee zemin, which the proprietors can afford to rent to them on easier terms than a farmer or zemindar, who pays an assessment for the lands held by him.　The consequences of this practice, if no restraint be imposed, will annually become more important.　To this it has been owing that the assets of a district, on forming the hustabood of it, have been found unequal to the revenue demanded by the Government.

IV.—BOARD OF COMMISSIONERS (*13th April 1808*).

APP. XVI.

REGULATION
XLIV OF 1793
DID NOT VITIATE
RYOT'S TITLE.

Para. 45.

East India
Revenue
Selections,
Vol. I, page 9.

(*a*). Had circumstances, however, appeared to us to admit of the settlement being declared . permanent, we should have insisted upon the adoption of a russud (progressive) jumma in those estates which are capable of great improvement; for otherwise the assessment in a few years would have become altogether unequal. The proprietors of estates containing much uncultivated land would have possessed the means of ruining their neighbours, whose estates were fully assessed, by inducing the ryots to quit such estates, for the purpose of undertaking the cultivation of waste lands at a low rent; and the public revenue would, in consequence, become less secure in particular instances (para. 24).

(*b*). The population being unequal to the entire cultivation of the lands, and the different estates possessing very different capacities, it would follow that the proprietors of estates lightly assessed, *or of estates containing much waste land*, would have the means of drawing away the ryots from estates fully assessed; and the public revenue assessed on the latter might not only become precarious in consequence, but the original injustice of an unequal assessment would be aggravated, to the ruin, perhaps, ultimately, of particular individuals (para. 219).

44. Lord Cornwallis violated the "law and constitution of India," by giving away waste lands to zemindars (Appendix XV). It was soon perceived, however, that the gift endangered the permanent settlement by stimulating zemindars to attract neighbours' ryots to the waste lands on their own estates; but as one wrong generates another, the authorities persevered in the original error, and restrained zemindars from issuing pottahs for more than ten years. Offending zemindars provoked this enactment; but such are the cross-purposes between legislators and lawyers, or such the devil's luck of zemindars, that Sir Barnes Peacock only saw in Regulation XLIV of 1793 that it magnified culprit zemindars and destroyed the rights of the ryots. It did no such thing. (See para. 13, *c*.)

45. The capital error was mitigated, not corrected, by Regulation IV of 1794, which directed the renewal of the ten years' pottahs at the established rates of the pergunnah for lands of the same quality and description. This tinkering in 1794 of regulations of a *permanent* settlement of 1793 was lamentable. No doubt all are liable to err; but a sense of this fallibility should at least prevent a wicked daring presumption, if we had the power, of declaring perpetual any act of our fallible judgment which affects myriads. Is there such sacredness in an error which has doomed millions to misery, that, in defiance of God, who commandeth us to do right, the hasty, erring declaration and acts of a rash presumption, which could not keep in the same mind for even two years, shall remain unalterable for ever?

App. XVI.

ZEMINDAR'S
STATUS, AS
UNDERSTOOD IN
THE GREAT
RENT CASE.

Para. 46.

46. In the great Rent Case, the *status* of the zemindars under the Regulations of 1793 was discussed by the Full Bench of the High Court. Mr. Justice Trevor's description of that status included, substantially, nearly all that the other judges said on the subject; his description, and certain other features of that status, noticed by some other judges, are as follows :—

I. MR. JUSTICE TREVOR—" Though recognised as actual proprietors of the soil, that is, owners of their estates, still zemindars and others entitled to a settlement were not recognised as being possessed of an absolute estate in their several zemindaries; there are other parties below them with rights and interests in the land requiring protection, just in the same way as the Government above them was declared to have a right and interest in it which it took care to protect by law; that the zemindar enjoys his estate subject to, and limited by, those rights and interests; and that the notion of an absolute estate in land is as alien from the regulation law as it is from the old Hindu and Mahomedan law of the country."

II. MR. JUSTICE CAMPBELL treats it " as clearly established that, by the terms of the permanent settlement, the zemindars were not made absolute and sole owners of the soil, but that there were only transferred to them all the rights of Government, *viz.*, the right to a certain proportion of the produce of every beegah held by the ryots, together with the right to profit by future increase of cultivation and the cultivation of more valuable articles of produce; it being further established that the khoodkasht or resident ryots retained a right of occupancy in the soil, subject only to the right of the zemindars to the certain proportion of the produce represented by the pergunnah or district rates."

III. MR. JUSTICE NORMAN—" These processes appear to me to show that, although the zemindars were by the regulations constituted owners of the land, such ownership was not absolute. The regulations which create a right of property in the zemindars do not recognise any absolute right in them to fix the rents of the land at their own discretion."

IV. MR. JUSTICE PHEAR—" I may say that, in my conception of the matter, the relation between the zemindar's right and the occupancy ryot's right is pretty much the same as that which obtains between the right of ownership of land in England and the servitude or easement which is termed *profit á prendre*; although I need hardly say the ryot's interest is greatly more extensive than a *profit á prendre*. It appears to me that the ryot's is the dominant, and the zemindar's the servient, right. Whatever the ryot has, the zemindar has all the rest which is necessary to complete ownership of the land : the zemindar's right amounts to the complete ownership of the land subject to the occupancy ryot's right; and the right of the village, if any, to the occupation and cultivation of the soil, to whatever extent these rights may in any given case reach. When these rights are ascertained, there must remain to the zemindar all rights and privileges of ownership which are not inconsistent with or obstructive of them. And, amongst other rights, it seems to me clear that he must have such a right as will enable him to keep the possession of the soil in those persons who are entitled to it, and to prevent it from being invaded by those who are not entitled to it."

The ryot's being the dominant right, the zemindar's is a limited interest, and the ryot has all the rest—see appendix XVII, para. 9.

V. MR. PHILLIPS (summed up on the same side of the question as follows) :—

(*a*). An opinion long prevailed that the Government had given the zemindar the property in the soil, and had rendered the ryot absolutely dependent upon him, except in so far as the ryot was protected by express legislation. On the other hand, some considered that the permanent settlement was not intended to convey such property in the soil, or to interfere with subordinate rights. Page 312.

(*b*). In the great Rent Case which was decided in 1865, the majority of the judges appear to have held the view that the right of the zemindar was not an absolute right to the soil, as against the subordinate holders; but that in that direction the rights of the zemindar were limited by the rights of those subordinate holders.

(*c*). And the cases now seem to have decided that a settlement with a person under the Bengal system does not establish in the person settled with a right to the land, if he did not already possess it; but that a settlement is an arrangement made by that person with the Government with respect to the revenue only. This, indeed, appears from the regulations themselves, which, while directing in the regulations for the decennial settlement that the settlement should be with the 'actual proprietors,' recognises that the actual possessor, and the person therefore actually settled with, may not be the proprietor; and that, consequently, the fact of settlement with a person under the regulations does not conclude the question of proprietorship, as between that person and the true proprietor. * * Page 316.

(*d*). It is remarked by Sir Henry Maine that the distinction between proprietary rights and rights which are not proprietary is, that the latter have their origin in a contract[1] of some kind with the holder of the former. We have seen that Lord Cornwallis was under the impression that the rights of the ryots might be treated in this way; but the regulations themselves save the rights of the ryots as they actually existed; and it is now the opinion of most authorities on the subject that the actual rights of the ryots were proprietary rights. They were not derived from, or carved out of, an original theoretically complete proprietary right of the zemindar, in the way that all interests in land in England are theoretically derived from, or carved out of, the fee-simple. As, therefore, the term 'actual proprietors' does not mean what might be supposed *primá facie*, but something less, and considering the way in which it is used in a mere enumeration of the persons to be settled with, and unaccompanied by any declaration in the regulations or proceedings relative to the decennial settlement of an intention to confer Page 318.

---

[1] *e. g.*, zemindars, not being proprietors, derived their right from a contract with the Government for the land revenue outside the ryots' share of the produce.

APP. XVI.

ZEMINDAR'S
STATUS, AS
UNDERSTOOD IN
THE GREAT
RENT CASE.

Para. 46, contd.
any proprietary right upon the zemindars which they did not otherwise possess, save the exemption from alterations in the assessment,
it seems to me, with the utmost submission to the authorities which
have been referred to, that there is no necessity of enlarging the
meaning of the term, beyond the actual proprietary right which did
exist, especially when, as we have seen, the terms used do not mean that
every person actually settled with is an actual proprietor in any sense
except that of being actual possessor.   It is further to be observed that,
in the proclamation of the permanent settlement, at a time when the
rights of the actual proprietors were put as high as they could be put,
the language used is somewhat different from that in the regulations
for the decennial settlement.   In these latter, the settlement was to be
made "with the actual proprietors of the soil, of whatever denomination,
whether zemindars, talukdars, or chowdries;" whereas, in the proclamation of the permanent settlement, the enumeration omits chowdries, and
inverts the order of the sentence, which runs, "all zemindars, independent
"talukdars, and other actual proprietors," thus abstaining from any
definition of the rights of the zemindars, &c., and reducing, according to
the ordinary rules of construction, the other "actual proprietors" to
persons in a similar position to that of the zemindars, whatever that was.

Page 319.
(e).   The result seems to be that, even if the zemindars were thought
to be absolute proprietors, they are not declared to be so, but the contrary; and that the term "actual proprietors of the soil" does not
mean absolute proprietors of the soil, as against the ryots; and that,
consequently, as the Government do not declare any intention of giving
up to the zemindars anything but the right to alter the assessment,
there is nothing to show that the terms used are meant to render the
zemindars absolute proprietors, as regards the Government, except in the
matter of permanency of revenue.   They were to take the Government
share[1] of the produce as their own, yielding a fixed assessment to the
Government in exchange; but, as I venture to submit, no other alteration was made in their position by the permanent settlement.

(f).   Of course a great practical change was made, because the rights
of the zemindars were recognised and secured, while those of the ryots
were left to take care of themselves; moreover, the zemindar, having
acquired the Government right in the revenue in perpetuity, was in an
advantageous position for absorbing all other rights.

47. On the other side of the question Sir Barnes Peacock
held that, under the permanent settlement, the zemindar
became proprietor of the soil, whilst the status of the ryot since
that settlement has depended upon contract.   The arguments
upon which Sir Barnes Peacock relied as proving that
the zemindar was proprietor, were the following:—

I. The property in the soil was never, before 1793, formally declared
to be vested in the landholders, *nor were they allowed to transfer such
rights as they did possess, or raise money upon the credit of their tenures,
without the previous sanction of Government.*

---

[1] *i. e.*, Government share, as limited by Lord Cornwallis.

Thus, until 1793, the zemindars clearly were not proprietors of the soil; and under the law and constitution of India,
which Parliament had enjoined should be observed in settling
the rights of all concerned, the State was not the proprietor
(Appendix V); it follows that the ryots were proprietors of
the land until 1793, and they were so under a custom more
ancient than law. It was not within Sir Barnes Peacock's
knowledge that, outside Ireland, millions of proprietors, with
rights consecrated by ancient custom, were ever disestablished
by statute in favour of other proprietors created by statute.

II. The State (which was not proprietor of the soil) did, in 1793,
declare the zemindars to be proprietors; because it was intended that
thereby they would effect improvements in agriculture, and provide
against famine by constructing embankments and irrigation works.

If the statutory right of the zemindar was created with
this object, then another statute should now annul it;
because every improvement in agriculture in Bengal has
been effected by ryots and European planters;—the zemindars
have done nothing; nor have they done anything to avert
famine: on the contrary, over a great part of Bengal and in
Behar they keep the ryots on the verge of famine by rack-
rents, insomuch that the poverty of the ryots in Behar and
Orissa greatly aggravated the pressure in those provinces of
the famines in 1866 and 1874. The many millions sterling
expended by Government during the famine of 1874 were
provided at the expense of the tax-payers in British India.

III. The following passage in the proclamation of the permanent
settlement declares the zemindars' title:—" The Governor General in
Council trusts that the proprietors of land, sensible of the benefits conferred upon them by the public assessment being fixed for ever, will exert
themselves in the cultivation of their lands, under the certainty that
they will enjoy exclusively the fruits of their own good management
and industry, and that no demand will ever be made upon them or their
heirs or successors for an augmentation of the public assessment in consequence of the improvement of their respective estates.

The zemindars, as stated by Sir Barnes Peacock, were not
proprietors of the land up to 1793; millions of ryots were.
The breath of Lord Cornwallis could not unmake these
millions, or destroy the custom, more ancient than law,
under which they transmitted their rights to their descendants,
and under which those descendants were continually acquiring
independent rights in the soil by cultivating waste, subject,
merely, to payment of the established pergunnah rate, which
pergunnah rate of rent was all the property in the waste
that the State had assigned to the zemindar (Appendix XV,

App. XVI.
ZEMINDAR'S
STATUS, AS
UNDERSTOOD IN
THE GREAT RENT
CASE.

Para. 47, contd.

paras. 5 and 7). Moreover, Lord Cornwallis spoke of the good management and industry of his proprietors of mushroom growth in the same breath in which he declared the legal fiction of their status as proprietors. Their good management, as a body, consisted in rack-renting ryots, and forcing on them the sweets of Huftum and Punjum;—their industry, in doing nothing, but letting the ryots do everything. ' As Lord Cornwallis' substantial reward for ideal qualities of ideal zemindars, the actual zemindars enjoy exclusively, and the ryots not at all, the fruits of the ryots' industry in Behar, and over a great part of Bengal and Orissa; though the faith of the State and of the nation was as solemnly pledged to the ryot as to the zemindar, that he should undisturbedly enjoy his dominant right in the fruits of those labours which, said the authors of the permanent settlement, are the riches of the State, in like manner as their predecessors in the Government only twenty years previously had said that "it ought to be remembered" (not a great effort for the memory of even a weak benevolence) "that the welfare and good of the whole was never intended to be sacrificed to the enriching of a few, perhaps worthless, individuals, who can show no pretence to these peculiar advantages, but a prostitution of their integrity to their avarice."

IV. The position that "the rights of those ryots, at least, whose tenures commenced since the date of the permanent settlement, depend not upon status but upon contract, and upon the laws and regulations which have been specifically enacted," Sir Barnes Peacock supported as follows :—

(a). Sections 54 and 55 of Regulation VIII of 1793 having stated that the zemindars and ryots should agree in concert respecting the amount of existing rents and *abwabs* which should be entered in a consolidated sum in pottahs which the zemindars were ordered to grant to the ryots, which consolidated sum was not to be augmented thereafter by fresh *abwabs*, the following provisions occur in sections 56, 57, and 60 :—

(b).—*Section 56 (quoted in full, in paragraph 12, section a).*

Where it is the established custom to vary the pottahs for lands, according to the produce, all particulars are to be specified ; and in the event of the species of produce being changed, *a new engagement shall be executed for the remaining term of the fresh lease, or for a longer term, if agreed on.* Further, it is expected that, *in time,* proprietors and ryots will find it for their mutual advantage to *enter into agreements in every instance* for a specific sum for a certain quantity of land, irrespective of produce.

This simply meant that every time the produce was varied, the ancient established rate for the new produce should

App. XVI.

———

ZEMINDAR'S
STATUS, AS
UNDERSTOOD IN
THE GREAT RENT
CASE.

———

Para. 47, contd.

be ascertained in concert, and be entered in a fresh pottah, and that, in time, zemindar and ryot might possibly agree at their option to strike an average of the ancient established rates for the several kinds of produce, for insertion in a pottah as the rate to be levied irrespectively of the kind of produce. The matter was not one of bargain or contract, for the established pergunnah rate limited the demand and the payment : what section 56 required was that, by arithmetic and other enquiry, the zemindar and ryot should agree respecting the amount that was to be entered in the pottah as the record of what the ryot had to pay in accordance with established custom, see para.

(c).—*Section 57 (quoted in para. 12, section b).*

The rents to be paid by the ryots, by whatever rule or custom they may be regulated, shall be specifically stated in the pottah.

Here, again, bargaining or contract was not contemplated; but simply a record of what the ryot had to pay in accordance with established custom.

(d).—*Section 60 (quoted in para. 12, section c).*

Conditionally protected leases to under-farmers and ryots, *made previous to the conclusion of the settlement,* and conditionally restrained zemindars from cancelling the pottahs of the khoodkasht ryots.

This, too, was not matter for contract or bargaining. The zemindars were restrained from levying, from any ryots old or new, more than the established pergunnah rate; but they were empowered to raise to that rate any who claimed to be assessed at a more favourable rate, but could not prove their title.

Sir Barnes Peacock continued :—

V. Regulation XLIV of 1793, section 2, restrained zemindars from granting pottahs to ryots for the cultivation of land for a term exceeding ten years, as a cheek upon a practice which had prevailed of granting such pottahs for a long term or in perpetuity at a fixed rent. This law remained in force until 1812; and therefore in the interval zemindars were not competent to create permanent sub-tenures.

It is shown in para. 42 that Regulation XLIV of 1793 was directed against malpractices of zemindars ; and that, as regards rent (the only matter for contracts between landlord and tenant in other countries), the Regulation restrained the zemindar from letting at less, and from demanding more than the established rate of the pergunnah. It further required him to renew leases at that established rate. The

APP. XVI.

ZEMINDAR'S
STATUS, AS
UNDERSTOOD IN
THE GREAT RENT
CASE.

Para. 47, contd.

elements of contract, and scope for it, were shut out; the Regulation XLIV of 1793 did not trench upon customary rights of the ryots; it simply provided that the record of what the ryot had to pay, conformably with those rights, should be a valid record for not more than ten years; after that period the rent which he had to pay, in accordance with established rates of the pergunnah, would be entered in a fresh record, thus providing (in an awkward, blundering way as regards the mass of ryots) for the comparatively few ryots, who, in the course of time, would be taking up waste land at low rates, rising progressively to the pergunnah rate. Accordingly, if there was room for the growth among the cultivating class of permanent rights of occupancy at the ancient established rates, independently of Regulation XLIV of 1793, nothing in that regulation interfered with such growth of custom.

48. Sir Barnes Peacock misapprehended the true character of the pottah, and that error vitiated his reasoning. It was a record, as to amount of rent, of rights which the ryots possessed independently of the pottah, and this, its character, even if not otherwise demonstrable (see, however, paras. 3, 4 and 9 sec. III), was evident from the power given to the ryot by the regulations to compel the zemindar, by a civil suit, to issue a pottah in accordance with the established rate of the pergunnah. As the pottah spoken of in the Regulations of 1793 was not a lease in the ordinary English sense, the rights of ryots were not derived through it from the zemindars. As the pottah was constituted by the Deed of the Permanent Settlement, a record of then existent ryot's rights, the rights necessarily existed outside the pottah, and independently of the zemindar.

49. Down to 1793, at any rate, the ryot's right to the land which he cultivated was determined, not by a pottah, but by (1st) the record, in the cutcherry of the village or pergunnah, of the ancient established rate of rent for land in that locality; (2nd) the payment of that rate by the ryot. The Regulations of 1793 recognised this custom by the provision in them for continuing the office of those Putwarries of whom Mr. Rocke, Member of the Board of Revenue, wrote in 1815 :—

" The Putwarries were, in fact, the depositaries of the local usages of the country, from whom it was always easy for the Revenue Officers of Government to collect correct information regarding the individual rights of the ryots, in cases of disputes between them and the zemindars or

App. XVI.

——

ZEMINDAR'S
STATUS, AS
UNDERSTOOD IN
THE GREAT
RENT CASE.

Para. 49, contd.

farmers. They were then considered the immediate servants of Government; but now, being dependent on the proprietors of the soil, the nature and intention of their original institution are naturally altered, and instead of being the protectors and guardians of the rights and privileges of the cultivators of the soil, they are become the zealous and interested partisans of the new proprietors. Of course little information can now be derived from that source, calculated to secure the ryots from the gripe of their new masters.

These two conditions being sufficient, namely, the village record of the ryot's pergunnah rate and his payments at that rate, the resident ryot held without any pottah from the zemindar; and so rooted was this custom in the traditions and feeling of the people, that the British Indian Association testified so late as 1859, that the great body of the ryots held, even in that day, without pottahs.

50. Of the two conditions which, as just stated, determined the ryot's title to the land which he occupied and cultivated, the established local rate of the pergunnah was the dominant or ruling, and, practically, the only real condition. Now (a) that local rate, as we have seen, was only confirmed and perpetuated by the Regulations of 1793 (paragraphs 24 and 25). Accordingly, (b) the charter of the ryot's rights was upheld, not destroyed, by the permanent settlement. We have also seen (paragraphs 36 to 40) that (c) the proprietorship vested in the zemindar was in merely a part of the Government's share of the produce of the soil; and that (d) the residents in a village were not disestablished, by the Regulations of 1793, from their right of cultivating waste lands in their village, subject only to payment of the established pergunnah rate for such lands, inasmuch as property in that rate only, and not in the waste lands, was made over to the zemindars (Appendix XV, paragraph 9). It follows that the ancient custom which had been handed down through centuries, under which hereditary rights of permanent occupancy, subject only to the payment of the established local rate, were being continually created through the cultivation of waste land in each village by its inhabitants, was not interrupted by the Regulations of 1793; but when we arrive at this conclusion, the foundation and the fabric of Sir Barnes Peacock's reasoning are destroyed.

51. Mr. Phillips adds, on the zemindar's side of the question—

Sir Barnes Peacock did not agree with the actual decision in this case, and seems to consider a greater right to belong to the zemindar. And a recent writer (Mr. Justice Phear in the *Calcutta Review* for 1874)

APP. XVI.

ZEMINDAR'S
STATUS, AS
UNDERSTOOD IN
THE GREAT
RENT CASE.

Para. 51, contd.

appears to consider that the zemindars have acquired larger rights than I have attributed to them. He says:—"A very important change was brought about by the legislation of 1793. The legislature then, for the first time, declared that the property in the soil was vested in the zemindars, and that they might alien or burden that property at their pleasure without the previously obtained sanction of Government; and the moment this declaration was made, obviously all subordinate tenures and holdings of whatever sort became also personal proprietary rights in the land, of greater or lesser degree, possessing each within itself also in greater or lesser degree powers of multiplication. When the zemindar's right had become in a certain sense an absolute right to the soil—not exclusive, because the legislature at the same time recognized rights on the side of the ryot—with complete powers of alienation, the rights of all subordinate holders were necessarily derivative therefrom, and enforcement of them immediately fell within the province of the public courts of justice."

52. The fallacies in these assumptions, that the ryot's became a derivative right from the zemindar's under the permanent settlement, and that any greater property in the soil than a portion of the Government's limited share of the produce became vested in the zemindar, have been indicated in the remarks on Sir Barnes Peacock's argument. But the absurd conclusions to which these assumptions lead may be indicated.

I. On 12th August 1765 the East India Company succeeded to the dewany of Bengal, Behar, and Orissa; on 28th August 1771 they "stood forth" as dewan; on 22nd March 1793 the permanent settlement took effect; up to 1765 the zemindars were not proprietors of the soil; millions of cultivators had a right of property in the land. No incidents of the acquisition of the dewany by the Company had entailed on the cultivators a confiscation of rights such as even conquest does not involve; on the contrary, the Company's Government during 1765 to 1793 laboured to assure the ryots of protection from tyranny and wrong; yet it is gravely averred that the legislators of 1793, without compensating the ryots for the destruction of their proprietary rights, swept away the verities which had sustained those rights, and substituted for them, in zemindars misbegotten of Lord Cornwallis' benevolence, John Does and Richard Roes through whom, as so-styled proprietors of the soil, the ryots were to derive their rights in despite (during more than two succeeding generations) of violence, perjury, and fraud, and with such help as the poor creatures could get from Stamp Acts and from the weakness, corruption, and inefficiency, for long, of the police and the civil courts. Great is the power of the law, but never before or since 1793 was it known that the proprietary rights

App. XVI.
———
ZEMINDAR'S
STATUS, AS
UNDERSTOOD IN
THE GREAT
RENT CASE.
———
Para. 51, contd.

of millions "obviously" ceased under a mere inference from a declaration (by those who had no power to confiscate) that a comparatively few rapacious officials were by a legal fiction proprietors of the land which was then held by millions of cultivators in right of a custom more ancient than law.

II. If a breath could thus make the zemindars proprietors without compensating the ryots, a breath can unmake them without compensating the zemindars. The rights of the millions of cultivating proprietors had been hallowed by the prescription of centuries; Lord Cornwallis' zemindars cannot plead the prescription of even a century. The offices in virtue of which they were declared proprietors in 1793 are now held by European officials who represent the rulers of Bengal,—more truly than ever did the zemindars,—in race, religion, education, character, and the feelings and instincts which make the English landed gentry as a class considerate to tenants and merciful to the poor. All the considerations which were put forth as justifying the wisdom and benevolence of Lord Cornwallis' settlement with zemindars, would justify a new proclamation declaring that the European officers of Government are the proprietors of the soil. The Government's word would, indeed, be broken to the zemindars of 1793 and their successors; but surely it was a bigger, blacker, more wicked lie, by far, to dispossess millions of proprietors by falsely proclaiming the zemindars as proprietors of the soil, in the sense in which Mr. Justice Phear understood the declaration, than it would be to now put forth as proprietors, European gentlemen who would leave the substantial fruits of property in larger measure with the cultivators of the soil. Truth, right, and humanity would be better attained thus, by reversing or unsaying the first fiction. We know, however, that these uncouth phrases, this absurd conclusion, are grossly misapplied to any work of the authors of the permanent settlement; and, accordingly, the declaration of Lord Cornwallis, that the zemindars were the proprietors of the soil, was obviously a mere legal fiction, which had a narrower meaning than Mr. Justice Phear attached to it.

53. The Regulations of 1793 show that the property vested in the zemindars was property in the Government's limited share of the produce, and those regulations, together with the minutes of Lord Cornwallis and Sir John Shore, show that the pottah which the ryot was empowered to demand from the zemindar, even by a civil suit, was designed as a record of the ryot's right. It has also appeared from the

App. XVI.

ZEMINDAR'S
STATUS, AS
UNDERSTOOD IN
THE GREAT
RENT CASE.

Para. 53, contd.

extracts in this Appendix, that the only rates of rent recognized by the Regulations of 1793 were the ancient established pergunnah rates, and other *reduced* rates. Higher than the pergunnah rates were not countenanced; on the contrary, the levy of fresh *abwabs*, that is, enhancement in the only form in which rents were increased under Native rule from a rise of prices, was strictly prohibited. In fine, as regards rent, the Regulations of 1793 made no provision for any subsequent revision or increase of a ryot's rent, after its entry, once, in a pottah, by mutual consent of the zemindar and ryot; and this was an advised omission, for the regulations only carried out, in this regard, what had been determined upon by the Government since 1769, and by Sir John Shore, Lord Cornwallis, and the Court of Directors, in their discussions of the permanent settlement.

54. It further appears that the custom, more ancient than law, under which the residents in a village acquired permanent occupancy right in waste land by bringing it under cultivation, subject to payment of the established pergunnah rate, was not abrogated, or put an end to, by the permanent settlement, inasmuch as the zemindar was debarred from charging more than the ancient pergunnah rate for any land in his zemindary; at the same time that he was bound to give a pottah at that rate to any resident cultivator who demanded it. Even pykasht or stranger ryots were protected so far that, if allowed to cultivate, no more than the pergunnah rate could be demanded from them, and on the expiration of the temporary lease they were entitled to renewal at the pergunnah rate.

55. Lord Cornwallis was familiar with the English copyhold tenure, according to which the tenant pays, like the khoodkasht ryot, a rent fixed by immemorial custom, and not liable to increase, while the only record of it, as with the khoodkasht ryot of 1793, was in the court roll of the minor, a copy of which, corresponding to the pottah deliverable to the khoodkasht ryot, constituted, to the copyholder, the sole record of his title. The analogy between the copyholder and the khoodkasht ryot fails so far that the zemindar was not the proprietor;—but in Lord Cornwallis's estimation he was, and from his Lordship's point of view the analogy was perfect; whence we are warranted in concluding, in confirmation of the view in this Appendix, *1stly*, that the pottah was designed as a mere record of a right which the ryot did not derive from the pottah; *2ndly*, that the rent specified in the pottah was not liable to increase.